Analyzing Elections

Analyzing Elections

REBECCA B. MORTON

PROFESSOR, WILF FAMILY DEPARTMENT
OF POLITICS
NEW YORK UNIVERSITY

THE NEW INSTITUTIONALISM IN
AMERICAN POLITICS SERIES

W·W·NORTON & COMPANY
New York   London

W. W. Norton & Company has been independent since its founding in 1923, when William Warder Norton and Mary D. Herter Norton first published lectures delivered at the People's Institute, the adult education division of New York City's Cooper Union. The Nortons soon expanded their program beyond the Institute, publishing books by celebrated academics from America and abroad. By mid-century, the two major pillars of Norton's publishing program—trade books and college texts—were firmly established. In the 1950s, the Norton family transferred control of the company to its employees, and today—with a staff of four hundred and a comparable number of trade, college, and professional titles published each year—W. W. Norton & Company stands as the largest and oldest publishing house owned wholly by its employees.

Manufacturing by the R. R. Donnelley & Sons, Inc.—Crawfordsville Division.

Book design by Jacques Chazaud.
Production manager: Ben Reynolds.
Composition by PennSet, Inc.
Drawn art by John McAusland.

Library of Congress Cataloging-in-Publication Data
Morton, Rebecca B., 1954–
    Analyzing elections / Rebecca Morton.
       p. cm.—(The new institutionalism in American politics)
    Includes bibliographical references and index.

ISBN 0-393-97829-X (pbk.)

    1. Elections—United States.   2. Voting—United States.   3. Political campaigns—United States. I. Title. II. Series.
  JK1976.M65 2005
  324.973—dc22

                                     2004061078

W. W. Norton & Company, Inc., 500 Fifth Avenue, New York, N.Y. 10110
wwnorton.com
W. W. Norton & Company Ltd., Castle House, 75/76 Wells Street,
London W1T 3QT

1 2 3 4 5 6 7 8 9 0

This book is dedicated to the memory of my grandmother, Archie Claire Holmes Hill, who as a local election commissioner spent many long nights counting votes.

Contents

Acknowledgments

I began this book in the late 1990s, while a faculty member at the University of Iowa, based on notes that I used in classes I taught there. Through the years, I have gained much insight from students there and in my classes at the University of Houston and New York University. I hope someday they (and, particularly, their teaching assistants) will forgive me for making them read and study the earlier drafts of this manuscript. This book would also not have been written without the encouragement and insight of my editor at Norton, Stephen Dunn. I have benefited from lengthy comments by Gary Jacobson and Scott Adler on earlier drafts as well as from comments by Paul Abramson, Eric Dickson, Morris Fiorina, Sandy Gordon, Chuck Shipan, David Stromberg, and Richard Winger. Quite a number of friends and colleagues have provided me with data and with insights into their work, particularly David Baron, Tim Besley, Chuck Cameron, Bob Erikson, Liz Gerber, Tim Groseclose, James Hamilton, Michael Herron, Jonathan Katz, Jeffrey Lewis, John Lott, Nolan McCarty, Jeff Milyo, Warren Mitofsky, Richard Niemi, Tom Palfrey, Keith Poole, Howard Rosenthal, Ken Shotts, Pev Squire, Koleman Strumpf, Stephen Voss, and Ken Williams. I appreciate greatly the opportunity to complete the final version of this manuscript while a scholar at the Center for the Study of Democratic Politics at Princeton University and the sabbatical I received from New York University. Two wonderful princesses of administration helped me manage my academic life through the period of writing—Diana Barnes and Diane Price. I also greatly appreciate the diligent copyediting of Abigail Winograd. But my biggest debt is to the two women who had to adjust their lives to the demands of this book in countless ways—my daughters, Renda and Charlotte.

Analyzing Elections

1

How Elections Rule American Politics

Bush versus Gore, September 11, and American Elections

Both the fall of 2000 and the fall of 2001 were momentous periods for U.S. citizens. In November 2000, an extremely rare event occurred, a virtually tied election involving millions of voters, whose outcome was debated for weeks, then finally resolved by the U.S. Supreme Court. In September 2001, terrorists attacked the World Trade Center in downtown Manhattan and the Pentagon in Washington, D.C., plunging the country into military conflict in Afghanistan and catalyzing a confrontation with Iraq, as well as bringing to the forefront of political debate issues of domestic security, immigration, civil liberties, and civil rights. From the perspective of today, the happenings at the end of 2000 seem almost trivial in comparison with those of the fall of 2001. Yet the events of November and December 2000 profoundly affected the response of the nation to the attacks in 2001. Because Republican George W. Bush had been elected in the presidential contest of 2000, he was the one who made the initial policy choices on how the United States would respond to the terrorist attack. Similarly, the officials in his administration (appointed with the consent of the Senate) were the ones making the initial policy decisions about how to deal with the terrorists (both domestically and internationally).

Statements by Al Gore, Bush's Democratic opponent in 2000, Massachusetts senator John Kerry and the other candidates for the 2004 Democratic presidential nomination, and other Democratic officials and party leaders suggest that the terrorist attacks would have been handled differently if

Gore had won the election. In particular, Democrats criticized Bush's response to the terrorist attack for quickly shifting its focus to Iraq and Saddam Hussein instead of remaining on Al Qaeda, the organization directly responsible for the attacks, and they expressed displeasure with some of the measures that administration officials such as Attorney General John Ashcroft took to uncover terrorist networks within the United States. Although a number of Democrats expressed support for the troops during the war with Iraq, they also argued against the war and Bush's policies in postwar Iraq. Questions were raised about the justifications for the war and whether enough effort was being expended to fight Al Qaeda. Massachusetts senator John Kerry, the 2004 Democratic presidential nominee, noted in a speech before firefighters in March 2004 that he believed Bush had "done too little [in the war on terror] and some things that he didn't have to. When the focus of the war on terror was appropriately in Afghanistan and on breaking Al Qaeda, President Bush shifted his focus to Iraq and to Saddam Hussein."[1]

Democrats also criticized the administration's policies on North Korea, which the Bush administration labeled part of an axis of evil.[2] Would a Democratic administration have pushed for a confrontation with Iraq? Would a Democratic administration have dealt with North Korea differently? Would a Democratic administration, in order to uncover domestic terrorist networks, have been as willing to investigate its citizens' library use or ask diving shops for lists of customers who had recently taken lessons?[3] Would a Democratic administration have pushed for a tax cut in the face of increased war and domestic antiterrorist expenditures?[4] Although we can never experience the counterfactual of a Democratic administration responding to the terrorist attacks of 2001 and the problems of North Korea in 2002 and 2003, the Democrats suggest that they would have handled things differently.

The occurrence of September 11 after the close presidential election, coupled with the success of President Bush in Afghanistan and public satisfaction with his ability to handle the terrorist threat, helped the Republican Party secure a majority in both houses of Congress in the midterm election of 2002, something that might not have happened if voters had been more concerned about domestic issues at the time of the election. Bush was able to use this majority to enact further tax cuts in the spring of 2002, thereby lowering the tax rates for many wealthy voters. If Gore had been elected in 2000 and capably handled the crises, the Democrats might have seen the same success in the 2002 elections but probably with different consequences for domestic policy.

The lesson from 2000 and its effects on American reactions to the terrorist attacks and American policy making is that elections dominate U.S. politics. The election calendar deeply influences the timing of public policy choices; economic decisions are affected by elections and electoral outcomes; fights over the right to vote and how votes are counted have historically resulted in some of our most serious political strife and significant court decisions; and considerable financial resources, effort, and time are demanded by the electoral process. Our elected officials seem driven by the next campaign, and every political event is interpreted by the media in the context of current or future campaigns. Despite claims of widespread cynicism about politics, low turnout, and high levels of voter apathy, almost all levels of American society are involved in elections, from Buddhist nuns in southern California to dairy farmers in Vermont. Understanding how elections work is crucial for understanding American politics and policy choices.

Actors and Institutions

Actors in American Elections

In this book, we investigate the American electoral process and the roles played by actors and institutions. In the 2000 presidential election, the principal actors were of course the voters, the candidates, the members of the Supreme Court of Florida and the Supreme Court of the United States, and the election officials in Florida and other states, as well as a host of party and elected officials and interest groups. In the chapters to come, we will meet many other actors in U.S. elections and hear their stories. Some of the people we will meet are elected officials, such as Dianne Feinstein, who successfully defeated a recall attempt while mayor of San Francisco and won a seat in the U.S. Senate; Jeb Bush, who had to learn to moderate himself on policy issues; Jesse Ventura, who challenged the two-party system and defeated it; Charlie Norwood, who tried to push through patients' rights legislation; Harold Washington, who became the first black mayor of Chicago; and so on. We will discuss interest group leaders like Betty Friedan, who helped mobilize the modern feminist movement, and Don Smith, a union leader in Detroit. We will meet Hollywood stars like Ben Affleck who actively campaign in elections. But we will also talk about individuals like Amanda Strom of St. Louis, who didn't believe her vote would make a difference, and Fannie Jeffrey, whose parents moved from Alabama in the early 1900s in order to have the right to vote that Strom did not use.

Electoral Institutions

The Electoral College However, focusing only on the actors and their choices would give us an incomplete view of American elections and how they influence American politics. Our electoral institutions—the rules that determine who votes, the geographic areas represented by the elected officials, the ways in which votes are counted, which public officials are chosen by election rather than appointment, and whether elected officials in one branch of government must compromise with officials in another branch of government to choose policy—play crucial roles in how elections dominate U.S. politics. For example, because we elect presidents through an electoral college system rather than by direct popular vote, the winner of the 2000 presidential election was not the winner of the popular vote. That is, although George W. Bush received 50,456,002 popular votes to Al Gore's 50,999,897, Bush won more electoral voters (271 to 266), and so he became president.

Separation of Powers Moreover, because we elect our president and our Congress in separate elections and because we have an independent judiciary and a federal structure of government with independently elected state and local officials, the outcome of a single election is unlikely to fully determine the policy choices of the government. Although Bush was the winner in 2000, in early 2001, when Vermont Republican senator James Jeffords declared his independence from the party and gave the Democrats majority control in the Senate, Bush and his party recognized that in order to enact policies he needed support from Senate Democrats. For instance, Bush initially opposed an independent commission to investigate the September 11 attacks, but he later agreed to such a commission because of pressure from members of Congress and other state and local elected officials. The legislation creating the commission was a carefully crafted compromise involving Democratic and Republican members of Congress and the president.[5]

A Federation of Electoral Institutions Furthermore, because of Jeffords's defection, Bush and the Republicans saw the Senate election of 2002 as an opportunity to change the balance of power in the Senate. They recognized that a congressional election held between presidential elections could seriously affect the extent to which a president can enact policies. Yet because only one third of the Senate was up for reelection, the balance of power in the nation and the types of policies that would be enacted hinged on contests in only the states with Senate elections.

One of the most contested of the 2002 Senate races was in Louisiana, where Democratic senator Mary Landrieu was up for reelection. In the November general election, Landrieu received only 46 percent of the vote, less than a majority, although she received more votes than any other candidate (a plurality). In some states that would have meant immediate victory, but in Louisiana, because Landrieu had less than 50 percent of the vote, she had to compete with her closest opponent in a runoff election. Moreover, Landrieu had faced not just one Republican opponent with sizable support but three Republican candidates (because Louisiana's elections are nonpartisan, with no party primaries or nominating conventions choosing one Republican candidate for the general election). Republican voters and party leaders were divided among these candidates, with the result that no one received as many votes as Landrieu, but Landrieu did not receive a majority.[6] But the Republicans still had a chance to defeat Landrieu in the December runoff, which meant that until the runoff, the actual number of Republicans and Democrats in the Senate in the coming term was uncertain. Landrieu did win in the runoff despite strong campaigning by Bush and other Republicans, who united in support of her opponent.

The feature of shared but limited power coupled with separate elections scheduled at different times in states with different electoral rules can fundamentally affect American public policies. Even though Landrieu won reelection, the Republicans won a majority in the Senate in 2002, winning seats previously held by Democrats in Georgia, Minnesota, and Missouri while losing a seat in Arkansas. If the Democrats had held on to at least two of those lost seats, Bush's ability to affect the agenda in Congress would have been reduced and his need to compromise on policy would have increased. National politics thus very much depends on state politics and state electoral rules and institutions.

Changes in Institutions

Differences in electoral institutions over time have also affected American politics in important ways. Before the passage of the Voting Rights Act of 1965, many southern states used poll taxes and literacy tests to make it difficult for African Americans to register to vote. White southern Democratic officials were more conservative than northern Democrats on civil rights and voting rights issues, while agreeing with their partisans on other issues, resulting in a de facto three-party system in Congress (Republicans, southern Democrats, and northern Democrats). After passage of the Voting Rights Act and increased voting by African Americans in the South (and in the North, where blacks were emboldened by the end of disenfranchisement in the South), either conservative Republicans replaced Democrats in southern congressional districts or southern Democrats became more liberal, depending on the size of the black voting population in each district. The passage of the Voting Rights Act, changing the rules on who could vote, thus affected the policy positions of members of both political parties.[7]

Thus, in myriad ways, the institutions that govern the electoral process in the United States affect which officials are elected and the policy choices that they make while in office. When most people think about institutions in American politics or the study of American institutions, they mean studying Congress, the presidency, the judiciary, or the executive branch. But without a thorough understanding of the role of electoral institutions, we cannot understand American elections.

Election Games

In order to understand how the interactions of actors and institutions work in the electoral process, we will sometimes use simple game-theory models of those connections. Game-theory models allow us to think carefully about the motivations of the actors in the election process and the institutional setup that the actors are embedded in. But the main value of the game-theory approach is that it allows us to consider the impact of actors' choices on the choices of other actors.

In most situations facing actors in elections, the choice an actor makes depends on not only the institutional rules governing the process but also the choices of other actors. For example, when Mary Landrieu decided whether to run for reelection, she had to consider not only whether she could achieve enough votes to meet Louisiana's majority requirement but also what sort of challengers she might face in the election and to what extent interest groups and other political actors would support those challengers. One challenger might be what we would call a strong challenger, like the governor, who has already won in a statewide contest and has a lot of support across the state. Another potential challenger might be a weak challenger, like a state legislator, who is largely unknown outside his or her home district and would have to work harder to convey to voters his or her positions on issues or raise financial resources from interest groups.

Mary Landrieu's likelihood of winning reelection would depend on which types of challengers she might face, and as a result her decision on whether to run for reelection is influenced by who she thinks might challenge her. Similarly, the weak and strong challengers' decisions on whether to run against Landrieu will depend on whether the others run and whether Landrieu herself chooses to run. The situation facing Landrieu and her potential challengers when Landrieu chooses whether to run for reelection and her potential challengers choose whether to compete is a *strategic* situation, where the best choice for an actor depends not only on the institutional constraint but also on the choices made by other actors and vice versa.

By setting up the strategic situation facing Landrieu and her potential challengers as a "game," we can consider how the choices act together in the electoral process, since we can then use knowledge that we have about games similar to that situation and theories about how individuals make choices in strategic situations in general. Sometimes this approach allows us to come up with understandings that are not obvious or intuitive until the strategic nature of a situation is laid out clearly. In chapter 11, for instance, we see that considering an election entry game between weak and strong challengers suggests the counterintuitive conclusion that weak challengers can benefit from using a strategy of taking on incumbents whereas strong challengers would rather wait until the contest is an open-seat race (one in which there is no incumbent).

Our study of the American electoral process will also involve, when it can, discussion of how well the analytical models of that process, these games, fit the reality of U.S. elections. For example, if we consider the decision to vote as a strategic choice of individual voters, game theory tells us that very few people should vote in large elections. Yet citizens do choose to participate; it is currently estimated that in November 2004 over 122 million people voted in the U.S. presidential election, 60.7 percent of the voters eligible to participate, far more than the individualistic game-theory approach would predict.[8] In the next chapter, we discuss some explanations for how to reconcile the empirical reality that voters do participate in elections with the conclusion drawn from individualistic game-theory models.

The Plan of the Book

Fundamentals: The Main Characters

This book is divided into five parts. Part I comprises the building blocks of our analysis of the American electoral process by studying the roles of the main actors—voters, candidates, and parties—and the institutional electoral process through which the actors move. In chapter 2, we begin our inquiry with perhaps one of the hardest and most studied questions in the electoral process—what motivates individual voters? We find that although the act of voting is irrational at an individual level, voters can be mobilized through the use of selective incentives, and we find that the decisions of those who mobilize voters are strategic and related to the federal structure of the electoral process. In chapter 3, we consider advances in those mobilization strategies in the 2004 election and how those strategies resulted in turnout levels that exceeded those of previous years; we also consider recent changes in the methods of voting, such as the use of early balloting, the Internet, and new registration procedures.

In chapter 4, we add candidates and the major political parties to our analysis. We discuss why, in a majority-rule system, candidates find it desirable to converge toward the center on issues but nevertheless also choose divergent positions while working within the major political parties. We find that the different procedures used by political parties to nominate candidates can affect how divergent the positions are. The popular media has made much of a polarized country divided into red states and blue states, that is, states that supported Republican president George Bush and states that supported Democratic candidates Al Gore and John Kerry. Voters who supported Bush are commonly considered very different—in terms of their preferences for the war in Iraq, abortion, religion, gay marriage, and so on—from those who supported Gore or Kerry.

In chapter 5, we consider whether the nation is polarized by partisanship. We discover that the picture is more complex than that presented in the media and that while elected officials and party activists in the two major parties have become more ideologically distant, a large number of voters are relatively centrist. We also consider how candidate and voter behaviors are affected when candidates differ in qualities over which voters are not divided (such as the ability to manage the economy or a war).

Money and the Mass Media

In Part II, we explore the sources and effects of campaign advertising and the mass media in the electoral process. In chapter 6, we examine the regulation of campaign finance and how it has affected campaigns and elections. We also discuss the motives of campaign contributors and the implications of those motives for elections and candidate choices. We discover that contributors reap advantages from giving to incumbents. In chapter 7, we investigate how campaign money influences voters and discover how even rational voters' decisions can be affected by the provision of information about candidates' policies or other qualities that voters care about. We learn that campaign advertising on behalf of challengers (by the candidates themselves or by other groups) can be more influential per dollar than that on behalf of incumbents.

In chapter 8, we investigate how the news media influences the information voters have about candidates and policies in elections. The mass media is criticized for either a liberal or a conservative bias and is thus believed to influence voters' choices in elections. We assess the empirical evidence of media bias and the possible reasons why political reporting might be biased. We observe that the demand for entertaining news, the preferences of advertisers, the nature of reporting, and the cost structure of media organizations can all lead to an ideological bias in reporting, but we also observe that consumers of political news can gain information even from biased sources.

Incomplete Information

Part III expands our understanding of elections by examining more extensively the ways in which voters and candidates deal with the lack of complete information in elections. In chapter 9, we examine how the lack of complete information about elected officials' policy decisions affects voters' and candidates' behavior. We see that voters have an incentive to use the electoral process to reward or punish elected officials for their decisions and therefore vote retrospectively rather than prospectively, and we see how retrospective voting affects the choices of some elected officials—regulators, prosecutors, and judges. We consider the extent to which retrospective voting affects elected officials' choices in how to manage the economy and finance government affairs. We also study how mechanisms of direct democracy (referenda and recall elections) provide voters with the opportunity to influence elected officials, even if they do not take advantage of them.

In chapter 10, we consider the problem of incomplete information about voters' preferences. We see how candidates and the news media attempt to measure voter preferences in order to predict election outcomes and gauge public opinion on issues. We find that while public opinion polls are the predominant method used, they are not the only or necessarily the best way to measure voter preferences. We discover that academic statisticians and social scientists have often worked with candidates, parties, and the media in their attempts to divine public opinion. But we also find that elected officials generally see public opinion as something that they influence as much as or more than it influences them.

Federal Elections

Part IV focuses on two particular types of federal elections: congressional (both Senate and House) and presidential. In chapter 11, we discuss congressional elections and find that the use of single-member districts, which must be redrawn after each census, to elect members of Congress fundamentally affects who is elected and, as a consequence, choices of congressional policy. We also consider candidates' decisions to run for Congress and what determines who wins the elections.

Presidential-election contests in U.S. politics are so complex that they comprise two chapters—in chapter 12, we examine the nomination process (presidential primaries), and in chapter 13, we consider the election itself. We learn that the use of individual state primaries and their scheduling affects which candidates are chosen as party nominees. We also see how the Electoral College affects how the major nominees compete for office. In chapter 13, we consider why voters might choose to have a divided government (that is, why they would vote for one major party to dominate Congress and the other to control the presidency) and why voters might be willing to have a unified government, as they were in 2004.

Minorities

Part V considers the important roles played by minor-party and independent candidates in U.S. elections and the complicated issue of minority representation through the electoral process. In chapter 14, we consider minor parties and independent candidates and discuss how those candidates can win even in a system built to favor the major parties and how their winning election can affect how policies change over time. In chapter 15, we review both the sad history of how minority voters were disenfranchised in the U.S. electoral system and the intricate issues involved in making sure that all voters are able to participate and work effectively through the electoral system to influence policy. The final chapter is brief, like this one, and attempts to provide a summary of what we know about U.S. elections (as explained in previous chapters) and what we don't know.

The Message of the Book

The final chapter also returns to what I call the message of the book. Many books about U.S. politics have a message. The message might be to explain some puzzle in American politics or contribute to the literature addressing an issue in American politics from an academic perspective—for example, Anna Harvey's *Votes without Leverage: Women in American Electoral Politics, 1920–1970*, seeks to explain why, although women received the right to vote in 1919, they did not have an effect on policy making until much later. The message might be to show the problems with a given perspective on American politics—for example, David Mayhew's *Electoral Realignments: A Critique of an American Genre* argues that the theory that there are periodic significant changes in U.S. elections, parties, and policy making that have a predictable aspect is without substantiation.

Other books emphasize a comprehensive understanding of a particular substantive part of American politics, with a more subtle message—for example, Keith Poole and Howard Rosenthal's *Congress: A Political-Economic History of Roll-Call Voting* provides a careful examination of roll-call voting in the U.S. Congress using current theory and empirical evidence. Their book has lots of details about how voting in Congress has changed over time, the types of issues that have polarized and united congressional voting, and current trends in congressional voting. The message is that we can—and how we can—use the combination of theory and empirical evidence to understand congressional voting. The purposive message of this book is similar—that current theory about the electoral process combined with empirical evidence can help us understand many aspects and features of American elections.

The choices I have made in writing this book not only influence the perspective of the U.S. electoral process I present but also convey another message. It would have been difficult to do otherwise, given the volume of research on the subject and the need to make sense of it. So the book also has the message of how I view the way American elections work. My perspective emphasizes, as noted above, electoral institutions. It emphasizes explanations of behavior grounded in the presumption that all the actors in the process are attempting to meet their individual goals in the best way they can. This presumption does not preclude the possibility that actors might sometimes make choices that, from an outsider's perspective, are less than rational or desirable due to limits on the information they have, the likely impact their individual choices will have on the outcome, the feelings they may have for particular candidates, or ideological biases, as will become clear in the coming chapters.

My perspective emphasizes that the American electoral process has serious flaws. Those flaws stem from problems in the lack of uniformity and clearness in voting procedures, continuing debates over voting rights and how votes should be aggregated geographically and in determining winners, the unequal distribution of resources across the participants, difficulties voters have in controlling elected officials' behavior in office, and difficulties elected officials have in understanding voters' preferences. In this sense, my perspective has a pessimistic side.

On the optimistic side, my perspective also emphasizes that the American electoral process—with difficulty because of the checks and balances in the government structure—gradually changes. The picture of the U.S. electoral process drawn in this book is, I believe, significantly different from what would have been found in a similar book written just twenty years ago and certainly for a similar book written forty years ago. We discuss some of those changes in the coming chapters—changes in voter mobilization and the process of voting, candidate nomination procedures, campaign finance regulation, terms of elected officials, measuring public opinion, and the design of legislative districts. We also discuss proposed changes—changes in the voting franchise, further regulation of campaign finance, presidential nominations, and the Electoral College. My perspective is not that these changes, if they occur, will lead to a perfect electoral process—that is impossible. And changes have risks: they might lead to instability and a greater disconnect between what we might want as an ideal and the reality. But the changing nature of the process gives those who are dissatisfied the opportunity to have the system better reflect their preferences, and that opportunity provides hope. It is my suspicion that the fact that the electoral process can be changed over time, albeit with difficulties and only gradually, is responsible for much long-run stability in U.S. politics.

A Note to the Reader

Decisions on what to cover in a book as well as how to order the material are arbitrary and often do not cover all the material a particular reader would like or in the order he or she prefers. To deal with those problems, I have included chapters on subjects that not everyone would discuss but some would like more information on, such as the mass media, public opinion, congressional and presidential elections, minor parties, and minority representation. In general, those chapters can be easily skipped or reordered with some minor explanations if the reader prefers. Because congressional elections have probably been more extensively studied than any other type of election, chapter 11, also includes a section on the relationship between political experience and the decision to compete for office, which some may want to read even if they omit the bulk of the chapter. Finally, until chapter 14, the book almost exclusively discusses the election process using single-dimensional models. If the reader is interested in how parties and

candidates locate themselves in more than one dimension and the paradox
of voting earlier, chapter 14 can be easily read any place after chapter 4,
again with some minor explanations.

Much of the academic research on the election process that is discussed in
this book uses mathematical techniques (both in developing formal models
and in statistical estimation) beyond the standard knowledge of many readers. Yet the intuition behind the work can generally be explained. This book
attempts to provide such nontechnical explanations—it attempts to make
accessible some of the latest work on elections without too much of the
mathematics. As such, I rely on many examples from the real world of the
electoral process coupled with fairly simple models and empirical analysis.
The simple models, of course, should never be considered a substitute for
the more rigorous analysis from which they are derived, and citations are
provided throughout the book to lead the reader to that work. The empirical analysis is also meant to be illustrative, and citations to more rigorous
evaluations of theories are provided as well, with the hope that interested
readers will turn to them. At the end of each chapter, I have included a few
study questions and problems that are designed not to force the reader to
regurgitate what is said in the chapters but to think further about the implications of the material presented in the chapter.

Finally, although I have attempted to cover much of the formal and empirical research on U.S. elections, this is one of the most extensive areas of
study in the discipline of political science. As a consequence, it is impossible
to cover all of this work, and I apologize to the scholars whose work I have
omitted or covered only lightly. My hope is that those who use this book
will be inspired to seek out this broad and interesting literature.

NOTES

1. David Stout, "Kerry Criticizes Bush Record on Terrorism," *New York Times*,
   March 15, 2004. For criticism from Gore, see Adam Nagorney, "Gore Says
   Bush's War on Terrorism Is Ineffective," *New York Times*, November 21, 2002.
   For other Democratic criticism of Bush's response to the terrorist attacks, see
   Kevin Sack, "Former President Carter Is 'Disappointed' in Bush," *The New York
   Times*, July 25, 2001; David Johnston and Eric Lichtblau, "Little Headway in
   Terrorism War, Democrats Say," *New York Times*, November 12, 2002; Susan
   Milligan and Elizabeth Neuffer, "Kennedy Criticizes Bush on Iraq Policy,"
   Boston Globe, September 28, 2002; and Eric Black, "Candidates Are Worlds
   Apart: Wellstone and Coleman Take Opposite Sides on Most Foreign Policy Is-
   sues," *Minneapolis Star Tribune*, October 20, 2002. Others argued that Demo-
   crats needed to criticize Bush's war on terrorism more explicitly, contending that
   the statements of Gore and Democrats were "weak"; see, for example, "Speech-
   less," *New Republic*, October 7, 2002. In 2003, both before and during the war
   with Iraq, Democratic criticism was mixed, some arguing against the war, others
   supporting it; see, for example, Jim VandeHei and Helen Dewar, "Democrats
   Lambaste Bush on Iraq," *Washington Post*, March 7, 2003; Christopher Craff,
   "Dean Says He Backs Troops, but Not Bush War Policies," *Manchester Union*

Leader, March 18, 2003; and Will Lester, "Democratic Leaders Tout War Support," *Associated Press Online*, April 9, 2003.

2. For Democratic criticism of Bush's foreign policy on North Korea, see David Westphal, "Bush Criticized for Response to N. Korea: Democrats Say Reactor Demands Greater Sense of Urgency," *Minneapolis Star Tribune*, February 7, 2003; Sonni Efron and Barbara Demick, "Democrats Say Focus Should Be on N. Korea," *Los Angeles Times*, March 6, 2003; and Matt Kelley, "Bush Sends Bombers to Guam to Keep Eye on North Korea: Democrats Demand U.S. Talk Directly to Pyongyang," *Ottawa Citizen*, March 6, 2003.

3. See Michael Moss and Ford Fessenden, "America under Surveillance: Privacy and Security; New Tools for Domestic Spying, and Qualms," *New York Times*, December 10, 2002; Jerry Seper, "Ashcroft's Assurance Is Sought on Privacy: 4 Democrats Fear Tracking System," *Washington Times*, January 14, 2003; and Mark Benjamin, "Democrats Blast Ashcroft Surveillance Plan," *United Press International*, February 10, 2003.

4. See "Democratic Hopefuls Debate War, Tax Cuts," *Associated Press*, May 4, 2003; David Welna, "Democrats Argue President Bush's Tax Cuts Will Inflate the Federal Budget Deficit," *All Things Considered*, NPR, January 10, 2003; and Janet Hook, "Democrats Enter Tax Break Battle," *Los Angeles Times*, January 7, 2003.

5. See Helen Dewar, "Deal Reached on 9/11 Commission: Bipartisan Panel to Probe What Led Up to Attacks," *Washington Post*, November 15, 2002.

6. Republican governor Mike Foster supported John Cooksey, whereas Bush and the National Republican Senatorial Committee supported Suzanne Terrell. See Bruce Alpert, "Landrieu Camp Breathing Easier with Foster Out," *New Orleans Times-Picayune*, August 25, 2002, and "NRSC Hoping to Force Landrieu into Runoff," *Bulletin's Frontrunner*, October 15, 2002.

7. See Poole and Rosenthal (1997) for a discussion of the changes in congressional voting in this period and Carmines and Stimson (1992) for a review of how the parties' policy positions on race changed during the period. Filer, Kenny, and Morton (1991) documented the effect of the Voting Rights Act on African American turnout.

8. Press release, Center for the Study of the American Electorate, January 14, 2005.

Part I

Fundamentals

~2~

Understanding Turnout

Three Things

This election is going to come down to three things: turnout, turnout, and turnout. Whoever gets their base to the polls is going to win.
Mike Madrid, political director of the California Republican Party, quoted in Richard L. Berke, "With Few Hot Issues, Parties Turn On the Ad Blitz to Prod Voters," *New York Times*, October 25, 1998

It's turnout, it's turnout, it's turnout.
Ron McCloud, chairman of the Kentucky State Democratic Party, quoted in R. W. Apple, Jr., "When the Race Is Tight, All the Talk Is of Turnout," *New York Times*, October 29, 1998

It should be no surprise that turnout is important in elections in American politics. In the 1998 congressional elections, political analysts recognized the weight of turnout on the outcome. Traditionally, midterm elections (elections that take place when there is no presidential race) have a low turnout, and 1998 appeared to be no exception. All the talk among political activists was how to get their supporters to the polls and their candidates elected.

In 2000 and 2002, turnout was again a fundamental issue. In the presidential contest of 2000, states such as Florida, where the election was close, received great attention from the candidates and the parties. The Democratic Party aggressively encouraged African American voters in the state, and the turnout rate among blacks was a record 72 percent. That helped make the race close in Florida, so close that the outcome in the state was resolved only by a Supreme Court ruling. However, 2002 was different. Some experts believed that George W. Bush's brother Jeb Bush won reelection as governor in 2002 because many of these black voters (who had participated in 2000) stayed home—the turnout rate in Florida in 2002 among blacks was only 43 percent.[1] Similarly, in California, incumbent governor Gray Davis, who was widely expected to win reelection, won by only 5 percent because of the low turnout of minority voters who had supported him strongly in previous elections. And in Texas, Democrats who were counting on minority voters to support their candidate for governor, Tony Sanchez (who is Latino), and their candidate for the senate, Ron Kirk (who is black) were unable to secure enough such votes to overcome the strong white vote for the Republican incumbent governor, Rick Perry, and the Republican candidate for the Senate, John Cornyn.

Both Democrats and Republicans began planning to increase voter turnout for the 2004 election almost as soon as the 2002 contest was concluded. At a November 2003 training session in Florida (the third in a series of twelve scheduled events), Bush campaign spokesman Reed Dickens told attendants: " 'This is not a pep rally. You're here to get homework for the next 12 months.' . . . Brett Doster, the executive director for Bush's Florida campaign, said he is telling Florida's 67 county party chairmen that they should aim for an 80 percent Republican turnout."[2] By the time Florida had its Democratic presidential primary, in March 2004, Massachusetts senator John Kerry had campaigned there vigorously, emphasizing the importance of turnout in 2004. The presidential primaries of 2004 also showed the importance of differences in turnout rates across voter groups. Earlier, in the Georgia Democratic primary, Kerry had managed to defeat North Carolina senator John Edwards (who had hoped to use his southern roots to win states like Georgia). With six out of ten African Americans supporting Kerry and blacks outnumbering whites at the polls, Edwards withdrew from the contest.[3]

The focus on turnout only intensified as the general presidential election approached. On Halloween Day in 2004, two days before the presidential election, President George W. Bush's campaign speech before an audience in Ashwaubenon, Wisconsin, across the street from the Green Bay Packers' Lambeau Field, had a clear message:

> We're here to ask for your vote and here to ask for your help. It is close to voting time. We have a duty in our democracy to vote, and so I'm asking you to get your friends and neighbors and remind them of that duty. Find your fellow Republicans and turn them out. Find independents and turn them out. Find discerning Democrats, and head them to the polls. And when you get them going to the polls, remind them if they want a safer America, a stronger America and a better America, to put me and Dick Cheney back in [the White House].[4]

On election day, John Kerry did four hours of thirty-eight consecutive TV interviews urging voters in swing states to turn out. Democratic spokesman Joe Lockhart noted that Democrats were "still convincing every voter to get to the polls, till the polls close and even after"; Tad Devine, a Democratic strategist, said that "as the evening wore on, the party was making calls farther and farther west, where polls were open in such states as Nevada and New Mexico."[5]

Turnout matters. If some voters are more likely to turn out in elections than others, then candidates and political parties preferred by the voters who turn out are more likely to be elected, as Sanchez, Kirk, and Edwards discovered. Abramson, Aldrich, and Rohde (2003) estimated that if turnout rates had been even across voters, Al Gore's share of the 2000 presidential vote would have been 1.8 percent higher, perhaps enough to change the electoral vote in Florida, given the closeness of the vote there.

In this chapter, we consider why voters participate and the role of turnout in American elections. We begin our study of turnout with three puzzles—a strange forty-five-year lag, the issue of declining turnout, and the paradox of not voting.

Three Puzzles

Puzzle 1: The Forty-Five-Year Lag

In 1919, the ratification of the Nineteenth Amendment gave women the right to vote in U.S. elections. The passage of the amendment was made possible by the concerted efforts of women's organizations, which had built substantial political clout. Soon after its passage, many believed that women's new right to participate would result in policy choices reflecting their preferences. If a large group of voters begins to participate in electoral politics, it seems obvious that we will see public policy that is more reflective of the new voters' preferences. Early on, some new measures suggested this was happening—as Harvey (1998, p. 4) reported, in 1921 a coalition of women's groups lobbied Congress to pass legislation providing grants to states for pre- and postnatal care for children. Yet this accomplishment and others like it seemed to quickly dissipate after 1924, and the landmark legislation passed in 1921 was not renewed when it expired in 1929.

The failures of women's organizations to influence policy continued. As Harvey pointed out, New Deal programs, although seemingly beneficial to women, were designed to please "the concerns of more political powerful groups such as labor unions" rather than women's organizations. Programs for women and children were largely restricted to "needy" families, while programs for male "breadwinners," like Social Security and unemployment insurance, provided universal coverage. Harvey concluded (p. 9): "After 1925, we simply do not see a sustained recognition of women as a significant group in policy making until 1970." Why the lag? Why did it take forty-five years for women's organizations to begin to affect public policy? Why did it take so long for their interests to be reflected in U.S. elections?[6]

Puzzle 2: Declining Voter Participation

In the 1998 and 2002 midterm elections—in which activists argued that turnout was everything—turnout was considered low. According to early estimates by the Committee for the Study of the American Electorate, turnout was only 36 percent in 1998, the lowest in any election since 1942, when the nation was at war. Abramson, Aldrich, and Rohde (2003) reported that in 2002 overall turnout was only slightly higher, at 39.3 percent. While turnout did reach a significant high in 2004, an estimated 60.7 percent, some commentators saw it as an aberration related to the specific nature of the contest rather than a sign of a reversal of the downward trend.[7] Curtis Gans of the Committee for the Study of the American Electorate contended: "Unless there is a continuation of the deeply-felt political divisions

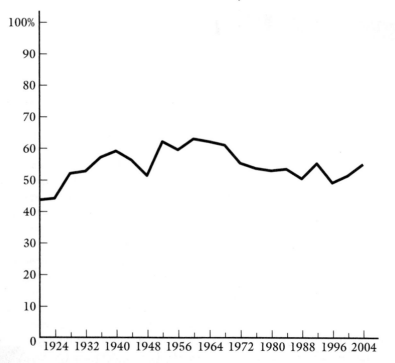

FIGURE 2.1
Voter Turnout in Presidential Elections, as Estimated by the U.S. Census Bureau, 1920–2004

Source: Abramson, Aldrich, and Rohde (2003), with figures for 2004 added.

FIGURE 2.2
Voter Turnout in Presidential Elections, Corrected for Ineligible Voters, 1952–2004

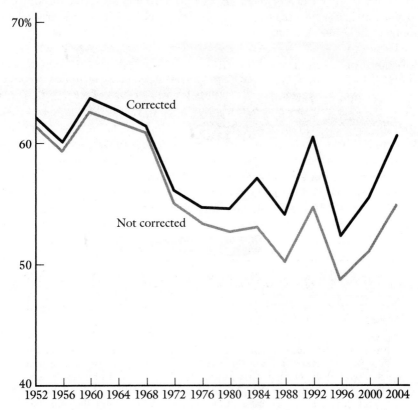

Source: McDonald and Popkin (2002), corrected for errors.

in the nation, the substantial turnout increase of 2004, of about the same magnitude as the turnout increase between the elections of 1988 and 1992, is likely, as in the earlier turnout rise, to prove temporary."[8] Figure 2.1 shows how turnout in presidential elections has changed over time as a percentage of those eligible to vote, as measured by the U.S. Census Bureau.

The turnout percentage of the population of eligible voters increased from 1920 to 1940, then declined during World War II, when a significant percentage of the population was in the military and voting and political participation were more difficult to manage. In the 1950s, turnout returned to prewar levels. Yet there was a significant decline in 1968, which (with the exception of jumps in 1992 and 2004) has continued without an obvious explanation. McDonald and Popkin (2001) contended that part of the alleged turnout decline is a result of errors in the measurement of the voting-age population. In particular, they demonstrate that the census includes in its estimates of eligible voters noncitizens who cannot vote and convicted felons who have lost the right, populations that have grown significantly since the 1960s. Figure 2.2 presents data from their research corrected for these errors. Even taking these errors into account, however, turnout did decline in 1968 and has returned to the levels of the 1950s and early 1960s only in the 2004 election.

Turnout is positively related to voters' income and education (which are of course positively related to each other as well [Abramson, Aldrich, and Rohde 2003]). For example, in the 2000 presidential election self-reported turnout rates of white voters with an income of less than $15,000 was approximately 39 percent, whereas for white voters with an income of $85,000 or more the rate was 85 percent. Similarly, white voters who are not high school graduates reported a turnout rate of 45 percent, whereas white voters with college degrees voted at a rate of 92.5 percent. The puzzle of participation is that since 1960 both education and real per capita income have risen, a phenomenon that suggests that turnout should be rising given the fact that voters who are more educated and have a higher income are more likely to vote in a single election. Why this inconsistency? Brody (1978) has labeled this the "puzzle of political participation."

Puzzle 3: The Paradox of Not Voting

Some Famous and Not-So-Famous Nonvoters

> Amanda Strom, 24, is a University of Missouri at St. Louis optometry student who registered to vote three years ago—but hasn't voted. She is an active volunteer, helping with a group that readies used prescription eyeglasses for donation to the poor. She volunteered this weekend for the "Sprint for Sight" in Forest Park to benefit the blind. But she's not persuaded that her vote would make a difference.
> Karen Branch-Brioso, *St. Louis Post-Dispatch*, March 16, 2003

Strom is just the kind of voter whom the Academy Award–winning actor Ben Affleck tried to reach in the 2000 election. Affleck campaigned for Al Gore, appearing at numerous events, trying to appeal to young, disaffected voters. It turned out, however, that Affleck, like Strom, did not vote in 2000, as reported by the online magazine *The Smoking Gun* on April 24, 2001, and apparently he had not voted since 1992. In response to queries, Affleck's spokesman cited a bureaucratic snafu that had prevented him from voting in New York, then his residence.[9] Affleck is not the only campaigner who has encouraged others to vote while not always following his or her own advice—in 2002 the governor of Minnesota, Jesse Ventura, while publicly pushing voters to participate, did not vote in his state's September 10 primary election: "Ventura spokesman John Wodele said the governor acknowledged not voting in the Sept. 10 primary. 'He regrets that he was not able to make it to the polls. He simply said his schedule got the best of him with all the other things going on that week and he couldn't make it there,' Wodele said." *Minneapolis Star Tribune* reporter Mark Brunswick found that Ventura had also failed to vote in the general election in 1996, even though he served as honorary campaign chairman for the independent candidate for the Senate that year.[10] Ventura has not been the only well-known elected official who has a history of not voting: former North Carolina senator and vice presidential candidate John Edwards did not always participate in elections prior to running for the U.S. Senate (Barone and Cohen 2003, p. 1190).

Voting is a costly act—mainly in terms of time, as Ventura's experience shows. If a voter, like Strom, does not believe that his or her vote will make a difference, it is hard to argue that he or she should spend the time and effort. When asked about the actor's failure to vote, Affleck's spokesman pointed out that "fortunately the candidates he supported carried New York State without his vote." Al Gore carried New York with 60.2 percent of the vote. Tim Penny, Ventura's preferred candidate in the primary election he failed to participate in, won with 96 percent of the vote. One of the things Ventura did that day instead of voting was attend a Minnesota Twins baseball game with a group from St. Joseph's Home for Children. It is hard not to think that his choice made sense and more of a difference in the lives of these children than the outcome of the primary, much like Strom's choice to help the poor with eyeglasses.

Expected Utility and the St. Petersburg Paradox We can represent the choice of a voter like Strom, Affleck, or Ventura by using the concepts of utility and expected utility. *Utility* is a nineteenth-century word that social scientists use to represent the satisfaction that individuals derive from different things they might experience or receive. Economists generally talk about the utility that consumers get from goods and services. Political scientists refer to the utility that voters can get from the government's different public policy choices. Social scientists assume that individuals prefer greater utility to less and wish to make choices that maximize their utility. We can think of Ventura as getting utility from various things—for example, attending the Twins game with the children from St. Joseph's Home, seeing Tim Penny elected in the primary as his party's nominee for governor, or seeing Penny's opponent in the primary, Bill Dahn, elected as his party's nominee for governor. We can label the various utilities, calling Ventura's utility from going to the Twins game U_T, Ventura's utility from Penny's election U_P, and Ventura's utility from Dahn's election U_D.

The concept of *expected utility* is slightly more complicated. It depends not only on the utility the individual receives from each possible outcome but also on the probability that each outcome will occur. We use the concept of expected utility to describe the satisfaction individuals get from many types of situations where the outcome is uncertain. For example, suppose that Ventura had bought a lottery ticket from which there was an 80 percent probability that he would win $5 and a 20 percent probability he would win $100. The expected monetary value of the ticket would be the probability of each outcome times each outcome summed; that is, the expected monetary value equals $0.8 \cdot \$5 + 0.2 \cdot \$100 = \$24$. Expected utility is calculated the same way, except instead of the monetary value of each outcome being multiplied by the probability of that outcome, we multiple the utility Ventura would get from the outcome by that probability; that is, Ventura's expected utility equals $0.8 \cdot$ (Ventura's utility from \$5) + $0.2 \cdot$ (Ventura's utility from \$100).

Why do we need to use utility instead of the actual dollar amounts—why not use just expected monetary value? Consider the St. Petersburg paradox, discussed by the mathematician Daniel Bernoulli in the eighteenth century. Suppose you can play a game (supposedly played in St. Petersburg, Russia, at this time) in which you flip a fair coin until it comes up tails, and the total number of flips, which we can call n, determines the prize, which equals $\$2^n$. So, for example, if you got tails on the first flip of the coin, your prize is $2; if you got heads on the first flip and tails on the second flip, your prize is $2 \cdot \$2 = \$4$; if you got heads on the first two flips and then tails on the third flip, your prize is $\$2 \cdot \$2 \cdot \$2 = \$8$—and so on. It turns out that this game can be played indefinitely and there are an infinite number of possible outcomes. The probability of each outcome is equal to 1 divided by 2^n. That is, the probability of getting tails on the first flip is $1/2$; the probability of getting heads on the first flip and then tails on the second flip is $(1/2) \cdot (1/2) = 1/4$; the probability of getting heads on the first two flips and then tails on the third flip is $(1/2) \cdot (1/2) \cdot (1/2) = 1/8$—and so on. Note that each flip is independent, so we can compute the probabilities in this fashion. What is the expected monetary value of the game? To get the monetary value of the game, we can just multiply the probabilities by each outcome and sum them up; that is, the expected monetary value equals $(1/2) \cdot \$2 + (1/4) \cdot \$4 + (1/8) \cdot \$8 + \ldots = \$1 + \$1 + \$1 + \ldots = \$$ infinity. Thus it turns out that the monetary value of the game, since it has an infinite number of possible outcomes, is equal to an infinite amount of money.

But would you pay an infinite amount of money to play this game? Most agree with Bernoulli that the game is not worth that amount of money and that the expected utility of the game is not equivalent to the expected monetary value. Therefore, because people generally do not make choices that maximize their expected monetary values, we use expected utility to represent individuals' satisfaction from uncertain outcomes rather than the expected monetary value from those outcomes. Moreover, in politics, when voters like Ventura are evaluating candidates in an election, their preferences are usually not easily quantified in terms of some monetary value, as in a lottery. Utility is a more general idea and can represent the satisfaction Ventura gets from the election of a candidate when the satisfaction is not necessarily monetary but is more reflective of the policy choices that the candidate can help influence if elected, policy choices like allowing or limiting the rights of gays to marry, for example.

The Expected Utility of Voting Expected utility is useful in calculating Ventura's *investment* benefits from voting. That is, when Ventura decides whether or not to vote, he is choosing between the election contest between Penny and Dahn if he doesn't vote and the election contest between Penny and Dahn if he does vote. Ventura's investment benefits from voting are the difference in his expected utility from the two possible contests (the contest between Penny and Dahn if he votes and the contest between Penny and Dahn if he doesn't vote). The appendix to this chapter shows how Ventura's expected-utility investment benefits of voting can be given as $\Delta P \cdot B$, where ΔP is the effect of Ventura's vote on Penny's election and B is the difference in Ventura's utility between the election of Penny and the election of Dahn, or $(U_P - U_D)$.

What is Ventura's cost of voting? As we noted earlier, his other option was to go to the Minnesota Twins game with the children from St. Joseph's Home, for which he would receive the utility equal to U_T, which is generally labeled as c for the cost of voting. Ventura should vote if the following is true:

$$\Delta P \cdot B > c \qquad\qquad \text{(Equation 1)}$$

The Probability of Being Decisive What can we say about the size of ΔP? In particular, what is the effect of Ventura's voting on the probability that Penny will win? Ventura's vote can change the probability that Penny will win in two cases: (1) when the election is a tie without Ventura's vote and his vote decides the outcome for Penny and (2) when the election is a one-vote win by Penny's opponent without Ventura's vote and his vote makes the election a tie. If Penny's opponent is winning by two votes or more without Ventura's vote or if Penny is winning by one vote or more, Ventura's vote does not matter and has no effect on the outcome. So unless the election is a tie or Penny's opponent is winning by one vote without Ventura's vote, $\Delta P \cdot B = 0$, regardless of the size of B.

Needless to say, many American elections are far from being decided by one vote, so in most elections $\Delta P \cdot B = 0$ and for any cost of voting, albeit very small, a rational voter should not vote. Even in 2004, when polls could not predict the outcome, the likelihood of a voter's vote affecting the outcome of the election was close to zero in nonbattleground states like New York (expected to go to Kerry easily) and Texas (expected to go to Bush easily), given that voters could make a difference only if they could change the outcome in the state in which they resided (because of the use of the electoral college to select presidents, as we will discuss in chapter 13). Participating in the presidential election was not rational for voters.

California secretary of state Bill Jones draws the following analogy to explain why it isn't rational to vote in an election that isn't close: "Would you buy a ticket to a World Series game if you knew who was going to win?"[11] Note that even though the 2000 presidential election was amazingly close nationally, because the relevant determinant of the winner was the electoral college's vote rather than the popular vote and Gore won Affleck's home state of New York with a large margin, winning New York's electoral votes whether Affleck voted or not, Affleck's vote was unlikely to have made a difference any more than Ventura's would have in the Minnesota primary.

Yet millions of Americans, unlike Strom, Affleck, and Ventura, do vote even when doing so is quite costly. In 2004, turnout was at record levels in Alabama and Georgia, states where it was predicted Bush would win easily. In 2002, the *Baltimore Sun* reported on Fannie Jeffrey, a voter who participated in that year's election when it would have been much easier to stay home:

> Despite a recently broken arm and an ensuing fall, despite knee surgery that makes standing in line to vote nearly impossible, despite aches and pains that might keep others in their retirement home on a chilly November morning, Jeffrey, 92, zipped herself into her winter coat and cast her ballot in person yesterday, continuing seven straight decades of going to the polls. "You want to keep it up, the voting—it's good to go and be a visible part of the community," says Jeffrey, a spirited former social worker whose discerning gaze still penetrates even behind fishbowl glasses. "As long as I can walk, I'll continue to vote."[12]

Turnout is amazingly high given the fact that so few elections are close. Why, when it is clearly not rational? Why is Jeffrey willing to vote even though it isn't rational? Why is she not like Ventura, Affleck, or Strom? This paradox is generally called the "paradox of not voting."[13]

Consumption versus Investment

We will begin our attempts to resolve our three puzzles with the last—the paradox of not voting, or why Fannie Jeffrey votes. Much ink has been used to try to explain why people vote.[14] One way to think of the paradox is that it emphasizes the investment benefits of voting (benefits that will accrue after the election) and ignores the consumption benefits of voting (present benefits from the act itself).[15] That is, voters may derive some benefits from the act of voting independent of the effect that the vote can possibly have on the outcome of the election. Voters may feel satisfaction or utility from fulfilling their "citizen duty" and participating in the democratic process. Fannie Jeffrey clearly sees voting as her responsibility; she needs to be "a visible part of the community."

To see how introducing the consumption benefits of voting changes our voting equation, define D as the consumption benefits that Jeffrey receives from the act of voting itself. Then it is possible that

$$\Delta P \cdot B + D > c \qquad \text{(Equation 2)}$$

Although appealing as an explanation for voting and fitting in well with stories such as Jeffrey's, this is not a very satisfactory solution to the paradox, as it is what researchers call *ad hoc*—it is like saying that the sun is in the sky because the sun is in the sky, or people vote because they like to vote. Saying that individuals vote because they like to doesn't help us much when we want to try to understand the forces that lead to more or less turnout over time (as in the puzzle of participation) or why giving the right to vote to a group of voters who do turn out does not always translate into a change in policy outcomes (like the forty-five-year lag). It may be a "theory" of why people vote, but it isn't a useful theory unless we have some understanding of what gives voters a "taste" for voting. Ideally, we would like to know why Jeffrey has such a strong "taste" for voting that it has gotten her to the polls for seventy years despite many difficulties, whereas Strom isn't even interested in elections and Affleck and Ventura sometimes vote and sometimes don't.

Togetherness: The Group Investment Benefits of Voting

Staying Home: Its Effect on Other Voters' Incentives

Ventura could safely stay away from the polls on primary day because he anticipated that many other Penny supporters would turn out; similarly, Affleck's bureaucratic snafu did not affect the outcome in New York in the 2000 election because many others did vote for his preferred candidates. Although they appeared to care more about the outcome of the election than Strom (because both were publicly campaigning for their candidates and engaging in other support besides voting), they could basically "free-ride" on the choices of other voters who they knew would turn out and vote as they wanted (we will see shortly how the temptation of free riding works).

If the "other" voters in Minnesota or New York had made the same calculation as Ventura or Affleck, however, then no one would have voted and a single voter could have affected the outcome. Thus, the investment benefits ($\Delta P \cdot B$) become huge as Ventura's and Affleck's individual votes can be decisive! There is a simulataneous relationship between individual voting decisions and the closeness of an election.[16] This simultaneity can mean that some rational voters who calculate the complex relationship between their decision to vote and others' decisions will vote for investment purposes (that is, rational turnout is not zero when the endogeneity is taken into account).

Nevertheless, at the individual level it is hard to imagine that voters consider the endogenous nature of their investment benefits—that their own choices and the choices of others influence these benefits—in making turnout calculations, because even when they recognize this endogeneity, the difference between the investment benefits and the costs is small. Yet for a group of like-minded voters, the calculation that the group can influence the outcome of the election and that other groups can similarly behave strategically is not difficult. Evidently, Ventura and Affleck knew that they were members of groups of like-minded voters and expected those groups would make such a calculation and largely vote. In fact, in their campaigning they attempted to sway groups of voters to choose as they would.

Mobilizing Groups of Voters

In Chicago The possibility that groups of like-minded voters can affect electoral outcomes is recognized by most political actors. In 1983, Harold Washington did the unthinkable—he became the first African American mayor of Chicago. He accomplished this feat by first winning the Democratic primary in a three-candidate race—against two white Irish candidates (from the machine that had ruled Chicago for over half a century). His success was extraordinary because no one, particularly his supporters, believed a black candidate could win in a majority white city like Chicago and one that had for so long been dominated by a cohesive political machine. As Grimshaw (1992, p. 170) related, there was a "widely held view" among both whites and blacks that Washington was unelectable. This meant that he had to persuade his supporters that they should turn out and that a vote for him would actually make a difference in the outcome.

Despite these obstacles, Washington entered the race anyway and worked hard to build support. Yet black voters continued to doubt his electability. They knew that both white candidates had a sizable backing, and they did not believe that Washington's faction would be large enough to make the race close. How could Washington convince these black voters (whom he needed) that he had a chance of winning and that their votes could make a difference? As Grimshaw reported, Washington held a large rally at a twelve-hundred-seat pavilion. If attendance had been low, Washington would have failed, but if attendance was high, the sight of the crowd would have helped convey the message that he did have the backing to make it worthwhile for his supporters to turn out. The make-or-break rally worked, as the pavilion was filled beyond its capacity. On election day, Washington turned out black voters in record numbers. He turned out black voters who had migrated from the South before the Supreme Court's 1966 ruling that outlawed state poll taxes (*Harper v. Virginia Board of Elections*). Individuals turned out who had probably never voted in their lives ("phone calls came in on election day inquiring about the amount of Chicago's poll tax," Grimshaw reported [p. 171]). They voted because after they had become convinced that

Washington had a chance, they expected that their vote as a group could make a difference.

In Georgia In the 1998 Georgia gubernatorial election, Roy E. Barnes also acknowledged the importance of black turnout and made considerable efforts to mobilize African American voters. The Georgia Democratic Party made three telephone calls and sent two mailings to thousands of black homes. Barnes went to four black churches the Sunday before the election, accompanied by black political leaders. Black support for Barnes was strong, and he won the election by 9 percent, with 90 percent of the black vote. Although only 27 percent of the state's registered voters were black, 29 percent of the voters in that election were black, as compared with 16 percent in 1994 and 25 percent in 1996.[17]

In 2002, however, when Barnes was up for reelection, Republicans turned the tide by turning out their own groups of supporters in record numbers, including white rural conservative fundamentalist Christian voters who were unhappy with Barnes but not generally politically involved. One Republican campaign manager described this group of voters as "people who typically don't turn out." Republican campaigners "recruited organizers and volunteers at Rotary Clubs and churches all over the state." The campaign manager argued that it was the "personal touch of 'neighbors calling neighbors' that made the difference." In contrast, Barnes was not able to get out the vote of the blacks he had mobilized in 1998, as they had been alienated by some of the choices he had made in office and by his lack of support for African American candidates. Barnes was defeated by Sonny Perdue, who became the first Republican governor in the state in 130 years by mobilizing new groups of voters who preferred him to Barnes.[18]

Across the Nation But blacks and rural white fundamentalist Christian voters in the South or elsewhere are not the only groups of voters who are especially targeted by appeals to vote as a group. In 1998, the AFL-CIO and other unions financed advertisements on Latino-oriented radio stations in New York and other large cities, sending out the message to turn out on election day. The efforts of the union to mobilize its members were partly modeled on efforts they had made in the 1997 New Jersey gubernatorial race. *The New York Times* reported that in New Jersey in 1997 the state's AFL-CIO "registered more than 10,000 union members." The union's president had stated: "We're getting on the phone, we're getting commitments and we're holding our members accountable."[19] In the 2000 presidential election, Michigan labor leaders worked hard to encourage members to vote. In Lansing, the Service Employees International Union (SEIU) called fifteen hundred union members an hour. In Flint, "Jessie Cloman, a city housing inspector, was setting up a 'mentoring' program in which 190 shop stewards have each been assigned 100 union members who have voted only once in the last six years."[20] Similarly, in Minnesota the union get-out-the-vote effort meant that union members cast 30 percent of the votes in 2000 although they represented only 17.7 percent of eligible voters.

For the 2004 presidential race, Steve Rosenthal, former political director of the AFL-CIO, formed a political action committee called America Coming Together (ACT). He used tactics that resulted in a rise in the percentage of voters labeling themselves members of labor households, from 19 percent to 26 percent from 1992 to 2002 (whereas unions represent only 13 percent of the workforce). *BusinessWeek*, in March 2004, reported on their efforts:

> ACT is hiring several thousand foot soldiers in 17 swing states, including Florida and Ohio. Guided by seasoned campaign officials and armed with handheld organizers loaded with voter lists of households likely to lean Democratic, the canvassers have started knocking on doors. They offer to register anyone who's not already signed up. . . . They also try to engage voters on key Democratic issues like jobs, health coverage, and education. Canvassers then build a profile of each person willing to listen, entering their positions and other information onto the handhelds to construct a database. Over the next eight months, ACT . . . plan[s] to contact each receptive voter 5 to 10 times.[21]

Other interest groups are involved in election mobilization efforts as well. For example, in the 2002 Senate race in Minnesota, interest groups like the U.S. Chamber of Commerce, the National Rifle Association, and advocates of both right to life and free choice had get-out-the-vote campaigns aimed at their members and supporters.[22]

Plainly at the group level, strategic concerns reflecting the investment benefits of voting matter in determining turnout levels. Black voters in Georgia turned out for Barnes in 1998, when they thought he was more likely than his opponent to make choices they preferred, and did not turn out in 2002, when they felt he had not been significantly effective in pursuing their interests. Turnout decisions—"getting out the vote"—are influenced by political elites like party leaders, candidates, union heads, and interest group leaders who recognize these strategic interests and go to particular groups of voters using group-based strategies to persuade them to go to the polls as a group. The implication is that somehow these group leaders induce their members to vote (and sometimes don't) in order to influence the outcome of the election strategically as a group. Whereas Fannie Jeffrey's devotion to voting is clear, it is also clear that she, too, was part of an organized effort to get out the vote—she rode in a bus to the polling place from her home in the Collington retirement community in Prince George's County, Maryland, with fifty other residents of the community. How do group leaders motivate voters like Fannie Jeffrey to be so devoted to voting?

Consumption and Citizen Duty Redux

Group Investment Benefits and the Collective-Action Problem

Getting voters to act as a group raises a further reason why voters may choose not to vote (which we alluded to earlier)-the "collective-action" or "free-rider" problem. That is, the group would benefit if as a collective it acted together; however, each individual in the group has an incentive to "defect," or "free-ride," and rely on the actions of others in the group, a phenomenon that can result in the group's failing to take the action desired. Affleck and Ventura could safely stay away from the polls because they knew that others who had similar preferences would vote.

Some Louisiana Voters To see how voting can be a problem of collective action, consider the following simple example with two voters in the 2002 Louisiana Senate runoff election discussed in chapter 1. We will consider a situation in which two voters acting together, Karen and Bruno, can change the outcome of the election to their benefit. We'll assume that their preferred candidate, Mary Landrieu, is expected to lose by one vote to her opponent, Suzanne Haik Terrell, if neither Karen nor Bruno votes. If both voters vote, however, then Landrieu wins for sure. If only one votes, then Landrieu is in a tie with Terrell (both have a 50 percent chance of winning).

Karen and Bruno prefer Landrieu to Terrell because the benefits they expect to get from Landrieu's election are greater than the ones they expect to get from Terrell's. We use utility to represent their preferences. Assume that if Landrieu wins, both Karen and Bruno receive 100 units of utility, and if Terrell wins, both receive 25 units of utility. The utility difference between what they get if their preferred candidate wins minus what they get if the other candidate wins then would be $100 - 25 = 75$, the B term in equation 1. If the election is a tie, then we need to calculate Karen and Bruno's expected utility. In that case, the probability of Landrieu's winning is 0.5 and the probability of Terrell's winning is also 0.5. Karen and Bruno's expected utility when the election is a tie is then equal to $(0.5) \cdot 100 + (0.5) \cdot 25 = 62.5$ utils (units of utility). That is, they expect to get 100 utils 50 percent of the time and 25 utils 50 percent of the time, which taken together gives them an expected utility of 62.5 utils. But if Karen or Bruno votes, he or she must each pay 50 utils, the cost of voting, c. Table 2.1 presents the utility payoffs received by Karen and Bruno for each of the four possible combinations of choices they could make. The first number in each cell is how much Karen will receive given her and Bruno's choices, and the second number is how much Bruno will receive given his and Karen's choices.

If both Karen and Bruno vote, then Landrieu wins for sure, and both will receive $100 - 50 = 50$ utils. If both do not vote, Terrell will win for sure, and each will receive $25 - 0 = 25$ utils. But if only one votes, then only one

Table 2.1
Payoff Matrix for Karen and Bruno

	Bruno's Choices	
Karen's Choices	Bruno votes for Landrieu.	Bruno does not vote.
Karen votes for Landrieu.	50, 50	12.5, 62.5
Karen does not vote.	62.5, 12.5	25, 25

must pay the cost of voting and they receive different units of utility. For example, if Karen votes and Bruno does not, the election is a tie, and Karen receives 62.5 – 50 = 12.5 utils, and Bruno receives 62.5 – 0 = 62.5. If Bruno votes and Karen does not, the election is also a tie, and Bruno receives 62.5 – 50 = 12.5 utils, and Karen receives 62.5 – 0 = 62.5 utils.

Nash Equilibrium and Voting What will Karen and Bruno do? They are in a strategic situation, a "game," and to figure out what they will do, we need to find what is called the Nash equilibrium of the game, a concept originated by Nobel Prize–winning mathematician John Nash.[23] A Nash equilibrium exists when each actor in a game is making the best choice given what the others in the game are doing. In order to find the Nash equilibrium (or equilibria, as sometimes there is more than one), we need to consider what the optimal responses are for Karen and Bruno, given what the other is doing.

First we will consider Karen. Suppose that she knows for sure that Bruno will vote. Clearly, then, Karen would prefer not to vote, since 62.5 utils is greater than 50 utils. So if Bruno is voting, Karen's optimal response is not to vote. Suppose that Karen knows for sure that Bruno is not voting. Now her comparison is between 25 and 12.5, and since 25 is greater, she should not vote. Therefore, regardless of what Bruno is doing, Karen should not vote. Similarly, if Bruno knows for sure that Karen is voting, he should not vote, and if he knows for sure that Karen is not voting, he should not vote. Therefore, regardless of what Karen is doing, in this game Bruno's optimal choice is also not to vote. The only equilibrium (where both are choosing optimally) is when neither votes, Terrell wins, and each receive 25 utils. Both Karen and Bruno would be better off if they both voted—each would receive 50 utils as compared with 25—yet the incentive to free-ride, or defect, when the other voted leads both to the equilibrium, where neither votes and each gets 25.

Karen and Bruno, then, will have difficulty acting collectively to elect Landrieu even though they both prefer to do so and both would benefit. Thus, although it is true that as a group the two voters can affect the outcome, leading to more utility for both, each has an incentive to free-ride even though that could lead to their least preferred outcome. For us to think about turnout as a group choice, we have to understand how groups are able to overcome these problems of collective action. How are groups able to motivate voters like Fannie Jeffrey to ignore the advantage of free riding?

Voting and Private Selective Incentives

Pastries and Raffles Although voters like Fannie Jeffrey have to take a bus and stand in line at the polls, sometimes voting comes to individuals, or at least is sweetened, with a payoff. In Wisconsin, the governor's race in 2002 was the most expensive in its history. Part of the money spent by the Democratic Party on behalf of their candidate, Jim Doyle, was used to pay for soda, kringle pastry, and quarters for use in a bingo game at the Dayton Residential Care Facility in Kenosha. After the game, the Democratic activists told residents they could vote upstairs by absentee ballot (unlike Jeffrey and other voters at the Collington retirement community, who had to take a bus on election day).[24] Whereas the Kenosha voters got bingo and snacks, members of Culinary Local 226 in Las Vegas in August 2000 were invited to a rally at two early-voting sites (we discuss in the next chapter how some states allow individuals to vote prior to election day at special locations), where they could vote for the union's preferred candidate and maybe win big bucks—union leaders noted that in 1998 they had spent a greater amount on hot dogs and sodas but were hoping this year's raffle prize of $3,000 might attract more voters.[25]

The Democrats at the Kenosha nursing home and the union leaders in Las Vegas used consumption benefits tied to the act of voting to induce their members to vote and conquer the problem of collective action. In the nineteenth century, and particularly before the advent of the secret ballot, many state and local political parties (often run as political machines) gave out consumption benefits to individuals in return for their votes (consumption benefits that came close to, and may have crossed the line separating them from, bribes). In 1905, George Washington Plunkitt of Tammany Hall (the old Democratic political machine in New York City) described how machine politics got out the vote by providing individualized benefits to their supporters (Riordon 1994, p. 64):

> If there's a family in my district in want I know it before the charitable societies do, and me and my men are first on the ground. . . . The consequence is that the poor look up to George W. Plunkitt as a father, come to him in trouble—and don't forget him on election day. Another thing, I can always get a job for a deservin' man. I make it a point to keep on the track of jobs, and it seldom happens that I don't have a few up my sleeve ready for use.

How do private selective incentives work to overcome the free-rider problem? Consider again the situation facing Karen and Bruno. Suppose they have a group leader like Plunkitt who gives them a chicken worth 25 utils if they vote. Their new payoffs from voting and not voting are given in table 2.2. If both Karen and Bruno vote for Landrieu, each gets $100 - 50 + 25 = 75$. That is, Landrieu wins, and they each get 100 utils, they pay 50 utils for voting, and they get 25 utils from the chicken Plunkitt gives each of them. If only one votes—say, Karen—then she gets 62.5 from the tie election minus the 50 utils from voting plus the 25 utils from Plunkitt's chicken, to equal 37.5 utils, and Bruno, who did not vote, receives 62.5 utils. If both do not vote, they again receive 25 utils.

TABLE 2.2
Payoff Matrix for Karen and Bruno with Private Selective Incentives

Karen's Choices	Bruno's Choices	
	Bruno votes for Landrieu.	Bruno does not vote.
Karen votes for Landrieu.	75, 75	37.5, 62.5
Karen does not vote.	62.5, 37.5	25, 25

Now the Nash equilibrium is for both to vote. To see this, consider Karen's optimal strategy if she knows for sure that Bruno is voting. If she votes, she gets 75 utils; if she doesn't, she gets 62.5 utils—so she should vote. What about her strategy if she knows for sure that Bruno is not voting? If she votes, she gets 37.5 utils; if she doesn't, she gets 25. Again, she should vote. Regardless of what Bruno is doing, Karen should vote. Similarly, if Bruno knows that Karen is voting, he should vote, and if Bruno knows for sure that Karen is not voting, he should vote, so Bruno should vote regardless of what Karen does. The only Nash equilibrium is for both Bruno and Karen to vote.

Bribery Kentucky Republican state representative Barbara Colter was cautious in her answers to the press about the May 2002 primary election that she lost. "It's very dangerous what we're talking about . . . and I've got children," she said. "Everybody was afraid. They had thugs running their campaigns."[26] What scared Colter were not only the individuals offering to buy votes for her, haul voters to the polls for her election, and include her name on a "ticket" of candidates who would get purchased votes but also the shooting incidents involving four people in the county clerk's race. Although buying votes with a case of liquor had a long history in the eastern part of the state, voters allegedly were giving away their votes in 2002 for a new currency, "a handful of OxyContin," a powerful painkiller, and drug dealers, not afraid of violence, were believed to be involved in vote buying. Whereas Plunkitt's chicken, the bingo game in Kenosha, and the lottery in Las Vegas may seem innocuous, vote "purchasing" using private selective incentive is a form of bribery and at its worse can mean that the election itself has been "purchased." Purchasing and selling votes directly with cash is illegal in all fifty states, although enforcement and penalties differ across the states.

Drawing the line between what is an illegal purchase of a vote and what is not is sometimes difficult. Both the Kenosha and the Las Vegas affairs were publicly criticized by opposition candidates as "vote buying," and in Wisconsin the Republican incumbent governor used the Kenosha event in his campaign ads to discredit his opponent as "crooked." In Kentucky, individuals have been indicted for vote buying in recent elections. In Kenosha, however, a special prosecutor declined to file charges, largely because there was no proof that "vote buying" had actually occurred. In Las Vegas, the district attorney said that the event "goes up to the line but doesn't cross the line." In Kenosha and in Las Vegas, although the events were clearly tied to the election and to voting (by absentee ballot in Kenosha and at early-voting locations in Las Vegas), an individual was not required to vote in order to receive the prize in the lottery or the kringles at the bingo game. According to the owner of the Dayton Residential Care Facility, only two individuals at the bingo game actually voted, and both denied "being induced by the bingo or any person in casting their votes."[27]

Because outright vote buying of the sort State Representative Colter was offered is illegal, most groups who provide private selective incentives do not require that the individuals vote in order to receive them. Moreover, with the widespread use of secret ballots, even just knowing that an individual votes does not ensure that he or she made the choice that the vote buying purchased. For example, in 1961, when Henry B. Gonzalez took on the white establishment in San Antonio to run for Congress, his Republican opponent, John Goode, visited the Chicano precincts where Gonzalez had strong support, providing ten kegs of beer and twenty-four hundred tamales. Yet he received only sixteen votes. Gonzalez noted: "They drink Goode's beer, they eat Goode's tamales, then go to the polls and vote for Gonzalez" (quoted in Rosales 2000, p. 72). Furthermore, private selective incentives cannot explain why Fannie Jeffrey voted, as she did not get to play bingo or receive kringle pastries or a lottery ticket. To understand Jeffrey and group mobilization today, we need to examine other selective incentives that groups can use.

Voting and Social Selective Incentives

The incentives for turning out that voters receive today are primarily social *and* related to their membership within groups that are recruiting them. Jeffrey went to the polls with her fellow residents as a group of fifty. It was a social activity, a day's event for the residents. The Kenosha and Las Vegas events were also not just about the treats and the lottery but about the chance to socialize as well. Furthermore, although the group leaders cannot observe how the individuals vote, they and other members of the group can observe who votes and who does not, and because of shared preferences, they can assume that the votes are in accord with what the group prefers. When interviewed about how she was voting, Fannie Jeffrey refused to reveal her choices. "It's my business!" she told the reporter. But many of the other bus riders said they had voted for Kathleen Kennedy Townsend, the Democratic candidate for governor (Robert F. Kennedy's daughter), and nodded their heads when Jeffrey did reveal that she had voted in the past for "all the Kennedys."

To see how social selective incentives for voting might work, suppose that Karen and Bruno care about whether they choose the same thing (that is, they socialize). Suppose that if *both* Karen and Bruno vote or they *both* do not vote, they get an additional amount of utility, 25 utils, from participating in a group activity. This is different from the utility they would get from the chicken from Plunkitt—it is utility that they get from acting together as a group in a social situation. If they choose differently, if either Karen votes and Bruno doesn't or Bruno votes and Karen doesn't, then neither gets added utility because they are not participating in a group activity. The new payoff matrix for the same pattern of voting with social selective incentives is given in table 2.3.

TABLE 2.3
Payoff Matrix for Karen and Bruno with Social Selective Incentives

Karen's Choices	Bruno's Choices	
	Bruno votes for Landrieu.	Bruno does not vote.
Karen votes for Landrieu.	75, 75	12.5, 62.5
Karen does not vote.	62.5, 12.5	50, 50

Notice how the payoff matrix differs from that in tables 2.1 and 2.2. If both vote, as in table 2.2, each gets 75 utils (100 from Landrieu's winning minus 50 for the cost of voting plus 25 for acting together). If one votes—say, Karen—and the other doesn't—say, Bruno—then Karen gets 12.5 utils (62.5 for the tie election minus 50 for the cost of voting), and Bruno gets 62.5. If neither votes, each gets 50 utils (25 from Terrell's winning plus 25 for acting as a group).

Now there are two possible Nash equilibria in the situation facing Karen and Bruno. Why? First, consider Karen's optimal strategy if Bruno is voting. In that case, she should vote, as 75 is greater than 62.5. But what should she do if she knows Bruno is not voting? Then she should not vote, as 50 is greater than 12.5. Similarly, Bruno should vote if Karen is voting and not vote if Karen is not voting. The game facing Bruno and Karen is a coordination game; they wish to coordinate on the same choice, either voting or not voting. The added utility from coordinating now makes voting as a group a rational decision but does not make it the only possibility. Voting as a group will be the outcome for Karen and Bruno if they coordinate on voting as a social activity. If they coordinate on not voting as a social activity, then participation for their group will be low.[28] The problem confronting group leaders, then, is to coordinate the group of voters on the voting equilibrium instead of on the nonvoting equilibrium.

Incentives and Voting Today

Family and Friends Not all twenty-four-year-olds in the twenty-first century have the same attitude toward voting as Amanda Strom of St. Louis, who chose not to vote because she did not believe it would make a difference. Nora Galowitch of Allentown, Pennsylvania, "eager to cast her very first ballot, barely beat the rush hour traffic" in order to vote on election day in November 2002. Galowitch, also twenty-four, had registered to vote in June 2002 "at the urging of her cousin, who took a semester off from college to work with a campaign in the gubernatorial race. Who did she vote for? 'It was Rendell [the Democratic gubernatorial candidate]. No doubt,' Galowitch said. 'My cousin would have kicked my butt if I didn't.' "[29] Galowitch's experience is not unusual. Harvey (1998, p. 37) reported that in "a nationwide 1983 ABC-Harvard survey, 37 percent of respondents and 41 percent of regular voters cited as a reason for voting the statement 'My friends and relatives almost always vote and I'd feel uncomfortable telling them I hadn't voted.' " Knack (1992, p. 139) reported that 42 percent of respondents in a 1990 survey answered yes to the question, "Do you have any friends, neighbors, or relatives who would be disappointed or angry with you if they knew you had not voted in this year's elections?" and those who answered yes were significantly more likely to vote than those who answered no. Of new voters in 2004, 61 percent reported that the reason they voted was because "my family or friends encouraged me to vote," according to a postelection poll conducted by the Shorenstein Center on the Press,

Politics, and Public Policy at the John F. Kennedy School of Government, Harvard University. As with Fannie Jeffrey, for many, voting is a social event.

At the individual level, voters often choose to vote based on individualized consumption benefits—benefits that are particularistic to the individual and today largely social (albeit sometimes sugared with private incentives, like pastries or lotteries). At the individual level, voters are not *directly* motivated necessarily by the investment benefits of their actions, but they may be motivated by the satisfaction they derive from participating in a group goal that is *indirectly* related to the investment benefits. Political leaders of groups of like-minded citizens, such as those in a particular ethnic group or in union or in some other interest group, recognize that for the group the level of turnout can affect the outcome of the election. They recognize that voting can be an equilibrium when it is a social activity. Group leaders then "mobilize" voters to participate by providing the selective, particularistic incentives to motivate their participation. When the investment benefits are high for the group, group leaders mobilize greater numbers of voters.

Purposive Benefits Finally, to some extent, group leaders use what interest group scholars have called purposive benefits, which are selective incentives that emphasize the investment benefits for the group in terms of group goals. Group leaders work to instill in voters the sense that additional utility comes from the group's achieving its goal, enough utility to overcome the incentive to free-ride. Purposive benefits, unlike social selective benefits, work like the private benefits provided by Plunkitt (the game facing two voters is similar to the situation illustrated by table 2.2), and the only equilibrium, if these purposive benefits work, is for both Karen and Bruno to vote. Leaders of the Las Vegas Culinary Workers Union not only used a lottery to motivate voters and a social gathering to give out the lottery, but they were also clear on how they expected their members to vote—against the incumbent—and why—because over union objections she had voted on the county commission to permit Wal-Mart to expand in the county.[30]

The Group Voting Equation In summary, groups use a combination of incentives, social and purposive, to mobilize voters. When voters are mobilized by a group, its leaders will choose a mobilization strategy that maximizes their expected utility. We can rewrite equation 1 in terms of the group leaders' mobilization decisions. That is, group leaders will mobilize voters as long as the following is true:

$$\Delta P_G \cdot B_G > c_G \qquad\qquad\qquad \text{(Equation 3)}$$

Where ΔP_G is the effect of mobilizing a group of voters on the election outcome, B_G is the difference in group benefits if the group's preferred candidate wins, and c_G is the cost to the group of mobilization. For the group, the effect of mobilizing on the election outcome can be large as the benefits can be, and in many cases the benefits can outweigh the group cost of mobilization. Notice that as the cost of voting for individuals increases, turnout decreases, because mobilization is more difficult. Similarly, if voters are mobilized by groups whose preferences are the same as theirs, equation 3 implies a positive relationship between turnout and both the investment benefits of voting and the probability that an election is close.

These predicted relationships among closeness, differences in candidates, the costs of voting, and the likelihood of turnout do at face value ring true: voters are more likely to participate when elections are expected to be close, candidates offer platforms that provide sharp differences, and the process of voting is easier. The high turnout in 2004 can be attributed to those factors—as noted above, Curtis Gans has argued that voting was high partly because of the deeply felt political divisions in the nation (that is, because of the utility differences that voters saw between the two candidates). Reviews of the debates between the candidates highlighted how often they clashed on the issues. As James O'Toole and Maeve Reston of the *Pittsburgh Post-Gazette* summarized the last debate: "The candidates disagreed on a broad array of issues, including the economy, gay marriage, abortion, health care, immigration and gun control."[31] The editors of *Newsday* opined: "These were important, interesting and possibly the most pivotal campaign debates in many years. The differences between President George W. Bush and Sen. John Kerry of Massachusetts couldn't have been more stark and substantial. In fact, the centerpiece of the debates was policy differences, not personality quirks."[32]

Voting Rationally and Turning Out Irrationally

Group Differences

If the group providing a voter with the selective incentive to vote is a group of like-minded voters, then by definition once the voter enters the voting booth, his or her preferences are the same as those of every other member of the group. If all the members of the Las Vegas Culinary Workers Union agree that the Wal-Mart expansion in their county is a bad thing and want to vote this preference, then voting as mobilized by their union means that that preference is translated into action at the voting booth even if an individual voter is really motivated mainly by the social gathering and the lottery. So theoretically, selective incentives can work positively to help a voter act on his or her preferences.

But what if the group providing a voter with the incentives is not so cohesive—what if the individual's investment-motivated choice between candidates is different from that of the group mobilizing him or her? We can think of two types of groups that can provide voters with selective incentives: office-seeking groups and benefit-seeking groups.[33] Generally, we think of office-seeking groups as political parties or groups of candidates that have been combined to maximize votes in order to get elected (in Kenosha, the Democratic Party organized the bingo game to mobilize voters) and benefit-seeking groups as interest groups, such as the Las Vegas Culinary Workers Union, civil rights groups, and women's groups such as NOW (National Organization for Women), which mobilize voters in order to seek certain policy outcomes.

Mobilization by Benefit-Seeking Groups

Ordinarily, benefit-seeking groups use their ability to provide voters for office-seeking groups so that the elected officials choose policy positions that please (or are perceived by the leaders to please) the members of the benefit-seeking group. In the 1998 elections in the South, where black votes made such a difference as in the Georgia gubernatorial race mentioned earlier, it was clear that African American leaders expected that their turnout would be rewarded. For example, in 1998, black South Carolina representative James E. Clyburn said of his newly elected governor, Jim Hodges: "He's a smart guy. . . . He knows where his margin of victory was, and I don't think there's going to be any problem getting our concerns addressed."[34] Benefit-seeking groups can also withhold votes from office seeking groups if they believe that the office-seeking groups is not following their preferences and that the cost of mobilization is not worth the return, as Roy Barnes discovered in Georgia in 2002, when he did not get the same support from black groups as he did in 1998 and ended up losing.[35]

Black voters in Georgia may have been dissatisfied with Barnes and may simply have withheld their support, but they did not take the option of forming a third party or supporting an independent candidate, as other benefit-seeking groups have done. By 1970 in Texas, Mexican Americans had achieved some success in electing representatives such as Henry Gonzalez. However, many saw themselves as largely ignored and segregated from politics by the major parties, and they chose to form a third party, La Raza Unida, and ran candidates for office, competing directly with the major parties. Their candidate for governor, Ramsey Muniz, gathered 214,118 votes (6 percent), which, although not a majority, nearly resulted in the Republican candidate's beating the Democratic favorite in an upset. La Raza succeeded in electing candidates to local offices in twenty-two Texas counties. Yet the party died out as its goals and its members became incorporated into the Democratic Party.[36]

Mobilization by Office-Seeking Groups

The examples above illustrate how benefit groups can mobilize voters either for office-seeking groups, receiving in return the benefits they want (as

Clyburn has done with black voters in South Carolina), or directly for their own candidates, inducing office-seeking groups to change their policies (as Mexican American activists did in Texas) in response to the new competition. If, by contrast, voters are mobilized by office-seeking groups that may not share all of their policy preferences, then they may not be making the same choices in the voting booth as they would if they were mobilized by benefit-seeking groups. Mexican American voters in Texas were mobilized by the major political parties before La Raza Unida. Author Robert Caro, in his noted biography of the early years of Lyndon Johnson, *The Path to Power*, tells how Johnson "sat in the city's [San Antonio] Plaza Hotel behind a table covered with five-dollar bills, peeling them off and handing them to Mexican-American men at a rate of five dollars a vote for each vote in their family" (p. 277).

Whereas Johnson's candidate at the time was a New Deal liberal, Maury Maverick, who worked to bring benefits to Mexican American voters,[37] Texas remained a largely segregated state, with Mexican Americans suffering significant discrimination for many years. Mexican American groups did begin to mobilize voters and elect candidates they preferred, as with Henry Gonzalez in 1961, and they took support away from white candidates who still used the old mobilization techniques. But it was not until the 1970s, when La Raza Unida formed and Mexican Americans challenged discriminatory electoral laws and conducted their own voter registration drives, that significant policy changes benefiting Mexican Americans began to occur within the state, a movement discussed more extensively in chapter 15.[38] If voters are not mobilized by groups seeking policy or benefit motivations, such as ending discriminatory practices in schools, but are mobilized instead to receive $5 bills given out by office seekers, then office-seeking groups have less reason to respond to them. The voters will base their choices on the consumption benefits since they have no electoral power to induce the office seekers to provide them with the collective benefits. Figure 2.3 illustrates these differences in mobilization and the mobilization process.

It is important to recognize that it isn't necessarily that the office-seeking groups are "evil" when they mobilize new groups of voters without providing group benefits. Office-seeking groups choose policy positions to respond to already mobilized benefit-seeking groups and through that process build a group of supporters. Changing policy would be costly to the office-seeking group. If new voters can be mobilized without changing overall policy, by providing the new voters with purely private consumption benefits unrelated to a collective investment benefit, then the office-seeking group can win new voters without losing the old voters.

During the nineteenth century and the era of political machines, some voters were mobilized solely by office-seeking groups that provided them with simple, tangible, private benefits that were often unrelated to a collective benefit for them as a group, as was the case with Mexican American voters mobilized by Johnson in the 1930s in Texas. In the Chicago machine

FIGURE 2.3
Voter Mobilization in U.S. Elections

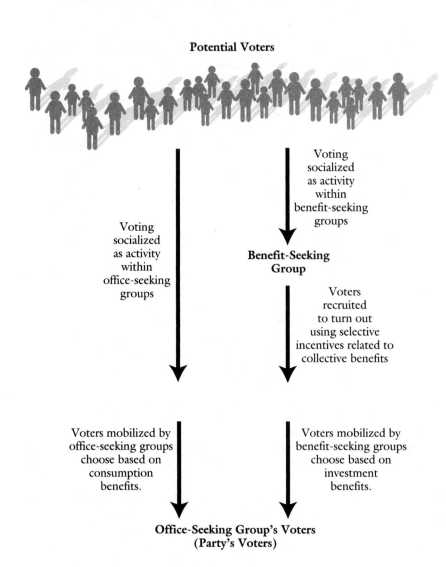

Potential Voters

Voting
socialized
as activity
within
office-seeking
groups

Voting
socialized
as activity
within
benefit-seeking
groups

**Benefit-Seeking
Group**

Voters
recruited
to turn out
using selective
incentives related to
collective benefits

Voters mobilized by
office-seeking groups
choose based on
consumption
benefits.

Voters mobilized by
benefit-seeking groups
choose based on
investment
benefits.

**Office-Seeking Group's Voters
(Party's Voters)**

era, experts argued that the machine could control a percentage of black votes in that fashion. Whitehead and Weisman (1974, p. 80) quoted former Chicago mayor Jane Byrne's campaign manager Don Rose: "The Organization owns a lock on a solid 20 percent of the black vote. This is the vote the machine would deliver for a George Wallace against Martin Luther King."[39] Unless a group of voters does have political leaders who perceive the collec-

tive benefits of the groups' voting power and use this to induce office seekers to note their voting strength, office seekers have less incentive to please
the group of voters in collective policy decisions. If only the office seekers
are mobilizing a group of voters, then collective benefits for the group are
not likely to be supplied.

What determines how voters are mobilized? How likely is it that voters
are mobilized by benefit-seeking groups versus office-seeking groups? To
address these questions further, we turn to our other puzzles, the forty-five-
year lag and the decline in political participation.

The Forty-Five-Year Lag Revisited

New Voters and Parties

We began this chapter with three puzzles. So far we have addressed only
one—puzzle 3, the paradox of not voting: we have developed an explanation for why voters may vote even when it appears that at the individual level
they are making an "irrational" decision. We can also now provide a possible
explanation for puzzle 1, the forty-five-year lag in women's groups' receiving policy benefits after such a promising start in the early 1920s. It lies in
the way women voters have been mobilized electorally over time. As Harvey
(1998, pp. 48–49) summarized: "Women's benefit-seeking organizations
first pursued and then dropped a strategy based on electoral mobilization;
women were then mobilized to vote as a group solely by the office-seeking
parties until the late 1960s, at which time women's benefit-seeking organizations once again sought to leverage women's votes into policy." Harvey
finds that as a consequence, policy concessions to women and party leadership roles for women also lagged.

Figure 2.4 illustrates the situation that some women's groups faced. We
can think of the graph as representing positions of the political parties and
women's groups. Along the horizontal axis, policy on the issues that divide
the two major parties is measured, with liberal positions on the left and conservative positions on the right. For example, the parties might be divided
over how much to spend on national defense or whether to lower or raise
tariffs on imported goods. (In later chapters, we discuss in more detail what
determines why some positions are liberal and some are conservative.) D
and R are the policy positions of the two major parties on these issues. The
vertical axis measures policy on the issues that divide women's groups and
the two major political parties. W is the average policy position of women's
groups. We assume that the women's groups are on average midway between the two major parties on the issues that divide the parties. If W mobi-
lizes the new women voters, then this group of voters will choose based on
the differences between women and the two major parties. The parties will
be forced to move closer to W in order to attract these voters. But if D and

R mobilize the new women voters, then this group of voters will divide along the issues that divide the major parties and make choices based on those differences, and there will be no pressure on the parties to choose policies favored by women's groups. Harvey argues that this is what happened when women were mobilized in the 1920s—they were mobilized by the major parties instead of by women's groups, and thus the parties had little incentive to move policy closer to the preferences of women's groups.

FIGURE 2.4
Positions of Women's Groups on Policy versus Positions of the Major Political Parties

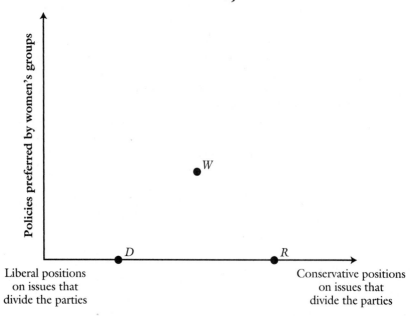

The Fixed Costs of Group Mobilization

Although the above analysis provides an answer to the puzzle of why policy choices of the political parties did not change much when women got the right to vote, it raises the question of why women's groups did not mobilize voters in the 1920s. The explanation lies in the difficulties involved. Although it seems clear that once a large group of voters is mobilized to vote their preferences, the group can then have an impact on policy, but the initial mobilization of a group of voters is not easy. It involves getting a large group of people to begin to choose irrationally at an individual level (engaging in a costly activity that has little personal benefit) to meet a group goal. This is the "fixed" cost for a group leader of beginning group-based activity.

For mobilization by a benefit-seeking group of like-minded voters to be worthwhile, it must generate a benefit level for the group that is sufficient to sustain the costs of the selective incentives provided to its members. For that to happen, the group has to be sizable enough, through the votes mobilized, to have an effect on electoral outcomes. That is, unless a group of voters can have an effect electorally, they cannot deliver any benefits by voting that can make selective social incentives profitable for the group. There is a minimum size of mobilized voters that is necessary for a group to have an electoral impact. Once a group reaches that size, however, the cost of mobilizing additional voters is small and decreases as the number of members increases. The reason the cost decreases is that the dynamic of mobilization works through the social networks established by the group—the more members, the more spread out the cost of the selective incentives in mobilizing those members.[40]

The situation facing a group mobilizing voters is like the problem facing a "public utility"—a company offering a service that has high fixed costs, such as an electric power plant, a cable television service, and so on. Most of the cost of generating electric power is in building the plant and providing the lines in the city or neighborhood by which customers can be connected to the plant. After the plant is built and the lines laid, the cost of adding customers is small in comparison. Similarly, mobilizing a new voter within an existing group of mobilized voters is cheap. Starting a new group of mobilized voters is expensive.

Harvey (1998) argued that the women's groups did try to mobilize voters after enfranchisement, but they were at a serious disadvantage when competing with already organized and developed office-seeking party organizations that also worked at mobilizing women voters. Although women's groups had established strong associations of their own during their drive to achieve suffrage, because of disenfranchisement these associations had not developed the procedures that would allow the group to express its preferences through the voting booth—procedures to select candidates, establish common agendas, and so on. Moreover, because of the efforts on behalf of suffrage, the office-seeking party organizations were aware of the benefits of mobilizing the new voters directly. Harvey notes that benefit-seeking groups often manage to mobilize voters prior to office-seeking groups because they have better information about the likely success of a mobilization effort (that is, they know whether it is possible to build a group large enough that the group benefits exceed the sum of the private costs). But in this case, women's groups did not have this advantage because office-seeking groups, having witnessed the drive for suffrage, were aware of the potential benefits of mobilizing women.

Once a group of voters is mobilized by one group, a competing group has to be able to provide a higher incentive to get that group of voters to make choices (turnout and voting decisions) for different motives. That is, if a group of voters, such as women, has been mobilized by an office-seeking group, like a party, to make choices that meet the party's interests, it is difficult to convince those voters to make choices that meet a benefit-seeking group's goals, which may be contrary to the wishes of the party. That is, it is difficult to socialize the voters to think of themselves as voting for different motives once they have established a social norm within the office-seeking group. And most important, it is more difficult than it would have been if the benefit-seeking group had acted before the office-seeking group. Because mobilization of women was carried out by office-seeking groups, it did not translate into policy benefits for women. Because the parties did not need to get the support of independent women's groups in order to get women's votes, the party did not need to provide women with policies in return for their votes.

The 1970s and Women

The Gender Gap and Mobilization In the 1970s, things began to change. In 1966, the National Organization for Women (NOW) was formed, and in 1968 its president, Betty Friedan, began to advocate an electoral strategy. In 1970, NOW and other women's groups began to form electoral coalitions. The consequence of the new mobilization by independent women's groups meant that the office-seeking groups needed to provide policies that advantaged the benefit-seeking groups. Policies that favored women began to see enactment again.

The parties began to realign themselves on women's issues from the 1970s on—that is, they began to move their policy positions. This change led to an oft-noticed "gender gap" in voting, in which women (particularly single women) are more likely to vote Democratic and white males are more likely to vote Republican. Abramson, Aldrich, and Rhode (2002, pp. 100–101) reported that in 1976 the male and female vote was split equally between the two presidential candidates, Jimmy Carter and Gerald Ford.

> But in every subsequent presidential election, women have been more likely to vote Democratic than men. The "gender gap" was 8 points in 1980, 6 points in 1984, 7 points in 1988, 4 points in 1992, and 11 points in 1996. According to the Voter News Service survey, 54 percent of female voters supported Gore, while 42 percent of the male voters did, a record gap of 12 percentage points.

In 2004, the gap narrowed somewhat, with 51 percent of women and 42 percent of men supporting Kerry.[41] Prior to the 1980s, however, gender differences in party support were not significant enough to notice. Then, as the Democratic Party began to support policies favored more by women's groups than by white males (for example, the equal rights amendment, equal pay, and affirmative action programs), voters responded to the change in the liberal-conservative dimension, and a gender gap between the parties developed.

Single Women and the Gender Gap Of course, there were other forces that facilitated the increased mobilization and may explain the change in how women vote. An alternative explanation of the changes is that women's preferences were not that different from men's when women were first given the right to vote, and so it did not matter how they were mobilized. Edlund and Pande (2002) argued that an increase in the number of women who are single and financially independent but in general poorer than men has resulted in an increase in the number of women who prefer left-leaning policies, which benefit those less financially well off. They point out that a similar situation has resulted in Europe—using survey data, they show that during the same period a gender gap emerged in Europe in which women are much more likely than men to vote for leftist parties. This suggests that the situation in which women's preferences differed from men's, as in figure 2.4, did not arise until recently. When Friedan began to recruit women as voters in a benefit-seeking group, their numbers were large enough that the parties (or at least the Democratic Party) responded by changing its policy positions. A poll by John Zogby taken before the 2004 election indicated that the division between single and married women in terms of party preferences would be larger in that election than the gender gap of previous elections has been, suggesting that single women have a greater preference for policies advocated by Democrats—abortion rights and greater financial and health security for lower-income workers—than married women. Zogby summarized: "That gap is enormous—married and single voters live not on different planets, but different solar systems, when it comes to their politics and values. Republicans have a problem with single voters, especially single women. The Democrats' problem is with married people, especially married women."[42] Zogby's predictions were borne out in the 2004 exit polls: 57 percent of single people voted for Kerry, and only 44 percent of married people voted for him. Kerry carried 62 percent of unmarried women but only 39 percent of married men.

Nevertheless, although the Democratic Party has been more friendly to these left-leaning women, both parties have supported more pro-women policies (in terms of restraints on sexual harassment, employment discrimination, and so on) since women have been mobilized by benefit-seeking groups than they did when they were mobilized by the parties directly. When left-leaning benefit-seeking women's groups began to mobilize women voters, similar efforts were made by conservative-leaning benefit-seeking women's groups as well, and social issues became more divisive for both parties.

We still have not answered all our questions (we may never) about the mobilization of women in American politics. One important question in particular remains: why did women's groups begin to mobilize in the 1970s? Although an increase in the number of single women is part of the answer, the increased mobilization by women's groups was reflective of a general trend of increasing mobilization by interest groups in that period. The answer is related to our third puzzle, the puzzle of declining participation.

The Final Puzzle—Why Did Turnout Decline in the 1970s?

The Decline of the Precinct Captain as Mr. Goodbar

In 1955, Richard J. Daley ran for mayor of Chicago in the Democratic primary. On the face of it, it seemed a tough time to try to become mayor of a major American city. After all, Daley's opponent was two-term incumbent Martin Kennelly. But Daley had an advantage. The Democratic machine had decided to drop Kennelly, and Daley was their man. The machine would get out the vote to elect him. *Chicago Tribune* columnist Mike Royko, in his popular book *Boss*, described the campaign (1971, pp. 89–91). Daley used party mobilization mechanisms (not much different from Plunkett's fifty years before) to become mayor and to remain in that position until his death in 1976. Yet during his years in office, campaigns changed throughout most of the country.[43] With the technological advances of the post–World War II period, candidates found themselves increasingly able to reach voters outside the political party and form their own independent organizations. Technological developments also changed the nature in which the selective social benefits of voting are conveyed. The process of mobilizing voters no longer revolved around the precinct captains cracking their whips. Royko described the old process in Chicago in 1955 (1971, p. 91): "The Skid Row winos, shaky with the bars being closed for election, came out and got their bottles of muscatel. The elderly were marched wheezing out of their nursing homes, the low-income whites were watched by the precinct captains as they left for work in the morning and reminded that they had to stop at the polling place."

In the late twentieth century, there were two major differences from the machine era in the way the mobilization of voters was conducted:

• Much mobilization occurred by telephone, targeted television and radio ads, and direct mail. Most important, it was candidate centered and, some suggest, issue centered. Although party-managed "get-out-the-vote" campaigns continued to use some face-to-face contact, more and more mobilization was concentrated on a candidate or an issue, *and* benefit-seeking groups played a larger role than before. Mobilization also became more capital intensive than labor intensive. Although undoubtedly much door-by-door canvassing continued, it was no longer the dominant way in which voters were reached and encouraged to turn out. Imai (2005) estimated that personal visits (the traditional method of campaigning) increases turnout by 9.2 percent on average, whereas telephone calls increase turnout 6.5 percent on average and mailings only 1.5 percent.[44]

- As voters' education levels increased and as voters became more prosperous, the appeal of the older selective incentives became less enticing than before, and the appeals of benefit-seeking groups, tied to collective benefits, became more attractive. Voters with higher levels of income require greater private incentives to participate, so recruitment using these methods is more costly. More educated voters can recognize the gains from acting as a collective and are more willing to do so for purposive benefits as well as social ones. Benefit-seeking groups can appeal to educated voters by pointing out the benefits of coordination as a group.

These changes in how voters are mobilized can help us understand why turnout declined in the United States after 1960. Rosenstone and Hansen (1993) estimated that approximately half of the decline can be explained by by the decrease in party mobilization and the change to interest group mobilization. Benefit-seeking groups have had larger roles in mobilization because they have been advantaged by the rise of candidate- and issue-centered campaigns and the technology that made them feasible, as well as by the existence of a more educated and less needy set of potential voters. These groups speak to voters on the issues that motivate them—they tie the selective benefits to the collective goal, providing purposive benefits, which these voters appreciate. Mobilization simply to please an office-centered party precinct captain in return for some current or future simple private favor has less import in a more technologically advanced, better-educated population. The social and selective incentives that motivate the political participation that interest groups such as women's organizations can offer to voters are more appealing in a more prosperous and better-informed electorate.

In general, however, this change has meant a decline in turnout. Rosenstone and Hansen (1993) noted that interest group mobilization has generally been focused on other types of political participation (writing letters to members of Congress, for example), a change, they suggest, that has led to a decline in turnout. Additionally, when voters switch from turning out for the motivations provided by office-seeking groups, which are less obviously tied to the individual's investment benefit from voting, to turning out for the motivations provided by benefit-seeking groups, which generally have explicit ties to an individual's investment benefit from voting, mobilization becomes partly a function of the contrast between the candidates or the parties in the election. We have argued that voters are mobilized to participate in elections through private, selective, and social incentives. Parties for many years worked successfully to provide such mobilization through private consumption benefits and social incentives as well. But as these consumption benefits have become replaced by more purposive benefits that are more directly tied to the collective benefits for voters by interest- or benefit-seeking groups, the paradox of not voting has become more difficult to overcome if voters see little difference between the parties or candidates. If a voter is not particularly interested in the collective benefit or believes that the group will act without him or her and she or he can "free-ride" on the votes of others, then the associated social or purposive incentive provided by a benefit-seeking group can be less valuable. Educated voters can figure out when they are being manipulated. In some cases, the advances in education and technology have provided favorable policies to groups that were not previously mobilized by benefit-seeking groups, like women, but in general fewer voters have been participating. The paradox of not voting to some extent explains the puzzle of declining participation.

The Advent of Television and the Decline of Turnout

Our explanation—that changes in mobilization can help explain the decline in turnout—links these changes with the technlogical advances of the period (particularly the rise of television). Gentzkow (2005) argued that the advent of television has had an informational effect on voters, which can also explain the decline in political participation. That is, television coverage of political matters and elections is more focused on presidential contests than on local and state races, whereas local and state newspapers cover both types of contests. If voters substitute television for reading newspapers, they receive less information about their choices in an election. Gentzkow contended that as voters become less informed about politics, they also become less likely to participate. The idea that an uninformed voter is best off *not* participating is simple to understand. Suppose that our voter Bruno in the Louisiana senatorial race does not know what the candidates' positions are or who would best serve his interests. He knows that there are other voters who do have that information and have similar preferences to his. If he votes randomly, he could possibly negate the votes of those who have information. Given that voting is costly, then he is better off abstaining. This idea has been labeled "the swing voter's curse" and has been formally explored in the work of Feddersen and Pesendorfer (1996, 1997, 1999).

Gentzkow compared participation levels in counties where television was introduced earlier with those counties that received television coverage later, controlling for differences in the counties that would also affect turnout. Gentzkow found that the effect could account for between a quarter and a half of the total decline in turnout since the 1950s. Supporting the informational story and the swing voter's curse argument, Gentzkow also found that the effect of television viewing was largest in midterm Congressional elections (when the president is not seeking reelection). In such races, newspaper coverage was extensive, but television coverage was almost nonexistent, so the advent of television has the strongest informational effect on voters.

Forcing a Square Peg into a Round Hole

Recall that the main point of the puzzle of participation is that because education and income are positively related to turnout in a single election and both have been rising since 1960, turnout should be increasing, even using the corrected data of McDonald and Popkin (2001; see figure 2.2), yet turnout declined in the 1960s and stayed relatively steady until 2004. One explanation of this puzzle is that the reasoning ignores the fact that a relationship between turnout and income or education in a single election is not the same as the relationship between turnout and income or education over time across elections. In cross-sectional studies in which education and income are positively related to turnout, we look only at the effect of a voter's relative income (the voter's income relative to the overall distribution of income across all voters) on whether he or she votes. But when income and education change over time, a voter's relative income and his or her absolute income (the voter's income in terms of purchasing power) vary.

Changes in relative and absolute income or education can have different effects on the costs and benefits of voting. An increase in absolute income or education (holding relative income or education constant) can increase the cost of voting, as voting is mainly an opportunity cost of time. As these variables increase, voters have greater opportunities with higher potential gains. Our earlier analysis also suggests that better-educated voters are less likely to be mobilized using private selective incentives. Thus, over time the effect of an increase in absolute income and education on turnout is an increase in the cost of voting (which is mainly time), which should reduce turnout.

On the other hand, relative income (a voter's position in the distribution of income) also affects the benefits of voting, but in a complicated fashion. That is, one of the aspects of government policy is redistributive—many government programs tax more wealthy individuals to provide services for poorer (or middle-class) individuals. For example, the government redistributes income when the estate tax is used or when there is a tax on high incomes to finance food stamps or welfare checks. If voters perceive that the two parties differ in the extent to which they engage in such redistribution, then a voter's investment benefits will depend on his or her position in the overall distribution of income.

That is, suppose one party prefers a lot of redistribution while the other party favors little or none. Voters at the extremes (either wealthy or poor) have more at stake in the election (wealthy voters stand to lose a lot if the redistributing party's candidates are elected, and poor voters stand to gain a lot) than voters in the middle, whose income is less likely to be affected by the election of one or the other party's candidates. As a result, those whose income is low or high relative to the overall distribution of income will have a greater investment benefit from voting than those whose income is largely unaffected by the redistribution. The implication is that as a voter moves up in terms of income distribution from very poor to wealthy, if we hold the cost of voting constant, the probability of voting decreases at first, as the voter's income approaches the middle of the distribution, but then it increases as the voter's position continues to increase and the voter becomes more wealthy than most of the rest of the population. Thus, there is a U-shaped relationship. Since education and income are closely related, we would expect education to have a similar effect.

Filer, Kenny, and Morton (1993) formalized this argument. They assumed that two candidates, labeled 1 and 2, each propose a redistribution platform based on the before-tax income of voters. The two candidates differ on the platforms—candidate 2 offers a redistributive platform that is more progressive than that of candidate 1 (a progressive tax schedule is one in which higher incomes are taxed at a higher rate) and provides more lump-sum transfers or benefits directly to voters. Thus, candidate 2 courts low-income voters and candidate 1 courts high-income voters. For a voter like, say, Karen, in our example above, the benefit in after-tax income will depend on which candidate is elected and how her income relates to the mean income in the distribution. Filer, Kenny, and Morton showed that the benefit to a voter like Karen from the election of her preferred candidate first increases as her before-tax income increases and then decreases to zero at a value of before-tax income, given in figure 2.5 by $\hat{y}$ which will be larger than the mean income, Y, but smaller and than the mean income plus the variance divided by the mean, given by y^* on the figure. The curve has its unusual shape because it is a rotated parabola—that is, in the figure, the benefits, measures on the vertical axis, are equal to the absolute value of the after-tax income difference. If the vertical axis instead measured the actual after-tax income difference, the curve would be a parabola with a minimum at $\bar{y}$.

If Karen's income is greater than $\hat{y}$, the benefit to her in after-tax income from the election of her preferred candidate increases again as her income increases. Karen then has the most at stake in the election if she has a low income or a high income relative to the mean income in the population. If her income is close to the mean, her after-tax income is not much affected by which candidate wins the election. Thus, Karen has a greater incentive to vote if her income is either high or low, relative to the mean income in the population, than she has if her income is around the mean.

The empirical studies of income or education and turnout have generally looked for a simple linear relationship between the two, and the positive relationship in the single-election studies may be the result of trying to force a U-shape into a single line. Moreover, it is empirically difficult to distinguish between the effect of a change in absolute real income on turnout (the cost effect) and the effect of a change in relative income on turnout (the benefit effect). When we look at the effect of income on voters' turnout choices over time, the two effects are mixed together. To really examine the relationships between these variables, we need to examine voting by the same group of individuals both over time and across voters and carefully estimate both the cost and the benefit effects, allowing the relationship to take a U

FIGURE 2.5
Benefits of Voting and Before-Tax Income

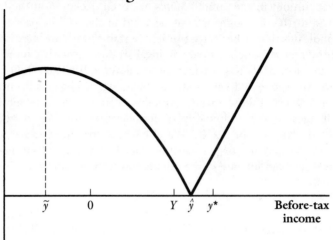

Source: Filer, Kenny, and Morton (1993).

shape. Filer, Kenny, and Morton, in an analysis of turnout in presidential elections from 1948 to 1980 at an aggregate level, provided some separation of the two effects of income on turnout decisions. They found that turnout does vary in a U-shaped fashion with position in the distribution of income, as predicted by the benefit effect, and that turnout declines with increases in absolute real income, as predicted by the cost effect. The apparent conflict in the relationship between income or education and turnout in a single election and over time may simply be a result of the researchers' treating the complexity too simply in the empirical estimation.

What We Know

At the end of this chapter and the coming chapters, I discuss what the chapter has revealed that we know and don't know about U.S. elections. Based on this chapter, we know that the individualized investment model of voting cannot by itself explain why voters participate in elections. Adding in groups helps but requires the assumption that the group can offer group members an incentive to participate. These selective incentives can be of three types: private consumption, social, or purposive. If voters are mobilized by benefit-seeking groups that have preferences similar to their own, the voters' choices in the voting booth are more likely to reflect their preferences on issues than they would if the voters were directly mobilized by office-seeking groups. Given the fixed costs of mobilizing a group of voters, however, mobilizing a group of new voters is difficult and limits the ability of latent groups of voters to exercise their preferences. We know, too, that the popular stylized fact that turnout in the United States has been declining in the last twenty years is a myth. Although turnout declined in the 1970s, proper measurement indicates that it has stayed relatively stable, with an increase in 2004. We know that although simple empirical studies show that more educated voters are more likely to participate, education can limit the ability of groups to mobilize voters, and we know that techological changes in mobilization have also affected how groups mobilize voters. Thus, rising education and changes in the technology of mobilization may be responsible for turnout declines in the 1970s. We also know that income has a complex effect on the benefits of participation—leading voters whose incomes are close to the mean income in the population to have the lowest incentive to participate.

What We Don't Know: Why Turnout Rebounded in 2004

In 2004, turnout was higher than it had been since 1968. Although the expected closeness of the election and the perceived differences between the two candidates were certainly reasons for expecting a high turnout, previous elections had been close (Bill Clinton never won with more than 50 percent of the vote), and issues had been stark before (for example, in 1980 the country faced double-digit inflation, and U.S. hostages were being held in Iran). In the next chapter, we consider the reasons for the turnout increase in 2004. We also examine recent developments in electoral institutions that govern the act of voting, such as early voting, advances in registration, and voting technology.

Study Questions and Problems

1. Suppose that the next senatorial election in California is a contest between incumbent Barbara Boxer and Governor Arnold Schwarzenegger. Your friend Thomas, who is a supporter of Boxer, would like to wager a private bet between the two of you. If Boxer wins, you will treat Thomas to dinner at Michael's restaurant in Los Angeles and if Schwarzenegger wins, Thomas will treat to dinner. The utility you would receive from dinner at Michael's with Thomas is 100 utils; the utility cost of paying for the dinner for the two of you is 80 utils. If you and Thomas go to dinner and split the bill the utility cost for you is 40 utils. What is the expected utility from taking the bet if Schwarzenegger's probability of winning is 25 percent? Should you take the bet? How high does Schwarzenegger's probability of winning

have to go for you to be willing to take the bet? Explain your answers.

2. Suppose that Karen, our Louisiana voter, receives extra utility from the expression of her preferences in the election outcome. That is, take the payoff to Karen and Bruno as illustrated in table 2.1, and assume that Karen receives an extra 25 utils whenever she votes and the candidate she votes for wins with a majority. What is the new payoff table for Karen and Bruno? Is Karen now more likely to vote than before? Is Bruno? Why or why not? How does your answer change if Bruno also receives an extra 25 utils whenever he votes and the candidate he votes for wins with a majority? Do you think expressive voting can explain turnout? Why or why not? How is expressive voting different from voting for selective incentives? How would you do an empirical test to determine which approach best explains voter turnout in the United States?

3. If voters do not care about the investment benefits of voting and vote only for consumption benefits, then is the concept of expected utility no longer relevant to explain their choices? Why or why not?

4. Suppose that the Constitution is amended to give the right to vote to noncitizens who have resided in the United States more than two years. Why does it matter whether these voters are mobilized by office-seeking or benefit-seeking groups? What factors are likely to affect how these voters may or may not be mobilized to participate? If these voters have incomes that are at the low end of the distribution of income, are they likely to participate more or less?

5. In this chapter, we discussed the paradox of not voting and the "free-rider" problem. Which one occurs because an individual looks at his or her choice as an individual choice? Which one occurs because an individual looks at his or her choice as a part of the decisions made by a group of similar individuals? In what other ways are these two problems in voting different? How are they similar?

Appendix to Chapter 2

The following analysis explains how equation 1 in this chapter is derived from expected utility. Ventura's benefit from voting depends on how voting will affect his expected utility from the election. Suppose that if Ventura votes, the probability that Penny wins is equal to P_V (the probability that Dahn wins is equal to $[1 - P_V]$), and if Ventura does not vote, the probability that Penny wins is equal to P_{NV} (the probability that Dahn wins is equal to $[1 - P_{NV}]$). Then if Ventura votes, his expected utility, $E_V(U)$, is given by equation 1A below, and if he doesn't vote, his expected utility, $E_{NV}(U)$, is given by equation 2A:

$$E_V(U) = P_V U_P + (1 - P_V) U_D \qquad \text{(Equation 1A)}$$
$$E_{NV}(U) = P_{NV} U_P + (1 - P_{NV}) U_D \qquad \text{(Equation (2A)}$$

Ventura's expected benefit from voting is the difference in his expected utility, the difference between $E_V(U)$ and $E_{NV}(U)$:

$$E_V(U) - E_{NV}(U) = P_V U_P + (1 - P_V) U_D - P_{NV} U_P - (1 - P_{NV}) U_D =$$
$$(P_V - P_{NV})(U_P - U_D) \qquad \text{(Equation 3A)}$$

Generally, we label the term $(P_V - P_{NV})\ \Delta P$, which is the effect of Ventura's vote on whether Penny is elected, and we label the term $(U_P - (U_D)\ B$, which is the difference in Ventura's utility between the election of Penny and the election of Dahn. We then can write the expected-utility benefits from voting for Ventura as the term $\Delta P \cdot B$, as in equation 1 in the chapter.

NOTES

1. Nevertheless, even a 100 percent turnout of blacks for Bush's opponent could not have overcome Bush's lead of 13 percent, as the black population is only 11 percent of the state. See Jim Yardley and Dana Canedy, "Some Democratic Losses Linked to White Defections," *New York Times*, November 9, 2002.
2. Brendan Farrington, "Bush-Cheney Training Activists for the 2004 Florida Campaign," Associated Press State & Local Wire, November 15, 2003.
3. Edwards received a similar percentage of white Democratic support in the state, but because whites made up a lower percentage of the voters who turned out, Kerry won. Eric Slater and Mark Z. Barabak, "The Race to the White House: Kerry Hopes to Rally African Americans; The Presumptive Democratic Presidential Nominee Must Persuade Blacks to Go to the Polls in Greater Numbers to Tilt the Race in His Favor," *Los Angeles Times*, March 9, 2004.
4. Tom Heinen, "Voters Guide 2004: Bush Sounds the Republican Trumpet; In Ashwaubenon, He Calls for Supporters to Rouse Friends, Neighbors to Vote," *Milwaukee Journal Sentinel*, October 31, 2004.
5. Philip Dine, "Kerry Relaxes in Hometown, Makes Final Appeal for Votes," *St. Louis Post-Dispatch*, November 3, 2004.
6. Some dispute the implication that women had little influence on policy after getting the right to vote. For example, Kenny and Lott (1999) contended that after women got the right to vote, government spending increased, reflecting the fact that women were "poorer" and benefited more from government spending programs. They examined the effects of women's suffrage in states that passed these measures before women were given the right to vote nationally. Although this may be true, we still have the puzzle of why women did not turn the right to vote into more equal treatment in general—that is, as Harvey pointed out, government policies continued to be biased in favor of males. Moreover, early women voters were not more likely to vote Democratic even though that party was more likely to advocate social welfare spending.
7. See Brian Faler, "Election Turnout in 2004 Was Highest Since 1968," *Washington Post*, January 15, 2005.
8. Curtis Gans, press release, Committee for the Study of the American Electorate, November 4, 2004.

9. *The Smoking Gun* reports that Affleck did register and vote in the November 2002 election in Los Angeles. See http://www.thesmokinggun.com/archive/affleck_doc.html.

10. Mark Brunswick, "Ventura Is among the Many Who Don't Go to the Polls: His Schedule on Primary Election Day Got the Best of Him, His Office Said," *Minneapolis Star Tribune*, October 2, 2002.

11. Quoted by John Wildermuth, *San Francisco Chronicle*, November 15, 2002.

12. Ellen Gamerman, "Ageless Devotion to Democracy: Hardships; On Election Day, the Will of Senior Voters Triumphs over Advanced Years and Physical Difficulties," *Baltimore Sun*, November 6, 2002.

13. See Downs (1957) and Riker and Ordeshook (1967). Some label this problem the "paradox of voting." However, a different problem (the tendency for majority rule to result in preference cycles, discussed in chapter 14) is also often called the paradox of voting. To distinguish between the two, I use the term "paradox of not voting." Of course, we are ignoring that even at the individual level the act of voting is strategic—that is, if all voters behaved "rationally," then no one would vote, and the effect of one vote would be sizable. Thus, if we assume that voters recognize the endogeneity of the turnout decision, then turnout would not be zero. We address these strategic concerns subsequently.

14. See Morton (1991) for a review.

15. See Downs (1957) and Riker and Ordeshook (1967).

16. See Palfrey and Rosenthal (1983, 1985) and Ledyard (1984).

17. Kevin Sack, "Democrats in Political Debt for Black Turnout in South," *New York Times*, November 6, 1998.

18. David M. Halbfinger, "Bush's Push, Eager Volunteers and Big Turnout Led to Georgia Sweep," *New York Times*, November 10, 2002.

19. Abby Goodnough, "In New Jersey, Getting Out the Vote(r) Is a Matter of Survival," *New York Times*, November 2, 1997.

20. Steven Greenhouse, "Michigan Unions Push Hard for Gore," *New York Times*, October 13, 2000.

21. Aaron Bernstein, Paula Dwyer, and Lorraine Woellert, "Inside the Dems' Shadow Party," *BusinessWeek*, March 22, 2004.

22. Greg Gordon and Tom Ford, "Voter Turnout Efforts Hit Peak: Interest Groups across the Spectrum Work to Energize Their Partisans," *Minneapolis Star Tribune*, November 5, 2002.

23. Nash is portrayed by Russell Crowe in the 2001 movie *A Beautiful Mind*.

24. "Owner of Care Facility Denies Vote-Buying," Associated Press State & Local Wire, October 31, 2002.

25. Jane Ann Morrison, "Kincaid Calls Union Event Vote Buying," *Las Vegas Review-Journal*, August 23, 2000.

26. "Authorities Investigate Vote-Buying Claims in Eastern Kentucky," Associated Press State & Local Wire, May 31, 2002.

27. One resident who could not legally vote since she was a convicted felon did ask for a ballot, but she did not vote, and her ballot was locked in the facility's office.

28. Notice that the situation for voters in table 2.3 is similar to the situation facing diners in restaurants when choosing to tip. In some societies, tipping is not a norm, while in others, like the United States, tipping is expected. In the United States, we have coordinated on the tipping equilibrium, while in some other countries, individuals have coordinated on a nontipping equilibrium. Some might argue that as a result, service is less effective in those countries where tipping does not occur, as the reward for service is less closely connected to the act of service.

29. Nicole Radzievich, "Valley Area Voters Flock to Polls as Hype, Governor's Race Turn Up Turnout: Polling Places See Steady Stream of People All Day Long," *Morning Call*, November 6, 2002.

30. There are, of course, many other theories that attempt to "solve" the paradox of not voting, as reviewed in Morton (1991). This research continues. For example, Feddersen and Sandroni (2002) considered how ethical considerations might explain how voters are motivated to act as a group without explicit mobilization by a leader. Schuessler (2000) and Overbye (1995) modeled voting as an expressive act, which can be related to social interaction. Bendor, Diermeier, and Ting (2003) modeled voting using an evolutionary approach, where voters myopically adapt their decision to vote over time.

31. James O'Toole and Maeve Reston, "Candidates Sharpen Domestic Differences: They Clash on Health Care, Gay Rights, Economy," *Pittsburgh Post-Gazette*, October 1, 2004.

32. "Reflecting on the Debates: Bush, Kerry Bobbed and Weaved, but Improved Process Benefits Voters," *Newsday*, October 15, 2004.

33. See Aldrich (1995) and Harvey (1998).

34. Sack, "Democrats in Political Debt." In the 2004 presidential nomination contest, Democratic candidates also recognized Clyburn's influence on black voters in South Carolina, who would make up nearly half of the Democratic votes in the South Carolina primary. In early May 2003, nine Democratic contenders attended a late-night fish fry given by Clyburn in Columbia. See Dan Balz, "Democrats Head to S.C. for First Debate: Nine Presidential Hopefuls Try to Gain Visibility, Draw Distinctions in '04 Field," *Washington Post*, May 3, 2003.

35. Clyburn's candidate, Hodges, also lost, although Clyburn blamed the election results on poor Democratic Party mobilization techniques. See George Will, "S. Carolina's Starring Role," *Chicago Sun-Times*, December 5, 2002.

36. Its gubernatorial candidate was sent to prison on drug charges. For the story of La Raza Unida, see the 1996 documentary *Chicano! History of the Mexican-American Civil Rights Movement*. See also Bob Richter, "Before There Was Clout, There Was Raza Unida," *San Antonio Express-News*, September 9, 2001. We discuss minor parties in U.S. elections in chapter 14 and minority representation in chapter 15.

37. Before entering politics, Johnson was a schoolteacher in a Mexican American school and worked to provide benefits to those voters as well, as Caro argues, when doing so fit with his political ambition.

38. Of course, Johnson's efforts were hugely accountable for the passage of the Voting Rights Act of 1965, which gave Mexican American litigants the ability to challenge many of those laws.

39. George Wallace campaigned for the presidency on a segregationist anti–civil rights platform, while Martin Luther King's contribution to the civil rights movement is well-known.

40. At some point, however, the costs will increase as there are usually at least some members of a group who find the act of voting so distasteful as to make the cost of mobilizing them prohibitive.

41. Marjorie Connelly, "How Americans Voted: A Political Portrait," *New York Times*, November 7, 2004.

42. Ralph Z. Hallow, "Americans Deeply Split over Politics," *Washington Times*, January 7, 2004.

43. Campaigns perhaps changed less in Chicago than elsewhere, as documented in the 1996 film *Vote for Me: Politics in America*, in which precinct workers are seen in acts not that much different from those practiced in the days of the senior mayor Daley. A recent *Chicago Sun-Times* exposé of gang involvement in

political campaigns shows that many of the same tactics used by Plunkitt in New York are still used by politically connected gang leaders in Chicago. See Frank Main and Carlos Sadovi, "Candidates Lean on Gang Members to Get Out the Vote," *Chicago Sun-Times*, December 22, 2002.

44. Imai used data from the field experiments of Gerber and Green (2004). Surprisingly, in their preliminary analysis of the data, Gerber and Green found that phone calls have a negative effect on turnout. Imai shows that the result is due to inappropriate statistical assumptions in the analysis of the data.

—3—

Trends in Voter Mobilization

Mobilization Strategies in the 2004 Election

Turnout increased significantly in 2004. Why did that happen? Was the cause changes in the mobilization strategies of parties and interest groups or institutional changes in the voting process? Parties did use different strategies to reach voters in 2004, and the voting process had been changed in response to problems experienced in 2000. Moreover, over the past decade, many states and localities have experimented with new registration and early-voting procedures. To answer this question, in this chapter we explore more expansively the mobilization effort in 2004 and the recent institutional changes in the voting process. We begin with the story of 2004.

The Republican Effort

Office-Seeking Mobilization Efforts Shortly after becoming president, George W. Bush started planning his reelection strategy. Bush and his campaign team calculated that given the divisive nature of the 2000 election controversy, the vast majority of voters were already committed to Bush or his opponent (at that time unknown) and that the Republicans would have little success in changing their minds. Therefore, instead of the usual practice of using 75 to 90 percent of their campaign resources on undecided voters, they decided to spend half their moneys on the mobilization of voters. In the 2002 elections, Republicans tested their mobilization strategies. What they found was that the traditional method of focusing on precincts based on the size of Republican support in the past missed a significant number of their potential voters, since only 15 percent of Republicans lived in such precincts. Pollster Matthew Dowd directed the Republican National Committee to hire consultants who used "expensive high-tech micro targeting to cherry-pick prospective Republicans who lived in majority Democratic neighborhoods. . . . Surveys of people . . . were then used to determine 'anger points' (late-term abortion, trial lawyer fees, estate taxes) that coincided with the Bush agenda for as many as 32 categories of voters, each identifiable by income, magazine subscriptions, favorite television shows and other 'flags.' "[1] They contacted these voters by the typical modern means of direct mail and telephone. But they also conducted "front-porch" visits. And their message emphasized issues about which they estimated these voters most cared. "We got a homogeneous group of new registered voters and stayed on them like dogs," said one Bush reelection official.[2] Bush budgeted $125 million, three times what was spent in 2000, on voter mobilization. His campaign used a volunteer army that Republican spokespersons claimed numbered 1.4 million people by election day. In Florida, Republicans used 109,000 volunteers to make three million voter contacts on election day and the five days before, in contrast to fewer than 10,000 volunteers making 77,000 contacts in 2000. Republicans used these volunteers to reach out to "what some of them called 'unreliable' or 'lazy' voters, a group of about 1.5 million people who were seen as unmotivated because they had participated in only one of the last three or four elections, or were newly registered to vote."[3]

Bush was directly involved in this party-directed mobilization effort. Admission to Bush campaign rallies required a ticket, usually color coded as to proximity to the president. According to news reports, Democrats and protesters were not welcome and were either refused tickets or evicted if recognized.[4] While criticized, such restrictions allowed Republicans to use the rallies to energize the faithful and allocate proximity to the president as an inducement to the stalwarts to mobilize other less committed or undecided voters. Eden Prairie, Minnesota, insurance agent Eric Larsen, his wife, and five children promised before a rally to knock on doors for the campaign afterward and were given special seats close to Bush. At a Bush visit to Wausau, Wisconsin,

> some of the 10,000 people who turned out agreed to work at phone banks inside a huge white tent. Volunteers who made 25 phone calls to registered Republicans would get a green dot sticker on their ticket, which would entitle them to stand close to the outdoor stage. Two hours before Bush arrived, all 250 cellphones provided by the campaign were being used, and a line of perhaps 20 people waited patiently for their turn. "A couple of phones have sprouted legs," said Wisconsin GOP spokesman Chris Lato. "But not many."[5]

Benefit-Seeking Mobilization Efforts

<u>Evangelical Voters</u> Republicans did more than build comprehensive voter lists and use party volunteers and rally participants to reach voters; they also mobilized groups of voters by reaching out to their leaders, particularly those with positions of authority in religious groups and churches. From the beginning of the Bush administration, the White House organized conference calls with evangelical religious leaders, which

> became a weekly ritual as the campaign heated up. Usually, the participants were Rove or Tim Goeglein, head of the White House Office of Public Liaison. Later Bush campaign chairman Ken Mehlman and Ralph Reed, former executive director of the Christian Coalition and the campaign's southeast regional coordinator, were often on the line. The religious leaders varied, but frequent participants included the Rev. Richard Land of the Southern Baptist Convention, psychologist James C. Dobson or others from the Colorado-based Focus on the Family, and Colson.[6]

In early June of 2004, Luke Bernstein, the coalitions coordinator for the Bush campaign in Pennsylvania, sent an e-mail message to many members of the clergy and others in the state, asking for their help in identifying volunteers in places of worship who could "help distribute general information to other supporters. . . . We plan to undertake activities such as distributing general information/updates or voter registration materials in a place accessible to the congregation."[7]

Pastor Tim Wilder of the First Baptist Church of Kissimmee, Osceola County, Florida, served as a grassroots evangelical mobilizer of voters. He described to Jennifer Ludden, host of National Public Radio's *All Things Considered*, how he attempted to reach voters:

> Well, we had two rallies here called Save America Now! rallies. We had one Christian Coalition–sponsored one here in our church during the weekday and then I preached the sermon the Sunday before the election on fighting for America, "Vote Our Values," but I'm a part of the Southern Baptist Convention and we really . . . geared things up at the . . . convention last year and talked about the importance of it. President Bush even spoke, not in person, but by live satellite . . . and we're one of the largest denominations in the United States. There's 16 million of us. We have an organization called VoteValues and, of course, James Dobson['s] Focus on Family and he sent out a pastor's kit to, I think, every pastor in the United States and it was how to talk to your people. A lot of the information I got for my sermon was from his materials and different things like that.[8]

In 2000, Osceola County had gone for Al Gore; in 2004, it went for Bush. Bush won 79 percent of the 26.5 million evangelical voters nationwide, according to exit polls.[9]

<u>Catholic Voters</u> The Republican campaign also took its message to Rome in an effort to reach Catholic voters in the United States. On June 4, 2004, President Bush met with the pope and other Vatican officials in the Vatican. *National Catholic Reporter* correspondent John L. Allen, Jr., quoted the recollections of an anonymous source:

> In his meeting with Cardinal Angelo Sodano and other Vatican officials, Bush said, "Not all American bishops are with me" on the cultural issues. The implication was that he hoped the Vatican would nudge them toward more explicit activism. Other sources in the meeting said that while they could not recall the president's exact words, he did pledge aggressive efforts on the cultural front, especially against gay marriage, and asked for the Vatican's help in encouraging the U.S. bishops to be more outspoken.[10]

Weekly conference calls from a White House representative were also held with prominent Catholic conservatives during Bush's first term. "To ramp up the Catholic campaign . . . the party dispatched its chairman, Ed Gillespie, and a roster of well-known Catholic Republicans on a speaking tour to Catholic groups throughout the swing states. The party has recruited an undisclosed number of Catholic field coordinators who earn $2,500 a month, along with up to $500 a month for expenses to increase conservative Catholic turnout."[11] During the fall campaign, a number of Catholic bishops, including Archbishop Charles J. Chaput of Denver, either explicitly endorsed Bush or made statements to the effect that voting for a candidate who did not oppose abortion, gay marriage, or stem-cell research would be a sin and must be confessed before receiving Communion. Chaput and other bishops organized voter registration drives, published editorials in their newsletters, and gave sermons on the importance of casting a vote in the election for a candidate with the appropriate cultural values.[12] According to exit polls, Bush won 52 percent of the 31 million Catholic voters, a gain over his percentage in 2000.[13]

<u>Amish Voters</u> Even small religious groups in battleground states received extra attention from the Republicans, such as the just over 100,000 Amish voters in Pennsylvania and Ohio. On July 9, 2004, President Bush met privately with thirty Amish leaders in Pennsylvania. The London *Daily Telegraph* reported that a Lancaster County local veterinarian, Wendell Stoltzfus, "was rushing to an emergency calving along the highway, moments before it was closed for the presidential motorcade. Marveling at the tens of thousands of locals lining the verge, he realized many were Amish. "It hit me right then. I knew they supported Bush's social values and beliefs, but very few of them were going to vote.' " Stoltzfus "single-handedly registered 800 Amish to vote. . . . A letter to Amish voters from Dr. Stoltzfus has been copied many times, and turned up in Amish businesses across the

county, making front-page news in the local newspaper, the *Intelligencer*.
. . . Dr. Stoltzfus . . . arranged a fleet of volunteers to drive Amish to the
polls who cannot make it by horse."[14] In Amish- and Mennonite-dominated
Leacock Township of Lancaster County, where in 2000 there were only one
thousand registered voters, more than eight hundred people had cast ballots
by three o'clock on election day, an estimated 100 percent increase in
turnout.

<u>Church and State</u> The Republican mobilization of evangelical, Catholic,
and Amish voters through their leaders was criticized during the campaign
as a violation of the constitutional separation of church and state. Clergy
members rightly worry that being overtly political might endanger their
churches' tax-exempt status. According to the tax code, churches and other
charitable organizations cannot engage in partisan politics, although their
leaders can speak out about social issues and register voters. The *Pittsburgh
Post-Gazette* reported that the Church at Pierce Creek in New York State
"lost its tax-exempt status after it took out a full page ad in 1992 encouraging people to vote against Bill Clinton. The Rev. Jerry Falwell's 'Old Time
Gospel Hour' lost its tax status over political activity."[15] It was as a result of
such events, Pastor Wilder related to Jennifer Ludden, that he was careful
never to explicitly endorse Bush. As Wilder stated: "I even told our people,
'Don't go into the voting booth as a Republican or Democrat. Go in the
voting booth as a born-again believer in Jesus Christ and vote your values.' " Yet Wilder admitted that he was not silent about what voting your
values meant to him: "If anybody probably read between the lines, they, of
course, knew how I felt. . . . If people ask me personally outside the pulpit,
I can tell them who I'm voting for and that kind of thing."

<u>Gun Control Activists</u> Another group of voters mobilized for the 2004 elec-
tion was those active in the anti-gun-control community. The National Rifle
Association ran an aggressive campaign, spending over $20 million on tele-
vision ads, billboards, radio advertising, leaflets, and voter mobilization
in support of Bush.[16] Such outreach seems to have affected the turnout of
voters like Dennis Meyer, owner of Shooting Star Archery in the
Chequamegon-Nicolet National Forest in Wisconsin, who declared: "If the
NRA tells me to do something, I do it. That's why I'm voting."[17] One vig-
orous gun-rights supporter is former New York City bar owner Bill Bunting.
Six years before, he and some friends had formed a political club to lobby
against gun control, and it had grown to become a group supporting Republican candidates. As Republican Party chairman in Pasco County,
Florida, Bunting surveyed voters to find out what issues mattered to them
and held events like a Fourth of July barbecue. By 2004, he had over four
hundred people working for him to mobilize voters for Bush. *The New York
Times* reported: "Bunting rented and borrowed six vans to drive voters to
the polls on Election Day." Bush won Pasco County by twenty thousand

votes even though the county had been dominated by Democrats prior to 2000.[18]

Top Down or Bottom Up? Bunting's experience of first starting a group focused on the issue of opposing gun control and then becoming part of the Republican mobilization effort is an example of how a significant portion of that effort was accomplished by group leaders who had begun to organize independently and, to some extent, prior to and at variance with the top-down centralized organization run by Karl Rove. In particular, a number of the religious leaders argue that the campaign followed their efforts rather than directing them and that their mobilization of voters led to campaign policy decisions. For example, eleven states had initiatives on the November ballots outlawing same-sex marriage, a move that some Democrats claimed was engineered by Rove and other Republicans to increase turnout for Bush on election day, but the state and religious leaders have argued otherwise. According to *The Washington Post*, Charles Colson "recalled a meeting early this year when Christian leaders warned White House aides that the marriage issue was likely to appear on state ballots and be a factor in the presidential election. 'The White House guys were kind of resisting it on the grounds that "We haven't decided what position we want to take on that," ' he said." Lori Viars of Ohio began a registration drive at churches on July 4. She recalled: "By the time the Bush campaign said, 'You should do voter registration through churches,' we were already doing that."[19]

Furthermore, the evidence is weak that Bush and Republican lobbying of the Catholic hierarchy were the source of vote mobilization of the Catholic bishops in the Bush campaign. John L. Allen, Jr., of the *National Catholic Reporter* contends that because of disagreement over the war in Iraq, many in the Vatican actually opposed Bush's reelection and that the Vatican was as divided as many American voters, with a slight majority in favor of Kerry.[20] Archbishop Chaput said that he had had no contact with the Republican Party or the Bush campaign, that his sole contact was his appointment to the U.S. Commission on International Religious Freedom, and that his communications director had formerly worked for the Bush administration. Chaput stated: "We are not with the Republican Party. They are with us."[21]

Bunting, Chaput, Colson, Stoltzfus, Viars, and Wilder mobilized voters in groups that already existed, where they were in positions of influence. They tied voting for Bush to the policies that voters within those groups supported. They believed that voting for Bush was likely to lead to those policies, and they used both the social incentive of acting as a group and the purposive incentive of achieving group policy goals to induce voters to turn out in the election. While we will have to analyze Bush's second term to determine whether their policy preferences were in fact supported by his administration, during the campaign (on February 24, 2004) Bush came out in support of a constitutional amendment to ban gay marriage. When the Senate voted on a bill relieving the gun industry of liability in civil suits with amendments that would have extended the assault-weapons ban, Bush announced that he would not sign any gun-liability bill with amendments, and it was defeated with his help in the Senate (on March 2). The assault-rifle ban subsequently expired, in September. When 206 members of the House of Representatives (including some in the Republican leadership) signed a letter asking President Bush to loosen federal restrictions on the funding of stem-cell research put in place by executive order in August 2001, the White House announced (on May 4) that it would not change the policy.

The Democratic Effort

Office-Seeking Mobilization Efforts Of course, Democratic organizations also ran extensive and sophisticated efforts to mobilize voters in 2004. Yet the effort led directly by the party was much smaller than that of the Republican machine. The Democratic Party had 250,000 volunteers, which came close to triple the number enlisted in 2000 but only 18 percent of those reportedly organized by the Republican Party, and it spent almost $60 million on mobilization, more than double the amount spent four years earlier but less than half that spent by the Republican Party.[22] Most of the real Democratic mobilization efforts were "farmed out" to outside groups formed for the purpose, such as Americans Coming Together (ACT), which was estimated to have spent $125 million on voter turnout efforts, and MoveOn.org (founded in 1998, during the Clinton impeachment trial), and to already existing Democratic organizations with long ties to the Democratic Party, such as labor unions and environmental groups. ACT workers used hand-held computer devices to record information they gathered on voters, which was later compiled into a database that could be used early in the campaign season to identify undecideds or people whose support for a candidate was "soft." As election day approached, the information was used more to identify known Kerry supporters and to get them to the polls. It is estimated that 140,000 ACT and MoveOn.org workers were involved in voter canvassing. On election day, ACT rented approximately five thousand vans to drive voters to the polls and armed its workers with "20,000 digital cameras to record instances of voter intimidation."[23]

Benefit-Seeking Mobilization Efforts

<u>Traditional Democratic Interest Groups</u> Policy-oriented interest groups also engaged in large programs to mobilize voters for Kerry. The AFL-CIO spent about $45 million on voter mobilization, about the same as in 2000, but had "far more volunteers and full-time workers, about 4,500 paid staff compared with 1,500 the last election," according to the *San Francisco Chronicle*. In all, 226,000 labor union members were anticipated to be involved in voter canvassing for Kerry.[24] The Sierra Club and the League of

Conservation Voters announced during the Democratic National Convention that they planned "an unprecedented voter mobilization effort . . . to hit over three million households in nine states using door-to-door canvassing, phone calls and emails."[25] At its annual convention in July, the National Education Association proclaimed a partnership with organizations such as MoveOn.org, the Association of Community Organizations for Reform Now (ACORN), and the Campaign for America's Future to mobilize voters.[26] Whereas these groups explicitly mobilized voters for Kerry, because of campaign finance laws (which we discuss in chapter 6)—that is, because their funding came from so-called soft money sources (sources not restricted by campaign finance regulations to certain limits on individual contributions)—they could not explicitly coordinate with the Kerry campaign and the Democratic Party, a situation that meant there was more duplication of effort.

Even more tenuously connected to the official Democratic mobilization effort were efforts of charities or officially nonpartisan groups that had tax-exempt status and had to worry about overtly endorsing candidates. Many nonpartisan charitable groups with liberal positions on issues became involved in mobilizing voters. Groups that targeted minority, homeless, and/or young voters were often groups that had advocated policy positions close to those supported by Kerry and had expressed criticism of the Bush administration. As with church leaders who supported Bush, leaders of these groups had to worry about how far they went in encouraging turnout at the same time they discussed the election. The NAACP's National Voter Fund focused on seven to nine states in the presidential election under the banner of "Empowerment 2004" and provided grants to state and local affiliates, with a goal of registering and mobilizing 250,000 new voters. The NAACP combined with six other organizations with a goal of spending $26 million on door-to-door and phone contacts, leaflets, and so on.[27] Its chairman, Julian Bond, compared the two candidates in general terms at the group's convention, but with a message about whom he supported: "The election this fall is a contest between two widely disparate views of who we are and what we believe. One view wants to march us backward through history—surrendering control of government to special interests, weakening democracy, giving religion veto power over science, curtailing civil liberties, despoiling the environment. The other view promises expanded democracy and giving the people, not plutocrats, control over their government."[28] Just before the election, news emerged that the IRS was investigating the NAACP's tax-exempt status because of Bond's speech; as of this writing, the investigation is ongoing.

The Youth Vote One group of potential voters that was hotly recruited during the election was young voters, aged eighteen to twenty-nine. Rock the Vote, a nonpartisan group founded in 1990 to fight censorship in music and later expanded to mobilize young voters, claimed 1.371 million entries on its Web site reflecting new registrations. The New Voters Project, supported in part by the nonpartisan, nonprofit Pew Charitable Trusts, exceeded its goal of registering 265,000 people aged eighteen to twenty-four in six battleground states.[29] According to the *New York Post*, on the day before the election and on election day, MTV aired over six hours per day "of election-themed programming including spot-coverage of young voters in several key swing states, about a dozen documentaries from the network's award-winning 'Choose or Lose' series and other election-related material."[30]

Whereas those efforts were nonpartisan, since polls showed that younger voters seemed predisposed to Kerry and anti-Bush, many Democratic activists and political pundits anticipated that votes would benefit Kerry. The number of voters aged eighteen to twenty-nine did increase in 2004, by approximately 4.6 million, but the percentage of voters in that age group was largely the same as in 2000 because turnout increased across the board. Exit polls by the Associated Press showed that Kerry received a larger percentage of young voters, 55 percent to Bush's 44 percent, which was greater than the percentage received by Al Gore in 2000 (48 percent). Those votes were not enough to overcome the votes for George W. Bush, however.

Were Republican Turnout Efforts Better?

Family and Friends versus Out-of-State Volunteers and Paid Employees After the election, a number of commentators argued that Bush won in part because of the differences in the mobilization strategies used by the two parties. This is somewhat surprising because the perception prior to the election was that historically Democrats had dedicated more resources to voter mobilization and had more experienced workers in that campaign and, as a result, would be more effective than Republicans. Curtis Gans of the Committee for the Study of the American Electorate argues that Democrats were less effective because John Kerry's campaign could not legally coordinate with the larger part of the mobilization effort run by ACT, MoveOn.org, and labor unions as well as nonpartisan groups such as the NAACP and that it was a mistake to "farm out" the mobilization effort to those groups rather than run it within the party and the campaign, as the Republicans did. Furthermore, ACT and MoveOn.org used more paid workers for the door-to-door contacts (paying them $75 on election day, for example), and whereas the Republican Party effort did have a paid staff and subsidized expenses of some volunteers, most were unpaid Republican converts who lived in the same general area as the voters. The commitment of the Democratic canvassers might have been less than the Republican volunteers, and that factor could have influenced voter mobilization efforts. Dan Balz and Thomas Edsall reported in *The Washington Post* on the day before the election that ACT canvassers were surprised to find working-class Democrats supporting Bush in Appleton, Wisconsin, and that one canvasser "was not sure how she will vote."[31] ACT did have volunteers like Daniel Menaker, executive editor in chief of Random House in New York, who spent a week of his vacation in Columbus, Ohio, mobilizing voters. But Menaker's efforts demonstrate what experts argued was a greater tendency of the Democrats to rely on out-of-state workers from New York and California to make up for in-state volunteers.[32]

Our analysis of selective social incentives suggests that the Republicans were right that mobilizing voters would be more effective if done by neighbors and members of existing groups that voters were already involved with and where voting could be tied to the preferences of the group. When Dr. Stoltzfus told the local Amish farmers how he thought they should vote and encouraged them to vote as a group, he could more credibly provide the voters with the purposive incentives to act and be directly involved in inducing the social incentives as well. When a paid canvasser from New York approached the same Pennsylvania voter, it was much more difficult for that worker to provide such incentives. However, it would be wrong to suggest that Democratic volunteers and paid canvassers, and even nonpartisan voter efforts, were unsuccessful in mobilizing voters and increasing turnout in 2004. Curtis Gans reported that Democratic turnout increased by 3.6 percentage points in the closely contested states. The problem for the Democrats was that the Republicans did slightly better, increasing their vote totals in those states by 4.4 percent. Even more significantly, Republican turnout in the other states increased 3.9 percent, and Democratic turnout in the other states increased only 1.5 percent.

Money Matters A big factor in Bush's and the Republicans' success was that unlike Kerry, Bush did not have to compete in the primaries and thus had $110 million available in March 2004 while Kerry's campaign had a debt of $5 million. Moreover, because Bush's campaign had begun to mobilize voters before the 2002 election, they had much more experience and expertise with the new technologies. Although the Democrats had the same computer data files that enabled the Republicans to reach voters, they did not have the time or the money to do the detailed research that was needed. Thomas Edsall and James Grimaldi of *The Washington Post* quoted one Democrat involved in mobilization in 2004: "Very few people understand how much work it takes to get this technology to actually produce political results. We are one election cycle behind them in this area."[33]

At this writing, it is too early to draw strong conclusions about the lessons from the two parties' voter mobilization efforts in 2004. No doubt the large turnout reflects the predicted closeness of the election and the stark differences between the candidates. On the day before the election, a *USA Today*/CNN/Gallup poll found that 90 percent of voters said that the stakes were higher in 2004 than in past elections and all but 2 percent of voters had made up their minds, with Bush and Kerry scoring "record high" strength-of-support ratings. Moreover, each candidate was rated "highly un-

favorable" by more voters than any other major-party candidate since Barry
Goldwater, the Republican nominee in 1964. In terms of our analysis in
chapter 2, these polls suggest that in 2004 the perceived utility difference
between the candidates for most voters, the B term in equations 1, 2, and 3,
was higher than that in previous elections, making it easier to motivate voters using purposive incentives.

It is unclear whether the turnout would have been as high and the mobilization as successful or as extensive if the election had not been predicted to
be so close or if the positions of the candidates had been more alike on the
issues. The higher Republican turnout may simply reflect an increasing conservatism on the part of the nationwide electorate. Republicans and Democrats did not return to the mobilization of the machine-politics era, but
theirs was an issue- and social-driven mobilization, offering voters social and
purposive selective incentives. The difference from previous years was that
both organizations offered those incentives far more efficiently and effectively than the party or conservative interest groups had in past elections,
and evidence suggests that the Republicans in particular did a good job of
mobilizing those voters.

The Good, the Bad, and the Institutions

In one sense, the analysis in chapter 2 is good news—when mobilization is
mainly by benefit-seeking groups, choices in the voting booth are more
likely to reflect voters' preferences. So if mobilization is more likely to be a
result of benefit-seeking group activity, that may be good for policy. What
can be good about black voters' turning out when their mobilizers brag that
they could get the voters to vote for George Wallace over Martin Luther
King, something, the mobilizers clearly imply, the voters would not do if
they chose according to their own preferences?

Nevertheless, the decline in participation in the 1960s suggests that a significant subset of voters who once participated stopped voting. Although
turnout has increased recently, there is still variation in participation rates
across groups of voters. The National Election Studies (NES) at the University of Michigan found that in the 2004 election, 60.4 percent of respondents with a high school diploma reported voting, while only 40.91 percent
of those without a diploma voted. Of respondents who reported that they
were of Latino descent, only 41.67 percent voted, while 70.27 percent of
non-Latino respondents voted. Of respondents with both parents born in
the United States, 69.91 percent voted, whereas 59.41 percent of those
with one parent born outside the United States participated. Almost 40 percent of the estimated eligible voters in the United States did not participate
in 2004. When groups of voters such as those do not participate in the same
numbers as members of other groups, their preferences may be ignored. Are
they disregarded? The degree to which those voters' preferences will be

overlooked will depend on their ability to form mobilized benefit-seeking groups if they so desire. If they can do so easily, then ignoring those voters can have consequences for the parties and other office seekers, and we can expect that they will not be disregarded. Hence, it could be that those voters are not mobilized because they are generally happy or indifferent about the policy outcomes. Alternatively, it could be that the cost of their mobilizing as a benefit-seeking group is prohibitive, and thus their preferences are being safely overlooked by office seekers.

Many researchers contend that to the extent that there are class inequalities, when mobilization of the population is low, class inequalities are multiplied because enough voters with less total income are less likely to be able to mobilize and so overcome the fixed costs they face. Office-seeking parties and candidates continue to allocate resources to please those who do participate, increasing the class inequalities and the cost of mobilizing. Rosenstone and Hansen (1993, p. 245) remarked that the U.S. history of disenfranchisement of blacks in the South makes it clear how differences in voting power can affect class inequalities: "Inequalities in participation led to inequalities in influence, which led to inequalities in policy outputs, which led to inequalities in resources, which led once more to inequalities in participation and the beginning of another vicious circle. Jim Crow . . . [laws in the South during this period limiting black civil and voting rights] was self-perpetuating because the disadvantaged did not—indeed, could not—participate." The logic is that if low-income and less-educated voters are not mobilized to the degree that high-income and more-educated voters are, then it is probable that inequality will increase through public policies that disadvantage those voters further, making it even more difficult for them to mobilize to change policy. If there are laws and policies that restrict the right to vote, as there were in the American South in the first half of the twentieth century, then mobilization can be even more difficult and policy change highly unlikely. The changes in civil rights and voting rights that did take place in the South in the latter half of the twentieth century are extraordinary in retrospect.

Ideally, some entrepreneur from a benefit-seeking group will recognize the potential benefits and mobilize the group. But such mobilization can take a long time and even involve bloodshed, as the civil rights movement demonstrates, and in the meantime the disadvantaged group is permanently scarred. How can such an outcome be prevented? One way is to use government policy—electoral institutions—to facilitate the efforts of benefit-seeking groups in mobilizing voters. One of the themes of this book is the importance of institutions in constraining and influencing political behavior. Institutions that increase the ability of benefit-seeking voters to mobilize as a group decrease the likelihood that those voters will be ignored.

Making Voting Cheap and Easy

Regardless of whether voters are motivated for investment benefits or consumption benefits, when the cost is high, they are less likely to vote. A major hurdle for voting in U.S. elections is the requirement that voters register in advance of the elections. Only North Dakota has no registration requirements, although some states, such as Minnesota, allow voters to register at the polls. Grimshaw (1992, p. 168) notes that Harold Washington's campaign in 1983 was partly successful because in the fall of 1982 a voter registration drive had "added about 125,000 black voters to the rolls, expanding the size of the black electorate by nearly 30 percent."

The Motor-Voter Bill

Recently a number of measures have been instituted to decrease the cost of voting by lowering the barriers to registration and otherwise countering factors that inhibit the act of voting. Most notably, in 1993 Congress enacted the National Voter Registration Act (the "motor-voter" law), which took effect January 1, 1995. The act requires that states establish three types of registration procedures:

- Individuals must be able to register to vote when they apply for a driver's license.
- Mail-in voter registration must be available, and the forms must be readily available to groups conducting registration drives.
- In-person registration must be available at various agencies, including all public assistance agencies and agencies that primarily serve the disabled. States were also encouraged to provide the opportunity to register at other agencies, such as schools, libraries, and various licensing bureaus.

There have been court challenges to the law, yet it has survived intact. Has it been successful? Certainly many voters have made use of its provisions. During the act's first year, 8 million citizens were enrolled or updated their registrations at motor vehicle agencies, 1.3 million registered at public assistance agencies, and 4.2 million registered by mail. Over 1.2 million voters were registered in both Florida and Texas.[34]

Nevertheless, it is not clear whether the law has significantly increased turnout. The first elections after its passage were not promising. There is some evidence that the influence of black voters in the 1998 and 2000 elections, as discussed earlier, is a consequence of the motor-voter law. For instance, *The New York Times* reported that "an analysis of selected precincts in the Atlanta area suggests that this year's higher black turnout may have been a windfall from increased voter registration under the motor voter law."[35] It remains to be seen whether the motor-voter act will have a consequential effect on voter turnout; the poor showing of minority voters in California, Florida, Texas, and Georgia discussed earlier suggests that the effect may be dissipating.[36]

One important caveat about easier voter registration is that the motor-voter act applies only to general elections, not to primaries. Many states have much more restrictive registration requirements for closed primaries (discussed more expansively in the next chapter). For example, in New York a voter must register one year in advance to vote in a particular party's primary. In general, primaries do have much lower levels of turnout than general elections. In the presidential primaries of 2000, only 4.85 percent of the voting-age population participated. This is not a good measure of participation, however, since the turnout rate in presidential primaries varies significantly across states, depending on when the primary is scheduled—in 2004, rates ranged from 29.9 percent in New Hampshire (the first primary in the sequence and widely regarded as more important than many of the others) to 6 percent in Texas, which held its primary after it was clear that John Kerry had secured the Democratic nomination. In contrast, turnout in the 2004 presidential election in New Hampshire was 70.5 percent compared with 53.9 percent in South Dakota. Turnout in congressional primaries nationwide in 2000 was only 12.8 percent of the voting-age population. This again varied signficantly by state, however, as many congressional incumbents face no competition. In 1990, for example, there were only 139 Democratic, and 118 Republican, congressional primaries—31.95 percent of the contests in the first case and 27.13 percent of the contests in the second.

Punching Out

Ballot Problems in 2000 The image was amazing. Broward County, Florida, election officials were peering at punch cards, trying to determine whether a vote had been cast for one candidate, for two candidates, or for no candidate. The world watched on television as the decisions of these local election officials in one state affected the outcome of the 2000 presidential election between George W. Bush and Albert Gore. The ballot was confusing, and the method of voting was fraught with errors. How could it be that the results of an election of this magnitude would depend on such flimsy technology? Furthermore, there were reports of other voting irregularities nationwide—individuals turned away at the polls even though they had registered and election officials unable to assist voters with their ballots. If those voters' votes had been counted correctly, would the outcome of the election have been different? Were some groups of voters more likely to be disenfranchised through problems with voting technology than other groups of voters? Trying to figure this out became a hot topic in the media and in academic research, with some evidence that Gore might have won

Florida if the errors had not occurred. For example, Herron and Sekhon (2003) analyzed the extent to which voters in Broward and Dade Counties engaged in overvoting—casting multiple votes for president on a single ballot. They found that precincts with large numbers of blacks, Latinos, and registered Democrats tended to have high rates of presidential overvoting, suggesting that those votes were less likely to be counted than the votes in predominantly white and Republican precincts. Similarly, Herron and Lewis (2004) studied whether there is evidence that the confusing butterfly ballot used in Palm Beach led Gore supporters to vote for Pat Buchanan by mistake. They found that Buchanan voters in Palm Beach voted on other races much more like Gore voters than did Buchanan voters in other Florida counties. They also found that the Buchanan voters on election day made significantly different balloting choices on other races than those who voted absentee, not using the butterfly ballot. Those results strongly suggest that the butterfly ballot did cause Gore voters in Palm Beach to vote for Buchanan; Wand and others (2001) and Herron and Lewis (2004) estimate that between twenty-five hundred and three thousand votes were lost to Gore due to the butterfly ballot.[37]

As with primary regulations, voting procedures—such as ballot design, equipment, precinct locations, and election officials—are decided by local and state governments with traditionally little federal involvement, a situation that has led to a wide variety of voting methods across states and across localities within states. Five types of voting equipment are used: hand-counted paper, mechanical-lever machines, punch-card ballots, optically scanned paper, and electronic voting machines. Researchers at California Institute of Technology and Massachusetts Institute of Technology estimated that 4 million to 6 million presidential votes were lost in 2000 and 1.5 million were not recorded because of problems with voting equipment. In addition, up to 3.5 million votes for senators and governors were lost over the last election cycle because of problems with technology. In general, the worst problems in voting were found to occur when voters used punch cards, lever machines, and electronic machines; the most reliable voting mechanisms were hand-counted and optically scanned paper ballots. Furthermore, they note that the U.S. Census Bureau reported that in the 2000 election 7.4 percent of registered voters who did not vote (3 million people) reported that trouble with registration was the main reason and that 2.8 percent of registered voters who did not vote (approximately 1 million people) reported that long lines or inconvenient hours or polling places were the main reason they did not vote.

The researchers recommended that optical-scanning ballot systems or any electronic voting system that has been proved to perform well in extensive tests replace punch cards, lever machines, and older electronic voting equipment. They also recommended more aggressive use of provisional ballots when a potential voter's registration status is challenged at the polling place (originally part of the motor-voter act). A voter who uses a provisional bal-

lot votes as other voters in the precinct do, but the ballot is sealed in a separate envelope, along with an affidavit from the voter declaring that he or
she is eligible to vote. After election day, the registration status is verified,
and if the voter should have been allowed to vote, the ballot is then counted
(otherwise it is discarded). If voters know that they can vote provisionally,
then worries about registration may be less likely to deter turnout on election day (Caltech-MIT Voting Technology Project 2002).

Helping America Vote In response to the controversy and reports such
as these, on October 29, 2002, President Bush signed the Help America
Vote Act (HAVA), a bipartisan bill from Congress sponsored by Representatives Steny Hoyer (Democrat from Maryland) and Bob Ney (Republican
from Ohio). The act requires that states upgrade their ballot machines and
make the polls more handicapped accessible, and it provided some resources
to help states in the effort. Florida has replaced all of its punch cards with
optical-scanning or new electronic voting equipment. Between 2000 and
2004, the use of electronic equipment increased nationwide from 12.5 percent to 29 percent and the use of optical scanning increased from 29 percent
to 32 percent. As of February 2004, however, 307 counties were thought to
be using the discredited technology. Kimball Brace, president of Election
Data Services, reported that an estimated 32 million voters (or 18 percent)
would use punch-card ballots in the 2004 presidential election (in particular,
in Illinois, Missouri, Ohio, Tennessee, and Utah).[38] Nevertheless, in a preliminary evaluation after the election, Stewart (2005) reported that improvements in voting technology led to an estimated reduction in voting
problems and approximately 1 million more voters having their votes
counted.

HAVA also instituted measures that stiffen rules on registration in federal
elections (which may be seen not as helping America vote but as lessening
fraud). That is, the act requires that each state create a computerized list of
registered voters; that those registering to vote for the first time in a federal
election provide a driver's license number, the last four digits of a Social Security number, or a statement that they have neither; and that those registering by mail to vote for the first time in a federal election provide a copy of
photo identification or proof of residency, such as a paycheck stub, bank
statement, or government document.

From Punches to Provisionals

On election day in 2004, new voter Nick Papa, a freshman at Kenyon College in Knox County, Ohio, got in line to vote at 4:30 P.M. The line was
long, and he was told that it might be six or seven hours before he got to
vote. At 1:30 A.M., he was still in line. Election officials offered him a paper
ballot, but he and other students in line rebelled and waited for the chance
to vote electronically.[39] While Papa had a chance to vote electronically,

155,337 voters in Ohio were given provisional ballots, as required by HAVA, because their names were not listed on the rolls or, in some cases, because the lines were too long to give them a chance to vote before the polls closed. Not counting those ballots, the final unofficial vote total of regular ballots gave President George W. Bush a 136,483-vote lead over Senator John Kerry on the morning of Wednesday, November 3.[40] The outcome in Ohio would determine the presidency. But Ohio state law required that the ballots first be checked to see if the voters were eligible "under state law," as required by HAVA, and would not be counted for eleven days. Moreover, Ohio state law allows military ballots to come in as many as ten days after the election as long as they are postmarked by election day. Should Kerry have waited until all the votes were counted on the small chance that he would get enough votes to win Ohio, or should he have conceded? He decided to concede, although the counting would go on.

Like Papa, seventy-year-old John L. Zalusky of Drum Point, Maryland was having a difficult time on election day. As a poll observer for the local Democratic Party, he found himself "removed from the polling site . . . by two Calvert County sheriff's officers and one Maryland State Police trooper after he complained that election judges were violating the law. The Calvert County Board of Elections had instructed poll workers not to hand out provisional ballots to people who were not listed in a state-wide database of registered voters." But Zalusky pointed out that this violated HAVA, and he was right. After a meeting with a Democratic lawyer that afternoon, the Calvert Board of Elections realized it had instructed the election judges incorrectly and quickly tried to contact voters who had been turned away. Zalusky and Democratic poll watcher Darlene M. Coco also complained because election judges had told voters that they could not cast ballots if they showed up at the wrong voting precinct. Coco was also asked to leave the polling place when she advised voters to demand a provisional ballot. Coco complained: "Some of these people had already gone to two or three polling places and were being turned away again. It is very disheartening. My understanding is that we should encourage people to vote."[41]

The battle over the rules governing provisional ballots had begun before election day. The House of Representatives had wanted HAVA to permit votes at the wrong precinct to be counted, but the Senate had not, and the resulting compromise was vague, leaving the decision to the states. Seventeen states would count such ballots, while twenty-seven states and the District of Columbia would not. As of early November 2004, state and federal judges in Colorado, Florida, Michigan, Missouri, and—notably—Ohio had ruled that a voter must be in his or her correct precinct for a provisional ballot to count.[42] Yet clearly many voters, election officials, and party leaders were confused about the rules governing provisional ballots on election day. While anecdotes like the one from Maryland have been reported, at this writing it is unclear whether problems with the interpretation of HAVA and state laws were significant in affecting vote totals. Preliminary research reviewed by Stewart (2005) shows no evidence that these problems had a systematic effect on the election.

Prior to election day, Ohio judges and other state and federal judges also considered whether to allow for challenges of voters at the polls. Republicans had challenged many new Democratic registrants as ineligible voters and made charges of voter fraud. Providing evidence of undeliverable mail to new voters at the addresses on their registration forms, Republicans argued that thousands of voters in battleground states should not be allowed to participate. While suits were brought prior to the election, in a number of cases Republicans announced that they would station volunteers to challenge voters at the polls and Democrats announced that they would have their own representatives at the polls as well to help defend new voters. Yet as of this writing, there is little evidence that extensive challenges were made against voters on election day. The debate over provisional ballots illustrates the continuing debates over the variation in electoral laws regulating voting machinery, voting procedures, counting procedures, voter registration, and so on, across states and whether such variation should be allowed.

Voting by Mail, at the Mall, on the Net . . .

Howard's Web In late November 2003, events in Michigan looked bad for Massachusetts senator John Kerry's effort to gain the Democratic presidential nomination. Michigan's presidential caucus was scheduled for February 7, just two weeks into the primary and caucus season, and 128 delegates were up for grabs (more than in any of the nine states where primaries preceded Michigan's on the calendar). But an October poll showed Kerry and Missouri congressman Richard Gephardt tied for third place, with only 13 percent of voters supporting each of them (former Vermont governor Howard Dean had 21 percent, retired army general Wesley Clark had 15 percent, Connecticut senator Joseph Lieberman had 12 percent, and the remaining candidates divided the rest of the support).[43] On Wednesday, November 12, SEIU and the American Federation of State, County, and Municipal Employees, with a combined membership of 105,000 voters in Michigan, endorsed Howard Dean.[44] And on Saturday, November 22, the national Democrats approved a plan by the Michigan Democratic Party to allow voters to participate in their caucus via the Internet.[45] Internet voting was expected to help Dean in particular: his poll numbers were significantly higher among those who would vote by Internet, and he had built a large support base using the Web and appealing to Web-savvy voters (Dean led with 25 percent of the voters who said they would like to vote online; no other candidate had more than 14 percent of that vote).[46] Could Kerry stop Dean from winning the biggest state of the first half of the primary season despite Dean's union support and Internet-using supporters?

Michigan's use of Internet voting was not the first in a presidential primary—39,942 Arizona Democrats had voted online in their 2000 presidential primary (almost half of the vote in the primary).[47] Internet voting is part of the general movement to extend the period over which an election takes place as well as expand the number of polling locations a voter can choose from (including, for example, satellite polling stations at malls) in order to make voting more convenient. In Michigan, Internet voting was a two-stage process. Voters first applied for a ballot, which was sent to them by mail with a unique user number and password. They could then either mark the ballot and mail it in or go online and vote using their user number and password. They could also vote in person at the caucus site.

A Day That Lasts Weeks Mail-in balloting like that available to Michigan voters began to take hold in the 1970s, when states began to liberalize their absentee-ballot laws. The enlargement of absentee-balloting privileges is part of the general expansion of the voting franchise that took place after the passage of the Voting Rights Act of 1965. But in a number of states, liberalized absentee balloting has evolved to an extended voting period. It began with a few local elections in which officials despaired of declining turnout and interest in special ballot measures. According to Magleby (1987), the first such completely mail-in balloting took place in Monterey County, California, for a small special district election in April 1977. Subsequently, other localities experimented with mail-in balloting—as maintained by Hamilton (1988), thousands of substate, often nonpartisan vote-by-mail elections had been held by 1988. Liberalization of early and mail-in balloting for voters at large occurred at the state level in the 1990s. At least twenty-one states had adopted these procedures by the end of 1998, although they are generally not mandated for counties but are options available to local election officials. According to the Caltech-MIT Voting Technology Project, the percentage of voters voting early nationwide has increased from 5 percent in the early 1980s to 14 percent in 2000. In 2004, thirty-five states had early voting, and many reported significant increases in the number of voters casting early ballots. The National Annenberg Election Survey at the University of Pennsylvania completed the week before the election found that 14 percent of registered voters had already voted, compared with 11 percent who had reported voting early at the same point in 2000.[48] Over 22 percent of respondents to the NES post-2004 election survey reported voting before election day, with over 73 percent of the early voters reporting that they had voted more than a week before election day. One third of early voters used a satellite voting location, while the rest voted by mail or absentee ballot.

Who Votes Early? The advantage of early voting is that it lowers the cost of participation: it is supposed to increase turnout. In Arizona, in the Democrats' first experiment with Internet voting, turnout was nearly eight times the level of 1996 and over twice that of 1992 (note, however, that the

1996 contest was uncontested). As with the motor-voter law, advocates hope that mail-in and early balloting will, in particular, increase turnout among voters who normally are less likely to participate—voters with low income and less education (although, the opposite has been predicted by some with respect to Internet voting since computer ownership and use increase with income and education). Unfortunately, the early evidence of non-Internet mail-in and early balloting does not support the hope. Oliver (1996) compared 1992 turnout levels across states as a function of absentee-voting eligibility, mobilization efforts, and types of voters. He concluded (p. 510) that liberalizing absentee voting has increased turnout, but not among those groups less likely to vote. Instead, the result has been an increase in turnout among registered voters, making their votes more "reliable"—less subject to the random factors that can affect turnout. Oliver also reported that the voters most likely to be so mobilized are elderly and Republican.

Stein (1998) compared election day with early voters in the 1994 Texas gubernatorial election and found (pp. 67–68) that in fact the voters who take advantage of early voting tend to be more ideological and more interested in politics. Stein pointed out that the results suggest that campaign officials are using early voting as a way of making sure they get out their core supporters at the beginning of the voting period and then using the remaining period to focus on swing voters and moderates. Consistent with this reasoning, Herron and Lewis (2004) compared actual absentee-vote choices by examining the ballots in ten Florida counties in the 2000 presidential election and those made on election day. They found that the choices on the absentee ballots across different elections (presidential, senatorial, congressional, and so on) are much more consistently partisan than the choices on the election day ballots. These results suggest that early voting may increase the political participation of partisan voters over time as campaign activists use the expanding period of voting to target different populations of voters at distinct times. Figure 3.1 presents the percentage of 2004 NES respondents who voted early by partisanship and when they voted (Oregon voters are omitted because all voting is conducted by mail in the state). Although both strong Republicans and strong Democrats were more likely than Independents to vote early, Republicans were in general much more likely to vote early. These results suggest that Republicans had made up their minds earlier than Democrats. Sometimes early voting frees party activists to have a negative effect on turnout totals. For example, Florida Republican volunteer Jim Kivlon, a title agent in Broward County, voted early so that he could "work as a poll-watcher Nov. 2 and prevent anyone from sneaking in a late vote. 'We want to make sure the election ends at 7 P.M.,' he said."[49]

Who Votes on the Internet? What about Internet voting? Does it affect who votes and/or increase turnout in general? Supporters in Michigan argued that Internet voting would empower younger voters who would be

FIGURE 3.1
Early Voting, 2004

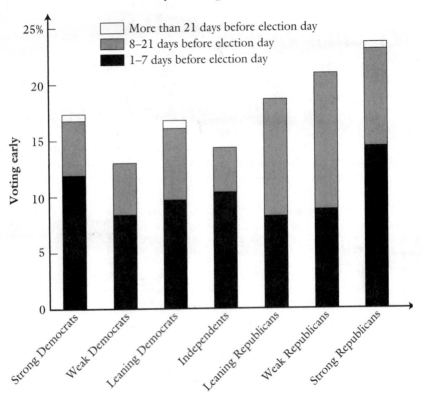

Source: National Election Studies.
Note: Oregon voters are not included.

more likely to vote on the Web. Pollster Ed Sarpolus predicted, "This might be the first election where the youth vote will determine the winner of the caucus and not the senior vote."[50] However, others objected that Internet voting would effectively hurt minority and low-income voters. All the candidates except Dean and Clark objected to the use of the Internet—as North Carolina senator John Edwards maintained, "Until we have closed this digital divide, Internet voting can have only one effect—disempowering the very poor and minority voters who have historically suffered discrimination at the polling place."[51] Yet supporters contended that these voters would not be negatively affected, since all voters would be able to vote early via mail-in ballots, and there were over fifteen hundred sites around the state where voters could get free Internet access. Mark Brewer, the executive chairman of the Michigan Democratic Party reasoned, "For the price of a 37-cent stamp, anyone in Michigan can vote from the comfort of their home."[52]

In Michigan, Internet voters were younger than regular caucus voters. The average Internet caucus voter was 48.5, while the average non-Internet caucus voter was 53.4. As we see in chapter 4, what matters in terms of influence in voting is the identity of the voter whose age is at the median of the distribution (that is, half the voters are older or the same age and half are younger or the same age). The median age for an Internet caucus voter was 51; the median age for a non-Internet caucus voter was 54. Figure 3.2 presents a graph of the age distribution of Internet and non-Internet caucus voters. Although the Internet did attract younger voters on average, the median age of the Michigan voting-age population, according to census figures, is still below that population—that is, the median age is approximately 44.[53] Moreover, given the limited amount of data, it is not possible to reach strong conclusions as to whether the voters who voted by Internet would not have voted anyway using a mail-in ballot or attending the caucus sites, given the competitiveness of the race for the White House at that time.

FIGURE 3.2
Distribution of Voting by Age and Internet Use in the Michigan Presidential Caucuses, 2004

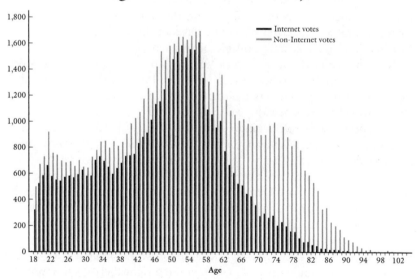

Source: Michigan Democratic Party.

Internet voting was planned to be available to approximately one hundred thousand U.S. citizens serving in the military and civilians living abroad for the presidential primaries and election of 2004 through the Secure Electronic Registration and Voting Experiment (SERVE). In 2000, almost one in three overseas armed forces personnel who registered to vote did not receive a ballot in time. After outside security experts criticized the program, however, the Defense Department decided to cancel it. Experts argued that hackers or terrorists could penetrate the system, change votes, and gather information about users. In particular, computer scientists were concerned about three major factors: (1) there is no way to verify that the vote recorded was the same as the one the voter cast, (2) it might be possible for hackers to determine how someone voted, and (3) stealth programs could gather data on voters who use public terminals.[54]

Bribery and Early Voting Beyond the technical issues of the security of using computers for voting, there is also a subtle change in the nature of voting when it is conducted via mail-in ballots or other mechanisms like the Internet, whereby voters make their choices outside a government office. As Lois Romano observed in *The Washington Post*, "The polling booth also guarantees privacy for voters. But when a person is filling out a ballot at home, they could be subject to intimidation. . . . It could become difficult or uncomfortable for a person to cast a different vote than her family."[55] If the act of voting is a function of social incentives, then when the act of voting is less private, mobilization of voters may increase. But when does a social selective incentive become a bribe? Moving voting into private spaces makes the distinction between fraud and the honest expression of preferences more difficult to determine. The incidents in Kenosha and Las Vegas, discussed in chapter 2, were possible because voting was easy to do by mail (in Kenosha) or at the mall (in Las Vegas). Most state and local laws prohibit electioneering at polling places, but when the polling place is a mall, it is easy for a Culinary Workers Union, for example, to hold a rally and a lottery at a mall to advance the cause of its preferred candidate or for the Democratic Party to hold a bingo game with voting upstairs when voting is by mail. Before the Michigan caucus, Public Broadcasting System media correspondent Terence Smith visited a geriatric center where Michigan SEIU communications director Bob Allison was training workers to vote electronically for Howard Dean. Allison related to Smith the benefits he saw from Internet voting: "The Internet to us has basically just been another tool that we've been able to use to get out and organize our members. I mean, ten years ago, we were going to work sites and we were getting people registered to vote. Today, we're able to go with laptops and we're able to essentially have them cast. . . . Get registered right there on the spot."[56]

Financing Turnout

One effect of campaign expenditures is to increase the probability that voters will turn out. How do campaign contributions enter into our explanation of why people vote? Campaign contributions clearly finance the expenditures of candidates and parties in mobilizing voters—the television and radio ads, the targeted mailings. Interest groups have a choice of providing campaign contributions or mobilizing voters directly. Interest groups who maximize expected utility will compare the expected benefits from giving to a campaign with that of mobilizing its own members. Both campaign spending and mobilization are investments a group makes in achieving policy outcomes. Groups vary in their capacities. Some interest groups with large numbers of members who can be easily reached and contacted (like unions) may find it cheaper to mobilize members directly than to give money for campaign ads. Mobilizing voters themselves is more likely to mean that they get their benefits, as discussed earlier in chapter 2.

Other interest groups may not have as many members, and/or mobilization of their members may be difficult logistically (as is the case for some business interests). These groups may find it easier to contribute money, which is used to mobilize voters. Alternatively, they may demobilize—use their resources to decrease the likelihood that their opposition votes. Reducing the opposition by one vote is equivalent to turning out an additional vote in support, and in some cases it may be cheaper. In the 2002 federal elections in Baltimore, an unsigned flyer appeared in minority neighborhoods declaring: "URGENT NOTICE. Come out to vote on November 6th. Before you come to vote make sure you pay your parking tickets, overdue rent and most important any warrants." Election day was actually November 5.[57] Finally, we would expect that interest groups, like other investors, will choose a diversity of methods given that the effect of each is uncertain and a diverse portfolio is less risky than investment in one type of strategy. So we would expect the AFL-CIO both to mobilize voters and to give campaign contributions to candidates or parties (which it does). In chapter 6, we discuss the use of campaign contributions in elections more expansively.

What We Know

This chapter, through its discussion of the mobilization strategies of 2004 and the problems with voting processes in 2000, illustrates how the differences in the process by which voters are induced to participate and how the process of participating itself can affect who wins elections. In 2004, Bush's campaign coordinated mobilization by the Republican Party and associated benefit groups, and both tended to use contacts with friends and neighbors, whereas Kerry's campaign used independent groups and contacts with paid and outside staffers. Kerry's campaign also had fewer financial resources. The preliminary evidence suggests that these factors contributed to Bush's victory. In 2000, the evidence suggests that the use of confusing ballots and old voting technologies contributed to Bush's victory in Florida and resulting win of the Electoral College. These factors can thus be significant in determining who wins elections that are predicted to be close. We know that recent changes in voting procedures—easier registration and early voting—may be increasing the participation of voters, although it is unclear whether these procedures encourage new voters to participate or simply make it easier to ensure that those who normally vote—partisans—do participate.

What We Don't Know: Candidates and Parties

In 2002, Governor Jeb Bush of Florida won reelection partly through the efforts of groups in the state to mobilize voters who supported his policies. Yet when he had first run for governor, he had lost because voters perceived him as an extreme conservative. In a state where both parties have strong support, his election the second time he ran and his reelection in 2002 are examples of the tension candidates face between moderation on policy to please voters in general elections and receiving the support and nomination of one of the major political parties. In the next chapter, we examine Jeb Bush's experience and this tension by considering the strategic choices of candidates and members of political parties in the election process.

Study Questions and Problems

1. Suppose Congress enacts the laws listed below. How would each of these pieces of legislation alone affect the mobilization strategies of the parties? of interest groups? How would each one affect turnout rates in U.S. elections? Explain.
    a. States and localities are required to allow voters to vote in presidential elections at any U.S. post office in the two weeks prior to election day regardless of where they are registered; however, voters must vote in their locality in other elections.
    b. Parties are prohibited from communicating with voters within three weeks of election day.
    c. Citizens who fail to vote on election day are fined $100.
2. Is it possible for Congress to pass legislation that would result in younger voters' turning out at the same rates as older voters? Why or why not? Can Congress pass legislation that would result in low-income and poorly educated voters' turning out at the same rates as high-income and better-educated voters? Why or why not?

NOTES

1. Thomas B. Edsall and James V. Grimaldi, "On Nov. 2, GOP Got More Bang for Its Billion, Analysis Shows," *Washington Post*, December 30, 2004.
2. Dan Balz and Thomas B. Edsall, "Unprecedented Efforts to Mobilize Voters Begin," *Washington Post*, November 1, 2004.

3. Abby Goodnough and Don Van Natta, "Bush Secured Victory in Florida by Veering from Beaten Path," *New York Times*, November 7, 2004.

4. For reports of refused admission and evictions from rallies, see, for example, in Robin Abcarian, "The Race for the White House: George W. Bush; Two Visions, Two Styles in One Race to the Finish," *Los Angeles Times*, October 23, 2004; Bridget Hall Grumet and Colleen Jenkins, "A George Bush Kind of Bash," *St. Petersburg Times*, October 20, 2004; Ken Herman, "Election 2004: Suit Alleges Protesters Are Muzzled at Bush Events: Professor Cites Kerry Contrast," *Atlanta Journal Constitution*, October 21, 2004; and Rick Ruggles, "Ticket Denial a Lesson in Politics," *Omaha World-Herald*, October 24, 2004.

5. Abcarian, "The Race for the White House."

6. Alan Cooperman and Thomas B. Edsall, "Evangelicals Say They Led Charge for the GOP," *Washington Post*, November 8, 2004. Rove is of course Republican strategist Karl Rove; Colson is Charles W. Colson, founder of the Prison Fellowship.

7. David D. Kirkpatrick, "Bush Campaign Seeking Help from Congregations," *New York Times*, June 3, 2004.

8. Tim Wilder, interview by Jennifer Ludden, *All Things Considered*, NPR, November 6, 2004.

9. Cooperman and Edsall, "Evangelicals Say They Led Charge for the GOP."

10. John L. Allen, Jr., "The Word from Rome: The Vatican and America," *National Catholic Reporter*, June 11, 2004.

11. David D. Kirkpatrick and Laurie Goodstein, "Group of Bishops Using Influence to Oppose Kerry," *New York Times*, October 12, 2004.

12. Kirkpatrick and Goodstein, "Group of Bishops Using Influence to Oppose Kerry."

13. In 1960, 80 percent of Catholics voted for John F. Kennedy, but now their voting is more reflective of current national trends, with a majority having supported both Reagan and Clinton. Gore received 50 percent of the Catholic vote in 2000, so Bush's gain from 2000 to 2004 was only a few percentage points. See Craig Gordon, "Catholic Voters: Matter of Faith Haunts Kerry," *Newsday*, October 20, 2004.

14. David Rennie, "Why the Amish Are Wheeling Out the Vote," London *Daily Telegraph*, October 28, 2004.

15. James O'Toole, "Bush Backers Create Storm in Church Plea," *Pittsburgh Post-Gazette*, June 4, 2004.

16. Yvonne Abraham, "NRA Ads Up the Ante Against Kerry," *Boston Globe*, October 15, 2004.

17. Anna Badkhen, "Hunters' Issues Could Decide Vote in Battleground States," *San Francisco Chronicle*, October 22, 2004.

18. Goodnough and Van Natta, "Bush Secured Victory in Florida."

19. Cooperman and Edsall, "Evangelicals Say They Led Charge for the GOP."

20. Ian Fisher, "In Vatican, Unease with Bush View with Qualms on Kerry," *New York Times*, October 24, 2004.

21. Kirkpatrick and Goodstein, "Group of Bishops Using Influence to Oppose Kerry."

22. Balz and Edsall, "Unprecedented Efforts to Mobilize Voters Begin."

23. James Rainey and Sam Howe Verhovek, "Thousands Are Deployed in Final Push," *Los Angeles Times*, October 31, 2004.

24. James Sterngold, "Unions Work to Make a Difference: Members Monitor Polls, Register Voters," *San Francisco Chronicle*, October 30, 2004.

25. "Environmentalists Rally against Bush Administration's Environmental Assault: Announce Unprecedented Three Million Household Voter Mobilization Effort," PR Newswire, July 29, 2004.

26. Phyllis Schlafly, "Political Activism Takes Center Stage for NEA," Copley News Service, July 20, 2004.

27. Ben Gose and Stephen G. Greene, "A Drive to Mobilize Voters," *Chronicle of Philanthropy*, July 22, 2004.

28. Tony Pugh, "IRS Probes NAACP Tax-Exemption: Legality of Bond Speech Criticizing Bush at Issue; Chief Accuses Feds of Playing Politics," *Pittsburgh Post-Gazette*, October 29, 2004.

29. Christine Laue, "Young Voters Find Their Voice with Stakes High, Electoral 'Sleeping Giant' Awakens," *Omaha World-Herald*, October 27, 2004.

30. Don Kaplan, "Punk Politics—Two Days before Election, MTV Rocks the Voters," *New York Post*, October 23, 2004. *Choose or Lose* was a series of nonpartisan specials on the policies of Bush and Kerry.

31. Balz and Edsall, "Unprecedented Efforts to Mobilize Voters Begin."

32. Liz Marlantes, "Final Factor: Who Will Turn Out Votes," *Christian Science Monitor*, November 1, 2004. Republicans relied on out-of-state volunteers as well.

33. Thomas B. Edsall and James V. Grimaldi, "On Nov. 2, GOP Got More Bang for Its Billion, Analysis Shows," *Washington Post*, December 30, 2004.

34. See National Motor Voter Coalition, 1996.

35. Kevin Sack, "Democrats in Political Debt," *New York Times*, November 6, 1998.

36. For analyses of the early effects of the motor voter act, see Wolfinger and Hoffman (2001) and Highton and Wolfinger (1998).

37. For other research on the effects of the ballot problems of 2000, see Lichtman (2003), Smith (2002), Herron and Sekhon (2003), Wolter et al. (2003), and Wand et al. (2001).

38. Delphine Soulas, "2000 Poll Problems May Return: Despite Act, Punch-Card Machines in Many States," *Washington Times*, February 15, 2004.

39. Dan Eggen and Jo Becker, "20 Crucial Electoral Votes May Be Stuck in Limbo: Clear Winner Could Take Weeks to Determine," *Washington Post*, November 3, 2004.

40. Mark Niquette, "Kerry's Concession a Numbers Game: Outstanding Votes Wouldn't Be Enough, He Decided," *Columbus Dispatch*, November 4, 2004.

41. Amit R. Paley, "Poll Watchers Face Challenges at Lusby Site," *Washington Post*, November 7, 2004.

42. Angie Cannon, "The Fix That Wasn't," *U.S. News & World Report*, November 8, 2004.

43. Kathy Barks Hoffman, "Dean Leads Other Democrats in State Presidential Poll," *Associated Press State & Local Wire*, October 10, 2003.

44. Helen Kennedy, "Labor of Love for Dean: 2 Key Unions Endorse Democrat," *New York Daily News*, November 13, 2003, and Ronald Brownstein, "Moves Expected to Bolster Dean Front-Runner Status," *Los Angeles Times*, November 8, 2003.

45. Nedra Pickler, "Democrats OK Michigan Internet Voting," Associated Press State & Local Wire, November 22, 2003.

46. Deirdre Shesgreen, "Internet Could Upend Michigan Race: Critics Say Online Voting Would Undercut Power of Blocs Such as Blacks, Labor," *St. Louis Post-Dispatch*, November 9, 2003.

47. Michael Doyle, "Voting on the Net: The Jury's Still Out; Is it a Boon to Democracy or a Promoter of Class Conflict?" *Minneapolis Star Tribune*, April 3, 2000.

48. Les Kjos, "Analysis: Early Voting Keeps Booming," United Press International, November 1, 2004.

49. Paul West, "Starting the Push to the Polls," *Baltimore Sun*, October 20, 2004.
50. Shesgreen, "Internet Could Upend Michigan Race."
51. Nedra Pickler, "Democratic Panel to Decide Fate of Michigan Democrats' Internet Voting Plan," Associated Press State & Local Wife, November 22, 2003.
52. Shesgreen, "Internet Could Upend Michigan Race."
53. The average age of the voting-age population is 45.9, close to the average age of the Michigan Internet voters.
54. The program would have been run by the Pentagon and would have been available to eligible voters whose home in the United States is in South Carolina, Hawaii, or some counties in Arkansas, Florida, Minnesota, North Carolina, Ohio, Pennsylvania, Utah, and Washington. See Anick Jesdanun, "Pentagon Cancels Internet Voting System for November," Associated Press, February 5, 2004.
55. Lois Romano, "Growing Use of Mail Voting Puts Its Stamp on Campaigns: Early Voters Are Targeted, Reducing Election Day Focus," *Washington Post*, November 29, 1998.
56. *The NewsHour with Jim Lehrer*, PBS, February 6, 2004.
57. Howard Libit and Tim Craig, "Allegations Fly as Election Day Nears," *Baltimore Sun*, November 4, 2002. I thank Gary Jacobson for pointing out this example.

4

Candidates, Primaries, and Ideological Divergence

Brothers in Office

In 1994, two brothers ran for governor in southern states, Jeb (John Ellis) Bush in Florida and future President George W. Bush in Texas. Political observers and family members expected Jeb, the younger brother, to be the "more astute politician" and were surprised when George W. won but Jeb lost. As *The New York Times* later reported, the results saddened the older brother:

> George W. Bush said that he has a photograph from his inauguration that he finds himself looking at every now and then. In it, he is taking the oath of office while, in the background, his father can be seen wiping away a tear. "And there, on the other side, is Jeb," he said. "He's looking happy and proud, but also something else, maybe a little sad, too. It's tough moment, tough for me to look at. I love my brother, you see."[1]

Why didn't both brothers win? Both brothers, Republicans, advocated conservative policies on many issues, such as welfare, education, and crime, and in 1994 Jeb Bush ran a campaign emphasizing those positions. He made no effort to appeal to moderate voters or minority voters who were worried about the effects of those policies—"when one black man asked him what he would do to help him, Bush replied, 'Probably nothing' " (Barone, Cohen, and Ujifusa 2001, p. 364). In contrast, George W. Bush worked hard to court minority and moderate voters and to explain how his positions might appeal to them. He received an endorsement from a coalition of

about forty Dallas-area African American, Asian American, and Latino entrepreneurs, lawyers, and executives.[2] He ran radio ads on black-oriented
stations accusing his opponent of giving less than 1 percent of state purchases and contracts to black-owned businesses and promising greater support for minority businesses.[3]

But Jeb apparently paid attention to his brother's experience—in 1998,
he ran for governor of Florida again and this time decisively defeated the
Democratic candidate, Lieutenant Governor Kenneth H. MacKay, Jr.,
55 percent to 45 percent.[4] In his second race, Jeb sought out black and
Latino voters unhappy with the Democratic Party, particularly over policies
favoring legalized abortion. He received endorsements from a black legislator and the mayor of Fort Lauderdale. Through these efforts, he won
14 percent of the black vote statewide in 1998, unusual for a Florida Republican.[5] He spoke in fluent Spanish about the Hispanic heritage of his
children, and his Mexican American wife, Columba, campaigned for him.
He emphasized positions that would appeal to more moderate voters in the
state. In 2002, when Jeb Bush was up for reelection, even in the face of a
strong Democratic opponent who had the support of the national party and
blacks' dissatisfaction with his policy choices while in office, the support he
had built among moderate whites and Cuban Americans helped him win.[6]
Jeb Bush's experience reflects what many believe is a truism about American
elections—moderation wins, and candidates for office are drawn to centrist
positions on issues in order to win.

Why Moderation Attracts in U.S. Elections

Voters' Preferences

In order to understand why candidates like Jeb Bush are drawn to moderate
positions, we need to examine the determinants of voter preferences on candidates' policy positions. In chapter 2, we introduced the concept of utility
as a measure of the satisfaction a voter like Jesse Ventura would derive from
the selection of his preferred candidate, Tim Penny, over Bill Dahn in the
Minnesota Independence Party primary. But although voters might prefer
one candidate over another based on a candidate's specific characteristics,
like personality, looks, accent, and so on, Jeb Bush changed his appeal to
minority voters not only by highlighting his wife's Hispanic heritage but
also by emphasizing policy positions that would appeal to those voters. With
the Urban League of Greater Miami, he founded and taught at a charter
school in a minority neighborhood. He lobbied the legislature to cut unemployment taxes in 1997. Moreover, Bush took advantage of the willingness
of minority voters in the state to support Republican positions on social issues. Democratic governor Lawton Chiles had vetoed such legislation as a
partial-birth abortion ban, school vouchers, and parental notification of

abortions, and black legislators had joined Republicans to overturn those vetoes. Bush reached out to these legislators and began to win over minority
voters. The utility that leaders of minority voters perceived they would get if
Bush was elected increased as Bush appeared to take and emphasize positions they approved of.

How did the utility of minority voters and their leaders change as Bush's
advocated policy positions changed? Consider, for example a minority voter
in Florida whom we will call Charlotte. Suppose we can represent along a
single line the policy positions that candidates choose, with liberal positions
on the left side of the line and conservative positions on the right of the line.
We can represent Charlotte's preferences on these issues by a line representing her utility, as shown in figure 4.1. Notice that Charlotte's utility, or

FIGURE 4.1
Charlotte's Utility Function from Policy

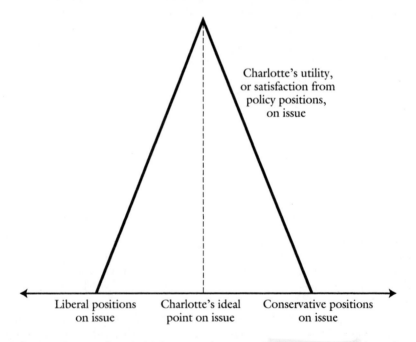

satisfaction from policy, is highest at what we call her ideal point. As policy
positions move away from this point, either to the left, becoming more liberal, or to the right, becoming more conservative, Charlotte's utility decreases. We assume that the effects on utility from movements away from
Charlotte's ideal point are symmetrical. Symmetry means, for example, that
if her ideal point is at 45, her utility from policy at 50 is equal to her utility
from policy at 40 (both 5 policy units away from her ideal point, 45).

We can place the candidates in the 1994 and 1998 Florida gubernatorial races on the policy dimension, as in figure 4.2. In 1994, Bush's opponent was incumbent governor Lawton Chiles, and in 1998, with Chiles unable to run again because of term limits, Bush's opponent was Kenneth MacKay, Chiles's lieutenant governor. We assume that Chiles (and, later, MacKay) had a position on policy issues equal to 30, 15 units away from Charlotte's ideal point. We assume that Bush in 1994 had a position on policy issues equal to 70, 25 units away from Charlotte's preferred position. Since Chiles was closer to Charlotte on policy, Charlotte received higher utility from the election of Chiles and would vote for him. In 1998, however, Bush moderated his position on issues, and he moved toward the center, to 57, now only 12 units away from Charlotte's ideal point. Assuming that MacKay was at the same position on the issues as Chiles, Charlotte now preferred Bush and would vote for him.

FIGURE 4.2
Charlotte's Preferences and Jeb Bush's Policy Positions

C is Charlotte's ideal point.
C-M is Chiles and MacKay's policy position.
B '98 is Bush's policy position in 1998.
B '94 is Bush's policy position in 1994.

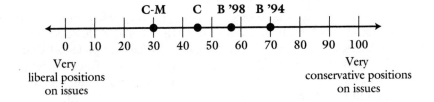

Why Jeb Bush Moved

In our simple model, Bush's move to a moderate position caused Charlotte to change her preference for the candidates. But Bush clearly moved not just because he wanted to get Charlotte's vote but in order to get elected, and getting elected surely means increasing one's votes. Why not move to a more conservative position instead? Or to an extremely liberal position? Why move toward the middle? In order to understand why Bush moved toward the middle, we have to make some assumptions about the policy preferences of the other voters as well as those of Charlotte.

We will assume that the other voters are like Charlotte in that they also have preferences for policy with a particular preferred position, or ideal point. And we will assume that each voter's utility from policy is highest when policy equals that point and declines symmetrically as it moves away from that point. Figure 4.3 presents an example of five such voters, Adam, Brigit, Charlotte, David, and Edith. The points A, B, C, D, and E represent their ideal points respectively. These voters' preferences for candidates, like Charlotte's, are determined by how close the candidates' policy positions are to their respective ideal points. Notice that Charlotte is the voter with the "median" ideal point—that is, one half of the other voters' ideal points are equal to or less than her ideal point, and one half of the other voters' ideal points are equal to or greater than her ideal point. Sometimes we call the voter with the median ideal point the median voter.

FIGURE 4.3
Five Voters' Ideal Points

A, B, C, D, and E are the voters' ideal points.

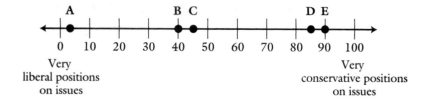

Figure 4.4 adds to the voters' ideal points the policy positions of Chiles/MacKay and Bush in 1994 and 1998. Consider the election of 1994. In that election, voters Adam, Brigit, and Charlotte preferred Chiles to Bush, and David and Edith preferred Bush to Chiles. Since Chiles received more votes, he won. Consider the election of 1998. Adam and Brigit still preferred the Democrat, now MacKay, and David and Edith still preferred Bush, but Charlotte now preferred Bush. Changing Charlotte's vote did change the outcome of the election.

Of course in a real election, there are many more voters. We could add more voters or think of these five as representing groups of voters in Florida who are then mobilized by their leaders to vote, as discussed in chapter 2. The logic of the simple example holds even as we expand the number of voters. That is, the candidate whose policy position is closest to the median voter's ideal point is going to win the election. This brings us to one of the fundamental theorems in political science—the median voter theorem.[7] According to the median voter theorem, if two candidates are competing for an office, if they care only about winning, if voters have preferences shaped like Charlotte's, and if all the voters turn out, then the candidates will choose policy positions equal to the median voter's ideal point. We can see this theorem in our five-voter example. Suppose that all Chiles/MacKay and Bush cared about was winning election. Then clearly the key is to be as close

FIGURE 4.4
Candidates' Positions and Five Voters' Ideal Points

A, B, C, D, and E are the voters' ideal points.

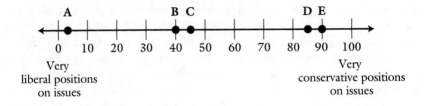

to the median voter's ideal point as possible because whoever is closest will win. Obviously, a candidate can get no closer than choosing the median voter's ideal point as his or her policy position. And once one candidate has chosen that position, the other candidate has no choice but to locate himself or herself at the same position; the best the other candidate can do is have an equal chance of winning if we assume that voters who are indifferent about the candidates choose randomly. Thus, candidates who care only about winning will converge on the median voter's ideal point.

Notice that the candidates converge on the median voter's ideal point no matter how the other voters' ideal points are arrayed along the line. Suppose that we have a large number of voters, say 101. Assume that 50 voters have ideal points at 10, 50 voters have ideal points at 80, and 1 voter, like Charlotte, has an ideal point at 45. In this case, even though almost half of the voters have ideal points at 10 and almost half have ideal points at 80, the candidates will still converge on Charlotte's ideal point. We can move the voters' ideal points along the policy line, but as long as the median voter's ideal point does not change, the candidates will still converge on that point. Thus, how the other voters' ideal points are distributed does not affect at all where the candidates will locate themselves as long as the median voter's ideal point stays unchanged. It does not matter whether the other voters are both very extreme in their ideal points or very moderate—*it is not the distribution of ideal points in terms of extremism that leads to moderation.*

In our example, with five voters, there is only one median voter, Charlotte. But if we had an even number of voters, then we could have two median voters. For example, suppose that we add a sixth voter, Frank, with an ideal point equal to 15. Now there are two voters whose ideal points are greater than or equal to one half of the other ideal points and less than or equal to one half of the other ideal points, those of Brigit and Charlotte. In this case, it turns out that the candidates will not necessarily converge on the same point, since any point between 40 and 45 will get at least half the votes. Candidates still converge, however, just not necessarily at the same point.

Moderation: Virtue or Vice?

Do Candidates Moderate?

Thirty years before Jeb Bush ran for governor of Florida, Republican senator Barry Goldwater ran for president. Goldwater was not interested in moderation. In fact, when Goldwater accepted the nomination of his party at the Republican National Convention in July 1964, he declared that "extremism in the defense of liberty is no vice . . . moderation in the pursuit of justice is no virtue."[8] Goldwater's unwillingness to moderate was spectacular—after his nomination, he purged moderate Republicans from his campaign staff and drove a number to support Lyndon Johnson, the Democratic candidate.[9] His loss was also spectacular (winning only six out of the fifty states and only 38.4 percent of the popular vote to Johnson's 61 percent). While Goldwater is an extreme example of a candidate who refused to court the median voter, the key reality of American elections is that candidates are generally different and offer distinct positions. Although Jeb Bush learned that he needed to choose more moderate positions and appeal to the median voter in order to win in 1994, his policy positions were still different from those advocated by MacKay, and neither candidate converged on the same policy position, as the median voter theorem would predict. Once in office, he passed the school voucher plan that Chiles had vetoed, got longer prison terms for crimes committed with guns, and reduced taxes by $1 billion, policies that Democrats opposed strongly.

Similarly, the policies promised by Jeb Bush's brother George in his 2004 reelection campaign were distinct from those offered by his opponent, Senator John Kerry. During the campaign, those differences became clear as the candidates engaged in three debates, the first watched by 62.5 million Americans and the remaining two receiving a television audience of about 50 million each. In terms of foreign policy, according to *The Christian Science Monitor,* "The war on terror is above all a matter of battling and reforming nation-states. Thus his 'axis of evil' was made up of three so-called rogue states—Saddam Hussein's Iraq, Iran, and North Korea—but did not include Al Qaeda. Kerry, meanwhile, is more focused on terrorist organizations and on international law-enforcement efforts to destroy them."[10] Their environmental proposals also were distinct, as reported in *The Christian Science Monitor,* with Bush leaning toward "loosening government regulations and favoring the marketplace to reduce pollution, while opening federal lands to more logging, mining, and especially oil and gas drilling. He's suspicious of international efforts to address issues like climate change." In contrast, Kerry was seen as a strong supporter of environmental laws "while advocating a faster pace toward renewable energy sources. He wants the US to engage more fully with the rest of the world on environmental issues that know no borders."[11]

On economic policy the differences were also stark—Bush advocated more tax cuts and tax credits and business-friendly economic policies, while Kerry argued for taking away corporate tax credits, which he claimed encouraged companies to move jobs outside the United States, raising the minimum wage, and expanding spending on poverty programs.[12] On health care, the two candidates offered vastly different ideological perspectives. According to *The Christian Science Monitor*:

> Kerry . . . takes a traditional Democratic approach. His proposals . . . would amount to a significant additional commitment of federal funds. Kerry would encourage employers to offer their workers health insurance by having the federal government reimburse them for 75 percent of the cost of their most expensive beneficiaries. . . . He would also create a new Congressional Health Plan that would allow both individuals and businesses to buy US-subsidized coverage. Kerry proposes to expand existing government safety-net programs.

In contrast, Bush proposed "plans that would cost much less. At the same time, he is pushing a more drastic change in the healthcare system—moving people away from employer-provided insurance to individually purchased insurance. Bush's plan to help cover the currently uninsured revolves around tax credits. . . . These tax credits could also be used to put money into Health Savings Accounts," which would allow individuals to take healthcare dollars from job to job.[13] In U.S. elections, candidates often do not converge and instead choose distinct positions on policy issues, as Bush and Kerry did in 2004.

What Do Voters Think?

There are a number of ways in which to see how candidates diverge on policy positions. One way is to consider voter evaluations of candidates. Do voters perceive that there is a difference between candidates? The NES asks voters to rate candidates for president (as well as other offices) on issue scales from 1 to 7. For example, one issue might be how the government should deal with crime. On one extreme (the liberal side) is the option "reduce crime by addressing social causes of crime," and on the other extreme (the conservative side) is the solution "reduce crime by catching, convicting, and punishing criminals." Voters are asked to estimate presidential candidates' positions on issues like that. So if a voter thought that George W. Bush, for example, strongly believed we should "reduce crime by addressing social causes of crime," the voter would rate Bush at 1. If the voter thought Bush's position was more moderate and between the two options, the voter would rate his position closer to 7. How do voters make these choices? Do voters perceive a difference? Abramson, Aldrich, and Rohde (2003) reported that in every presidential election from 1980 to 2000, the respondents who have answered these questions have on average rated the

Democratic candidate as more liberal and the Republican candidate as more conservative than the policy position of the average voter on every issue scale tested. Of course, many respondents do not answer all of these questions, reflecting the fact that many are uninformed about candidates' positions, something we address further in chapters 8 and 9.

What Do Candidates Say About Their Positions?

Are voters' perceptions about candidates' differences supported by the candidates' positions during campaigns? Project Vote Smart, a public interest group, has surveyed candidates for elected office on their positions on many issues. Their surveys show significant differences between Republicans and Democrats. Figure 4.5 presents data on the percentage of Republican and Democrat congressional candidates in 1996 who agreed with the legalization of abortion, passage of a constitutional amendment requiring an annual balanced budget, and a strengthened Clean Air Act. As the figure shows, there are significant differences between the percentage of Republicans and the percentage of Democrats who agreed with these positions. Republicans are much more likely than Democrats to disapprove of legalizing abortion, favor a balanced-budget amendment, and oppose a strengthened Clean Air Act. These answers and the others compiled by Project Vote Smart show that the differences between congressional candidates by party are also evident when examining the positions of members of Congress by party.

How Do Candidates Choose after the Elections?

Although candidates may advocate different positions, once in office they may not be as different from the opposition, and thus they may moderate more. One way to determine whether this is true is to look at the voting behavior of members of the House of Representatives and the Senate by party affiliation. Poole and Rosenthal (1997) conducted such a study.

Figures 4.6 and 4.7 present the smoothed frequency of different policy positions by party affiliation according to voting records for the 108th (2003–2004) Congress along with the particular records of several noted members of the House and the Senate, as computed by Poole and Rosenthal.[14] Voting records are measured on a scale from −1, which is the most liberal voting record, to +1, which is the most conservative voting record. The smoothed frequency curves are like histograms; that is, if you take any two policy points, the area under the curve between those two points is the percentage of party members who have voting records in that policy range. As the figures show, almost all Democrats have more liberal voting records than Republicans. In the House, California representative Maxine Waters has one of the most liberal voting records, and Ron Paul of Texas has the most conservative voting record. In the Senate, Russ Feingold of Wisconsin is the most liberal and Don Nickles of Oklahoma, the most conservative. At

FIGURE 4.5
Reported Positions on Issues by Congressional Candidates, 1996

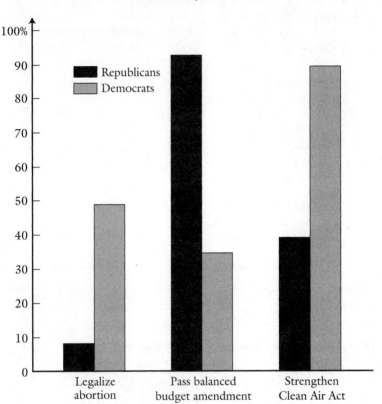

Source: Project Vote Smart.

the other extreme, there are some moderates, like Republican representative Connie Morella of Maryland, Republican representative Ralph Hall of Texas (a Democrat until 2003), Republican senator Lincoln Chafee of Rhode Island, and Democratic senator Ben Nelson of Nebraska. Note that the leaders in both the House and the Senate have voting records relatively close to the median of their parties in that body (House Democratic leader Nancy Pelosi is furthest from her party's median voter).

Later in this chapter we will discuss some of the factors that explain why both Chafee and Nickles can be Republicans yet have such divergent positions. The important fact to note for now is that while some moderates exist, such as Chafee, clearly the median Democrat and median Republican representative and senator have quite different policy positions, and the distributions by party overlap very little. Poole and Rosenthal also measured

FIGURE 4.6

Distribution of House Voting Records, 108th Congress, 2003–2004

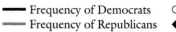

━━ Frequency of Democrats	○ Nancy Pelosi	◇ Dennis Hastert
━━ Frequency of Republicans	◆ Dick Gephardt	■ George W. Bush
● Maxine Waters	✕ Democratic median	△ Ron Paul
	□ Republican median	

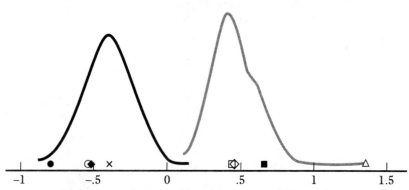

Voting records on the liberal-conservative dimension

Source: Keith Poole and Howard Rosenthal, http://voteview.com/dwnl.htm.

FIGURE 4.7

Distribution of Senate Voting Records, 108th Congress, 2003–2004

━━ Frequency of Democrats	○ Tom Daschle	□ Republican median
━━ Frequency of Republicans	◆ Democratic median	◇ Bill Frist
● Russ Feingold	+ Ben Nelson	■ George W. Bush
✕ John Kerry	▲ Lincoln Chafee	△ Don Nickles

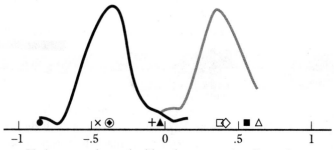

Voting records on the liberal-conservative dimension

Source: Keith Poole and Howard Rosenthal, http://voteview.com/dwnl.htm.

FIGURE 4.8
Policy Positions of Presidents, Eisenhower to George W. Bush

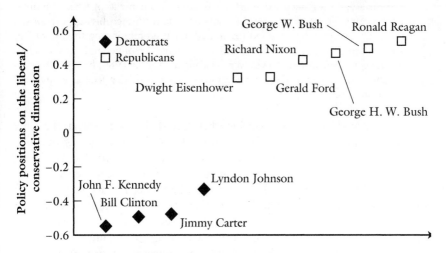

Source: Keith Poole and Howard Rosenthal, http://voteview.com/dwnl.htm.

the policy position of President George W. Bush by assuming he votes favorably on those bills he endorses formally, which is in general a more conservative position than that of his party's median representative or senator. Figure 4.8 presents the policy positions of the last ten presidents as measured by Poole and Rosenthal. Republican presidents have consistently supported more conservative policies while Democratic presidents have supported more liberal policies.

In summary, there is a lot of evidence that candidates do not converge on policy positions in American elections despite the attraction of moderation. Voters perceive the candidates as different, candidates espouse different positions, and they make different choices while in office. Moreover, the party of a candidate is a major predictor of the policy position that a candidate will espouse and the policies he or she will vote for while in office.

A Battle for the Left

Not only do candidates diverge in policy positions in U.S. elections, but often candidates in the same party also battle over which of them is more extreme or more divergent from the other party's candidates. The contest between Bill Bradley and Al Gore for the 2000 presidential nomination of the Democratic Party provides an example. In one of the debates between the two, Bradley was particularly infuriated. "That's not true," he reportedly "shot back" at Al Gore. What irritated Bradley was Gore's claim to have always supported abortion rights. Bradley knew that in 1977, Tennessee congressman Al Gore had

> voted for a ban on federal for abortions for poor women except when the pregnant woman's life was in danger. . . . In 1978, he reaffirmed his support for the Medicaid abortion ban and voted for an additional prohibition on the use of Defense Department money for abortions for military personnel and their families, again except when women's lives were in danger. And in 1980, he voted to prohibit the use of federal money for abortion services under federal employees' health insurance.[15]

Gore did cast some votes during this period that activists at the time considered "pro-choice," and he was not part of the campaign of the time to pass a constitutional amendment to ban abortion. In August 1984, however, he wrote to one constituent that it was his "deep personal conviction that abortion is wrong" and to another, "Let me assure you that I share your belief that innocent human life must be protected and I have an open mind on how to further this goal."[16] Yet in the fall of 2000, campaigning for the presidency, Al Gore was a staunch defender of abortion rights, claiming that while he may have been concerned about federal funding of abortion in the past, that didn't matter and he had always supported abortion rights fully, thus maddening Bradley. Why did Bradley care so much?

Bradley cared because in order to secure the Democratic nomination for the presidency, he had to face Al Gore in a series of Democratic Party primary contests for delegates to the National Democratic Convention. An important segment of the party's voters are feminists and members of abortion rights groups, and both Bradley and Gore wanted their support. As *The New York Times* reported during the campaign, "The two men have been wrestling for the support of just about every left-leaning Democratic group, including labor unions, abortion rights advocates, environmentalists, and African-Americans."[17]

How Parties Affect Candidates' Positions

Both Bradley and Gore knew that to win the presidential nomination of the Democratic Party, they needed to compete in presidential primaries and therefore win the support of the party members who would vote in those primaries. That meant going to all of the active groups in the party whose members vote in the primaries, many of which are seen as the core of the more "liberal" wing of the party, such as the Progressive Caucus, abortion rights organizations, and African American leaders. Similarly, the candidates for the Republican presidential nomination had to compete in primaries and appeal for support from all of that party's active groups whose members vote in the primary, many of which are seen as the core of the more "conservative" wing of the party, such as right-to-life organizations, the Christian Coalition, and supporters of Bob Jones University in South Carolina. Does this explain why candidates from our two major parties diverge on policy?

Parties and Ballot Access

It is important to understand the advantages of candidates of major parties as compared with the advantages of candidates of minor parties or candidates who choose to run outside an organized political party (as an independent). The Constitution delegates most of the regulation of elections to the states. Figure 4.9 illustrates how the flow of voters and candidates moves through state electoral institutions.

Voter flows are illustrated on the left side and candidate flows are described on the right side. There are two flows of candidates—candidates who compete for a party's nomination in the general election and candidates who enter the general election as independents. For a candidate to appear on a ballot as an independent, she or he must satisfy state laws governing ballot access. These laws can differ significantly across states. For example, in Tennessee an independent candidate for Congress need only supply a petition signed by twenty-five registered voters, but in North Carolina an independent candidate must have the signatures of 5 percent of the registered voters in the district, a threshold that can be as high as ten thousand to fifteen thousand names.

The requirements involved in declaring one's candidacy for a party's nomination also vary by state, according to whether the party is classified by the state as a major party or a minor party. In New Mexico, for instance, to compete for a major party's nomination for Congress, a candidate must have a petition signed by at least 3 percent of the party's vote for governor within the congressional district at the last primary, and to compete as a minor-party candidate, one must submit a petition signed by at least 0.5 percent of the gubernatorial or presidential vote at the last election within the district. While the percentage of the vote is less for minor-party candidates, the signature requirements facing minor-party candidates are in effect greater because the percentage is applied to the general election rather than the primary. In contrast, South Carolina has no petition requirements for candidates for any party's nomination regardless of party status.

What determines whether a party is major or minor? States usually designate parties as major if their candidates have historically received a given percentage of the votes in general elections. Typically, major parties have automatic access to run candidates in general elections, and minor parties have more restricted access, but this, too, depends on the state. In Alaska, for example, there are four classifications of parties—qualified, limited, new

FIGURE 4.9
Flow of Voters and Candidates through
State Electoral Institutions

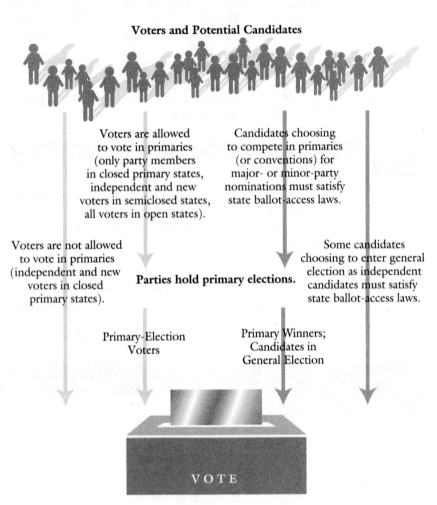

Voters and Potential Candidates

Voters are allowed
to vote in primaries
(only party members
in closed primary states,
independent and new
voters in semiclosed states,
all voters in open states).

Candidates choosing
to compete in primaries
(or conventions) for
major- or minor-party
nominations must satisfy
state ballot-access laws.

Voters are not allowed
to vote in primaries
(independent and new
voters in closed
primary states).

Parties hold primary elections.

Some candidates
choosing to enter general
election as independent
candidates must satisfy
state ballot-access laws.

Primary-Election
Voters

Primary Winners;
Candidates in
General Election

VOTE

General election determines winners

limited, and minor/new party. Qualified parties are parties that received at
least 3 percent of the vote in the previous gubernatorial election, limited
parties are parties that are organized within the state only for presidential
elections and received at least 3 percent of the vote in the last presidential
election, new limited parties must submit a petition signed by at least 1 percent of the vote in the last presidential election, and minor/new parties
must submit a petition signed by at least 1 percent of the statewide vote in
the last election. Like Alaska, most states make similar distinctions and re-

quirements for a party to have automatic status for its candidates in general elections; only Mississippi places no requirements on political parties.

These differences can affect the competitiveness of a state's elections. That is, in states with lower barriers, we would expect more candidates running for office and more incumbents retiring from office. Ansolabehere and Gerber (1996) found just that—in the 1980s, states with the highest barriers had triple the number of uncontested races compared with states that have the lowest barriers, and retirement rates for members of Congress from states with low ballot-access barriers were about three times higher than the rates for members of Congress who represented states with high ballot-access barriers.

Most important for our understanding of candidates' choices in policy positions, the ballot-access laws make it easier for candidates to choose to run within a major political party than to work outside it, particularly if a candidate wishes to run for the presidency, in which ballot access is needed across the states. Many of the ballot-access laws give special status to the existing major parties or are based on past vote totals. That is one reason candidates find it optimal to run for major-party nominations as their first step in achieving elected office. For example, Bill Frist, a heart surgeon who in 2003 was the Republican majority leader in the Senate, first decided to run for the Senate from Tennessee in 1993 (his first try at elected office). The governor, Ned McWherter, a Democrat who had appointed Frist to a statewide commission, asked him "What are you?" and Frist answered, "Well, I'm not sure." McWherter recalls telling Frist, "Well you got to make up your mind. This is a two party system." David Grann reports that friends of Frist state that he did "research" on which party label was more likely to get him elected and decided that he had a better chance as a Republican.[18] Running as an independent or as a minor-party candidate was apparently not considered by Frist (although we consider that option in chapter 14). Similarly, when North Carolina lawyer John Edwards began to think about running for the U.S. Senate, he could not recall in which party he had registered to vote. But he chose to run as a Democrat because of his strong disagreement with the stance of incumbent Republican senator Lauch Faircloth, who had a voting record that was as conservative as Jesse Helms's and was a strong critic of Democratic president Bill Clinton (Barone and Cohen 2003, p. 1190).

Other factors, which we discuss later, are also important reasons why the two major parties dominate U.S. elections—among them our use of winner-take-all elections and elected officials' desire for higher office (upward political mobility). Some candidates, like Jesse Ventura and his fellow Independence Party members, choose to work outside the major parties; variations in state electoral laws explain why some may find that the best choice. However, most aspects of U.S. elections, such as ballot-access laws, mean that the vast majority of candidates for elected office in the United States will compete in a major party's primary in order to get a major-party nomination. How does this competition work?

How Primaries Work

The first southern state to hold a Democratic presidential primary in 2004 was South Carolina. Because they were voting not long after New Hampshire and Iowa, South Carolina voters could choose to influence the fate of the nine candidates on the ballot (although Missouri representative Richard Gephardt had already withdrawn from the race, his name was still on the ballot). Polls predicted that the race would be between two men. North Carolina senator John Edwards hoped to get a win based on his status as a native son. Massachusetts senator John Kerry hoped to build on his previous wins in Iowa and New Hampshire. The other presidential candidates hoped to keep their candidacies alive. Their fates hinged on the voters in the primary, like fifty-five-year-old political science instructor Bob Peter of Seneca, sixty-two-year-old textile worker Roger Ruff in Prosperity, Clemson University student George Hollman, and forty-five-year-old accountant Jana Jayroe in Little Mountain. While most of South Carolina's voters had made up their minds, an estimated 9 percent were still undecided two days before the election. What determined how they would vote and who would win in the primary?[19]

In order to answer this question, we consider a simple model of how primary elections work. Suppose that there are seven voters, Adam, Sona, Charlotte, David, Edith, Frank, and Matt. Adam, Sona, and Charlotte are members of the Democratic Party, and Edith, Frank, and Matt are members of the Republican Party. David is not a member of either party; he is registered as an independent or nonaffiliated. Assume that there are three candi-

FIGURE 4.10
Candidate Competition in a Primary

A, S, C, D, E, F, and **M** are the ideal points of Adam, Sona, Charlotte, David, Edith, Frank, and Matt, respectively. Adam, Sona, and Charlotte are members of the Democratic Party; Edith, Frank, and Matt are members of the Republican Party; David is unaffiliated.
Bradley's policy position is at 30,
Gore's policy position is at 55,
and **Bush's** policy position is at 70.

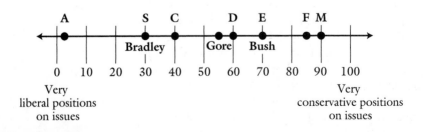

dates: Bush, who is the Republican frontrunner, is generally expected to be the Republican Party's nominee, and has a policy position equal to 70; Bradley, a Democrat whose policy position is equal to 30; and Gore, a Democrat whose policy position is equal to 55.[20] Figure 4.10 presents the voters' ideal points and the candidates' policy positions.

We will assume that the primary elections are "pure-closed" primaries—that is, only party members are allowed to vote in their respective party's primary. (Not all states use this type of primary system, and later we discuss how different systems might affect candidates' policy positions.) In a pure-closed primary, the voters registered as Democrats or Republicans decide which candidates should represent their party in the general election. In the Democrat Party's primary, only Adam, Sona, and Charlotte can vote, while in the Republican Party's primary only Edith, Frank, and Matt can vote. In the general election, all seven voters can vote. Notice that in the Democrat Party's primary, Sona is the median voter, while in the Republican Party's primary Frank is the median voter. David is the median voter in the general election.

Who will win the Democratic Party's primary? Bradley's policy position is equal to the ideal point of the median voter in the party (Sona) and would seem the obvious winner. But if the Democratic voters selected Bradley, they would clearly be behaving myopically. That is, in the general election, Bradley would face Bush and Bush would surely defeat Bradley because Bush's policy position of 70 is closer to that of the median voter in the general election, David (whose ideal point is 60). In contrast, Gore's policy position, at 55 in our example, while further from Sona's ideal point, will defeat Bush in the general election, as it is closer to David's ideal point of 60. Sona receives higher utility from Gore's policy position than from Bush's (which she would receive if she voted for Bradley in the primary). So Sona should vote for Gore over Bradley even though Bradley's policy position is closer to her ideal point. Sona should vote for Gore over Bradley because in our example he is more "electable."

What about Bush, then? Would Bush change his policy position? Clearly he will find it attractive to choose a position closer to David's ideal point. Interestingly, the closed primary system does not prevent the candidates from being attracted to the ideal point of the median voter in the general election. Bush, Bradley, and Gore all will be drawn to centrist positions since they recognize that those positions increase the likelihood of their winning the general election, and the voters in their respective party primaries also recognize that more moderate candidates are more likely to win the general election. A primary system does not in itself lead to extreme candidates in the general election—moderation still attracts. However, our analysis is missing an important reason for candidate divergence—uncertainty.

Uncertainty and Extremism

ledian Voter?

ʼarolina's 2004 Democratic presidential primary, Bob Peter, Jana
ɪd George Hollman were concerned about electability, as was Sona
in oↄ example. Jayroe had considered voting for Edwards or Kerry and
noted that she certainly wanted a Democrat to win who could win in November. However, she felt that both Kerry and Edwards had taken positions
that were too far from her preferences and so chose Howard Dean despite
his low poll numbers. In contrast, Peter concluded that Kerry had the best
chance of winning against Bush in 2004, and although he had originally
supported retired army general Wesley Clark, he decided to switch his vote
to Kerry. And Hollman planned to drive home to Greenville, South Carolina, to vote for Edwards because "he represents the best chance of
Democrats to beat Bush. He represents Southern values. He can win the
South."[21] How could Jayroe, Hollman, and Peter, who all claimed to care
about electability, reach different conclusions about which candidate they
should vote for?

In the simple primary-election example discussed earlier, candidates Gore,
Bush, and Bradley converged on the ideal point of the median voter because
they knew precisely where that point was. But in a real election, that is unlikely to be the case. In real elections, unexpected factors may affect who actually votes on election day, and it therefore affects the determination of the
true median voter in the electorate. For example, bad weather in one region
on the day of a presidential election may affect the distribution of preferences of the voters who participate in the election—and the location of the
median voter's ideal point if that region's voters' preferences are different
from those in the rest of the nation. In Missouri's 2004 Democratic presidential primary, held on the same day as South Carolina's, despite being
relatively early in the primary season, turnout was low—considered pitiful—
largely because of recent snowstorms. Such storms could affect rural voters
more than urban ones since the distance to a polling location is farther and
the trip to the polls more difficult. Kerry, who won Missouri, had greater
support in urban areas while Edwards, who came in second, had stronger
support outside the cities, so arguably Edwards might have done better if
the weather had not been a factor. County Democratic elections director
Judy Taylor of Missouri said of the low turnout and the weather, "We're
just not New Hampshire people. We're just not used to winter."[22] Even if
turnout were predictable or unlikely to affect the outcome, other factors can
create uncertainty in elections. Candidates may be unable to measure voters'
preferences on issues precisely, and this may lead them to be uncertain as to
the location of the median voter's ideal point. As we discussed in chapter 3,
millions of votes are lost because of problems with voting equipment and

ballot design, problems that candidates can rarely anticipate or control. Uncertainty is out there. If there is uncertainty about the median voter's ideal point, then it is difficult for candidates to converge on a common point—moreover, they may not find that such convergence is the way to win the most votes given such uncertainty. Can uncertainty lead candidates in pure-closed primaries to choose divergent (more extreme) positions?

An Example of Uncertainty

Assume in our simple example that both Bradley and Gore care only about winning. But now neither the candidates nor the voters are certain about the identity of the median voter. Suppose there is a 50 percent chance that the median voter is David, whose ideal point is at 65, and a 50 percent chance that the median voter is Deborah, whose ideal point is at 55. Where is the best place for a candidate to locate himself to win the Democratic Party primary in that case? The candidates care only about winning. But the voters in the Democratic Party are clearly ideologically different from the voters in the general election and from the voters in the Republican Party. In order to understand where either Bradley or Gore might locate himself, we can examine how Sona, the median voter in the Democratic Party primary, will choose. We know that if a candidate can appeal to Sona, he will win the primary. Candidates Bradley and Gore will act as if they were trying to match Sona's most preferred outcome. The candidates, who care only about winning, must adopt the preferences of Sona in order to win their party's primary.

Sona's Preferences in an Uncertain World

Candidates Bradley and Gore now want to achieve Sona's most preferred outcome. With uncertainty about the median voter's ideal point, however, the best strategy for achieving their aim is not so clear. Recall that we have assumed Sona receives utility from different policy positions and her ideal point is really the policy position that gives her the highest utility. Just as we graphed Charlotte's preferences in figure 4.1, so we can graph Sona's utility as a function of policy; see figure 4.11. Table 4.1 presents the utility numbers from figure 4.11. At point 30, Sona's ideal point, her utility is equal to 500 utils, and it declines as policy moves away from that point. For example, at 25 and 35, Sona receives 495 utils; at 20 and 40, 485 utils; at 15 and 45, 470 utils; and so on. Note that the decreases in Sona's utility increase as we move away from her ideal point—her utility function has a concave shape (from 30 to 35, utility declines by 5 utils; from 35 to 40, it declines by 10 utils; and from 40 to 45, by 15 utils; and so on).

Whereas the utility curve in figure 4.11 tells us Sona's value for different policy positions, when there is uncertainty about those outcomes, as in an election in which there is uncertainty about who the median voter will be,

TABLE 4.1
Sona's Utility from Policy

Policy Position	Sona's Utility
10	450
15	470
20	485
25	495
30	500
35	495
40	485
45	470
50	450
55	425
60	395
65	360
70	320
75	275
80	225
85	170
90	110

we need to determine Sona's expected utility. Recall from chapter 2 that expected utility takes into account the probability that something happens as well as the utility that Sona gets if it happens. For example, in a two-candidate election—say, with candidates 1 and 2—where P equals the probability that candidate 1 wins, $1 - P$ equals the probability that candidate 2 wins, U_1 equals the utility that Sona gets from candidate 1, and U_2 equals the utility that Sona gets from candidate 2; then Sona's expected utility equals $P \cdot U_1 + (1 - P)U_2$.

FIGURE 4.11
Sona's Utility from Policy

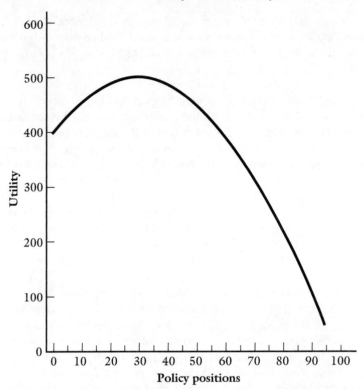

Suppose Bradley and Gore are located at 45 and 65, respectively, as in figure 4.12. Which candidate is better for Sona? As was the case earlier, what Sona considers is how each candidate would do in the general election with Bush. Consider a contest between Gore and Bush—in this case, since Gore is at 65 and Bush is at 70, regardless of whether the median voter is Deborah or David, Gore will win because his policy position is closer to that of both voters. In a contest between Bradley and Bush, however, Bradley wins when Deborah is the median voter, and Bush wins when David is the median voter. We can use the basic expected-utility formula to compare Sona's expected utility from voting for Bradley with her expected utility from voting for Gore:

Sona's expected utility from a contest between Gore and Bush = (probability Gore wins) · (utility Sona receives if Gore wins) + (probability Bush wins) · (utility Sona receives if Bush wins) = (1) · (360) + (0) · (320) = 360

What is Sona's expected utility from a contest between Bradley and Bush? The expected utility is calculated the same way:

Sona's expected utility from a contest between Bradley and Bush = (probability Bradley wins) · (utility Sona receives if Bradley wins) + (probability Bush wins) · (utility Sona receives if Bush wins) = $(0.5) \cdot (470) + (0.5) \cdot (320) = 395$

Sona's expected utility from a general-election contest between Bradley and Bush is greater than her expected utility from a general-election contest between Gore and Bush, and Sona will vote for Bradley. It is important to note that Sona does not vote for Bradley simply because he is closer to her ideal point. Suppose Gore moved from 65 to 30, Sona's ideal point, while Bradley stayed at 45. Then although Sona would receive higher utility if Gore wins, Gore would lose the contest with Bush because he is further than Bush from the median voter's ideal point even if Deborah is the median voter in the general election. Therefore, extremism is not always the best strategy, as Goldwater learned in 1964.

Note that our simple example can help explain why voters like Jayroe, Peter, and Hollman, who all cared about electability, still made different choices in the 2004 South Carolina Democratic presidential primary. These voters wanted to choose someone who could defeat George Bush and who, if elected, would make policy choices they liked. Jayroe saw both Kerry's and Edwards's policy positions as too far from her own ideal point to justify her voting for them in place of Dean, who she believed had a chance of beating Bush. Peter was willing to change his vote from Clark to Kerry in order to choose someone with a better chance of beating Bush since he believed both would be better as president than Bush. And Hollman chose Edwards because he felt Edwards was the best candidate and because he believed Edwards could beat Bush.

Why Doesn't George Bush Moderate?

Our analysis in the simple example assumes that there is no competition in the Republican Party, as in the 2004 election. Why doesn't Bush choose a position closer to 55 in order to win the median voter's vote? Bush will not converge because he will similarly try to appeal to the median voter in the Republican Party. Moving closer to 55 may increase his probability of winning, but it would lower the expected utility the Republican Party's median voter would receive. The Republican Party's median voter prefers a candidate who does not converge completely, just as the Democratic Party's median voter preferred Bradley over Gore in figure 4.12. If Bush moderates, he might find himself facing an opponent for the Republican nomination, someone with positions that increase the expected utility of the median voter in the Republican Party. As with the Democratic Party's median voter,

FIGURE 4.12
Effect of Uncertainty in a Primary Election

The ideal point of **Sona,** the median voter in the Democratic primary, is at 30. **Bradley's** policy position is at 45, **Gore's** is at 65, and **Bush's** is at 70. Fifty percent of the time, the median voter in the general election is **Deborah,** whose ideal point is at 55, and fifty percent of the time the median voter in the general election is **David,** whose ideal point is at 65.

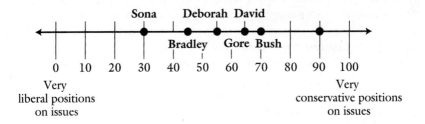

however, the Republican Party's median voter will not prefer extremism for extremism's sake—the Republican Party's median voter will recognize that the ability to win the general election also matters. The competition in the primaries leads to candidates who choose positions that maximize the expected utility of the median voters in their party's primaries, and when there is uncertainty about the location of the median voter's ideal point in the general election, the candidates will choose divergent positions.[23]

The uncertainty about the choices of voters on election day coupled with the need to get a major party's nomination causes candidates to diverge on policy positions. Bradley and Gore competed for the attention of the liberal wing of the Democratic Party because of this combination of factors. This also explains somewhat the inability of John McCain, who was generally seen as more moderate than George W. Bush, to defeat Bush in the contest for the nomination of the Republican Party in 2000.

Variations in Primary Systems

If You Don't Like the Rules . . .

In 1992, Tom Campbell lost the California Republican primary for the Senate to Bruce Herschensohn, who then lost to Barbara Boxer in the general election. The race between Boxer and Herschensohn was a contest between known extremists on the left and right (Boxer is generally rated as one of the most liberal members of the Senate, and Herschensohn was a backer of a flat tax, offshore drilling, and restrictions on abortion). At the time, it was not obvious which of the extremists would win. California had voted Republican for president in all but one election from 1952 to 1988, and Herschensohn had worked for Nixon and had been a strong supporter of Reagan, both Republican presidents from California. But in 1992, after the controversy over the nomination of Clarence Thomas to the Supreme Court, there was renewed emphasis on women's issues, and Boxer had built strong support among Democrats, who had been making gains in the state. A revelation at the end of the campaign that Herschensohn had visited nude-dancer nightclubs helped Boxer with voters on the fence, and she defeated him, 48 percent to 43 percent.[24] Campbell, a law professor at Stanford University and a more moderate Republican—a supporter of abortion rights, for example—was convinced he would have defeated Boxer if he had won the Republican nomination, and other moderates agreed.

From Campbell's perspective, the source of his failure was California's use of the pure-closed primary, in which only voters registered as members of a party can vote in that party's primary. Campbell believed that if independents and moderate Democrats could have voted for him, he would have defeated Herschensohn in the primary and then gone on to defeat Boxer. A movement developed in California to change the rules, to open up the primary system. In 1996, voters in the state passed a referendum changing the state's primary system, and in 2000 Campbell entered the Republican primary for the Senate again under the new rules—and won the primary.

Types of Primaries

In our earlier analysis, we assumed that the primary the candidates were competing in was pure-closed. As Campbell's experience demonstrates, however, the way in which voters are involved in parties' primaries varies significantly by state, like ballot-access laws and voting technology. There are six types of primary-election systems: pure-closed, semi-closed, semi-open, pure-open, blanket, and nonpartisan.[25] The titles of each system give some clues as to how the systems vary in voter participation. In general, in pure-closed primary systems, voters register their party affiliation in advance. Voters who affiliate as Democrats can vote only in the Democratic primary, and so on. Voters who do not choose a party affiliation in advance are not allowed to vote in the primary election at all. States diverge in how early voters must declare their party affiliation. In New Hampshire, for example, voters need to declare affiliation with a party only ten days in advance, while in New York new voters must declare their affiliation as much as one year in advance. Semi-closed primary systems are closed but allow new or unaffiliated voters to vote in a party's primary without declaring their affiliation in advance.

Open primary systems allow voters to decide on election day which party's primary they will participate in. Open primaries differ from one another, however, in the extent to which voters must declare a party affiliation in order to vote in a party's primary on election day. In semi-open primaries, they must publicly declare their affiliation; in pure-open primaries, they choose in secret the primary in which they will vote. South Carolina's Democratic presidential primary was semi-open in that any registered voter regardless of party affiliation could participate, but voters had to sign an oath stating, "I consider myself to be a Democrat," before casting a ballot. In pure-open primaries, the secrecy is maintained by giving voters ballots for all the parties' primaries at once but allowing them to choose only one party's primary in which to vote secretly.

Typically, however, there is more than one nomination contest on a ballot. For example, voters may be choosing a party's nominee for governor as well as lieutenant governor, for senator as well as representative. In standard semi-open or pure-open primaries, a voter's choice of party primary will apply to all the nomination contests on the ballot. But in blanket (sometimes called juggle) systems, voters can choose contest by contest which party's primary to vote in—perhaps voting in the Democratic primary for governor and the Republican primary for lieutenant governor.

Who Chooses Primary Systems, Voters or Parties?

As noted above, in 1996 voters in California changed their primary system from pure-closed to blanket. The political parties challenged the change, however, and in 2000 the U.S. Supreme Court, in *California Democratic Party et al. v. Jones, Secretary of State of California, et al.*, ruled the new law unconstitutional (this ruling was made in June, after Campbell won the March 2000 blanket primary). The Court ruled that a state cannot force a political party to allow nonparty members to vote in their primaries unless the party chooses to do so—forcing the political party to allow nonmembers to vote when the party rules do not permit them to is a violation of the political party's constitutional right of freedom of association. Thus, a state cannot require a political party to have an open primary unless the party wishes to. The same is true for closed primaries. Connecticut's election law required pure-closed primaries, and in 1984 the Republican Party wished to hold a semi-closed primary, allowing independents to participate. The law was challenged, and in *Tashjian v. Republican Party of Connecticut*, the Supreme Court ruled that the party's associational rights were violated by Connecticut's pure-closed primary law. Thus, a state cannot keep a political party from allowing nonparty members to participate in its primary.[26]

In some states, then, different political parties hold different types of primaries. Moreover, the California ruling has led to some discussion of challenges to open primaries in other states and other plans for change. Nevertheless, a significant number of states (including for example, Iowa and Minnesota) still use semi-open and open primaries, and these states are unlikely to change their systems in the near future. As of the fall of 2005, thirteen states are using pure-closed primaries: Arizona, Connecticut,

Delaware, Florida, Kentucky, Maryland, Nevada, New Mexico, New York, Oregon (Democrats only), Pennsylvania, South Dakota, and West Virginia (Democrats only). Sixteen states have semi-closed primary systems: Alaska (with some minor parties sharing a joint ballot but the Republican primary closed), California (which allows parties the option of letting unaffiliated voters participate), Colorado, Kansas, Maine, Massachusetts, New Hampshire (with new voters choosing a party at the polls), New Jersey, North Carolina, Oklahoma, Oregon (Republicans only), Rhode Island, and West Virginia (Republicans only). Semi-open primaries are used in fourteen states: Alabama, Arkansas, Georgia, Illinois, Indiana, Iowa, Mississippi, Missouri, Ohio, South Carolina, Tennessee, Texas, Virginia, and Wyoming. Pure-open primaries are used in nine states: Hawaii, Idaho, Michigan, Minnesota, Montana, North Dakota, Utah, Vermont, and Wisconsin.

If you were counting, you would have realized that we left out three states. Parties in Louisiana and Washington State do not have primary elections at all, and the general elections are considered nonpartisan. Although they are the only states to hold completely nonpartisan statewide elections, nonpartisan elections are used for many local contests and for some statewide special elections. Nebraska uses semi-closed primaries for elections to the House of Representatives and the Senate and closed primaries for all statewide offices but nonpartisan elections for the state legislature. Table 4.2 summarizes the differences in primary-election systems.

Opening Primaries and Party Control

Wisconsin's Customs

How do these variations affect our conclusions above about the causes of divergence? That is, in states whose primary systems are less closed party, elites are less able to dominate voting in primaries. A less closed primary system will affect the identity of the median voter in the primary and may affect the degree of policy divergence that candidates find desirable. For example, independents can vote in semi-closed primaries. If their ideal points are likely to be in the middle, more moderate than the ideal points of voters who are members of a party, then if they vote in the primary, the median voter in the primary will be closer to the median voter in the general election. In open primaries, the trend toward moderation can be amplified if moderate voters from the other party "cross over" party lines when they vote. We call this type of crossover voting sincere because the voters are voting for the candidate closest to them ideologically. This is the type of crossover voting that Tom Campbell thought would allow him to win the Republican nomination in 1992. Besley and Case (2003) showed that for the even-year elections from 1950 to 1998, turnout in states with open primaries was one to two percentage points higher than in those with closed primaries, controlling for

TABLE 4.2
Primary Systems and Participation Rules

Primary Type	Participation Rules
Pure Closed	Voters must declare party affiliation in advance of the primary election and can vote only in that party's primary.
Semi-closed	Voting is restricted to voters who have declared their party affiliation in advance and to new and/or independent (nonaffiliated voters) who choose which primary to vote in on election day.
Semi-open	Voters can choose which party's primary to vote in on election day regardless of their party affiliation but must declare their choice publicly.
Pure Open	Voters can choose privately which party's primary to vote in on election day regardless of their party affiliation.
Blanket	Voters can choose which party's primary to vote in *by office* on election day regardless of their party affiliation.
No Primaries or Nonpartisan Elections	Voters choose between all the candidates for an office regardless of their or the candidates' party affiliation. In some cases, if no candidate receives more than a set percentage (usually 50 percent) of the vote, the two candidates with the most votes face each other in a runoff election. In other cases, the two candidates with the most votes face each other in a second election regardless of the size of the vote in the first election.

other factors that also affect turnout, suggesting that open primaries do attract voters who would not participate in primaries that require party affiliation in advance.

Does sincere crossover voting actually take place? Although measuring crossover voting is difficult, much anecdotal evidence exists. Consider the situation in Wisconsin, with pure-open primaries, in the first half of the twentieth century. For nearly thirty years, the La Follette family dominated the state government. They were Republicans, but a large portion of their support came from Democrats and even Socialists because of their liberal policies. Wisconsin was virtually a one-party state at the time, and Democrats had little chance of winning. As Berdahl (1942, p. 39) reported, "The La Follette group always had to battle the conservative Republicans for control of that party, but usually won because Democrats, having no fight in their own party and little chance of success in the election, participated in considerable numbers in the Republican primary on the side of the La Follettes." Sincere crossover voting of Democrats did advantage candidates in the Republican Party who were more moderate. It also allowed the Republican Party to continue to dominate Wisconsin politics. But national politics began to intervene as the candidacy of Franklin D. Roosevelt revived the Democratic Party nationally, and Wisconsin Democrats began to feel hopeful. In the fall of 1932, most Democrats chose to support Democratic candidates, and La Follette lost control of the Republican Party.

Are Candidates More Moderate in More Open Primary Systems?

Figure 4.13 presents a summary of how primary systems affect the positions of members of Congress, using scores calculated by Americans for Democratic Action (ADA), a liberal interest group that evaluates members based on how often they vote for bills preferred by the organization. The ADA picks a set of votes on bills as proxies for the liberalness or conservativeness of members of Congress. If a member votes the way the ADA prefers on all of those bills, the member receives a score of 100; if a member votes against the way the ADA prefers on all of those bills, the member receives a 0.[27] The ADA scores in the figure are recast on a 50-point scale, with 0 representing extremism (high ADA scores for Democrats, low ADA scores for Republicans) and 50 representing moderation (low ADA scores for Democrats, high ADA scores for Republicans). The bars represent the average recast ADA score for members of Congress elected from states with each type of primary system. As the figure shows, semi-closed and open primary systems yield more moderate members of Congress. The effect, however, may simply result from differences in the median voters in the states, so a more sophisticated study is needed.

Gerber and Morton (1998) and Kanthak and Morton (2001) calculated how primary systems affect the policy choices of members of Congress relative to voters' preferences in the members' congressional districts, measured by examining the demographics of the districts and the way constituents voted in presidential elections. In a statistical analysis of the data, they demonstrated that states with semi-closed and semi-open primaries do select more moderate members of Congress than states with pure-closed systems; in states with pure-open primaries, however, the effect is less pronounced. Besley and Case (2003) considered whether open primaries tend to produce state-level elected officials who are closer in ideology to their constituents than those officials elected in states with closed primaries. They also found that officials selected in open primaries are significantly more likely to have positions closer to the authors' estimate of the officials' voters' preferences (considering semi-closed primaries together with closed primaries).

Tom Campbell's Enemy—Insincerity

Chris Lato, the Republican Party spokesman in Wisconsin, got a number of questions from Republican Party members prior to the Democratic presi-

FIGURE 4.13

Extremism of Congress Members by Type of Primary System, 1982–90

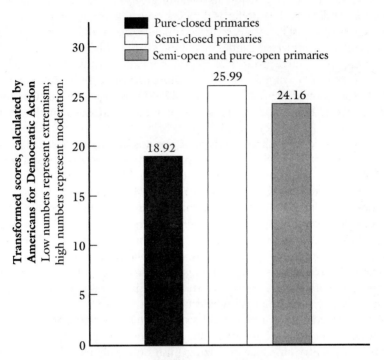

Source: Gerber and Morton (1998) and Kanthak and Morton (2001).

dential primary on February 17, 2004. With George W. Bush not facing a contest for the Republican Party nomination and Wisconsin allowing crossover voting, they wanted to know how they could best use their votes "to pave an easy victory for Bush." According to Amy Rinard of the *Milwaukee Journal Sentinel*, who interviewed several Republicans who voted in the Democratic primary, they "were quite candid about their strategy to use Wisconsin's open primary to try to add more votes to a Democratic candidate they felt could hand the easiest victory to President Bush." At least 10 percent of the voters in the Wisconsin primary were Republicans, with more votes cast in the Democratic primary in some Republican strongholds than there were voters registered as Democrats.[28]

The story of Wisconsin in 2004 is one reason pure-open primaries may not lead to much moderation—not all crossover voting is like that in Wisconsin in the 1920s. Crossover voting may be nonsincere—that is, voters in one party may strategically cross over to vote for a candidate in the other party who they believe their favored candidate is likely to defeat in the general election. In our example from the Bradley-Gore contest in 2000, Republican voters who believed that Bush had a better chance against Gore than Bradley may have found it desirable to cross over and vote for Gore if their state had an open primary.

As we saw in chapter 2, just mobilizing groups of like-minded voters to vote for candidates they prefer is difficult; hence, getting voters to vote for candidates they dislike in a party they generally don't affiliate with in order to benefit their preferred candidate is much more difficult. However, there are examples of such group strategic manipulation from the political machine era, when "paying for votes" was more prevalent. In New Jersey in the 1930s, for example, Berdahl (1942, pp. 42–43) noted, "The participation of Democrats in Republican primaries became so traditional that these 'one-day Republicans,' as they were called, were openly bid for by the managers of the respective Republican candidates, and this in turn encouraged deals of various kinds between the respective party leaders or bosses." According to the observers, the New Jersey "one-day Republicans" were not crossing over sincerely to vote for a candidate they preferred but were crossing over for one they thought their own nominee was more likely to defeat. Although probably infrequent, the potential for this type of involvement is one factor that led party leaders in California to challenge their open-primary law. Chris Lato, the Wisconsin Republican Party spokesman, saw a different danger in the strategy of nonsincere crossover voting. As he noted, "Crossover voting is this nifty idea that's out there and a lot of people like to speculate on what impact it could have. But it's not something the party has encouraged." Rinard reported Lato's conclusion—that it was better not to prolong the contest between the Democrats, as they were "trooping across the country en masse criticizing Bush on a daily basis followed by an army of reporters. 'It will be good to have just one candidate on the other side,' said Lato. . . . 'It's not going to be an easy race.' "[29]

Ambition, Ideology, and Divergence

Upward Political Mobility

Our analysis of how ballot-access laws and primary elections work provides an explanation of the policy divergence we see in U.S. elections—the fact that Democrats and Republicans are different from each other. Because there is always some uncertainty about independent voters' preferences and future choices, ambitious candidates who care nothing about policy in itself but wish to be the nominees of one of the major parties tend to choose positions that diverge from the median voters' ideal point and move toward the party elite's ideal point. However, this control by party elites can be mitigated in states with looser ballot-access rules and more open primary systems. Candidates' positions can also vary to reflect state and local variations in ideology.

Yet even in localities and states with less formal party influence or where the ideological preferences of voters are more conservative or more liberal than the national average, the influence of national or state major parties can be strong because of elected officials' ambitions for higher office. When Tom Campbell ran for the U.S. Senate, he was a member of Congress. Most elected officials in the United States don't run for just one office. City council members run for the state legislature. State legislators run for Congress or governor or other statewide offices. Members of the House of Representatives run for the Senate or for governor or for other state offices. Governors, House members, and senators run for president. While occasionally we elect a Dwight Eisenhower—someone with no experience in an elected office—most of our elected officials have such experience; professional wrestler Jesse Ventura, for example, was a local elected official before becoming governor of Minnesota. Retired army general Wesley Clark, who had no previous elected experience, failed in his attempt to win the Democratic presidential nomination in 2004.

Table 4.3 lists the New York members of the House of Representatives elected in 1998 and their previous jobs. Of the thirty-one representatives, only three had not held government positions prior to running for Congress (Carolyn McCarthy, Sue Kelly, and Amo Houghton). Most had been state legislators: twelve had been members of the New York State Assembly, and three had been members of the New York State Senate. Ten had held local or regional political office. Two had held executive positions in state government, and one had been a staff member in Congress. For many, this upward mobility continues even after they leave Congress. Between 1960 and 1990, nearly 40 percent of the voluntary retirees from the House of Representatives left to seek higher political office despite the fact that most members view serving in the House as a career in itself.[30] We call this tendency upward political mobility. It is evident that many of our elected officials see political office as a career in which one moves up the ladder of the political hierarchy.

TABLE 4.3
Jobs Previously Held by the
New York Congressional Delegation, 1998

Member of Congress	Party	District	Position before Running for Congress
Michael P. Forbes	R	1	Regional director of U.S. Chamber of Commerce (Formerly staff assistant to U.S. senator and U.S. representative, administrative aide to U.S. representative)
Rick Lazio	R	2	County legislator
Peter T. King	R	3	County comptroller
Carolyn McCarthy	D	4	Gun-control activist

TABLE **4.3** (*cont.*)
Jobs Previously Held by the
New York Congressional Delegation, 1998

Member of Congress	Party	District	Position before Runninbg for Congress
Gary L. Ackerman	D	5	State senator
Gregory Meeks	D	6	State assembly member
Joseph Crowley	D	7	State assembly member
Jerrold Nadler	D	8	State assembly member
Anthony Weiner	D	9	City council member
Edolphus Towns	D	10	Deputy borough president
Major R. Owens	D	11	State senator
Nydia M. Valázquez	R	12	Secretary of Puerto Rico Department of Community Affairs in the United States (formerly city council member)
Vito Fossella	R	13	City council member
Carolyn B. Maloney	D	14	City council member
Charles Rangel	D	15	State assembly member
José Serrano	D	16	State assembly member
Eliot L. Engel	D	17	State assembly member
Nita M. Lowey	D	18	Assistant secretary of state
Sue W. Kelly	R	19	College professor
Benjamin A. Gilman	R	20	State assembly member
Michael R. McNulty	D	21	State assembly member
John Sweeney	R	22	Deputy secretary to governor
Sherwood L. Boehlert	R	23	County executive
John M. McHugh	R	24	State senator
James T. Walsh	R	25	Syracuse Common Council President
Maurice D. Hinchey	D	26	State assembly member
Thomas Reynolds	R	27	Minority leader of state assembly
Louise M. Slaughter	D	28	State assembly member
John J. LaFalce	D	29	State assembly member
Jack Quinn	R	30	Town supervisor
Amory Houghton	R	31	Chairman and CEO of glass works company

Political Mobility and Party Influence

The desire for upward mobility reinforces the need for candidates to win support from the political elites within their parties at higher levels as they seek higher office. Consider, for example, how ambition to seek a position in the Senate might influence the policy choices a candidate makes in the House of Representatives. A member of the House, in running for reelection, has to face the voters in his or her district (which for some small states is in fact the entire state). Our analysis suggests that the House member, when running for reelection, will need to make policy choices in order to please the median voter of his or her party in his or her district. But a candidate for the Senate must choose a policy position to please his or her party median in the state. The party median in a single congressional district may be different from the party median in the state. Our examination would imply that a member of the House who has policy positions closer to his or her state's party median should be more likely to attempt to run for the Senate.

Francis, Kenny, Morton, and Schmidt (1996) investigated this hypothesis. They investigated the relationship between how close the policy position of a member of the House of Representatives is to his or her party and the likelihood that a member of the House of Representatives will compete for the nomination of his or her party in the Senate. That relationship is shown in figure 4.14. The policy positions of members of the House were measured using ADA scores, and the party positions were estimated using past senatorial positions and demographic information from the states. As the figure demonstrates, both House members who are more extreme than their party and those who are more moderate are less likely to run for their party's nomination to the Senate.

FIGURE **4.14**
Congress Members Who Run for the Senate by Distance from Their Party's Position, in Forty-one States with Two-Party Competition, 1960–88

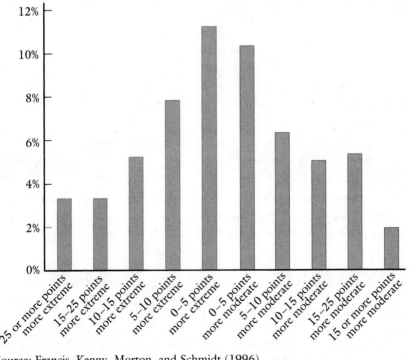

Source: Francis, Kenny, Morton, and Schmidt (1996).

The relationship reported here demonstrates how parties influence candidates' positions through progressive ambition. House members who wish to seek higher office are more likely to seek to achieve that ambition if they have chosen policy positions close to their party's statewide position. A similar relationship exists for local and state elected officials—progressive ambition for a higher position encourages them to make policy choices at local and state levels to please party elites at higher levels. Thus, the influence of party elites electorally extends beyond a single race, influencing choices that politically ambitious officials make at lower-level offices. This means that electorally driven party differences at higher levels will influence the policy choices of elected officials at lower levels if the lower-level elected officials wish to seek higher office. Party-driven and electorally driven policy divergence for governor will influence the choices of elected party members in the state legislature or as mayor. Similarly, party-driven and electorally driven policy divergence for president will influence the choices elected party members make as governor or senator.

Note that in our analysis we are assuming that voters and party elites look to past policy decisions of those who have served in office as a guide to future policy choices of elected officials and that voters choose retrospectively based on the decisions of elected officials rather than prospectively based only on the promises that elected officials make about their future choices. In chapter 9, we discuss why voters and party elites might find it optimal to use a retrospective voting strategy.

What We Know

We know that the majority-rule nature of most U.S. elections rewards candidates who moderate extremist policies and that the candidate who most appeals to the median voter in an election is the one who is most likely to win. We also know, however, that through the process of choosing nominees, members of political parties can induce candidates to choose positions closer to their preferences, further from the preferences of the median voter. Differences in the extent to which nonparty members can participate in these processes also affects candidate positions. Finally, the desire for upward political mobility can influence the positions candidates take on issues as they attempt to build a record that pleases future voters.

What We Don't Know: Red States versus Blue States

On election day 2004, *The Washington Post* reported:

Red and blue . . . have become . . . shorthand for an entire sociopolitical worldview. A "red state" bespeaks not just a Republican majority but an entire geography (rectangular borders in the country's midsection), an iconography (Bush in a cowboy hat), and a series of cultural clichés (churches and NASCAR). "Blue states" suggest something on, and of, the coastal extremes, urban and latte-drinking. Red states—to reduce the stereotypes to an even more vulgar level—are a little bit country, blues are a little more rock-and-roll.[31]

When did states get colors? And how did those colors become a shorthand for describing the residents and partisan politics? Is the nation divided and polarized? In the next chapter, we answer these questions.

Study Questions and Problems

1. Suppose that Fred, Simran, Marco, Melanie, Marisa, and Gerard have the utility functions over policy given in table 4.4. Suppose, further, that there are two candidates in the election, Gulenay and Tony, who are choosing policy positions in order to win election. What policy positions should Gulenay and Tony choose, and why?

TABLE 4.4
Voters' Utility from Policy

Policy Position	Fred's Utility	Simran's Utility	Marco's Utility	Melanie's Utility	Marisa's Utility	Gerard's Utility
10	450	500	425	110	0	100
15	470	495	450	170	10	300
20	485	485	470	225	20	490
25	495	470	485	275	30	660
30	500	450	495	320	40	830
35	495	425	500	360	50	990
40	485	395	495	395	60	1,140
45	470	360	485	425	70	1,280
50	450	320	470	450	80	1,400
55	425	275	450	470	90	1,500
60	395	225	425	485	100	1,590
65	360	170	395	495	110	1,670
70	320	110	360	500	120	1,740
75	275	50	320	495	130	1,800
80	225	0	275	485	140	1,740
85	170	0	225	470	150	1,670
90	110	0	170	450	160	1,590

2. Suppose that in question 1, Fred and Simran are members of the Democratic Party, Marisa and Gerard are members of the Republican

Party, and Marco and Melanie are not members of either party. Suppose that Gulenay and Tony are candidates for the Republican Party nomination and that the Democratic candidate is Taylor, whose policy position is at 50.

a. Assume that the parties conduct closed primaries. What policy positions should Gulenay and Tony choose, and why?

b. For the following questions, assume that there is a 75 percent chance that Marco does not vote in the general election, and assume that Marco never votes in a primary.

 i. Would Tony and Gulenay locate at the same policy positions as in question 2a? Why or why not?

 ii. Suppose that the Republican Party decides to have a semi-closed primary, allowing independent voters as well as their own party members to participate in the primary. Melanie decides to vote in the primary with Marisa and Gerard. Would Tony and Gulenay locate at the same policy positions as in question 2a? Why or why not?

 iii. Suppose that the Republican Party decides to have an open primary, allowing any voters to participate. Melanie, Fred, and Simran all decide to vote in the Republican primary with Marisa and Gerard. Would Tom and Gulenay locate in the same policy positions as in question 2a? Why or why not?

NOTES

1. Rick Lyman and Mireya Navarro, "George W. and Jeb Bush Are Easily Elected Governors in Texas and Florida," *New York Times*, November 4, 1998.

2. Robbie Morganfield and John Makeig, "Minority Coalition Gives Endorsement to Bush," *Houston Chronicle*, November 3, 1994.

3. R. G. Ratcliffe and Robbie Morganfield, "Richards, Bush Slug It Out for Minorities' Support," *Houston Chronicle*, October 29, 1994.

4. His brother George W. also won reelection, 69 percent to 31 percent, and of course went on to win the 2000 and 2004 presidential elections.

5. Wes Allison, "Bush, McBride Didn't Draw Black Voters," *St. Petersburg Times*, November 8, 2002.

6. African American support for Jeb Bush was low (6 percent of the vote in predominantly black precincts), but turnout in predominantly black precincts was low in general, 43 percent as compared with 54 percent statewide. See Allison, "Bush, McBride Didn't Draw Black Voters."

7. See Hotelling (1929) for the seminal work on this theorem.

8. *New York Times*, November 1, 1964.

9. *New York Times*, November 4, 1964.

10. Howard LaFranchi, "At Odds: Very Different Worldviews," *Christian Science Monitor*, October 20, 2004.

11. Brad Knickerbocker, "Cheaper vs. Cleaner: Big Differences," *Christian Science Monitor*, September 28, 2004.

12. Ron Scherer, "Divide over Managing US's Wallet," *Christian Science Monitor*, October 6, 2004.

13. Peter Grier, "Rival Views of the Government's Role," *Christian Science Monitor*, October 1, 2004.

14. Keith Poole and Howard Rosenthal maintain a Web site, http://voteview.com/dwnl.htm, with analyses of congressional voting that is updated after every Congress.

15. Robin Toner, "The 2000 Campaign: The Abortion Issue; Shifting Views over Abortion Fog Gore Race," *New York Times*, February 25, 2000.

16. Toner, "Shifting Views over Abortion Fog Gore Race."

17. James Dao, "Gore-Bradley Race Places Left at Front and Center among Democrats," *New York Times*, October 27, 1999.

18. See David Grann, "The Price of Power," *New York Times Magazine*, May 11, 2003, p. 53. Frist did not register to vote until he was thirty-six years old. As Tennessee has open primaries, registration by party is not required in order to vote in the primaries, something we will discuss shortly.

19. Matt Kempner, "Campaign 2004: S.C. Undecideds Waver, Then Choose," *Atlanta Journal Constitution*, February 3, 2004.

20. In the 2000 presidential election, Bush did of course face competition, notably from John McCain. For now, however, we will consider the case in which there is competition in only one party; later we will consider the implications of competition in both parties.

21. Kempner, "S.C. Undecideds Waver, Then Choose."

22. Jo Mannies, "Urban Voters Give Kerry Victory, Edwards Does Well in Rural Areas," *St. Louis Post-Dispatch*, February 4, 2004.

23. The formal analysis that explains the role of policy preferences of elites coupled with uncertainty in candidate divergence is found in the work of Wittman (1977) and Calvert (1985).

24. Minor-party candidates got the remaining vote. In chapter 14, we discuss in more detail such candidacies and their effects on elections.

25. Note that these are the primary systems as used in nonpresidential elections. In some cases, states with open primary systems used a closed primary structure for the selection of delegates in presidential primaries (as in California in 2000, where the presidential primary was "open" to all voters, but only party members' votes counted in the selection of presidential candidates).

26. As of this writing, the Connecticut Republican Party has never actually held a semi-closed primary. Note that while these two Supreme Court rulings appear to give parties complete power to determine who participates in their primaries, there are limits. White primaries, in which participation was restricted to white voters, used in a number of southern states in the first half of the twentieth century, were declared unconstitutional in *Smith v. Allwright* (1944) because "when a State prescribes an election process that gives a special role to political parties, the parties' discriminatory action becomes state action under the Fifteenth Amendment," which guarantees to racial minorities the right to vote. We discuss this ruling in more detail in chapter 15.

27. Sometimes members of Congress miss votes due to absences. The ADA counts an absence as a vote for conservatism. This was corrected for in the analysis of the data.

28. Amy Rinard, "Election Day Crossover Finds Few Republican Adherents," *Milwaukee Journal Sentinel*, February 22, 2004.

29. Rinard, "Election Day Crossover Finds Few Republican Adherents."

30. See Schansberg (1994, table 1).

31. Paul Farhl, "Elephants Are Red, Donkeys Are Blue: Color Is Sweet, So Their States We Hue," *Washington Post*, November 2, 2004.

~5~

Polarized over Policy or Voting on Valence?

A War between the States?

Red and Blue

On NBC's *Today* show a week before the 2000 election, Matt Lauer and Tim Russert discussed their projections of each state's voting, using a map and color scheme in which states projected for George W. Bush were colored red and those for Al Gore were colored blue. According to *The Washington Post*, Russert asked Lauer, in the first recorded reference to red states and blue states, "So how does [Bush] get those remaining electoral red states, if you will?"[1] During the weeks after the election, those terms solidified, becoming a way of describing the closeness of the election contest and the relatively even division of the country's electorate during the weeks of the election dispute. The evidence of division was strong. In the 1996 election, Bill Clinton had won the presidency with just 49.2 percent of the vote. In both 1996 and 1998, Republicans had won the House of Representatives with 48.9 percent of the vote, and they had won it with 48.3 percent in 2000. And Gore won the popular vote in 2000 with 48.4 percent. The last time a presidential candidate had won with a majority of the popular vote was 1988. The presidential elections of 1992, 1996, and 2000 constituted the longest stretch of close elections in one hundred years. In 2000, during the weeks of endless discussion of the election while the nation awaited court decisions on disputed ballots, news commentators and pundits needed a way to describe a country that was so evenly divided, and the red-blue shorthand worked well. As *The Washington Post* reported, almost everyone used it. David Letterman joked that one way to solve the country's woes was to "make George W. Bush president of the red states and Al Gore head of the blue ones."[2]

The view of an America divided into red and blue states expanded after the election dispute and despite the temporarily unifying effect of the terrorist attacks of September 11. While Republicans kept control of the House of Representatives in 2002, they did so with only 50.9 percent of the vote, demonstrating that at the ballot box Americans remained evenly divided between the parties. As the 2004 presidential election approached, polls showed an election too close to call. Pollsters and pundits began to explore and debate the sources of the extreme parity between the two political parties, and increasingly the red and blue states were described almost as if the residents in them lived in different cultures. Toward the end of 2003, the Pew Research Center released a report titled *The 2004 Political Landscape: Evenly Divided and Increasingly Polarized*, which was widely cited in the media. In a series of articles in *The Christian Science Monitor* published during the summer of 2004, staff writer Liz Marlantes wrote, "The nation's political divide has not only stuck but, if anything, seems to be intensifying."[3] In early January 2004, the *O'Leary Report* and Zogby International released poll results comparing voters in states that went for Gore with voters in states that went for Bush. Citing figures showing that a greater percentage of voters in blue states supported abortion and gay marriage than those in red states and that a greater percentage of red-state voters described themselves as "born again" and owned guns than did voters in blue states, the accompanying press release contended that the results revealed "two different, yet parallel universes."[4]

News-media reporters looking for a good story to interest readers contrasted communities and individuals in the two states that fit these stereotypes. For example, Newhouse News Service's commentator Mark O'Keefe's compared blue-state voter Gregg Steiner of Huntington Beach, California, who is Jewish and thinks religion should be kept out of politics, with red-state voter Dorothy Wallis of Baton Rouge, Louisiana, a born-again Christian who "likes the way President Bush frames issues, particularly the war on terrorism, in religious terms."[5] And the 2004 exit polls seemed to confirm that there were indeed cultural differences between the supporters of Kerry and Bush, as summarized in tables 5.1 and 5.2. In particular, evangelical and born-again Christians were more likely to have voted for Bush, as were voters who attend church at least weekly, gun owners, whites (especially white males), married people with children, suburban and rural voters, voters with high incomes, and those voters who oppose legal recognition of same-sex couples. Jews were more like to vote for Kerry, as were nonwhite voters (especially nonwhite women), young voters, voters with low incomes, urban voters, union members, gay, lesbian, or bisexual voters, and those who believe abortion should be always or mostly legal. These poll results seem to confirm the idea that if you lived in a state that supported Bush, you were indeed very different from someone who lived in a state that supported Kerry. Even state-level differences in fighting the West Nile virus, spread by mosquitoes, were described using the symbols. In an editorial in *The Hartford Courant* on Connecticut's lax attitude toward fighting the West Nile virus through aggressive mosquito control, Laurence D. Cohen remarked half seriously, "The red states are inclined to execute their killer mosquitoes, while the blue states tend to call the Mosquito Civil Liberties Union and talk and talk until the mosquitoes die of old age."[6]

TABLE 5.1
Breakdown of Voters' Choices for President by Segment of the Electorate, Based on Exit Polls, 2004

Segment of Electorate	Candidate (% of vote)		
	Bush	Kerry	Nader
White men	62	37	0
White women	55	44	0
Nonwhite men	30	67	1
Non-White Women	24	75	1
Men and women aged 18–29	45	54	0
Men and women aged 30–44	53	46	1
Men and women aged 45–59	51	48	0
Men and women aged 60 and older	54	46	0
Voters with income under $15,000	36	63	0
Voters with income from $15,000 to $29,999	42	57	0
Voters with income from $30,000 to $49,999	49	50	0
Voters with income from $50,000 to $74,999	56	43	0
Voters with income from $75,000 to $99,999	55	45	0
Voters with income from $100,000 to $149,999	57	42	1
Voters with income from $150,000 to $199,999	58	42	0
Voters with income of $200,000 or more	63	35	1
Union members	38	61	1
Urban voters	45	54	0
Suburban voters	52	47	0
Rural voters	57	42	0
Married voters with children	59	40	1
Gay, lesbian, or bisexual voters	23	77	0
Gun owners	63	36	1
Democrats	11	89	0
Republicans	93	6	0
Independents	48	49	1
Liberals	13	85	1
Moderates	45	54	0

Conservatives	84	15	0
Protestants	59	40	0
Catholics	52	47	0
Jews	25	74	0
Voters of other religions	23	74	1
Voters with no religious affiliation	31	67	1
White evangelical/born-again voters	78	21	0
Voters who attend church weekly or more often	61	39	0

Source: *New York Times*, November 5, 2004.

TABLE 5.2
Breakdown of Voters' Choices for President by Issues, Based on Exit Polls, 2004

	Candidate (% of vote)		
Issues and Segment of Electorate	*Bush*	*Kerry*	*Nader*
Policy Toward Same-Sex Couples			
Voters favoring legal marriage (25%)	22	77	1
Voters favoring civil unions (35%)	52	47	0
Voters favoring no legal recognition (37%)	70	29	0
Position on Abortion			
Voters favoring always legal abortions (21%)	25	73	1
Voters favoring mostly legal abortions (34%)	38	61	0
Voters favoring mostly illegal abortions (26%)	73	26	0
Voters favoring always illegal abortions (16%)	77	22	0
Position on Decision to Go to War in Iraq			
Voters approving of decision (51%)	85	14	0
Voters disapproving of decision (45%)	12	87	0

Source: *New York Times*, November 5, 2004.

A Purple Nation?

Similarities across the States Some states are pretty large, containing both rural and urban regions, NASCAR lovers and latte drinkers, making them a mix of red and blue. As a result, some of the differences between red and blue states cited by the Zogby poll, while they exist, are not statistically significant (for example, in a subsequent, February 2004, poll of red- versus blue-state voters, Zogby found that 52 percent of red-state voters supported a constitutional amendment to ban gay marriage, compared with a very similar 50 percent of blue-state voters).[7] Fiorina, Abrams, and Pope (2005) analyzed data from an extensive Pew survey of voters just prior to the 2000 election. Table 5.3 presents a selection of statements they studied. Although they found that preferences for the candidates did vary significantly between red- and blue-state residents, on many other dimensions the differences were not significant. Fiorina, Abrams, and Pope also analyzed responses of only those who reported voting in the 2000 election, as surveyed by the National Election Studies (a selection of which are also listed in table 5.3). Although slightly greater differences showed up between actual voters in the two types of states, on many issues these distinctions were not large. Among those protesting the wholesale division of states into red and blue was Illinois senator-elect Barack Obama. In his keynote address to the Democratic National Convention in Boston, on July 27, 2004, Obama said:

> The pundits like to slice-and-dice our country into Red States and Blue States; Red States for Republicans, Blue States for Democrats. But I've got news for them, too. We worship an awesome God in the Blue States, and we don't like federal agents poking around our libraries in the Red States. We coach Little League in the Blue States and have gay friends in the Red States.[8]

TABLE 5.3
Voters Agreeing with Statements in Pew Survey, August 2000, and NES Survey, 2000

Survey Statements	Blue-State Respondents (%)	Red-State Respondents (%)
Pew Survey of Residents		
Government is almost always wasteful and inefficient.	39	44
Discrimination is main reason blacks cannot get ahead.	25	21
Corporations make too much profit.	44	43
Government should use budget surplus to cut taxes.	14	14
Government should do whatever it takes to protect the environment.	70	64
Do you favor partial privatization of Social Security?	69	71
Are you very involved in church activities?	21	29
Religion is very important in my life.	62	74
Do you favor abolition of inheritance tax?	70	72
Homosexuality should be accepted by society (agree strongly).	41	31
Homosexuality should be accepted by society (agree not strongly).	16	14

NES Survey of Voters

Immigration should decrease.	41	43
Do you attend church regularly?	50	65
Goverement should allow homosexual adoption.	52	40
Government should favor environment over jobs.	43	42
Do you favor stricter gun control?	64	52
Blacks should get preferences in hiring.	13	14
Do you favor death penalty?	70	77

Source: Fiorina, Abrams, and Pope (2005).

Canceling Out Not only does survey evidence show that there are similarities across states among the majority of voters, but most states also have elected officials who come from both major political parties, some even representing the same constituents. Every state has at least three elected officials who are elected statewide, two senators and one governor. Since these officials face the same constituency as presidential candidates in the state, superficially we might think they would all be from the party with the majority of supporters in the state in general and the party that wins the state's presidential vote. Yet that is not the case. In the summer of 2004, only sixteen out of the fifty states had two senators and a governor from the same party as the state's vote for president in 2000. Louisiana, a red presidential state, had a Democratic governor and two Democratic senators.[9] In November 2004, George Bush won 59 percent of the vote in Montana, but the voters in the state selected a Democrat for governor and Democratic majorities in both houses of the state legislature, resulting in unified Democratic control in the state for the first time since 1977. In Colorado, where registered Republicans exceed registered Democrats by 186,000, Bush won with 51 percent of the vote. Yet at the same time, Democrats won control of both houses of the state legislature for the first time since 1960. Democratic brothers Ken and John Salazar took over formerly Republican U.S. Senate and House seats. Three of the five ballot issues increasing the size of government, opposed by Republicans, passed in metro Denver and statewide. While Montana, Colorado, and Louisiana may seem atypical, it is not unusual for candidates from both parties to receive majorities almost simultaneously in the same state.

Sometimes when a state elects both Republicans and Democrats to offices at the federal level each can make choices that effectively negate the other's choices. For example, Iowa Republican senator Chuck Grassley votes 100 percent of the time the way the National Right to Life Committee (an anti-abortion interest group) prefers on bills it considers important, but his vote gets canceled out by Iowa Democratic senator Tom Harkin, who never votes its way. Grassley was first elected to the Senate in 1980 and was re-elected most recently in 2004; Harkin was first elected in 1984 and was re-elected most recently in 2002. Neither senator has varied much over these years on his abortion position. Moreover, abortion is not the only thing they disagree about. According to the National Hispanic Leadership Agenda, Grassley never supports bills it approves, and Harkin approves them 100 percent of the time, further canceling each other out. The National Rifle Association also says Harkin is a 0 but Grassley is a 100. The canceling of each other's votes is not absolute—the League of Conservation Voters says that Harkin votes its way 89 percent of the time while Grassley does 11 percent of the time. Similar differences exist in all states with divided senate delegations, with the Democratic senator always having a higher ADA score than the Republican.

Why might voters in a state like Iowa put up with two senators who cancel each other out in this fashion? If the strength of the two major parties is about evenly divided and party elites are influencing the nomination process, we might expect a median voter whose preferences are in the middle, between the two parties' elites, to balance out one party's senator with another in order to "moderate" between the two parties.[10] This theory of split ticket voting is called the moderating-voter theory.

State and Local Issues If voters side with one political party on national issues but with the other on local and state issues, then they also may split their votes between the parties. This might explain why Iowans voted for Bush in 2004 but currently have a Democratic governor. Changes in the mobilization of voters from party to candidate, discussed in chapter 2, have made it easier for voters to evaluate a party's candidates for local and state offices as distinct from their evaluation of presidential candidates for that party. Consider, for example, Arvada, Colorado, Republican voters Kevin and Julie Smith, who voted for Bush and the Republican U.S. Senate candidate Pete Coors. But for the state legislature they voted Democratic because they were unhappy with the state Republican agenda. Julie Redson-Smith explained: "With the way that everything being Republican was running was that they had their own agenda with the voucher systems, with the Pledge of Allegiance, with all of these things that they were trying to do. And that wasn't what the people wanted to do. People wanted a change."[11] In a postmortem of his party's failure to provide policy options that appealed to voters in the state and local contests, Colorado's Republican president of the state senate in 2004, John Andrews, remarked: "Their [the Democrats] motive for winning was to get in there and do things. Ours, it often seemed, was merely to stay in there. . . . Democrats talked about making Colorado a better state, about not letting Republicans cut cherished programs, and about the GOP's supposed obsession with 'gays, guns, and God.' . . . Other than denying their charges and hurling some back, we pretty much punted."[12]

Variations in Party Positions across States When Jeb Bush attended the exclusive private boarding school Phillips Academy in Andover, Massachusetts, one of his classmates was future Rhode Island Republican senator

Lincoln Chafee. Yet the old-school ties did not prevent Chafee from challenging many policies of Jeb's brother President George W. Bush and joining a small number of Republicans who voted with Democrats against Bush's tax proposals. (Recall from figure 4.7 that Chafee has a relatively moderate voting record compared with that of other members of his party.) On Sunday, April 27, 2002, Chafee appeared on the CBS news program *Face the Nation* opposite one of Bush's Republican supporters in the Senate, Lindsey Graham of South Carolina. Confronted with the apparent "family feud" between the Republican senators, Graham noted that he understood the reason behind Chafee's position on the issue: "I'll be the first to admit, Lincoln, that I couldn't get elected in Rhode Island."[13]

The differences between Chafee and Graham point to a reality: while we can talk about the median or average Republican or Democrat, there is variation across states within political parties about what should be the right policy choice. Like Chafee, Republicans and Democrats in northern states tend to be more liberal than their counterparts in southern states (like Graham). Thus, supporters of Bush (or Kerry) in two states that that are both red (or blue) may have different ideal points over the policy space even though they agree on the same presidential candidate. That is, in one red state Republican voters may have a median ideal point for policy that is more conservative than both Bush's and Kerry's but closer to Bush's while in another red state Republicans voters may have a median ideal point for policy that is more moderate than Bush's, but closer to Bush's position than to Kerry's. In summary, the survey evidence shows that the majority of voters in red states and blue states have a lot of similarities. And the party affiliations and voting records of elected officials show that (1) few states are really purely red or blue but are more a mix of both colors and (2) even states defined as red or blue by presidential vote vary in hue, that is, in preferences within the range of liberal and conservative positions represented by the national party.

Counting Counties As Fiorina, Abrams, and Pope's research reached the media in the summer of 2004, a number of reports noted the problems and difficulties of using the state color symbols. But this recognition reduced only slightly the extent to which the nation was viewed as polarized geographically, divided into two quite different preference groups that were far apart on the issues and growing further apart. Increasingly, news reporters and pundits began to divide the nation by communities within states and found distinctions larger than those across states. For example, reporter John Wildermuth wrote in the *San Francisco Chronicle* after the 2004 election, "Geography was a determining factor in how California voted. . . . Most inland counties outside the Bay Area voted for President Bush, with his strongest support in the far northeastern corner of the state. But these were offset by votes for Democrat John Kerry in the more populous counties of the Bay Area, coastal/Northern California and Los Angeles."[14] The day before the 2004 election, *Milwaukee Journal Sentinel* writer Alan J. Borsuk noted:

> Consider this fact: In the presidential race between Al Gore and George W. Bush four years ago, no county in Wisconsin had as close a margin as did the state as a whole. In other words, almost every county was clearly red or blue. It was the state as a whole that was essentially tied. To be specific, the statewide difference was 0.2%, or 5,708 votes out of 2.6 million cast. But in 52 of the state's 72 counties, the outcome was decided by 5 or more percentage points. In only four counties, all with relatively low populations, was the margin less than 2 percentage points.[15]

In an analysis of all U.S. counties, *Austin American-Statesman* writer Bill Bishop examined the percentage of landslide counties, defined as those in which one presidential candidate received at least 60 percent of the vote. From 1948 to 1976, this percentage declined, but since 1976 it has risen and now is at its highest point in the post–World War II years, at 48.3 percent, compared with 26.8 percent in 1976. Bishop concluded:

> The nation in 2004 became more politically polarized than during any presidential contest since World War II. . . . The contours of that divide fell along stark geographic lines: Democrats concentrating in dense urban areas and inner suburbs, Republicans expanding in exurbia and rural America. . . . Voters on average are less likely to live among neighbors who supported a different candidate for president. Communities are more homogenous, more single minded."[16]

In 2003, on the weekend after Thanksgiving, November 29–30, John McLaughlin, the host of the syndicated television talk show *The McLaughlin Group*, used numbers from the 2003 Pew survey to summarize the view of an America becoming more polarized by partisan views:

> On this Thanksgiving, did you notice that the talk around the dinner table over turkey was a bit more heated than usual? It may be due to the fact that America is as partisan and polarized as it has ever been on political and social issues. How far apart are we? Item: Is military strength the best way to ensure peace? Republicans: yes, 69 percent. Democrats: yes, 44 percent. That gap, 25 points, is the widest gap since the question was asked by Pew 16 years ago. . . . Item: Should government guarantee every citizen food and shelter? Yes: Democrats, 81 percent; Republicans: 46 percent yes—a whopping 35 percent difference.[17]

In our analysis of how candidates and voters interact in the electoral process, we have seen that while there are forces that push candidates toward moderation in the general election, uncertainty about the location of the median voter's ideal point, the need to secure a major party's nomination for ballot access, along with the desire for upward mobility, cause candidates to diverge in their policy choices toward the preferences of party elites. Thus, we understand the forces behind divergence between candidates in policy choices. We have also noted, in chapter 3, that cursory evidence suggests that turnout was higher in 2004 partly because voters saw the choices between the two candidates as distinct and consequential. But we haven't said much about what the actual distribution of voters' preferences in U.S. elections is like. Is McLaughlin right? Have U.S. voters become more polarized?

The Arguments behind the Polarized View: A Closer Look

The arguments that voters are more polarized rest on five stylized facts: (1) national elections now are unusually close as compared with those of previous years; (2) voting in counties and other substate geographic areas is increasingly lopsided in favor of one party or the other; (3) elected officials from the two major parties seem more doctrinaire and extreme than previously and appear less willing to compromise and create bipartisan coalitions to pass legislation; (4) Republican and Democratic identifiers are expressing preferences in surveys that suggest more divisions over issues between parties than before; and (5) voters are polarized by cultural and social issues, as evidenced in exit polls, and those issues are now framing the choices voters are making in elections. We consider below each of these stylized facts and whether they imply an increasing polarization of the electorate.

Do Close National Elections Imply a Polarized Electorate?

Fiorina, Abrams, and Pope (2005) point out that the existence of close elections, with party support divided almost evenly, does not necessarily mean that the electorate is polarized. To see why this is so, we need to define what we mean by polarization of voters' preferences. Consider the hypothetical distribution of voter ideal points in Figure 5.1. At each policy position the curve gives us a measure of the frequency with which voters have ideal points at that policy point. We say that this distribution is bimodal, which means that it has two "local" maximums or, in not exactly correct mathematical terms, two pseudomodes or pseudo-most-likely points.[18] That is, notice that as policies move from the most liberal extreme on the far left, the frequency of voters' ideal points first increases and reaches a maximum (which we call a local maximum since it is not necessarily the global maximum point on the curve) and then decreases. At the ideal points of voters in the middle, between liberal and conservative, the number of voters is much smaller. Then, as policy becomes more conservative, the curve increases again, reaching a second local maximum, declining as policy becomes more and more conservative. The electorate is polarized, with few voters in the middle. It is also evenly divided, with almost equal numbers of voters whose ideal points are close to each party's policy position, although this is certainly not required for an electorate to be polarized. Notice the similarity between this figure and figures 4.6 and 4.7, which present the distribution of voters' ideal points in the U.S. House of Representatives and Senate, as estimated by Poole and Rosenthal. Congress is clearly polarized.

FIGURE 5.1
A Divided Polarized Electorate

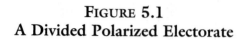

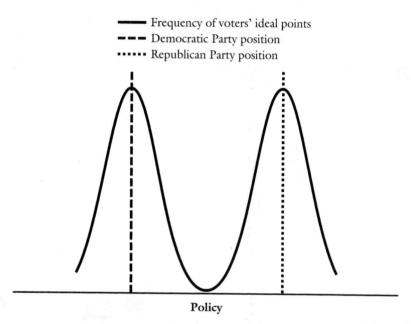

Policy

In figure 5.2, the electorate is similarly divided but not at all polarized; the majority of voters' ideal points are between the two party positions, and there is a single mode, or most popular ideal point, which also happens to be the median. The fact that the major parties are splitting the vote almost evenly would exist under both situations, yet in one, voters are polarized, and in the other voters are not. Closely divided elections in themselves cannot tell us whether the electorate is polarized. The problem with trying to make inferences about the polarization of the electorate based on the closeness of an election is that because an election is a binary choice, just knowing the percentage of the vote does not tell us anything about how far or close the voters' ideal points are from or to the candidates' policy positions or how they are distributed generally. All we can say is that the candidates have located such that the voters as a whole are indifferent and the election is tied. The recent period of especially competitive national elections may simply reflect candidates locating at positions that more evenly divide the population as a whole than they did in previous years. As we discuss in more detail in chapter 13, because most states allocate Electoral College votes using a winner-take-all system, elections are often closer in terms of the popular vote than the electoral vote, and what is reported or recorded historically as an overwhelming or landslide victory in electoral votes is often far from that in terms of the popular-vote margin. Since 1880, in only five of the thirty-two presidential elections has the winner achieved a popular-vote victory of 60 percent or more, and in those cases, he has never received more than a little over 60 percent. The last such election was in 1972, when Richard Nixon defeated George McGovern.

FIGURE 5.2
A Divided Nonpolarized Electorate, 2004

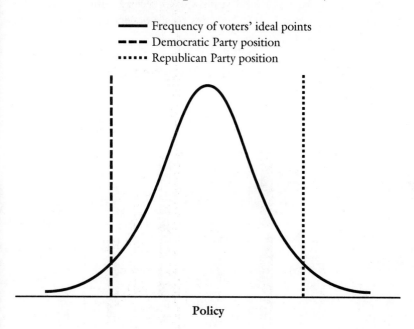

——— Frequency of voters' ideal points
– – – Democratic Party position
•••••• Republican Party position

Policy

Does an Increase in Landslide Counties Imply a More Polarized Electorate?

Are More Voters Living in Landslide Counties? Although Bishop's data, mentioned earlier, suggests that the number of landslide counties is increasing, a more careful analysis presents a complicated picture. Klinker (2004) examined county voting patterns from 1840 to 2000 and found that only 36 percent of voters in 2000 lived in landslide counties. Moreover, he pointed out (p. 3) that because Republican voters "tend to be concentrated in a large number of relatively small counties, the numbers of landslide counties and the number of voters in them is closely related to the performance of Republican presidential candidates." Since George W. Bush did well in 2000 and 2004, the number of landslide counties would naturally be higher. Furthermore, even if landslide counties are increasing, the increase may also reflect increased polarization of candidates, not voters. To see how this can be true, consider the following "hypothetical" Wisconsin.

A Hypothetical Wisconsin As noted above, the margin between the two presidential candidates in Wisconsin in 2000 was closer than the margin in any county in the state. Figure 5.3 provides an example of a distribution of voters' ideal points in a hypothetical state with two counties. The situation it presents is similar to that in Wisconsin, where the electorate as a whole is polarized. Suppose that there are two candidates, Andrea and Boris, who locate at 45 and 55, respectively. Andrea would receive approximately 82.5 percent of the vote in county 1, and Boris would receive approximately the same percentage in county 2. Both counties would be landslide counties, yet

FIGURE 5.3
Hypothetical State with a Polarized Electorate

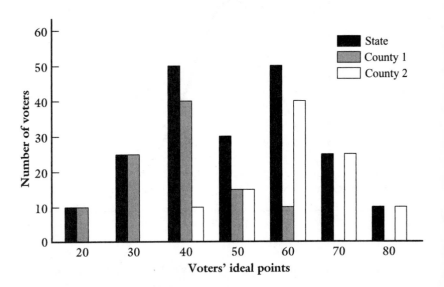

in the state as a whole the election would be virtually tied. The evidence that candidates are winning the counties by landslides seems to support, from this example, the inference that the electorate in the state is polarized.

Yet consider another hypothetical state, represented in figure 5.4. In this state, there are more voters with ideal points at 50, but the counties are in fact slightly more lopsided than in the previous figure (in figure 5.3, county 1 has some voters whose ideal points are at 60 and county 2 has some whose ideal points are at 40, which is not the case in figure 5.4). The voters are sorted better by county according to their ideological preferences. Suppose again that voters in the state were choosing between Andrea and Boris. Andrea would receive 87.5 percent of the vote in county 1, and Boris would

FIGURE 5.4
Hypothetical State with a Nonpolarized Electorate

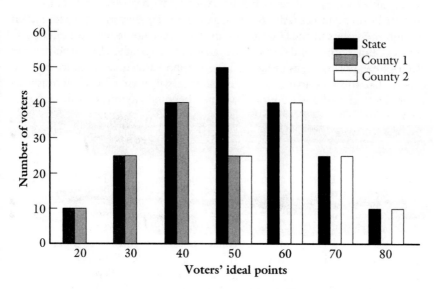

receive a similar percentage in county 2. Both counties have landslides in this example—in fact, more so than in the previous example—yet the state as a whole is not polarized.

Our simple analysis shows that just knowing that landslide counties are increasing does not necessarily imply that the electorate as a whole is polarized, since sorting of voters ideologically could have the same effect. It is difficult to measure whether such sorting is occurring, but it is not unreasonable to assume that if factors that are related to the type of community that an individual prefers are positively related with the way an individual votes, then if that relation is becoming stronger, ideological sorting is occurring as voters choose to live in communities they prefer independent of their public policy preferences. It is not that voters are moving to communities where they know they will find fellow partisans but that their fellow partisans have similar preferences on which types of communities they like. Consider, for example, Californian Katherine Lopez, who moved to a more rural community prior to the 2004 election. Lopez remarked, "It doesn't feel very Democratic out here. . . . It's more conservative, and there's a big Christian community out here."[19]

But we don't actually need voters to move to show that in nonpolarized electorates we can see an increase in landslide counties. The same effect can occur because candidates themselves have distinguished their policy positions better. For example, suppose that initially both Andrea and Boris had chosen policy positions at 50, the position of the general electorate's median

voter. All voters would be indifferent toward the two candidates even if they
had located in communities where voters are similar in their preferences on
policy, and each candidate would be expected to receive 50 percent of the
vote in both examples. All counties would be competitive and close even
though the voters in the counties might have very homogenous policy preferences. But if the candidates move apart ideologically, then whether the
electorate is polarized, as in figure 5.3, or nonpolarized, as in figure 5.4, we
expect that the vote margins in the counties will increase even though no
voters have moved and counties have not become any more homogeneous
than before. Thus, candidates becoming more polarized could cause an increase in the number of people living in landslide counties even though the
electorate's preferences are unchanged and no one has moved.

Parties, Candidates, and Policy Choices over Time Has there been a
recent change in the policy positions of national candidates such that the
candidates are further apart and thus voters are less likely to be indifferent
toward them, resulting in more landslide counties? Unfortunately, we have
very little data on the positions of challengers in elections over time, but we
do have detailed information on the voting records of members of Congress, which has been used by Poole and Rosenthal (1997) to construct policy positions for these members and for some presidents, as discussed in
chapter 4 and illustrated in figures 4.6–4.8. Figure 5.5 presents the different
party medians in the House of Representatives from 1879 to 2004. Estimates for presidential positions are also graphed. Figure 5.6 presents the difference in the party medians over the same period, and Figure 5.7 presents
the entire distribution of voting by major-party members for selected Congresses during the post–World War II period. Poole and Rosenthal were
able to create these estimated positions over time because of the overlapping
nature of congressional tenure. That is, each year that Congress is in session
there are members from previous Congresses and members who will serve in
future Congresses. This allows Poole and Rosenthal to compute policy positions that can be compared over time for periods for which the major parties
are relatively stable with overlapping generations within parties. It is not
possible, however, to use these estimates to compare, for example, the policy positions of Federalists in the first Congress with Republicans in Congress currently, but it is reasonable to compare positions over the twentieth
century.

As the figures show, after World War I, the parties began a long trend of
moving toward the center and closer together, which stabilized from the
1940s until the early 1970s. The distribution of voting choices during
1947–49 was in fact unimodal. Both Republicans and Democrats appear to
have moderated their positions, and one Republican president, Dwight
Eisenhower, chose particularly moderate positions on issues during this period. But beginning in the early 1970s, the parties in Congress began to diverge again, to polarize. Note the Democrats' movement to the left from

FIGURE 5.5

Party Medians in Congress and Presidential Positions, 1879–2003

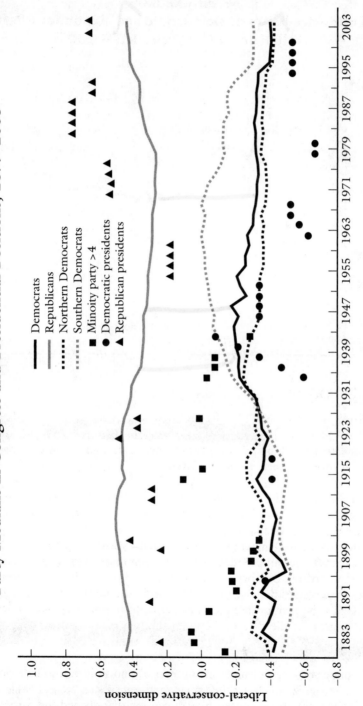

Source: Based on Poole and Rosenthal (1997).

FIGURE 5.6
Difference between Democratic and Republican Party
Medians in Congress, 1879–2003

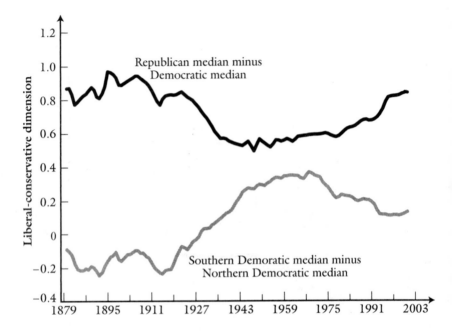

Source: Based on Poole and Rosenthal (1997).

1947–49 to 1979–81, the Republicans' movement to the right from 1979–81 to 2003–04, and the relative disappearance of moderate members. By the late 1990s, the parties had polarized, although they were not as divided as they had been in the late 1890s.

The North-South Democratic Coalition Why did the moderation begin to occur in the 1930s and '40s, and how was it sustained for so long? We can see that the moderation was clearly related to a division between northern and southern Democrats—until the mid-1930s, when Franklin Delano Roosevelt was elected president, southern Democrats were slightly more liberal than northern Democrats. But southern Democrats became increasingly more conservative than northern Democrats over time, such that by the mid-1960s the division between northern and southern Democrats was almost as great as the division between the two major parties. The median southern Democrat was slightly closer to the median Republican than to the median northern Democrat.

To understand the changes in southern Democratic voting behavior, we need to recognize that over the time period some issues are not easily classified in the main liberal-conservative dimension that divided the parties, par-

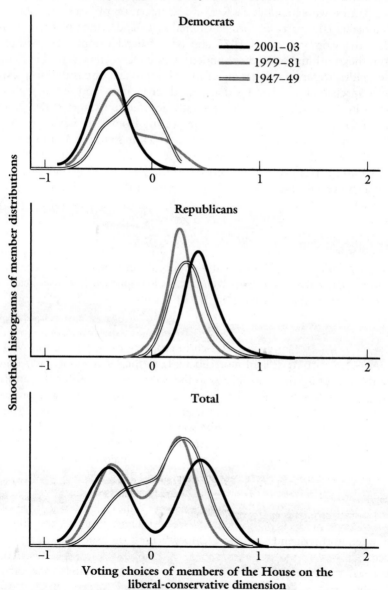

FIGURE 5.7
**Changing Distribution of Voting in Congress
by Major-Party Affiliation**

Democrats

2001–03
1979–81
1947–49

Republicans

Total

Voting choices of members of the House on the
liberal-conservative dimension

Source: Based on Poole and Rosenthal (1997).

ticularly the issue of civil rights and voting rights for blacks. After the Civil War ended, Republicans continued to propose measures to ensure civil rights and voting rights for blacks, and during Reconstruction blacks were able to participate in politics and achieve elected office in the South. Civil rights and voting rights for blacks in the South was an issue that divided the two parties, with Republicans favoring participation of blacks in politics and Democrats (the party of former Confederates and sympathizers) opposed. After the Compromise of 1877 and after federal troops were withdrawn from the South the same year, southern white Democrats were able to begin the gradual disenfranchisement of blacks, a process discussed more expansively in chapter 15. During that period, civil rights and voting rights for blacks in the South were no longer hotly debated in Congress. Being liberal meant favoring the redistribution of wealth from rich whites to poorer whites, many of whom lived in the South. Thus southern Democrats were slightly more liberal than northern Democrats in their voting behavior.

As more African Americans moved to the North during and after World War I, however, liberal policies began to mean the redistribution of wealth to blacks as well as poor whites, especially with the advent of the large New Deal aid programs. Southern and northern Democrats began to separate, with southern Democrats becoming more conservative. There is some evidence that the rise in the conservatism of southern Democrats was a combination of the racial prejudice and economic interests of the elite in the South—richer white southern Democrats also opposed liberal policies such as a minimum-wage law passed in 1938 because such policies lessened economic advantages of southern labor.[20] Why didn't these southern Democrats join the Republican Party, given their increasing conservatism, whatever their motives? As discussed in chapters 14 and 15, until 1964 the Republican Party remained more liberal than the Democratic Party on civil rights and voting rights for blacks in the South. Since the Republican Party, the party of Abraham Lincoln, continued to be the party that represented those few African Americans who were able to participate in politics in the South, it was unthinkable for white southerners opposed to black participation to make such a switch. Southern Democrats also held significant positions of leadership in Congress by forming the majority in a coalition with northern Democrats. By being in the majority, southern Democrats were able to hold positions of authority within Congress and control the agenda, preventing the passage of legislation on civil rights and voting rights or allowing only the passage of weak measures.[21] Thus, although the difference between northern and southern Democrats grew on issues of economics and race, southern Democrats simply voted in coalitions with Republicans on issues when they disagreed with northern Democrats rather than officially switching parties. Congress operated as a three-party legislature, with southern Democrats choosing by issue which side to support.

Moderation also occurred among Republicans during this period. Partly this was a reaction to the crisis of the Great Depression and the desire for more liberal policies across the country to deal with the crisis. During World War II and the subsequent cold war, nationally elected officials from both parties agreed on many choices facing the country. Of note is the relative disappearance of minor-party members of Congress as the two major parties moderated. From 1879 to 1941, a number of Congresses had five or more representatives who were members of minor parties, like the Progressives. The median minor-party member is shown for these years in figure 5.5. These medians are always more moderate than the two major parties.[22] Yet as Democrats and Republicans began to choose more moderate policies, the minor-party members began to cease achieving office. While minor-party members and independents have served in the House since 1941, there have always been fewer than five in any given Congress.

The Rise of Southern Republicans How did polarization in Congress begin to increase again? In the 1964 presidential election, as explained in chapter 14, Democrats and Republicans switched their positions on civil rights and voting rights, and with a majority of Democrats in Congress, a southern Democratic president, Lyndon Johnson, passed the Civil Rights Act of 1964 and the Voting Rights Act of 1965. During the late 1960s and throughout the 1970s and 1980s, as blacks were again able to vote in the South in large numbers, the Democratic Party was their party of choice, and conservative white Democratic House members either switched to the Republican Party or were replaced by more liberal Democrats in districts where black votes could be consequential or by Republicans where black votes were not consequential. As a result, the division within the Democratic Party became less pronounced, particularly in the 1990s as Republicans gained a majority in the House of Representatives and a number of remaining southern Democrats switched parties or were defeated.

The switch on civil rights and voting rights was not the only factor behind the increasing polarization. The Republican Party began to adopt more conservative positions on social issues, such as abortion, gay marriage, school vouchers, and so on, while Democrats took more liberal positions on those issues. Liberal northern Republicans began to be replaced by either more conservative Republicans or liberal Democrats. While the replacement of southern conservative Democrats certainly had an impact on the increasing polarization, the continued rise in polarization during the 1990s suggests that something more has been going on to cause elected officials from the two parties to choose more divergent positions. When Poole and Rosenthal analyzed changes in congressional policy choices without southern representatives in their estimation, they found polarization increasing over time.[23] Why this has happened is something we will come back to at the end of this section.

In conclusion, the evidence suggests that the parties in Congress had become much more polarized by 2004. Such polarization of elected officials could explain why more people are living in landslide counties. As voters have to make choices that are more distinct in terms of policy consequences, and as voters' preferences over these policies have become more homogeneous within counties than across the country, we would expect that the difference in vote shares between the parties would rise in counties even if voters' preferences for policies are unimodal and not polarized and the degree of homogeneity of voters' preferences in counties has stayed constant. Thus, the evidence that more people live in landslide counties does not mean that the electorate is becoming more polarized and more so geographically.

Reverse Logic—Does Polarization of Elected Officials Imply Polarization of the Electorate?

In November 2003, Republicans in Congress were more frustrated with Democrats than usual. They didn't have enough of a majority to pass the energy and Medicare legislation they wanted or to confirm presidential judicial appointments. The Republicans decided to schedule a thirty-hour-long debate to force Democrats to discuss the issues. But the debate only led to more acrimony. As Senator Tom Harkin of Iowa remarked: "Republicans just want to make up the rules as they go, change them to fit the times and the circumstances, to change their arguments, sanctimonious hypocrisy, partisan politics, double standards." Senator Don Nickles of Oklahoma responded: "It is not right to be coming down and mentioning senators by name and use words like *sanctimonious hypocrisy* and impugning the senators' motives."[24] As the presidential campaign heated up in 2004, battles between Democrats and Republicans in Washington continued. When senators and their official president, Vice President Richard Cheney, gathered for a formal portrait in June 2004, Senator Patrick Leahy of Vermont walked over to the Republican side of the room. Cheney turned away from Leahy, who had recently publicly claimed that Cheney's former company, Halliburton, was receiving special favors from the government. Leahy joked that Cheney was unwilling to talk to Democrats. Cheney and Leahy then had a fiery exchange, with Cheney stalking off, "using an obscene phrase to describe what he thought Mr. Leahy should do."[25] Such interactions are not just in the Senate. In the session after the November 2004 election, Democratic House leader Nancy Pelosi called Republican House majority leader Tom DeLay " 'not only unethical but delusional' while DeLay charged 'she has violated federal law.' "[26]

These incidents are just two examples of what many observers have described as an atmosphere of greater bickering and less bipartisanship among elected officials. In an interview with *Time* magazine in November 2004, retiring Republican senator Don Nickles of Oklahoma remarked: "In the past few years, the Senate has become probably more partisan than I think a lot of us like to see."[27] Democratic Senator Joseph Lieberman of Connecticut bemoaned: "It used to be you ran for office and in the first few months you could get something done. Now it's a constant campaign, a constant partisanship."[28]

If elected officials from the two parties are more polarized and are choosing positions to please voters, shouldn't we infer that voters are more polarized? Not necessarily. Recall that earlier in the chapter we noted that the median voter result holds regardless of whether the electorate as a whole is polarized. But we also found that because elected officials have to balance out the preferences of political elites with those of the voters in the general electorate (and median voters' preferences may be less clear to the candidate), in order to secure ballot access as a party nominee or move up to a higher political office, the candidates will diverge in policy. If political elites are becoming more polarized, then that polarization could result in the greater polarization of candidates. Surveys do seem to show growing differences between partisans, as McLaughlin noted.

But doesn't polarization of the candidates and the elites mean that voters in general elections are themselves more polarized? Wouldn't the movement apart of the political elites be a response to a general movement apart of voters in terms of policy preferences, since elites are just a subset of voters themselves? For the reverse logic to hold—for candidate polarization to mean a polarized electorate—all three groups must have polarized: elected officials, elites who select the nominees, and voters in the general election who choose the winners. So far we have seen strong evidence of polarization in Congress. We suspect that political elites are also polarized since theoretically their polarization would explain what we see in Congress, and some survey evidence seems to suggest that elites are indeed polarized (although we have not yet fully explored the evidence on elite polarization). And we don't know whether elite polarization, if it exists, is related to voter polarization theoretically or empirically. So the answer to the question of whether the stylized fact of greater polarization of elected officials means that voters are polarized depends on our answer to the question about whether the fourth stylized fact (that there has been a polarization of Republican and Democrat partisans) means voter polarization. We consider that question next.

Do Greater Preference Differences between Republicans and Democrats Imply a More Polarized Electorate?

Two factors can cause an increase in the difference between Republican and Democratic survey respondents while the distribution of total voter preferences remains the same: (1) moderate party members leave the party and become independent or unaffiliated and (2) ideological sorting by party members increases. First we consider the impact of a rising number of independents, and then we look at the ideological sorting.

A Hypothetical Mid-twentieth-Century Electorate Consider figure 5.8, which shows a hypothetical distribution of voters, all of whom are members of one of the major political parties. While more Democrats than Republicans have ideal points below 50, the median in the electorate, and more

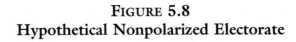

FIGURE 5.8
Hypothetical Nonpolarized Electorate

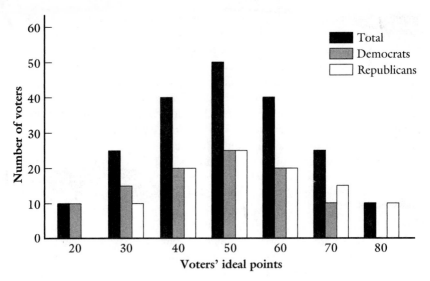

Republicans than Democrats have ideal points above 50, there is a lot of overlap in membership such that there are liberal Republicans (with ideal points below 50) and conservative Democrats (with ideal points above 50). Although such a configuration of party members may seem odd to observers in the twenty-first century, it was relatively close to the case in the middle of the twentieth century. Just as southern Democrats in Congress were closer to the median congressional Republican than their northern Democrat counterparts, most southern white voters, although conservative on many issues, saw themselves as members of the Democratic Party. The Republican Party was virtually nonexistent in the South for local and state elections until the last decades of the century. White southern Democrats often called themselves yellow dog Democrats because they would supposedly vote for a yellow dog if he or she were a Democratic candidate. Similarly, in the North where voters were generally more liberal than the nation as a whole, a number of Republican voters' preferences for policy were liberal compared with the preferences of the average Republican nationwide.

We can see evidence of the heterogeneous nature of the national parties by looking at ideological survey data from the NES toward the end of this period. In presidential-election years, the NES asks respondents to rate various groups and individuals in society on a 100-point scale. These scales are called thermometer ratings. A rating of 0 means that the respondent has a very cold or unfavorable feeling about the group, but if the respondent rates the group at 100, he or she has a very warm or favorable feeling about the group. Respondents are asked to rate liberals and conservatives in this fashion. Using these ratings, the NES then constructs a general 100-point liberal-conservative rating for each respondent, with 0 representing the most liberal position and 100 the most conservative position. These ratings give us more information about how voters see themselves in terms of the liberal-conservative dimension than just a response as to whether they are liberal or conservative, since we can estimate a fuller range of opinions. Figure 5.9 presents the distributions of these ratings for respondents by partisanship in 1970, the first year for which such measures are accurate.[29] Voters are asked to declare partisanship on a 7-point integer scale where 1 is considered a strong Democrat, 2 a weak Democrat, 3 a leaning Democrat (an independent who leans toward the Democratic Party), 4 an independent, 5 a leaning Republican, 6 a weak Republican, and 7 a strong Republican. It is clear from the figures that there were many self-declared Democrats in 1970 who saw themselves as conservatives rather than liberals and somewhat fewer self-declared Republicans who saw themselves as liberals rather than conservatives. Thus, our hypothetical configuration of voters' preferences in figure 5.8 is not an unreasonable view of the electorate.

Becoming Independent In our hypothetical distribution, if you were to survey Democrats and Republicans as to their policy preferences, both the median Democrat and the median Republican would have an ideal point at

FIGURE 5.9
Voter Ideology in NES Survey, 1970

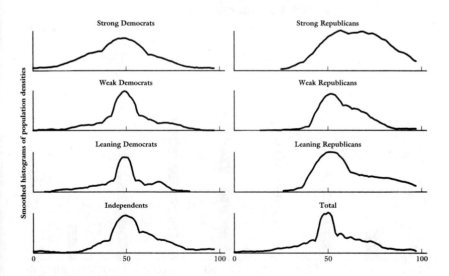

Source: National Election Studies.

50 and thus their preferences on issues would sound very similar. For example, suppose the policy question on which voters have ideal points is government spending for the poor. Let 40 represent a proposed increase in spending on these programs and 60 represent the status quo of spending. If you quizzed voters, you would find that approximately 57.5 percent of Democrats and 42.5 percent of Republicans would prefer the proposal, an ideological difference of 15 percentage point between the parties. What happens if voters in the middle range or some voters whose ideology most clashes with their partisanship choose to be independents and drop their partisan inclinations, as in figure 5.10? Notice that now the median ideal point in the Democratic Party is at 40 and the median in the Republican Party is at 60. The shift of some voters to independents caused party members to be more extreme even though the distribution of preferences in the electorate itself did not change. What happens if we quiz voters now on the proposal? Now two thirds of Democrats prefer the proposal and only one third of Republicans do, a 33.3 percent difference! Yet the distribution of voters' ideal points in the electorate has not changed at all, even though Republicans and Democrats are further apart ideologically.

Movements of moderate or ideologically dissimilar party members to independent status could explain the growing difference between Democrats and Republicans in survey responses cited by Pew and referred to by John McLaughlin above. Has such a movement taken place? Since 1952, the NES has asked voters their partisan inclinations every two years. In figure 5.11

FIGURE 5.10
Hypothetical Nonpolarized Electorate
with Independent Voters

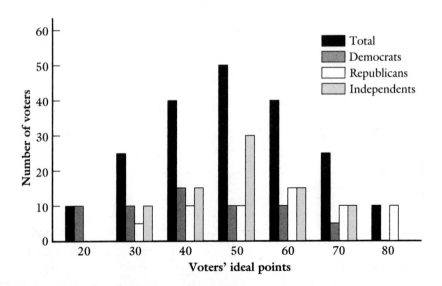

the distribution of responses is presented over time. The percentage of voters declaring themselves independent did increase from 1964 to 1978; however, the period from 1978 to 2004 shows a small increase in self-declared partisanship. An increase in the number of independents can perhaps explain the movement of Democrats from the mid-'60s to the late '70s but does not explain movements of Republicans since 1978.

Ideological Sorting

<u>Measuring Voters' Preferences over Time</u> While moderate voters moving from partisanship to independent status can obviously make party members more extreme on average even though the electorate has not changed, if voters in addition sort better ideologically by partisanship affiliation, we can expect that party members are even more extreme. Consider the hypothetical distribution of voters in figure 5.12. Now no Democrat (or Republican) has an ideal point greater (or less) than 50. If we quizzed these voters on whether they sup-

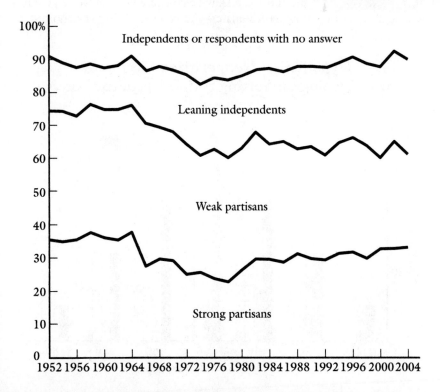

FIGURE 5.11
Self-Declared Party Identification in NES Surveys,
1952–2002

ported the proposal, we would find that 91.67 percent of Democrats were supporters and only 8.33 percent of Republicans were, a huge ideological disparity. Yet the electorate is still as nonpolarized as it was in figure 5.10.

Are those who declared a party affiliation sorting ideologically more now than previously? Have party members polarized while the overall electorate's distribution of preferences has remained unchanged? Answering this question turns out to be difficult, even though the NES and other organizations have surveyed voters repeatedly on a number of different issues, candidates, groups, and so on, during the period. The first difficulty is that most long-running opinion polls ask binary questions, which cannot tell us much about the intensity of individual preferences, as our simple examples show. Thus, we need to look at questions that give respondents a range of alternatives or a large number of issues, both of which the NES does provide. However, NES data suffer from a second problem—over time, issues and variables that the NES and other surveyors ask voters change. The majority of questions have to do with specifics of the current election or political climate. For example, early NES surveys asked respondents about busing, the Vietnam War, and their opinions of Lyndon Johnson. Current NES surveys ask voters about abortion, gay marriage, and terrorism. While some questions are relatively constant, many that have to do with current political events, such as a respondent's preferences in an election and his or her opinions of candidates or incumbents, and those can truly be compared only if we can control for the changes over time in candidates' and incumbents' policy choices.[30]

FIGURE 5.12
Hypothetical Nonpolarized Electorate
with Ideological Sorting and Independent Voters

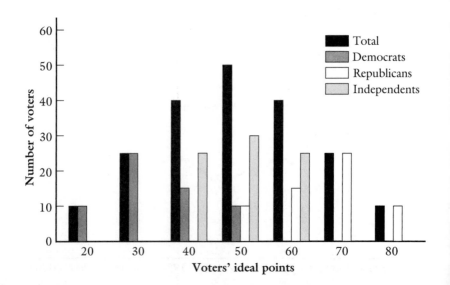

A similar problem of course exists in the examination of congressional voting, since the issues before Congress also change, yet we have argued that we can compare members of Congress over time using Poole and Rosenthal's scores, which are based on congressional voting on these changing issues. Why? Because members of Congress typically serve for more than one term, overlapping the terms of members from previous and future years. This situation allows Poole and Rosenthal to construct estimates of members' ideal points that can be compared over time given our relatively stable party systems.[31] But NES generally surveys a randomly selected group of respondents, which varies from year to year. Since it is extremely costly to follow a group of truly representative respondents over time, only a few studies of public opinion have done so, and none are comprehensive enough or repeated frequently enough for a long enough time to allow us to draw conclusions about U.S. voters' preferences that we could use to compute the same kind of time series of distributions of voters' ideal points that Poole and Rosenthal construct for members of Congress.[32]

The Evidence Given these serious caveats, in figure 5.13 we compare the ideological sorting of partisans over time with the liberal-conservative thermometer question we examined in figure 5.9 by contrasting the distribution of partisans in 2002 and 1980 with that in 1970. There is some small visual evidence of ideological sorting. Conservative Democrats, particularly conservative strong Democrats, and liberal Republicans, particularly liberal strong Republicans, grew less prevalent even during the years when the percentage of independents remained relatively constant. Moderate partisans make up most of the increase, although there is some small evidence of slight increases in the frequency of extremists in both parties. Independents and the population as a whole have become more moderate. Recalling our caveats, this seemingly moderating effect for voters might be simply a reaction to the polarized nature of the positions of elected officials. If voters now view liberal and conservative in terms of more extreme policy choices than they did in 1970, then they may be more likely to view themselves as moderates, while strong partisans may be viewing themselves as more extreme to fit in with their new views of liberal and conservative, so we cannot say for certain that ideological sorting has occurred. Nevertheless, the evidence is consistent with ideological sorting by partisanship. Statistical comparisons of the means of these distributions over time show that in general the mean response in 2002 is not significantly different from that in 1970 for all types of voters except strong partisans, for whom there is a small effect on the mean response, suggesting that they are slightly more extreme than before.[33]

More sophisticated studies of NES data as well as data from other surveys over time have produced similar results. In particular, DiMaggio, Evans, and Bryson (1996) examined the vast array of U.S. public opinion surveys from 1972 to 1994, and Evans (2003) expanded the data to 2000. These re-

FIGURE 5.13

Self-Declared Partisanship of NES Survey Respondents:
Liberal-Conservative Thermometer Ratings over Time

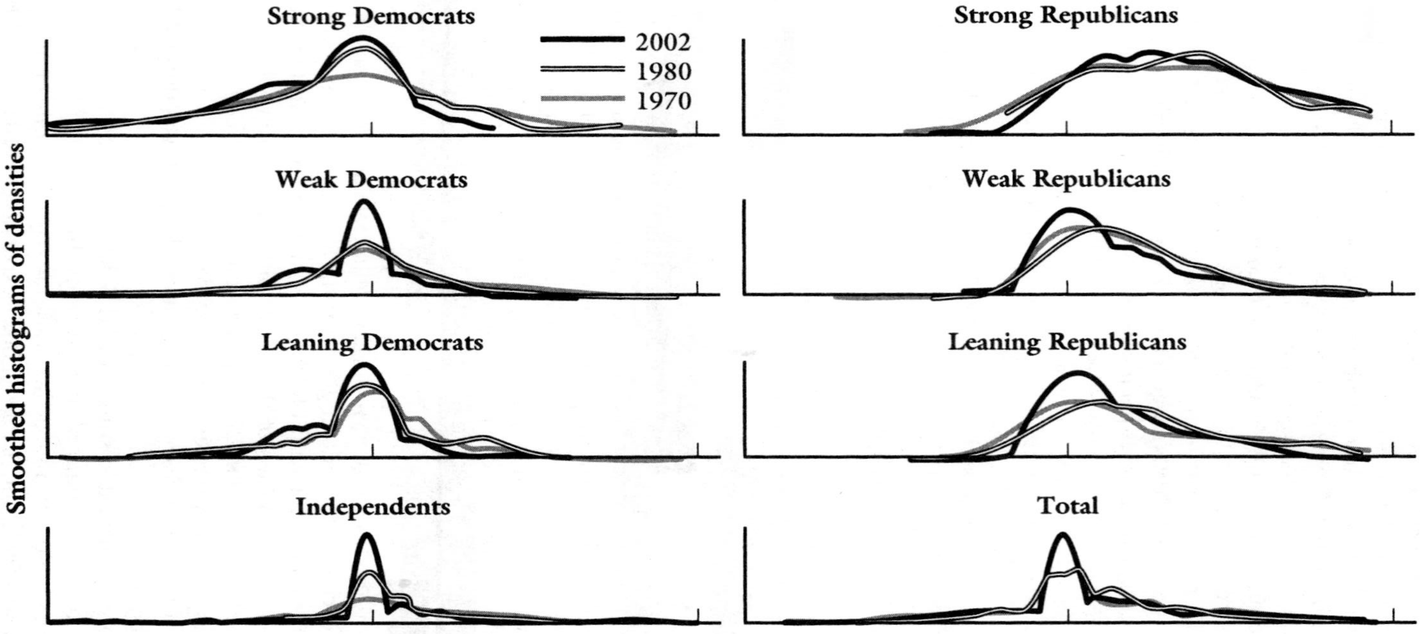

Strong Republicans

Weak Republicans

Leaning Republicans

Total

2002
1980
1970

Strong Democrats

Weak Democrats

Leaning Democrats

Independents

Smoothed histograms of densities

Source: National Election Studies.
Note: Ranges are from 0 for most liberal to 100 for most conservative.

searchers used a variety of measures intended to capture changes in the shapes of voters' preferences. They found instead growing polarization in the population as a whole and evidence of public opinion convergence across age categories, educational attainment, racial and ethnic groups, religious affiliation, and geographic residence on many issues, except those of abortion and sexuality, where they found evidence of some polarization (a subject we address in the next subsection). The researchers also found increasing polarization between the opinions of Democrats and Republicans, supporting the suggestion that the growing difference in survey responses between members of the two parties is a consequence of better ideological sorting. Evans (p. 87) summarizes:

> It is now clear that the primary instances of between-group polarization are between people who are somehow identified with politics, not with their gender, religion, race, or some other identity. Note that it is not the marginally politically involved who are polarizing—such as voters—but those who identify with partisan labels in the political system—people who label themselves liberals or conservatives, Democrats or Republicans.

Thus we find evidence of increasing polarization of political elites even though there is minor evidence of polarization of the general public. The increasing polarization of political elites can help us understand the increase in polarization in Congress, even controlling for the changes that occurred as the Democratic Party abandoned its conservative positions on civil rights and voting rights for blacks. As political elites, who are involved in candidate nomination processes, become more polarized, as noted above, we would expect candidates to diverge more in their policy choices. But so far the evidence of the polarization of elected officials and political elites does not seem to imply that voters as a whole have become more polarized.

Is Cultural and Social Polarization Causing Political Polarization?

On the 2003 Thanksgiving-weekend show of *The McLaughlin Group*, guest Pat Buchanan gave his own interpretation of host John McLaughlin's vision of a polarized America: "John, the key thing now is not simply divisions on war or peace. Morally, culturally, socially, about right and wrong, whether it's abortion or gay marriage, this country is as polarized and divided and deeply divided as it's been since the Civil War."[34] Many pundits noted that when voters were asked what they saw as the most important issue in exit polls during the 2004 election, the most frequent response (22 percent) was moral values. Certainly in chapter 3 we found that groups opposed to abortion and same-sex marriage were extremely active in the 2004 presidential campaign and mobilized significant numbers of voters to support Bush based on those matters. Given the evidence of polarization on issues of abortion and sexuality found by DiMaggio, Evans, and Bryson (1996) and

Evans (2003), perhaps if we looked more specifically at those issues, we would find a polarized country in which voters are increasingly choosing on those issues. It might be that by looking at the general concept of ideology, we are missing a polarization that is occurring at a cultural level.

Same-Sex Marriage First, consider the issue of civil rights for gay men and lesbians, particularly same-sex marriage, which was much discussed during the 2004 campaign. While same-sex marriage was specifically addressed by the NES only in the 2004 survey, the NES has asked respondents since 1984 to rate gay men and lesbians using thermometer ratings of feelings. Figure 5.14 presents a comparison of those ratings by partisan affiliation for the years 1984, 1994, and 2004. It appears that in 1984 and 1994 the general public was polarized on the issue of gay men and lesbians, with modal values close to 0 and close to 50. But the polarization was across partisan groups, particularly in 1984. Strong and weak partisans (particularly strong Democrats and weak Republicans) were internally polarized on sexuality. But that polarization had lessened significantly by 2004. In particular, the population as a whole does not appear polarized, but is centered around 50. We also see signs of ideological sorting on the issue, with Democrats more likely to give gay men and lesbians ratings above 50 and Republicans more likely to give them ratings below 50. The trend from 1984 has been an ideological sorting over gay men and lesbians and a decreasing polarization in the electorate at large, with most respondents in the middle. While feelings about gay men and lesbians do appear to divide Democrats and Republicans, the majority of voters are not polarized.

How do we reconcile the evidence in figure 5.14 with the exit-poll evidence that supporters (or opponents) of same-sex marriage are overwhelming in favor of Bush (or Kerry), as shown in Table 5.2b? The presentation of the exit-poll numbers in the table (matching the presentation in the news media) biases the perception of a polarized electorate. It is true that 70 percent of those who oppose any legal recognition of same-sex marriage support Bush. For example, Decatur, Illinois, factory worker Mike Johnson explained: "I can't vote for a party that supports homosexuality and abortion."[35] Yet those voters are just a bare majority of Bush's supporters, 52 percent. Bush's supporters were almost evenly divided on the issue, with 48 percent supporting some sort of recognition (11 percent supported marriage, 37 percent supported civil unions). One of the gay-marriage supporters who voted for Bush was twenty-five-year-old Crissy Hill of Coon Rapids, Minnesota. Similarly, while 77 percent of those who favored allowing gay marriage voted for Kerry, they are only a little over 41 percent of Kerry voters, including Crissy's thirty-year-old sister, Mary Hill. Both sisters favored same-sex marriage but voted for different candidates for president because of differences in their views on the Iraq war.[36]

Further evidence that same-sex marriage was not the deciding factor in many voters' decision is that unlike Mary, close to 60 percent of Kerry voters opposed

FIGURE 5.14

Self-Declared Partisanship of NES Survey Respondents:
Thermometer Ratings of Feelings toward Gay Men and Lesbians over Time

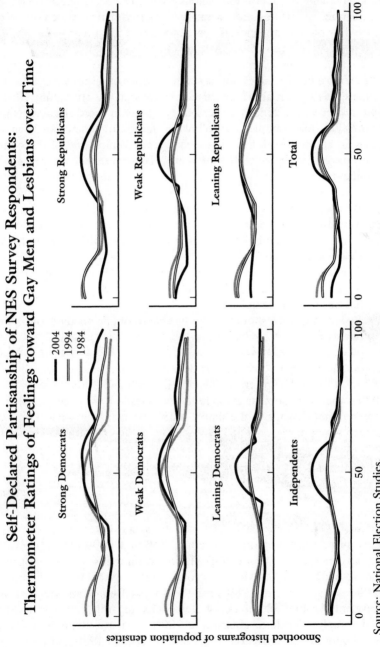

Source: National Election Studies.
Note: Ranges are from 0 for cold feelings to 100 for warm.

gay marriage (over 23 percent opposed any legal recognition, and over 35 percent were willing to support civil unions only). In Ohio, where a ban on same-sex marriage was also on the ballot, the majority of the 60 percent of black voters who voted for the ban also voted for Kerry. Thus, supporters for Kerry, like those for Bush, were divided on the issue of same-sex marriage.

Abortion The NES does not have a time series of responses evaluating individuals' feelings on abortion-related groups that we can compare.[37] Since 1980, however, the NES has asked respondents in most elections (though not in 2002, for example) the following question: "There has been some discussion about abortion during recent years. Which one of the opinions on this page best agrees with your view?" These were the options given to respondents:

1. By law, abortion should never be permitted.
2. The law should permit abortion only in case of rape, incest, or danger to the woman's life, but only after the need for the abortion has been clearly established.
3. The law should permit abortion for reasons other than rape, incest, or danger to the woman's life, but only after the need for the abortion has been clearly established.
4. By law, a woman should always be able to obtain an abortion as a matter of choice.

Figures 5.15 and 5.16 compare the distribution of responses over time from 1980 to 2004 and by partisan affiliation in 1980 and 2004.

While the most popular answers to the question are responses 2 and 4, giving a bimodal shape to the simple distribution, answer 4 has received the plurality of responses, and the combination of 3 and 4 has received the majority of responses for the entire twenty-year period. So although there is some evidence of polarization in the general population on the issue, it is not a disagreement between those who would outlaw abortion completely and those who favor complete legality but a disagreement over whether to allow abortion only in the special cases of rape, incest or danger to the woman's life. The bimodal character of the data exists in varying degrees in almost all partisan categories for both 1980 and 2004. There is evidence that party members have ideologically sorted on the issue. The clear modal response of Democrats (whether strong, weak, or leaning) to the question in 2004 was 4, while in 1980 strong and weak Democrats had been more ambivalent. Around 50 percent of Democrats, regardless of type, most preferred complete legalized abortion in 2004. Similarly, Republicans became more supportive of restrictions on abortion between 1980 and 2004.

How does the NES survey evidence fit with the exit-poll data on the abortion issue when they are broken down by Bush and Kerry supporters in

FIGURE 5.15
Responses to NES Abortion-Legality Question, 1980–2004

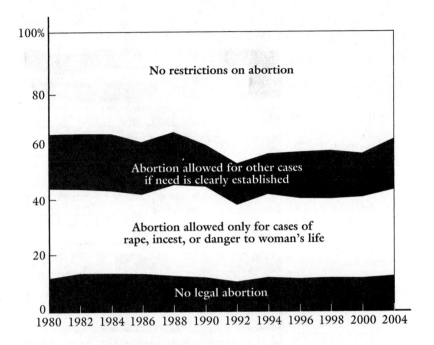

Source: National Election Studies.
Note: The question was not asked in the 2002 survey.

table 5.2? Interestingly, the exit-poll data are not bimodal. One big difference in the exit-poll data is that the question is worded differently. Instead
of giving respondents the specifics of the middle-of-the-road options 2 and
3, the exit polls simply ask voters whether abortion should be always legal,
mostly legal, mostly illegal, or always illegal. This wording leaves to the respondent the interpretation of the types of limits he or she would place on
abortion, the meaning of "mostly legal" and "mostly illegal." In 2004, the
distribution of responses was 21, 34, 26, and 16 percent, respectively, with
a clear modal and median response at mostly legal. In 2000, the percentages
were roughly the same, with 23, 33, 27, and 13 percent, respectively. The
difference in the distribution of responses between the exit polls and
the NES surveys suggests that the specificity of the abortion questions in the
NES survey may be the cause of some of the bimodality that we observe.
The suggestion, then, is that the specificity that the NES attaches to the
middle-of-the-road options is not equivalent to voters' views on those op-

FIGURE 5.16
Responses to NES Abortion Legality Question by Party Affiliation, 1980 and 2004

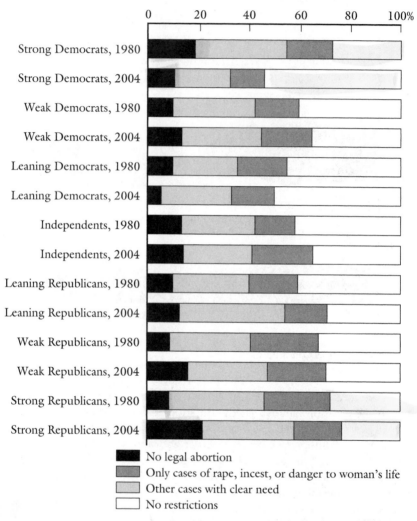

Source: National Election Studies.

tions. In fact, respondents who say "mostly legal" may have something in mind that is more pro-abortion than that described by the NES in option 3 and, as a result, may choose "always legal" instead.

How do the supporters of the two candidates in 2004 break down in terms of their abortion preferences? Kerry's voters do strongly espouse legal abortion—33 percent back making abortion always legal, and almost 45 percent support mostly legal abortion, for a total of almost 78 percent. About 14.5 percent of Kerry's followers want to make abortion mostly illegal, and 7.5 percent prefer making abortion always illegal, for a total of a 22 percent. Conversely, the majority of Bush supporters favor making abortion illegal. Yet they are slightly more divided. Almost 11 percent of Bush voters believe abortion should be always legal, and 26 percent believe it should be mostly legal, for a total of 37 percent. A little over 38 percent of Bush supporters believe abortion should be mostly illegal, and 26 percent favor making all abortion illegal, for a total of 63 percent. Bush's followers do not seem as strongly opposed to abortion as Kerry's voters are in favor of it. Evans (2003) also noted the internal divisions of Republicans on abortion and other cultural issues (p. 86): "While the two groups [Democrats and Republican identifiers] are separating in their mean opinion, the Republicans are becoming increasingly internally polarized over feelings toward the poor, feelings toward liberals, and abortion."

In conclusion, the evidence on sexuality and abortion provides little support for the view of a nation deeply polarized in a way that dominates the choices the majority of voters make in elections. While the data show some ideological sorting on these issues over time, there is also a suggestion that among partisans and even political elites there are also internal divisions.

Exploiting Internal Divisions "This is one election I believe you have an obligation to choose according to your moral beliefs," black Cleveland Heights, Ohio, resident Carol Upshur warned the congregation at the New Spirit Revival Center. Upshur "criticized Kerry's stance on same-sex unions and abortion, even graphically describing how a partial-birth abortion is performed. She reminded churchgoers that the new president would appoint several Supreme Court justices, leaving an imprint on the nation's laws." Upshur used to be a Democrat, but, she noted, "I was so burdened over the way I felt our Democratic Party has taken us for granted for years, and it was never so apparent as this year."[38] Upshur's conversion was just one example of how Republicans made an effort to appeal to Democratic voters on cultural issues, particularly religious African Americans who supported bans on gay marriage and abortion. As noted in chapter 3, the Bush campaign engaged in a massive get-out-the-vote effort using extensive research in an attempt to reach Republican-leaning voters in Democratic precincts, with messages targeted on issues they predicted those voters cared about. In previous campaigns, Republicans would call potential voters with a tape-recorded message from Ronald Reagan or a similar personage on the generic importance of voting. In 2004, a voter concerned about abortion would hear "if you don't come out and vote, the number of abortions next year is going to go up."[39] In an after-the-election post-mortem, Democratic National Committee chairman Terence R. McAuliffe concluded: "They [the Republicans] came into Democratic areas with very specific targeted messages to take Democratic voters away from us."[40]

A number of Democrats have begun a postelection effort to soften their position on abortion. Donna Brazile, the manager of Al Gore's campaign in 2000, noted: "All these issues that put us into the extreme and not the mainstream really hurt us with the heartland of the country. Even I have trouble explaining to my family that we are not about killing babies."[41] Nevada senator Harry Reid, an abortion opponent, was chosen to be the new Democratic minority leader, replacing Tom Daschle, who lost his bid for reelection.

But Republican divisions on cultural issues also showed during the campaign, and Republicans likewise worried that Democrats were exploiting them. As noted in chapter 3, groups opposed to same-sex marriage pushed the issue with Republicans before Bush and his administration were sure of their opinion. Moderate Republicans who have liberal positions on abortion and gay rights, such as California governor Arnold Schwarzenegger and New York City mayor Michael Bloomberg, spoke at the Republican National Convention. At a campaign rally just prior to the convention, Vice President Cheney was asked by a questioner, "I would like to know, sir, from your heart—I don't want to know what your advisers say, or even what your top adviser thinks—but I need to know: What do you think about homosexual marriages?" Cheney answered, "Lynne and I have a gay daughter, so it's an issue our family is very familiar with." He continued, saying that he opposed a constitutional amendment to ban same-sex marriage, and he remarked, "Freedom means freedom for everyone." But he concluded by declaring that the president sets the policy for the administration.[42]

Did Kerry try to use the divisions among Republicans? In the last presidential debate of the campaign, moderator Bob Schieffer of CBS asked Bush whether he believed that homosexuality was a matter of choice. Bush stated that he did not know, but Kerry suggested, "I think if you were to talk to Dick Cheney's daughter, who is a lesbian, she would tell you that she's being who she was, she's being who she was born as." Cheney and his wife, Lynne, reacted angrily to Kerry's reference to their daughter. "This is not a good man. What a cheap and tawdry political trick," Lynne Cheney declared. Conservative Christian activist and former presidential candidate Gary Bauer explained the concern of Republicans: "I think it is part of a strategy to suppress traditional-values voters, to knock 1 or 2 percent off in some rural areas by causing people to turn on the president."[43] If this was the reason for mentioning Cheney's daughter, the strategy backfired, as post-debate polls showed that 64 percent of likely voters felt that Kerry's comment was "inappropriate."[44]

The 2004 campaign demonstrated not just that some voters did choose to vote based on divisions over same-sex marriage and abortion. It illustrated as well not only the fine line that both Democrats and Republicans face in choosing a position on these moral issues because of current internal divisions but also the opportunity such internal divisions can give their opponents. In 2004, it appears that the Republicans were more successful in attracting unhappy socially conservative Democrats than the Democrats were in suggesting to social conservatives that Republicans were not committed to socially conservative policies.

Are Moral-Issues Voters Choosing against Their Economic Interests?

What's the Matter with Kansas?

The poorest county in America isn't in Appalachia or the Deep South. It is on the Great Plains, a region of struggling ranchers and dying farm towns, and in the election of 2000 the Republican candidate for president, George W. Bush, carried it by a majority of greater than 80 percent. This puzzled me when I first read about it, as it puzzles many of the people I know. For us it is the Democrats that are the party of the workers, of the poor, of the weak and the victimized. . . . When I told a friend of mine about that impoverished High Plains county so enamored of President Bush, she was perplexed. "How can anyone who has ever worked for someone else vote Republican?" she asked. How could so many people get it so wrong?

Thus begins journalist Thomas Frank's recent book, *What's the Matter with Kansas?* (2004, p. 1). One of the puzzling things about the division of the country into red and blue states is that even though the standard wisdom, as Frank notes, is that Democrats support economic policies that benefit the poor (higher minimum wages, redistributive social programs, and progressive income taxation) and that Republicans support economic policies that benefit the rich (lower minimum wages, fewer redistributive social programs, and flatter income tax schedules), blue states have higher per capita income than red states. Even if we conclude, as our data shows, that voters are not polarized, why do we seem to find poor voters voting against their economic interests, voting on moral values instead? Are voters more concerned about moral values and cultural issues than their economic well-being?

Income and Partisanship

Part of the answer to this puzzle is that the stylized fact is wrong—that is, low-income voters, even those who care about moral values and religious issues, are not more likely to vote Republican than Democratic. The exit-poll results from 2004, reported in table 5.1, show that this is true—63 percent of voters whose income is below $15,000 voted for Kerry, and the same percentage of voters whose income is above $200,000 voted for Bush. In fact, as income increases, the support for Bush increases almost linearly and the support for Kerry decreases. Bush's support from voters whose income is below $50,000 is less than 50 percent. The effect is true with respect to partisanship as well. McCarty, Poole, and Rosenthal (2005) extensively exam-

FIGURE 5.17
Republican Identification by Belief in the Bible and Income in NES Survey, 2004

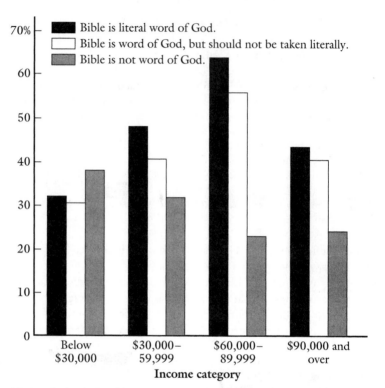

Source: National Election Studies.

ined the relationship between income and partisanship using NES data from 1952 to 2002 and Pew data for the 1990s and 2000s. They found (p. 130):

> High income Americans have consistently, over the second half of the twentieth century, been more prone to identify with and vote for the Republican party than have low income Americans, who have sided with the Democrats. The impact of income persists when controlling for other demographics, and the impact's magnitude is important. Moreover, there has been a rather substantial transformation in the economic basis of the American party system. In the 1990s, income was far more important than it had been in the 1950s.

The effect that McCarty, Poole, and Rosenthal found is also true for voters who supposedly are supporting Republicans on the cultural issues—evangelical voters. In 2004, the NES asked respondents about their beliefs about the Bible—specifically, the NES asked respondents, "Which of these

FIGURE 5.18
Support for Bush in Presidential Election by Belief in the Bible and Income, 2004

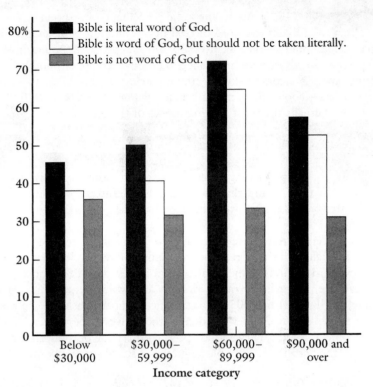

Source: National Election Studies.

statements comes closest to describing your feelings about the Bible? You can just give me the number of your choice." The choices were the Bible is the actual word of God and is to be taken literally, word for word; the Bible is the word of God but not everything in it should be taken literally, word for word; and the Bible is a book written by men and is not the word of God. Figures 5.17 and 5.18 break down the responses to these questions by household income, vote choice in the 2004 presidential election, and partisanship.

Only a little over 30 percent of respondents who state that the Bible is the actual word of God and should be taken literally but have a household income below $30,000 identify as Republican, compared with over 60 percent of the respondents who believe similarly but have a household income between $60,000 and 89,999 and over 40 percent of those with a household income over $90,000. Similarly, only about 45 percent of those respondents who believe the Bible should be taken literally as the word of

God but have an income below $30,000 voted for Bush, compared to over 70 percent of the respondents who believe similarly and have a household income between $60,000 and 89,999. Note that the effect of income is stronger for those who believe that the Bible should be taken literally than for those who do not. About the same percentage of respondents who believe that the Bible is the word of God but should not be taken literally and have a household income below $30,000 identify as Republican—around 30 percent—as those who believe it should be taken literally and have a similar income. As income increases, these voters are more likely to identify as Republicans—about 55 percent when income is between $60,000 and $89,999. Perhaps the most striking aspect of the figures is how, as income increases among those who do not believe the Bible is the word of God, support for the Republicans and Bush decreases and the fact that, as income increases beyond $90,000, support for the Republicans and Bush falls for all types of respondents. Evangelicals appear much more responsive to income concerns in their voting than nonevangelicals. Instead of asking, "What's the matter with Kansas?" we should perhaps ask, "What's the matter with Wall Street?"

The preceding results are from just one NES survey, and we might question the small numbers of respondents (only 182 responded that the Bible is not the word of God). Other analysis however, supports the conclusion that low-income evangelical voters identify and vote Democratic. McCarty, Poole, and Rosenthal (2005) also examined the partisanship of Pew respondents from 1997 to 2004 who identify themselves as born-again Christians by income and race. They found (p. 126) that "for born-agains and evangelicals, the percentage Republican increases steeply with income."

Ecological Inference and the Kansas Puzzle Yet, as we noted earlier, there seems to be a contradiction between the observed relationship between average income at the state and county level and these results—that is, the higher the average income of a state or county, the more likely it is that the state or county will support Democrats. How can those results be reconciled? The problem is with drawing an inference about how individual voters behave based on aggregate choices. Such inferences suffer from an *ecological fallacy*—generalizing from the aggregate to the individual. For example, consider how the votes of low- and high-income voters are distributed between Bush and Kerry in the hypothetical states shown in tables 5.4 and 5.5. In both states, 60 percent of voters are low income and 60 percent of voters supported Bush. In the table 5.4, 100 percent of low-income voters voted for Bush, but in table 5.5 only 33.3 percent (one third) of low-income voters supported Bush. It is impossible to know just by looking at the aggregate vote totals by state what the percentage of support for Bush is among low-income voters.

TABLE 5.4
Hypothetical State 1

	Low Income (%)	High Income (%)	Total (%)
Voted for Bush	60	0	60
Voted for Kerry	0	40	40
Total	60	40	100

TABLE 5.5
Hypothetical State 2

	Low Income (%)	High Income (%)	Total (%)
Voted for Bush	20	40	60
Voted for Kerry	40	0	40
Total	60	40	100

Putting the Evidence Together

Our analysis of the data shows that the stylized facts do not support a theory of a nation polarized by moral values but that, instead, voters are concerned with economic issues as much as if not more than they are about cultural issues. In fact, the stylized facts suggest a different theory: that political elites—partisans—became more polarized in terms of the meaning of *liberal* and *conservative* and, to some degree, in terms of cultural issues like same-sex marriage and abortion in the last decades of the twentieth century. We also find that elected officials are similarly more polarized. These two phenomena occurring at the same time make sense. Most candidates seeking political office in the United States will do so by first seeking the nomination of a major political party. If the elites in the party have preferences that are more extreme than the electorate and there is uncertainty about the general electorate's preferences, the candidates will diverge toward the preferences of the elites. Yet this does not mean that the general electorate itself has become polarized, and in fact when we examine preferences of voters as a whole, we see little evidence of polarization over time. Nevertheless, what explains the apparent increasing polarization of party elites and elected officials? In the next section, we consider one possible explanation that has been offered by McCarty, Poole, and Rosenthal—the rise in immigration.

Income Inequality, Immigration, and Polarization

Increasing Income Inequality and Polarization of the Parties

During the same period that the parties have become polarized, income inequality has risen significantly. As McCarty, Poole, and Rosenthal (2005, p. 20) reported, "In 1967, the household in the 95th percentile of the income distribution had 6.0 times the income of someone in the 25th percentile. By 2003, the disparity had increased to 8.6." Figure 5.19 shows how the Gini ratio—a measure of household income inequality calculated by the U.S. Census Bureau—has changed from 1967 to 2003. When income is equal across households, the coefficient equals 0; if one family has all the income, the coefficient equals 1. As the figure shows, income inequality has risen throughout the period.

McCarty, Poole, and Rosenthal argued that the increase in inequality can help explain the increase in polarization. As the dispersion in income has increased, voters on either end of the distribution of income (high and low) have grown further apart in terms of their preferences on economic policies, particularly redistributive ones. We discussed in chapter 2—recall figure 2.5—that as a voter's position on the income distribution changes, what he or she has at stake in terms of redistribution also changes. That is, suppose that an issue before the government is changing the Social Security program. One solution is to raise the payroll-tax ceiling currently used to fund the program—income above the ceiling is not taxed. It is straightforward to see that the voters who would be most affected by such a change would be those whose income is at either end of the income distribution— the more wealthy a voter, the more likely he or she will be negatively affected by a tax increase, and the poorer a voter, the more likely he or she will benefit from the additional financing from a tax increase without having to pay for it. If the separation between these types of voters in terms of income is increasing, then their stake in elections is similarly increasing. Assuming that Republicans are largely supported by high-income voters and Democrats by low-income voters, then rising income inequality can explain why there might be increased polarization of partisans on economic issues. Given that voters whose income is in the middle have less at stake in elections and thus benefit less from participation in the process, then participation in choosing candidates will be dominated more by the voters who are at the extremes of the income distribution. Thus, as the income inequality increases, there are more voters at the extremes who see elections as having a potentially greater effect on their after-tax income, and candidates will respond more to those voters.

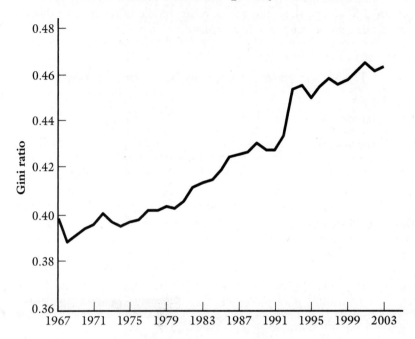

FIGURE 5.19
Household Income Inequality, 1967–2003

Immigration and the Persistence of Income Inequality

The rise in income inequality suggests another puzzle. Normally a rise in income inequality would mean a reduction in the median voter's position on the income distribution. That is, as income inequality increases, the percentage of households with lower income levels increases and the percentage of households with higher income levels decreases, lowering the position of the median on the income distribution. As the median voter's income declines, we would expect larger numbers of voters who would pursue economic policies that are redistributive.[45] Yet although income inequality has risen in the United States, redistributive measures like raising the minimum wage and increasing taxes for social programs have not received support, as documented by McCarty, Poole, and Rosenthal (2005).

Why is that the case? Recall from chapter 3 that there has been a significant growth in noncitizens in the United States since the passage of the Immigration and Nationality Amendments of 1965. These noncitizens generally cannot vote.[46] McCarty, Poole, and Rosenthal showed that the growth in low-income earners has been primarily among noncitizens. They found that the median family income of noncitizens fell from 82 percent of the median income of voters in 1972 to 65 percent in 2000. In fact, the researchers found that the median income of voters in the United States has stayed relatively constant in recent years. Thus they argued that policies that would reduce income inequality do not receive popular support. As we saw in figure 2.5, voters whose income is in the middle of the income distribution do not gain or lose much from redistributive policies.

Do Voters Base Choices on Issues or Abilities?

Where Bush and Kerry Agreed

Both Crissy and Mary Hill supported same-sex marriage but split their votes for president. Crissy said she admired Bush and wanted him to finish the job in Iraq while Mary did not like the way the war was going.[47] Yet there wasn't much evidence during the campaign that either candidate had different plans for dealing with Iraq or terrorists or foreign policy more generally; both claimed that they planned to strengthen the military, work with allies, bring peace to the Middle East, maintain a hard line with North Korea, reduce dependence on Middle Eastern oil, help train Iraqi forces and encourage democracy in Iraq, and bring American troops home as quickly as possible. As James Lindsay, director of studies for the Council on Foreign Relations, concluded prior to the election, "They might not be in the same ZIP Code, but they're in the same area code."[48]

The disagreement was over who would be best in accomplishing these goals, whose strategies or abilities would be most effective given the evidence from Bush's and Kerry's records and their plans for the years ahead. In their first debate, the two candidates were asked to define the greatest threat to national security. Kerry quickly answered:

> Nuclear proliferation. Nuclear proliferation. . . . Now there are terrorists trying to get their hands on that stuff today. And this president, I regret to say, has secured less nuclear material in the last two years, since 9/11, than we did in the two years preceding 9/11. We have to do this job. And to do the job you can't cut the money for it. The president actually cut the money for it. You have to put the money into it and the funding and the leadership. . . . We're going to make it clear to the world that we're serious about containing nuclear proliferation.[49]

When given his chance to respond, Bush joined in, agreeing with Kerry about what was the greatest threat:

> Actually, we've increasing funding for, for dealing with nuclear proliferation. About 35 percent since I've been the president. . . . I agree with my opponent that the biggest threat facing this country is weapons of mass destruction in the hands of a terrorist network. And that's why we've put proliferation as one of the centerpieces of a multiprong strategy to make the country safer. My administra-

tion started what's called the proliferation security initiative. . . . And we've been effective.[50]

While certainly there were differences in the strategies the candidates proposed to deal with problems like Iraq and nuclear proliferation—for instance, Kerry advocated shutting down U.S. missile silos as a source of nuclear proliferation while Bush argued that they were important as a defensive tool in bargaining—in general, the two candidates' agreement on the priority of solving these problems reflected a country of voters also concerned with these issues. Although the emphasis on which ones were most important in voters' minds varied, 71 percent of voters in exit polls said they were worried about terrorism. The issue was not whether the country should defend itself against terrorism but who, as president, would be best in doing so.

Nonpolicy Matters

Because of these worries about terrorism, for many voters in 2004, like Crissy and Mary Hill, the positions of the two candidates on same-sex marriage or abortion or other traditional issues that divide the parties were not the reasons for their votes. For example, *Boston Globe* reporter Joan Vennochi quoted an anonymous Bush supporter in Massachusetts:

> I'm for gay marriage and stem cell research. While I initially supported the war in Iraq, I now see it as a tragic mistake. . . . Long ago, I gave up the idea that presidents actually do anything to make public schools better or healthcare more affordable. For me, this election was all about homeland security and the war in Iraq. Kerry never sold me on how he would do a better job with either one. To this day, I don't understand his positions on the war, or what his plan was to bring home the troops. . . . Not so with Bush. I always felt I knew where he stood, what he believed in, and the direction he wanted to take the country. Even though we didn't see eye-to-eye on most things, I liked the clarity of Bush's convictions and willingness to stand up for them.[51]

In contrast, seventy-two-year-old retired prep-school teacher Robert Dealy of Fredericksburg, Virginia, who had voted for every Republican candidate for president since Ronald Reagan, told the *Richmond Times-Dispatch*: "The current president has had four years to make things work, but on foreign policy and Iraq, he has failed. Ideology aside, it's just a matter of competence."[52] Both the anonymous Massachusetts voter and Robert Dealy based their choices not so much on the policies advocated by the candidates but on the candidates' personal qualities—their leadership ability, their convictions, and their competence in dealing with the war in Iraq and terrorism. The voters disagreed on which candidate was better in terms of those qualities, yet they generally agreed that having those qualities was desirable, and both were willing to forgo voting for a candidate whose policies they agreed with in order to vote for the candidate whose nonpolicy aspects they found more appealing.

Our emphasis so far has been on understanding the relationship between voters and candidates in terms of policy choices when voters disagree on the ultimate goals, things like same-sex marriage, abortion, taxation, and so forth. One of the early critics of simplistic position-taking models of politics like the one we have discussed in this chapter, Donald Stokes, argued in 1963 (pp. 372–73):

> The corruption issue of 1952 did not find the Democrats taking one position and the Republicans another. And neither were some voters in favor of corruption while others were against it. If we are to speak of a dimension at all, both parties and all voters were located at a single point—the position of virtue in government. To be sure, enough evidence of malfeasance had turned up in the Democratic administration so that many voters felt the party had strayed from full virtue. But throwing the rascals out is very different from choosing between two or more parties on the basis of their advocacy of alternatives of government action.

Using a term originated by Kurt Lewin, Stokes labeled these sorts of issues "valence issues," explaining (p. 373) that he meant issues

> that merely involve the linking of the parties with some condition that is positively or negatively valued by the electorate. If the condition is past or present ("You never had it so good," "800 million people have gone behind the Iron Curtain"), the argument turns on where the credit or blame ought to be assigned. But if the condition is a future or potential one, the argument turns on which party, given possession of the government, is the more likely to bring it about.

Stokes then went on to argue that in many elections, particularly those for for president, valence issues are the main determinant of individual votes.

Modeling Valence Issues

Can we incorporate valence issues into our simple model of candidates' position taking? The simplest way to do it is to add to voter utility from the outcome of an election the utility voters receive from such valence issues, as in Groseclose (2001). Of course if two candidates have equal valence qualities, then the results that we have found so far will be unchanged. Valence issues can affect how an individual votes when the utility from the valence issue for one candidate is higher than that for his or her opponent. To see how this works, consider the utility that a voter named Edward receives from Bush and Kerry, illustrated in figure 5.20. Edward perceives Bush as more reliable in fighting terrorism. The utility Edward gets from Bush's election for every policy position Bush might take is the higher curve, and the utility Edward gets from Kerry's election for every policy position Kerry

FIGURE 5.20
Edward's Utility from Bush and Kerry, 2004

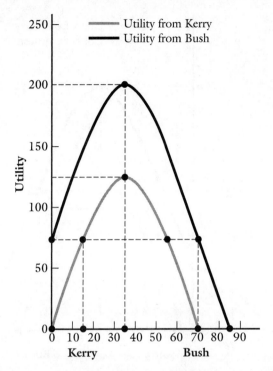

might take is the lower curve. The vertical distance between the two curves is 75 utils, which is the additional utility Edward receives from the election of Bush regardless of his policy position, because Edward sees Bush as more capable. For example, if Bush's policy position is at 35, Edward's ideal point, Edward receives 200 units of utility; but if Kerry's policy position is at 35, Edward receives only 125 utils. Similarly, if Bush's policy position is at 70 (as it is in the figure), Edward receives 75 utils; but if Kerry is at 70, Edward receives 0 utils.

From our analysis, it is clear that if Bush and Kerry adopt the same policy position, Edward will always prefer Bush. Suppose, however, that the candidates have to choose policy positions in order to please party elites, as we discussed earlier in this chapter, and Bush locates at 70 and Kerry at 15, as shown in figure 5.20. Note that although Bush is further from Edward's ideal point than Kerry, Edward is indifferent toward Kerry and Bush; both give Edward 75 utils. In contrast, consider the utility function that might represent our anonymous voter in Massachusetts, whom we will call Helen. Helen's utility function is like Edward's, but her ideal point is at 40, not 35, as shown in figure 5.21. However, even though Kerry's policy position is closer to her ideal point, she prefers Bush. She receives 100 utils from Bush

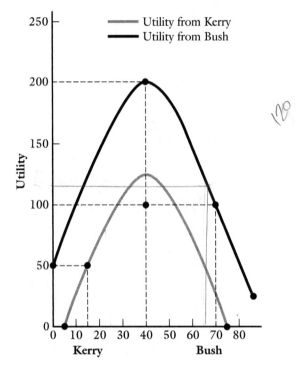

FIGURE 5.21
Helen's Utility from Bush and Kerry, 2004

Note: Helen prefers Kerry although Bush's policy is closer to her ideal point.

and 50 utils from Kerry. Groseclose (2001) called voters like Helen *Stokes voters*. Any voter with a utility function like Edward's or Helen's but with an ideal point between 35 and 45 will prefer Bush even though Kerry's policy position is closer to the voter's ideal point. Groseclose labeled the region between 50 and 45 the *Stokes region*. The Stokes region becomes larger as the candidates' positions on issues get closer. For example, suppose that Bush is at 60 and Kerry is at 35. In that case, any voter whose ideal point is between 35 and 60 will prefer Bush to Kerry. This is not surprising; as the candidates moderate, we would expect voters to be more likely to base their votes on valence issues.

Therefore, when voters receive valence utility, they are willing to vote for candidates whose policy positions are further from their ideal point, as our anonymous Bush voter in Massachusetts was. Does this mean that a candidate with a valence advantage can afford to choose a more extreme position than one who does not have a valence advantage? Groseclose (2001) solved the game between two candidates when they are choosing positions in order to please the policy preferences of party elites, they are uncertain about the location of the median voter's ideal point, and voters are receiving extra valence utility from one of the candidates. He found that adding a valence issue leads to a greater divergence between candidates in terms of policy compared with a situation in which no valence issue exists and that the size of the divergence between the candidates increases with the size of the utility voters receive from the valence issue. Interestingly, when the utility voters receive from the valence issue is small, the candidate who is advantaged chooses more moderate positions than before, while the candidate who is disadvantaged chooses more extreme positions than before. But when the size of the utility from the valence becomes large, both candidates become more extreme than before, although, surprisingly, the disadvantaged candidate is always more extreme than the advantaged candidate.

These results seem counterintuitive. Why doesn't the advantaged candidate choose the more extreme position, and why does he or she moderate when the valence utility is small? Why is it that the disadvantaged candidate always chooses the more extreme position? The key is that by moving to an extreme position, the disadvantaged candidate can reduce the advantages of valence for his or her opponent. So for the disadvantaged candidate, moving to a more extreme position can both serve his or her party elites and reduce the number of Stokes voters. The disadvantaged candidate does not gain from moderation as much as he or she does when a valence dimension does not exist and is less likely to moderate with a valence issue. The advantaged candidate, on the other hand, faces conflicting incentives; he or she would like to move to a moderate position to increase the number of Stokes voters but at the same time wants to please his or her party elites, who have more extreme preferences. Thus with small valence advantages, the advantaged candidate moves to a more moderate position to increase the number of Stokes voters; but as valence utility increases, the advantaged candidate can become more extreme without losing as many Stokes voters. Yet the advantaged candidate is always less extreme than the disadvantaged candidate because of the conflicting motives.[53] Valence issues, then, can result in candidates' taking more extreme positions and are an additional force causing divergence and polarization between candidates. Given the divergence, however, the candidate who has the valence advantage is also going to be more moderate on policy.

Valence and Actual Elections

Groseclose's results are empirically supported. Fiorina (1973) has found that incumbent members of Congress who have won with big margins of victory (and thus might be argued to have some valence advantage with voters) are more likely to moderate their positions than those with small margins. Ansolabehere, Snyder, and Stewart (2001), using data on candidates' positions in congressional races, found that high-quality challengers select more moderate positions than low-quality challengers (measuring quality in terms of the candidate's background and expertise).

Can our analysis of valence issues help us understand the election of 2004? Exit polls suggest that there were individuals, like our anonymous Massachusetts voter and Crissy Hill, who disagreed with Bush's policy positions but voted for him because they felt he was better at managing foreign policy than Kerry. While there were also voters like Robert Dealy, who had the opposite point of view, 58 percent of voters said that they trusted Bush to handle terrorism, while only 40 percent said they trusted Kerry. This is despite the fact that 52 percent of voters felt that the war in Iraq was going badly and only a bare majority, 53 percent, approved of how Bush was handling the job as president (Bill Clinton's job-approval rating when he left the presidency in 2001 was 65 percent; Ronald Reagan's in 1989 was 64 percent; Dwight Eisenhower's in 1961 was 59 percent). Retired teacher Sue Martin of Jefferson City, Missouri, summed up her reasons for voting for Bush: "I think we need to stay with him, let him finish what he's trying to do. His presidency has been so influenced by 9–11 that he really hasn't had an opportunity to focus carefully on the country. Bush is just a man of integrity, and I really question whether Kerry is."[54] Bush did seem to have a small valence-issue advantage on terrorism with a slight majority of voters, which did help him attract some Stokes voters and win an extremely close election.

What We Know

The evidence suggests that U.S. voters are not polarized on cultural issues. Partisan elites do appear to be more polarized on these issues. Elected officials are significantly more polarized on measures of overall liberalism and conservatism. Growing income inequality, coupled with the reality, as noted in chapter 2, such that the benefits of participating electorally are greatest for those whose incomes are at the extremes of the distribution of income, provides an explanation for the growing polarization of elites and elected officials, as argued by McCarty, Poole, and Rosenthal. We also know that when voters value valence issues—nonpolicy factors—which evidence suggests they often do, candidates choose more extreme positions on divisive policies.

What We Don't Know: What Money Does

So far, we have yet to mention much about how interest groups and campaign contributions affect elections beyond mobilization or how voters might handle a lack of information about elected officials' policy positions. As we noted earlier, for the 2000 Senate race, the Republican Party in California used a blanket primary system and Tom Campbell won the nomination. But he had to win the general election, and for that contest it turned out that money, not type of primary system, was important. In the next chapter, we explore why.

Study Questions and Problems

1. Is it possible for a state that has two counties to have polarized voter preferences when each county has voters who are nonpolarized? Use graphs in your answer.
2. Is it possible for the electorate to be polarized but for the two major parties to be nonpolarized? Use graphs in your answer.
3. In this chapter, we considered two reasons why candidates might diverge on policy positions—candidates' having to please party elites in primaries and candidates' having valence-issue advantages. How are those two explanations similar? How are they different? Suppose you want to empirically determine which of these theories can best explain how the two major political parties have diverged on policy positions over time. How would you do so? What sort of evidence would you look for?

NOTES

1. Paul Farhi, "Elephants Are Red, Donkeys Are Blue: Color Is Sweet, So Their States We Hue," *Washington Post*, November 2, 2004.
2. Farhi, "Elephants Are Red, Donkeys Are Blue."
3. Liz Marlantes, "Inside Red-and-Blue America," *Christian Science Monitor*, July 14, 2004.
4. Zogby International, America Culturally Divided: Blue vs. Red States, Democrats vs. Republicans—Two Separate Nations, New O'Leary Report/Zogby Poll Reveals, January 6, 2004, http://www.zogby.com/news/ReadNews .dbm?ID=775.
5. Mark O'Keefe, "Presidential Politics Confronts a Values Divide in Red and Blue America," Newhouse News Service, January 20, 2004.
6. Laurence D. Cohen, "When It Comes to Pest Control, Better Red Than Dead," *Hartford Courant*, September 22, 2004.
7. Zogby International, Bush Leads in Red States, Kerry Ahead in Blue States, February 18, 2004, http://www.zogby.com/news/021804.html.
8. "Barack Obama's remarks at the Democratic convention," *USA Today*, July 27, 2004, http://www.usatoday.com/news/politicselections/nation/president/ 2004-07-27-obama-speech-text_x.htm.
9. The retirement of Senator John Breaux resulted in the election of a Republican in November 2004.
10. In chapter 10, we discuss the incentive for moderate voters to create such a balance between the two parties in their votes for president and Congress.
11. "How Voters in Colorado Split Their Tickets in the Last Election," *All Things Considered*, NPR, December 21, 2004.
12. John Andrews, "What the Hell Happened in Colorado? Why Republicans Held the State for Bush and Lost Everything Else on the Ballot," *Weekly Standard*, December 6, 2004.

13. John Mulligan, "Chafee Stands Firm against Tax-Cut Plan," *Providence Journal-Bulletin*, April 28, 2003.
14. John Wildermuth, "Red State, Blue State," *San Francisco Chronicle*, November 7, 2004.
15. Alan J. Borsuk, "Red, Blue, and a Bit Bruised: A Divided Wisconsin Looks Beyond the Vote," *Milwaukee Journal Sentinel*, November 1, 2004.
16. Bill Bishop, "The Great Divide: An Utterly Polarizing U.S. Election," *Austin American-Statesman*, December 4, 2004.
17. Federal News Service, December 1, 2003.
18. Technically, a mode is the most likely point, so for a distribution to have two modes, the two local maximums must be exactly equal. That is not necessary for us to call a distribution bimodal.
19. Wildermuth, "Red State, Blue State."
20. See Poole and Rosenthal (1997), chapter 5.
21. Blacks in the North, who were enfranchised, began to switch to the Democratic Party and elect Democrats during the 1930s in response to the liberal economic policies of northern Democrats. Robert Caro's multivolume biography of Lyndon Johnson, in which he describes Johnson's years in the House and the Senate during this period, provides a useful window on how southern members of Congress were able to control the legislative agenda. In chapter 15, we discuss how the South disenfranchised black voters after Reconstruction was ended by the Compromise of 1877.
22. On some issues that did not fit well within the standard liberal-conservative dimension, the Progressives were more liberal than both major parties. In chapter 14, we discuss the role of minor parties and how their candidates can affect policy changes over time in terms of more than one spatial dimension.
23. Of course, taking out the South in terms of the empirical analysis does not control for the fact that those in Congress are taking positions with the South in the real world. Empirically it is difficult to estimate the counterfactual of a country without the impact of conservative southern Democrats when the choices we analyze are made by actors who are not choosing in the hypothesized counterfactual world.
24. As quoted on *Talk of the Nation*, NPR, November 17, 2003.
25. Richard W. Stephenson, "Cheney Owns Up to Profanity Incident and Says He 'Felt Better Afterwards,' " *New York Times*, June 26, 2004.
26. David Lightman, " 'Constant Partisanship' Bogging Down Congress," *Hartford Courant*, November 23, 2004.
27. Michael Duffy and Douglas Waller, "What We'll Miss and What We Won't," *Time*, November 29, 2004.
28. Lightman, " 'Constant Partisanship' Bogging Down Congress."
29. While the NES began asking these questions in 1964, from 1964 to 1968 respondents who answered "don't know" were coded as moderates, thereby overstating the percentage of moderates in the population and making comparisons over time with data from these periods problematic.
30. See Fiorina, Abrams, and Pope (2005) for a discussion of the identification problem in using this data to make inferences about changes in voters' preferences when there is no control for the changes in candidates' positions.
31. The ideal points that Poole and Rosenthal estimate for members are dynamic—that is, they are allowed to change over time. For more information on the procedures behind this estimation, see http://www.voteview.com/dwnl.htm.
32. One noteworthy longitudinal study that might be of use is of a class of high school seniors, including parents and later children. See Jennings and Stoker (1997). In this study, a national sample of high school seniors and their parents were surveyed in 1965, and surveys of the same individuals were conducted in

1973, 1982, and 1997. However, because the original sample was not representative of the electorate in 1965 (there were only two selected age cohorts), we cannot use this sample to draw inferences about the distribution of ideal points in the population as a whole in 1965 compared with the distribution as a whole in 1997.

33. See also Fiorina, Abrams, and Pope (2005) for an examination of changes over time in mean responses according to whether a respondent is a partisan and, in particular, an "active" partisan in terms of participating in a greater number of political events during an election year. They found some small evidence that activists have become more extreme in ideological views over time, but they have found little change in ordinary voters.

34. Federal News Service, December 1, 2003.

35. Jan Dennis, "Some Say Bush's Showing Signals Right Turn in Downtown Illinois," Associated Press State & Local Wire, December 19, 2004.

36. Eric Black and Dane Smith, "The Myth of Red and Blue," *Minneapolis Star Tribune*, September 19, 2004.

37. The closest is a thermometer rating on the women's liberation movement. Examination of those ratings show changes very similar to those for gay men and lesbians in terms of moderation by most respondents, with some sorting by strong Democrat or Republican.

38. Olivera Perkins and Margaret Bernstein, "Both Parties Take Heart from Black Voters' Turnout," *Cleveland Plain Dealer*, November 7, 2004.

39. Thomas B. Edsall and James V. Grimaldi, "On Nov. 2, GOP Got More Bang for Its Billion, Analysis Shows," *Washington Post*, December 30, 2004.

40. Dan Balz, "DNC Chief Advises Learning from GOP," *Washington Post*, December 11, 2004.

41. Adam Nagourney, "Democrats Weigh De-emphasizing Abortion as an Issue," *New York Times*, December 24, 2004.

42. Susan Page, "Cheney Says He Opposes Marriage Amendment," *USA Today*, August 25, 2004.

43. David Stout, "Cheney Criticizes Kerry for Mentioning Daughter," *New York Times*, October 15, 2004.

44. Richard Morin, "Singling Out Mary Cheney Wrong, Most Say: 2 in 3 Polled Find Kerry's Comment 'Inappropriate,' " *Washington Post*, October 17, 2004.

45. See Foley (1967), Romer (1975), Roberts (1977), Meltzer and Richard (1981), and Bolton and Roland (1997).

46. Some localities allow noncitizens to vote in local school board elections. A measure to allow such voting was defeated by voters in San Francisco in 2004.

47. Black and Smith, "The Myth of Red and Blue."

48. Maura Reynolds, "The Race for the White House: Foreign Policy Divide Is Slim for Bush, Kerry," *Los Angeles Times*, September 30, 2004.

49. "Transcript of the Candidates' First Debate in the Presidential Campaign," *New York Times*, October 1, 2004.

50. "Transcript of the Candidates' First Debate in the Presidential Campaign."

51. Joan Vennochi, "An Election Day Secret," *Boston Globe*, December 7, 2004.

52. Pamela Stallsmith, "Voters Split over Future," *Richmond Times-Dispatch*, November 3, 2004.

53. For a multidimensional model of candidates' spatial location with a valence dimension, see Ansolabehere and Snyder (2000). Other spatial voting models that incorporate a valence dimension are described by Aragones and Palfrey (2002), Londregan and Romer (1993), Feld and Grofman (1991), and Berger, Munger, and Potthoff (2000).

54. "Feelings Run Strong Among Missouri Voters," Associated Press State & Local Wire, November 2, 2004.

Part II

Money and the Mass Media

6

How Campaigns Are Financed

Memorandum for the President
From: Harold Ickes
In order to raise an additional $3,000,000 to permit the Democratic National Committee to produce and air generic tv/radio spots as soon as Congress adjourns, . . . I request that you telephone Vernon Jordan, Senator Rockefeller and Bernard Schwartz either today or tomorrow. You should ask them if they will call ten to twelve CEO/business people who are very supportive of the Administration . . . to have breakfast with you, as well as with Messrs. Jordan, Rockefeller and Schwartz, very late this week or very early next week.

The purpose of the breakfast would be for you to express your appreciation for all they have done to support the administration, to impress them with the need to raise $3,000,000 within the next two weeks . . . and to ask them, if they, in turn, would undertake to raise that amount of money.

"The Ickes Files: Please Send Us a Check Now,"
New York Times, March 2, 1997

The Desperate Man

An incumbent president was up for reelection. He had won the presidential nomination easily enough at his party's convention, and the campaign had started out well, giving him a good lead over his opposition. But in one of the states that he counted on and needed, his campaign was in trouble. The party's state committee had told him that it needed funds from the national committee, but the national committee was out of funds. The desperate president "summoned a group of monied men . . . to a hush-hush White House breakfast, where he told them that if they gave him the money he needed they'd have nothing to fear from him during his second term."[1]

This president was not Bill Clinton, and the year was not 1995, when Harold Ickes wrote his memorandum. The president was Theodore Roosevelt, the year was 1904, and the state in which the campaign faced trouble was Roosevelt's home state of New York. The moneyed men were Edward Henry Harriman, Hamilton McKown Twombly, Henry Clay Frick, and Thomas Lamont. And evidence suggests that financiers and railroad magnates like Harriman, Twombly, Frick, and Lamont did contribute mightily to the campaign—72 percent of the contributions were reportedly from corporations. According to Harriman (as quoted by Lukas [1998, p. 392]), the money given to Roosevelt in response to his request "enabled the New York State Committee to continue its work, with the result that at least 50,000 votes were turned in the city of New York alone, making a difference of 100,000 votes in the general result." Moreover, Harriman did not just expect that Roosevelt would turn a blind eye to the business dealings that had faced the scrutiny and impediments of government regulators; he also expected that his friend and ally Chauncey M. Depew (who was worried about his reelection bid for the Senate) would be appointed ambassador to France after the election.[2]

What about the breakfast that Ickes was trying to arrange? Clinton was as desperate as Roosevelt. In 1994, the Republicans had won a majority of the seats in the House of Representatives for the first time in forty years. The Republicans' success meant that the Democrats no longer controlled Congress, and many pundits began to pronounce Clinton's presidency a one-term wonder. Did Clinton's breakfast similarly involve promises of favors? Schwartz, like Harriman, had begun his career in New York's financial district. Harriman owned railroads, and Schwartz owns Loral Space and Communications. In 1994, Schwartz wrote a check for $100,000 to the Democratic National Committee, and two months later he joined Secretary of Commerce Ronald Brown on a trip to China. Schwartz denied there was a relationship between the check and the trip. "On the plane, Schwartz said he asked Brown if he could arrange a private meeting with Zhu Gao Feng, the vice minister of China's Ministry of Post and Telecommunications. In a meeting with Chinese telecommunications officials, Brown publicly praised Loral's Globalstar cellular telephone system." Loral eventually landed an agreement with China that earned the company $250 million annually. Schwartz denied that the contribution and the contract were connected and was cleared by Charles G. LaBella, the prosecutor investigating campaign finance violations.[3] In 1997, Schwartz was the largest individual contributor to the Democratic Party. From 1991 to 2003, he contributed $5.6 million to Democratic candidates.[4]

To be fair, Republican leaders also have strong ties to those who donate large sums of money. *The Washington Post* reports a number of examples of both Republican and Democratic leaders who have provided big campaign contributors with access and influence. For instance, according to the *Post*, on October 27, 1995, Republican National Committee chairman Haley Barbour "sent a letter to [Bob] Dole, who was the Senate majority leader, asking him to meet with then–Pfizer chief executive Williams C. Steele Jr. The pharmaceutical company had given $100,000 to the GOP committee."[5]

Questions about the influence of campaign contributions are not limited to the federal government. After Jeb Bush was reelected governor of Florida, he began a process of privatizing the state government in order to reduce costs and government size. In that process, however, many of the private companies given government contracts had been big Republican donors in 2002. "If you look at the contract you can almost tell who it's written for if you look at the contributors' list," charged Cindy Hall, president of the Florida AFL-CIO.[6]

From before Teddy Roosevelt to the present, campaign contributions and moneyed men (and now women) have played important roles in U.S. elections.[7] In this chapter, we examine how campaign contributions and paid advertising are involved in electoral politics. First, we discuss who the contributors are and how they make their contributions.

Who Makes Contributions?

As of March 2004, thirty-three-year-old Houston lawyer Paul Dickerson had not given any money to George Bush's 2004 reelection campaign. He is not a multimillionaire, a high-powered executive of a major business, or even a partner in his law firm. Yet he had attended campaign "appreciation" events at the president's Crawford, Texas, ranch and on Ellis Island, in New York Harbor. At an event in Houston attended by the first president Bush, Dickerson was tapped for the honor of introducing the former president. Had the Bush family wasted their time on Dickerson? Hardly. Dickerson is one of 187 "Rangers," each of whom raised $200,000 from individual contributors to the president's reelection campaign. How did Dickerson become so important to the Bush campaign?

Interest Groups

When most people think of campaign contributions, they think of organized interest groups, not people like Paul Dickerson. Organized interest groups are certainly important in campaigns, as we saw in chapter 2; groups like the AFL-CIO are heavily involved in mobilizing voters for elections. They also contribute money to election campaigns. There are two basic types of interest groups—economic and noneconomic. Economic interest groups represent four kinds of economic interests—business (for example, the Chamber of Commerce), labor (for example, the American Federation of Labor and Congress of Industrial Organizations, or AFL-CIO), agriculture (for example, the National Farmers Union), and professional (for example, the American Medical Association, or AMA). Noneconomic interest groups take three forms—general public interest groups (for example, the League of Women Voters), single-issue groups (such as the National Rifle Association, or NRA), and ideological groups (like the Christian Coalition).

Organized interest groups generally work to affect U.S. politics at all levels of government, from mobilizing voters and other kinds of involvement in political campaigns to lobbying members of Congress and the president to pass legislation or take actions preferred by the group, lobbying members of the bureaucracy who are sometimes delegated by Congress and the president to make policy decisions, and using the courts to attempt to overturn policies or decisions they do not prefer. Whether interest groups take actions as a group in elections or after elections, their members must be willing to provide both physical and financial resources to underwrite those efforts. With a few exceptions (union members who work in a closed shop, where union membership is required of all employees), membership in interest groups is voluntary. As we saw in chapter 2, when a group of individuals wishes to take a common action that benefits all members and the members have the opportunity to choose whether to participate, each member (or potential member) has an incentive to free-ride on the actions of the others. Organized interest groups therefore face a problem of collective action.

How do organized interest groups overcome their collective-action problems? In general, most groups use selective benefits, as we saw in the mobilization of votes in elections. Many of the selective benefits that these groups provide are social or purposive or both, as with voter mobilization. But interest groups, because they often require more of members than just voting, also provide informational and material benefits. Informational benefits are things like special newsletters, periodicals, training programs, conferences, and so on. For example, U.S. Term Limits publishes an online newsletter called *No Uncertain Terms* and, on its Web site, commentary under the heading "Commonsense." Material benefits are things like goods and services, even money. The American Association of Retired Persons (AARP) provides members with insurance and discount purchasing programs.

Organized interest groups provide campaign contributions through the political action committees, or PACs, that many of them form. A PAC is a private group whose purpose is to raise and distribute money for use in election campaigns. Just as with interest groups, PACs come in two types—economic and noneconomic—and face a potential collective-action problem. PACs can also be either "connected" or "nonconnected." Connected PACs are formally connected to an interest group, corporation, labor union, or other existing entity and can draw on the resources and members of that entity to fund its organizational costs. Gais (1996) found that in 1992, 71 percent of PACs were connected. Nonconnected PACs are independent and must attract outside contributors to pay their expenses. As a result, connected PACs have an easier time with the potential collective-action problem, since they already have a membership and resources.

PACs versus Individuals and Collective Action

Although PAC contributions are the most talked about form of campaign contribution and some evidence suggests that they are overstated in the news media, a greater portion (the majority) of campaign spending comes from individual contributions raised by people like Paul Dickerson.[8] For example, the Federal Election Commission (FEC), in its report on contributions to congressional candidates for the 2002 election, as of March 31, 2002, stated: "Contributions from individuals totaled $250.6 million and continue to be the largest source of receipts for Congressional candidates, representing 58.2% of all fundraising as of March 31. PAC contributions totaled $121.1 million or 28.1% while candidates themselves contributed or loaned a total of $37.8 million which was 8.8% of all receipts." The remaining amounts were from other candidates or from party committees.

How did Dickerson get involved in raising individual contributions for Bush? As it happens, he went to college with Travis Thomas, the Bush campaign's national finance director. At a barbecue in the summer of 2003, Thomas persuaded Dickerson to become a volunteer fund-raiser for the campaign and commit himself to trying to raise $100,000. Dickerson recalled: "A bunch of us are at a time in our careers when friends help us out. I figured I'm his buddy and I should help him out." Dickerson already had a talent for networking, according to friends (with a Christmas-card list of over 350 names).[9]

Yet Dickerson's experience shows that while the majority of contributions are from individuals, those contributions are sometimes given through an intermediary who is serving as a volunteer fund-raiser for the candidate. The Bush campaign assigned tracking numbers to fund-raisers committed to raising $100,000, and contributions that bore a tracking number were credited to the respective fund-raiser. Such contributions were usually generated at or in conjunction with "events" attended by Bush; his wife, Laura; or other members of his family or the administration, such as Vice President Cheney. Big fund-raisers like Dickerson then recruited others (starting with friends and family and building up to cold calls to strangers) to commit themselves to raising smaller amounts, such as $5,000, $10,000, or $25,000 by selling tickets to the events, and so on, in return for being listed as a "host" of the event on its program. The contributions were logged with Dickerson's tracking number. *The New York Times* reported: " 'It's friends of friends of friends of friends, like a daisy chain,' said Jeanne L. Phillips, a veteran fund-raiser for the Bush campaign in Texas and a former United States ambassador. 'We go hand to hand and neighbor to neighbor. We ask everybody.' "[10]

The Internet and Campaign Finance

When the campaign finance reports came out in July for the second quarter of 2003, many experts were shocked. Former Vermont governor Howard Dean had raised more money than Senators John Kerry, John Edwards, and Joseph Lieberman and Representative Richard Gephardt (who had been expected to be a strong leader in fund-raising, with his ties to organized labor). Dean had raised $7.5 million from 59,000 contributors.[11] How did he do it?

On the Internet. But while many use the Internet in campaigns (Dickerson had an e-mail address just for the Bush-Cheney campaign, which he used to contact potential contributors), Dean allowed online supporters to become an active part of the campaign. Doing so meant losing some control. He allowed supporters to build their own Web pages and to post largely uncensored messages on an online campaign diary that campaign staffers used to communicate with online supporters. Online supporters became active freelance fund-raisers, like Bush's Rangers, but they were a more fluid, changing group of individuals communicating mainly through the Web. Dean said about his online supporters: "They would never support you if you just sent e-mail and told them what the daily message is."[12]

Other candidates have followed Dean's lead in trying to expand use of the Web to attract contributions. Supporters of retired army general Wesley Clark used the Web to raise $2 million to draft him into the campaign. "It's tough to keep up with the demand," Ben Green said. "We're getting inquiries daily, as opposed to once a month or once a week." Green's firm, Crossroads Strategies, has handled Web-based campaigns for Senators John Kerry and Hillary Rodham Clinton and others.[13]

The stories of Bush's Rangers and Dean's online supporters show how unorganized individual campaign contributions can be combined in ways that can mean a sizable difference in a campaign and how individuals can realize they are working as a group. For example, the "Democratic National Committee . . . e-mailed an advertisement to 1.4 million Democrats that called for an investigation into claims that White House aides had leaked the name of a Central Intelligence Agency agent. It then asked supporters to finance a drive to put the ad on television. The committee raised enough money to air the ad in Pennsylvania."[14]

Federal Campaign Finance Regulations

Early Regulation and the Creation of the Federal Election Commission

Dickerson and other Rangers for Bush had helped him build a campaign chest of $160 million dollars by March 2004, almost as much as both the former president Bush and Bill Clinton had spent in the 1992 election. Both

George W. Bush and John Kerry opted out of public financing during the primaries, and thus there was no limit on the sum each could raise. However, federal regulations limited how much their contributors could give and the candidates were required to publicly report what they received. How did these regulations on campaign finance come about? For many years, campaign financing was unregulated. Then, in 1907, corporations and banks were forbidden to give money to presidential and congressional candidates, and unions were included later. Congress passed the Federal Corrupt Practices Act of 1910, revised in 1925, in an attempt to limit contributions of individuals. However, the limits placed on contributions were so unrealistically low that no one was ever prosecuted. Then, with the rise of the national media and use of the media in campaigns during the 1950s and 1960s, pressure built to regulate campaign finance. Congress passed the Federal Election Campaign Act of 1971 (FECA), which was amended in 1974 and provided for partial public funding of presidential campaigns and required full public reporting and strict limits on all contributions and expenditures in federal elections. The FEC was created to collect and provide the information as well as enforce the law.

Nevertheless, the law was controversial—in particular, limiting campaign contributions is contended by some to be an unconstitutional infringement of the right to free speech. Senator James Buckley (whom we discuss in more detail in chapter 14), among others, challenged the law, and in 1976, in *Buckley v. Valeo*, the Supreme Court declared that spending limits and ceilings on how much of their own money candidates could spend, as well as how much others could spend to agitate for or against candidates independent of a candidate's campaign, were unconstitutional. Limits on individual and party contributions to candidates were also declared constitutional. In 1979, however, Congress amended the FECA to allow party organizations to engage in unlimited campaign spending for state and local party building and mobilization of voters. In 1996, in *Colorado Republican Federal Campaign Committee v. Federal Election Commission*, the Court ruled that party organizations were not subject to limits on spending for other reasons as well. Money spent by the parties in that fashion, as well as money spent by groups or individuals independent of candidates, has been called soft money—money that is not subject to FECA regulation—while money spent by the candidates and parties to promote a candidate in a particular election has been labeled hard money—money that is subject to FECA regulation. Under the court rulings, however, almost anything related to a campaign could be paid for with soft money as long as it was not an ad explicitly telling voters to vote for a particular candidate.

The Rise of Soft Money

A result of these rulings was an increased use of soft money by parties and other spending by interest groups and individuals in campaigns that focused on the advocacy of issues instead of candidates and thus were not subject to federal regulation. Table 6.1 presents a summary of hard and soft money raised by the national political parties for elections from 1991 to 2000. As the data show, both types of campaign money increased, with soft money increasing as a percentage of the total (the presidential election years of 1992, 1996, and 2000 generated higher spending levels than the nonpresidential election years). Although during this period the national Republican Party raised a larger amount of money, both hard and soft, than the Democrats, a greater percentage of the Democratic resources came from soft money.

Table 6.1
National Major-Party Fund-Raising, 1991–2000

	1999–2000	*1997–98*	*1995–96*	*1993–94*	*1991–92*
Democrats					
Hard Money	$275.2	$160.0	$221.6	$139.1	$177.7
	(52.9%)	(63.3%)	(64.1%)	(73.9%)	(83.0%)
Soft Money	$245.2	$92.8	$123.9	$49.1	$36.3
	(47.1%)	(36.7%)	(36.9%)	(26.1%)	(17.0%)
Total	$520.4	$252.8	$345.5	$188.2	$214.0
Republicans					
Hard Money	$465.8	$285.0	$416.5	$245.6	$267.3
	(65.0%)	(68.4%)	(75.1%)	(82.4%)	(84.3%)
Soft Money	$249.9	$131.6	$138.2	$52.5	$49.8
	(35.0%)	(31.6%)	(24.9%)	(17.6%)	(15.7%)
Total	$715.7	$416.6	$554.7	$298.1	$317.1
Grand Total	$1,236.1	$669.4	$900.2	$486.3	$531.1

Source: Federal Election Commission, May 15, 2001.
Note: Amounts are in millions of dollars. Percentages appear below dollar amounts.

Soft money obviously allowed parties and interest groups to spend more in elections than was permitted under federal regulations as long as the moneys were not used expressly to advocate a particular candidate in a particular election. In many cases, however, it was difficult to determine where advocacy began. Should a get-out-the-vote drive by a state party before a general election in which the party's candidate needed a high turnout to win be viewed as unrelated to the candidate's campaign simply because voters were recruited by the party rather than the candidate? Should a message funded by a businessman criticizing a congressional incumbent be viewed as unrelated to the incumbent's challenger's campaign simply because it does not mention the election taking place the next day or the challenger's name? In surveys and focus groups, voters in the 2000 election saw both types of efforts as equivalent to explicit campaign advertising.[15] The soft-money loophole suggested to many that the FECA regulations limiting campaign contributions had been effectively eliminated and could be reinstated in actuality only by regulating soft money.

In March of 2002, Congress passed, and President Bush signed, the Bipartisan Campaign Reform Act (BCRA) of 2002 (also called the McCain-Feingold act, after the two senators who sponsored the bill). This act limits the size of contributions and requires full public disclosure of the sources of moneys that go directly to candidates as well as the soft money previously spent by parties. Specifically, in congressional elections individuals may give no more than $2,000 per candidate per campaign, with primary, runoff, and general-election campaigns considered separately. Nonparty PACs are limited to contributions of $5,000 per candidate per campaign, and parties may give no more than $5,000 to a candidate for the House of Representatives and no more than $17,500 to a candidate for the Senate. The $2,000 individual contribution limit also applies to candidates in presidential primaries and to presidential candidates who accept public funds for the general election. Note that the limits were increased from those set by FECA. Contributions from foreign sources are illegal in federal elections. The new law was immediately challenged and reviewed by the Supreme Court in *McConnell v. Federal Election Commission* (2003). The Supreme Court rejected most of the challenges and upheld all of the major provisions.

The Provisions of BCRA

BCRA regulates soft money in five principal ways:

1. National parties are prohibited from soliciting, receiving, or transferring or directing to another person or committee any funds that do not comply with FECA's dollar limitations, source prohibitions, and disclosure requirements.
2. State and local parties are prohibited from using soft money to finance federal election activities, which are defined as
   a. voter registration activities within 120 days of a regularly scheduled election for federal office
   b. voter identification, get-out-the-vote activity, or generic campaign activity conducted in connection with an election in which a candidate for federal office appears on the ballot
   c. public communications that refer to a clearly identified candidate for federal office and promote or oppose that candidate

    d. services provided by party staffers who spend more than 25 percent of their time working in connection with a federal election
3. Political parties are prohibited from soliciting funds for or donating funds to tax-exempt organizations that participate financially in federal elections.
4. Federal candidates and office holders are prohibited from soliciting, receiving, spending, transferring, or directing soft money in connection with any election for federal, state, or local office.
5. State and local candidates and office holders are prohibited from spending soft money on public communications that support or oppose federal candidates.

BCRA also created a new legal category of communication—electioneering communication. Such communication is subject to federal disclosure regulation, and corporations and unions are banned from directly financing it if it is a broadcast, cable, or satellite communication that fulfills each of the following conditions: (1) it refers to a clearly identified federal candidate, (2) it is publicly distributed to a television station, radio station, cable-television system, or satellite system for a fee, and (3) the communication is distributed within sixty days of a general election or thirty days of a primary election for a federal office.

The Millionaires' Amendment

Howard Dean's ability to raise money on the Internet seemed to translate into electoral support in the fall of 2003 as the first caucuses and primaries of the presidential nomination season approached. A poll in Iowa taken during the Thanksgiving period showed Dean with 29 percent of the vote, Gephardt with 21 percent, and Kerry in third place, with 18 percent. Kerry was out of money. But that didn't mean he was out of the race. He would lend the money to his campaign if he had to, and he did. He shopped for a mortgage on his home on Louisburg Square in Boston and lent his campaign $850,000. Overall, he ended up using $3.5 million in personal cash to keep the campaign going to February 2004.[16] Would Kerry have been able to stay in the campaign without the ability to make such sizable loans using his own resources? What does this mean for potential candidates who don't have the capability to make such loans or don't have valuable houses to mortgage?

    At the same time that Kerry was spending his own money trying to win the Democratic presidential nomination, former securities trader Blair Hull, worth about $500 million, was using his largesse to try to win the Democratic nomination to run for the Senate from Illinois in a race to fill the seat of retiring first-term Republican senator Peter Fitzgerald. By late February 2004, he had spent over $20 million and was ahead in the polls. But he lost to a young state senator, Barack Obama. Obama benefited from negative information that emerged about Hull (like Affleck and Ventura—see chapter 2—he hadn't bothered to vote in recent elections, and his ex-wife had sought a civil order of protection against him). However, Obama also benefited from one of the provisions of BCRA, the so-called millionaires' amendment, sponsored by Illinois senator Dick Durbin. The millionaires' amendment limits the amount that self-funded candidates can spend on their own campaigns based on the voting-age population of the election district. In addition, for candidates who face self-funded challengers, it raises the limit on individual contributions up to $12,000, depending on how much of his or her own money the self-funded candidate spends. As a result, Obama was able to raise $3 million from 480 individual donors who contributed more than the standard limit of $2,000. Without the millionaires' amendment, these donors could have contributed a total of only $960,000—the millionaires' amendment allowed Obama to get more than $2 million extra, which was more than one third of his total campaign spending.[17] Even with the millionaires' amendment, Obama spent about one sixth as much as Hull—yet he won with 53 percent of the vote (Hull came in third). Being able to finance oneself does not ensure victory.

Was BCRA successful? Whether it was or not, BCRA did change the way in which political parties and candidates raised money in 2004. Both political parties, restricted to hard-money donations, were able to raise more in hard dollars than they raised in hard and soft dollars combined in 2000. Thus, political fund-raising by candidates and parties was more broad based than in previous years, with the political parties and candidates relying more on small donations than on large, individual contributions. But BCRA definitely did not lead to a reduction in the amount candidates and their party organizations spent. According to the FEC, more than $1 billion was spent in the 2004 campaign by the presidential candidates and the national conventions, 56 percent more than was spent during the 2000 campaign.[18]

Shadows in the Law

A camera zooms out from a picture of billowing smokestacks to reveal a factory with Chinese writing on it. "During the past three years, it's true George W. Bush has created more jobs. Unfortunately, they were created in places like China," a voice says. The video of the factory was shown in seventeen states in March of 2004. But this was not an ad by John Kerry, the Democratic presidential candidate, who was frantically trying to raise money after having largely depleted his reserves during the hectic primary season. Kerry, while running some ads of his own, didn't have the resources to match the ads being run by Bush with the $159 million the president had raised in the last nine months. In the first two weeks of March, Bush's campaign spent nearly $20 million on campaign ads against Kerry, while Kerry spent just under $2 million during the same period. So others were running ads for the Democrat. This ad was paid for by a new group called the Media

Fund, started by Harold Ickes and using soft money (with large contributions from George Soros, who, like Bernard Schwartz, has historically been a big campaign contributor for the Democrats). Republicans and Bush were angry about the ads. Hadn't BCRA outlawed this kind of thing? " 'This is another example of bitter partisan groups blatantly using illegal soft money to create a shadow Democratic Party in order to defeat President Bush,' said Scott Stanzel, a Bush campaign spokesman."[19]

The Media Fund was not the only group using soft money in this fashion. At the same time that its ad came out, a similar group also receiving funds from Soros, MoveOn.org, revealed ads criticizing Bush's decision to go to war against Iraq. In the 2004 election, according to a report by the Center for Public Integrity, 257 groups spent over $550 million, compared with approximately $286 million spent in 2002. While most of the expenditures were in support of Democratic candidates (76 percent for presidential-election spending, 55.64 percent for congressional-election spending), the ads of one particular Republican group motivated by Kerry's anti-war testimony during the Vietnam era had a huge impact. On April 4, 2004, nine Vietnam veterans called by retired Navy rear admiral Roy Hoffman—who had commanded Kerry in Vietnam and had been negatively portrayed in Douglas Brinkley's biography of Kerry, *Tour of Duty* (2004), which relied strongly on Kerry's diaries—met at a Dallas public relations firm to form the Swift Boat Veterans for Truth. The veterans felt that the accounts of bravery in the biography were inaccurate and that the incidents for which Kerry had been awarded medals did not happen as reported. They produced a series of television ads and a book, *Unfit for Command* (O'Neill and Corsi 2004), in a campaign called by Senator John McCain "dishonest and dishonorable."[20]

Are these ads legal? It turns out that BCRA does allow for some corporations organized under sections 501(c)(4) and 527 of the Internal Revenue Code to run such ads using soft money. However, this exception does not apply to a "targeted communication"—a broadcast, cable, or television ad that promotes or opposes a candidate and is broadcast to the candidate's constituency. Yet there is also a loophole here, as well as one for organizations that are created for political, not business, purposes, that do not have shareholders or other persons affiliated with it who have a claim on the corporation's assets or earnings, and that do not accept contributions from business corporations.[21] So it would appear that these so-called 527 organizations just might be exempt from the BCRA's limitation on soft money.

Still, they may *not* be exempt. Senators John McCain and Russell Feingold pointed out during the campaign that any group whose *major purpose* is to influence federal elections and receives contributions or spends at least $1,000 for that purpose is required by the FECA to register with the FEC as a political committee and be subject to the contribution limits. What is the major purpose of organizations like MoveOn.org and Swift Boat Veterans for Truth under federal law? Are they "shadow parties" that should be regulated, as McCain argues, or are they simply organized for general political purposes, not explicitly or only to influence elections? Since McCain and Feingold wrote the Bipartisan Campaign Reform Act, how is it that they are now unhappy with it?

The problem from the point of view of the BCRA supporters in Congress is that the FEC has failed to implement the act appropriately and has allowed the 527 loophole to exist. McCain complained in an editorial two days after the 2004 election: "The FEC is a failed agency with overtly partisan commissioners who oppose both new and longstanding campaign finance statutes."[22] Representatives Christopher Shays and Marty Meehan have filed a lawsuit against the FEC for failing to force 527s to register as political committees, and McCain and Feingold have sponsored new legislation, the 527 Reform Act. As of this writing, the suit against the FEC is in the courts, and the legislation has not been brought to the floor of the Senate.

While McCain and Feingold have complained that the FEC's allowing 527 groups to evade the campaign limits takes the teeth out of the BCRA, the fact that the campaigns could not coordinate with 527s did mean that the BCRA limited the influence of soft money in 2004. That is, Kerry's campaign relied more on 527 efforts than Bush's campaign and was not able to mobilize voters as effectively as Bush's campaign (as discussed in chapter 3). And as we discuss in the next chapter, the wall between the 527 groups and Kerry's campaign also limited his ability to respond to negative ads from Bush and his 527 groups. Thus, although the 527 groups did allow for the use of soft money in the election, the separation between the 527 groups and the official hard-money-driven campaigns gave the advantage to the candidate who relied more on hard money—in this case, Bush.

The 527 groups were not the only outside influences in the 2004 election. Two privately funded documentaries produced independently received considerable criticism during the election campaign as unregulated advertising, *Fahrenheit 9/11* and *Stolen Honor: Wounds That Never Heal*. (We discuss these films and the effect of the mass media on the election process in chapter 8.) Regardless of whether the efforts to control 527s succeed, there can be no doubt that campaign money—hard money like that raised by Paul Dickerson and contributed online and by PACs—will continue to play a major role in elections. In order to understand that role, we need to have a theory about why people make campaign contributions and how contributions influence electoral outcomes. We consider these questions in the next section.

Giving to Elect or to Receive?

There are two major questions that any theory of campaign contributions in politics must answer:

- What are the contributors' motives? That is, why are campaign contributions made?

• How does campaign money influence voters' choices and electoral outcomes?

The motive behind campaign contributions may be thought of in one of two ways—as policy or electorally induced or as service induced. Policy-induced or electorally induced campaign contributions are given in order to elect a candidate such that the overall policy outcome will be closer to the contributors' preferences.[23] Service-induced campaign contributions are given to secure special favors or services for the contributor from an official once he or she has been elected. Often these favors or services are simply the ability to directly communicate with or otherwise lobby an elected official—to gain "access" to the official.

Our examples from the beginning of this chapter present both types of motivations and show that they are intricately related. Harriman claimed he expected a favor or service if Roosevelt was elected, and some suspect that Schwartz's contacts with the Chinese were set up because he was a big contributor to Clinton's campaign. But both Harriman and Schwartz made contributions to help elect candidates they preferred in order to influence overall policy outcomes. Harriman, a stalwart Republican, faced a dilemma in that Roosevelt was more progressive than the mainstream Republicans (later breaking away to form the Progressive "Bull Moose" Party) and Roosevelt's 1904 opponent, Alton B. Parker, was a conservative Democrat. But even "the spokesmen of high finance supported Roosevelt in the persuasion that 'the impulsive candidate of the party of conservatism' was preferable to 'the conservative candidate of the party which the business interests regard as permanently and dangerously impulsive.' "[24]

Schwartz is a longtime Democrat. "His grandfather was a Tammany Hall functionary who died while campaigning for Democrats. Schwartz's political sensibilities were shaped by the party that sent his family a turkey and two bags of coal every holiday season and the policies of President Roosevelt."[25] Clearly, Schwartz supported Clinton in part for ideological reasons.

There are also multiple answers to the second question about campaign contributions above: How do campaign contributions influence voters' choices and electoral outcomes? In races with more than two candidates—for example, the Louisiana Senate race we discussed in chapter 1, in which the Democrat, Landrieu, faced more than one Republican challenger—campaign contributions can act as a coordination mechanism for voters, signally which of the challengers has received the significant support and may be more likely to win. (We discuss the role of coordination in multicandidate elections in chapter 14.)

But campaign contributions must be doing more than just allowing voters to coordinate, since candidates desire campaign contributions in two-candidate contests as well, and contributions seem to have some effect on voting behavior in these races. Voters may be influenced by campaign spending in that it provides them with information. Or the advertising generated by the money may affect voters' preferences for the candidates by altering their views along some nonpolicy or valence dimension. Or campaign spending may simply be used to increase the ability of voters to vote on election day (by providing voters with rides to the polls, and so on), leading to an increase in turnout or participation.

Interest groups and campaign contributions are complex phenomena, and that complexity is one reason we have waited until now to bring them into our analysis. Getting a handle on the intricacies of their operation is difficult. The easiest way to go about it is to start small and think carefully about one part of the way they are involved in elections and gradually add other parts. We'll take that strategy. Thus, we are going to leave aside how voters are influenced by campaign contributions and focus on one type of motivation for making campaign contributions—policy-induced contributions.

In this chapter, we "black-box" how campaign contributions influence voters by simply assuming that campaign contributions do increase a candidate's total votes in an election. Then we consider the other type of campaign contribution—service induced. Finally, in the next chapter, we open the black box and examine how voters might be influenced by campaign contributions.

Giving to Elect

What Are "Black-Boxed" Voters?

A simple way to think about the influence of campaign contributions on elections is to consider that the probability of a candidate's election is based on the share of campaign contributions he or she receives. For example, suppose there are two candidates, Barbara Boxer and Bruce Herschensohn, as in the 1992 California Senate election discussed in chapter 4. Boxer has campaign contributions equal to X_B, and Herschensohn has campaign contributions equal to X_H. We want to assume that the candidate with the most money is most likely to win. So we want to come up with a way to make the probability of winning depend on who has the most money.

An easy way to do this is just to assume that the probability that Boxer will win, which we will call P_B, is equal to $X_B/(X_B + X_H)$, and the probability that Herschensohn will win, which we will call P_H, is equal to $X_H/(X_B + X_H)$. We assume that if both X_B and $X_H = 0$, then $P_B = P_H = 0.5$ (or 50 percent). So if the candidates have equal amounts of money, the election is a toss-up. Notice that using this simple formula, if Boxer has more money than Herschensohn, Boxer has a higher probability of winning. If Boxer has all the money, her probability of winning is 100 percent, or 1; if Herschensohn has all the money, then Boxer's probability of winning is 0 percent, or 0. Notice that $P_B = 1 - P_H$; for example, if Boxer's probability of winning is 75 percent, then Herschensohn's is 25 percent. The implicit assumption is that voters respond to campaign contributions and that the larger the share of contributions a candidate has, the greater the probability he or she will win. Remember that we are ignoring parties and voters just for a little while and will add them to the equation later.

We will assume that candidates want to maximize their probability of winning, which is, then, the same as maximizing their share of campaign contributions. We will also assume that candidates choose policy positions in a single-dimensional space, as in chapter 4. But now the candidates are choosing positions in order to generate campaign contributions, which then generate votes (the process through which we have black-boxed).

How Policy-Motivated Campaign Contributions Work

The Expected Utility of Contributing Policy-Motivated or electorally motivated contributors care about policy by definition. In May 2003, Florida lawyer Thomas A. Culmo, a partner at Culmo and Culmo in Miami and president of the Dade County Trial Lawyers Association, was angry about some of the public policies President George W. Bush was advocating—in particular, his proposal to cap pain-and-suffering damages in medical malpractice cases. As a result, Culmo and other lawyers were looking ahead to the 2004 election, looking to provide campaign money for the Democratic candidates who hoped to win their party's nomination and defeat Bush. He predicted that other lawyers would also become involved in providing Democrats with moneys as well as raising funds from others: "I think we're seeing lawyers increasing their intensity both financially and timewise."[26]

We can think of contributors like Culmo as having utility functions over policy, much as we discussed in terms of voters in chapter 4. They, too, have an ideal point for policy, and as policy moves away from that ideal point, their utility or satisfaction from the policy declines. Contributors, however, do not give their votes to the candidates; they give money. And they have different amounts of money to give—different budgets. Suppose, for example, that the Sierra Club is considering contributing to the election, with the ideal point shown in figure 6.1 and the utility shown in table 6.2. Assume that the Sierra Club has $2,000 it can give to the candidates. In figure 6.1, Boxer is located at 50, and Herschensohn is located at 60 (Herschensohn advocated offshore oil drilling, and Boxer opposed it). How will the Sierra Club distribute its money? It is going to make contributions in order to maximize its expected utility (as discussed in chapter 2). That is, the Sierra Club wants to maximize the following:

Sierra Club's Expected Utility = $P_B \cdot 185 + P_H \cdot 170$

One thing is obvious—the Sierra Club will give to only one candidate. In order to see why this is true, suppose that the Sierra Club gives equally to

Boxer and Herschensohn. Assume that there are no other contributions. The probability that each candidate will win is equal to 0.5 since $X_B = X_H$, or the election is a toss-up. The Sierra Club's expected utility equals = $0.5 \cdot 185 + 0.5 \cdot 170 = 177.5$.

TABLE 6.2
Sierra Club's Utility from Policy

Policy Position	Sierra Club's Utility
0	170
10	185
20	195
30	200
40	195
50	185
60	170
70	150
80	125
90	95
100	60

FIGURE 6.1
Candidates' Positions and Contributor's Ideal Point

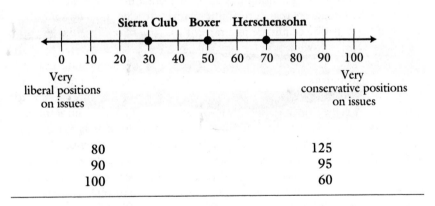

Is the Sierra Club behaving rationally? Suppose it gave the entire $2,000 to Boxer? Then Boxer has $2,000 and Herschensohn has $0 (assuming there are no other contributions). The probability that Boxer will win is now equal to 1, while the probability that Herschensohn will win is 0. The Sierra Club's expected utility will increase to $(1) \cdot 185 + (0) \cdot 170 = 185$, which is greater than 177.5. It is straightforward to show that even if both candidates are receiving other contributions, the Sierra Club will always receive a higher expected utility by giving to Boxer exclusively.[27]

Are Contributions Large Enough to Make a Difference? Our example is of course extreme because it assumes that the Sierra Club's campaign contributions are large enough to influence the outcome of the election. But the majority of campaign contributions come from individuals in small amounts. Ansolabehere, de Figueiredo, and Snyder (2003) estimated that the average individual contribution is only $115. Big individual contributors were limited at this time to $2,000 per campaign per candidate and $1,000 per year per candidate. For even small electoral campaigns that total hundreds of thousands of dollars, it is hard to imagine that an individual giving a campaign contribution expects his or her contribution to be pivotal. Ansolabehere, de Figueiredo, and Snyder contended that this suggests that campaign contributions are primarily consumption driven, much as individual voters are sometimes argued to vote for expressive or consumption purposes.

However, as we discussed in the introduction to this chapter, there is evidence that individual campaign contributions are given in a coordinated fashion by entrepreneurs like Dickerson who use their family and friends much as groups use selective incentives in order to motivate voters, as we discussed in chapter 2. For example, contributors get to participate in and be listed as "hosts" of events with the candidate and/or his surrogates. Candidates' organizations and fund-raisers use these selective incentives, joined with purposive incentives, to persuade individuals to contribute as a group— a group that can be large enough to affect the outcome of the election.

Our analysis suggests that contributions given to elect favored candidates are given to only one candidate in a race. Is this true? In the 1992 presidential election, only approximately 10.5 percent of the contributors to the Bush and Clinton campaigns gave to both candidates, suggesting that it is rare for contributors to give to more than one candidate in an election.[28] However, contributors sometimes give to Republicans in one race—say, for governor—and to Democrats in another—say, for president. And joint contributions like those may have increased with the role of soft money. The Supreme Court noted in *McConnell v. Federal Election Commission* that "in 1996 and 2000 more than half of the top 50 soft-money donors gave substantial sums to both major national parties." But were these contributors giving to elect a candidate, as in our Sierra Club example? The Supreme Court majority did not seem to think so. The justices quoted former Arkansas senator Dale Bumpers, who said, "Giving money to both parties, the Republicans and Democrats, makes no sense at all unless the donor feels he or she is buying access." How does buying access work?

Giving to Receive

What Is Received?

In our analysis, we examine contributors who give campaign moneys in order to elect the candidate who is closest to their preferences. But often the contributors are interested not in overall candidates' policy positions but in special favors or influence that a contribution might give them in the future, as Harriman was reported to have expected and some argue Schwartz expected as well. Contributors don't typically relate the quid pro quos they arrange for contributions (it is no accident that we have to go back to the early twentieth century to find Harriman's frank revelation of his quid pro quo contribution to Roosevelt). However, the general access that contributors get to elected officials is fairly obvious. For example, Florida plaintiff attorney Ira Leesfield was an early contributor to Bill Clinton's campaign in 1992.

> Later, because of his relationship with Clinton, Leesfield . . . got to stand close to Clinton, Yitzhak Rabin and Yasser Arafat when the Israeli and Palestinian leaders signed the historic peace accords in 1993. When President Clinton hosted a white-tie state dinner at the White House for King Juan Carlos of Spain, Leesfield was there—sitting between Barbara Walters and Meg Ryan. Leesfield fondly recalls sleeping in the Lincoln bedroom, serving on two presidential commissions and brunching with Clinton and Barbra Streisand at the actress's Malibu home during the 2000 Democratic National Convention. He even gave the president a Yom Kippur passage on repentance—called "On Turning"—that Clinton read at the National Prayer Day breakfast in 1998 as part of his mea culpa for the Monica Lewinsky affair.[29]

Bumpers and the Supreme Court majority in *McConnell* believe that the giving of soft money to both political parties suggests that contributions are given in return for something—quid pro quo favors or, at a minimum, access in a way that the average individual cannot receive—and not just to elect a preferred candidate. How do these motives affect how contributors and politicians behave?

When interest groups give contributions with the expectation that there will be a service rendered in the future, a quid pro quo, then the contributor is giving campaign moneys in order to receive a private good from the candidate once he or she is elected. One way to think of the political service or favor is as one of many such "private" goods that the contributor can purchase with his or her campaign contribution.[30] These goods are small enough in magnitude that they do not generate much opposition from other supporters or voters (like a small subsidy for a manufacturer of a new fuel substitute or a small grant to a university for a research program on students' math skills). The contribution is the "price" of the service.

We can think of the service as the return that the contributor receives on his or her "investment" in the candidate. An interest group can make a lot of investments that would yield a return in the private market and presumably could evaluate investments in candidates much as it would an investment in the private market. For example, Harriman invested in Roosevelt's campaign with the expectation that his ally Depew would receive an ambassadorship and that his business interests would be advantaged by Roosevelt's administration, leading to greater profits for him. He could have taken the moneys he gave Roosevelt and used them to expand his railroad holdings or build a new factory. Those investments would have yielded a given return and greater profits. When he gave the money to Roosevelt, he expected that the return from the investment would at least equal, if not exceed, the return that he could receive from those alternatives.

For What Price?

How much would Harriman be willing to give Roosevelt? We can call the present monetary value of the favors that Harriman expects to receive s. That is, s is how much the favors are worth if Harriman has to pay for their equivalent in the private market. Let P_R equal the probability that Roosevelt will be elected. Then the expected monetary value of the favors would be that probability times the monetary value of the favors, $P_R \cdot s$, which is the expected benefit Harriman would get from contributing to Roosevelt's campaign. That is, if Harriman knows for sure that Roosevelt will win, he can be sure of getting s. If Harriman knows for sure that Roosevelt will lose, he can be sure of getting 0. Note that s, what Roosevelt is offering, stays the same. But Harriman's expectation of what he will get depends on the probability of Roosevelt's winning.

Harriman will be willing to contribute campaign contributions, which we call c, such that $c \le P_R \cdot s$. That is, Harriman will contribute as long as the cost of contributing is less than or equal to the benefit he expects to receive. If Roosevelt is not elected, Harriman's contribution to Roosevelt gets him 0 favors; Harriman receives no utility or satisfaction from the election of Parker, Roosevelt's opponent (we assume for the moment that Harriman gives only to Roosevelt).

How much, then, can Roosevelt demand from Harriman for his services? At most, Roosevelt can demand $P_R \cdot s$—this is the highest "price" that Harriman is willing to pay, since any price above that would mean Harriman would be receiving less in the future than he is paying for today.

We can think of each elected official as having a fixed stock of favors that he or she can offer to contributors. For example, there are only so many ambassadorships that Roosevelt could offer to his supporters once elected, there is a fixed amount of money for tax breaks, and so on. We can call the monetary value of the stock of favors that a candidate will have once elected S, where S = the sum of the s's for each contributor. That is, if there are two contributors, then $S = s_1 + s_2$; if there are three contributors, $S = s_1 + s_2 + s_3$; if there are four contributors, $S = s_1 + s_2 + s_3 + s_4$, and so on. How much, then, will the elected official receive in total campaign contributions if all campaign contributions are motivated by the private favors that can be given out once elected? How much should Roosevelt receive? Suppose there are two contributors. Then Roosevelt should receive $X_R = P_R \cdot s_1 + P_R \cdot s_2 = P_R \cdot (s_1 + s_2) = P_R \cdot S$; in general, for any number of contributors, Roosevelt should receive $X_R = P_R \cdot S$. This result suggests an empirical relationship between campaign contributions and the probability of winning—the higher a candidate's probability of winning, the greater the campaign contributions that candidate should receive, since the stock of services is fixed.

Enforcing the Contract

The Problems of Enforcing an Illegal Contract "Tell me what I've got to do, but I've got to have money from him. . . . I'm on my knees begging," Clark County, Nevada, commissioner Erin Kenny told an associate of a high-profile strip-club owner, Michael Galardi, in Las Vegas just before the November 2002 election. In return for the money, she would help the owner crush his rivals in the industry and defeat new rules on illicit sexual activities at the clubs. The *Los Angeles Times* reported Galardi as saying that "if Kenny came through for him on an upcoming vote, he would 'take her to a local automobile dealership and buy her a Denali' pickup." But someone was listening in and observing her actions as Kenny made her bargain—the FBI. Kenny accepted a plea deal in July 2003.[31]

Our analysis of service-induced campaign contributions assumes that a legal contract can exist between the elected official and the contributor. Actually, such a contract does not generally exist, and if it did and was discovered, the elected officials and the contributors would, like Kenny and Galardi, face criminal charges. It is a fact of American elections that some elected officials do explicitly trade votes or other specific promised benefits for campaign contributions or personal goods like cars and that many of them and their contributors—like Kenny and Galardi—are caught and prosecuted. Hence, elected officials are going to avoid making explicit promises, promising instead to provide access and favors in a more generic, vague sense. Moreover, elected officials are really under no obligation to fulfill their side of a bargain even if they make explicit promises; they can easily take the money and run.

Interestingly, such a violation of the unwritten contract appears to have occurred between Harriman and Roosevelt. Roosevelt did not give Depew the ambassadorship that he had promised. He also did not bestow the favors that the industrialists expected, and after his election he continued his battles against the "malefactors of great wealth" leading Henry Clay Frick to state, "We bought the son of a bitch and then he didn't stay bought."[32]

Incumbents and Contract Enforcement Roosevelt chose not to run again in 1908, and although he did run in 1912 as a Progressive, he did not seek contributions from the railroad men again (at least not Harriman). Since many incumbents do plan to run again and are engaged in a repeated game with their contributors, reneging on promised services is not likely to maximize their probability of winning in the future. Oftentimes elected officials take out loans to finance campaigns, repaying them later with postelection contributions—which is one reason Kerry lent personal money to his campaign, money he hoped to pay back one day. Contributions to pay back loans can be tied more closely to services, since the elected official is already in office. The loser, of course, can have a more difficult time repaying such loans, although in that instance party connections can help.

Alternatively, incumbents may provide services while in office in return for contributions to future campaigns. Nevertheless, the legal limitation on bribery is a real constraint on the ability of contributors to force candidates to provide services, as they constrain incumbents from demanding contributions for services already provided. The legal constraint, interestingly, advantages incumbents in raising campaign contributions, since they can more easily tie the contribution to the service provided at the time of the exchange. Challengers must give only contingent contracts.

Double Dipping Redux

"Contributing to the wrong party can 'buy you enemies. People often don't remember who gave them contributions. But they remember who gave to their opponents,' " noted Congressman Thomas M. Davis III of Virginia, chairman of the National Republican Congressional Committee.[33] When incumbent Democratic governor of California Gray Davis was worried about the possibility of facing former Los Angeles mayor Richard Riordan in his reelection attempt in 2002, he "played rough with his own wealthy donors, many of whom were also social friends of Riordan." His top political adviser, Garry South, recalled, "We were very clear with people that it was an unfriendly act to the governor of California to give money to Dick Riordan."[34]

The fact that elected officials can renege on promised services implies that they can to some extent enforce a requirement that contributors give to only one candidate in a race. Contributors may want to give to the other candidates in the race when their contributions are service induced. After all, the contributors don't care a great deal who is elected when their contributions are service induced—if they are mainly looking for a favor or access or maintaining contacts that they have developed over the years. For example, Florida lawyer Joseph P. Klock, Jr., helped George W. Bush in 2000 when he represented Florida secretary of state Katherine Harris before the Florida Supreme Court and the U.S. Supreme Court in the dispute over Florida's vote count, and he planned to be an active fund-raiser for Bush in 2004, but he gave the maximum individual campaign contribution to both Senator Bob Graham and Representative Richard Gephardt in their quest for the Democratic presidential nomination. Nonetheless, a candidate certainly does not want to reward a contributor who gives to both candidates in the same race. That is, a contributor who gives to two candidates in the same race is not helping either candidate win because the money balances out. Why would candidates want to reward contributors who help their opponents just as much as they help them? Klock was clear that he would back only Bush in the general election.[35]

Of course, to the extent that it is difficult for candidates or parties to monitor campaign contributions made through donations of soft money, it is probably no surprise that we see more double dipping in this case. Nevertheless, even when contributors are giving to receive, to the extent that candidates and parties can observe contributions, double dipping is discouraged.

Evidence on Quid Pro Quo Contributions

The Size Issue Redux

As with electorally motivated contributions, some researchers contend that contributions cannot be given for access or quid pro quo services in the future because most contributions are so small, as discussed earlier. Yet many purchases made for investment involve small amounts of money, so size in itself is not evidence against the argument that contributions are given for investment. Consumers often make purchases of a few hundred dollars for goods and services that they expect to use in the future and are concerned with the durability of the product. Furthermore, those most likely to be contributing with the expectation of receiving for services or access often make contributions of the maximum amount allowed. In a study of over sixteen hundred top five executives from fifteen hundred Standard and Poor's firms, Gordon, Hafer, and Landa (2005) found that more than half of the contributions made by these executives to candidates in particular races were at the legal maximum. These executives overwhelmingly gave to incumbents—over 97 percent of the contributions in races with an incumbent seeking reelection were given to the incumbent—further suggesting that the contributions are not for consumption motives alone. Gordon, Hafer, and Landa also found that the executives whose compensation was dependent on their firm's performance were more likely to give campaign contributions than were those whose compensation was largely determined by salary alone. If the campaign contributions were given primarily for consumption purposes, we would expect that the structure of the compensation would not affect the willingness of executives to contribute.

The Elusive Connection between Policy and Money

Although the evidence on how executives contribute to campaigns suggests that the money is given to candidates in return for expected services, many political science researchers have tried to find a connection between explicit policy making and campaign contributions. Usually their studies examine voting in Congress on particular pieces of legislation. According to the review by Ansolabehere, de Figueiredo, and Snyder (2003), the evidence is weak. Yet is this the right connection to look for? Is it really roll-call votes that contributions are buying? In some cases, yes, but in most cases the access granted by giving is exhibited in the more preliminary stages of policy making, when elected officials choose which policies to push and which to deemphasize, how much time to spend on a topic, and so on. The obvious outright purchase of votes for money typically does not need to take place if influence affects what is voted on in the first place. Furthermore, much of what affects contributors is the way in which policy making is implemented rather than the voting choice. In an interesting study, Gordon and Hafer (2005) examined the relationship between inspections at nuclear power plants and campaign contributions by nuclear power companies. They found that the greater the size of a nuclear power company's campaign contributions to candidates for federal office, the less likely the company's plant would be inspected, controlling for other factors that affect inspection rates.

As Gordon, Hafer, and Landa (2005) pointed out, we can also think of these contributions for access or services as similar to purchasing insurance—a purchase made in case the contributor needs government access or service, much as consumers purchase insurance in case of fire or flood. The contributor may on average never require the access or service from the candidate as the event the contributor is insuring against (government policy he or she dislikes) does not on average occur.

Finally, if we want to see if there is an empirical relationship between contributions and government policies, ideally we would compare how much access a contributor receives without a contribution with how much he or she receives after making a contribution. When we compare a cross section of individuals who have contributed with a cross section of those who have not, we are making a different comparison. That is, in equilibrium those who have not contributed may be receiving the policy services they desire or are possible for them to receive. Hence, the policy making that noncontributors receive and the policy making that contributors receive may seem unaffected by the contribution even when the policy making a contributor receives is affected by whether he or she makes a contribution. The policy making a noncontributor receives is not a good proxy for the policy making a contributor would receive if he or she did not contribute.

In summary, an examination of contribution strategies by executives suggests that the contributions are given for quid pro quo access or services, and there is evidence that some policy choices at the implementation stage are influenced by contributions. Furthermore, because contributions may be seen as insurance against unlikely policies and because it is difficult to assess policy making in the absence of contributions, it is very difficult to find a link between contributions and policy making. Hence, the absence of such a link is not evidence that all contributions are given just for consumption.

Coordination and the Decisiveness of Money

A Game between Contributors

On July 15, 1998, Geraldine Ferraro's campaign for the Democratic nomination for Senator from New York reported that Ferraro had raised barely $2 million, much less than the other major candidate in the race, Charles Schumer, who had raised $11 million. Interestingly, Ferraro's lack of fundraising occurred despite the fact that there were few substantive differences between the candidates in the primary to explain the imbalance in support. A *New York Times* editorial the following Saturday suggested that the lack of fund-raising reflected contributors' perception that Ferraro was likely to lose. Ferraro later lost the primary to Schumer, justifying contributors' expectations.

Ferraro's failure is an example of the impact of service- or favor-induced campaign contributions on elections, which we have so far ignored. That is, in a two-candidate race contributors are most likely to give to the candidate with the higher probability of winning. This means that if contributors see one candidate having even a small electoral advantage and the contributors are giving for favors or access, then the candidate with the perceived advantage can receive most of the campaign contributions, leaving his or her opponent with few resources.

To see how this can happen, consider the following simple example. Suppose that our two candidates for the 2000 California Senate race discussed in chapter 4, Campbell and Feinstein, can offer the same level of service to contributors. Assume that there are two contributors who are making contributions in order to get access, the AOL Time Warner PAC and the California Association of Winegrape Growers (CAWG) PAC. Both PACs would like to receive favors or services from whoever is elected.[36] Assume, further, that the candidates always fulfill their service commitments (there is no reneging) and candidates reward only service-induced campaign contributions given to them exclusively. The candidates choose policy positions that maximize the expected utility of the median voter in their respective parties. There are no electorally induced campaign contributions; therefore, all contributors care nothing about policy; they care only about the private services they can receive. Assume that Feinstein is the incumbent, and if campaign spending by the two candidates is equal, Feinstein, as the incumbent, has a slightly higher probability of winning; that is, Feinstein will win with a probability of 52 percent (with equal contributions, Campbell is expected to win with a probability of 48 percent).

Suppose that each group has $2,000 to spend and that the candidate who is elected can provide services worth a total of $5,000 after the election, which he or she will give to contributors. Table 6.3 presents the payoffs to the two PACs from the contributions. The four cells in the bottom right give the payoffs for each of the four possible combinations of contributions. The first number in each cell is the amount AOL Time Warner will expect to receive given the choices of the two interest groups associated with that cell, and the second number in each cell is the amount the CAWG will expect to receive given the choices of the two interest groups associated with that cell. If both PACs give to Campbell, his probability of winning will be 100 percent and the contributors will split the $5,000 in services (they will be in the bottom far right cell in the table). But this is not an equilibrium. Because Feinstein has an advantage, both AOL Time Warner and the CAWG have an incentive to give to Feinstein if they think the other is giving to Campbell. That is, suppose that AOL Time Warner gives to Feinstein and the CAWG gives to Campbell (this is the cell in the row above the one in the bottom far right). While the contributions are equal, because Feinstein is the incumbent and has an advantage, she is more likely to win, and the CAWG will expect to receive $(0.48) \cdot (\$5,000) = \$2,400$, but AOL Time Warner will receive $(0.52) \cdot (\$5,000) = \$2,600$ in services alone. Similarly, the CAWG, if it believes that AOL Time Warner is giving to Campbell, will want to give to Feinstein to get the greater amount of services.

TABLE 6.3
Payoff Matrix for Game Facing Service-Induced Contributors

		California Association of Winegrape Growers' Choices	
		Gives $2,000 to Feinstein	Gives $2,000 to Campbell
AOL Time Warner's Choices	Gives $2,000 to Feinstein	$2,500, $2,500	$2,600, $2,400
	Gives $2,000 to Campbell	$2,400, $2,600	$2,500, $2,500

But neither of these scenarios is an equilibrium for the two groups. For example, if AOL Time Warner is known to be giving to Feinstein, the CAWG will want to give to Feinstein too ($2,500 is greater than $2,400); similarly, if the CAWG is known to be giving to Feinstein, AOL Time Warner will want to give to her too. The only equilibrium in this game, where all contributions are service induced and one candidate has an advantage, is for both groups to give to the candidate who is perceived to have an electoral advantage in a close race, even though the advantage is small. In fact, this is what happened in the election: both AOL Time Warner and the

CAWG gave to Feinstein but did not give to Campbell. The results in this game would be even more unbalanced if Feinstein, as the incumbent, is perceived to have more services to offer than Campbell.

Do Votes Follow Money, or Does Money Follow Votes?

In the Ferraro-Schumer race, commentators argued that contributors believed that Ferraro had less of a connection to voters than Schumer. Contributors formed an expectation that Ferraro was more likely to lose, and given that expectation, they chose to contribute to Schumer, reinforcing the expectation. Feinstein, in the 2000 California Senate race, gathered $10.3 million to Campbell's $4.8 million. Before the race for the general election began, she was widely expected to be the winner in the general election, having gathered 51 percent of all votes cast in the open primary to Campbell's 23 percent of the entire primary vote (combining the votes in both parties). Of course, we have already noted that incumbents do have an advantage in tying services to contributions and may be able to generate contributions more easily to begin with. The edge, then, can attract more contributions, leading to a significant monetary advantage for incumbents. This prediction is borne out empirically. Abramson, Aldrich, and Rohde (2003) reported that incumbents in Congress receive significantly more campaign contributions than challengers. In 2000, the ratio of incumbent to challenger campaign spending was $2.87 to $1. There is also evidence that as challengers' spending increases (approaching incumbents' spending levels), the incumbents' share of the vote declines, as demonstrated in table 6.4.

TABLE 6.4
Incumbent's Share of the Vote in Congressional Elections, by Challenger's Campaign Spending, 2000

Challenger's Spending (thousands of dollars)	Incumbent's Share of the Two Major Parties' Vote (%)				
	70% or more	60–69%	55–59%	Less than 55%	Total
25 or less	53.0	45.5	1.5	0.0	100
26–75	19.0	79.3	0.0	1.7	100
76–199	8.6	57.1	31.4	2.9	100
200–399	7.5	45.0	42.5	5.0	100
400 or more	1.4	19.7	26.8	52.1	100
All spending	26.3	47.0	14.5	12.1	100

Source: Abramson, Aldrich, and Rohde (2003, p. 216).

A simple interpretation of these figures would suggest that as campaign spending by challengers increases, vote shares for incumbents decline, reflecting an influence on voters. Our analysis above suggests, however, that when contributors anticipate that incumbents are in close races, they are more likely to give to challengers. So the causal relationship between challengers' campaign spending and their share of the vote may be the reverse of that suggested by the simple analysis. The truth is that the relationship between campaign spending and the votes candidates receive is reciprocal: when candidates have more campaign resources, they are likely to have a greater vote share, but a high expected vote share is also likely to generate more contributions, particularly when contributions are service or favor induced.

Policy versus Service Redux

Our analysis of service-induced campaign contributions suggests implications different from those of our analysis of electorally induced campaign contributions. That is, when contributions are service induced, contributions focus on who is likely to win rather than on the candidates' policy positions. Contributions are positive regardless of who will win. No doubt campaign contributions in general, as with Roosevelt, Clinton, Feinstein, Campbell, Ferraro, and Schumer above, are mixtures of the two. The more similar candidates are in policy, the more likely contributors are motivated by services or favors. Thus, we would expect that service-induced contributions are more prevalent and decisive in primary elections like that between Schumer and Ferraro, whereas both types are factors in general elections like the contest between Feinstein and Campbell. Service-induced campaign contributions are also more likely to be given to incumbents, both because they have an advantage in tying service to contributions and because incumbency can serve as a focal point for the coordination of contributions across contributors. It should be no surprise that by the end of March 2004, incumbent president George W. Bush had raised almost as much money in campaign contributions as the combined spending of the two major presidential candidates in 1992. In general elections, contributors have both motives and may influence the policy choices of the candidates, who may find themselves seeking contributions by choosing positions closer to those of the interest groups with the most money.

Nevertheless, even in general elections, contributors may be giving in return for service or access more often than for electoral motives. That is, when an interest group's motives are electoral, the group is contributing to the production of a "public good" in that all those who prefer the candidate receiving the contributions benefit even if they are not contributing to that candidate. Interest group contributors with electoral motives have an incentive to free-ride on contributors with the same motives, a collective-action problem across contributors with similar preferences in a given election. To solve that collective-action problem, candidates who desire electorally motivated contributions may well use access or services as private selective benefits, but with ties to policy, to get interest groups to contribute. Some scholars contend that candidates do in fact engage in "shake-down" tactics, pressuring potential contributors by threatening to withhold access or services.[37]

What We Know

We know that recent changes in campaign finance regulation have altered some of the strategies used in gathering and spending campaign money but do not appear to have reduced the role of money in elections. We know that contributors give campaign contributions to affect election outcomes and in return for expected services, favors, or access. Although contributors may give to both major political parties across races, contributors generally give to only one candidate in a particular election contest. Moreover, contributors who give for expected services would like to coordinate on a common candidate, and that gives incumbents significant advantages in raising campaign money. Some contributions are also no doubt given purely for consumption. However, the evidence of the coordination of contributors into groups with like-minded preferences and the relationships between contributors' personal benefits and their contribution decisions suggests that contributions are given for investment motives.

What We Don't Know: Opening Up the Black Box

A Pew poll in early September 2004 found that 50 percent of adults were following the Swift Boat Veterans' ads "very closely" or "fairly closely." The Center for the Study of Elections and Democracy at Brigham Young University surveyed voters in the latter half of September 2004 about both Bush and Kerry's military service. Seventy-six percent of the respondents mentioned issues or concerns that had been advanced by the Swift Boat Veterans. While 30 percent mentioned the Swift Boat Veterans' criticism of Kerry, only 5 percent mentioned ads run by veterans who came to Kerry's defense. So far we have ignored the process by which campaign money affects voters. Are negative ads like the ones aired by the Swift Boat Veterans effective? In the next chapter, we investigate how campaign money influences voters.

Study Questions and Problems

1. Suppose that Tim is a candidate for mayor of Denver. He is wealthy and has decided that he is willing to spend up to $1 million on campaign advertising and other campaign expenditures. His opponent is Magdalena, who is the incumbent and does not have the same resources. Magdalena can offer a stock of favors or services to contributors in return for campaign moneys, however. Magdalena, as the incumbent, has a large advantage with voters, who are quite happy with her. That is, if Tim and Magdalena spend equal amounts of money on campaigning, she will win with a 75 percent probability. But for every $10,000 Tim spends over what she spends, the probability that Magdalena wins is reduced by 1 percent (voters' preferences are black-boxed).

    a. What will determine whether Tim will be able to defeat Magdalena? That is, under what circumstances can Magdalena win, and under what circumstances can Tim win? Explain your answer.

    b. How does your answer change if Tim also promises favors or services after the election to contributors in return? Explain.

    c. Are the voters in question 1a rational? That is, does it make sense for them to support Magdalena when she and Tim expend the same amount of resources in the campaign? Explain your answer.

2. Show that if all campaign contributions are given for electoral motives, voters are blacked-boxed, and interest groups are willing to contribute to any candidate who is closest to them, then two candidates in the same race will converge on policy positions. Will there be campaign contributions in such a case? Does this mean that contributions are not electorally motivated? Explain.

Notes

1. See Lukas (1998, pp. 392–93).
2. As Lukas (1998) discussed, Theodore Roosevelt denied that the promise had been made. Edmund Morris, in his noted biography *Theodore Rex* (2001), does not mention the incident.
3. Jill Abramson and Don Van Natta, Jr., "Clinton-Loral: Anatomy of a Mutually Rewarding Relationship," *New York Times*, May 24, 1998. Abramson and Van Natta summarize the way in which Schwartz lobbied the president to approve Loral's launching a satellite over the objections of other administration officials. They report: "After Clinton was sworn into office in 1993, Schwartz cherished his many invitations to the White House. But he cited one perk that eluded him. 'I'd give my eye-teeth to stay in the Lincoln Bedroom,' he said." Concerns over security leaks about Loral's dealings led to a congressional inquiry. Specifically, telecommunications technology used by Chinese civilians can also be used by the Chinese military. Republicans charged that Loral's laxity in ensuring the security of the security of the design secrets that could benefit the the Chinese military resulted in leaks of those secrets to the military. See also Vernon Loeb,

"Back Channels: The Intelligence Community; More Money, Less Disclosure,"
Washington Post, May 30, 2000.

4. Recent business downturns may have reduced Schwartz's largesse. Loral filed
for chapter 11 bankruptcy protection on July 15, 2003. As of this writing,
Schwartz maintains that the company hopes to emerge from bankruptcy protection by the end of 2005. Christopher Scinta, "Loral Plans to Exit Chapter 11,"
Chattanooga Times Free Press, March 18, 2004.

5. Juliet Eilperin, "Old Memos Detail Link of Money to Influence," *Washington
Post*, May 17, 2003. More recently the financial ties between Vice President
Richard Cheney and his former company, Halliburton, have come under attack
since Halliburton was awarded a number of lucrative contracts to rebuild in Iraq
without going through the standard bidding process.

6. Joni James, "Free Market Fever," *St. Petersburg Times*, February 22, 2004.

7. For a good, readable history of presidential campaigning, see Troy (1996).

8. Ansolabehere, Snowberg, and Snyder (2004) present evidence of the overstate-
ment of the role of contributions from PACs in the news media. We discuss this
evidence further in the next chapter.

9. Glenn Justice, "Newcomers Provide Fuel for Bush Money Machine," *New York
Times*, March 14, 2004.

10. Justice, "Newcomers Provide Fuel for Bush Money Machine."

11. Adam Nagourney and Michael Janofsky, "Dean's Surge in Fund-Raising Forces
Rivals to Reassess Him," *New York Times*, July 3, 2003. John Kerry raised $6
million; John Edwards and Joseph Lieberman each raised $5 million; Richard
Gephardt, $4.5 million; Bob Graham, slightly under $3 million; Dennis
Kucinich, slightly more than $1 million; and Carol Moseley-Braun, $150,000.
Al Sharpton's campaign finance figures were unavailable.

12. Nagourney and Janofsky, "Dean's Surge in Fund-Raising Forces Rivals to Reassess Him."

13. Glenn Justice, "Howard Dean's Internet Push: Where Will It Lead? *New York
Times*, November 2, 2003.

14. Justice, "Howard Dean's Internet Push."

15. See Magleby (n.d.).

16. Wayne Woodlief, "If Kerry Can't Do It in Iowa, He's Finished," *Boston Herald*,
December 21, 2003, and Sharon Theimer, "Personal Loans Helped Kerry Campaign Survive as Primaries Began," Associated Press, February 21, 2004.

17. Interestingly, Durbin sponsored the amendment partly in response to Fitzger-
ald's use of his own moneys to defeat Democratic incumbent senator Carol
Moseley-Braun in 1998 and partly in response to the competition he had faced
from millionaires in securing office, as discussed later in this chapter. See
Christopher Hayes, "McCain-Feingold Helps Little Guy," *CBSNews.com*,
March 17, 2004, http://www.cbsnews.com/stories/2004/03/17/opinion/
main60689 0.shtml.

18. "2004 Presidential Campaign Financial Activity Summarized," Federal Election
Commission, press release, February 3, 2005.

19. Liz Sidoti, "New Ads Assail Bush on Economy, Iraq War," Associated Press,
March 17, 2004, and Jim Rutenberg, "90-Day Strategy by Bush's Aides to Define Kerry," *The New York Times*, March 20, 2004.

20. See Pamela Colloff, "When the Swift Boat Veterans for Truth Capsized John
Kerry's Presidential Campaign, Much of the Unfriendly Fire Came From
Texas," *Texas Monthly*, January 2005. The principal spokesman for the new
group was John O'Neill, who had debated Kerry in 1971 on *The Dick Cavett
Show*. O'Neill concluded after the election: "What motivated me, and a lot of
other guys at that meeting in Dallas, . . . was his own Senate testimony in 1971,
in which he claimed atrocities were being committed on a day-to-day basis in

Vietnam. . . . Hearing his testimony was one of the most shocking moments of my entire life. . . . It felt like a total betrayal."

21. In *FEC v. Massachusetts Citizens for Life, Inc.* (1986), the Supreme Court ruled that these types of corporations could not constitutionally be prohibited from using corporate treasury funds in federal elections.

22. John McCain, "Paying for Campaigns: McCain Eyes Next Target," *USA Today*, November 4, 2004.

23. Usually this means giving to the candidate closest to the contributor ideologically, but it is not the case if the contributor believes that that candidate has little chance of winning. Then the contributor may give strategically to a less preferred alternative candidate to prevent an even less desirable candidate from winning.

24. See Lukas (1998). Interestingly, Harriman's son W. Averell Harriman later became the Democratic governor of New York, as well as ambassador to the Soviet Union and England. He and his wife, Pamela Beryl Digby Churchill Hayward Harriman (a onetime ambassador to France), were credited with reinvigorating the Democratic Party during a period of decline.

25. Abramson and Van Natta, "Clinton-Loral: Anatomy of a Mutually Rewarding Relationship." Here, President Roosevelt is FDR, not TR.

26. Matthew Haggman, "Oval Office Dreams: Driven by Ideology, Friendship and Visions of Clout, South Florida Lawyers Are Hitting the Phones to Raise Money for Presidential Candidates," *Broward Daily Business Review*, May 19, 2003.

27. For formal models of policy-induced campaign contributions where both voters' and contributors' choices are endogenized, see Austen-Smith (1987) and Cameron and Enelow (1989). This literature is reviewed in Morton and Cameron (1991). For more recent work taking this approach, see Coate (2004a).

28. See, for example, the literature reviewed in Morton and Cameron (1991).

29. Haggman, "Oval Office Dreams."

30. We mean *private* in the sense that the goods are divisible and depletable, not that they are produced in the private sector. See Baron (1989) and Snyder (1989) for examples of service-induced campaign contributions models in which voters are black-boxed as we assume is the case here. This formal work analyzing service-induced campaign contributions is reviewed in Morton and Cameron (1991). For formal models of campaign contributions in elections in which both voters' and contributors' choices are endogenized, see Ashworth (2003), Coate (2004a,b), and Prat (2002).

31. John Johnson, "The Talk of Las Vegas Is Operation G-String: Current and Former County Officials Are Accused of Taking Bribes from a Strip-Club Owner," *Los Angeles Times*, December 21, 2003, and Carri Geer Thevenot, "Judge Rules Attorney Can Represent Malone," *Las Vegas Review-Journal*, January 5, 2005.

32. See Lukas (1998, p. 392).

33. Jim VandeHei, "Controlled Access: GOP Activists Are Monitoring Lobbyists' Politics," *Washington Post*, national weekly ed., June 17–23, 2002.

34. John W. Wildermuth, "Riordan Alarmed Davis the Most: Consultants Dissect Race for Governor," *San Francisco Chronicle*, January 12, 2003.

35. Haggman, "Oval Office Dreams."

36. Morton and Myerson (2003) formalized the coordination problem facing contributors.

37. See for example Sorauf (1992).

~7~

How Campaign Money Affects Voters

I n the 2002 Republican Illinois primary contest for the U.S. Senate nomination, two millionaires, Chicago lawyer and businessman John Cox
and Aurora dairy magnate Jim Oberweis, each spent at least $1 million of
their own cash and were defeated by Illinois state representative Jim Durkin,
a Westchester, Illinois, Republican who spent only $300,000.[1] So spending
more does not mean winning. So far we have simply assumed that more
campaign spending means more votes. This is not always true, however—
while candidates who are "big spenders" often win (as did millionaire Mark
Warner in the 2001 Virginia gubernatorial race and Mike Bloomberg in the
2001 New York mayoral race), money does not ensure victory, as Stephen
Forbes, one unsuccessful wealthy candidate for the presidency learned, as
did Blair Hull in the 2004 Illinois Senate Democratic primary. Nevertheless,
candidates seek money and use money to attempt to influence voters. The
average incumbent member of Congress spent over $500,000 in the 2002
election. How might that money be used to influence voters?

Inside the Black Box: Indirect Influences

Campaign spending can influence voters in many ways. Some are indirect,
impressing voters with the amount of money a candidate has amassed or
using funds to provide voters with incentives to turn out. Others are

direct, using ads to communicate directly with voters about candidates' policy positions or valence qualities. We will first discuss the indirect methods through which campaign spending can influence voters and, then we will discuss the direct ones. There are three indirect methods:

- Mobilization—campaign contributions are used to provide incentives to increase the probability that a candidate's supporters turn out on election day.
- Coordination—levels of campaign spending can serve as a coordination mechanism for voters in contests in which there are more than two candidates.
- Signals of candidates' "ability"—levels of campaign spending might serve as a signal to voters from contributors, who know the candidates' abilities more directly.

In chapters 2, and 3 we examined how campaign contributions may work to mobilize voters. Here we investigate the other two ways in which campaign spending can indirectly affect voters.

Coordination

Star Power California Republican state senator Tom McClintock had solid conservative credentials and a lot of support for his run for the governorship in California's 2003 recall election. By contrast, the popular and well-known actor Arnold Schwarzenegger was also running as a Republican. The election was a winner-take-all race with all possible candidates from all possible parties involved, 135 of them (we discuss some of the reasons for the recall election in chapter 9). With no primary before the election, Republican voters did not get to decide on the one candidate the party would support. In contrast, the Democrats had managed to restrict the number of entrants from their party such that there was only one perceived viable Democrat in the race, Lieutenant Governor Cruz Bustamante.

Republican Party leaders first declined to endorse anyone at their state convention; California state Republican chairman Duf Sundheim said that the party leaders were like parents and could not choose between their children. But the grassroots members of the party were not happy. Forty-two of fifty-six Republican county leaders voted to endorse Schwarzenegger. Republican Alameda County chairman Jim Hartman summarized the Republicans' reasoning: "This is a two-person race and Arnold Schwarzenegger is the candidate we should unify behind on Oct. 7 or risk a Bustamante governorship." As a consequence, the state Republican Party board decided to endorse Schwarzenegger after all. Sundheim urged "Republicans to consider their decision carefully because 'we don't want them to waste their vote.' "[2]

Republicans were not the only ones choosing Schwarzenegger over

McClintock. The California Taxpayers' Association, an interest group representing corporate taxpayers, had never endorsed a candidate in its seventy-seven-year history. Now it endorsed Schwarzenegger in order to defeat Bustamante. The *Los Angeles Times* reported: "Asked why the group had chosen Schwarzenegger over McClintock, who has pledged that he would not raise taxes under any circumstances, McCarthy said: 'I think it was simply a matter of their perception that Arnold Schwarzenegger was the most viable candidate with the greatest potential of winning.' "[3] Schwarzenegger did win, with 48.6 percent of the vote to Bustamante's 31.5 percent and McClintock's 13.5 percent.

Most of our discussion has focused on two-candidate races, but oftentimes more than two candidates run in an election, particularly in primaries (although rarely 135, as in California in 2003). When Tom Campbell ran for the Republican nomination for the Senate in California in 1992, he faced not only Bruce Herschensohn but also Sonny Bono, and many believed that he lost in part because Bono took away some of his support. If that is true, then Republican voters who preferred either Campbell or Bono to Herschensohn would have been better off if they had been able to coordinate their vote, choosing either Bono or Campbell, rather than splitting their vote. (In chapter 14, we discuss in greater detail the motives for coordination in races with more than two candidates.) Voters have a greater desire to coordinate their vote and choose a common candidate when they see that doing so prevents a worse outcome than that of splitting their vote. Campaign contributions and endorsements by such interest groups as the California Taxpayers' Association can serve as a coordination mechanism for voters in primary-election contests where party labels are not able to serve that purpose.[4]

The Interaction of Service-Induced Contributions and Coordinating Voters As noted earlier, contributors who are making donations in return for services or favors are particularly interested in coordinating their efforts on behalf of a common candidate. Since such contributors often coordinate their efforts on behalf of incumbents, who are better able to provide such services, if voters are using those contributions as a mechanism to coordinate their votes as well, the advantage to the incumbents is even greater. To the extent that both voters and contributors use campaign contributions to coordinate, candidates who are able to raise money early are also at an advantage—and that is one reason for the first name of the PAC that attempts to help elect pro-choice Democratic female candidates: *Emily*, in Emily's List, stands for "Early Money Is Like Yeast."

Many have contended that for the Republican nomination for president in 2000, the desire for early coordination of both primary voters and contributors was the major reason for George W. Bush's success in getting the nomination despite a number of strong challengers. Twelve Republicans had declared their candidacy, including several who had held major federal offices in previous administrations (Lamar Alexander, Pat Buchanan, Elizabeth Dole), a former vice president (Dan Quayle), three former and current senators (Orrin Hatch, Robert Smith, John McCain), and a member of the House of Representatives (John Kasich), plus a number of non-Washington politicians who were noted public figures (Gary Bauer, Stephen Forbes, Alan Keyes). Bush was able to rise above the pack partly because of campaign contributions. For example, he announced in July 1999, over a year before the election, that he had already raised $36.3 million. Before the primaries began, the only competitors remaining were Bauer, Forbes, Hatch, Keyes, and McCain. Only McCain showed any strength against Bush, but he was unable to build enough support to keep Bush from the nomination. The story of Bush's success in securing the nomination reads like a blueprint for how voters and contributors use early poll results, endorsements, and campaign contributions to coordinate their efforts on behalf of a common candidate in primaries when ideological differences are relatively insignificant.[5]

Although Bush's experience in the 2000 Republican contest for the presidential nomination suggests voters' use of campaign contributions to coordinate their votes, a very different story unfolded in the 2004 Democratic contest for the presidential nomination. Despite having a lead in campaign finance going into the Iowa caucuses and the New Hampshire primary and despite a number of high-profile endorsements from former nominee Al Gore and Iowa Senator Tom Harkin, Howard Dean came in third behind John Kerry (who had to borrow money to stay in the race) and John Edwards. In New Hampshire, Dean again found himself behind Kerry, this time in second place, but given his nearby Vermont roots, such as showing was seen as less than expected. Other factors besides coordinating votes on behalf of the biggest spender played out in Kerry's wins in Iowa and New Hampshire. (We discuss those factors in more detail in chapter 12.)

Signals of Candidates' Abilities

Yvonne Howard, a first-grade teacher in Warner, New Hampshire, displayed a campaign sign for former Vermont governor Howard Dean in her yard for weeks before 2004's first-in-the-nation Democratic primary. "I even gave him money, although I didn't tell my husband," she related. But Dean's scream during his concession speech after losing the Iowa caucus caused her to change her mind. The *Los Angeles Times* reported: " 'I was solidly for Dean until last Monday night,' she said. 'But I was embarrassed. . . . I thought when he becomes president he is going to hit tougher situations than coming in third in the Iowa [caucuses]. If he's going to fly off the handle, I'm not sure that he's the man who would best handle the job.' "[6]

Voters like Howard care about a candidate's ability to "handle the job," a valence issue like those discussed in chapter 5. While Dean's scream very publicly revealed to Howard something about his abilities that disturbed her, in most cases the average voter doesn't have the opportunity for the kind of contact with a candidate that can help him or her judge the candidate's abilities sufficiently. But contributors, with the access they are granted, do. Bush supporter Florida lawyer Joseph Klock had such close contact when he worked with Bush in the Florida vote dispute, and Klock was impressed, a reason he gave for supporting Bush in 2004: "President Bush has got guts and integrity. I can never think of a situation where the guy lied." On the other hand, a partner in Klock's law firm, Alvin Davis, chose to support Senator Joseph Lieberman, who was a good friend of his at Yale Law School. Davis summarized his choice: "He is smart, very conscientious, not beholden to anyone. And I know him, so I know what I am getting."[7]

Because contributors have this firsthand knowledge of candidates, campaign contributions may serve to signal information that contributors have on candidates' "abilities" or valence issues that is unavailable to voters.[8] Campaign contributors spend time with candidates (typically one of the services or favors they receive in return for their contributions) and thus may "know" the candidates better than voters do, and they may know their capabilities in valence-issue areas. Voters, even when they know that candidates may be giving away services or favors or making policy choices to attract contributions, may see the size of the contributions as mattering if they are indifferent about the candidates on those issues where the candidates' policy positions do diverge. This influence on voters is more likely to be effective when a problem facing the country is perceived as significant and there is little disagreement by the public and interest groups about how the problem should be handled. If voters do perceive campaign contributions as a positive signal, candidates, if they are uncertain about the policy preferences of the median voter, may be drawn to make the choices preferred by the interest groups in order to attract campaign contributions, and those choices then send a double message. We address this problem of "moral hazard" in chapter 9.

Inside the Black Box: Direct Influences

So far we have discussed ways in which campaign spending indirectly affects voters, but campaign spending principally finances efforts by candidates to engage in direct communication with voters, either through television or mail or by financing rallies and campaign events. Through these methods of communication, information is conveyed to voters about candidates' policy positions; more personal, nonpolicy information is conveyed as well. The Swift Boat Veterans for Truth used their ads to discredit John Kerry's Vietnam War message, and from the survey evidence, voters did gain information from those ads. Through such information, then, campaign contributions can influence voters directly. We discuss four ways in which this influence occurs:

- Impressionability—campaign messages and events may affect some voters' psychological attachment to candidates (an attachment independent of policy preferences).
- Reducing uncertainty—campaign messages and events can provide voters with information about candidates' policy positions, making the voters less uncertain and increasing the probability that a risk-averse voter will vote for the candidate.
- Agenda setting—candidates can choose to provide information on a particular set of issues, establishing those issues as important for the voter in his or her decision making.
- Negative advertising—candidates can use campaign messages and events to convey information about their opponent (about policy or about non-policy characteristics) that they believe will reduce the probability that a voter will support the opponent.

Impressionability

Psychological Influences Before the 2004 Georgia Democratic presidential primary, two voters varied in their preferences, but their reasons were very similar, as reported by *The New York Times*:

> "Edwards has a boyish charm that's very appealing," said Sandra Johnson, who was baby-sitting her niece in a mall. "I think he can relate to ordinary people, so I'm with him." But Bryan Paden, 37, a police officer, had a very different feel. "It's about my sense of the candidate as a person," Mr. Paden said. "At first I thought John Edwards had the 'look' of a president. But lately I've just gotten a good feel about John Kerry. He seems approachable, a good listener, someone I can trust."[9]

Most psychological views of campaign advertising and the effects of other campaign events suggest that they influence voters' "affect," or psychological evaluation of the candidate, the feelings that both Sandra Johnson and Bryan Paden had about Kerry and Edwards. Advertisements might also convey information about nonpolicy or valence issues, making voters perceive candidates as more likable.

There is a major problem with this assumption, however. Campaign spending in itself sends a message—it implies that the contributor is receiving something. With policy-induced or electorally induced contributions, candidates are choosing positions on policy close to the position of the contributor; with service- or favor-induced contributions, candidates are giving favors to contributors, favors that no doubt mean there will be fewer favors or services for noncontributors (that is, most voters). Thus, seeing that a candidate is receiving a great amount in contributions should imply that a voter favors a candidate less, not more (unless the voter is sure that his or her preferences are the same as those of the contributors).

Rational Impressionable Voters One way to resolve this problem is to assume that voters do recognize the negative implications of campaign spending but also receive some tiny positive utility from voting for a candidate who advertises more. That is, suppose voters receive an unspecified psychological value from voting for a candidate who is more familiar and has sent out positive messages about himself or herself on television or through other campaign advertising, regardless of the candidate's policy positions. The voter receives some warm and fuzzy feeling by voting for a candidate who has a friendly face and demeanor, support from his or her family, and so on, as conveyed through campaign advertising or campaign events. We call these voters rational impressionable voters.[10]

Note that the additional utility that rational impressionable voters receive from campaign advertising by a candidate, the warm and fuzzy feeling, may be extremely small but still have a sizable effect on the electoral outcome. That is, if a fully informed voter is indifferent about the choice between two candidates in terms of policy issues (knowing contributions' probable impact on policy) but is impressionable, he or she will end up choosing to vote for the candidate who has advertised more. Thus, even if voters are impressionable only at the margin—that is, this effect of campaign advertising on voters plays only a tiny role in the voters' overall utility calculations—if the median voter is indifferent about candidates, he or she will end up choosing to vote for the candidate who has spent more money on campaign advertising. When voters are rational impressionable and candidates choose policy positions that the median voter is indifferent between, campaign advertising can have a sizable impact on electoral outcomes. The implication is that a large real-world effect of campaign advertising on voters' behavior does not mean that voters' impressionability dominates their policy concerns because they may simply see candidates as equivalent on policy positions and get some very tiny utility from voting for the candidate who has spent more.

A second implication of the assumption that voters are rational but impressionable is that the effect of campaign spending on those voters' choices that occur because of such impressionability is likely to be more significant in elections in which candidates are more ideologically similar and policy differences are less significant for many voters (a situation that is similar to the coordination effect of money). This is likely to be true in primary elections and in general elections in which a large number of voters are indifferent toward the candidates. Moreover, impressionability is likely to be more important if voters are less informed about candidates' policy positions and the link between campaign contributions and candidates' choices. Finally, if voters are impressionable and candidates are uncertain about the policy preferences of the median voter in the general election (see the discussion in chapter 4), then candidates will find it attractive to try to use campaign advertising to influence voter "affect" in this manner.

Reducing Uncertainty

Stepping Off the Pedestal Probably the most remarkable aspect of Arnold Schwarzenegger's victory over Cruz Bustamante and Tom McClintock in the 2003 California gubernatorial race was the fact that when Schwarzenegger's campaign began, voters were very uncertain about him. And he did not help matters much. In his early appearances on television, he was vague on policy issues and on what he would do as governor, and his aides treated him as a movie star, not a candidate. He claimed to be against raising taxes and in favor of cutting government spending. But his announced economic adviser, billionaire investor Warren Buffet, suggested that property taxes were too low. Polls showed that Schwarzenegger's support was declining as he campaigned.

Things began to turn around when Schwarzenegger brought on Mike Murphy, who had managed Jeb Bush's gubernatorial campaign and John McCain's run for the presidency. Murphy got the candidate to give extensive interviews and field questions in small public forums on public policy issues. The campaign issued detailed position papers—"on workers' compensation, the economy, the state's building and construction code, education, the environment." Dan Schnur, who ran former baseball commissioner Peter Uberoff's campaign in the race, noted: "I don't think Mike cares that much what the workers' compensation proposal said. What he cared about is that Arnold was addressing the issues, and that voters understood that. Mike understood that the biggest credibility hurdle that a celebrity candidate would face was knowledge of public policy."[11] Six days before the election, Schwarzenegger announced a ten-step plan for his first one hundred days in office and declared that if the state legislature didn't agree, he would go to the voters through the initiative process (a process we discuss in chapter 9). He announced: "I am not here today to talk about campaigning. I'm here today to talk about governing."[12]

While much is written about voters' "feelings" for candidates and how their reactions to screams or good looks affect their choices in elections, many candidates do spend a considerable amount of their campaign resources talking about policy and their policy positions. Such talk and expenditures are not examples of candidates acting irrationally. The information can affect voters' preferences for the candidates, particularly if voters believe the information and it reduces uncertainty about the candidates' policy positions or changes the voters' perceptions of those policy positions.[13]

Utility and Risk Aversion For example, suppose that a voter called Renda has utility for policy that is given by table 7.1. Renda's utility function is similar to Sona's in chapter 4; that is, if we were to graph it, it would have a concave shape. But since Renda is uncertain about the candidates' policy positions, we need to discuss her expected utility. In chapter 2, we introduced the concept of expected utility and how voters evaluate the effect of voting on their expected utility when deciding whether to turn out. In chapter 4, we used the concept of expected utility to discuss how uncertainty about the ideal point of the median voter in the general election affects the policy positions that candidates choose. Now we need the concept of expected utility to see how changing the degree of uncertainty that a voter has about a candidate's policy position can increase the voter's expected utility.

TABLE 7.1
Renda's Utility from Policy

Policy Position	Renda's Utility
0	185
10	225
20	260
30	280
40	295
50	315
60	310
70	315
80	295
90	280
100	260

First, recall how expected utility works in a general sense. Suppose Renda had a chance to buy a lottery ticket with a price of $50.90. Assume that there is a 10 percent, or one-tenth, chance she will win the lottery of $500 and a 90 percent chance she will lose the lottery and get a $1 consolation price. Notice that the lottery has an expected dollar prize of $0.1 \cdot 500 + 0.9 \cdot 1 = \$50.90$, which is the same as the price of the ticket. Renda's expected utility from the lottery is equal to the sum of the probabilities of each possible outcome times the utility she would get from each outcome. Let's suppose that Renda's utility from $500 for certain (not in a lottery) is equal to 10 utils, her utility from $50.90 for certain (not in a lottery) is equal to 5 utils, and her utility from $1 for certain is equal to 1 util. Her expected utility from the lottery is equal to the sum of the probability of getting each of these amounts times the utility she would get if she had these amounts of money for certain. Her expected utility equals $0.1 \cdot 10 + 0.9 \cdot 1 = 1.9$ utils. Her expected utility from the lottery, 1.9 utils, is less than the utility she would get if she got the cash value of the lottery for certain, 5 utils. We call Renda risk averse because she prefers the certain monetary equivalent of the lottery to the lottery. If Renda's utility from $50.90 was equal to 1.9 utils, we would call her risk neutral because she would be indifferent between the sure or certain monetary equivalent of the lottery and the lottery itself.

If Renda's utility from $50.90 was less than 1.9 utils, we would call her risk seeking because she would prefer the lottery to its certain monetary equivalent.

Risk Aversion and Campaign Information We have assumed that Renda receives utility from different policy positions and that her ideal point is really the policy position that gives her the highest utility. Similar to Charlotte's preferences in chapter 4 (figure 4.1), Renda's utility can be graphed as a function of policy (see figure 7.1). At point 60, Renda's ideal point, Renda's utility is equal to 320 utils, and it declines as a candidate's policy moves away from 60. For example, at 50 and 70, Renda receives 315 utils; at 40 and 80, 295 utils; at 30 and 90, 280 utils; and so on. Note that the decreases in Renda's utility increase as we move away from her ideal point, 60—the utility function has a concave shape (from 60 to 70, utility declines by 5 utils; from 70 to 80, it declines by 10 utils; from 80 to 90, by 15 utils; and so on). Renda's utility function shows that she is risk averse, whereas Charlotte's shows that she is risk neutral. You can see this by comparing the utility Renda would get from a 50/50 lottery between two policy choices on the same side of her ideal point—say, between 20 and 40 with the utility she would receive from 30 (which is the expected outcome of a 50/50 lottery between 20 and 40). For policy for sure at 30, Renda would receive utility equal to 280. Her expected utility from a 50/50 lottery between 20 and 40 would be equal to $(0.5) \cdot (260) + (0.5) \cdot (295) = 277.5$, which is less than 280. Thus, Renda is risk averse.

Because Renda is risk averse, more precise information about a candidate's policy position can increase her expected utility from that candidates' winning. How does this work? Recall that we have assumed that Renda knows that a candidate's policy position is somewhere between 100 and 70—such that there is one-fourth probability that the candidate is at 100, one-fourth probability that the candidate is at 90, one-fourth probability that the candidate is at 80, and one-fourth probability that the candidate is at 70. Renda's expected utility from that candidate's winning is $(1/4) \cdot 305 + (1/4) \cdot 295 + (1/4) \cdot 280 + (1/4) \cdot 260 = 285$. Now suppose that through campaign advertising financed by campaign contributions she finds out that the candidate is for certain at 80. Renda's utility from a sure win by the candidate is equal to 295, which is higher than her utility when she was uncertain about the candidate's position.

Interestingly, when the candidate's position was less certain, it was possible (in Renda's mind) that the candidate would be located closer to her than he or she actually was. But because Renda is risk averse, Renda's expected utility from a candidate who is less "risky" is higher than her utility from the risky one who might be closer but also might be further away. When voters are risk averse, then if campaign advertising makes the candidates' positions more precise, the voters may be more willing to vote for them as campaign spending increases, even if the spending decreases the probability that the

FIGURE 7.1
Renda's Utility from Policy

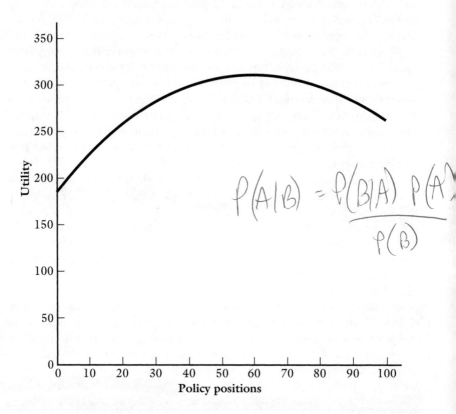

candidates' policy positions are close to the voters' ideal point. Thus as Schwarzenegger provided voters with more information about his policy positions during the campaign, even if some voters found those positions less desirable than the positions they believed he might hold, the reduction in uncertainty about his policy increased the utility they perceived they would gain from his winning.[14]

Agenda Setting

Stephen Moore, the president of Club for Growth, a conservative activists group that supports Republicans, was concerned in February 2004 about President George W. Bush's reelection prospects. A Pew poll released on February 19 showed that the percentage of voters concerned about the growing federal deficit and the failure to find weapons of mass destruction in Iraq was increasing. Although the Pew poll showed Bush tied with Kerry if the general election was between those two, a poll by CNN showed Kerry with a 12 percentage point lead. Bush had appeared on the NBC television show *Meet the Press* to try to defend his policies on Iraq, but the performance had been deemed weak. *The Boston Globe* reported Moore as saying, "I would describe the mood among conservatives right now as frightened." The report continued: " 'For the first time,' said a top staff member for a GOP senator, 'some Republicans are facing the prospect that the president could lose.' " Conservatives were concerned not only about Bush's reelection prospects but also about some of his policies—in particular, the federal deficit. The *Globe* reported: "Grover Norquist, president of Americans for Tax Reform, a conservative group that advocates lower taxes, . . . agreed with other Republicans who are concerned about Bush's spending. They see the rising deficit and rising spending and want to change course, he said. 'People recognize they're in a pot of water and it's getting hot.' "[15]

In the midst of the rising concern about the deficit, Iraq, and the poor poll numbers, President Bush made an announcement. He called for a constitutional amendment to ban same-sex marriage. A ruling by the Massachusetts Supreme Court declaring that it was unconstitutional to restrict gays to civil unions and the granting of marriage licenses to large numbers of gay couples in San Francisco had energized social conservatives to push Bush aggressively for an endorsement of a constitutional gay-marriage ban (discussed in chapter 3). In conversations with Bush aide Karl Rove, some groups were even threatening to withhold their votes on election day.[16] Previously, Bush had said the decision on gay marriage should be left to the states.[17] Senators Kerry and Edwards (still opposing each other in the Democratic primaries), when immediately asked to comment on the issue, announced their opposition to the amendment and denounced the president for playing politics with the Constitution. Why the reversal on gay marriage to please conservatives and gain votes? Why not some other issue, such as the deficit?

Reducing the deficit would mean cutting either federal programs or Bush's signature tax cuts. Bush was facing pressure from fiscal conservatives to veto a popular transportation bill. In contrast, according to a Pew poll at the time, 34 percent of those surveyed said they would not vote for a candidate who supported gay marriage even if they agreed with the candidate on most other issues. For Republicans and evangelicals, that number was even higher: 55 percent for evangelicals and 50 percent for Republicans. However, only 6 percent said they would refuse to vote for a candidate who opposed gay marriage if they agreed with him or her on most other questions.[18] By taking a stand against gay marriage, Bush forced the issue into the presidential campaign agenda. He forced Kerry, the presumed nominee of the Democrats, to come out against the ban, suggesting to the public that the senator from the state of Massachusetts, whose supreme court had recently ruled in favor of gay marriage, was implicitly also in favor of gay marriage. Bush both shored up wavering social conservative voters and made it more difficult for Kerry to attract support from Republicans and evangelicals. Furthermore, as we saw in chapter 3, Bush's decision to campaign on same-sex marriage and abortion allowed him to exploit internal divisions within Democrats.

Not only can candidates use campaign resources to reveal information about their policy positions, thus attempting to reduce voter uncertainty, but they can also, by being precise on some issues and vague on others, make some issues more important in a voter's decision making as the differences between candidates on those issues become clearer than their positions on the other issues. Prior to Bush's support of the constitutional gay-marriage ban, there was uncertainty about both Bush's and Kerry's views on public policy with respect to the issue. Bush had said that the issue should be left to the states and supported the Defense of Marriage Act, which defines marriage as a union between a man and a woman and allows states to refuse to recognize gay marriages performed in other states. Kerry had said that he favored civil unions but was against gay marriage even though he had voted against the Defense of Marriage Act. Although Kerry's position was in one sense more liberal, in another sense it could be argued that Bush's position was more liberal since it allowed for gay marriages if a state approved it. By taking an explicit stand against gay marriage nationwide, Bush reversed his previous position, reduced uncertainty about his position, and forced Kerry's view to appear more liberal. By being more precise on the issue of gay marriage, the utility difference between the candidates on that issue became more pronounced, and voters were more likely to choose between the candidates based on their position on gay marriage than they were on other issues where the differences between the candidates was less clear. Given the information available to them about the candidates' policy positions, voters who cared about gay marriage were responding rationally when they placed a greater weight on the gay-marriage issue in making their voting decision.

Negative Advertising

" 'Dean's always attacking everybody and then they all attack back,' said an exasperated Cindy Anderson, 39, a Des Moines resident. . . . 'It's like a bunch of little kids playing badly together.' "[19] Anderson summed up the tone of many of the campaign ads, speeches, and mailings that dominated the Democratic candidates' campaign for support in the Iowa Democratic presidential caucuses of 2004. Pundits agreed that it was an especially negative campaign, and some argued that the negative advertising worked to hurt Howard Dean and Richard Gephardt, both of whom used it heavily (although the winner, Kerry, also sent out some negative mailings).

What is negative advertising? The candidates defended their ads in Iowa as simply telling the truth—Howard Dean remarked on the NBC *Today* show: "Actually, my ads were not particularly negative. All they did was point out that Senator Edwards and Senator Kerry and Dick supported the war and I didn't. I think that's a reasonable ad to have."[20] A voter in Iowa asked Kerry about the negativity of his message during one public meeting, and Kerry responded: "What's happening is that we are getting closer to the election, there's a greater urgency to say to you 'Here are the distortions.' If I don't tell you, who will?"[21] Just as candidates try to convey information about their own policy positions in campaign messages, so, too, do they try to convey information about their opponents in an effort to affect voter utility—either creating uncertainty about those positions if doing so will decrease the probability a voter will vote for their opponent or reducing uncertainty if they believe doing so will paint the opponent as further from the voters ideologically.

However, negative advertising also sends a message about the candidate whom the ads are supposed to benefit. If voters care about qualities such as temperament, honesty, and so on, then negative advertising can work to undermine voters' perceptions of those qualities. In the race for the Democratic nomination for president, North Carolina senator John Edwards incorporated into his campaign the theme that he would engage in only positive campaigning (although on occasion he also broke this pledge by pointing out "truths" about his opponents). This sent a message about him as a person, one that can appeal to rational impressionable voters. For example, retired public health official Ruth Balster from Cedar Rapids, Iowa, noted: "I think it helped Edwards because he was above the fray."[22]

In late March 2004, the Bush reelection team decided to do some "truth telling" about John Kerry. In a *New York Times*/CBS News poll taken from March 10 to March 14, more than 40 percent of voters surveyed said they were either undecided or did not know enough about John Kerry when asked if they had a favorable or unfavorable opinion of him. The Bush campaign saw the uncertainty among voters as a chance to define Kerry as someone who would raise taxes and weaken the fight on terrorism and was too unsteady to lead the nation in a time of war. "It's easiest to define somebody when they're ill-defined, and John Kerry's ill-defined," reasoned Mark McKinnon, Bush's head media strategist. *The New York Times* reported that Bush's "advisors contended that that [defining Kerry] would be relatively easy to do because impressions of him are so ill-formed with many voters. 'He peels like an onion,' said an associate of Mr. Bush. 'People aren't like, "I really believe in this guy and I'm not willing to accept the information." They accept it very easily. With some candidates there's a hard shell. With him there's a soft skin.' "[23]

As noted in chapter 3, Bush's campaign had money in the bank for such ads while Kerry's was in debt from the primaries and desperately raising money. The Democratic 527 groups did respond to the ads, but because officially they could not coordinate with Kerry, Kerry could not play a visible role in the response, directly challenging the negative information. According to the National Annenberg Election Survey, Kerry's positive ratings in battleground states fell from 40 to 35 percent, and his negative ratings rose from 24 to 36 percent. Similarly, when the Swift Boat Veterans ran their negative ads in August 2004, Kerry's campaign did not control the resources necessary to fully respond. Harold Ickes, who ran the Media Fund, a 527 group, felt unable to counter the ads at the time because they concerned "a matter so personal to Senator Kerry, so much within his knowledge. Who knew what the facts were?"[24] Because Kerry relied more on the 527 groups for advertising than Bush did and because the BCRA prohibited Kerry's campaign from coordinating with Democratic 527 groups to respond to negative advertising, the negative advertising against Kerry was particularly effective in 2004.

Empirical Evidence on Campaign Advertising

Does Campaign Advertising Work?

The Early Evidence Sociologist Paul Lazarsfeld at Columbia University had a theory about how voters used the media in elections. He argued that the media worked through a two-step flow of communication. He saw voters as divided into two groups—opinion leaders, who took an interest in public events and information from the media to form their views, and their followers, whose attitudes and preferences were influenced by the leaders. Surveying voters repeatedly during the 1940 election in Elmira, New York, and Erie County, Ohio, Lazarsfeld and his collaborators found that in general what happened during the campaign had very little effect on the voters. The opinion leaders already had significant levels of information, and the campaign did not change their minds. The voters followed the leaders. The campaigns were irrelevant, the researchers concluded.[25]

The researchers decided that the decisions of most voters in their sample were determined by factors that were independent of the voters' exposure to campaign advertising, such as demographic characteristics, which were unchanging. Further research using the NES surveys in the years that followed showed that voters' choices were indeed heavily influenced by their partisan identification and demographic characteristics. There seemed to be little room for campaign advertisements to change voters' choices given the strength of the effects of these other factors.[26] More recent work has agreed with this finding.[27] Over time, more sophisticated analyses of national election outcomes began to use aggregate historical data to predict how voters would choose in elections, and this work (which we address more expansively in chapter 10) showed that information about the economy and political conditions that was available before election campaigns even began could predict well how an election would end up.[28] Given that election outcomes can be predicted in advance, before campaigns, and voters' decisions are so heavily influenced by factors independent of campaign advertising, many political scientists concluded that campaigns must not have much of an effect on the outcome.

Are Candidates and Supporters Really Irrational?

<u>Evidence in Support of an Effect</u> Although these aggregate studies based on survey data found little effect of campaigns on voters' behavior, other research found evidence suggestive of an effect. First, experimental laboratory studies of individuals' exposure to campaign ads show that individuals' preferences can be influenced. While generally these studies used hypothetical candidates and elections, the experiments did involve real individuals who gave real responses that were then affected by the experimental manipulations.[29]

Second, there is evidence that campaign ads in real elections affect voters' levels of information, suggesting that ads must be influential. Early work by Atkin and others (1973) and Atkin and Heald (1976) found that voters were more likely to be informed about candidates if they had seen television ads. Brians and Wattenberg (1996) found that survey respondents who recall campaign advertisements, compared with those who read newspapers or watch television news, are more likely to know a candidate's issue positions.

Third, there is growing evidence that voters are influenced by campaign spending in congressional races, particularly spending by challengers. Figure 7.2 shows campaign spending in the 2000 congressional elections involving an incumbent, in terms of the predicted probability that voters' will recall incumbents' and challengers' names as a function of their campaign spending. The campaign spending of both incumbents and challengers increases the ability of voters to recall their names, although, not surprisingly, the effect is stronger for challengers than incumbents.

<u>The Effect of Competition</u> How can we reconcile the evidence of an effect on voters' information levels found in experiments with the slight effect found in aggregate studies of presidential campaigns? First, note that the aggregate studies do find some effect; it is just small. In the 1984 presidential election, in which Ronald Reagan clearly had an advantage in terms of valence issues, as discussed in chapter 5, Markus (1988) found that campaign advertising affected the vote outcome by 3 percent, which in a closer race (as in 2004 or 2000), could have affected the electoral outcome.

Second, in presidential campaigns, the strategic competition between candidates might result in what has been labeled a balanced informational environment such that neither candidate has a perceptible advantage, as discussed in Bartels (1992), Gelman and King (1993), and Zaller (1992). Gelman and King (1993) concluded that campaigns "enlighten" voters so that they choose based on objective economic and political factors that are not affected by campaign events. Thus, finding little aggregate effect on either voters or the election outcome could simply result from the competi-

FIGURE 7.2

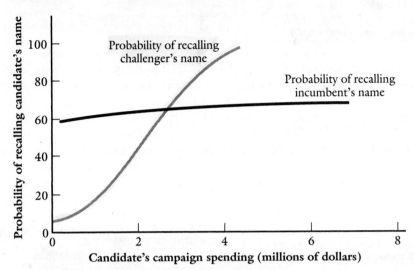

Source: Federal Election Commission (campaign-spending data) and National Election Studies (voter data).
Note: The NES did not ask about this in 2002, and the 2004 data are not yet available.

tion of ads in which each candidate attempts to balance the other and strategically chooses ads that do so. In order to determine whether ads do in fact influence elections, it would be necessary to control for the strategic behavior of the candidates in their advertising and those cross effects. Statistically this is difficult using data from real elections, partly because until recently political scientists have not had even somewhat comprehensive data sets on campaign advertisements by both candidates in elections or sufficient data on voters' television-viewing habits and their decisions. Thus, we should be careful about putting too much weight on aggregate studies, given these limitations.

Shaw (1999) presented an interesting attempt to control for the cross effects of advertising in presidential elections. He examined the effect of differences in presidential candidates' campaign advertising in states in terms of the candidates' vote share. For example, suppose in the presidential contest in 2004 Kerry and Bush had advertised the same amount in Florida. We would expect that the advertising of each candidate would have offset that of the other and that there would have been little effect of either candidate's advertising on the difference in votes won by both candidates in the state. But if Kerry had increased his advertising in Florida and Bush had not increased his, and campaign advertising affects voters, we expect that Kerry's vote share in Florida would have increased. Shaw tested this expectation using data on campaign advertising in the 1988, 1992, and 1996 presidential elections. He found that when a candidate advertised more than his or her opponent in a state, the candidate's vote share in that state was likely to be higher than it would have been if he or she had advertised the same amount as his or her opponent. This finding suggests that advertising is influencing voters. Shaw also found that the greater the number of undecided voters in the state, the stronger the effect, as measured in the September polls, suggesting that advertising influences how voters ultimately choose.

What Types of Ads Work?

While showing that campaign advertising truly affects electoral outcomes is not straightforward, we can gather a lot of information about how candidates see advertisements as working by studying the choices they make in advertising. We've discussed multiple ways in which campaign advertising can influence voters. In particular, we've argued that sometimes campaign advertising is all about nonpolicy issues (when it is a coordination device for voters, serves as a signal to voters about valence issues, or influences rational impressionable voters' perceptions of the candidates on valence issues) and other times it is informative in terms of policy stances candidates take (when it reduces voters' uncertainty about candidates' policy positions or defines the policy issues that will be prominent in voters' choices). Furthermore, sometimes campaign advertising is positive (favoring a particular candidate) and other times negative (opposing a particular candidate). How often is campaign advertising about policy or valence issues? How often is it negative? Do candidates, parties, and interest groups run different types of ads?

Policy versus Valence in Ads Surprisingly, a sizable portion of ads are about policy issues, more than are about valence issues. Jamieson (1996) analyzed prominent ads in presidential elections from 1952 to 2000 and found that policy issues are more prevalent than messages relating to a candidate's personal qualities (such as leadership, trustworthiness, compassion). West (2000), in a study of the 2000 election, found that 60 percent of ads contained messages pertaining to domestic policy matters and only 31 percent mentioned a candidate's personal qualities. Spillotes and Vavreck (2002), in a study of over one thousand ads by 290 candidates in 153 elections in thirty-seven states in 1998, found that in 92 percent of the ads, candidates mentioned issues and 52 percent of the ads were predominantly issue driven. Although most of the discussion of issues was vague, according to their analysis, a significant minority of the candidates, 32 percent, made at least one ad that could be classified as adopting a specific position on an issue. Thus, the evidence suggests that the majority of ads are about policy, although not overwhelmingly so, as a significant minority does not mention policy issues.

It is useful to distinguish between advertisements about policies that have substance—that is, that give voters verifiable information about a candidate's position, allowing the voter or other interested parties to check the facts—and ads that simply claim that the candidate has or will take a given position on a policy issue but provide no way for the claim to be verified. For example, consider the ads in figures 7.3, 7.4, and 7.5. These are storyboards from congressional campaigns in 2000 tracked by the Campaign Media Analysis Group (CMAG) or, more specifically, the company's Ad Detector product.[30] As you can see in figure 7.3, an ad for incumbent Georgia congressman Mac Collins presents valence information but tells voters nothing substantive about Collins's policy choices as a member of Congress. In contrast, figure 7.4 presents an ad for incumbent Arkansas congressman

FIGURE 7.3
Television Ad for Mac Collins for Congress, 2000

[Woman 1]: "He's honest. If he says it, believe it." [Man 1]: "I've never known him to waste money—his or anybody else's."

[Woman 2]: "His faith is important to him and so is his family."

[Man 2]: "He's not afraid of hard work." [Woman 3]: "He understands people because he listens."

[Announcer]: "Integrity. Commitment.

Common sense." [Woman 4]: "Matt Collins." [Man 4]: "Matt Collins."

[Woman 5]: "Matt Collins." [Announcer]: "Keep Matt Collins representing us

in the United States Congress." [Man 5] "Back Matt."

Source: Campaign Media Analysis Group (CMAG), http://www.politicsontv.com.
Note: CMAG incorrectly recorded Collins's first name as Matt.

FIGURE 7.4
Television Ad for Marion Berry for Congress, 2000

[Berry]: "There is no rhyme or reason about the way that prescription drug manufacturers in this country

price their products. In one case that I remember well, prices of

the medicine for a month's supply went from $6 to $120

in one month. It created tremendous hardship

for people and we had a great outcry—'Why is this company doing this?

Why would they want to do this to us?' That is why I introduced a bill

that would reduce the cost of prescription medicine by as much as 40%. [ANNOUNCER: Paid for by Marion Berry for Congress]

Source: Campaign Media Analysis Group, http://www.politicsontv.com.

Marion Berry that gives factual information about a bill Berry had introduced in Congress to reduce the cost of prescription medicine. Note that not all ads of substance contain positive messages, as figure 7.5 shows. In this ad, information is provided about the votes of incumbent Kentucky congresswoman Anne Northrup, with the suggestion to viewers that the votes were not in their interest. While these three ads are about incumbents, if a challenger has previous elective experience, then challengers may also air positive ads with verifiable substance and incumbentsain negative substantive ads on challengers.

How often do candidates advertise verifiable substance about their records or the records of their opponents? Table 7.2 summarizes the extent

FIGURE 7.5
Television Ad for Anne Northrup for Congress, 2000

[Announcer]: "With all this back and forth about Anne Northrup's record it's hard to know what to believe. But I got on the Internet

and looked up Anne Northrup's voting record for myself. Turns out Anne

Northup did vote against a real patient's bill of rights. Denying you

the ability to sue your HMO. And I also learned Northup voted against

allowing women to choose their ob-gyn for their primary care physician.

If you want to know Anne Northup's real record get on the Internet

and check the facts for yourself.
[Paid for by Kentucky Democratic Party]

Source: Campaign Media Analysis Group, http://www.politicsontv.com.

to which congressional incumbents and challengers advertised substance in the 2000 elections in which an incumbent ran, using the CMAG data.[31] The Ad Detector found ads by either incumbents or challengers in only one third (131) of the 399 congressional races with an incumbent in the continental United States. In 11 of those contests only the challenger advertised, while in 53 of them only the incumbent advertised. Incumbents ran slightly more ads with no substance than with either positive or negative substance. In contrast, challengers ran slightly more ads with either negative or positive substance than ads with no substance. Not surprisingly, the rarest type of ad was a substance ad for a challenger, reflecting the fact that challengers typically have less experience on which to base substance advertising.

TABLE 7.2
Congressional Candidates' Advertisements
by Substance, 2000

Types of Ad	Number of Contests with Ads	Average Number of Ads per Contest	Standard Deviation in Ads per Contest	Smallest Number of Ads	Largest Number of Ads
Positive-substance ads on incumbent	62	438.5	495.82	12	2,605
Negative-substance ads on incumbent	53	776.79	839.25	5	3,357
Nonsubstance ads on incumbent	106	587.28	762.73	8	3,621
Positive-substance ads on challenger	26	312.65	305.97	14	1,516
Negative-substance ads on challenger	33	537.85	539.41	7	1,974
Nonsubstance ads on challenger	74	934.85	1,409.25	4	6,791

Source: Campaign Media Analysis Group, http://www.politicsontv.com.

Candidates' Advertising Choices We would expect that the further a candidate's record is from the ideal point of the median voter in the district, the less the candidates will advertise positive verifiable substance. That is, if a candidate's record is far from the ideal point of the median voter in his or her district, then giving false information can do damage if someone discovers the falsehood. Giving truthful information, if believed, will only reduce the probability that the median voter will support the candidate. Similarly, we would expect that the closer a candidate's opponents' record is to the ideal point of the median voter in his or her district, the less likely the candidate will advertise negative verifiable substance. Furthermore, we might expect that the further a candidate's record is from the median voter's ideal point in his or her district, the more likely the candidate will advertise messages that are primarily nonsubstantive—that is, about valence issues, like that in figure 7.3.

Are these predictions true? We can estimate the relationship between the number of ads of each type a candidate airs as a function of his or her (or his or her opponent's) distance from the median voter in his or her district. Figure 7.6 presents these estimated relationships using data on campaign advertisements from CMAG for the congressional races in 2000 combined with an estimate of the distance between the incumbent's voting record in Congress (measured by Poole and Rosenthal, as discussed in chapter 4) and an estimate of the median voter's ideal point in the district.[32] As the figure shows, there is little relationship between the number of positive-substance ads by incumbents and how far the incumbent is from the median voter in his or her district. However, incumbents are more likely to run negative-substance ads about their challengers and ads without substance as their voting records move further from the median voter's ideal point. Similarly, the further the incumbent is from his or her median voter, the more the challenger runs both negative-substance and positive-substance ads, to the extent that doing so is possible. The evidence suggests that candidates do use verifiable substance in their ads strategically.

The Effect of Substance Advertisements on Voters Are voters affected by all this advertising? If the advertising affects voters, we would expect that it would affect their probability of approving incumbent members of Congress as measured by the NES in 2000. We can estimate the predicted probability

FIGURE 7.6
Substance in Congressional Campaign Ads, 2000

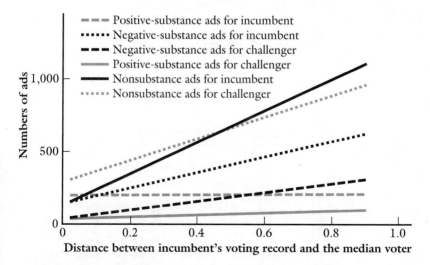

Source: Campaign Media Analysis Group, http://politicsontv.com, and Keith Poole and Howard Rosenthal, http://voteview.com/dwnl.htm., and Abrajano and Morton (2005).

FIGURE 7.7
Effect of Substance in Ads on Predicted Probability
of Approval of Incumbent Congress Members, 2000

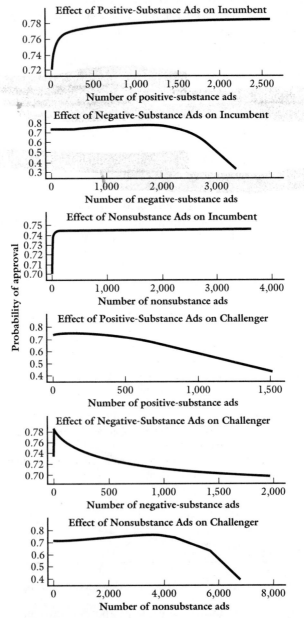

Source: Campaign Media Analysis Group. http://www.politicsontv.com, and National Election Studies, and Abrajano and Morton (2005).

as a function of the quantity of each type of ad run in congressional campaigns in which ads were run. The data are limited and not carefully representative of each congressional district, and only the relationship between positive-substance ads on the incumbent and the predicted probability is statistically significant, so the analysis should be interpreted with caution. However, such an estimate does show that approval of incumbents significantly increases with the number of positive-substance ads run by the incumbent, decreases with the number of all types of ads run by the challenger, as well as negative-substance ads run by the incumbent about the challenger, and is only slightly affected positively by the number of nonsubstance ads run by the incumbent.[33] Figure 7.7 presents these estimated relationships.

Note that challengers clearly benefit most if they can run positive-substance ads about themselves—one thousand ads with positive substance about the challenger can reduce the predicted probability that a voter will approve the incumbent Congress member from a little over 10 percent (holding all other things constant), while the same number of negative-substance ads about the incumbent or nonsubstance ads has a very slightly positive effect on the predicted probability a voter will approve the incumbent. Whereas ads with positive substance or no substance run by an incumbent can increase the predicted probability that a voter will approve the incumbent, the change is smaller and has a significantly diminishing effect. Lau and Pomper (2002) examined the dialogue in campaigns and NES voter evaluations and 143 U.S. Senate elections from 1988 to 1998 in which an incumbent ran for reelection. They found a similar result: conditional on the opponent's strategy, negative campaigning is relatively effective for challengers, while positive campaigning is more effective for incumbents.

In summary, both incumbents and challengers appear to benefit from advertising positive substance about their records, although for incumbents the effect is smaller and requires fewer ads. Negative-substance ads about incumbents and nonsubstance ads about challengers can benefit challengers when a sizable number are aired. Nonsubstance ads about incumbents benefit incumbents little, and negative-substance ads about challengers appear to hurt incumbents.

Who Sponsors Substance Ads? As discussed above, one of the problems the Kerry campaign faced in 2004 was that a significant portion of its advertising was conducted by 527 groups financed by soft money and legally prevented from coordinating with the candidate. In retrospect, it is clear that Kerry should have responded to some of the negative ads by Bush's campaign earlier and to a greater extent, but the 527 groups focused on more positive messages. Furthermore, the evidence suggests that Kerry also was hurt by the ads run by a Bush 527 group, the Swift Boat Veterans for Truth. Are interest groups more likely to run negative ads? Do interest groups provide less substance than candidates and parties, or more substance? More generally, to what extent do ads differ by substance depending on who pays for them?

CMAG also provides information on the sponsors of the ads in 2000. Table 7.3 presents a summary of the types of ads run by the three types of sponsors in the 2000 congressional elections involving an incumbent: candidates, parties, and interest groups. Most ads had no substance, while the fewest ads had positive substance (reflecting the fact that few challengers ran ads with positive substance). Candidates sponsored the majority of the ads. Interestingly, negative-substance ads were most likely to be run by candidates, then by parties, and last by interest groups, although parties ran more negative-substance ads than any other type of ads (29 percent of all party ads). Interest group ads are about equally divided between the three types. Interest groups appear less likely to run negative ads (17 percent of all interest group ads) compared with parties and candidates, and a higher percentage of interest group ads have positive substance (50 percent of all interest group ads). Hence, the evidence suggests that interest group ads are actually more positive in nature and more substantive than ads run by candidates and parties.

TABLE 7.3
Congressional Candidates' Advertisements by Substance and Sponsor, 2000

Type of Ad	Sponsor of Ad (%)			
	Candidate	Party	Interest Group	Total
Nonsubstance ads	32	7	7	47
Positive-substance ads	8	1	8	17
Negative-substance ads	19	12	6	37
Total	59	20	22	100

Source: Campaign Media Analysis Group, http://www.politicsontv.com.
Note: Each cell represents the percentage of ads run by incumbents and challengers in congressional races in 2000 in which an incumbent ran and the sponsor of the ad was detected. Totals may be different from the sum because of rounding.

What We Know

We know that campaign expenditures, by paying for campaign advertising, can affect voters in many ways: indirectly—through mobilization and coordination and by signaling candidates' qualities—and directly—by affecting voters' feelings about candidates, reducing voters' uncertainty about candidates' positions, affecting the issues that determine how voters choose in an election, and providing negative information about a candidate's challenger. Empirical evidence suggests that candidates advertise strategically—candidates who have records that are closest to their voters' preferences are more likely to discuss those records, and if their opponents' records are far from voters' preferences, they are more likely to advertise negative information about their opponents. Challengers benefit from campaign advertising more than incumbents but tend to have fewer resources with which to engage in advertising, giving well-known incumbents an advantage.

What We Don't Know: Other Sources of Information

Michael Moore's documentary attacking George W. Bush's policy in Iraq and Afghanistan, *Fahrenheit 9/11*, received considerable attention and grossed $119 million, the most ever for a documentary. Of particular debate was whether ads for the movie were a violation of BCRA since they showed highlights from the film that were critical of Bush. The FEC unanimously ruled in August 2004 that the ads were not a breach of federal regulations. But *Fahrenheit 9/11* was not the only political documentary to draw criticism from the campaigns in 2004. *Stolen Honor: Wounds That Never Heal*, former *Washington Times* journalist Carlton Sherwood's anti-Kerry documentary highlighting the effect of Kerry's anti–Vietnam War testimony on U.S. prisoners of war in Vietnam, did not receive a similar major release and financial support but became news when the Sinclair Broadcast Group announced that it would preempt regular programming to air the documentary in prime time on all sixty-two of its television stations, many of which were in swing states. The decision by the company was highly criticized, and advertisers threatened to boycott. In response, Sinclair aired a documentary called *A POW Story: Politics, Pressure, and the Media*, which focused primarily on the story behind the decision to air the documentary, including five minutes of the film as well as pro-Kerry statements. The weekend before the election, the cable network Pax aired *Stolen Honor* ten times, and Dish Network offered it on a pay-per-view basis the day before the election.

While campaign advertisements are one source of information available to voters during campaigns, the mass media, through documentaries and reports on television and radio and in newspapers, provide voters with much of the information that they have about candidates and the issues in elections. Is the mass media biased? And if so, how would that affect voters in elections? We consider these questions in the next chapter.

Study Questions and Problems

1. Archie's utility from policy on different levels of defense spending is given in table 7.4. Suppose Archie thinks there is a 10 percent chance

John Kerry will spend $20 trillion on defense and a 90 percent chance Kerry will spend $60 trillion. He also thinks there is a one-half chance George W. Bush will spend $70 trillion and a one-half chance Bush will spend $90 trillion.

a. Given his uncertainty, which candidate does Archie prefer on the issue of defense spending?

b. Suppose Archie finds out for sure that Bush will spend $75 trillion. Which candidate does Archie prefer on the issue of defense spending?

c. How does your answer to question 1a change if Kerry convinces Archie that Bush will spend $90 trillion?

TABLE 7.4
Archie's Utility From Policy on Defense Spending

Defense Spending (trillions of dollars)	Archie's Utility
20	0
25	5
30	75
35	135
40	185
45	225
50	260
55	280
60	295
65	305
70	310
75	305
80	295
85	280
90	260

2. Suppose that Archie in question 1 bases his vote on the candidates' positions on defense spending and abortion. That is, his utility from a candidate's winning is equal to the utility he receives from the candidate's position on defense spending plus the utility he receives from the candidate's position on abortion. He receives 100 utils if the candidate is going to restrict abortions and 0 utility if the candidate is not going to change government policy on abortion.

a. Does your answer to question 1 (all three parts) change if Archie thinks that both Bush and Kerry are unlikely to change government policy on abortion? Explain.

b. Does your answer to question 1 (all three parts) change if Archie thinks that Bush is likely to restrict abortion but Kerry is not? Explain.

NOTES

1. Even though Durkin was successful, his experience was probably one reason he sponsored the millionaires' amendment to the BCRA, discussed in chapter 6.
2. Joe Mathews, Daryl Kelley, and Mitchell Landsberg, "GOP Council Backs Actor: Endorsements from the State Party and a Group of Business Taxpayers Accompany an Apparent Schwarzenegger Surge; Huffington May Quit," *Los Angeles Times*, September 30, 2003.
3. Mathews, Kelley, and Landsberg, "GOP Council Backs Actor." McCarthy is Larry McCarthy, president of the association.
4. For a discussion of how voters might use campaign contributions to coordinate in multicandidate elections, see Myerson and Weber (1993). Myerson, Rietz, and Weber (1998) demonstrated in laboratory experiments how such coordination can occur.
5. See Abramson, Aldrich, and Rohde (2003, pp. 23–24).
6. Ronald Brownstein, "Kerry Showing Strength across Board in N.H.," *Los Angeles Times*, January 24, 2004.
7. Matthew Haggman, "Oval Office Dreams: Driven by Ideology, Friendship and Visions of Clout, South Florida Lawyers Are Hitting The Phones to Raise Money for Presidential Candidates," *Broward Daily Business Review*, May 19, 2003.
8. For an exposition of the signaling model of campaign contributions, see Gerber (1996), Grossman and Helpman (1999) and Prat (2002).
9. Elisabeth Rosenthal, "With Decision at Hand, Many Voters Turn to Instinct," *New York Times*, February 29, 2004.
10. Morton and Myerson (2003) formalized rational impressionable voters; see also Grossman and Helpman (1999) and Prat (2002).
11. Joe Matthews, "From Novice to Governor in Two Months: How Schwarzenegger Did It," *New York Newsday*, October 12, 2003.
12. Joe Mathews and Greg Jones, "Acting As If It's in the Bag: Six Days before the Vote, Schwarzenegger Touts a Plan for His First 100 Days in Office; His Governor-Elect Tone Infuriates Davis Aides," *Los Angeles Times*, October 2, 2003.
13. See Austen-Smith (1987).
14. Alvarez (1997) examined voter uncertainty in elections. He found that voters did penalize candidates who were insufficiently clear about their positions.
15. Wayne Washington, "The GOP Faithful: Republicans Waiting for Bush to Sharpen His Focus," *Boston Globe*, February 20, 2004.
16. Bill Walsh, "Bush Takes Hard Line on Gay Marriage: Rivals Say Move Is a Political Stunt," *New Orleans Times-Picayune*, February 25, 2004.
17. In an interview with CNN's Larry King during the 2000 election, Bush was asked about gay marriage:

    "If a state were voting on gay marriage, you would suggest to that state not to approve it?" CNN's Larry King asked Bush during a Republican primary debate in South Carolina. "The state can do what they want to do. Don't try to trap me in this state's issues," Bush answered. White House spokesman Scott McClellan denied Tuesday that the president has switched his position. Bush had been referring to states' authority to approve civil unions, not gay marriage, the spokesman said.

Bennett Roth and Patty Reinert, "Bush Urges Gay Marriage Amendment: Proposed Constitutional Ban Sets Up U.S. Debate," *Houston Chronicle*, February 25, 2004.

18. Ken Fireman, "Bush's Stance Not Risky to Him," *New York Newsday*, February 28, 2004.

19. Deirdre Shesgreen, "Iowa Voters Feel Buried in Mudslinging," *St. Louis Post-Dispatch*, January 9, 2004.

20. Bob Dart, "Negative Ads Hurt Dean and Gephardt in Iowa," Cox News Service, January 20, 2004.

21. Shesgreen, "Iowa Voters Feel Buried in Mudslinging."

22. Shesgreen, "Iowa Voters Feel Buried in Mudslinging."

23. Jim Rutenberg, "90-Day Strategy by Bush's Aides to Define Kerry," *New York Times*, March 20, 2004.

24. Thomas B. Edsall and James V. Grimaldi, "On Nov. 2, GOP Got More Bang for Its Billion, Analysis Shows," *Washington Post*, December 30, 2004.

25. Berelson, Lazarsfeld, and McPhee (1954) and Lazarsfeld, Berelson, and Gaudet (1944).

26. See Campbell et al. (1960).

27. See Bartels (1992), Finkel (1993), and Markus (1988).

28. See Abramowitz (1988), Campbell (1992), Fair (1996), Lewis-Beck and Rice (1992), and Rosenstone (1983).

29. See, for example, Ansolabehere et al. (1994), Ansolabehere and Iyengar (1995), Garramone et al. (1990), Kahn and Geer (1994), and Noggle and Kaid (2000).

30. These materials are based on work supported by the Pew Charitable Trusts under a grant to the Brennan Center for Justice at New York University School of Law and a subsequent subcontract to the Department of Political Science at the University of Wisconsin at Madison. For more information regarding the data, refer to Ridout et al. (2002).

31. In 2000, CMAG monitored the satellite transmissions of the national network (ABC, CBS, NBC, and Fox) as well as the transmissions of twenty-five national cable networks such as CNN, TBS, and ESPN. The advertisements were monitored in the top seventy-five media markets. While there are over two hundred media markets in the U.S., the seventy-five selected cover more than 80 percent of the U.S. population.

32. The median voter's ideal point is estimated using demographic and political information from the district. For more information, see Abrajano and Morton (2005).

33. See Abrajano and Morton (2005) for more information.

8

The Mass Media and Voters' Information

Candidate Information and the Media

The Temperature of the Media

On the Fox News Channel on Tuesday, September 14, 2004, Sean Hannity began the *Hannity and Colmes* interview show with the following statement: "There you have it. Only 49 days until George W. Bush continues his duties as president of the United States. But it seems like some in the news media, that they want to keep that from happening and they want to do it at any cost."[1] Hannity was referring to the Wednesday, September 8 broadcast of *60 Minutes*, on which anchorman Dan Rather claimed to have access to memos from the national guard that impugned George W. Bush's record of service during the Vietnam War. Immediately, the documents, available from CBS.com, were given intense scrutiny by conservative bloggers like Mike Krempasky of Greensburg, Pennsylvania, one of the founders of the Web site Rathergate.com. It turned out that the bloggers discovered that the documents might not be what they claimed to be and the facts had not been checked adequately. By September 20, Dan Rather had apologized on the prime-time *CBS Evening News* show: "We made a mistake in judgment and for that I am sorry."[2] Conservative commentators pounced on the episode as an example of an obvious liberal bias that had led to slipshod journalistic standards. For example, Pat Buchanan argued in an editorial in the Pittsburgh *Tribune-Review*: "It was pride and blind hatred of the right that led him [Dan Rather] to commit a journalistic atrocity that will end up killing not the president's re-election, but his own reputation and career."[3]

The CBS News story on the national guard memos was just one of several controversies over the role of the mass media in the presidential election of 2004. The debate over the failure of CBS News to adequately research the guard memos, the *Fahrenheit 9/11* advertisements, and the broadcast of the documentary about the documentary *Stolen Honor* illustrate the tension in a society in which freedom of the press is considered a hallmark but perceptions of bias and the influence of the media on a public making political choices worries many. A number of recent books have argued, using anecdotal evidence, that the media is biased, from Goldberg (2002) and Coulter (2002) claiming a left-wing bias to Alterman (2003) and Franken (2003) asserting a right-wing bias. There is evidence that journalists are more likely to be liberals. Only 7 percent of national journalists surveyed by Pew in March and April of 2004 described themselves as conservatives, while 34 percent described themselves as liberals and 54 percent as moderates. Eighty-eight percent of the national press felt that homosexuals should be accepted by society, rather than discouraged, compared with 51 percent in the general public.[4] *The New York Times* reported that only 8 percent of Washington correspondents supported George W. Bush in 2004.[5]

It isn't only writers of books on politics who think that the media is biased. Pew surveyed registered voters in late October 2004 concerning their views of the media's coverage of the presidential election. They found that 50 percent of respondents thought that most newspaper reporters and TV journalists wanted to see Kerry win the election and 58 percent felt that members of the news media often let their political preferences influence the way they reported the news (with 32 percent reporting that they thought such influence occurred sometimes). Furthermore, 37 percent of voters (52 percent of Republicans) felt the coverage was unfair to George W. Bush, and 27 percent of voters (26 percent of Democrats) felt the coverage was unfair to John Kerry.[6] Journalists themselves are divided on whether the news media is biased. When asked by Pew whether the criticism that journalists let their ideological views show too often was valid, nearly half, 46 percent, of top national editors and reporters agreed. Interestingly, while the Pew numbers show a public that is more likely to perceive the news media as having a liberal bias, news-media professionals perceive a more conservative bias. Thirty-eight percent of national news-media members felt that there were news organizations that were too liberal (20 percent particularly mentioned *The New York Times*), while 82 percent felt there were some that were especially conservative (62 percent particularly mentioned Fox News).[7] Are these perceptions correct? Is the media biased? And if so, is there a liberal bias, a conservative bias, or both?

The Mass Media and Voters' Information

Campaign advertisements, financed by a candidate's campaign or supporters, are a way in which candidates and their supporters attempt to communicate with voters through the mass media. But much of what is said (or is not said) about candidates in the mass media is determined by the producers of news programs on television and radio, the publishers of newspapers, and producers of other mass-media products, such as movies, Internet Web sites, and so on. How much do these information sources affect voters?

There is evidence that the more voters are exposed to the mass media, the more likely they are to be informed about candidates. For example, the NES asks voters whether they saw, heard, or read about campaigns on television, radio, or newspapers. Figure 8.1 presents the percentages of voters who could recall the names of congressional incumbents and their challengers as a function of the number of different types of mass media they reported using in 2000. Notice that for both types of candidates, an increase in media exposure increases the probability that a voter can recall their name, although for challengers the effect is most pronounced when respondents use all three sources.

While this evidence is simplistic, the relevant research is not. Bartels (1993) conducted an extensive study of mass-media exposure using surveys

FIGURE 8.1
Voters' Recollection of Congressional Candidates' Names as a Function of Media Exposure, 2000

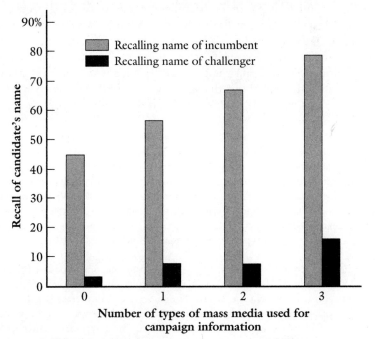

Source: National Election Studies.

of voters taken four times during and after the 1980 presidential election. He found that exposure to the mass media had a significant effect on a variety of measures of voters' preferences in the presidential race. For example, the maximum exposure to television news coverage of the campaign affected voters' approval ratings of incumbent president Jimmy Carter by about 6 percent, and the maximum exposure to newspaper coverage of the campaign affected these ratings by almost 2.5 percent (the maximum exposure was actually quite small in terms of the voter's time commitment). Hence, exposure to the mass media affects voters' knowledge of candidates and their preferences for candidates.

A Biased Information Source?

Defining Media Bias

Before we determine whether the media is biased, we need to define what we mean by media bias. Bias can happen in many ways. Journalists can blatantly falsify information that is supportive of their bias. Less transparently, they can fail to check adequately whether the information they want to report is true while overzealously double-checking information they dislike. This is what Dan Rather and CBS News were accused of doing. Journalists can present some facts prominently and contradictory facts less prominently or not at all. Journalists can frame the way in which facts are presented so that they seem to support one view of the world over an alternative view. To see how framing and selecting facts can influence how information is conveyed, consider two opening paragraphs of essentially the same length, published on the same day about the same event by different newspapers (the first quotation is from *The Seattle Times* and the second is from the *Las Vegas Review-Journal*):

> The former chief U.S. weapons inspector in Iraq issued a broad critique of U.S. intelligence gathering yesterday, saying the U.S. government was simply "wrong" to conclude before the war that Iraq was maintaining major stockpiles of weapons of mass destruction. Testifying before the Senate Armed Services Committee, David Kay said that contrary to earlier claims by President Bush and his Cabinet, Iraqi leader Saddam Hussein did not possess "large stockpiles" of chemical and biological weapons and was not actively pursuing nuclear weapons.[8]

> After hearing testimony Wednesday by former U.S. weapons inspector David Kay, Sen. John Ensign said he still is convinced that President Bush's decision to invade Iraq was correct. Kay told the Senate Armed Services Committee that he did not find any weapons of mass destruction after the war and was wrong in believing beforehand of the existence of such weapons in Iraq. But Kay added that Iraq clearly was violating United Nations resolutions requiring disclosure of weapons activities. "There will always be unresolved ambiguity here," Kay said.[9]

The first statement emphasizes the failure to find weapons of mass destruction (WMDs) and the fact that Bush and his cabinet had claimed they existed, and it puts the word *wrong* in quotation marks; the second statement emphasizes that the senator from Nevada believed Kay's testimony supported Bush's decision, that Iraq was violating UN resolutions, and that there was continued uncertainty over whether WMDs existed in Iraq, and it does not put the word *wrong* in quotation marks. Even the headlines say very different things. The first article has a headline quoting Kay—"It Turns Out We Were All Wrong"—while the second headline highlights Ensign's interpretation—"Ensign, Gibbons Say Kay's Words Affirm Bush's Actions." Both present biased views of the event, in which Kay did both say that the intelligence was wrong and defend the Bush administration and cabinet against the criticism that they had pressured the intelligence agencies to provide false information.

We define media bias as occurring when members of the news media use their news choices in a way that is not perfectly truthful given the information and resources available to the news organization and thus we include all of these types of biases. Yet this is an incomplete definition because it ignores the fact that with regard to political information, media bias has a direction as well as a size. Dan Rather wasn't just accused of having a bias but was accused of having a liberal bias. We define a bias as liberal (or conservative) if the way in which the truth is altered is seen as supporting a view of the world that liberals (or conservatives) prefer.

Measuring Media Bias

Just the Facts, Ma'am While anecdotes suggest that media bias exists, how widespread is it? Has it changed over time? Is it liberal, conservative, or balanced? To answer these questions, we need to have an objective measure of media bias. Since we have defined media bias as an alteration of the truth, ideally we want some measure of the truth that we can compare to media coverage. We also need to be able to quantify what is meant by a liberal (or conservative) view of the world in order to measure the direction of the bias. One easy way to measure a deviation from the truth is to examine how the media reports quantifiable data, such as presidential-approval ratings or economic statistics. There are two ways in which the media might bias such data—reporting it only when it potentially benefits the perspective of liberals (or conservatives) or framing the presentation of the data to potentially benefit liberals (or conservatives).

Four studies have taken this route:

1. Ansolabehere, Snowberg, and Snyder (2004) compared the reporting on campaign expenditures, contributions, or receipts from 1996 to 2000 in the five U.S. newspapers with the largest circulation to the information

available from the FEC. That is, they used the data as reported in the media in individual stories to estimate what is contained in the publicly available campaign reports. Interestingly, they found that the newspapers' figures aggregated in this fashion exceed the comparable FEC figures by as much as eight times. They also found that the press focuses excessively on soft money and corporate contributions although the majority of campaign contributions are both hard money and from individuals. Furthermore, the biased reporting seems to have an effect on voters' information—survey respondents, particularly better-educated ones who read newspapers, are more likely to overstate the amount of money spent and perceive that soft money and corporations are more involved in campaign finance than is actually the case. While insightful and illustrative of an issue in media bias that we discuss in the next section, this study does not make clear whether the bias involved is liberal or conservative. In fact, the Democrats received a greater percentage of soft money and corporate donations during this period, and as we have seen, the regulation of such moneys in 2004 had a more negative effect on the Democrats' ability to mobilize and motivate voters, given that reliance, than it had on the Republicans' ability to mobilize and motivate.

2. Groeling and Kernell (1998) considered the decisions of the television networks to report presidential-approval polls as a function of whether the approval ratings are declining or not. They focused on whether the networks are more likely to emphasize declining approval ratings (bad news) over rising ones (good news). They found at best weak evidence of a tendency to produce bad news more often than good. They did not examine whether there is a partisan or ideological dimension to the reporting, primarily because the time period they examined (1990–95) covers only two presidents (George H. W. Bush and Bill Clinton), and it is impossible to separate partisan and ideological differences from idiosyncratic personal differences between the two.

3. Lott and Hassert (2004) examined media bias in the reporting of a variety of economic statistics from 1991 to 2004 (they examined a much smaller set of newspapers during previous years). However, they did not test whether information was withheld or revealed, as in Groeling and Kernel, or truthful, as in Ansolabehere, Snowberg, and Snyder, but they examined whether the headlines of newspapers whose content was available from LexisNexis at the time these economic figures were released reported them positively or negatively. For example, a negative headline on the release of data on the number of new jobs in the economy might read as one did in the January 8, 2005, issue of *The New York Times*—"Jobs Picture Shows Some Signs of Life"—or a positive headline on the same statistics might read as one did in a story in the *Los Angeles Times* from the same day—"Job Growth in 2004 Best Since 1999." Technically, Lott and Hassert's study is not an evaluation of the "truth" of the reporting since they did not have an estimate of how the information should be revealed, although they did have a clear understanding of the fact to be reported (the statistic). They found

that in the aggregate newspapers presented economic statistics more positively under Clinton's administration than they did during the administrations of either George H. W. Bush or George W. Bush, even controlling for the better economic conditions during the Clinton years. The *Chicago Tribune*, Associated Press, *New York Times*, *Wall Street Journal*, and *Washington Post* tend to be the least likely to report positive news during Republican administrations. Not all the newspapers demonstrated a Democratic bias, however. For example, the *Houston Chronicle* (George H. W. Bush's hometown paper) had a slight Republican bias, and the *Los Angeles Times* (Ronald Reagan's hometown paper) presented figures more positively during Reagan's administration than during Clinton's.

4. In contrast to Lott and Hassert's study, Niven (2001) examined the reporting on one particular economic statistic, unemployment, from February 1989 to September 1999 in 150 newspapers, considering at least two papers from every state. He analyzed news stories on the unemployment rate for whether they explicitly mentioned the incumbent president positively, neutrally, or negatively, and he coded news stories on a three-point scale (1 was positive, 2 was neutral, 3 was negative). He found no significant differences in the coverage of George H. W. Bush and Bill Clinton on unemployment; the average coverage for Bush was 2.3 while the average for Clinton was 2.2, suggesting no bias in the reporting on unemployment. He did find that the media coverage is more likely to occur when the unemployment rate is high, suggesting that the media is more likely to cover bad news.

Measuring Ideological Placement Although the ideal way of measuring bias is by comparing "truth" to reporting, requiring a measure of the "truth" severely limits the extent to which we can measure bias, particularly in areas where the public is likely to be least informed or there is a great deal of uncertainty about the truth that may never be resolved. We already noted that Lott and Hassert did not attempt to define a truthful way for reporters to present statistics on economics. But the problem is deeper than that for a number of important issues. For example, George W. Bush, after his reelection in 2004, began to push for privatization of Social Security. He claimed that Social Security was in financial straits and that privatization was needed to keep the program afloat. He also argued that privatization was better for retirees in the long run, allowing them to achieve higher returns on their investments. Democrats contended that Social Security was not in financial trouble and that privatization hurts retirees. Who was right? Both had plenty of statistics and facts to support their point of view. Given that we can never have two different countries under exactly the same conditions running alternative plans, we can never know who was ultimately right. The presentation of facts and information on this issue is arguably more potentially consequential to voters than is the presentation of economic growth rates or presidential-approval ratings.

Groseclose and Milyo (2003) contended that defining and measuring bias as a deviation from the truth suggests a negative connotation to what may simply be a reporter's marshaling of the facts in a manner that makes ideological sense to him or her and others in the public but may imply a view of the world that is either more liberal or more conservative than the current median voter's view. Thus, measuring bias only as a deviation from a known truth misses a significant part of the ideological nature of reporting. How can we deal with this problem if we want to measure bias? A number of researchers have taken the approach of estimating the ideological bias of various media sources by measuring the ideological makeup of their readers. For example, Sutter (2004) showed that as a region becomes more liberal, the consumption of the newsmagazines *Time, Newsweek*, and *U.S. News and World Report* increases. Hamilton (2004) provided an ideological rating for news outlets by the ideology of their readers as measured by Pew and the ratings that consumers assign to the outlets. He found that Fox News is considered one of the most conservative outlets and that magazines such as *The Atlantic, The New Yorker*, and *Harper's* are rated most liberal. Hamilton also found that conservatives are more likely to see the media as biased than liberals are, which, he maintained, suggests an overall liberal bias in the media.

Although these indirect measures are indicative of a biased media, they do not prove that the reporting is actually biased or, if it is, biased in the direction of voter ideology unless we know for sure that voters choose media that has biases similar to their ideological preferences. Most studies of media bias look for balance in terms of coverage; that is, the assumption is that if a report or a news outlet gives equal weight to two opposing viewpoints, then the media outlet is unbiased. These types of analyses provide mixed results. Lowry and Shidler (1995) analyzed sound bites about candidates during the 1992 presidential election and found that they were significantly more negative toward Republicans than Democrats. However, Domke et al. (1997) analyzed a random sample of 12,215 news stories during the 1996 presidential campaign and found that the ratio of positive to negative stories was 1.8 for Bill Clinton and 1.7 for his opponent, Bob Dole.

An alternative to checking for balance is comparing the reporting of the news with the versions of reality presented by liberals and conservatives. If news reports sound the same as a known liberal (or conservative) public official speaking on the issue, we can classify the news organization producing the reports as having a liberal (or conservative) bias. How can we make such a comparison? Groseclose and Milyo (2003) devised a clever way. For major media outlets such as *The New York Times* and the Fox News show *Special Report*, they estimated scores similar to those given by Americans for Democratic Action to members of Congress. They first counted up all the times the media outlets cited various think tanks and policy groups. They excluded editorial statements and opinion pieces such as letters to the editor, book reviews, and so on, since it is possible for the news pages to have a liberal (or conservative) bias while the editorial and opinion page has a conservative (or liberal) perspective.[10] They then compared these counts with the times that members of Congress cited the same groups in their speeches in the House of Representatives and the Senate, and they used the comparison to estimate where the media outlets would be if they were making a speech in the House or the Senate and thus constructed an ADA score for each media outlet from that comparison.[11] To understand the process, suppose that there are just two groups cited in congressional speeches and the media: the Thoughtful Think Tank (TTT) and the Particular Policy Program (PPP). Suppose that *Special Report* mentions TTT twice as often as PPP. We assign to Fox the ADA score that is assigned to a member of Congress who also cites TTT twice as often as PPP. That member might be, for example, Republican senator Susan Collins from Maine. Then we conclude that Fox News has a similar bias in ideology as Collins demonstrates in the Senate.[12]

Figure 8.2 presents the scores of the various news organizations measured by Groseclose and Milyo as compared with the estimated ADA scores of selected members of Congress. The analysis shows that the most liberal media outlet turns out to be the news pages of *The Wall Street Journal*, at 85.1, which is close to Senator John Kerry and the average Democrat in Congress. Next in line are *The New York Times* and *CBS Evening News*, both at 73.7, and the *Los Angeles Times*, at 70. Most of the remaining news outlets have ADA scores ranging between 55 and 67, with PBS's *NewsHour* at 55.8. Only two news outlets have scores below 40, Fox's *Special Report* at 39.4 and *The Washington Times* at 35.4. Note that there are no news outlets more conservative than the average Republican legislator.

Although it is clear from Groseclose and Milyo's analysis that the media has a range of ideological perspectives, it is not so clear, if we accept the ADA measures, that the media overall has a liberal or conservative bias without some measure of the median voter in the electorate. Most of the news outlets appear in the range of moderate members of Congress, such as former senator John Breaux of Louisiana, who was known for his bipartisanship. Is the appropriate estimate of the median voter the median in the Congress? Groseclose and Milyo noted that there are a number of problems with assuming that the median in Congress is the median in the electorate. For example, small states are overrepresented in the Senate, and District of Columbia voters have no representation. To deal with these and other disconnects between the policy positions of members of Congress and the median voters in the electorate as a whole, they created a mythical Congress, a mirror of the electorate, assuming that each member of Congress accurately represented the median voter in his or her district, and then estimated the mean voter's ideal point for the mythical Congress at 50.1 (they used both median and mean but focused more on the mean because the median fluctuates more with changes in control of Congress). They then concluded that most media outlets are more liberal than the average American voter. Furthermore, they compared the distance between outlets and their estimate

IDEOLOGICAL SCORE

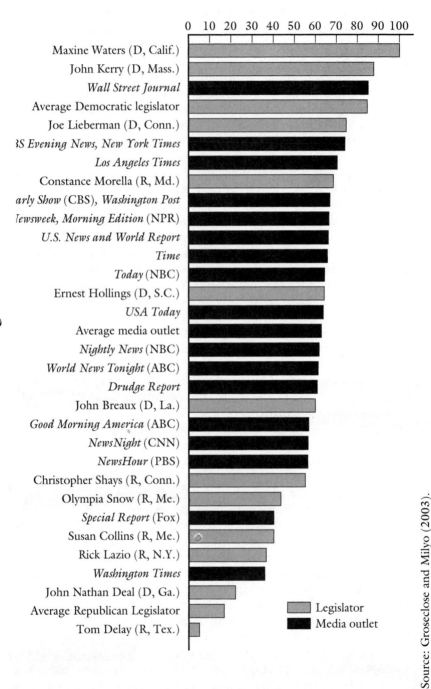

Source: Groseclose and Milyo (2003).

of the average voter as a measure of extremism so that they could consider which is more extreme, *The Washington Times* and Fox's *Special Report* or *CBS Evening News* and *The New York Times*. They found that the liberal media outlets are more extreme (farther from their estimate of the median voter) than the conservative ones.

Media Bias as Agenda Control In our discussion so far, we have focused on media bias as the selective use and presentation of facts relevant to an issue. But an alternative way of thinking of bias is that there are a set of issues to choose from in reporting, rather than a set of facts, and a media bias can occur by the media's emphasizing issues that benefit particular candidates or parties. As we noted in chapter 7, one way in which candidates can use campaign advertising to influence voters is by emphasizing particular issues and taking stances on those issues. We observed that George W. Bush took a more conservative position on the issue of gay marriage when the situation in Iraq began to deteriorate, and survey evidence suggested that a significant percentage of voters would support him on that issue over other concerns. If there are issues on which one party is closer to the median voter than the other party, then we might expect that party to want voters to weight that issue highly in their choice of candidates. Alternatively, we can think of some issues before voters as primarily valence issues (as discussed in chapter 5), and we can suppose that voters perceive that political parties have valence advantages on different issues. From the voters' perspective, we can think of some issues as more advantageous to one party. Petrocik (1996) argued that some issues are therefore "owned" by particular parties. He showed that these "owned" issues tend to be emphasized by candidates in their speeches and when Democratic (or Republican) issues are salient, more Democrats (or Republicans) vote, fewer Republicans (or Democrats) vote, and independents swing toward the Democrats (or the Republicans).

If issues are indeed owned, then the strategic choices in covering issues may influence the salience of them for voters. Puglisi (2004) examined this question by studying the coverage of issues in *The New York Times* from 1946 to 1994. Since Petrocik's data analysis of issue ownership considered only a short time period (1988 to 1991), Puglisi first collected a much more extensive data set on issue ownership. While there are variations over time in the distribution of issues, Democrats are perceived to have advantages in civil rights (particularly from 1964 on), welfare, and health care, whereas Republicans are perceived to have advantages in law and crime (from 1972 on, with the exception of 1976 and 1992) and defense (with the exception of 1964 and 1980). Puglisi found (controlling for other factors that might influence news coverage) that *The New York Times* gives more emphasis to issues owned by the Democrats during presidential campaigns when the incumbent president is a Republican, suggesting that *The New York Times* does demonstrate some partisan bias. He also found that when there is no presidential campaign under way, the *Times* covers more Democratic issues when the incumbent president is a Democrat.

The studies of Ansolabehere, Snowberg, and Snyder; Groeling and Kernell; Lott and Hassert; Niven; Sutter; Hamilton; Groseclose and Milyo; and Puglisi provide a general picture of bias in reporting. There is evidence that most national media outlets have a liberal bias, although the extent of the bias varies by outlet and several outlets have a clearly measurable conservative bias. Given that biases exist, what are their sources? Do biases affect voters' behavior in elections and as a consequence public policy?

The Sources and Effects of Media Bias

Media Demand and Supply

We considered both the supply and the demand sides of campaign spending; that is, we first considered the motivations behind the supply of contributions in terms of why contributors give money to candidates, and then we analyzed the demand side, or the uses for campaign spending by candidates to reach voters. The market for political information similarly has both supply and demand sides. On the supply side, we need to think about issues like the cost of producing news, the wages of journalists, changes in technology, and so on.

The demand side is a bit more complicated. Who exactly are the demanders of the mass media? While the answer to this question seems straightforward—the purchasers of newspapers, the viewers of television news reports, the listeners of radio news programs—the news media's revenues are primarily from advertisers or sponsors rather than the actual consumers of the news, a situation that is unlike most other industries, where demand and revenue are directly connected. Advertisers pay for programs they hope will reach the segment of the public they wish will see their ads. Some news organizations are nonprofit, publicly supported organizations, which seek a mixture of corporate sponsors and contributions from individuals who use the media and have particular preferences for programming. This means that it is not always desirable for the mass media to reach a large audience, just a "good" audience, one that is either attractive to advertisers or likely to generate support from sponsors. For example, the television show *Gunsmoke*, which had a large number of viewers, was canceled because its audience was too old and too rural and thus not attractive to advertisers (Barnouw 1979, p. 69).

We can think of the demand side of the market for political information as having two stages: first, a news-media organization, such as CBS News or National Public Radio (NPR), determines the optimal demand group for its product given the preferences of advertisers or sponsors that pay for the product, and second, a news-media organization chooses how to present its product to that demand group or audience in order to maximize the number reached. We begin our analysis by looking at the second, or bottom, stage. That is, we assume that a news-media organization has already determined an audience (for example, we might say that CBS News has decided it wants to appeal to affluent individuals who buy SUVs because doing so will lead to higher revenue) and desires to maximize the number of individuals in the group who use their news product. We consider what factors are likely to lead to media bias as CBS News attempts to appeal to its audience. Then we consider what factors might lead CBS News to choose SUV purchasers as their audience and whether those factors are likely to lead to media bias. As we investigate both of these stages, we will see that supply-side factors are also important in leading to media bias.

The Audience as a Source of Media Bias

What Do Readers, Listeners, Viewers Want? When we think of the demand side of the media, we are considering the factors that influence the extent to which individuals seek out political news. At one extreme, we can think of consumers of news as rational individuals who desire to get the most accurate, unbiased information possible. For some things, like purchasing a car or choosing whether to purchase a stock, individuals want accurate information so that they can maximize their expected utility. They want to know the safety records of the automobiles or the expected profit of the company issuing the stock. At another extreme, we can think of consumers of news as looking for entertainment in the news itself, as something that they find interesting, compelling, or enjoyable independent of what information they gather. Whether or not the information is biased does not bother them since the main value is its entertainment rather than its content. Psychologists have shown that individuals generally like to hear confirmation of their beliefs, so news consumers may also enjoy hearing news that is biased if the bias confirms their beliefs.[13] We define the first extreme as the *investment* benefits from news, since the consumer is acquiring news in order to make a decision and wants that news to be unbiased, and we define the second extreme as the *consumption* benefits from news, since the consumer is gaining utility from the news itself, not the information it provides about the future, and is willing to tolerate a bias and might even prefer one.

We assume that consumers of political information have both motives. They want to make informed political decisions in the future and therefore want accurate, unbiased information. But they enjoy the consumption benefits of news as well. Because of the small probability that one person's vote or political action individually has an effect on the group choice, the individual investment benefits might be quite small and the consumption benefits more sizable and determinant. For example, a conservative radio listener named Janice has a choice of hearing the day's political news from Bob Edwards (formerly the host of *Morning Edition* on NPR) or conservative commentator Rush Limbaugh. Janice thinks that the news presented on NPR is relatively balanced but that Limbaugh has a definite conservative bias and doesn't reveal all the facts. Yet she enjoys hearing someone present her point of view strongly, which Limbaugh's reporting allows him to do. Janice also knows that Edwards injects humor into his news summaries only occasionally, but Limbaugh often does, plus he plays lively music and invites calls from listeners, who say surprising things. Because the investment benefits of Janice's political decisions are small and Limbaugh is more entertaining and she likes hearing support for her views, she might rather hear her news from Limbaugh than from Edwards.

The Effect of Competition If most people are like Janice, then news outlets will seek to meet that demand. Does this mean that the news that individuals receive will be biased and that the public will have little knowledge of the truth? Not necessarily. Mullainathan and Shleifer (2005) demonstrated that when voters prefer biased news, as Janice does, the likelihood of an overall bias of total information will depend on the distribution of voters' biases. The more heterogeneous the biases of the news-purchasing public, the more unbiased the overall news coverage will be, even though individual news organizations might be biased. *The Seattle Times* interpretation of David Kay's testimony before the Senate, emphasizing the failure of the Bush administration, will be balanced by the interpretation of the *Las Vegas Review-Journal*, focusing on Kay's defense of Bush.

How does this work? Suppose the story reported in the news media is about Bush's service in the national guard. If the population of news buyers is diverse, with some biased toward seeing Bush's service in a favorable light and an almost equal number wishing to see Bush's service in an unfavorable light, then the competition of media outlets will result in the provision of accurate information. CBS News was forced to correct its story on Bush's service, which was based on inaccurate documents. Conservative bloggers served as a check on CBS because public opinion was sufficiently diverse and therefore there was a demand for an alternative viewpoint. Similarly, Mullainathan and Shleifer argue that during the Bill Clinton–Monica Lewinsky scandal, the competition among different biased news outlets led to an overall accurate interpretation of events. As we noted above, Hamilton (2004) and Sutter (2004) provided evidence that readers do sort themselves according to different media outlets, as Mullainathan and Shleifer predicted. According to a Pew survey of media use in June 2004, 35 percent of Republicans regularly watch Fox News, compared with 21 percent of Democrats; similarly, 28 percent of Democrats watch CNN regularly, compared with 19 percent of Republicans.[14] Not surprisingly, in a post-2004-election survey, Pew found that 70 percent of voters whose major source of news was Fox News preferred Bush, while only 26 percent of viewers of CNN did.[15]

When Competition Fails Yet while the coverage of Bush's national guard service and the Clinton-Lewinsky scandal may have arguably been fair on balance because of competition among biased media, the news media went through an unusual period of soul searching throughout 2004 over a different story, on which there had been little disagreement. On August 12, 2004, *The Washington Post* published a three-thousand-word front-page article criticizing its own news coverage on the issue of whether Iraq had WMDs. Executive editor Leonard Downie, Jr., summarized: "We were so focused on trying to figure out what the administration was doing that we were not giving the same play to people who said it wouldn't be a good idea to go to war and were questioning the administration's rationale. Not enough of those stories were put on the front page."[16] Earlier, on May 26, editors of *The New York Times* produced a similar mea culpa. They wrote: "We have found a number of instances of coverage that was not as rigorous as it should have been. In some cases, information that was controversial then, and seems questionable now, was insufficiently qualified or allowed to stand unchallenged. Looking back, we wish we had been more aggressive in re-examining the claims as new evidence emerged—or failed to emerge."[17] But outlets viewed as liberal were not the only ones to retract their support for the reasons for going to war in Iraq. In March 2003, before the Iraq war began, Fox News host Bill O'Reilly of *The O'Reilly Factor* had promised Charles Gibson of ABC's *Good Morning America*: "If the Americans go in and overthrow Saddam Hussein and it's clean, he has nothing, I will apologize to the nation and I will not trust the Bush administration again." On February 11, 2004, before the *Times* and the *Post* issued their retractions, O'Reilly kept his promise, stating on *Good Morning America*, "I was wrong. I'm not pleased about it at all. And I think all Americans should be concerned about this."

Why was the coverage so unbalanced that at least three major news outlets, including a media personality who presumably had a bias in favor of the administration, felt compelled to retract earlier statements? Mullainathan and Shleifer (2005) predicted that one-sided bias can occur when there is general public agreement on a particular biased view of an issue. This may explain the biased reporting on Iraq. In general, the American public favored force against Iraq. Even before September 11, when Clinton conducted military strikes against Iraq, a Pew survey on December 22, 1998, reported that 75 percent of the public approved of the action and only 20 percent disapproved. The support for military action in the Middle East rose after the September 11 attacks. A *USA Today*/CNN/Gallup poll conducted the weekend of September 15–16, 2001, found that 41 percent of Americans placed a great deal of blame for the attacks on Iraq, and 32 percent placed a moderate amount of blame on Iraq.[18] In mid-September 2001, 82 percent of Pew respondents favored military action, including ground troops, to retaliate against those responsible for the terrorist attacks. A *Newsweek* poll published on October 13, 2001, reported that 81 percent

ıns approved the use of direct military action against Iraqi leader
Iussein. When news organizations began to write stories about
e in terrorism and possession of WMDs toward the end of 2001
ughout 2002, the American public was largely predisposed to see
l Saddam Hussein as a threat and to blame them for the terrorist attacks. Therefore, Mullainathan and Shleifer's theory provides one explanation for the bias in reporting on the possibility of Saddam Hussein's
possession of WMDs—because of the homogeneity in opinion and voters'
preference for information that fit their given, largely homogeneous interpretation of the truth and was entertaining, the news coverage might have
been less critical and more biased in favor of military action.

Problems with the Consumption Theory of Media Bias The assumption
that most consumers of political news are like Janice—mainly making
choices based on entertainment and confirmation value rather than to gain
information—seems reasonable, given the small investment benefits in information acquisition when individuals make decisions on public policies in
voting and so on and helps explain why the news media might provide bias.
Yet there are some problems with this explanation. According to the theory
biased reporting occurs because people have a taste for it, much as we might
explain voting as occurring because people like to participate politically. But
as we saw in chapter 2, assuming that voters participate in elections purely
because of exogenous tastes for such an activity does not get us far in answering the bigger questions about voter turnout. Similarly, the theory of
demand-driven bias does not explain why individuals have biased views of
the world or why some voters prefer the bias at Fox News to the relatively
reduced bias at NPR (as measured by Groseclose and Milyo) but others
have the opposite preference, besides simply saying that people have different tastes. Ideally, we would like to be able to answer these questions.

We also would like to answer questions about how media bias varies over
time. In the mid–nineteenth century, the American press was extremely partisan.[19] Newspapers were closely affiliated with political parties. Yet by the
beginning of the twentieth century, the American press was arguably much
less partisan and less biased. Why did the change occur? If we assume bias is
primarily a psychologically determined taste, we can't explain the change. Is
the American press again becoming more partisan as elected officials and
party elites have polarized (as discussed in chapter 4)? And if so, why? We
need to move beyond assuming a taste for bias to answer this question as
well.

There is also a factual problem with the assumption that biases are a response to consumer demand since it does not fit what most people say
about their news-consumption preferences. Table 8.1 presents the results of
a 2004 Pew survey that asked respondents what things about the news they
liked. The most popular aspect of the news is the presentation of debates between people with differing points of view (55 percent of all respondents

like news that does so), while a minority, only 36 percent, prefer news that shares their point of view. This suggests that the majority of consumers want a diversity of views, not just one biased presentation. A sizable majority, 87 percent, prefer news that they can use in their daily life, which implies that they are seeking news for investment purposes (to make better decisions) rather than consumption (to be entertained). Moreover, 53 percent agree with the statement "I often don't trust what news organizations are saying," and 48 percent believe people who decide on news content are "out of touch." If consumers of the news wanted biased reporting and sought news outlets that presented news that confirmed their views, then we would expect the majority to trust what news organizations are saying and to think that those who are providing the news are "in touch" with them. Clearly, that is not what they think.

TABLE 8.1
Aspects of the News That Consumers Like

Aspect of the News	Respondents Who Like It (%)	Respondents Who Dislike It (%)	Respondents Who Are Indifferent (%)
Presents debates between people with differing points of view	55	6	38
Has reporters and anchors with pleasant personalities	53	3	43
Includes ordinary Americans giving their views	49	7	43
Makes the news enjoyable and entertaining	48	6	45
Is sometimes funny	46	6	47
Has in-depth interviews with political leaders and policy makers	46	9	44
Stirs your emotions	29	12	56
Shares your point of view on politics and issues			
All respondents	36	5	58
Respondents with low political knowledge	18	7	71
Respondents with moderate political knowledge	35	5	59
Respondents with high political knowledge	42	3	53

Agree or disagree with the statement	Respondents Who Agree (%)	Respondents Who Disagree (%)	Respondents Who Are Not Sure (%)
"Want the news to contain information that is helpful in my daily life"	87	11	2

Source: Pew Research Center Report, June 8, 2004.
Note: Totals are approximate.

Finally, there is a lot of evidence that although most news consumers did hold the view that Iraq was dangerous, was involved with terrorists, and had WMDs, the same news consumers were extremely motivated to gather accurate and unbiased information about the world situation, making it less likely that a demand for bias can explain the tendency of the media to bias its reporting on the issue. In mid-September 2001, Pew reported that 96 percent of news consumers were following stories on the terrorists' attacks closely. The percentage remained high (in the high 80s low 90s) throughout the fall of 2001. In comparison, in a 1997 summary of ten years of respondents' interest in various issues, only 57 percent reported following presidential campaigns and elections closely (the 1988, 1992, and 1996 presidential campaigns), 49 percent reported following major sports events closely (the 1996 Summer Olympics in Atlanta, the 1992 Winter Olympics, and the 1988 World Series), and 42 percent reported following celebrity scandals (Jim Bakker's guilty verdict, Mike Tyson's rape trial, and the banishment of Pete Rose from baseball).[20] The same surveys after the terrorist attacks found a marked rise in the number of respondents worried about a terrorist attack—in August 1998, 29 percent were not worried at all about a terrorist attack (the remaining percentage had some degree of worry). But after the attacks, the number dropped over ten percentage points, remaining lower for the rest of the fall. Consumers wanted information about terrorism because they worried about the consequences. Given the intense interest of consumers in information on terrorism, their desire to have information they could use, and their worries at the time, it seems unlikely that consumption benefits drove their choices such that they preferred biased information and that that would explain the reporting on Iraq.

Therefore, we consider some other sources of media bias, assuming that individuals prefer unbiased, accurate information. By assuming that all voters prefer unbiased information and are consuming news for investment purposes, we can focus on nonconsumer-demand sources of bias. It is important to remember, however, that in the real world we fully expect both factors are involved in media demand and that there is a real demand for bias in response to the psychological and consumption benefits, as discussed above, just as such concerns cannot explain many aspects of the media bias we observe such as consumers complaints about media bias and changing partisanship of the media over time. We take the modeling strategy of disregarding these motivations so that we can better determine the sources of biased information beyond consumer demand.

Journalists as a Source of Media Bias

Private Decisions and Political Information We begin our examination of the nonconsumer-demand sources of media bias by considering the motivations of journalists. Baron (2004) provided an interesting model of journalists as a source of media bias. In it, there are three basic players: consumers, journalists, and owners. Consumers use the news media to help them make a private decision when their utility from that decision depends on an uncertain political matter. For example, suppose that in October 2004, Arthur is deciding whether to buy a new car and would really like to purchase a Hummer H2, an SUV modeled after a military vehicle commonly called the Humvee. But he is worried about gas prices. His dealer says that the Hummer gets only eight to ten miles per gallon. He could get a Ford Expedition, which gets fourteen to nineteen miles per gallon, or he could wait until April 2005, as he has heard that Toyota is going to come out with a sport-utility vehicle that is supposed to get compact-car gas mileage, the Lexus RX 400h.[21] But he wants to take a camping vacation in the Southwest during the winter holidays and drive through rural areas where he would need an SUV. And his old non-SUV needs a lot of repairs if it is going to make it until April. He figures if gas prices are going to rise significantly, he should wait, repair his old car, and postpone the vacation; if gas prices are going to stay relatively constant, he should buy the Expedition; and if they are going to go down, he should splurge now and buy the Hummer.

Arthur expects gas prices will depend on who wins the 2004 presidential election, and he figures that both candidates are equally likely to win. Gas prices rose during the spring and summer, breaking records, with the national average at $1.82.[22] Arthur figures that if Bush stays in office, gas prices will stay at about that level, and he would probably be best off with the Ford Expedition, which would give him a utility level of 75. But he is not sure what would happen if Kerry wins. He figures that if Kerry wins, gas prices might fall, since Kerry wants to stop adding to the strategic reserves and lobby OPEC, as well as engage in other measures to lower prices, and he has campaigned on the issue of lowering gas prices.[23] If prices are going to be lower, Arthur could buy the Hummer, which would give him 100 utils. But Bush has said that Kerry would raise gas taxes and has pointed out that Kerry voted for gas-tax increases eleven times in the Senate.[24] So gas prices might rise if Kerry raises taxes, in which case Arthur should wait until 2005, repairing his old car and altering his vacation plans, which would mean a utility level of 10.

We can think of there being two states of the world if Kerry wins, one in which he does not raise taxes, he enacts his other policies, and gas prices are lower, and one in which he does raise taxes and gas prices are higher. Suppose that both states of the world are believed by the general public to be equally likely; that is, the prior general perception is that there is a 50/50 chance that Kerry will raise gas taxes.[25] We can imagine that there are lots of different consumers like Arthur who are making private consumption decisions before an election for which they are gathering information about whether Kerry will raise gas taxes. For example, Charlotte and Dimitri might, like Arthur, see their utility from gas prices under Bush as 75 utils and their utility if Kerry does not raise taxes as 100. But Charlotte's utility if gas taxes are raised is 50 utils, while Dimitri's is 60 utils, as shown in table 8.2.

TABLE 8.2
Some Utility Payoffs from Bush's and Kerry's Election

	State of the World If Kerry Is Elected	
	Kerry raises gas taxes.	Kerry does not raise gas taxes.
Arthur's, Charlotte's, and Dimitri's Utility If Bush Wins	75	75
Arthur's Utility If Kerry Wins	10	100
Charlotte's Utility If Kerry Wins	50	100
Dimitri's Utility If Kerry Wins	60	100

If we assume that voters' preferences in the election are purely a function of their personal concerns, given the prior public perceptions, Arthur will support Bush because his expected utility if Kerry wins is $= 0.5 \cdot (100) + 0.5 \cdot (10) = 55$ utils, while his expected utility if Bush wins is 75 utils. Charlotte is indifferent in choosing between Bush and Kerry because her expected utility if Kerry wins is $= 0.5 \cdot (100) + 0.5 \cdot (50) = 75$ utils, the same as she will get if Bush wins, while Dimitri's expected utility is higher under Kerry, $0.5 \cdot (100) + 0.5 \cdot (60) = 80 > 75$.

Notice that in Baron's model, as well as in Stromberg (2004a), Arthur, Charlotte, and Dimitri would like to have information about whether Kerry will raise gas taxes because they want to make better individual private decisions for the future. In this way, it is rational for them to want information relevant to the election regardless of whether their vote will be consequential. Unlike the investment benefits from voting, their investment benefits from acquiring political information are dependent not on the probability that their participation in political decisions is decisive but on the relationship between their private decisions and political matters—those who feel that politics can have a sizable impact on the consequences of their private decisions will want to have the most political information.

Thus, the demand for political information can have an investment component even if the demand derived from the effect of one's individual political-participation decision is likely to be small, as noted above. The role of groups (benefit and office seeking) that helped us resolve the paradox of not voting in chapter 2 might also explain individual investment demand for political information beyond that desired for private decisions. Clearly the set of individuals who have roles as group leaders have an incentive to be informed about politics so that they can lead their groups to make better political decisions. Hence, leaders in the community who mobilize voters (as discussed in chapter 3), such as Pastor Timothy Wilder and Michigan labor union member Bob Allison, receive significant investment benefits from being informed. At the individual-member level, purposive incentives used by benefit-seeking groups to motivate voters (discussed in chapter 2) tie individual utility to the effects of political outcomes on a group as a whole. As a consequence, individuals who have internalized such incentives might also perceive a greater investment benefit in being knowledgeable about politics even if their individuals vote are not consequential. We could think of Arthur's, Charlotte's, and Dimitri's utility from different gas prices as personal preferences on energy policy, and Dimitri's higher utility from higher gas prices could reflect those preferences. Accordingly, investment motives for gaining political information should not be ruled out simply because of the paradox of not voting.

Enter a Journalist Wishing to Write a Story Now let's add a journalist for a major newspaper, Kanchan. She covers domestic policy for the newspaper. A source she knows suggests that there is a high probability that Kerry has a secret plan to raise gas taxes, but the source's information is not verifiable. Kanchan tries to find verifiable information. Obviously, if Kerry has no secret plan, she will not find the evidence. So we will call the probability that Kanchan finds evidence given that Kerry has a secret plan $\Pr(E|No\ Plan) = 0$, and we will call the probability that Kanchan finds no evidence given that Kerry has no secret plan $\Pr(No\ E|No\ Plan) = 1$. But if Kerry has a secret plan, she might find evidence or she might not. Given the limitations of resources and time, if Kanchan finds no evidence, she can never be sure Kerry does not have a secret plan because she can never know whether she simply failed to find evidence that did exist. Let's assume that if Kerry has a secret plan, the probability that Kanchan finds verifiable information is 60 percent and the probability that she doesn't is 40 percent, as in Table 8.3. That is, $\Pr(E|Plan) = .6$ and $\Pr(No\ E|Plan) = .4$. We call this the quality of Kanchan's news organization, the time and resources she has to investigate the story and the sources she has available to her.

The asymmetry in what Kanchan can discover about the truth provides a useful insight into the difficulty of a lot of investigative news reporting. Suppose the question to be investigated were whether medical care in large city hospitals is safe. If Kanchan did not find evidence of problems with medical care, she could still not conclude that medical care is safe, since she might be looking at the wrong aspects of health care. Moreover, there is nonverifiable information (like the original source on Kerry) that she can tell a story about. That is, there are claims by individuals that they have suffered or had medical problems, but these claims are not verified. For any difficult, uncertain issue before the public that Kanchan would like to write about, like the

TABLE 8.3
Kanchan's Probability of Finding Verifiable Information

	Kerry has a secret plan to raise gas taxes: P(*Plan*) = 0.5.	Kerry does not have a secret plan to raise gas taxes: P(*No Plan*) = 0.5	Probability of Finding Evidence of Plan
Kanchan finds verifiable information.	P(E|*Plan*) = 0.6	P(E|*No Plan*) = 0	P(E) = (0.5)(0.6) + (0.5)(0) = 0.3
Kanchan does not find verifiable information.	P(*No E*|*Plan*) = 0.4	P(*No E*|*No Plan*) = 1	P(*No E*) = (0.5)(0.4) + (0.5)(1) = 0.7

safety of medical care or a candidate's plans for taxes, proving a negative can almost never be done with certainty, whereas if she finds some positive verifiable information, she has a story worth telling.

After searching for evidence and determining whether she can find some or not, Kanchan writes a story. If she finds evidence, she can either reveal the evidence or hide it; if she does not find evidence, she can either focus on the non verifiable information she has, making it sound better than it is, or reveal that she found no verifiable information.

Kanchan's Preferences Let's assume that Kanchan would prefer to write a story saying that Kerry has a secret plan. We assume she has such a preference for ideological reasons. That is, she believes that Bush is a better president than Kerry would be, independent of what happens with oil prices. As a specialist in domestic policy, she has become impressed with the Bush administration's programs in education and national security and would like to see the administration stay in office. She also has a lot of friends in the administration, and she would like to support them. She knows that the election is expected to be close and that if she could reveal that Kerry had a secret plan to raise gas taxes, the information might change the outcome of the election. Notice that Kanchan does not have a biased prior perception on the probability that Kerry's election will lead to an increase in gas prices; before she begins her research, she, like Arthur, Charlotte, and Dimitri, thinks that the probability is 50/50. But she would like to be able to write that she found evidence that Kerry will raise gas taxes in order to try to influence the views of Arthur, Charlotte, and Dimitri because she would like Bush to defeat Kerry.[26]

Given Kanchan's preference for writing a story about finding evidence, if she does find evidence, she will definitely write the story. But what if she doesn't find evidence? She knows that there is still a probability that Kerry will raise gas taxes. What is that probability? We assume that she updates her estimate that Kerry will raise gas taxes, using Bayes's rule, attributed to the eighteenth-century English minister Thomas Bayes. Bayes's rule allows one to calculate the conditional probability of an event given evidence. That is, suppose we are interested in finding out whether A is true given that we know B. The probability of the joint event of A and B together is equal to the probability of A given B times the probability of B, or $\Pr(A,B) = \Pr(A|B)P(B)$. We also know that the probability of this joint event is equal to the probability of B given A times the probability of A, or $\Pr(A,B) = \Pr(B|A)P(A)$. Combining terms, we can show that the probability of A given B is equal to the probability of B given A times the probability of A divided by the probability of B, or $\Pr(A|B) = \Pr(B|A)P(A)/P(B)$. Thus, Bayes's rule makes it possible to estimate conditional probabilities of things unknown given the probabilities of things known. We can calculate the probability that Kerry will raise gas taxes given that no evidence is found by multiplying the probability that we find no evidence given Kerry will raise gas taxes times the probability that Kerry will raise gas taxes divided by the probability of finding no evidence. That is, $\Pr(Plan|No\ E) = \Pr(No\ E|Plan)\Pr(Plan)/\Pr(No\ E) = (0.4)(0.5)/0.7 = 0.2857$. So there is a 29 percent chance that even though Kanchan found no evidence, Kerry will raise gas taxes.

Will Kanchan claim to have verifiable information even though she does not? While fabricating evidence sounds extreme, we could think of this more as reporting facts in a biased manner such that they suggest evidence that does not exist. Such fabrication can be quite subtle but powerful in terms of framing. For example, she might quote sources and present information that she knows is not credible. The independent panel reviewing the *60 Minutes Wednesday* story on Bush's national guard service noted that there was evidence that the source of the memos used in the reports, retired Texas national guard lieutenant colonel Bill Burkett, was not credible, given conflicting statements he had given to the press in 2000.[27] The review panel also found that the statement made by Dan Rather on the program about the memos—"We consulted a handwriting analyst and document expert who believes the material is authentic"—had no factual support since the analyst referred to did not authenticate the documents but had said only that he thought the signature on one document was authentic, with qualifications.[28]

Or Kanchan might color the presentation of information that she does find to make it sound highly likely that Kerry will raise gas taxes. For example, *60 Minutes Wednesday* presented an interview with former Texas national guard lieutenant Robert Strong, who had left the guard several months before the memos were written, had served 180 miles away from the place where Bush was stationed, and had said that he had no evidence that Bush had avoided service in Vietnam by joining the guard. *60 Minutes* presented Strong simply as someone who had served in the national guard during the Vietnam War and as a friend and colleague of the alleged memo author before airing general statements Strong made about well-connected young men using the guard to avoid service in Vietnam, suggesting that Strong did know the same was true about Bush. Yet prior to the airing of the interview, *60 Minutes* producer Mary Mapes had information from a number of credible sources that Bush had volunteered for service in Vietnam while in the guard but had been turned down in favor of more experienced pilots.[29] Thus, there is a degree to which Kanchan can try to present noncredible or incomplete information as evidence. We call this the discretion she has in writing her story. The more discretion she has, the more she can make it sound like she has evidence. We assume that the owner of the news outlet determines how much discretion Kanchan has. We can think of the discretion she has as the percentage of the time the owner lets her publish a story without having fully checked the facts. The greater the percentage of the time she can do that, the more discretion she has. Let's say that Kanchan has a degree of discretion of 20 percent; that is, 20 percent of the time she can claim to have evidence when she does not.

It is important to recognize that Kanchan might see herself as balanced. After all, even though she found no verifiable evidence, there is still a probability that Kerry will raise gas taxes since she knows that Kerry has voted in the Senate to raise gas taxes, and so by suggesting that there is such a possibility she might not be seen as lying. She may persuade herself that the evidence she found is persuasive and credible. Both CBS producer Mary Mapes and anchor Dan Rather told the panel of investigators that after CBS News apologized for airing unsubstantiated claims about Bush's national guard service, they continued to believe the memos were real. Rather remarked that he believed the content of the documents was true because "the facts are right on the money."[30] In support of such thinking, Patterson and Donsbach (1996) presented journalists from five Western democracies with news situations and asked them to make decisions about story content and headlines. They then compared their decisions with the journalists' self-identified ideology. They found that the journalists often made decisions that colored the facts to suit their ideological preferences without consciously being aware of their intentions.

Kanchan Writes Her Story In summary, Kanchan can thus write two types of stories, one that says she cannot find evidence and one that says she has found it. If she finds evidence, she reports it. If she does not find evidence, 20 percent of the time she will claim that she did find evidence and 80 percent of the time she will report she did not. What are Arthur, Charlotte, and Dimitri likely to think of the story? Much the way Kanchan considers whether or not she finds evidence and updates her ideas about whether Kerry will raise gas taxes using Bayes's rule, Arthur, Charlotte, and Dimitri can take Kanchan's story and update their ideas about whether Kerry will raise gas taxes. Assume they know Kanchan is biased in favor of reporting evidence. Suppose Kanchan writes a news report stating that she cannot find evidence that Kerry will raise gas taxes. Arthur, Charlotte, and Dimitri know that she is telling the truth and that the fact she did not find evidence means that the probability that Kerry will raise gas taxes is less than what they had thought before. If they know the quality of Kanchan's news organization, they can calculate that probability to be 29 percent.

But things are more complicated if Kanchan writes a news report in which she claims to have evidence that Kerry will raise gas taxes. Arthur, Charlotte, and Dimitri know that sometimes Kanchan is telling the truth when she claims to have evidence that Kerry will raise gas taxes and sometimes not because they know she is biased in favor of Bush. They also know that even if Kanchan is not telling the truth, Kerry may still be planning to raise gas taxes. It turns out that if they take all this into account, the probability that Kerry will raise gas taxes if Kanchan writes that it is so is greater than 0.5, which is what they thought before, as long as Kanchan does not have 100 percent discretion. In our example, given the quality of Kanchan's news organization and her degree of discretion, the probability that Kerry will raise gas taxes if Kanchan writes a story claiming to have evidence he will is approximately 77 percent. That is, using Bayes's rule, $\Pr(Plan|Story\ Claims\ Evidence) = \Pr(Plan)[(P(E|Plan) + \Pr(No\ E|Plan)(0.2)]/[\Pr(E) + \Pr(No\ E)(0.2)] = 0.5[0.6 + (0.4)(0.2)]/[(0.3) + (0.7)(0.2)] = 0.7727$. So if Kanchan writes a story saying there is no evidence, Arthur, Charlotte, and Dimitri can revise their expectation such that there is now a 29 percent chance Kerry will raise gas taxes and a 71 percent chance he will not raise gas prices. If Kanchan writes a story saying there is evidence, Arthur, Charlotte, and Dimitri can revise their expectation such that there is now a 77 percent chance Kerry will raise gas taxes and a 23 percent chance he will not raise gas taxes. Even though Kanchan has discretion and is biased, her news reporting can influence Arthur's Charlotte's and Dimitri's expectations.

Arthur, Charlotte, and Dimitri Choose Kanchan can influence their expectations, but will she also influence their preferences in the presidential election? Before Kanchan wrote her story Arthur, Charlotte, and Dimitri thought the probability Kerry would raise gas taxes was 50 percent. Arthur supported Bush, Charlotte was indifferent, and Dimitri supported Kerry. If Kanchan writes that she has no evidence, Dimitri will still support Kerry, since his expected utility is higher under Kerry than under Bush: $75 <(0.29)(60) + (0.71)(100) = 88.4$. However, now Charlotte also supports Kerry, since her expected utility is higher under Kerry than under Bush: $75 < (0.29)(50) + (0.71)(100) = 85.5$. What about Arthur? Arthur is still in favor of Bush, since $75 < (0.29)(10) > (0.71)(100) = 73.9$. So only Charlotte's preferences change as a result of the information.

If we think of the expected utility that a consumer such as Arthur, Charlotte, or Dimitri receives from increased gas taxes under Kerry as a measure of how favorable they are to increased gas taxes, we can imagine that with the new information there is a consumer who is now indifferent toward the choice between Kerry and Bush, given Kanchan's story of no evidence. That is, a consumer whose expected utility from higher gas taxes under Kerry = 75 − (0.71)(100)]/(0.29) = 13.79 utils would be indifferent about choosing between Bush and Kerry. A consumer whose utility from higher gas taxes under Kerry is less than 13.79 will, like Arthur, support Bush after reading Kanchan's story stating there is no evidence that Kerry will raise taxes, and a consumer whose utility from higher gas taxes under Kerry is greater than 13.79 will, like Charlotte, support Kerry after reading Kanchan's story. Notice that any consumer whose utility from higher gas taxes under Kerry is between 13.79 and 50 will now favor Kerry over Bush, given Kanchan's story that there is no evidence. Figure 8.3 shows the effect of Kanchan's reporting that she found no evidence on support for Kerry.

FIGURE 8.3
Effect of Kanchan's Story about Finding No Evidence That Kerry Will Raise Gas Taxes

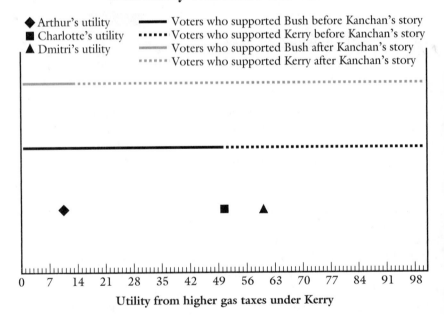

What if Kanchan writes that she has evidence? The information does not change Arthur's preference, as 75 > (0.77)(10) + (0.23)(100) = 30.7. But now both Charlotte and Dimitri favor Bush, as 75 > (0.77)(60) + (0.23)(100) = 69.2 > (0.77)(50) + (0.23)(100) = 61.5. We can again figure out the expected utility from Kerry's raising gas taxes for a consumer who is indifferent between Bush and Kerry given Kanchan's story as [75 − (0.23)(100)]/(0.77) = 67.53. Any consumer whose utility from higher gas taxes under Kerry is less than 67.53 will support Bush after reading Kanchan's story of finding evidence, and anyone with utility greater than 67.53 will support Kerry. Notice that Kanchan's reporting of evidence changes the preference of those whose utility is between 50 and 67.53 from Kerry to Bush. Figure 8.4 shows the effect of Kanchan's reporting that she found evidence of Kerry's plan to raise gas taxes.

Notice that there are consumers who are unaffected by either story. For example, Arthur will support Bush regardless of what Kanchan writes. Certainly consumers who get more utility if Kerry raises gas taxes than the 75 utils they expect to get from gas prices under Bush will never find themselves influenced by Kanchan's story to support Bush. But even those who perceive gas taxes as costly will not be influenced by Kanchan's story. Consider a consumer named Riley whose utility if Kerry raises gas taxes is 70. For

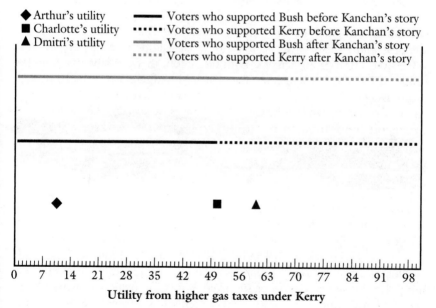

FIGURE 8.4
Effect on Kanchan's Story about Finding Evidence That Kerry Will Raise Gas Taxes When She Has Discretion in Reporting

Utility from higher gas taxes under Kerry

Riley, as for Arthur, there is no payoff to reading Kanchan's news report because he will still prefer Kerry to Bush: $75 < (0.77)(70) + (0.23)(100) = 76.9$.

How does Kanchan's ability to use discretion affect consumers overall? If Kanchan was forced to report truthfully, then if she wrote that she found evidence, consumers could update their probability that Kerry had a secret plan to raise gas taxes to 100 percent, and now as long as the utility from Kerry's raising gas taxes is less than 75, a consumer will support Bush. Figure 8.5 presents the scenario when Kanchan does not have any discretion and finds evidence. Riley's preferences would change if Kanchan claimed to have evidence and she had no discretion. Riley would benefit from the report and would be willing to read it. Discretion, then, reduces the value of reading the news for consumers like Riley and hence reduces the likelihood they will read the news. The more discretion Kanchan has, the less likely consumers are going to want to read her reports, particularly consumers with low utility losses from increased gas taxes. Discretion reduces the informativeness of stories that claim to be based on evidence and the benefit of gathering information to verify evidence.

Given that discretion decreases readership, why would Kanchan want to exercise it? The key is that Kanchan needs to have an effect on only the median voter in the electorate. As long as Kanchan's report increases the likelihood that the median voter supports Bush, she has been successful from her perspective. So if the median voter's expected utility from Kerry's raising taxes is less than 67.53, her reporting with discretion is effective even if voters like Riley remain opposed. Plus, by having discretion, Kanchan is more likely to write a story claiming evidence since 20 percent of the time when she has no evidence she will write such a story. That is, with no discretion the probability that she can write a story that will increase support for Bush = $0.5 \cdot 0.6 = 0.3$ or 30 percent. With discretion, that probability = $0.5 \cdot 0.6 + 0.5 \cdot 0.2 = 0.4$ or 40 percent. Thus, by having discretion she is 10 percent more likely to be able to write a story that will increase support for Bush, and as a consequence she increases her chances of swaying the median voter to support Bush. In summary, discretion reduces the number of consumers who find using the media valuable but increases the chances that Kanchan can write stories that support her preferences and as a result increases the probability that the median voter will support her preferences.[31]

The Owner and the Competition Our story makes sense so far, but what about the owner? Why would the owner allow Kanchan discretion if it reduces readership and, presumably, profits? The owner of course could have ideological preferences as well and hire Kanchan as a consequence if he or she is willing to take the loss in profit in return for a gain in utility from influencing policy in a direction he or she likes. But many owners of news outlets claim to present unbiased news, market themselves as objective sources, and are owned by large corporations. So why allow for reporters to have discretion? Baron (2004) showed that the fact that journalists receive utility from discretion allows owners to pay them lower wages, which can be greater than the cost in revenue from bias. Furthermore, we expect that reporters who have ideological preferences and want discretion to influence voters are also more motivated to gather information on public policy issues and as a consequence are more diligent reporters. It is difficult for news outlets to monitor

FIGURE 8.5

Effect of Kanchan's Story of Finding Evidence That Kerry Will Raise Gas Taxes When She Does Not Have Discretion in Reporting

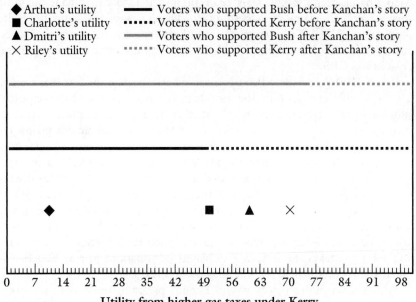

◆ Arthur's utility   ——— Voters who supported Bush before Kanchan's story
■ Charlotte's utility   •••••• Voters who supported Kerry before Kanchan's story
▲ Dmitri's utility   ——— Voters who supported Bush after Kanchan's story
✕ Riley's utility   •••••• Voters who supported Kerry after Kanchan's story

0   7   14   21   28   35   42   49   56   63   70   77   84   91   98

Utility from higher gas taxes under Kerry

their reporters since most of reporters' work is done off-site, meeting with sources, conducting research, and visiting other countries and other parts of the United States. For example, former *New York Times* reporter Jayson Blair falsely claimed to be reporting from other parts of the country while sitting in his Manhattan apartment, and only after repeated discrepancies and evidence of plagiarism did his editors discover that he was failing to do his reporting job, causing a major scandal at the newspaper and eventually resulting in the resignation of two top editors.[32] Thus, owners may find it optimal to allow for discretion if it is attractive to reporters who are diligent and receive consumption utility from learning about a particular subject area that interests them. Discretion may be a small price to pay for the loss to the paper from having reporters who are not motivated to do their jobs.

What happens if a news outlet faces competition? Can competition drive newspapers to present less biased news by forcing them to reduce the discretion they allow their journalists? On the contrary, competition may force owners to allow discretion in order to get what is widely perceived as a possible story first if their competitors also use discretion. When *60 Minutes* producer Mary Mapes pursued the story on Bush's service in the national guard in August 2004, she e-mailed her superiors: "There is a bit of a storm brewing in Austin re the Bush stuff. Many many reporters from various print outlets (Harpers, Vanity Fair, NY Times mag., etc) all chasing the Bush National Guard stuff again. It is much more intense than it was four years ago and there is a strong general feeling that this time, there is blood in the water."[33] The day after Dan Rather reported on the controversial memos that Mapes had gotten for him, *USA Today* published a story that made the same unsubstantiated claims.[34] According to Mapes's superiors, she used the forthcoming *USA Today* story as one of the reasons the story should be rushed at CBS.[35] Interestingly, USA Today did not receive the same general criticism as CBS.[36]

Baron (2004) considered competition when two news outlets bias stories. He shows that competition does not drive out bias because of the opportunity for news outlets to segment the market by presenting different types of biases and discretion and thus take advantage of the benefits of giving reporters discretion (lower wages and harder-working employees). To see how the news outlets can segment the market, assume that Rudolfo, a reporter for a competing news outlet, is biased in favor of Kerry. He uses his discretion to understate the probability that Kerry will raise gas taxes. When Rudolfo reports that Kerry will not raise gas taxes, sometimes he is giving biased information, just as Kanchan sometimes gives biased information when she claims Kerry will raise gas taxes. When Rudolfo reports that Kerry will raise gas taxes, he is giving unbiased information, just as Kanchan is when she reports that Kerry will not raise gas taxes.

Which news outlet's story would Dimitri prefer to read? With no story, given the prior probability, Dimitri supports Kerry. A story by either Kanchan or Rudolfo saying that there is no evidence that Kerry will raise gas taxes will not change Dimitri's mind and only confirms his support for Kerry, so accuracy is not important to him when the story is that Kerry will not raise gas taxes. A story suggesting Kerry will raise gas taxes could change his mind, but it is important to him that the story be as accurate as possible, since whether it will change his mind depends on just how probable it is that Kerry will raise gas taxes. Rudolfo is more likely to give an accurate report in this case, so Dimitri will prefer to read Rudolfo's story.

Similarly, suppose a consumer named Tanisha has a utility level of 40 from Kerry's raising gas taxes, as in figures 8.3–8.5. With no story, given the prior probability, Tanisha supports Bush. A story by either Rudolfo or Kanchan claiming Kerry will raise gas taxes only confirms her support for Bush, so accuracy is not important to her when the story is that Kerry will raise gas taxes. A story suggesting that Kerry will not raise gas taxes could change her mind, but it is important to her that the story be as accurate as possible, since whether it changes her mind depends on what the probability is. Kanchan is more likely to give an accurate report in this case, so Tanisha will prefer to read her story.

Notice that Dimitri, who is ex ante a Kerry supporter, is reading the story from the news outlet that is biased toward Kerry, and Tanisha, who is ex ante a Bush supporter, is reading the story from the news outlet that is biased toward Bush, but both are looking for the best unbiased information that is useful for them, information that might change their ex ante preferences. If Bill O'Reilly of Fox News is biased toward the Iraq war, then his viewers are going to be more likely to favor the war, and thus his announcement that there were no WMDs in Iraq is much more meaningful to his readers than is an article in *The New York Times*, which the evidence of the empirical research reviewed above suggests might be biased in the opposite direction. In seeking out unbiased information that they find useful, they choose news outlets with biases that conform to their individual ex ante preferences. They do so not for entertainment or because they psychologically want news that conforms to their initial preferences but because the news they can get that might have a consequential effect on their expected utility from the source biased toward their ex ante preferences is likely to be more accurate than the news they can get from the source biased against their ex ante preferences.[37] Hence, Baron's model can help explain the survey data suggesting that individuals would like unbiased reports, see the media as biased, and are more likely to choose media sources whose biases fit their own.

Does Baron's model help us understand the mass media's admitted lack of objective coverage of the reasons for going to war with Iraq, discussed above? There is evidence that specialists in foreign affairs in U.S. politics are in general more concerned about foreign policy matters than the U.S. public and more favorable to intervention internationally. For thirty years, the Chicago Council on Foreign Relations has surveyed the public and leaders with foreign policy power, specialization, and expertise. The leaders represent a random sample of administration officials in the Departments of State, Treasury, and Commerce and other federal departments and agencies dealing with foreign policy; members of the House and Senate or, mostly, their senior staff members with committee responsibilities in foreign affairs; senior business executives from Fortune 1,000 firms who deal with international matters; university administrators and academics who teach in the area of international relations; presidents of major organizations or large interest groups active in foreign affairs; presidents of the largest labor unions; religious leaders; and journalists and editorial staffers who handle international news.

In its 2002 report, the council analyzed the differences in leader and public opinion on foreign policy issues from 1974 to 2002.[38] They found persistent differences between the opinions of leaders and the public on foreign policy. They found that leaders have consistently been more supportive of the United States' assuming an active part in world affairs, are less committed to international cooperation, and are less alarmed about international threats. They found that the public places a higher priority on domestic programs than on foreign policy programs, is more concerned about domestic security, has a greater aversion to putting troops at risk, and is more supportive of safe-guarding jobs and well-being at home. While journalists who specialize in foreign affairs are only a subset of the leaders surveyed, the other leaders do comprise the general set of individuals that such journalists would use as sources, and so on. If foreign affairs journalists and their sources have a greater preference for international intervention and are less concerned about domestic affairs than the public, as the report suggests, then their preferences might result in a bias in reporting that is favorable to international intervention. These biases might explain why the press failed to be objective in its early coverage of the evidence of Iraq's production of WMDs and relationship to terrorist attacks on the West.

Technology and Advertisers as Sources of Bias

We now have two justifications for media bias: (1) when consumers want news that is largely entertainment and confirms biases that already exist, news outlets will provide biased news, and (2) when consumers are looking for unbiased news, news outlets that wish to hire journalists who will work for lower wages and are more dedicated to their jobs will allow reporters the discretion to bias the news. In both cases, we expect that news outlets will bias the news in directions that favor ex ante preferences of their audiences. Both justifications help explain why we might observe media bias and variation across media outlets in the degree of bias as well as the tendency of consumers to use media outlets whose biases confirm their ex ante preferences.

However, the empirical evidence that we reviewed above suggests that currently the mass media has an overall liberal bias. Moreover, evidence suggests that the extent to which the news media has taken on a partisan bias and provided political information has changed substantially over time. Neither justification explains these stylized facts. To explain them, we need to look at the roles played by technology and advertisers in the provision of political information via the mass media. These two factors interact to create a particular environment of mass media provision of political information that has varied over time. We will examine how changes in technology and advertising led to the existence of a mass media ostensibly independent of partisanship and explicit bias and conclude with a discussion of both a possible cause for an overall liberal bias and the current bias diversity in news outlets.

The Decline of Partisan Newspapers In the 1870s, 74.3 percent of the circulation of newspapers in the fifty largest cities in the United States was covered by those papers that had not just an ideological bias but also an explicit partisan connection, often in the newspaper's name (54.5 percent of the circulation was covered by Republican newspapers while 32.6 percent was covered by Democratic ones). Partisan newspapers were a way of communicating the party message to voters, and they received direct financial support from party organizations. But a change was taking place. By 1990, partisan papers made up only 46.6 percent of circulation (31.7 percent Republican, 14.9 percent Democratic). Independent newspapers made up the rest, explicitly declaring their intention to be objective and take stances independent of a particular party. They drew on advertising for their revenue and reached wider audiences.[39] Today almost all news outlets claim to be independent. What caused the rise of an independent media?

To understand the change, we need to understand the nature of the technology of mass media production. There are two types of costs in the production of goods: fixed and variable. In newspaper production, fixed costs are things like printing presses and buildings; variable costs are things like newsprint, reporters, delivery personnel, and so on. In early news production, printing presses were not very sophisticated and not too expensive but were costly to operate. Fixed costs and variable costs were not that different. Thus, it was relatively easy to set up a newspaper (fixed costs were low) but costly to increase circulation (variable costs were high). But, as reviewed in Hamilton (2004), in the nineteenth century advances in technology resulted in much more efficient printing presses, lowering variable costs. The presses were also much more costly to purchase, so fixed costs increased. This meant that it cost little for a newspaper with a modern printing press to add an additional customer, and thus increasing circulation became much more feasible (and desirable, since it helped defray the now larger fixed costs of the printing press). Furthermore, newspapers began to see a rise in advertising revenue because during this period national products began to emerge, with manufacturers attempting to reach large mass markets. Advertisers were willing to pay for newspapers with a wide circulation. Having an explicit partisan affiliation limited circulation and the newspapers' ability to gain this revenue. Although party organizations continued to support many newspapers, increasingly publishers saw advantages to forgoing those contributions, expanding their circulation beyond the members of a particular party, and gaining advertising revenue by increasing circulation. Eventually it became the norm for newspapers and most other media outlets to be independent and appear objective so that they could attract a wide audience, a norm that today in large part governs many major news outlets. Similarly, radio and television are also media outlets with high fixed costs but almost negligible variable costs. Thus, such outlets largely desire to reach the broadest market possible and have generally claimed a nonpartisan, independent label in order to do so.

There are a few notable exceptions to the norm of independence, such as opinion-focused newsmagazines like *The New Republic* and *The Weekly Standard*. In recent years, agencies in the federal government have supplied local television stations with canned reports that present government programs in a positive light.[40] In January 2005, Armstrong Williams, a conservative commentator and columnist, revealed that he was paid $240,000 by the U.S. Department of Education to promote the No Child Left Behind Act, and Howard Dean's campaign reported that it had paid two bloggers for their efforts in the Democratic primaries. However, these instances of supplying obviously biased news reports and paying journalists have been heavily criticized as violations of a well-understood norm.[41]

The Importance of Young Women The independence and norm of objectivity of news outlets have not meant that news coverage is completely unbiased today, as the empirical evidence we have reviewed so far suggests. But Hamilton (2004) contended that the rise of advertising as a source of revenue and the desire to reach a wide audience can explain why there seems to be an overall liberal bias in television news. He showed that television news programs compete to reach young consumers, particularly those aged eighteen to thirty-four. According to Hamilton (p. 161): this competition for advertising dollars in the news media increased significantly during the last thirty years of the twentieth century and was encouraged by changes in both the ownership of the media and public policies: "As the founders of the networks disappeared from ownership control, as the FCC [Federal Communications Commission] partially deregulated television, and as networks became part of conglomerates that were not first and foremost media companies, the focus on generating profits from news increased." The independent panel reviewing the CBS story on Bush national guard service noted that *60 Minutes Wednesday* "was created to appeal to a 'younger and jazzier' demographic group than the original 60 Minutes audience."[42]

Young women in particular are seen as valuable as audience members because they control many of the purchases in households. But they also tend to be marginal viewers of the news and therefore the least reliable audience, so more effort must be made to reach them. Thus, Hamilton argues that national news programs choose to emphasize issues, and stances on those issues, that appeal to young women, assuming they can also keep reliable older viewers. Since women aged eighteen to thirty-four tend to be more liberal than the general population, he suggests that news programs have a liberal bias. Hamilton also contends that the news has become more "soft," covering topics that younger individuals find more interesting. Hamilton shows that between 1968 and 1998 the television networks increased their coverage of entertainers and sports figures and reduced their coverage of votes in the Senate and House that were considered important by Congressional Quarterly and liberal and conservative lobbying groups. This might reflect the fact that younger viewers, who have less income and wealth, are less likely to see public policies as having a consequential effect on their individual private decisions and to consume news as entertainment rather than as investment (or as an investment in making entertainment decisions, such as whether to see a particular movie, buy a compact disc, or watch a football game, where public policy and politics are not considered relevant).

But as we have seen, not all news outlets have a liberal bias. Recent changes in the technology of news production might have caused some increase in the diversity of bias across news outlets. Furthermore, consumers are watching more news programs than before. According to Media Dynamics (2001, p. 244), adults in households with televisions watched an average of 133 minutes per week of newscasts and prime-time newsmagazines in the early 1970s but 349 minutes in the late 1990s. With the advent of cable and Internet news sources, the number of competitors for an individual news outlet's programs has increased, reducing the market share any particular news program can command. Thus, there is less of a cost to a news organization of not appealing widely, whereas it is more effective to focus instead on the news preferences of a particular group. Furthermore, technological changes have reduced both the fixed and the variable costs of conveying information, making it much cheaper to reach any given audience. However, it is still too early to assess the impact of the recent technological changes on the extent to which news outlets will become more or less biased in their presentation of political information.

Incomplete Information as a Source of Media Bias

In the explanations of media bias that we have explored so far, media bias results because of ideological preferences either of the readers or of the journalists, reporters, or owners. Gentzkow and Shapiro (2005) offer an explanation for media bias that does not rely on such ideological preferences. To understand their explanation, suppose that there are two types of news sources, high-quality news sources and low-quality news sources. Assume that consumers of the news want an unbiased news source that is high quality. But they do not know for sure which news source is high quality—all claim to produce high-quality news and there is no way for consumers to verify news outlets' types. Gentzkow and Shapiro show that consumers who use Bayesian updating will infer that a news outlet is of higher quality when its reports conform to the consumer's prior expectations about the world. This gives news outlets an incentive to slant their reporting to fit consumer's prior expectations in order to build a reputation for being a high-quality news source. As in Baron's model, in Gentzkow and Shapiro's model consumers still gain from using the biased information source but are worse off as a consequence since their information is biased. And as in the work of Mullainathan and Shleifer, if consumers have conflicting priors about the state of the world, news media outlets will offer different biases, and competition from independent media outlets can reduce overall bias.

What We Know

We know that evidence suggests some bias in the mass media reporting on elections, although compared with the media in previous periods in U.S. history, the media now is less biased, primarily because of technological changes in how information is provided. Technological changes currently taking place, such as the rise of Internet communications and cable television, may be reversing the trend and leading to an increase in bias. Current biases in the media may also be the result of voters' increased consumption demand for biased sources, the biases of journalists who have discretion in how they report stories, or advertisers' wishes to reach a particular market. The good news is that although there is evidence of media bias, voters who wish to seek out unbiased information can benefit from the biased information. Furthermore, even if voters desire biased information, if there is heterogeneity in the voters' biases, the aggregate or overall level of information will be unbiased.

What We Don't Know: A Referendum on Whom?

"The important thing to remember is that the American people see George Bush as the steward of a bad economy, the leader who led them to war under false pretenses," said Stephanie Cutter, a spokesperson for John Kerry. Kerry's campaign saw the Bush campaign's efforts to define him as an attempt to "turn the election into a referendum on Mr. Kerry rather than one about the president."[43] Part of the problem facing voters during the 2004 election was uncertainty not just about who Kerry was but also about how to judge Bush's performance. Was Bush responsible for the economy and the apparent loss of jobs as of March 2004? Had Bush made the right decisions with respect to pursuing terrorist suspects and going to war with Iraq? Would Kerry do better or worse?

For voters, the answers to these questions depend on both information they have and, most important, a lot of information they typically do not have. The problem is even more difficult when it comes to war and national security, since revealing too much information may endanger the nation and its allies. We've seen how campaign advertising and the mass media play a role in providing voters with a lot of information. But we've seen that campaign advertising can often contain little of substance, particularly if an incumbent does not face a challenger who advertises. We've also seen that the information provided to individuals through supposedly objective news outlets can be biased and that unless voters have private reasons for wanting political information, are leaders of groups involved in elections, or have internalized group motives, they have little incentive to seek out unbiased political information.

In the next chapter, we consider how the distribution of political information across voters can affect the public policy choices of elected officials. We also investigate the electoral institutions (term limits, recall elections, initiatives, and referenda) by which voters with limited information often try to control elected officials and their policy choices.

Study Questions and Problems

1. Suppose that in our example with Kanchan, she has no discretion in how she reports the evidence she finds. How does that affect who reads her stories? Explain.

2. Suppose that instead of thinking of Kanchan as a journalist, we think of her as a documentary film producer, like Michael Moore.

   a. Does our analysis of Kanchan's choices and voters' reactions explain why some voters might be willing to pay to see documentaries like *Fahrenheit 9/11* and *Stolen Honor*, which they expect will be biased presentations of the facts? Explain.

   b. Using our analysis, will the documentaries attract the same audiences? Why or why not?

   c. Using our analysis, can the documentaries affect election outcomes? Why or why not?

   d. Technological advances have decreased significantly the cost of making documentaries as well as the number of outlets over which they can be broadcast. Is that likely to mean more documentaries like *Fahrenheit 9/11* and *Stolen Honor* will be part of campaigns? Is this a good or bad thing for voters' information? Explain your answer.

3. Suppose that Kanchan would like to see Kerry elected and would like to write a story saying that Bush has a secret plan to eliminate the Social Security program. Assume that voters' preferences for the elimination of Social Security are those in table 8.4 and they will vote for the candidate who provides them with the highest expected utility. Voters and Kanchan think ex ante that there is a 30 percent chance that Kerry will eliminate Social Security and a 40 percent chance that Bush will. Kanchan expects that if Bush has a plan, she has a 50 percent chance of finding evidence. Kanchan has 20 percent discretion in how she reports the evidence she finds.

   a. If Kanchan does not find evidence of a plan after investigating, what is the probability that Bush has a plan?

   b. How do the voters' preferences for Bush and Kerry change if Kanchan writes that she does not find any evidence of a plan?

   c. How do the voters' preferences for Bush and Kerry change if Kanchan writes that she does find evidence of a plan?

TABLE 8.4
Some Utility Payoffs from Social Security

	Utility If Social Security Is Eliminated	Utility If Social Security Is Not Eliminated
Arthur's Utility	10	120
Charlotte's Utility	30	120
Dimitri's Utility	50	120
Sandy's Utility	75	120
Cathy's Utility	100	120
Shigeo's Utility	150	120

4. Suppose Kanchan is going to investigate the likelihood that one of the leaders in the war-torn region of Darfur, Sudan, has managed to escape to South America, where he is avoiding prosecution. She expects ex ante that there is an 80 percent chance that the leader has escaped. Furthermore, if he has escaped and she investigates, she has a 50 percent chance of finding evidence. She again has 20 percent discretion in how she reports the evidence she finds. In this case, however, voters are not likely to change their preferences for the candidates in the election based on the story, although they would read the story for entertainment value if Kanchan found evidence. They will not read a story that reports no evidence.
   a. Suppose Kanchan writes a story saying that she found no evidence. What would a reader think is the probability that the leader has escaped?
   b. Suppose Kanchan reports that she found evidence. What will voters think is the probability that the leader has escaped? Explain your answer.
   c. If Kanchan does not find evidence, do you think she will have an incentive to write a story saying that she did even though the story is unlikely to affect voters' preferences in the election? Explain.
5. Suppose that Kanchan can choose whether to investigate the possibility that Bush has a secret plan to eliminate Social Security (as in item 3 above) or the possibility that the Sudanese leader has escaped (as in item 4). Kanchan expects that if she writes that she has found evidence in either story, she will receive a pay increase worth 100 utils. She would also like to see Kerry elected. Assume that the cost of investigating both stories is the same. Which story will Kanchan investigate, and why? Explain your answer.
6. Suppose that voters seeking unbiased information use two competing biased media sources for information during an election campaign.

One source is biased in favor of the Democratic candidate, and the other source is biased in favor of the Republican candidate. Will those voters be more or less informed than voters who have only one unbiased source of information? Explain your answer.

NOTES

1. "Is National Guard Story Evidence of Bias?" *Hannity and Colmes*, Fox News Channel, September 14, 2004.
2. David Bauder, "CBS, Rather 'Regret Mistake in Judgment,' " *Pittsburgh Tribune-Review*, September 21, 2004.
3. Pat Buchanan, "Dan Rather: The Final Days," *Pittsburgh Tribune-Review*, September 18, 2004.
4. Pew Research Center, *How Journalists See Journalists in 2004*, May 23, 2004.
5. John Tierney, "Finding Biases on the Bus," *New York Times*, August 1, 2004.
6. Pew Research Center, "Voters Impressed with Campaign," news release, October 24, 2004.
7. Pew Research Center, *How Journalists See Journalists*.
8. " 'It Turns Out We Were All Wrong' About Iraqi Weapons, Kay Testifies," *Seattle Times*, January 29, 2004.
9. Tony Batt, "Ensign, Gibbons Say Kay's Words Affirm Bush's Actions," *Las Vegas Review-Journal*, January 29, 2004.
10. For example, *The Wall Street Journal* is well-known for having an extremely conservative editorial page but a news section that is considered liberal and viewed by liberals as accurate. See, for example, Irvine and Kincaid (2001).
11. Groseclose and Milyo (2003) used ADA scores constructed using the method described in Groseclose, Levitt, and Snyder (1999) so that the scores could be compared across time and chambers, as with Poole and Rosenthal's scores.
12. Groseclose and Milyo omitted instances in which members of Congress or the media criticized a think tank or used an ideological label for it. For example, they omitted statements of the following sort: "even the liberal American Civil Liberties Union thinks." When they included such statements the scores became more moderate. They contended that such statements are actually used in a biased way; that is, *The New York Times* tends to label only conservative think tanks, while Fox News labels only liberal think tanks. Thus, they argued, the labels are an implicit criticism of the think tank rather than a positive citation.
13. See, for example, Graber (1984) and Severin and Tankard (1992). Mullainathan and Shleifer (2005) reviewed this literature.
14. Pew Research Center, "News Audiences Increasingly Polarized," Pew Research Center Biennial News Consumption Survey, June 8, 2004.
15. The Pew results are available in numerous summaries at http://people-press.org/
16. Howard Kurtz, "The Post on WMDs: An Inside Story; Prewar Articles Questioning Threat Often Didn't Make Front Page," *Washington Post*, August 12, 2004.
17. "The Times and Iraq," *New York Times*, May 26, 2004.
18. "Poll Shows Solid Backing for Bush's Handling of Attack," *USA Today*, September 17, 2001.
19. See Hamilton (2004).
20. Pew Research Center, "Ten Years of the Pew News Interest Index," May 17, 1997.
21. For gas mileage reports on SUVs, see Paul Wilborn, "No SUV Backlash for Hummer Owners," Associated Press, February 3, 2003, and for the anticipation

of Lexus's new low-gas-mileage SUV, see Danny Hakim, "Green de Luxe," *New York Times*, October 27, 2004.

22. Dan Oldenburg, "Caught over a Barrel: Soaring Gas Prices Have Motorists' Wallets Running on Empty," *Washington Post*, May 4, 2004.

23. Josh Gerstein, "Kerry and Bush Trade Charges on Gas Prices," *New York Sun*, March 31, 2004.

24. Gerstein, "Kerry and Bush Trade Charges on Gas Prices."

25. In Mullainathan and Shleifer (2005), consumers are assumed to have different biased prior perceptions of the world, and while gaining better information reduces their losses from uncertainty, they pay a utility cost for being exposed to information that is at variance with those perceptions. Here we assume that no one is biased on the issue; all have the same prior perceptions.

26. Baron (2004) also posited that journalists prefer to write stories that are biased because if they do, they are more likely to publish the stories and reap ultimate rewards, such as book contracts, interviews on talk shows, and the like, leading to prominence in the field. However, for this to be true, there must be consumer demand for these sorts of stories independent of their information value, which sounds very similar to a demand-driven bias, as discussed previously. This is probably also a reason why journalists prefer to write biased stories, but if it is, the source is consumer demand for the stories rather than journalistic preferences.

27. Dick Thornburgh and Louis D. Boccardi, *Report of the Independent Review Panel on the September 8, 2004*, 60 Minutes Wednesday *Segment "For the Record" Concerning President Bush's Texas Air National Guard Service*, Kirkpatrick and Lockhard Nicholson Graham, January 5, 2005, http://www.image.cbsnews.com/htdocs/pdf/complete_report/CBS_Report.pdf. See pp. 49–51.

28. Thornburgh and Boccardi, *Report of the Independent Review Panel.*

29. Thornburgh and Boccardi, *Report of the Independent Review Panel.*

30. Quoted in Thornburgh and Boccardi, *Report of the Independent Review Panel,* pp. 218 and 225.

31. The presentation of Baron's model here is different from the main application he posits. That is, Baron suggests that journalists engage in what he calls private politics; that is, Kanchan may prefer that individuals purchase fewer SUVs because she worries about the effects of energy consumption on the environment. Public politics involves lobbying the government to enact policies that reduce gas-guzzling SUV consumption and encourage more consumption of hybrid vehicles. In contrast, private politics is trying to discourage citizens from choosing individually not to purchase gas-guzzling SUVs under an existing government policy. According to this interpretation, if Kanchan uses her discretion to engage in private politics, she might be more likely to publicize information that would reduce the probability that Arthur would want to buy a gas-guzzling SUV. She is not trying to indirectly affect a public decision, such as an election outcome, that may have a public policy effect, but she is trying to directly affect individual private decisions, which collectively can lead to a similar outcome.

32. Mark Jurkowitz, "Two Top Editors Resign at Times in Blair Fallout," *Boston Globe*, June 6, 2003.

33. Quoted in Thornburgh and Boccardi, *Report of the Independent Review Panel,* p. 68.

34. See Dave Moniz and Jim Drinkard, "Guard Commander's Memos Criticize Bush," *USA Today*, September 9, 2004.

35. Thornburgh and Boccardi, *Report of the Independent Review Panel*, p. 107.

36. Thornburgh and Boccardi, *Report of the Independent Review Panel*, p. 222.

37. Bovitz, Druckman, and Lupia (2002) contended that media bias is unlikely un-

less all three actors in media production—owners, journalists, and consumers—have common biased preferences. However, their model does not allow for owners paying journalists lower wages by giving them discretion, and the information assumptions in the model limit the ability of consumers to gain from information sources that are biased against their ex ante preferences. Under the more general assumptions in Baron's model, owners do not need to be ideological, nor do all three actors need to have common preferences.

38. Chicago Council on Foreign Relations, *Worldviews 2002: American Public Opinion and Foreign Policy.*
39. See Hamilton (2004).
40. See Robert Pear, "U.S. Videos, for TV News, Come under Scrutiny," *New York Times,* March 15, 2004.
41. See Stuart Elliott, "An Undisclosed Paid Endorsement Ignites a Debate in the Public Relations Industry," *New York Times,* January 12, 2005, and *Wall Street Journal,* January 14, 2005.
42. Thornburgh and Boccardi, *Report of the Independent Review Panel,* p. 34.
43. Jim Rutenberg, "90-Day Strategy by Bush's Aides to Define Kerry," *New York Times,* March 20, 2004.

Part III

The Problems of Incomplete Information in Elections

9

Controlling the Behavior of Elected Officials

William Goodling's Unusual Election

Rep. William F. Goodling (R-Pa.) looked uncomfortable. Surrounded by Christian and ideological conservatives supporting his besieged bid for a 13th term, Goodling, a moderate of the old school, plaintively told the gathering in the second-floor meeting room of the York Christian School: "This has been the most unusual election I've ever been through in my life. I don't understand. I'm still trying to figure out what is really going on."

Thomas B. Edsall, *Washington Post*, May 12, 1998

What was unusual about Goodling's election? For one of the few times since he was first elected in 1974, replacing his father, who had retired, Goodling was facing a serious fight. It is no surprise that he was perplexed. After all, in 1992 he had managed to get reelected despite having 430 overdrafts at the bank of the House of Representatives, totaling $188,000, a sum that would have led to the defeat of some of his colleagues in Congress. Since then, the voters and his party had seemed happy with his record in Congress. Moreover, with Republicans in the majority after Newt Gingrich's success in 1994, Goodling had become chairman of the Committee on Education and the Workforce and was thus in a position of power within the House, which should have had appeal to his voters. But in May 1998, Goodling looked to be in danger of not even winning renomination much less reelection. Why?

The voters deciding Goodling's fate were considering a question that has

291

faced voters in American elections repeatedly. Should they reelect an incumbent with clout, power, and prestige who can ably deliver the policies they want? "You don't bench champions. . . . Just let him do his job and continue," argued one of his supporters. Or should they throw him out and try someone new and less powerful because Goodling was "as removed from the people as was the royalty of Europe. . . . He's accepted special interest paid junkets to the four corners of the world"[1] (according to his opponents advertisements)?

A Return to Citizen Legislators

In 1997, 40 percent of Maine's state legislators were new. In 1998, two thirds of the Michigan house, one half of the Arkansas house, and one third of the Oregon house were replaced. This is surprising because in general, incumbents in state legislative elections win over 90 percent of their races.[2] The reason is not that voters were suddenly voting less for incumbents but that incumbents were no longer allowed to run because of the imposition of term limits.

The change was attracting new people to politics. In Arkansas, for example, term limits induced Jack Norton, a sixty-four-year-old chicken farmer, and Mary Beth Green, a forty-one-year-old speech pathologist and mother of five, to run for the state legislature. Voters in Arkansas and other states with new legislative term limits had decided that they didn't want incumbents in state legislatures to have a chance at reelection. Norton and Green were vying to replace a state representative who was chairman of the Joint Budget Committee and had served for twenty-four years. *The Washington Post* reported: "Popular Rep. Edward S. Thicksten delivered to his rural district countless paved roads, nutrition programs for the elderly, funding for a local community college and an adult education center."[3] Arkansas voters were avoiding the decision that Goodling's constituents faced by preventing incumbents from running again. Thicksten was forced to retire because of the new term-limits law. Why did Arkansas voters chosen to institute a system that prevented incumbents from running again? To answer this question, we need to explore further how much voters know and do not know about incumbents' policy choices.

The Secret World of Incumbents

Was 9/11 Predictable?

In March 2004, former counterterrorism coordinator for Presidents Bill Clinton and George W. Bush, Richard A. Clarke, published a book, *Against All Enemies: Inside America's War on Terror*, in which he claimed that neither president did enough to counter terrorism prior to 9/11 and that the Bush administration ignored the threat of Al Qaeda (the group behind the terrorist attacks of 9/11) to go to war against Iraq. Clarke claimed he called for a cabinet meeting in January 2001 to discuss Al Qaeda but his request was ignored to focus on missile defense and Iraq. In an interview on CBS's *60 Minutes*, Clarke remarked: "He ignored terrorism for months, when maybe we could have done something to stop 9/11. Maybe. We'll never know."[4] Furthermore, according to *The New York Times*, Clarke contended that Bush mounted "a lackluster, bureaucratic and politicized response to the attacks. . . . Mr. Clarke also alleges . . . that Mr. Bush and others in his small inner circle tried to intimidate him and other officials into finding a link between Iraq and Al Qaeda despite the intelligence community's repeated determinations that no significant connections existed."[5]

Bush administration officials went on morning talk shows, granted interviews to reporters, and wrote op-ed pieces in major newspapers to argue against Clarke's claims. The White House released a point-by-point rebuttal. In particular, the statement noted "that the president told national security adviser Condoleezza Rice early in his administration he was 'tired of swatting flies' and wanted to go on the offense against al Qaeda, rather than simply waiting to respond." In a guest column in *The Washington Post*, Rice wrote: "Before Sept. 11, we closely monitored threats to our nation. President Bush revived the practice of meeting with the director of the CIA every day—meetings that I attended. And I personally met with [CIA director] George Tenet regularly and frequently reviewed aspects of the counterterrorism effort." On ABC's *Good Morning America*, Rice recalled that after 9/11, Bush was

> concerned about against whom we were going to retaliate. He wanted to know whether or not Iraq, given our history with Iraq, given that Iraq had tried to assassinate former President Bush, whether Iraq was behind the attack. Dick Clarke wasn't in every meeting. The president was talking about al-Qaeda with George Tenet. . . . He was talking about al-Qaeda with Donald Rumsfeld. He talked about al-Qaeda with me.[6]

Whose version of the administration's work on terrorism prior to and after 9/11 is correct? White House communications director Dan Bartlett dismissed Clarke's accusations as "politically motivated" and said that the book's timing, when Bush's reelection campaign was just beginning, showed that it was "more about politics than policy."[7] If the 2004 presidential election was a referendum on Bush's record in office, then voters would care whose version of the administration's response to terrorist threats is correct. Whereas voters knew a lot about Bush and his performance in office, there was a lot that individual voters in the 2004 election did not know about the president's choices behind closed doors in meetings with his aides, foreign leaders, members of Congress, or his cabinet—and as Clarke's and Rice's comments show, there were different versions of what went on. How do voters deal with such uncertainty? And in any case, shouldn't voters look to the future rather than to the past? Shouldn't they have based their choice on what they expected either Bush in a second term or Kerry in a first term would accomplish instead of focusing on the events prior to 9/11 (especially given that Clarke faulted both Clinton and Bush)?

Travelgate

In January 1996, President Bill Clinton's former director of administration, David Watkins, appeared before a congressional committee. According to *The Washington Post*, Watkins testified

> that he felt tremendous pressure coming from President Clinton and first lady Hillary Rodham Clinton to fire seven members of the White House travel office in the early days of the administration. But he insisted that neither of the Clintons directly ordered him to dismiss the longtime employees. Watkins . . . took responsibility for the firings but said "there would have been a great price to pay—perhaps my removal from the White House" had he refused to do so. The pressure, he said, was generated mainly by the first lady and came to him through two intermediaries—the late deputy White House counsel Vincent Foster and Hollywood producer Harry Thomason, a friend of the Clintons.[8]

Why were the employees of the travel office fired? According to Clinton critics, the firings were an effort to replace good workers with a group of cronies from Arkansas, and they were done by defaming the names of the workers and misusing the FBI. The former travel office director, Billy Dale, was investigated by the FBI on charges of embezzlement and acquitted. And evidence suggests that one reason White House counsel Vincent Foster committed suicide was his concern that Hillary Clinton would be blamed for the firings. Were there genuine problems in the travel office, justifying the firings and the replacements, as the Clintons argued? Did Watkins just act on his own? Or were the firings an effort by corrupt politicians to try to use some of the spoils of government to benefit their friends, as their critics suggested?

What Voters May Not Know about Incumbents

Our analysis up till now has examined voters' and candidates' choices assuming that candidates' policy positions before an election fully represent their choices after the election. That isn't always the case, however. Incumbents do not have complete control over policy once in office. Random factors—like sudden upturns or downturns in the economy in response to oil embargoes or droughts in other countries, the bombing of U.S. embassies and the taking of American hostages abroad, and bad intelligence supplied by our allies—can influence the political outcomes even when an elected official is making his or her best effort to do what voters want. Furthermore, incumbents rely on staff members who may make choices on their own that could hurt or help them in their job. Finally, candidates may change their minds about what they intend to do policywise, or they may have lied about their policy intentions during the elections and make choices voters cannot observe that lead to different policy outcomes from those promised. Voters face a problem, therefore: how can they be sure that the candidates they have elected are making the choices they prefer?

There are two types of information about candidates' choices in office that even voters who are informed or act *as if* they are informed are unlikely to have when voting, and each type creates a problem:

- the moral-hazard problem, in which information about the effort a candidate expends once in office is hidden
- the adverse-selection problem, in which information about a candidate's true policy preferences is hidden.

The Moral-Hazard Problem

Hidden Information about the Actions of Elected Officials Moral hazard exists in many relationships. A classic example of moral hazard is when an insurance company offers fire insurance to a smoker. If the smoker does not smoke in bed, the chance of a fire is much lower than if the smoker does smoke in bed. The insurance company cannot monitor the smoker to determine whether he or she smokes in bed—thus the insurer faces a moral-hazard problem in determining which rate to charge the smoker. Should the insurance company charge the smoker a higher rate, assuming he or she will smoke in bed even if there is the possibility that the smoker will not? Should the insurance company assume that the smoker does not smoke in bed and charge a lower rate?

How would a moral-hazard problem appear in an election? As insurance companies cannot monitor smokers' habits, so voters cannot monitor the day-to-day activities of their elected officials, their incumbents. A voter does not know how much time a representative is spending running the government and how much time he or she is spending on vacations at the beach or on junkets abroad or helping out cronies with jobs and government resources. A voter does not know when an incumbent is trying to fire good employees on trumped-up charges so that his or her own friends can have the job or whether the employees should be fired and replaced with more reliable ones that the incumbent knows can do a better job. These moral-hazard issues were brought up by William Goodling's opponents in his congressional race and by Bill Clinton's opponents in his 1996 reelection campaign. And in 2004, Richard Clarke accused the Bush administration of not devoting enough resources and time to fighting terrorism.

A Simple Example Consider a simple example of the moral-hazard problem. Suppose there is an existing status quo level of policy equal to SQ. We can think of this as perhaps the status quo level of national defense against terrorism right after September 11, 2001. After the attacks, voters preferred a greater level of national defense to protect the country against terrorism, point M, which is greater than SQ, as illustrated in figure 9.1. While the events of 9/11 provide a natural explanation for why voters might prefer a change in a status quo, there are other situations in which a shift in preferences can occur. For instance, SQ may be a level of education provided to students in a city. Previously the education provided was sufficient for the graduates of the education system to get good jobs, but a decrease in manufacturing in the area now implies that more students need college-preparatory courses and voters prefer higher standards for graduation. Another example might be an SQ that is a level of enforcement of tax laws in a state. An unexpected revenue shortfall means that to maintain existing public services, either more taxes must be raised or the existing tax laws must be better enforced, and voters prefer to see the laws better enforced. Notice that in those cases, the assumption is that voters agree on the correct policy outcome.

In figure 9.1, $SQ = 50$ and $M = 75$. Suppose that voters then elect a candidate—say, Agatha—who promises to try to implement policy equal to M—to move policy from SQ to M. Agatha does not care about policy—all she cares about is getting elected. She receives 100 units of utility if she is elected and 0 units of utility if she is not elected.

FIGURE 9.1
Example of Moral Hazard

SQ is the status quo policy. Voters would like policy changed to **M**.
The new policy, **P**, = **SQ** + **E** + **R**.
E is the effort that **A** (the elected official) chooses.
R is a random factor that is unpredictable when **A** chooses her **E**.
If **R** is positive and equal to **R+**, the new policy is at **P+**.
But if **R** is negative, equal to **R−**, then the new policy is at **P−**.

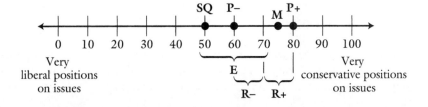

But moving policy from SQ to M depends on two things—Agatha's effort (E) in policy making (reorganizing the distribution of resources for investigating terrorism if she is the president; holding hearings, writing legislation, and discovering facts if she is a member of Congress) and factors she has no control over (for example, difficulty with getting information about terrorist activities from other governments, unexpected numbers of students with learning disabilities in the community, the unexpected movement of tax cheaters to other countries, where they are difficult to catch). We will call these random factors R. R could have a positive effect on policy, making it easier for policy to approach M, or R could have a negative effect. The problem is that R is unpredictable and largely unobservable by voters, and incumbents cannot predict R when they choose their levels of effort. So the ultimate policy that will be implemented if Agatha is elected is equal to P, which is the sum of SQ, E, and R:

$$P = SQ + E + R$$

Notice that if R is high, Agatha does not need to put much effort into changing policy. But if R is negative, Agatha needs to expend more effort. Figure 9.1 illustrates some sample values of R, given E and the way P is determined. In figure 9.1, Agatha puts forth an effort equal to 20. When $R = ZS-10$, the resulting new policy is $P = 50 + 20 - 10 = 60$. But when R equals +10, the resulting new policy is $P = 50 + 20 + 10 = 80$.

Agatha does not know what R will be when she chooses E. Furthermore, E is costly to Agatha. Why is that? It may be because Agatha would prefer to spend her time on other issues, or perhaps she would prefer taking vacations to the beach or junkets to foreign countries to investigate policy on this issue. Assume that for every unit of E that Agatha expends, she must pay 2 utils. So in our example, Agatha loses 40 utils by expending effort equal to 20. Agatha's utility, then, from serving in office is $100 - 40 = 60$. Finally, voters are unable to measure E or R. All voters ever observe is P.

Given the situation facing Agatha, what value of E should she choose? Suppose Agatha is going to serve only one term. Clearly, then, her utility-maximizing choice is an E equal to 0. Because voters never observe R, she can always claim that it is because of the value of R that her policy did not come close to M, not because of her lack of effort, or she can take credit if R does benefit her. However, rational voters know that Agatha will choose an $E = 0$ because they realize that she has no incentive to expend effort. So they expect that E will equal 0, and that is the essence of the moral-hazard problem in elections—Agatha has no incentive to put forth effort once elected, and voters have zero expectations of Agatha's effort.

Of course, most elected officials would find the suggestion that they prefer foreign junkets to policy making offensive, especially during a major crisis, such as the one that occurred after 9/11. But assuming that politicians like policy making is like saying that people vote because they like voting—neither explanation helps us understand politics and elections very much. Moreover, if we assume that candidates like Agatha care about policy, we come to our second problem of hidden information.

The Adverse-Selection Problem

Hidden Information about Elected Officials' Motives Like moral hazard, adverse selection exists in many relationships. An example of adverse selection occurs when consumers buy products without knowing their quality. For example, a carmaker may produce two types of cars—low quality and high quality. On the outside and for simple inspections, it is difficult for the consumer to determine whether he or she has a low-quality car (a lemon). What should the consumer do?

An adverse-selection problem can be manifested in elections when candidates have their own policy preferences or when they have incentives to choose policies that are different from those they promised to promote during their campaign (to please special interests, for example). The adverse-selection problem occurs because voters do not know what type of elected official they have chosen, just as consumers may not know what the quality of the car they are buying. That is, voters may know what a candidate has promised to do but not what he or she intends to do or what he or she actually does in office. Unfortunately, there is no way to make politicians tell the truth about their policies. In 1998, for example, the Washington State Supreme Court struck down a law that banned false political advertising because it infringed on free speech.[9]

Adverse selection was also an issue in Goodling's unusual election. His opponent in the Republican primary, Charles Gerow, criticized Goodling for not choosing conservative policies—"for failing to support full implementation of the anti-missile defense system, for opposing the death penalty and for supporting the 1997 budget agreement."[10] And it was an issue when Richard Clarke accused the Bush administration of having a private preference for invading Iraq, as it was when Clinton's critics accused him of using the travel office to please special interests.

A Simple Example In moral-hazard situations, it is clear where policy should move—in which direction: all voters in our earlier example agreed that SQ should move to M. But what if candidates care not only about being elected but also about actual policy choices, either because they have their own preferences or because they would like to please special interest groups who are not representative of voters' preferences.[11]

Suppose in the example above, in which all voters prefer that policy move to M, that some candidates have other preferences. Some candidates, like Isabel, prefer that policy stay at SQ. Perhaps she prefers that policy stay at SQ because she likes SQ more than M. Or perhaps she would like to please some special interest group that prefers SQ to M. Candidates like Isabel with a private preference for SQ over M we call SQ types. Other candidates are like Étienne and prefer M over SQ. Étienne may have this preference because of "noble" motives—that is, he likes to please voters, or he, too, would like to please some special interest group that happens to have the same preferences as voters. We call candidates like Étienne M types. We assume that if policy is at SQ, Isabel receives the most utility, which declines as policy moves away from SQ, while Étienne receives the most utility at M, which declines as policy moves away from M.

Thus, in contrast to the candidates in the moral-hazard problem, these candidates receive utility not from being elected but from choosing policy they prefer. We continue to assume that policy making is costly; that is, for every unit of effort a candidate expends—either Isabel or Étienne—he or she loses 2 utils. Clearly, if Isabel is elected, she will not expend effort to move policy to M. In contrast, if Étienne is elected, he will attempt to move policy toward M. The problem for voters is that they do not know which candidates are SQ types and which are M types when they vote. Suppose that the election is between Isabel and Étienne. Voters know it is possible that either or both candidates are SQ types. But during the campaign, both candidates claim to be M types. If voters decide to vote for Isabel, she will not expend any effort. Moreover, because of the random factor, voters cannot tell based solely on the final outcome whether Isabel is an SQ type or an M type.

Controlling Incumbents by Getting Information

How can voters solve the problems of moral hazard and adverse selection? Ideally, the best solution is for voters to acquire information about incumbents' policy preferences or tendencies to take various actions. Yet because acquiring information is costly and the effect of an individual's actions are small, voters have little incentive to seek out such information. Nevertheless, in chapters 7 and 8 we have seen that election campaigns often provide voters with information in order to influence their preferences, and we have seen that voters can use that information to increase their knowledge of the candidates' policies. Is it possible that the information voters receive is sufficient to allow them to ensure that they not vote for candidates who will not expend effort or have policy preferences that are contrary to theirs?

Campaign Advertising and Voters' Information on Incumbents

In chapters 7 and 8, we discussed how information about elected officials is conveyed through campaign advertising and the mass media. Campaign advertisements sometimes do provide voters with substantive, verifiable information about candidates. Do they provide voters with enough information to solve the problems of moral hazard and adverse selection? Although campaign spending is sizable in U.S. elections, many candidates for elective offices, such as those running for the state legislature in Arkansas, engage in little campaign advertising. Stratmann (n.d.) analyzed campaign contributions in thirty-seven states in 1996, 1998, and 2000.[12] He found that in open-seat races the average candidate raises $80,000. But in races with an incumbent, challengers raise on average only a little over $22,000, while incumbents raise on average almost $88,000.

As we saw in chapter 7, in congressional races sizable spending by challengers is necessary for voters to even recall a challenger's name, and campaign advertising with substance about an incumbent's record is likely only when an incumbent faces a challenger who advertises significantly. Given how low challengers' campaign spending is in state legislative races, the evidence suggests that in many cases we cannot expect that campaign advertising is providing voters with much information about incumbents' choices in elective office. Although there is more spending in races for higher offices, as we saw in chapter 7, the majority of congressional races saw little campaign advertising. Thus, except for the few high-visibility elective offices—like that of president, governor, or senator—we would expect that campaign advertising rarely provides voters with extensive substantive information about incumbents' policy choices.

The Mass Media and Voters' Information on Incumbents

What about the mass media? How much information about incumbents' behavior do voters gain from the media, and can they use the information to control for problems of moral hazard and adverse selection? As we saw in chapter 8, it is possible for voters to gain information even from biased media sources, and evidence suggests that they do learn from the mass media during presidential campaigns. But how much information does the mass media provide to voters about elected officials in lower-level offices?

Arnold (2004) extensively examined the local mass media coverage of a random selection of members of Congress. He found a large variation in the amount of detail in the media reports, with some coverage quite thorough but other coverage only cursory. The most coverage comes when an incumbent is in a competitive race and campaign spending is extensive, suggesting that mass media coverage generally follows the same trend as campaign advertising. Moreover, the findings suggest that the mass media does not provide voters with much detailed information about the majority of members of Congress. Although to my knowledge a similar study of state and local officials has not been conducted, it seems reasonable to assume that the news media spends even less time discussing what those incumbents are doing in office.

Inequalities in Voters' Information

The evidence above suggests that voters do not receive enough information from the mass media or campaign advertising to accurately know what elected officials are up to. But another important implication of voters' lack of information is that the information is unequally distributed. Husted, Kenny, and Morton (1995) considered the accuracy of voters' information about their senators' policy positions by comparing voters' estimates in NES surveys with interest group measures of the senators' voting records. They found that education, gender, race, and income significantly affect the accuracy of voters' information about their senators. Thus, not only are voters largely uninformed, but some voters are more uninformed than others.

Controlling Elected Officials on the Basis of Little Information

Getting Cues from Others

Perhaps it isn't necessary for voters to be informed. That is, if voters choose as if they were informed, it doesn't matter whether they actually have the information or not. How might voters choose as if they were informed? Downs (1957), Popkin (1991), and Riker (1988) posited that voters can use simple cues like party labels in order to infer candidates' policy positions on issues. Snyder and Ting (2002) formalized this argument. However, such information would be quite coarse and would not tell voters much about how an individual incumbent might deviate from his or her party's position on issues. The implication is that the party controls the elected officials. But our analysis of policy choices of members of Congress in chapter 4 shows that there is a wide diversity within political parties, with some Democrats, like Joe Lieberman, choosing relatively moderate positions while others, like Maxine Waters, choose more extreme positions. Even within the same political jurisdiction and party we can see variation in policy choices. For example, in 2002 both of Arizona's senators, John McCain and Jon Kyl, were Republicans, yet the ADA gave McCain a 20 (making him a relative moderate) and Kyl a 0. Just knowing that an incumbent is a Democrat (or a Republican) cannot tell voters where he or she is within the range of positions that Democrats (or Republicans) usually choose. Moreover, in Goodling's race, the main competition was in the primary, from fellow Republicans. Party labels would hardly have helped voters in evaluating him in comparison with his opponents.

While party labels may be too coarse to signal to uninformed voters what incumbents have done in office, if voters are mobilized by benefit-seeking groups, as discussed in chapter 2, they might act as if they were informed if the group leaders are informed about incumbents' choices in office and mobilize the voters to act accordingly. Alternatively, uninformed voters may be able to act as if they were informed if they can observe how informed voters choose in elections and have some information about informed voters' preferences.[13]

Retrospective Voting

Another way in which voters might control the behavior of elected officials when they do not have information is through retrospective voting. That is, if voters choose between candidates based on past behavior, elected officials might be induced to make the choices the voters prefer, even if the voters do not have high levels of information about those choices. Thus retrospective voting can be used to control for both moral-hazard and adverse-selection problems. To see how this works, we will first consider using retrospective voting to control for moral hazard-problems and then consider its use to control for adverse-selection problems.

Solving the Moral-Hazard Problem Let's return to our example of Agatha. Remember that Agatha cares only about being elected and sees policy making as costly. Once elected, Agatha would expend 0 effort trying to move policy to M. But now assume that Agatha has an opponent, Ben, who has the same preferences as Agatha. Also assume that there are two periods, as shown in figure 9.2. In period 1, Agatha and Ben make promises about the effort they are going to expend in office. Then voters choose one candi-

FIGURE 9.2
Retrospective Voting and Moral Hazard

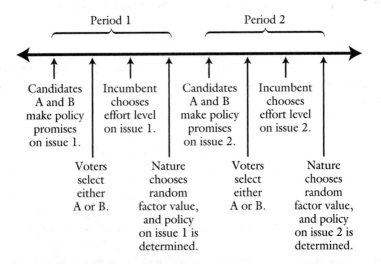

date, who becomes the incumbent. The incumbent chooses E, and nature chooses R. $P = SQ + E + R$. Voters observe only P, not E or R.

In period 2, the incumbent is up for reelection and faces a challenger, the defeated candidate in the first election. Now voters care about a different issue (which we will call issue 2)—that is, they would like to see the status quo changed on a different issue. Both the incumbent and her challenger make promises about the effort they will expend to change policy, and again, because these two candidates are exactly alike, they make exactly the same promises. The same sequence of events occurs: one candidate is elected, the incumbent then chooses an effort level, nature chooses a random-factor value, voters observe the policy position. The process continues indefinitely.

Consider the situation facing voters in the election at the beginning of period 2. Because the candidates are exactly alike, voters are indifferent. They have no reason to expect that Agatha is any different from Ben and vice versa. Voters in each election could just toss a coin and vote randomly. But if they voted randomly, what effort levels would Agatha and Ben choose if elected? Both would choose effort levels equal to 0 if elected—there is no payoff from choosing anything else.

Suppose instead that voters choose retrospectively, based on the policy they observed during the previous period. For example, suppose that in period 1, Agatha is elected. Agatha is now the incumbent. Agatha would like to be reelected in period 2. Suppose she knows that voters will be more willing to vote for her if they observe policy on issue 1 that is closer to their preferences. Voters are not choosing prospectively because they perceive little difference between Agatha and Ben on future issues; they are voting retrospectively based on the outcome of past policy. Agatha now has an incentive to choose a positive effort level.

Of course, because of R, the random factor that nature determines, voters never know exactly how much effort an incumbent has expended. So tying the probability that voters will choose an incumbent for another term to observed policy may reward some incumbents who expended little effort and punish others who expended much. On average, however, because voters vote retrospectively and incumbents want to be reelected, incumbents will have more of an incentive to expend effort than they would if voters ignored their past choices. It is important to note that although voters are choosing retrospectively, they are making this decision because they want to have an effect on *future* effort levels. If candidates anticipate that voters will use retrospective voting strategies, the candidates are more likely to fulfill effort-level promises.[14]

Solving the Adverse-Selection Problem   Can retrospective voting also help solve the adverse-selection problem? Let's return to our example of Isabel and Étienne and extend it to more than one period as well. As with Agatha and Ben, in period 1, both Isabel and Étienne will make promises to move policy to M, and because voters do not know the candidates' private preferences, they will choose one candidate randomly. In period 2, the incumbent is up for reelection. We assume that as with Agatha and Ben, there is now a second issue on which voters would like to see a policy change. On issue 2, Étienne has the same preferences as the voters whereas Isabel does not. Isabel and Étienne both want to be reelected so that they can make policy on this issue. We assume, as with Agatha and Ben, that the process continues indefinitely.

What happens if voters choose retrospectively in subsequent periods based on the policy choices incumbents make? Would such a strategy force a candidate like Isabel to choose as Étienne has chosen if she becomes the incumbent? Doing so is costly for Isabel because she would on average have to expend effort and on average policy would move further from her ideal point. If Isabel values being reelected, she might be willing to pay that cost. But if she doesn't value being reelected, retrospective voting will not induce her to choose policies that voters like. But retrospective voting can make it less likely that Isabel would run for office in the first place. When voters choose retrospectively, Isabel's cumulative value of achieving and staying in office is less than Étienne's. Since running for office is costly, retrospectively voting can lead candidates like Isabel to choose not to run and help voters increase their likelihood of selecting candidates like Étienne.[15]

Empirical Evidence

We have discussed two mechanisms by which voters with low levels of information can control elected officials: they can use simple cues or endorsements from informed policy leaders, and they can vote retrospectively to induce incumbents to expend effort in policy making and to lessen incumbents' incentive to run when their policy preferences are contrary to voters'. Do these mechanisms work? If they worked, we would be able to make three predictions: (1) there would be little difference between the choices of uninformed and informed voters; (2) voters' possession of information would have little effect on whether their policy choices were enacted by elected officials; and (3) fewer incumbents who made policy choices contrary to voters' preferences would be elected or run for reelection.

Prediction 1: How Uninformed Voters Choose Bartels (1996) considered the first empirical prediction. He examined voters' choices in presidential elections as reported in NES data as a function of how informed a voter was and his or her demographic characteristics. For given demographic characteristics, he compared the choices of voters who, according to interviewers, had very high levels of information as compared with those with low levels of information. He found significant differences in the choices of high- and low-information voters and in general found that low-information voters were more likely to vote Democratic and to vote for incumbents in presidential elections. He estimated that Democrats received 2 percent more votes and incumbents received almost 5 percent more votes when not all voters were fully informed, compared with what the Democrats would have received if all voters were fully informed.

Bartels also found that the extent to which voters chose as if they were informed varied according to demographic group. High-information female voters were much more likely to vote Democratic than low-information female voters. Similarly, low-information Protestants were less likely to vote Democratic. Catholics had the opposite tendencies, with high-information Catholics more likely to vote Republican. In contrast, African Americans and high-income voters chose the same way regardless of whether they had low or high information levels (African Americans were more likely to vote Democratic; high-income voters were more likely to vote Republican). Bartels's evidence suggests that uninformed African Americans and high-income voters are better able to act as if they were informed. Bartels's evidence suggests that for some groups of voters, information appears to matter and thus uninformed voters in those groups do not appear to be mobilized according to their interests or are not using informed voters' choices as a guide, yet an alternative explanation is that low and high levels of information correspond to unmeasured preference differences that are not captured by demographic characteristics.

Prediction 2: Information and Policy Stromberg (forthcoming) presented evidence on the second prediction. He examined the effect of the expansion of radio stations during the New Deal on the federal government's spending. He found that counties with many radio listeners received more relief funds, controlling for differences in county wealth and unemployment. If voters in counties with poor information sources (that is, less radio coverage in Stromberg's analysis) had been able to make inferences about government spending levels based on the preferences of informed voters or were mobilized by more informed groups leaders, we should not have seen such an effect. Thus, the evidence suggests that information does matter in how voters choose, voters who are uninformed do not appear to vote as if they were informed, and policy outcomes change as the availability of information increases. These results suggest that moral-hazard and adverse-selection problems exist in U.S. elections—voters with low levels of information are unable to fully control incumbents' behavior.

Prediction 3: Retrospective Voting The picture is not so simple, however, that is, our third prediction is supported: voters do appear to use retrospective voting to control problems of moral hazard and adverse selection. Much campaign advertising concerns the records and accomplishments of candidates in previous positions or, for incumbents, in previous terms. We noted in chapter 4 that when candidates seek upward political mobility, voters appear to evaluate them based on their choices in previous elective positions. In particular, voters appear to evaluate incumbents retrospectively based on the outcome of economic policy.[16] Retrospective voting in response to the outcome of economic policy can have important effects on the economic choices that candidates make, as we see in the next section.

Retrospective Voting and the Economy

Taxes and Spending

Republicans and Tax Increases When Republican governor Bob Riley took office in Alabama in 2002, the per capita state and local tax burden (including property, sales, and income taxes) was $2,117, the lowest in the nation (the U.S. average was $3,100). Yet the income level at which a four-person family started to pay state income taxes was $4,600, also the lowest in the nation (the national average was $19,512), reflecting a tax structure that was above the national average in terms of the percentage paid by the poor. Furthermore, 87 percent of the tax revenue raised was earmarked for specific programs and thus left very little discretion for the state government to provide voters with new services. Riley proposed, and the legislature passed, a massive overhaul of the system and an increase in taxes to be placed before voters in a referendum.

Many Republicans in the state and nation were aghast. Marty Connors, the Alabama Republican Party chairman, puzzled: "I'm caught between desperately trying to help the governor and maintaining consistencies in Republican policy. It's very difficult to have on one side of my desk talking points from the president on why we have to have tax cuts, and on the other side, talking points from the governor on why we have to have tax increases."[17] Former Republican House majority leader Dick Armey, who worked with Riley when both served in Congress, announced that he would go to the state and campaign against the tax measures. According to a news report, "Tuscaloosa businessman Stan Pate, who has paid for signs and ads opposing Riley's plan, said he offered to fly Armey to Alabama before the Sept. 9 vote. 'Armey is a true Republican. You are not going to see him pulling a stunt like Riley has pulled on the party,' Pate said."[18] Political pundits suggested that Riley was risking his political future on his tax plan.

Riley may have gotten his inspiration from a smaller but equally controversial overhaul of the tax system passed by referendum in Louisiana in 2002, which reduced the state's sales tax (whose burden falls more heavily on low-income citizens, who spend a larger percentage of their income) and increased the state's income tax. It certainly wasn't the first time a tax-structure change had been pushed in Louisiana—former governor Buddy Roemer had tried unsuccessfully to pass a comprehensive change like Riley's in 1989. In Louisiana, the tax plan was pushed by a state legislator, Republican Victor Stelly, who announced during the campaign that he would not seek reelection or another elective office in order to convince voters that his goal in pushing the plan was sincere and not related to achieving elective office. Stelly noted: "The first thing people are asking me is, 'Are you getting name recognition for something? What are you going to run for?' "[19] But Stelly noted that he did not see himself as a viable candidate for any office he might want and he had accomplished what he wanted in the state legislature, whether his tax plan passed or not.

Why Punish Tax Increases? Although voters in Alabama and Louisiana may have preferred lower taxes than voters nationwide, Peltzman (1992) found that permanent increases in the size of government are punished by voters in gubernatorial elections nationwide. Convincing voters to change tax schedules that might increase their tax burden is difficult for elected officials and can lead to failure at reelection time, as Buddy Roemer discovered and many expected Riley would find out in Alabama. In 1992, when Democrat Bill Clinton challenged the first president George Bush, his campaign's motto was "It's the economy, stupid," and Bush's failure to win reelection was widely connected to his reneging on his promise not to raise taxes. In one sense, an aversion to government size may seem slightly irrational on the part of voters, for services cannot be provided without resources and whereas some may prefer no government at all, most voters want some government services. But if tax increases are correlated with incompetence or corruption (problems of moral hazard), then the relationship Peltzman observed may reflect retrospective voting to control for moral hazard.

When Do Voters Punish Tax Increases? Besley and Case (1995) investigated whether voters use cross-state comparisons to evaluate the success of incumbent governors. If economic shocks are correlated across states by region, then voters can compare how they are doing with how their neighboring states are doing and thus better measure the extent to which incumbents are engaging in behavior they dislike. If their governor increases taxes and the governors of other states don't, voters perceive their governor as incompetent or engaging in excessive spending, whereas if the governors of nearby states increase taxes and their governor doesn't, voters perceive their governor as especially competent and capable of controlling of spending. Governors who want to increase taxes also benefit if voters see other states increasing taxes—the suggestion is that a tax increase is necessary to fund needed services.

It made sense for Riley to try a tax change if voters knew about Louisiana's tax change. Supporting this argument, Besley and Case found that a governor is more likely to be defeated in a reelection bid if he or she increases taxes but is more likely to win reelection if his geographic neighbors increase taxes. Note that when voters perceive moral-hazard problems, they may also punish the incumbent's party even if the incumbent is not running. Using exit polls in gubernatorial elections, Niemi, Stanley, and Vogel (1995) found that voters are less likely to support an incumbent party's candidate when taxes have been increased during the previous term and that state-level income also affects voters' decisions.

Perhaps luckily, then, for the Republicans in Alabama, Riley's controversial tax plan was defeated. Riley changed his tune and said that the voters had spoken—they wanted reform in spending, not new taxes. At the 2004 winter meeting of the executive committee of the Alabama Republican Party, Riley announced: "We're doing what the people of Alabama wanted. We're going to make it the most cost-effective, the most efficient government in the United States." Republicans in Alabama, looking forward to being united for the next eletion, in general forgave Riley for his tax-increase plan. "A lot of healing has gone on," said Republican state representative Mac Gipson. "We need to be solidified in future elections."[20]

Retrospective Voting and Cycles

The Incentive to Manipulate President George W. Bush was speaking in Pittsburgh in early December 2003, and his subject was the nation's economy: "The American economy is strong and it is getting stronger. Perhaps you saw the fact that the third-quarter annualized growth numbers were . . . the fastest pace in nearly 20 years."[21] Bush had reason to be happy—he knew that the state of the economy would be an issue in the upcoming 2004 presidential election, whether he made it one or not. By all accounts, when he took office, the economy was beginning a recession. Bush had labeled it the Clinton recession, with the goal of claiming credit for a recovery.[22] Empirical evidence suggests that voters choose retrospectively in presidential elections, just as they do in gubernatorial elections, based on the state of the economy.[23]

If voters choose retrospectively and are operating within short time frames, it might make sense for incumbents up for reelection, like Bush in 2004 or Clinton in 1996, to use the economy to try to influence voters' choices. That is, if voters mainly consider their own economic condition or that of the country as their criterion for evaluating an incumbent, then manipulating the economy might benefit the incumbent. For example, an incumbent president may want to increase spending or reduce taxes or increase the money supply (which would ease credit and expand the economy) prior to an election, bearing the burden for the expansion after the election. The idea that business cycles may be politically influenced is an old one.[24]

However, is this rational for voters? Voters should anticipate that elected officials are engaging in this behavior and discount such efforts. To the extent that voters are myopic, such cycles might occur. But there are two explanations for political business cycles in which voters are rational. One explanation relates to the moral-hazard and adverse-selection problems facing voters. Suppose that voters know that some incumbents are more competent at managing the economy than others but cannot tell for sure, based on the state of the economy, whether it is the incumbent's choices that are responsible or just luck. But by manipulating the economy prior to the election, the incumbent can reveal that he or she has the ability to manage the economy and should be reelected. Voters are not fooled by the manipulation but are able to infer from the success the incumbent's abilities.[25]

The Effects of Electoral Uncertainty and Partisan Preferences When elected officials have partisan preferences over macroeconomic policies, uncertainty about who will win the election can cause a political business cycle with rational voters as well. Such a cycle is a postelection effect on the economy.[26] To see how this works, for example, suppose voters anticipated that if Bush were reelected, inflation would be low and employment would not increase much, but if Kerry were elected, both inflation and unemployment would increase. Because the outcome of the election was uncertain beforehand, they didn't know for sure what the economy would be like afterward. Yet voters must make economic decisions based on expected prices and employment, which are an average of the two parties' positions based on the predicted outcome of the election. Once the election occurs, however, they alter these decisions in response to the positions of the elected party, thus affecting the economy. When Bush was elected, they revised their predictions on inflation and employment, changing their economic decisions on investing and so on, and if Kerry had been elected they would have revised their predictions on inflation and employment upward, similarly changing their economic decisions on investing and so on. Thus, after an election, the economy either booms or falls as a consequence of the resolution of the uncertainty.

Empirical Evidence on Electoral Cycles The empirical evidence on whether political business cycles occur which examines the effect of elections on aggregate economic outcomes is mixed.[27] A different way to test the theory is to examine the assumptions made about voters. The models assume that voters can distinguish between politically created cycles and those caused by exogenous factors. Wolfers (2002) provided an interesting test of whether voters can judge incumbents' abilities when the economy is affected by business-cycle forces. He examined the extent to which governors are reelected on the basis of state economy, controlling for cyclical forces. He found evidence that voters use a general rule of thumb and evaluate an incumbent based on how his or her state's economy performed relative to the national economy; thus, voters do not reward or punish incumbent governors for national economic events. Voters are influenced by state-level cycles, however, even when it is unlikely that their governor is responsible for the upturn or downturn in the state economy. Wolfers found, for example, that in states where the economy is positively affected by oil-price increases (such as Alaska, Texas, and Wyoming), governors are rewarded for booms associated with those price increases, while in states where the economy is negatively affected by oil-price increases (such as Indiana and Michigan), governors are punished for downturns associated with the price increases. Thus, his research suggests that voters are somewhat sophisticated: they do not reward or punish governors for the effects of national cycles, but they sometimes punish or reward governors for economic factors they cannot control.

Retrospective Voting and Parties

In our discussion of retrospective voting, we have assumed that the voters whom the incumbents must please to secure reelection are the voters in the general election. But Goodling's difficulties were in the Republican Party primary. In Pennsylvania, Goodling's state, primaries are closed. So Gerow, Goodling's opponent, was trying to persuade Republican voters, not the entire electorate, to throw out Goodling based on Goodling's past behavior. We have seen that the two major political parties are different in policy—voters perceive they are different, candidates for office choose different policy positions, and once elected, they make different policy choices. Moreover, if voters are choosing in such a way as to balance the parties, even moderate voters may prefer a candidate who is more extreme, to balance out an already elected official whose position is also extreme (moderating between the parties is discussed in chapter 4).

In figures 9.3 and 9.4, the percentage of senators who run for reelection and win is shown according to the distance of their positions from those preferred by the voters in their state's party from 1960 to 1990, as estimated by Schmidt, Kenny, and Morton (1996). The policy positions are measured on a 100-point scale based on the scores assigned these senators by the ADA. As we noted in chapter 4, the scores show a significant difference between Democrats and Republicans. For example, the average ADA score for Republican members of Congress from 1982 to 1990 was 17.17, while the average ADA score for Democratic members of Congress during that period was 74.09.[28]

In figures 9.3 and 9.4, Schmidt, Kenny, and Morton measured how close an incumbent senator's ADA score was to the score they estimated was the senator's party position in his or her state on the ADA scale. If an incumbent was 0 to 5 points from the party's voters, his or her adjusted ADA score was 5 or fewer points from that preferred by the voters in the party, as estimated by the researchers. If an incumbent was 25 or more points from his or her party's voters, his or her adjusted ADA score was 25 or more points from the point preferred by the voters in the party.

As the two figures demonstrate, both incumbents who were more ex-

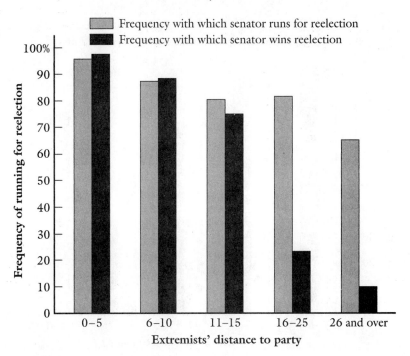

FIGURE 9.3

Frequency with Which Senators Run for Reelection and Win, for Senators Whose Positions Are More Extreme Than Those of the Voters in Their party in Their State, 1960–90

Source: Schmidt, Kenny, and Morton (1996).

treme than their party's voters and those who were more moderate were less likely to run for reelection or win reelection. The relationship is particularly close for the likelihood that an incumbent could win. Incumbents were much more likely to win if their voting positions were close to the position preferred by the voters in their party. This suggests strongly that voters do choose retrospectively. Moreover, the relationship reported here further demonstrates how parties influence candidates' positions. In chapter 4, we saw how, when candidates must first secure nomination in a primary before becoming a candidate in the general election and there is uncertainty about the location of the median voter in the electorate, the successful candidates will choose divergent positions. Our analysis shows that when voters choose retrospectively, they evaluate incumbents based on their closeness to their party's voters. Interestingly, moderation does not necessarily secure reelection, and becoming more moderate can decrease an incumbent's chance for reelection, rather than enhance it.[29]

FIGURE 9.4
Frequency with Which Senators Run for Reelection and Win, for Senators Whose Positions Are More Moderate Than Those of the Voters in Their Party in Their State, 1960–90

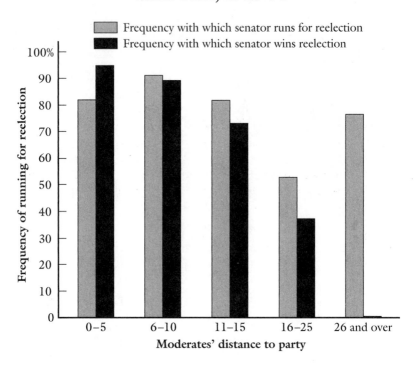

Source: Schmidt, Kenny, and Morton (1996).

Should Incumbency Be Limited?

The History of Term Limits

As we noted above, Representative Goodling considered the contest he faced in 1998 highly unusual. It wasn't just that his opponent in the primary was strong and articulate but also that he had support from a unique interest group, U.S. Term Limits, and its sister organization, Americans for Limited Terms. Term limits for elected offices in the United States have been debated since the American Revolution and are not unusual. Presidents have been prevented from serving more than two terms since 1951, with the passage of the Twenty-second Amendment to the Constitution. In fact, Goodling had pledged to support a constitutional amendment limiting

House members to three terms—six years in office. But he later voted against the measure and in favor of one allowing six terms—twelve years in office. One reason for the opposition of U.S. Term Limits to Goodling was his changed stance on the constitutional amendment.

Most states have term limits on executive offices like that for governor; some have had them for many years—since before the Civil War. Figure 9.5 shows states with term limits on governors and the year in which the limits were enacted. It is noteworthy that sixteen of the thirty-eight states with limits on gubernatorial terms passed the measures in the 1990s. At the same time, many of these states also passed term limits for legislative offices, as illustrated in Figure 9.6. As the figure shows, legislative term limits are completely a post-1990 phenomenon. Often these laws were designed to apply to members of Congress; in 1995, however, in *U.S. Term Limits, Inc., v. Thornton*, the Supreme Court declared their application to Congress unconstitutional because the Constitution sets forth the requirements for membership in Congress and changing those requirements (for example, by preventing someone from running for office because he or she has already served a number of terms) requires a constitutional amendment.

FIGURE 9.5
States with Gubernatorial Term Limits and Year Limit Was Enacted

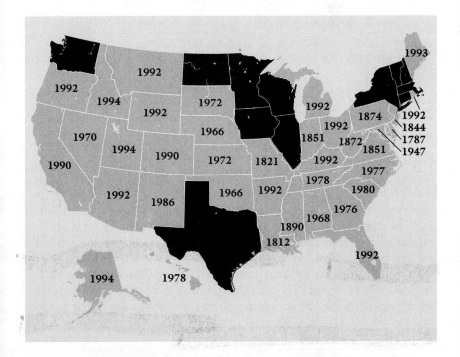

FIGURE 9.6
States with Legislative Term Limits and Year Limit Was Enacted

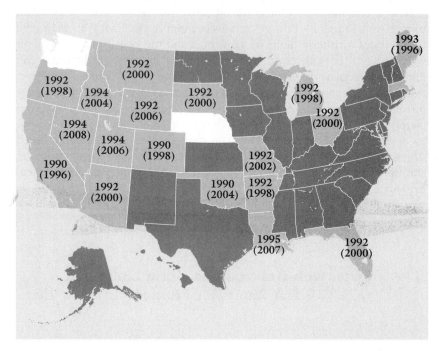

Notes: Dates in parentheses refer to the year in which the limit became effective in the House. Light-colored states passed limits, but they were annulled by state supreme courts.

Reasons for Term Limits

The Effect of Time on Incumbents' Behavior Why would voters want to enact term limits? After all, the analysis above suggests that voters can and do use a retrospective voting strategy to encourage incumbents to choose policy positions they prefer. Retrospective voting can help alleviate the twin voter information problems of moral hazard and adverse selection when incumbents run for reelection. But if term limits prevent incumbents from running for reelection, voters cannot use a retrospective strategy to solve those problems. However, retrospective voting does not appear to be successful all the time. As we discussed earlier, the extent to which voters are informed affects how they choose and the outcome of policy. If retrospective voting worked perfectly, we would not expect to find such an effect. Moreover, Wolfers's evidence suggests that voters tend to wrongly reward or punish incumbents based on economic factors.

Furthermore, problems of moral hazard and adverse selection may increase with the time an incumbent remains in office. Just as voters can "learn" about candidates during a campaign, so incumbents can learn while in office. We have assumed that voters cannot observe an incumbent's effort level because of random factors that affect ultimate policy outcomes. But incumbents who serve longer terms may learn more about those random factors. If an incumbent can anticipate their true size and direction, he or she can use the information to put forth less effort or make choices closer to those of his or her own preferences or the preferences of contributors. Thus, incumbents' knowledge of the government process can allow them to advocate legislation that benefits them in ways that voters cannot successfully monitor. On the other hand, many argue that when terms are limited, because there is less time for elected officials to learn how government works, they increase their reliance on nonelected staff members and interest group lobbyists who can control information and policy decisions.

Difficulties with Using Retrospective Voting Even if having incumbents learn how to "shirk" is harmful, why can't voters just adjust their retrospective voting strategies to account for this effect? That may not be so easy. Why would it be difficult for voters to use a retrospective voting strategy? First, because incumbents have an advantage over challengers that is independent of the advantage from retrospective voting (their ability to raise campaign resources), retrospective voting may not be as effective a method of solving moral-hazard and adverse-selection problems. The longer an incumbent has served in office, the easier it is for him or her to raise service- or favor-induced campaign contributions, because of an ability to provide such services while in office and because of the benefits to contributors from coordinating on incumbents. These advantages lessen the ability of voters to use retrospective voting as an evaluative mechanism and can increase with the length of the term.

Second, not all voters may have the same skills at processing information that may be necessary for retrospective voting to be effective. As noted earlier, Husted, Kenny, and Morton (1995) found that better-educated voters are less likely to make errors in estimating their senators' voting records. Coupled with Bartels's evidence (1996) that uninformed voters do not choose as if they were informed, this suggests that if most voters are less educated, it may make more sense to use term limits as a control over incumbents rather than retrospective voting.

Third, even if voters do have the skills to process the information or can use cues provided by benefit-seeking group leaders, as mentioned earlier, the ability to communicate information to voters varies across jurisdictions. More rural jurisdictions have fewer newspapers and television stations, making communication more difficult. This notion is supported by Stromberg's findings (2004b) that these voters are less likely to receive government benefits. Adams and Kenny (1986) also found support for this explanation of

the use of term limits when they examined the states that used gubernatorial term limits as of the mid-1980s. In general, term limits at that time were
more prevalent in rural states and places where educational levels are lower.
Gubernatorial term limits were also more prevalent in states that have four-
year terms for governor than in states with two-year terms.[30]

The Puzzle of the Increase in Term Limits

Service-Induced Campaign Contributions as an Explanation

Yet there is a problem with this explanation—it does not seem to explain
why there was a movement for instituting legislative term limits and an increase in states using gubernatorial term limits in the 1990s. As Francis and
Kenny (1999, p. 76) remarked concerning the advent of legislative term
limits: "The answer cannot lie in legislative term length or in voter education. There have been very few changes in the last 40 years in the length of
terms for the state house or senate. And educational attainment has risen,
which should actually reduce the need for term limits."

As noted earlier, however, voters may turn to term limits if an incumbent
has an electoral advantage independent of voters' retrospective evaluations.
If incumbents have greater campaign contributions and can use them to
sway impressionable voters, then even if other voters attempt to use retrospective voting strategies, the mechanism may not be as successful in weed-
ing out bad incumbents as it would be otherwise. There has been a growth
in campaign expenditures in all election races, perhaps reflecting an increased use of service-induced campaign contributions, which voters may
see as detrimental. Although we argued that the costs of these services are
widely dispersed and thus difficult to organize against, voters may use a
term-limit measure to control for their use. Furthermore, in recent years
there has been a rise in the professionalism of state legislatures, which some
have argued has also led to a reduction in competitiveness in elections.[31]
Hence, the increased demand for term limits for legislators and governors
covered may simply be a reflection of this increase.

Daniel and Lott (1997) found that in California, legislative term limits
substantially reduced campaign expenditures and increased the competitiveness of the races even before the limits became effective. Moncrief, Niemi,
and Powell (2004) investigated the degree of competitiveness in state legislatures as a function of the term-limit structure across states. They found
that term limits have increased competitiveness when other factors that can
affect competitiveness are controlled for. This suggests that because incumbents are less able to promise favors and services, campaign contributions
fell, and contributors did not have the same advantage from coordinating
their contributions on behalf of an incumbent who would soon be out of office on account of term limits.

Partisanship

There are other explanations for the rise in term limits—some have argued that the movement simply reflects attempts by Republicans and conservatives (the main proponents) to change the partisan control of legislatures. Certainly many Republicans who supported term limits when Republicans were the minority party in Congress (pre-1994), as Goodling did, changed their tune once Republicans won a majority in the House of Representatives. With the decrease in support among Republicans, the movement lost much of its steam.[32]

Nevertheless, advocates of term limits argue that the new legislators—like Jack Norton in Arkansas—will be more like citizen representatives rather than the career politicians they replaced. Have term limits had this effect? Carey, Niemi, and Powell (1998), surveying state legislators in 1995, found that there were no systematic differences in the professional backgrounds, education levels, income levels, or ideologies between legislators elected in states with term limits and those elected in states without them. The electoral success of African Americans and religious fundamentalist candidates were not significantly different either, although states with term limits did demonstrate greater success for women candidates. Carey, Niemi, and Powell did find that legislators in states with term limits spent less time securing "pork"—benefits specific to their districts—than legislators in states without term limits, a difference that may reflect a decline in service- or favor-induced campaign contributions.

Voters' Changing the Electoral Calendar

Too Clever

Keeping a Challenger off the Ballot In December 2001, California Democratic incumbent governor Gray Davis was worried about his chances for reelection. Voters in California were unhappy with his job performance, particularly his handling of the state's energy crisis. Polls reported that only 38 percent of voters approved of his record. Although Davis was glad no other Democrat would challenge him in the March primary, polls suggested that one of the candidates for the Republican nomination, former Los Angeles mayor Richard Riordan, would beat him in the general election by 7 percentage points. Riordan was likely to win the primary—polls predicted he would win 42 percent of the Republican primary votes to 19 percent for Bill Jones and only 5 percent for William E. Simon (with the remainder undecided). A race against either Jones or Simon would be much easier for Davis, who was predicted to win in either potential matchup.[33] What to do?

Davis decided to campaign early against Riordan, spending $10 million before the primary. As we noted in chapter 6, he conveyed to his contributors that he would view it an "unfriendly act" if they gave money to Riordan. He found a video clip in which pro-choice Riordan called abortion "murder" on a public-access cable television program. His campaign adviser, Garry South, related: "We knew the ad would be relatively fatal. It hit him both ways. The pro-life people thought he had changed his strongly held beliefs for crass political purposes. The pro-choice people just thought he was a liar."[34] Davis successfully helped conservative businessman Bill Simon defeat Riordan and then attacked Simon as an "incompetent" and "crooked" businessman, winning reelection with 47.3 percent of the vote to Simon's 42.4 percent (with minor-party and independent candidates taking the remaining votes).

The Consequences Yet voters' unhappiness with Davis and Republicans' unhappiness with his tactics during the primary unraveled the governor's success. His vote totals were hardly impressive as an incumbent; when he ran in 1998, he'd received 58 percent of the vote. And as it would happen, California is one of eighteen states in which voters can demand a recall election by having a petition signed by a given percentage of registered voters, forcing a potential change in leadership between regularly scheduled elections.[35] In February 2003, some Republicans and some conservative interest groups started a petition drive to recall the governor. The state faced a severe budget deficit, and Davis needed Republican state legislators to vote in favor of his proposed solutions.[36] But Republicans remained intransigent—refusing to increase taxes as Davis desired. Republicans who had voted with Davis on the last budget had not been reelected, and those who were left saw the potential of his being replaced in a recall election. In early July, the leaders of the recall drive announced that they had amassed more than the required 12 percent of registered voters on their petitions. A *Los Angeles Times* poll reported that only 22 percent of voters approved of the governor's job performance, and 51 percent would vote to recall the governor.[37] As we saw in chapter 7, the Davis recall was successful, and Arnold Schwarzenegger replaced him as governor.

When Davis first heard about the recall attempt, he was dismissive. Most recall efforts fail. During the period of time that California has allowed for the recall of state officials (since 1911), only 7 of the 117 attempts had made it to the ballot before Schwarzenegger defeated Davis (all for state legislators), and only four officials had been recalled. In all the states that provide for a recall, only one other governor has ever been recalled (Lynn J. Frazier of North Dakota, in 1921).[38] Why, then, do some states have such procedures, and why, if they rarely succeed, are they attempted? When can they be successful?

Recall Elections

Procedures Although typically considered one of the processes by which Americans engage in "direct democracy" (the others being initiatives and referenda, discussed later), recall elections are distinctive in that voters can use them to exert control over incumbent elected officials during their terms. If voters believe that an incumbent has made unacceptable choices and that a replacement could do better, the recall election allows them to petition for a vote on whether the incumbent should finish out his or her term. The rules on how recalls are conducted vary by state and locality but in general require first that voters file a petition signed by a minimum percentage of registered voters and then, if the election is held, that a majority of the voters vote in favor of the recall (in some cases a supermajority is required, and there may be specific grounds, such as corruption, that are subject to judicial review). The way a recalled official is replaced also varies—in some states, the vacant office is filled in the way that unexpectedly vacant offices are normally filled (by appointment or special election); in other states, as in California, voters vote for a replacement at the same time that they vote on the recall of the official.

Costs Recall elections can be quite costly for their proponents because achieving the number of signatures on a petition requires time-consuming canvassing of voters and ensuring that the signatures and the petitions have valid information, all undertaken within a given time period. In 1961, when blacks in Los Angeles attempted to recall white city council member Joe Hollingsworth, who had been appointed to fill a vacant seat over their objections, nearly half of the signatures were declared invalid by the city clerk. They had only ten days in which to gather more signatures, which they did, only to have the clerk invalidate the petition for failing to include required information about the individuals circulating the petition, thus leaving them insufficient time to regather signatures.[39] Moreover, the cost of a special election can be burdensome (if one is necessary, sometimes recall elections are scheduled at the same time as regular elections for other offices in a state or locality). Senator Dianne Feinstein, when she was mayor of San Francisco, defeated a recall effort in large part by criticizing her opponents for frivolously wasting public moneys only six months before she would face reelection.[40]

Benefits Why go to the trouble of a recall, given these costs? For African American leaders in Los Angeles, the recall attempt was part of a general process of trying to achieve political office for blacks in the city. At the time of the city council vacancy, no African American had been elected to the city council even though blacks constituted almost 15 percent of the city's population, and African Americans believed they should have representation on the fifteen-member council. The movement to recall the appointed white council member was seen as part of a general strategy to increase black voter registration and activism in order for African Americans to achieve elected office. Their efforts no doubt influenced the appointment of Gilbert Lindsay to a seat that opened subsequently and his election to the seat in 1963. The voters they mobilized helped Tom Bradley defeat Hollingsworth and in 1973 become the first black mayor of Los Angeles (serving for two decades) and the second black mayor of a majority-white city. The recall effort, then, was hardly a failure.[41]

Using a recall effort, as blacks did in Los Angeles, to mobilize voters for future elections can backfire if the process reveals that the cause has little support. When Mayor Dianne Feinstein of San Francisco sponsored a gun-control measure, the White Panthers, a group who described themselves as "Communist, Marxist, Leninist, Maoist, Castroist,"[42] failed miserably to recall Feinstein and in fact helped her reelection and her future campaign for the U.S. Senate by giving her much publicity. As *The Washington Post* noted after the recall election: "Feinstein . . . is now a certified national leader of the Democratic Party. As she proved in her remarkable 4-to-1 victory, she is an accomplished, effective politician. There are currently no Democratic women in the Senate or the Statehouses; the . . . Democrats need Dianne Feinstein." After the recall victory, Feinstein herself concluded about her chances for getting reelected, "Anybody who files against me is going to get creamed."[43]

Why would a group of voters like the White Panthers attempt a recall, given its likely failure and the consequence of such failure? From the perspective of the outside observer, it would seem foolish, given the low probability of success, yet from the point of view of the group of like-minded voters, if the utility payoff from winning is sizable and expected to have some long-term effects—such as mobilization on issues they support, like reductions in gun control—then the expected utility from challenging an incumbent through a recall may be worth the cost. For groups opposed to an incumbent, a recall election, as an explicit referendum on the incumbent's record, means that an incumbent who can manage to win reelection by calling a challenger less qualified has a more difficult time when there is no explicit challenger to demonize. The incumbent has more difficulty making the election about the challenger (as Davis did with Simon and Bush did with Kerry). A group that wishes to see an incumbent defeated but does not anticipate having a candidate able to defeat the incumbent in the near future (either because the incumbent is recently elected, as with Davis, or because the group lacks visible qualified candidates willing to run) may find it desirable to push for a recall. Note that this strategy is more difficult in the California system, where voters choose a replacement at the same time as they vote to recall the incumbent, than in other jurisdictions, where there is a separate contest later to determine who will replace the recalled official.

Effects We also would expect that states allowing recall elections would show a greater difference in elected officials' behavior as compared with states without recalls. Two of the four recalled state legislators in California's history were Republican state assembly members who cut deals with Democrats; both were defeated in 1995 in their heavily Republican districts. It is probably not surprising that Republicans in the state assembly were wary of engaging in similar alliances with Davis in 2003. Although recalls are rare, the potential for their use no doubt can affect the choices of elected officials. In July 2003, some Texans unhappy with Republican governor Rick Perry started a recall drive of their own on the Internet. Yet because Texas has no recall process for state or county officials (though some cities have one), the only way to forcibly remove the governor prior to the next election is by an impeachment by the state legislature (dominated by Republicans in 2003). Referring to California's problems, Perry reportedly remarked, "I get up every day and thank God I don't live in California."[44]

If the potential for use of the recall does affect elected officials' behavior in office, then we would expect that elected officials in states where recalls are an option would be more likely to choose positions close to the median voters in their electorates. However, recall provisions tend to exist along with mechanisms of direct democracy such as initiatives and referenda. These mechanisms can have a similar effect on elected officials, as we will see in the next section. Empirical evidence suggests that elected officials do choose policies closer to those of their electorate in states with these provisions, but disentangling the evidence to determine whether it is because of the potential for recall or because of the potential for referenda or initiatives is difficult.

Referenda and Initiatives

California in the 1970s

The tax proposals of Alabama governor Riley and Louisiana state legislator Stelly required passage not only by the legislatures in their states but also by the voters directly, in referenda. In some cases, however, measures like those are proposed directly by voters through petition. Although elected officials in Alabama and Louisiana in the early twenty-first century were worried about the tax measures put before voters, elected officials in California were appalled in June 1978 when activists Howard Jarvis and Paul Gann got on the ballot Proposition 13, which promised to cut property taxes in half and provide strict state constitutional limits on the amount of future increases. Former governor Edmund G. (Pat) Brown, father of then-governor Jerry Brown, who opposed the measure, called it "Communist." Los Angeles mayor Tom Bradley said it would "hit the city [Los Angeles] like a neutron bomb, leaving some city facilities standing virtually empty and human services devastated." The president of Los Angeles Chamber of Commerce, Howard Allen, described the measure as a "fraud on the taxpayer that will

cause fiscal chaos, massive unemployment, and disruption of the economy."
San Francisco's board of supervisors threatened to fire fifty-five hundred city
employees, raise bus fares, and cut funding for hospitals and libraries.[45]

Proposition 13 passed, and California did not fall into the ocean. Yet the
proposition did fundamentally affect much of the way in which California
funds public services. In education, California's per-pupil-spending rank
went from eighteenth in the country in 1977 to forty-second in 1995–96. It
also changed the level of government at which the distribution of state revenue is determined—before passage, local governments could determine
their own property tax rates and thus controlled their budgets directly, but
after its passage they needed to seek aid from the state legislature.[46] Some
elected officials believed that the proposition's passage was the result of a
political mistake on the part of Governor Jerry Brown. While voters were ex-
periencing record tax increases (voter Ernie Dynda noted that the property
tax on his home had increased from $800 in 1974 to $2,000 in 1978),[47]
Brown allowed a state surplus of $3 billion to accumulate, according to
then–state treasurer Jess Unruh.[48] Although Brown and the legislature be-
latedly passed their own alternative tax proposition, which was on the ballot
with Proposition 13, the measure failed.

The Effects of Direct Democracy

Theory The failure of Brown and the California legislature to anticipate
the extent of voters' unhappiness with the tax system led to voting on and
passage of the initiative. The lesson is that if elected officials know that referenda and initiatives can be used to implement policies that are close to
voters' preferences, they should enact those policies before voters act for
themselves. Thus, the threat of initiatives and referenda, like the threat of recall elections, can induce politicians to choose policy positions closer to
those preferred by the median voters in their electorates.[49] Furthermore, initiatives and referenda allow voters to disentangle issues that are bundled together when they vote for candidates. That is, suppose the bare majority of
voters in a state are pro-choice but hold conservative positions on other issues, such as government spending, gun control, and so on. If they have to
choose between an anti-abortion conservative and a pro-choice liberal, they
need to make a choice as to which issues are paramount in their decision. If
voters can use the initiative process to enact pro-choice measures, then they
can enact policies on particular issues closer to their own preferences.[50]

Sometimes elected officials may prefer to allow measures to be enacted via
initiatives rather than tackle them through legislation. Matsusaka (1992)
contended that highly technical controversial issues tend to be considered
by the public via initiative so that legislators can avoid taking positions on
them. As we discussed in chapter 7, it may be difficult for voters to express opinions on complex issues or to induce elected officials to follow their

preferences on those issues through public opinion polls. Initiatives and referenda can be a way of forcing both the public and elected officials to take positions. Matsusaka and McCarty (2001) argued that initiatives can also reveal to elected officials voters' policy preferences and the strength of those preferences. So in some cases, elected officials may encourage voters to consider policies via direct democracy.

Evidence In 2003, twenty-three states had some form of direct democracy through initiative or referendum.[51] If the presence of direct democracy does lead to policies closer to those preferred by the median voter in the electorates in which they are used, a comparison of states with and without direct democracy should show a difference. Bowler and Donovan (2002) found evidence that voters in states with direct democracy are more likely to believe that government is responsive to them than voters in states without these procedures. Gerber (1999) considered the relationship between public opinion on parental-consent abortion laws and the death penalty and laws enacted. She found that states with laws allowing for initiatives were more likely to have laws on those two issues that reflected public opinion than states that did not allow for initiatives. Notice that it is the threat of the initiative that forces the legislature to enact laws closer to public opinion, not whether the initiative is used or not.[52]

Elected versus Appointed Officials

Electing Prosecutors

A Prosecutor's Mistake In 1996, Dominican immigrant Milton Lantigua was released from prison after serving five years of a twenty-year term for fatally shooting a man on a Bronx, New York, street. He was released because the state appeals court had discovered that the prosecution in his case had allowed its chief witness to perjure herself and had not revealed the existence of a second witness. The court called the errors "especially egregious." Lantigua was awarded $300,000 in damages from New York State and is currently suing New York City for violating his civil rights. The prosecutor in the case, who left the district attorney's office prior to the reversal, denies wrongdoing but could not comment at this writing because of the civil suit. Senior aides to the Bronx district attorney's office called the prosecutor's error an "honest mistake." *The New York Times* reported: "Mr. Lantigua, who is now 33, suggests he has paid too great a price for the prosecution's errors. 'They don't want to say they made a mistake,' he said."[53]

Retrospective Voting Using Conviction Rates Like the Bronx district attorney, over 95 percent of state and local prosecuting attorneys who deal with felonies in the United States are elected. Yet few other countries elect prosecutors. How does electing prosecutors affect the way crimes are investigated and prosecuted in the United States? When prosecutors face reelection, they often advertise their conviction rates, as noted by Gordon and Huber (2002). Should they? Should voters use conviction rates to evaluate prosecutors retrospectively? Or is that likely to lead to the conviction of the innocent in order to increase reelection prospects? Gordon and Huber cleverly demonstrate how votes' use of conviction rates retrospectively can induce elected prosecutors to expend the effort to gather information about whether a potentially guilty defendant is actually guilty or not.

How does that work? Cases brought to prosecutors have three possible outcomes—conviction, acquittal, or dropped charges. Consider a prosecutor, Michele, who has to decide whether to prosecute Doug. She has information that suggests whether or not Doug is guilty, but the information is incomplete. That is, Michele perceives that there is a probability, x, that Doug is guilty and a probability, $1 - x$, that he is innocent. If Michele investigates further, however, she can find out more reliably whether Doug is guilty. If Michele does not investigate further, then the probability that she will convict Doug is also given by x (the probability that Doug will be acquitted is $1 - x$). If Michele does investigate and finds that Doug is guilty, she can go to trial and win for sure, and if she finds out that he is innocent, she can drop the case without going to trial. Unlike the situation in Lantigua's case, here Gordon and Huber assumed that any information the prosecutor discovers will be revealed to Doug's attorney.

Assume that voters want Michele to expend the effort to investigate cases, but voters observe only the information about the case revealed in the newspaper (which is the same as the value of x) and the outcome of the case (conviction, acquittal, or dropped charges). Note that if an acquittal occurs, it is obvious to the voters that Michele has "shirked," because if she had gathered sufficient information, she would have dropped the case. Thus, voters rationally should never reward elected prosecutors for acquittals.

If voters increase the value they place on convictions, what is the effect? Michele will investigate cases that she normally would have failed to investigate because the only way to increase her conviction rate is to gather information (that is, her conviction rate approaches 1 when she uses the new information to drop all cases in which acquittals would occur and prosecutes all defendants who are known to be guilty). It makes sense for voters to examine conviction rates as a control over the moral-hazard problem facing prosecutors.

Of course, rewarding conviction rates does little good if the prosecutor is corrupt or lax with the rules, as the New York State Court of Appeals ruled was the case in the Bronx. In fact, rewarding convictions is likely to increase the incentive for prosecutors to violate the law, particularly if it is difficult for the public to monitor violations of the law by prosecutors. A national study found that "state and local prosecutors stretched, bent or broke rules so badly in more than 2,000 cases since 1970 that appellate judges dismissed criminal charges, reversed convictions or reduced sentences."[54] If voters do not punish prosecutors who engage in this sort of behavior, solving one moral-hazard problem (forcing prosecutors to gather information) simply leads to another (the violation of judicial rules).

Electing Judges

A Judge's Mistake A man accused of a notorious murder was acquitted in Oregon in 1911, and the populace believed that the circuit judge in charge of the case had given instructions to the jury that were biased in favor of the defendant. Some decided to take action and circulated a recall petition against the circuit judge (Oregon was the first state to pass recall provisions, in 1908) even though the instructions he had used had been given in another case, one that had led to a conviction, and had been supported by the state supreme court. A local newspaper favorable to the use of the recall bewailed its attempted use to control judges' legal decisions:

> In exercising the recall in such an instance, the electors of the second district, would, in effect, assume all the functions of one of the coordinate branches of state government of Oregon, setting aside the judiciary for a moment and making each elector in the second district a super supreme judge, exercising power above the judiciary and above the constitution itself. . . . The people are not in position to pass upon the legal questions involved.[55]

Are judges and judicial decisions different? Should they be subject to recall elections? Should they be elected at all?

Retrospective Voting Using Underpunishment Rates In thirty-nine states, trial judges stand for election and periodically stand for reelection. Yet voters probably know little about them; usually they are chosen in non-partisan elections. What voters know is sentencing behavior. How is this knowledge likely to affect judges' behavior? Some voters may prefer that judges be lenient in sentencing, whereas other voters may prefer that all convicted criminals serve long sentences. So voters face an adverse-selection problem as well as a moral-hazard problem. They want judges who have the same policy preferences as they have with respect to sentencing (adverse selection), but they also want judges to mete out punishments that are commensurate with the crime—that is, they do not want judges to make mistakes by expending too little effort (moral hazard). Huber and Gordon (2004) pointed out that errors of underpunishment are more likely to be observed than errors of overpunishment because convicted criminals will always claim that they have been sentenced too harshly, whereas voters are likely to notice when someone who appears to them to be highly guilty (as in Oregon in 1911) has been released or lightly sentenced. California state supreme court justice Rose Bird lost her seat in 1986 when voters criticized her unwillingness to support the death penalty in cases in which the rest of the court approved it.

How does voters' retrospective voting affect judicial behavior? Huber and Gordon contended that as elections for trial judges near, we should expect that all judges, regardless of their constituents' preferences for punishment, should choose higher sentences for all crimes. Because the main mistake voters can readily observe is underpunishment, overpunishment has few negative consequences, particularly close to elections, since discovering such errors takes more time. Huber and Gordon investigated whether this was the case by examining information on sentencing, judges, and constituents in cases before elected trial judges in Pennsylvania from 1990 to 1999. They found that controlling for other factors that can affect sentences, trial judges do become more punitive as they approach reelection. They noted, however, that their results do not mean that the process of electing judges is necessarily more problematic than that of appointing them. Any periodic review of judges might lead to the same sort of behavior. Moreover, their evidence shows that judges do respond to voters' preferences for sentencing, suggesting that the electoral mechanism does influence judicial behavior.

Electing Regulators

What about electing regulators? Whereas the majority of state and local business regulators are appointed by elected officials, in a number of states they are directly elected. Besley and Coate (2004) showed that the election of regulators, like the use of referenda and initiatives, results in a disentangling of the choices having to do with regulation from other issues, potentially benefiting voters. They argued that parties may want to choose regulatory policies that are pro-business in order to gain campaign contributions. Because the positions on regulation are bundled with other issues that voters care about and that divide the parties, voters cannot use the election mechanism to control regulatory policies. But if they elect regulators independently, then the regulators have an incentive to choose pro-consumer policies. Besley and Coate found some empirical evidence that supports this argument—that is, public utility regulators in states in which they are elected make choices that appear to benefit voters (at least in the short run; it is unclear what happens to investment in energy in the long run).

What We Know

We know that voters face a difficult problem in controlling elected officials' behavior. Elected officials may choose not to make choices voters prefer because they would rather not work hard—moral hazard. Or elected officials may choose not to make choices voters prefer because they have their own preferences—adverse selection. Voters cannot easily measure elected officials' actual behavior and thus cannot always make sure that those problems will not exist. Inequalities in information about policies can make this problem more consequential for some voters. Uninformed voters do not always choose as informed voters do. The expansion of information also affects public policy, suggesting further that information matters and the fact that some voters are less informed than others implies that their preferences may not be as well represented as those of better-informed voters.

On the positive side, we found evidence that voters do tend to use retrospective voting strategies to control for these problems. In particular, they choose retrospectively based on the state of the economy, which can encourage elected officials to make choices about the economy that may cause cycles in the economy. Voters also reward or punish incumbents, sometimes for economic outcomes over which the officials had little control. Evidence suggests that voters choose retrospectively when they vote in judicial and prosecutorial elections and that judges' and prosecutors' choices in office are influenced by elections and the election calendar. Yet despite the evidence suggesting that voters use retrospective voting, there has been an increase in limits on elected officials' terms, which may be related to the fact that retrospective voting is not always successful and a belief that career politicians are more likely to engage in undesirable behavior, or it may simply reflect an effort to change the partisan composition of legislatures. Voters also use recall elections to control elected officials. Finally, voters use referenda and initiatives to encourage elected officials to make choices they prefer on particular issues or directly elect regulators whose primary responsibility is defined by a particular issue.

What We Don't Know: What Voters Want

Ola Babcock Miller was Iowa's first female secretary of state. Just before she took office, in 1933, the son of a close friend was killed in an automobile accident. She therefore decided to do something about highway safety. At the time, the motor vehicle department, which was within her jurisdiction, consisted of fifteen employees whose job was to make sure the department received payment for driver's licenses. Miller decided to add to their duties the enforcement of road-safety regulations. She assigned each worker a set of counties and instructed him to look for unsafe vehicles and drivers and to warn or ticket them if necessary. She and her employees gave speeches at high schools, clubs, and other organizations. She issued them uniforms, which they had to pay for themselves. Her efforts paid off. Although the national highway death and accident toll increased by 17 percent between 1933 and 1934, in Iowa it decreased by almost 15 percent. In 1935, the Iowa legislature formalized Miller's efforts by establishing the Iowa State Highway Safety Patrol of fifty-three men and a training camp for recruits.[56]

Although Miller's accomplishments were remarkable, even more note-worthy was her electoral success. She first ran for office as a Democrat in 1932, when Republicans dominated the state government. The party had placed her name on the ballot as a thank-you for her efforts in support of her late husband, Alex Miller, the party's unsuccessful candidate for governor in 1926, and she called her candidacy "a martyrdom for the cause." But in 1932, with the economy in a depression, retrospective voters opted for a change, electing FDR along with other Democrats, including Miller. In 1934, when she was up for reelection, voters pleased with her highway-safety measures gave her more votes than any other previously elected Iowa official. But another reason she was so successful in her reelection bid was that she had some help figuring out what voters wanted. Her daughter Ophelia had married a marketing executive who was interested in measuring public opinion and wanted to try his hand at surveying voters in an election. His name was George Gallup. In chapter 10, we consider the difficulties that candidates for office have in figuring out voters' preferences and the ways in which pollsters like Gallup are involved in U.S. elections.

Study Questions and Problems

1. Suppose Justin is a candidate for governor of Connecticut. He believes that it is inappropriate for the government to regulate highway speed limits and that individuals should be free to drive at whatever speed they desire. But he knows that the majority of voters support speed regulation, so he keeps his opinion to himself. Justin would also like to have a long-term political career.

   a. Is this a problem of moral hazard or adverse selection? Explain your answer. Give an example of each type of problem.

   b. Assume that voters can observe Justin's actions after the election. If elected, will Justin use his power to reduce enforcement of the speed limit in Connecticut? Why or why not?

   c. Would your answer to item 1a change if Justin were elected governor of West Virginia (which has term limits)? Why or why not?

   d. Suppose voters can monitor Justin's enforcement of the speed limit only by measuring how many speeders are caught, but they have no way of determining how many speeders are allowed to break the law and only rarely find out when Justin is wrongly accusing someone of speeding. How would these factors affect Justin's behavior if he were governor of Connecticut? Explain.

   e. Suppose that Justin is governor of North Dakota, which has recall elections but no term limits. Are these conditions likely to affect your answer to 1a or to 1c? Why or why not?

2. Many political pundits complain that ballot initiatives in California are unreasonably complex and that voters therefore lack information

about the measures and so are often duped into approving measures that benefit special interest groups. Does this reasoning make sense? Why or why not?

3. Suppose that Justin, as governor of Connecticut, would like to improve the state's education system but knows this can only be done with a tax increase. He knows that voters would also like to see an improvement in education but they think that taxes are already too high. What factors would determine whether or not he would try to raise taxes? Explain your answer.

4. You have been asked to help write a new constitution for the state of Washington, which regulates the prices and services of Internet service providers in the state. Some experts have proposed that the state set up a separate regulatory commission for Internet providers rather than regulate these companies through an executive agency by means of laws passed by the state legislature. Do you think that is a good idea? Why or why not?

NOTES

1. Thomas B. Edsall, "Coming to Term Limits: Incumbent Goodling's 13th House Campaign Has Become an Issue Itself as Special Interest Money Floods Pa. District," *Washington Post*, May 12, 1998.
2. See Jewell and Breaux (1988, 1991).
3. Lois Romano, "Term Limits Give Neophytes Legs to Run," *Washington Post*, May 28, 1998.
4. "White House Dismisses Former Advisor's Charges," CNN.com, March 21, 2004, http://www.cnn.com/2004/US/03/21/bush.terror/index.html.
5. Judith Miller, "Former Terrorism Official Faults White House on 9/11," *New York Times*, March 22, 2004.
6. Ted Bridis, "White House Hits Back at Former Counterterrorism Aide," Associated Press, March 22, 2004.
7. Miller, "Former Terrorism Official Faults White House on 9/11."
8. Toni Locy and Susan Schmidt, "Ex-Aide Tells of Pressure for Travel Office Firings," *Washington Post*, January 18, 1996.
9. R. Drummond Ayres, "What If Politicians Could Tell No Lies," *New York Times*, February 28, 1999.
10. Edsall, "Coming to Term Limits."
11. Alternatively, an adverse-selection problem can exist when candidates vary in capabilities.
12. Stratmann examined only those states in which legislators are selected in single-member districts and all are elected simultaneously. He also omitted Louisiana because of the state's use of nonpartisan elections and Alabama, Delaware, Iowa, and South Dakota because of limited data. He omitted Mississippi and Virginia because they did not have state contests in the years he examined.
13. See McKelvey and Ordeshook (1985).
14. For a formal analysis of how voters can use retrospective voting to control the moral-hazard problem, see Austen-Smith and Banks (1989) and Banks and Sundaram (1993).
15. For a formal analysis of how retrospective voting can be used to control adverse-selection problems in elections, see Banks and Duggan (2000).

16. See, for example, Fiorina (1981).
17. David M. Halbfinger, "G.O.P. Chief's Idea for Raising Alabama: Taxes," *New York Times*, June 4, 2003.
18. Phillip Rawls, "Dick Armey Plans Trip to Alabama to Oppose Riley's Tax Plan," Associated Press State & Local Wire, June 18, 2003.
19. Patrick Courreges, "Tax-Swap Proponent Vic Stelly Says He Won't Seek Re-election," *Baton Rouge State-Times/Morning Advocate*, July 13, 2002.
20. Kim Chandler, "Republicans Emphasize Unity: Say Division over Riley Tax Plan behind Them," *Birmingham News*, February 22, 2004.
21. Thomas DeFrank, "Bullish on Reelection, White House Savors Economic Tea Leaves," *New York Daily News*, December 4, 2003.
22. Even Clinton economic adviser Gene Spurling noted that the economy was beginning a recession when Bush took the reins, as remarked in an interview on the Fox News show *Hannity and Colmes*, January 7, 2003.
23. See Kramer (1971) and the discussion in chapter 10.
24. The literature is reviewed in Alesina and Rosenthal (1995).
25. See Cukierman and Meltzer (1986), Rogoff and Sibert (1988), Persson and Tabellini (1990), and Rogoff (1990). Political business cycles can also occur with rational voters when elected officials are forced to choose policies that constrain future investment and consumption choices because of the inherent multidimensionality of these choices. See Boylan, Ledyard, and McKelvey (1996) and Boylan and McKelvey (1995).
26. See Alesina, Londregan, and Rosenthal (1993).
27. Again, see Alesina, Londregan, and Rosenthal (1993).
28. As noted in chapter 4, when members of Congress miss votes due to absences, the ADA counts the absence as a vote for conservatism. Again, the authors corrected for this in their analysis of the data.
29. One alternative explanation for why moderates may be less successful is that even though they are close to the median voter in their district, they are not members of the party that dominates the district and are thus independent of ideology: they have trouble winning, and they have chosen moderate positions in an attempt to win (albeit unsuccessfully). I thank Gary Jacobson for pointing this out.
30. See also Grofman and Sutherland (1996) as well.
31. See Moncrief, Niemi, and Powell (2004).
32. Katharine Q. Seelye, "Term-Limits Advocates Take a Bad Thrashing," *New York Times*, May 21, 1998.
33. Emily Bazar, "Poll: Riordan Leads Davis by 7 Points," Scripps Howard News Service, December 13, 2001.
34. John W. Wildermuth, "Riordan Alarmed Davis the Most: Consultants Dissect Race for Governor," *San Francisco Chronicle*, January 12, 2003.
35. For detailed (although somewhat out-of-date) information on recall procedures, see Zimmerman (1986). The Council of State Governments, in Lexington, Ky., and at http://www.csg.org, provides the current rules on recall by state.
36. Although Democrats controlled both state legislative bodies, a supermajority is needed to pass tax increases in California.
37. Gregg Jones and Evan Halper, "Recall Backers Assert Victory in Signature Drive," *Los Angeles Times*, July 8, 2003.
38. Jim Puzzanghera, "History of Recall Gives Fuel to Both Sides," *San Jose Mercury News*, July 13, 2003. Arizona governor Evan Mecham was impeached before a recall election, which would have likely led to his removal from office as well.
39. See Patterson (1969).
40. Mark Shields, "Feinstein and the Democrats," *Washington Post*, April 29, 1983.

41. In 1961, Latinos were already serving on the Los Angeles City Council. To some extent, however, blacks replaced them in districts in which both groups had sizable populations, and from 1962 to 1984, no Latinos served on the council. In the later 1960s, Bradley and Latino leaders attempted to increase the size of the city council to facilitate the election of more minority candidates, but the proposal was defeated by voters. See Kousser (1999, pp. 90–91). Issues of minority representation in elections are discussed in chapter 14.

42. Wallace Turner, "Fringe Group Forces Ouster Vote on Coast Mayor," *New York Times*, February 9, 1983.

43. Mark Shields, "Feinstein and the Democrats."

44. As reported in Paul Burka and Patricia Kilday Hart, "The Best and the Worst Legislators, 2003." *Texas Monthly*, July 2003. Burka and Hart also noted that Hilary McLean, the chief deputy press secretary to Davis, replied, "I'm sure there are millions of Californians who wake up every day and are glad of that too."

45. Lou Cannon, "1978: The Year the States Cut Taxes," *Washington Post*, April 17, 1978.

46. John Wildermuth, "Prop. 13—The People's Revolution," *San Francisco Chronicle*, May 20, 1998.

47. Quoted in Wildermuth, "Prop. 13—The People's Revolution."

48. Quoted in Cannon, "1978: The Year the States Cut Taxes."

49. See Gerber (1996, 1999).

50. See Besley and Coate (1997).

51. Gerber (1999) describes these processes in detail.

52. Gerber (1999) also found that between states with initiatives and those without there are significant policy differences on a number of other issues. In addition, researchers have considered whether initiatives reduce the size of government. The evidence on this is mixed; see Besley and Case (2003) for a review of the literature.

53. Andrea Elliott and Benjamin Weiser, "When Prosecutors Err, Others Pay the Price: Disciplinary Action Is Rare after Misconduct or Mistakes," *New York Times*, March 21, 2004.

54. Michael J. Sniffen, "First National Study Finds Thousands of Cases of Misconduct by Local Prosecutors," Associated Press State & Local Wire, June 25, 2003.

55. Quoted in Barnett (1912).

56. See Eric Bakker, "Renaming the Old Historical Building in Recognition of Ola Babcock Miller," Iowa Official Register, 1999–2000, http://publications.iowa.gov/archive/00000135/01/executive/1-9.

~10~

Measuring
Public Opinion

Psephology Failures

"It's not even going to be close," declared University of Iowa professor Michael Lewis-Beck to *Washington Post* reporter Robert Kaiser when he predicted in May of 2000 that Al Gore would win 56.2 percent of the two-party vote in the upcoming presidential election. And he was not alone; Kaiser reported that political scientists across the country predicted a Gore victory of between 55 and 60 percent.[1] On election night, things seemed to be going in Gore's favor. At 8:02 P.M., ABC anchor Peter Jennings announced that his network was going to call the state of Florida for Al Gore, as CBS, CNN, Fox News, and the Associated Press (AP) had a few minutes before. Jennings remarked: "Give him [Gore] the first big state momentum of the evening. This is the biggest state where the race has been close, the fourth biggest electoral prize."[2] Pundits were beginning to suggest that the election would be decided before the 11 P.M. news. But a couple of months later, George W. Bush became president, and Al Gore took a vacation and grew a beard.

How could so many political scientists have been so wrong? And why did the mass media feel comfortable declaring Florida for Gore at 8 P.M. on election day, just one hour after polls had closed in the state? In fact, political scientists were involved in the media's decisions on election night, just as they often help analyze and predict election results (a number had cautioned against the early call in Florida).[3] Why is the prediction of elections so interesting to academics when failures like these can happen? Forecasting elections provides a public service; it can both help those who need to make decisions that are affected by who wins the election (like Arthur in chapter 8) and make it easier for those involved in mobilizing voters to anticipate the impact of their efforts. But political scientists are also interested in forecasting and predicting elections for what they can learn about their theories of voters' and candidates' behavior. Coleman, Heau, Peabody, and Rigsby (1964, p. 420) contended: "Their interest for the producer is that of an intellectual game: unlike most problems in social science, this one provides a direct test, a moment of truth, once the complete returns are in." Mitofsky and Edelman (2002, p. 176) pointed out: "Elections provide a unique opportunity for an empirical evaluation of the statistical methods used. They are one of the only applications where the population is counted soon after the estimates are made. If other applications were subjected to the same scrutiny there is no telling what improvements might be made in statistical methods." Predicting elections thus allows political scientists to test theories in an irrefutable way. Plus, the academics can do so as part of a live television production or while reading about the research in *The Washington Post*.

In 1948, British academic Ronald McCallum was searching for a new word to describe an area of study that had become his focus since 1945. He turned to a classics scholar, W.F.M. Hardie, for a word to describe "the study of elections." Hardie suggested using the Greek word for pebble, *psephos*, as the basis for the word, since Athenians had voted with pebbles, and so McCallum coined the term *psephology*.[4] In the United States, the term has evolved to refer to using numbers not only to understand but also to predict elections. Psephologists are not just political scientists but pollsters, economists, sociologists, statisticians, and many others interested and involved in politics.[5] During elections, psephologists undertake three tasks: forecasting the election outcome, trying to keep track of opinion changes during the campaign, and helping the news media report the election results quickly. Although the three tasks are slightly different, they all involve using data from past elections, voter demographics, and/or measures of voters' choices in the months leading up to the election to try to figure out who will win.

In this chapter, we will see how psephologists use these data to engage in these tasks and why their efforts sometimes lead to failures, as in 2000. We will also investigate the complicated statistical issues involved. We study these tasks in roughly the historical order in which each one became prominent. We begin, therefore, with the use of polls and betting markets by psephologists to predict elections. Then we discuss how psephologists project winners on election night, using early returns and polls. We conclude our analysis of election predictions with a discussion of long-term election-forecasting models derived more directly from theories of elections.

In this chapter, we also consider more generally how elected officials use public opinion polls in deciding what voters want. We find a complex picture, in which elected officials often seek out polls and information about public opinion and sometimes pander to public opinion. At the same time, elected officials see public opinion as malleable—something they can lead as well as follow. Finally, we consider some of the serious measurement problems in using public opinion polls and surveys to estimate voters' preferences on complex issues and how those problems may lead to some voters' preferences being ignored.

Public Opinion Polls and Elections

How Am I Doing?

Mayor Edward Koch of New York City was campaigning at a shopping mall in the early 1980s and approached a woman. "How am I doing?" he asked her.[6] Koch became famous for the line, but his question is the one that worries any elected official seeking reelection or higher office. If voters are choosing retrospectively, then whether an incumbent wins or not depends on what voters think of his or her record. We've talked a lot about voters' uncertainty about candidates' positions, and we've mentioned that uncertainty about voters' preferences can explain why candidates from different political parties choose divergent positions. But candidates who hold elective office would like to know what voters think about their record and what their chances are for reelection. Many psephologists work for candidates and political parties who are trying to find out—as Koch was—how they are doing.

The first election predictions were surveys by candidates like Koch. Beginning in the 1700s, candidates started to keep poll books of who voted and how.[7] During the 1800s, such canvassing became regular and organized by political parties. A window onto their efforts can be found in the July 9, 1828, issue of the *U.S. Telegraph*, which contains a report by Andrew Jackson's Ohio organization on its predictions about Jackson's success in the coming election. Kernell (2000) has analyzed these predictions and found that they come within 1.5 percentage points of the actual vote. In the early age of machine politics, figuring out voters' preferences was not that difficult since ballots were not secret and precinct-level party officials could have a fairly accurate grasp of voters' intentions. As Kernell (p. 573) notes: during this period

> elections would be won or lost on the efforts of numerous party workers dispersed across the electorate who assiduously sought out the candidate's supporters and escorted them to the polls with the party's ballot in hand. In these labor-intensive campaigns decided by turnout, those best suited to reveal an electorate's tendencies to vote and to favor their candidate were not some randomly selected sample of voters, but rather the party workers whose efforts would be directly reflected at the ballot box.

According to Hamilton (1984), political parties were spending millions of dollars in the late 1890s in these canvassing efforts.

The News Media and the Advent of the Independent Poll

In chapter 8, we saw how consumers like Arthur have a private interest in wanting to know about a candidate's policy positions in order to make decisions that affect their future. If Arthur had known for sure that Kerry would raise gas taxes, his decision about buying a car would have depended crucially on his prediction of the election outcome. Therefore, he would have wanted to know how that outcome would affect his choices. In chapter 9, we discussed how a business cycle might occur because in advance of an election individuals must make business decisions on wages and so on that will be affected by the result of the election. Thus it should be no surprise that the public is interested in predictions about elections and that a sizable portion of media coverage during campaigns is devoted to the horse race.[8] The first recorded straw polls published by newspapers appeared during the 1824 election in the *Harrisburg Pennsylvanian* and the *Raleigh Star*. In the 1896 election, the *Chicago Record* spent over $60,000 to mail postcard ballots to each registered voter in Chicago and to a random sample of one vote out of every eight in twelve midwestern states; 250,000 ballots were returned.

In the next three decades, straw polls run by newspapers became extremely popular and were conducted by the Hearst newspapers, the *New York Herald*, *Cincinnati Enquirer*, *Columbus Dispatch*, *Chicago Tribune*, *Omaha World-Herald*, and *Des Moines Tribune*, as well as many others. One reason why these mass media polls expanded was that during this period, which saw growth in the government sector and the national economy, the outcomes of elections became more consequential to a greater number of voters. It was also becoming more difficult for party workers to predict elections. At the end of the nineteenth century and at the beginning of the twentieth, states began to exercise control over ballot access, when elections were held, and the use of secret ballots. Thus, party workers became less sure of how individuals would vote. With a growth in population, the uncertainty increased.

In the early mass media polls, the presumption was that the best way to get a good prediction of an election outcome was to contact as many voters as possible. That had certainly been the goal of the political parties, which coupled canvassing with mobilization. It was also the view of academic statisticians of the time, such as Karl Pearson (1857–1936). Pearson advanced the idea that the things we observe in the real world are never exact. For example, on election day November 4, 2008, we can measure the percentage of the U.S. voting population who vote for the Democratic candidate. But what we measure is not a constant but something that varies. Some of the variation is predictable and depends on the policy positions of the candidates, their valence qualities, and the voters' preferences. Other factors are less predictable: some supporters may find that they unexpectedly cannot take the time to vote because of work or family demands. Others will be ill, and still others may happen to make small, unpredictable errors when entering their votes or be confused about their designated polling place. If there are more than two candidates on the ballot, some supporters may choose to vote for their second choice because they think he or she has a better chance of winning. Finally, machines and people can make errors in calculating the votes once they are cast, and some individuals might even engage in fraud, thereby misrepresenting a candidate's support. While some of the variation in the election day value is systematic and predictable, other parts of it are random. It is important to note that if we could run the election simultaneously in an identical country, we could get a different value for the percentage of votes for the Democratic candidate because of the randomness. Thus, what pollsters are trying to estimate is not some fixed quantity but one observation of a random variable.

Pearson was one of the first statisticians to realize this inherit uncertainty in observables. If what we observe is not fixed, then how can we describe what we observe? He had a solution: he recognized that there were parameters that described random variables like the support for the Democratic candidate in 2008. The distribution of possible values has a mean, or central value, around which the measurements scatter and a standard deviation, or a degree of variation in how far most of the measurements scatter around the mean.[9] The mean equals the sum of the observations divided by the number of observations. The standard deviation is the square root of the variance, and the variance is equal to the average squared difference between the mean and an observation. Thus, the farther the observations are from the mean, the greater the variance and, correspondingly, the standard deviation.

If we want to predict the percentage of votes that the Democratic candidate will receive on election day 2008, we cannot predict the exact value because of the inherit randomness. But we can come up with a prediction of the parameters that describe the distribution of observed values. That is, we can estimate the mean and the standard deviation and thus have some idea of what we are probably going to observe on election day. We can survey a sample of voters who are likely to be in the population of those who will choose on election day and use the information we get from that survey to calculate what is called the sample mean and the sample standard deviation, which we can use as estimates of the mean and the standard deviation of the support for the Democratic candidate. Pearson, and other statisticians at the time, believed that with a large enough sample of voters, it is possible to figure out the true values of the mean and the standard deviation.[10]

It should be no surprise that those involved in such statistical applications as trying to predict elections would also think that the larger the sample, the closer the prediction would be to the mean, or central value, of what would happen on election day. The *Literary Digest*, a popular magazine with a large national subscription base, seemed like a natural for generating a large enough sample to predict elections, and beginning in 1916 the weekly magazine began a mail-in straw poll on presidential elections, using names drawn from automobile-registration lists and telephone directories. The *Digest* sent these ballots to a reputed one third of all the households in the United States, nearly 20 million. In 1932, it predicted the presidential election within a couple of percentage points.

Opportunity versus Representative Samples

In the 1920s, two Iowans began to think about ways of measuring public opinion. Elmo Roper operated a jewelry store in Creston, Iowa, but not very successfully.[11] He figured that he needed to have a better idea of what consumers wanted, so he began to measure the determinants of consumers' preferences by surveying consumers. Just a few prairie stops away by train from Creston, George Gallup, a professor and graduate student at the University of Iowa, was experimenting with new ways of measuring newspaper readership for the region by interviewing readers. By the early 1930s, both Roper and Gallup were in New York City, in the growing marketing industry, already the home of market researcher Archibald Crossley, who had worked on the *Literary Digest* poll in the 1920s and had subsequently set up his own firm.

As the 1936 election approached, each of these men—Crossley, Gallup, and Roper—decided to challenge the *Digest*. They noticed that its sample was what we today call an opportunity sample—that is, the data were easily gathered but not necessarily representative. In other words, it was easy to construct a list of individuals from automobile-registration and telephone lists. But if there were systematic differences between how those who did not own automobiles or have telephones would vote and those who did, the prediction would have a large error. The sample mean would be a biased predictor of the actual mean.

Crossley, Gallup, and Roper recognized, as statisticians such as R. A. Fisher, P. C. Mahalanobis, and Jerzy Neyman were beginning to note, that it was more important that a sample be representative that it be large in order to estimate the mean.[12] Moreover, it is not possible to know precisely the true value of the mean—all that is possible is to come up with an estimate of the mean from a sample. The gain from having a larger sample is not much if a sample is not representative but simply the easiest one to collect. As the 1936 election approached, the pollsters suspected that the *Literary Digest*'s opportunity sample would predict a win by Republican Alf Landon by underestimating the support for incumbent president Franklin D. Roosevelt. The *Digest*'s survey had worked in the recent elections because the classes had not been greatly divided in their choice for the presidential candidates. But FDR had chosen liberal policies, which had put off previous conservative Republican supporters, who were more likely than more moderate voters to own automobiles and telephones—and be surveyed by the *Digest*. Yet the pollsters knew through some preliminary surveys that FDR still had a strong base in the population. Gallup, who had a syndicated newspaper column about his new public opinion polls, "America Speaks," predicted not only that the *Digest*'s survey would be wrong but also that it would be wrong by 19 percent. He promised to refund the payments he had received for the column to the newspapers if he was wrong. Famously, the three new pollsters were right, and the *Literary Digest* was soon out of business (the *Digest* was wrong by 18 percent).[13]

Truman Trumps the Pollsters

Yet the three pollsters had failures, too. In 1948, all three predicted that Republican Thomas Dewey would defeat incumbent president Harry Truman by 5 to 15 percent. The *Chicago Daily Tribune*, putting its faith in the pollsters' predictions and early election returns, ran its now-famous early-edition headline, "Dewey Defeats Truman," which Truman, having won by 4.4 percent, gleefully displayed for photographers. What had gone wrong?

The most widely given reason for the bad predictions was that the pollsters had stopped questioning too early. As discussed in chapter 7, noted sociologist Paul Lazarsfeld had researched voters in Erie County, Ohio, and Elmira, New York, in the three previous elections and reached the conclusion that elections were decided before Labor Day. Roper's September 9 poll showed Dewey with a lead of 52.2 to 37.1 percent, and after talking to Lazarsfeld, he announced he would do no more polling during the campaign. "It's all over but the oathing," Roper wrote in the October issue of *Fortune* magazine.[14] In his last column before the election, Gallup wrote, "Gov. Dewey will win the Presidential election with a substantial majority of electoral votes."[15] The results on November 2 were starkly different, Truman received 49.6 percent to Dewey's 45.1 percent. Lazarfeld's theory was one of the first by a political scientist to be put to the strong test of an election result.[16]

The second problem with the polls was the way in which the pollsters allocated undecided voters. The presumption at the time was that the undecided would distribute their votes in the same percentages as those who had already decided. Pollsters subsequently recognized that undecided voters may have different preferences, and they began to think more carefully about how to predict their choices. According to Gallup, 8.7 percent of voters were still undecided when he finished polling, and most of them were Democrats. The subjects he interviewed from October 15 to 25 were given a postcard on which to report their final decision and asked to mail it to him after the election. The postcards were coded by serial numbers that matched the interviews. Gallup later reported that the majority of the undecided had voted for Truman.[17] The pollsters' solution to this problem was to poll up to election day (and during, as we will discuss shortly) and to ask more detailed questions of undecided voters.

Quota Sampling

The third problem with the 1948 polls was in the selection of the sample. The pollsters had used quota sampling. Gallup had done a lot of research and decided that there were five key determinants of public opinion: age, sex, income, region, and race. Using information from the census about the distribution of these demographics, he sought to get a sample of the population with the same distribution. Interviewers were given quotas—find so many people of this age, so many women, and so on. Gallup also chose quotas to represent not the voting-age population as a whole but the various types who had turned out in previous presidential elections, since his main focus was on predicting elections. Because women, southerners, and African Americans voted in much smaller percentages of the population, Gallup surveyed fewer of those individuals than were represented in the population. Roper's sample tended to be more representative of the census.[18] There were two difficulties with the quota sampling, however: (1) quotas were not sensitive to changes in the determinants of voting over time and depended on the accuracy of existing research was on the determinants of voters' preferences and (2) interviewers often filled their quotas opportunistically, in a way that affected the answers they received.

The first difficulty arose because quota sampling works only if the pollsters avoids any bias by accurately determining the optimal distribution of quotas in advance of the poll. To do so, pollsters need to know part of the answer ahead of time—they need to know for sure that the determinants they believe are important really are important. For example, suppose a pollster decides, based on information from previous elections, that women and men vote alike. She makes no distinction by gender, therefore; she figures income and ethnicity are more important. So when she gives her interviewers a quota, she tells them that filling their quotas by gender does not matter but they should make sure to have so many subjects from different income and ethnic groups. Suppose, then, that the interviewers find it easier to interview men and so come up with a sample that is disproportionately male. For elections prior to the 1970s, that would have not affected results much, since women then did vote the same way men did, as we discussed in chapter 2. In the 1970s, however, a gender gap began to emerge. If the pollster does not have the foresight to see the potential for the gender gap, her estimates of the vote will be biased.

Research by statisticians such as Neyman and Mahalanobis, coupled with the work of Morris Hansen and William Hurwitz at the U.S. Census Bureau, had compared quota sampling to probability sampling, which involves taking a random draw from the entire population.[19] If a true random draw is taken from the entire population, then each individual is equally likely to be selected. Therefore, there is no bias in the sample that is selected, and the predictions we make from it are unbiased predictions of the true population statistics. If our pollster had instead told interviewers to randomly choose between men and women, she would have been able to capture the change in preferences as it occurred; she would not have had to figure out the correct quotas in order to make sure that she got a representative sample. Statisticians showed in the 1930s that a true random draw from a population is more likely to yield a representative sample than one from quota sampling.

The second difficulty with the pollsters' use of quota sampling was in the interview process. Evidence shows that interviewers did not select randomly within a quota and sometimes, to save time, interviewed groups of respondents together.[20] An interviewer might be told to interview ten white men over forty in a particular neighborhood of known average income. But the interviewer had a lot of discretion within those quotas, and that discretion could affect the responses to the polls. Given a choice, interviewers tended to pick subjects who were more educated, friendlier, better dressed, and so on, leading to biased results. Education was particularly problematic because it was not a quota category, so interviewers were free to select respondents regardless of how well educated they were. Berensky (2004) reported that according to the 1940 census, about 10 percent of the population had at least some college education, whereas 30 percent of respondents in the 1940 Gallup poll did, a problem that existed in many other surveys of the 1930s and 1940s. This problem was compounded if interviewers chose to save time by interviewing groups of respondents at once. In that situation, respondents may be less willing to state their true preferences if they disagree with others. Polling organizations were aware of both of these problems and did attempt to circumvent them, albeit not completely successfully.

Why did the pollsters continue to use quota sampling even though they were aware of some of the problems? One reason was probably cost and ease of organization. Even today true random sampling is infeasible. Opinion polls that use probability-based sampling, like those conducted by the NES, use a stratified method—a modified multistage method in which random assignment is used in each stage of the process, and statistical methods are used to control for the procedures in the sampling design that can cause bias. Interviewers are not allowed discretion in choosing respondents.

But the early pollsters also chose quota methods because they did not trust that a small random sample could be representative—they did not trust the statistical theory and felt that because their samples were not large, they had to hard-wire representativeness into them via quotas.[21] After the 1948 election, pollsters gradually moved to probability-based sampling, although they continued to believe that quota-based sampling was not the source of the failure in the election; they believed that the sources were the failure to conduct polls sufficiently close to election day, to accurately allocate independent voters, and to control for variations in turnout.[22]

Evaluating Recent Preelection Polls

How have polls done in predicting elections since 1948? Traugott (2001) evaluated the prediction performance of preelection polls from 1956 to 2000. Following Mitofsky (1998), he used two standards for evaluating their performance: (1) the average absolute difference between the poll estimate for each of the leading candidates and (2) the absolute value of the difference between the margin separating the two leading candidates in the poll and the difference in their margin in the actual vote. According to the first measure, the polls have averaged a 1.9 percentage point error, and according to the second measure they have averaged a 3.4 percentage point error. Figure 10.1 presents these errors over time. In comparison, in 1948 the pollsters made a 4.9 percent average error in predicting the leading candidate's percentage of the vote and a 12.9 percent average error in predicting the margin of victory. Although the polls have never reached the level of error of 1948, the higher error in predicting the margin of victory is significant since it reflects a tendency to make greater errors in predicting the closeness of elections. Moreover, the figure shows very little change in accuracy since 1956. In 2000, the polls had on average a 4 percentage point margin, whereas Gore's margin on election day was 0.5 percent. Moreover, the vast majority of polls, fourteen out of nineteen, predicted a Bush win, while only three estimated a tie and two estimated a Gore lead. Thus the polls seemed to overestimate Bush's vote. At this writing, it is not possible to evaluate the 2004 polls fully; they ranged from a tied race (Fox News, *USA Today*/CNN/Gallup, American Research Group) to a Bush win of 6 percentage points (*Newsweek*), suggesting a better ability to predict the actual vote margin in 2004 than in 2000.

The Problem of Nonresponse

Early public opinion polls, like the straw polls run by the *Literary Digest*, were conducted by mail. One of Gallup's innovations in polling was to contact voters in person, in face-to-face interviews. Such contact was necessary to attempt to draw a random sample from the population. As Tourangeau (2004) reported, as late as 1963, 20 percent of U.S. households still did not have telephone service. Once phone service became nearly universal, there were statistical problems with simply trying to use phone directories to choose a random sample. For example, 30 percent of numbers are unlisted. The obvious solution was to use full random-digit dialing (RDD), in which random endings are added to active area code—prefix combinations. However, it turns out that only about 25 percent of the

FIGURE 10.1
Errors in Poll Predictions, 1956–2000 Compared to 1948

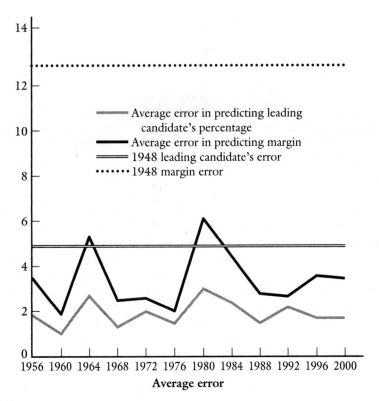

Source: Traugott (2001).

numbers reached this way are working residential numbers. Moreover, non-working numbers ring just like working ones, so the cost of conducting surveys by telephone using full RDD is quite high, given the number of interviews generated. These problems were solved in 1978 by the use of statistical methods, and a modified method of RDD was adopted by survey researchers.[23] Reaching respondents by telephone became a mainstay of survey researchers.

Yet telephone surveys also have problems. The growth of telephone ownership appears to have peaked, with about 4 percent of U.S. households remaining without phone service. In addition, a growing percentage of the population is foreign born, non-English-speaking, or elderly. If survey responses are gathered from someone in those categories, they typically involve a surrogate and thus may not reflect the respondent's true preferences. Furthermore, a growing number of households are using cell phones as a substitute for landline phone service. Because owners of cell phones pay to receive a call, it is difficult to make cell phones a mainstay of telephone surveys. Finally, the expansion in telephone surveys and marketing has resulted in consumers' reacting negatively and demanding devices such as caller ID and otherwise screening unwanted calls. The increased use of these devices is emblematic of a growing tendency to choose not to participate in surveys, as documented by Tourangeau (2004). Thus, telephone surveys are increasingly reaching a smaller segment of the population.

How can researchers deal with these problems? The principal method is to weight the data that is gathered to account for nonresponses by different populations. For example, if women are less likely to participate in surveys than men, then women's responses are given a higher weight than men's responses. The weights are constructed so that the demographics of the weighted-survey respondents resemble the demographics of the population, as estimated by the census. This sort of weighting is also used for making estimates based on in-person interviews as well as to control for the necessity of surveying in clusters.

To see how weighting can work, assume that in the population there are equal numbers of men and women. Further assume that 75 percent of men prefer Bush to Kerry, and the other 25 percent prefer Kerry to Bush. Assume that the percentages for women are the opposite: 75 percent of women prefer Kerry to Bush, and 25 percent prefer Bush to Kerry. Suppose that women are more likely not to respond to a survey, so if a researcher took a random survey, the sample would consist of 75 percent men and only 25 percent women. Assuming that the sample is randomly drawn across Kerry and Bush supporters by gender, an unweighted sample would yield an estimate that 62.5 percent of the population supports Bush, whereas in reality only 50 percent of the population does. If in contrast the sample were weighted to reflect the fact that nonresponse is higher among women, the estimate would be less biased and closer to the true percentage.

The problem with this approach to nonresponse, however, is that there may be factors having nothing to do with measurable demographics that determine whether an individual chooses to volunteer for a survey, and those factors may also affect the individual preferences in a systematic fashion. For example, suppose not just that women are less likely to participate in a survey but also that women who are ideologically opposed to participating in surveys, considering them an intrusion on their privacy, are more likely to favor abortion rights. These women are also less likely to prefer Bush because they favor abortion rights. The researcher gathers more data on men than on women and more of the women he surveys are opposed to abortion and in favor of Bush than are the women in the population. The researcher recognizes that he has gathered more data on men than on women and weights the data accordingly. But he does not recognize that the women in the survey are more likely to vote for Bush than the women in the general population. He does not know this because he does not get a chance to ask those women their preferences. The demographic weights will reduce some of the bias in the survey as long as some women who support Kerry do participate. The weighting cannot eliminate all of the bias, however. Thus, weighting cannot solve the researcher's problem if the factors that determine nonresponse are both not measurable and related to the preferences the survey researcher is attempting to estimate.

What to do? Most researchers see the only solution as increasing the likelihood of reaching nonresponders through the use of incentives and the like. Another alternative is to use theories from social psychology about individual behavior to model analytically the choice to respond. Both solutions have limitations, and so there is always the potential that nonresponse to surveys can lead to systematic misestimations of voters' preferences.

Polling on the Web

Advantages of the Internet As Internet use has grown, more and more researchers have turned to the Internet to measure public opinion. Obviously the Internet's nature allows a researcher to provide the respondent with unique and elaborate visual and audio content and to gather data almost instantly. Furthermore, some analysts suggest that respondents might be willing to reveal information on the Internet that they would be less willing to report over the phone or in person. And because Internet surveys have a much lower marginal cost than telephone surveys, they are better able to reach rare populations of subjects that are often too costly to reach using traditional methods. As Berrens and others (2003, p. 5) pointed out, "If one were interested in identifying a sample of people who have volunteered in political campaigns to learn more about the motivations for this type of political participation, Internet sampling might be feasible where RDD would be prohibitively expensive." Finally, the lower marginal cost also means that Internet surveys can be conducted using much larger sample sizes than surveys using telephone or in-person interviews.

Although estimates of Internet use vary and coverage is expanding, most researchers recognize that if 4 percent of households do not have telephone service, a much larger percentage does not have Internet access. Thus, samples drawn from Internet users are essentially opportunity samples and suffer from the problems described earlier. Internet pollsters have taken two approaches to dealing with the problem: (1) using RDD techniques to recruit households to a panel of respondents who are then provided with Internet service in order to participate in the surveys and (2) choosing to work with a self-selected sample of respondents and analyzing the data with statistical techniques designed to deal with the nonrepresentative nature of the sample.

Probability Sampling The first approach has been taken by Knowledge Networks (KN), a company founded by two Stanford University political scientists, Norman Nie and Douglas Rivers. While within the probability-sampling tradition, because of the necessity of providing subjects with Internet capability, KN works with a panel of respondents rather than randomly drawing a new sample for each survey, as is typical of most telephone surveys. Nonresponse rates are higher, since the requirements for respondents' participation is higher than that for a telephone survey. Respondents must voluntarily spend time at the Internet device. KN is limited to recruiting subjects from areas with potential for the kind of Internet service the company uses, Web TV, which encompasses 84 percent of the nation's households. Although 56 percent of those contacted by KN agreed to join its survey panel, only about 45 percent end up taking a given survey, leading to an overall response rate of 25 percent.[24] KN does have information on subjects who drop out at different stages, which it can use to attempt to statistically control for the nonrepresentativeness of the sample (procedures we discuss in more detail below with respect to the other types of Internet surveying method). Nevertheless, the size of the panel is large compared with most other surveys with over 100,000 members.

Volunteer Sampling The second approach to Internet surveying has been taken by Harris Interactive (HI), the polling firm that is the successor to the Harris poll, first created by former John F. Kennedy pollster Lou Harris in the 1960s. Instead of attempting to build a representative sample, HI advertises for volunteers widely, using advertisements, sweepstakes, surveys, and product registrations. Through this process, HI has built an extremely large panel—over 7 million adults. Although the sample is large, given that it is consciously nonrepresentative, are the results meaningful? Is this just a Web version of the *Literary Digest* poll?

HI deals with this problem through a particular type of weighting of responses, called propensity weights, as described in Berrens and others (2003), Taylor (1999), and Taylor and others (2001). Propensity weights are different from the standard sampling weights discussed earlier in that rather than use just demographic weights, they use information gathered in surveys from those individuals who choose not to participate to control for how the tendency to participate might affect an individual's response to a survey. Berrens and others (2003, p. 6) described the process:

> The propensity weighting involves adding attitudinal and behavioral questions to RDD telephone and Internet surveys being conducted contemporaneously. . . . The telephone and Internet data are merged and the attitudinal questions and standard demographic variables are used to predict the probability of being in one sample rather than the other. These probabilities, or propensities, then serve as the basis for weighting the Internet sample so that its pattern of covariates, including the attitudinal and behavioral questions, match those in the telephone sample.

As Berrens and others (2003, p. 6) noted, "One might expect that people who join panels after visiting a Web page would tend to be more inquisitive about politics than people randomly selected from the population, even after controlling for standard demographic characteristics." Theoretically, then, the researcher would expect that the propensity to participate in an Internet survey would be related to the individuals' tendency to gather information in general, as by reading books, consulting with friends, or watching television news. The researcher can combine telephone and Internet surveys to estimate the propensity to participate in the Internet survey as a function of those variables. Then those propensities can be used to weight the observations in the Internet survey so that those observations more accurately reflect the sample that would have been generated by a telephone survey. If it is true that people who are more likely to gather information are more likely to volunteer for an Internet survey, then the weights on their responses to the Internet-survey questions should be lower than the weights on the responses of those who are less likely to gather information but volunteer for the Internet survey.

This procedure can provide an accurate weighting if the following assumptions are true: (1) the factors that the researcher hypothesizes are related to willingness to participate are indeed so related and (2) the hypothesized determinants of the propensity to participate do not discriminate perfectly—that is, the theory is not perfect. Why can't the theory be perfect? Recall our example of standard survey weighting, in which we assumed that women who favored abortion rights were less willing to respond to surveys. As we noted, as long as some of those women responded, weighting could reduce the bias in the survey. Suppose, now, that most of those women are willing to participate in a telephone survey but are not as willing to participate in an Internet survey. As long as some of them participate in both, propensity weighting can correct for the bias. But if none of the women who favor abortion rights are willing to participate in the Internet experiment, the propensity weighting cannot correct for the bias.

Internet Surveys and Election Prediction How well do Internet surveys predict elections? Since Internet surveys are relatively new, the evidence is quite limited. However, both KN and HI report some success. KN conducted surveys during the 2003 California recall election and provided more accurate estimates of Schwarzenegger's vote than other polls. Schwarzenegger received 49 percent of the vote. KN predicted he would receive 43 percent, the Field poll predicted 38 percent, and both the Gallup and the *Los Angeles Times* polls predicted 40 percent. KN's press release suggested that respondents may have been reluctant to tell telephone interviewers they would vote for the actor but were willing to do so on the Internet.[25]

Taylor and others (2001, p. 2) reported on HI's predictions in the 2000 presidential election:

In the national vote for president, only two polls correctly showed that the two candidates tied (the final results were 48% for both Bush and Gore)—the Harris

Interactive online poll and the Harris Interactive telephone poll. . . . Our predictions for the 26 Senate races were also quite accurate. We made only one incorrect forecast and our average error was 2.2% for the two main candidates. Our predictions for the seven governors' elections were even more accurate. Our average error was 1.9% on the two main candidates.

Show Me the Money

The Election-Gambling Business

Crossley, Gallup, and Roper were not the only ones convinced that FDR would win reelection in 1936. Nor was Roper the only one to bet money (receipts from his newspaper column) on the outcome. On September 24, 1936, *The New York Times* reported that $2.5 million had been wagered, with most of the money placed on Roosevelt, with odds of 8 to 5 in the president's favor. Of the bets that had been placed by that date, 134 had been placed by women, and 104 of those had been in FDR's favor. Such betting was quite open, conducted by specialist firms of betting commissioners who operated on Wall Street as well as by the curb market that existed on Broadway. Betting commissioners would hold the stakes of both parties and charge a 5 percent commission on winnings.[26]

As Rhode and Strumpf (2004) pointed out, newspapers often published the odds given by the betting commissioners; in 1896, 1900, 1904, 1916, and 1924 *The New York Times*, the *Sun*, and the *World* provided almost daily quotes from early October to election day. Markets also existed in Philadelphia, Chicago, Baltimore, Los Angeles, St. Louis, and even Butte, Montana.[27] Over time, however, these markets became less public. Rhode and Strumpf speculated on a number of factors that might have caused the apparent disappearance, such as discouragement by financial firms, increased surveillance by legal authorities, increased competition from opportunities to gamble in other areas, and the advent of the scientific polls. Nevertheless, there exists evidence of betting on U.S. elections throughout history.[28] Recently, betting on elections has become popular at offshore Internet sites. The November 14, 2004, *Boston Herald* reported that an online betting company had already set up odds on the 2008 presidential election. According to the *Herald*, the company favored Republicans over Democrats and gave former New York City mayor Rudolph Giuliani a 5-to-1 chance of winning (compared to a 1-out-of-7 chance for Arizona senator John McCain and a 1-out-of-24 chance for Illinois Senator Barack Obama).

Academic Gamblers

Whereas the private commercial betting on U.S. elections is either offshore or underground, in 1988 University of Iowa economists Robert Forsythe,

Forrest Nelson, and George Neumann and political scientist Jack Wright (1992) created a betting market for the presidential election for research purposes, the Iowa Electronic Markets or IEM. These researchers and later collaborators have conducted markets for federal elections, state elections, and elections worldwide as well as other prediction markets.[29]

The contracts in the IEM election markets are generally either winner-take-all or vote share.[30] In a winner-take-all market, individuals purchase contracts that are bets on whether particular candidates win the election. Suppose Arthur buys a winner-take-all contract on Barack Obama in the 2008 presidential race. If Obama wins, Arthur receives $1 for the contract; if Obama loses Arthur receives nothing. If Arthur is risk neutral, we would expect that he would be willing to buy a contract as long as the price of the contract is less than or equal to his perception of the probability that Obama will win—that is, the expected value of the contract for Arthur is equal to his belief about the probability that Obama will win times $1, and if the price is less than that, he expects to earn money from the bet.

How does Arthur buy the contract? He can buy it in two ways. He can place a bid naming the price he is willing to pay for the contract and specifying a time during which he is willing to pay that price. If during that time period a seller is willing to sell at that price or lower, the exchange is automatically executed. Alternatively, he can place a purchase order to buy at the current market price, and if a contract is available at the current market's lowest price, the exchange is executed. Arthur can sell contracts similarly. He can name a price he is willing to sell the contract for and specify a time limit. If during the specified time period a buyer is willing to buy at that price or higher, the exchange is automatically executed. Alternatively, he can place a sell order to sell at the current market price, and if there is a purchaser at the current highest market price, the exchange is executed.

In a vote-share market, individuals purchase contracts that are bets on the vote shares the candidates will receive in the election. Suppose Obama is the Democratic nominee for president in the 2008 race and Arthur buys a vote-share contract on him. If Obama gets 49 percent of the two-party vote, Arthur will receive $.49 for the contract. If Arthur is risk neutral, we would expect he would be willing to buy a contract as long as the price of the contract is less than or equal to the vote share he expects Obama will receive in the 2008 election. The mechanics of buying and selling vote-share contracts is the same as that for winner-take-all contracts. Table 10.1 summarizes how each kind of contract works.

TABLE 10.1
Winner-Take-All and Vote-Share Contracts in Experimental Election Markets

Contract	Example	Details	Expectation
Winner-take-all	Contract pays $1 if Barack Obama wins 2008 presidential election.	Contract costs $P	P should represent the market's belief about the probability that Obama will win.
Vote share	Contract pays $.01 for every percentage point of the popular vote won by Barack Obama in the 2008 presidential election.	Contract pays $1 times the percentage of votes Obama receives.	The mean value of the percentage of the vote should be the market's expectation of the percentage of votes Obama will receive.

In the markets, consumers can always purchase a bundle of the contracts for all candidates for $1. New contracts enter the market only through bundles, so the researchers do not make or lose any money on the market. For example, suppose that there are two candidates in a market, Barack Obama and Rudy Giuliani. It is always possible for Arthur to purchase one contract on Obama and one on Giuliani in a bundle for $1. Similarly, it is always possible for Arthur to sell the two contracts together for as high a price as he can get. Thus, the researchers give consumers an incentive through arbitrage to constrain the prices up to $1 for all the candidates. If, for example, the sum of the market prices of the two contracts is less than $1, Arthur has an incentive to buy a bundle and sell it to the researchers, and if the sum of the market prices of the two contracts is greater than $1, Arthur has an incentive to buy a bundle from the researchers and sell it on the market. IEM does not charge a commission, but there is a one-time account registration fee of $5. Traders' accounts must have a minimum of $5 and may not exceed $500.

Both academic and nonacademic traders participate in the IEM; in the 2004 presidential-election markets, nonacademic traders constituted 44 percent of the vote-share market and 64 percent of the winner-take-all market. The traders are not a representative sample of the American population. Respondents to an anonymous survey of traders in the 2004 presidential market were 95 percent male, 90 percent white, and 89 percent college educated. Sixty percent had a household income greater than $75,000 and 95 percent said they planned to vote. However, they were more representative of partisan divisions in the country: 37.5 percent reported that they were Democrats, and 35.5 percent reported that they were Republicans (previous markets had been overwhelmingly Republican).[31]

Notice that if the market aggregates information in an unbiased manner, it can provide unbiased predictions about the outcome of an election. In the winner-take-all market, the market price of an Obama contract at any time is the market's prediction about the probability that Obama will win at that point. Similarly, in the vote-share market, the market price of an Obama contract at any time is the vote share Obama is expected to receive at that point.

The existence of betting markets on elections raises three important questions: (1) Why do individuals buy shares in these markets or bet on elections more generally; what are their goals? (2) Can these markets be manipulated? (3) How well do these markets predict electoral outcomes?

What Motivates Bettors?

Some of the traders in the IEM were robots set up to automatically take advantage of arbitrage opportunities and were involved in 21 percent of the trades. The rest were individuals making real decisions over time. In our example, we assumed that Arthur's goal was to make money and that he would make a trade if his private beliefs about the outcome of the election were different from what was reflected by the market prices. Arthur may also bet even if he thinks the prices are accurate, as a way to hedge against anticipated losses that might be a consequence of the election. For example, if Arthur thinks that an Obama win will mean lower real income for him compared with a Giuliani win, then he might bet on Obama so that if Obama wins, his total losses are less.

Arthur might also purchase contracts as a form of entertainment or to express his political preferences. Rhode and Strumpf (2004) reported that during the latter half of the nineteenth century and at the beginning of the twentieth, it was common for bettors to bet on their preferred candidates and to publicly and literally eat crow when they lost. Forsythe, Rietz, and Ross (1999) found that individual IEM traders' choices are correlated to their self-declared party identification. In general, the IEM traders do not appear to be fully rational. They frequently "leave money on the table"—that is, trade in ways that do not take advantage of the best available prices.[32] Therefore, Arthur might be willing to purchase contracts in order to show support for his favored candidate even if he thinks that the price is greater than the expected value of the contract. Sometimes hedging may be used to defray these kinds of expressive purchases. On October 26, 1936, *The Washington Post* reported that heavy Republican bettors on Alf Landon were hedging by accepting puts on low-grade utility stocks (that is, selling their options on them), which were expected to rise if Landon won and fall if Roosevelt won. Rhode and Strumpf (2004) reported that partisans would bet in opposition to their preferences if there was a change in the odds against their favored candidate, on whom they had already placed bets.

If participants are betting for investment purposes, then a market can exist only if voters have different beliefs about the candidates' chances. In a world of incomplete information in which the contest is between Obama and Giuliani and Arthur has precise positive information on the size of Obama's support but only vague information about Giuliani's and Charlotte has precise positive information on Giuliani's support but only vague information on Obama's, both bettors may think their candidate has a greater than 50 percent chance of winning and be willing to trade. Hence, if participants are more likely to know about their own party's candidate, purchases that appear to be expressive may reflect these information differences. The purchases may also be based on incorrect, biased beliefs similar to those that might motivate readers to seek out biased media outlets for news, as discussed in chapter 8. Berg and Rietz (2004) reported that when they asked traders in 2004, "Regardless of your preferences, who do you think will receive the most popular votes in the upcoming U.S. presidential election?" 68 percent of Democrats reported that they believed Kerry would win compared with only 5 percent of Republicans. Furthermore, traders tend to be overconfident in their own information. When asked, "Relative to other traders, how informed do you believe you were about the 2004 presidential election?" Eighty-nine percent said they were more informed than others.

Can Bettors Manipulate the Markets and Affect Elections?

Rhode and Strumpf (2004) reported that in the latter half of the nineteenth century and in the early part of the twentieth, there were charges that partisans were trying to influence the betting markets. It was usually claimed that partisans were trying to increase the odds in favor of their preferred candidate in the hope of depressing turnout for the opposition. Partisan newspapers (discussed in chapter 8) tended to present the results that were favorable to their party. There were also frequent reports of party officials' betting in the market, and mention was made of bettors' party affiliations. Thus, the fact that party officials were involved was not secret. The fact that both sides were involved in such matters suggests that it was unlikely that one side successfully manipulated the results. Recall the conclusion of Mullainathan and Shleifer (2005) that competition between biased but heterogeneous media outlets can lead to overall unbiased information.

What about the modern experimental markets? During the 1996 Republican primaries, Patrick Buchanan's Web site listed trading on the IEM as a way to support the candidate. Wolfers and Leigh (2002) reported that in an Australian market for regional elections, candidates created bets on themselves at long odds to create a "buzz." And according to Berg and Rietz (2005), several political blogs claimed that the IEM prices were being manipulated during the 2004 election, and several individuals sent e-mail messages to the IEM office, claiming that George Soros was manipulating IEM prices. Berg and Rietz found little evidence that manipulation of the market occurred, however, partly because manipulation is extremely costly and complicated. They explain:

> As an example, consider the trades of an individual trader that appears to be responsible for transient price movement on February 27, 1996, in the 1996 Republican Convention market [the market for the Republican nomination]. That trader's actions contributed to a $0.04 increase in Buchanan's price. But the actions were also costly, at least in the short-run. The trader spent $348 purchasing Buchanan constracts while later in the day selling at least some of those contracts for $98. The trader also apparently recognized that because contracts are tied together through bundles, manipulating the price of one contract would also require the manipulator to move prices in other contracts (so that prices stay in sync with one another). This generated a need for additional trading adding to the complexity of executing a manipulation strategy.

The ability to manipulate a betting market on elections depends on how thin the market is (how few traders there are) and the ability of traders to act without bias to take advantage of those willing to lose money in such an effort. So far, the evidence suggests that manipulation has not been successful.

How Well Do the Markets Predict Elections?

Like political polls during an election campaign, the prices in the election markets vary. Berg and Rietz (2005) showed how the prices react to information. For example, a false rumor of a Kerry affair with an intern mentioned in the *Drudge Report* caused a temporary price decrease for Kerry's stock. The closer to election day, the better the prediction of the market compared to the actual result. Thus, the price that is most likely to predict the election will be the one recorded the day before. The lesson here is much like the one Crossley, Gallup, and Roper learned—that predictions from polls taken in advance can be problematic. The election-eve forecast for the two-party vote share based on the closing prices for George W. Bush in the IEM 2000 market was 52.3 percent (Bush actually received less than 50 percent of the vote) and for the IEM 2004 market it was 51.4 percent (which was close to the actual percentage of 51.6). Berg and Rietz (2005), comparing election-eve vote-share predictions in presidential-election markets conducted from 1988 to 2004 with actual outcomes, found that the average absolute percentage error is 1.33 percent, which is at least as good as or better than that of most public opinion polls (the Gallup election-eve error for 1988 to 2000 was 2.2 percent). Berg, Nelson, and Rietz (2003) found that a comparison of polls with IEM forecasts show that IEM prices are closer to the actual vote share in 76 percent of the cases.

What about the commercial betting markets? As with the IEM markets,

Rhode and Strumpf (2004) found that the odds became closer to the actual result the closer the bet was placed to the election. They also found that in the markets from 1884 to 1940 the mid-October betting favorite won eleven times (73 percent of the time). In three elections from 1884 to 1892, the odds were basically even. Only in 1916 did the predicted loser, Woodrow Wilson, win. During World War II, the betting continued, and in 1944 the odds were 3 to 1 in favor of Roosevelt.[33]

Did the betting markets beat the polls in predicting the 1948 election? Fortunately for one flamboyant Louisianian, no. In 1948, James Brocato of New Orleans, popularly known as Diamond Jim Moran, a former fighter and bodyguard of the late former governor Huey Long and owner of a popular French Quarter restaurant, bet $10,000 that Truman would win although the odds were 20 to 1. He made off with $200,000. Brocato's odds, while high, did reflect the market's opinion that Dewey would win, although there is evidence that the view narrowed as the election approached. In early October, *The New York Times* reported that St. Louis had given Dewey a 15-to-1 chance of winning, and in late October the *Los Angeles Times* reported bets of $20,000 to $5,000 that Truman would lose.[34] The fact that in 1948 the betting market had its first failure at predicting a presidential election since 1916 supports Gallup's postelection argument that the two contests were similar.[35] Gallup pointed out that in both cases the Democratic candidate (Wilson in 1916 and Truman in 1948) won the presidency by barely winning California and lost the major northeastern states of New York and Pennsylvania. The wins were dependent on the choices of voters in the South, Midwest, and West Coast. It may be that the betting markets and Gallup's polling sample were biased against picking up the preferences of these voters sufficiently to predict the outcome. It also may be the case that by 1948 the betting market was beginning to follow the polls.

Election Night and Projecting Winners

The Exit-Poll Problem in 2004

The afternoon of election day 2004 was not a happy time for White House senior adviser Karl Rove. "I was sick," Rove later told *The Washington Post*. He had just been told the exit-poll numbers, and they showed Kerry in the lead. "But then I was angry when I started seeing the numbers. None of them made any sense." White House communications director Dan Bartlett recalled: "It was like a punch in the gut."[36] The preliminary numbers showed that Bush was 20 points behind in Pennsylvania and losing in every other contested state.[37] And Rove wasn't the only one reading the numbers: "Web sites such as slate.com, drudgereport.com and dailykos.com . . . were posting excerpts from early exit-poll reports. . . . Those postings were then e-mailed around, meaning that potentially millions of people were getting at least glimpses of the information."[38] Fox News anchor Brit Humes announced that exit-poll rumors on the Internet suggested that things looked "brighter on the Kerry side than the Bush side."[39] The stock market plunged nearly 100 points.[40]

Yet later in the evening, it became clear that Bush would do much better than the polls suggested. The next day, Kerry conceded the election. What happened? The failure was particularly annoying since most believed that the problems of 2000, when the networks made projections about states that they later were forced to retract (discussed above), had led to better efforts on the part of the news media to report accurately on the election. To understand the exit-poll problems of 2004 (and the problems of 2000), we need to examine the process by which news outlets report election results and how that process has evolved.

Tabulating the Vote in Federal Elections

Reporting the outcome of a U.S. federal election is not easy, primarily because the country is a federation, with each state having its own electoral procedures and laws, as we discussed earlier. U.S. citizens do not vote in one single election but in fifty different elections under fifty different legal systems that govern when polls close, how votes are counted, where they are stored, how they are reported to the media, and so on. Initially, all that was required at the federal level was a report of the vote of the members of the Electoral College, not a report of the popular vote. As a consequence, there is no official record of the popular vote for elections prior to 1824. While eventually the federal government began to collect states' popular-vote totals, the certified official records are not available for months after an election. For most of U.S. history, if a national news outlet wanted to report the results of federal elections it needed to have an organization with reporters stationed in every state who could get the vote totals in a timely manner and provide them to their national office. It is no wonder that in early years, sometimes weeks would past before election results would be known and published in newspapers. The advent of the telegraph meant that it was possible for newspapers to get election returns and determine the winner in races on election night when the outcome was not extremely close. But the cost for individual newspapers was high (particularly in the first half of the nineteenth century), and newspapers formed associations such as the AP to help compile the results across the country.[41]

On election night, the major newspapers would host large outdoor events with entertainment. They would hang huge canvases on which they posted the results as they became known and used light signals to spread the results throughout the area. In 1896, "a great canvass map of the country" was drawn on the upper stories of the Herald Tribune Building in New York City as the results came in, and the *New York Sun* used a stereopticon to enumerate the states that had gone for McKinley.[42] In 1916, the *Chicago*

Daily Tribune announced it would use light signals to inform citizens of the election results as they came in: "Stationary upright beam—white, result in doubt; green, Hughes leading; red, Wilson leading. White beam circling horizon—steady sweep, Hughes elected; zigzag sweep, Wilson elected."[43]

In 1920, things began to change for the newspapers as the first regular radio broadcasts began, significantly, with an inaugural program on the election returns that reached an estimated one hundred to five thousand listeners using homemade receivers, since none had yet been produced for the retail market.[44] No longer did voters need to congregate close to newspaper offices in order to hear the results as they came in (although the outdoor events continued to take place through the 1940s). In 1924, the election returns "were broadcast coast-to-coast on more than 400 stations to more than 20,000,000 people tuned in on home receivers."[45] By 1936, radio broadcasts of election returns had become quite elaborate, and for the first time Gallup representatives were part of the broadcast on CBS. In later years, Elmo Roper also took part in radio broadcasts. In 1948, returns were broadcast by television stations. During this period, the methods the radio networks used to gather and analyze the election returns were similar to those used by the newspapers, and essentially the radio stations used the returns gathered by the newspapers.

When Tabulations Don't Meet Deadlines

While the focus of these efforts was vote tabulation and reporting, since newspapers had to publish something the next day, election coverage also often meant projecting a winner before the final results were available. Thus the *Chicago Daily Tribune*, based on polls and early returns, could confidently produce a "Dewey Defeats Truman" headline even though the possibility existed that it would be wrong. In 1916, the *San Francisco Chronicle* had similarly proclaimed the day after the election that Wilson had been defeated. Littlewood (1998) reported that in 1883 the editor and publisher of *The Boston Globe*, General Charles H. Taylor, began to use "key precincts" to project the outcome of the election. Essentially his reporters picked out precincts that were representative of social and ethnic characteristics that they thought were important, studied the past voting patterns of those precincts, and then projected the statewide vote based on the precincts that reported first. While it was possible for the *Globe* to do this for Massachusetts, it was not until the age of television and computer technology that we see this type of detailed projection taking place on election night on a national scale.

UNIVAC Predicts

In 1952, the star political interpreter on CBS's television broadcast of the election returns was not George Gallup or Elmo Roper but UNIVAC.

UNIVAC, designed by the Remington Rand Corporation, stands for *universal automatic computer* and was the first American commercial computer. Researchers at Remington Rand had written a program that would make a prediction about the election based on previous election results and the results from precincts in states as they were reported. The program estimated a simple linear regression equation similar to the following:

$$VOTE \; FOR \; EISENHOWER \; IN \; PRECINCT = CONSTANT + (SLOPE)$$
$$\cdot \; (\text{Past Vote for Republicans in Precinct}) + ERROR.[46]$$

Using the data, the computer estimated the values of *CONSTANT* and *SLOPE* so that the squared difference between each observation and the regression line was minimized, giving the best linear fit to the data. Then the parameters, *CONSTANT* and *SLOPE*, and the data from the past in the other precincts could be used to estimate the vote for Eisenhower in those precincts for which results had not yet been reported, and a total estimate could be calculated. The computer was in Philadelphia, at the Remington Rand factory, where researchers had just finished testing it. The CBS News reporters phoned the data to Philadelphia, where data-entry clerks entered it in triplicate via key-to-tape machines (three versions were entered in order to catch errors in data entry). At 8:30 P.M. (two hours after the polls had closed in New York), with about 5 percent of the vote reported, UNIVAC predicted that Eisenhower would win forty-three states with 438 electoral votes and 32,815,049 popular votes.[47]

UNIVAC was censured. The people involved with the prediction could not believe the results. They had expected a close election. They decided not to tell the television audience since they were not used to the idea of calling an election based on such a small sample of the vote. To give the reporters something to talk about, the statisticians in Philadelphia fed the machine some fake data, making its estimates closer to the expected results. Finally, at 11:10 P.M., the humans gave up, put the correct data in (with the additional data accumulated in the meantime), and let UNIVAC predict. UNIVAC predicted that Eisenhower would get forty states. The final result was that Eisenhower won thirty-nine states with 442 electoral votes and 33,936,252 popular votes. Around midnight, when it was clear from the raw vote tabulations that Eisenshower was going to win big and other news outlets were declaring him the winner, the engineer in charge of Remington Rand's new product development division went on camera and apologized to CBS's viewers: "A mistake was made. But the mistake was human. We were wrong and UNIVAC was right. Next time we'll leave it alone."[48]

In the years that followed, the national networks gradually moved from less talk about vote tabulations to more projection, analysis, and interpretation based on computer projections. Networks also began a race to be the first to project the winners. In 1960, ABC and CBS announced they would name a winner by 6 P.M. and 7 P.M., respectively. They did, projecting that

Nixon would win, only to have to reverse their projections between 8 and 9 P.M.[49] According to Polsby and Wildavsky (1971), CBS used an estimation procedure that compared the electoral returns to the returns at the same time in 1956 in order to control for biases in the sample of available returns. But because Kansas had introduced a faster method of counting votes, its votes came in at the same time as Connecticut's, and thus the Republican vote totals were overstated, leading to the wrong call. Following the advice of Princeton statistician John Tukey, NBC did not declare Nixon a winner.[50]

Early Projections and Voters

Do early projections affect voters and electoral outcomes? Clearly, if voters believe the outcome is no longer in doubt, they have less of an incentive to participate. NBC projected a Nixon win in 1972, at 8:30 P.M. and a Reagan win in 1980 at 8 P.M., eastern standard time, when many people still had not voted in western states. Did those early calls depress turnout in the West? Wolfinger and Linquiti (1981) studied the 1972 election using the current population survey, which asked respondents whether and when they had voted. They compared the turnout decisions with the decisions on voting in 1974 and contended that turnout decreased by 2.7 percent in the Pacific states. They also argued that the early call may have led to the defeat of incumbent California Democratic Congressman James Corman. Frankovic (2003) pointed out that since the study compared turnout in a presidential contest with turnout in a nonpresidential contest, it may have overestimated the extent of later voting, since in presidential contests voters tend to vote earlier in the day and that the information from voters is self-reported and overstates turnout in general.

Jackson (1983) and Delli Carpini (1984) studied the 1980 election. Jackson used data from the NES 1980 survey to determine whether the reports reduced voter participation. He found that hearing news of the projected outcome decreased the likelihood of voting by those who had not yet voted and that the effect was stronger for Republicans, who were more likely to vote late on election day. Frankovic (2003) argued that because the survey was conducted months after the election, the voters' memories are suspect. She pointed out that one fourth of the respondents claimed to have heard projections of the outcome before they were announced, and one fifth claimed to have heard Jimmy Carter's concession speech before it was delivered. Traugott (1992) also has criticized the study as inconclusive because of the small number of voters. Delli Carpini (1984) examined the effect of the early call on the vote totals in congressional races as well as the presidential contest and found that there was a small effect on vote totals. He contended that as many as fourteen races were affected by the early call. Moreover, he found that higher-income, white-collar, and better-educated voters were more likely to be affected by the early call.

Surprisingly little analysis of early election calls has examined contests from 1980 to 2000. After the 2000 election, there were a number of studies by Republican partisans, which claimed that the early Gore call in Florida decreased voter turnout in the western part of the state. However, as reviewed by Frankovic (2001), there are statistical problems with the studies: the results are not significant and use suspect data. Moreover, the network calls were made just ten minutes before polls closed in the western part of the state; thus it is highly unlikely that the calls significantly affected turnout. Most of those involved in network election-night reporting argue that the effects of early projections are minimal and that the best solution is to institute a nationwide uniform poll-closing law, as noted in Franovic (2001). Under the present system, 85 percent of voters turn out before any projections are made. Moreover the increasing use of absentee and mail-in voting, as in Oregon, is likely to lessen the effect.

Sampling Precincts

While most of the news media has focused on the use of computers in election reporting, computer projections are only as good as the work of the programmers and statisticians, as the problems that CBS ran into in 1960 demonstrate. Impressed with Louis Harris's polling for John Kennedy during the 1960 contest, CBS formed a partnership with him and IBM in 1961. Harris introduced a more scientific approach to choosing which precincts' data to use for projections. He selectively chose precincts using quota-sampling methods. Joseph Waksberg described in an interview in 1998 how the data from the sampled precincts was gathered: "People were stationed at the selected precincts, and when the polls closed at the end of the day, the backs of the machines were opened or the ballots were counted by hand. When the counts became available they were called in and entered into a computer in New York."[51]

While at first Harris's approach worked well, in 1966 he made two big errors. In Maryland and Georgia, the governors' races were between Democratic candidates who were more conservative on civil rights than the Republican candidates, so black voters who had previously voted Democratic now voted Republican. When Harris's analysts saw these early results in predominantly black precincts, they thought the results were mistakes in the data and threw out the observations, predicting big wins by the Democratic candidates, although in both states the Republicans won a plurality of the vote.[52] Harris's error in throwing out the observations shows the problems with selecting observations on the basis of whether they made a priori sense and using a nonrandom way to determine which precincts would be included in the sample.

In 1967, CBS hired statisticians Warren Mitofsky and Murray Edelman, who had worked with Hansen and Hurwitz at the Census Bureau on random sampling, and enlisted their former boss, Joseph Waksberg, as a consultant. Mitofsky and Edelman instituted stratified probability-based sampling similar to that used by the NES in surveys (as discussed above).[53] From 1967 to 1988, CBS used those procedures. From 1990 to 2004, all the networks worked together in cooperative ventures, using the methods designed by Mitofsky and Edelman. As Waksberg recalled in 1998, CBS's new hires were determined that the network should adopt probability sampling:

> Having been trained by Hansen and Hurwitz, we said they had to introduce probability sampling and stick to it. Quality control was still necessary to detect data errors, but before rejecting data, you had to find out whether they reflected errors, flukes, or indicated something was happening. Also, if there were major problems, you should take a conservative position, and take this into account by increasing your estimate of the margin of error in the system.

That is, instead of throwing out the data from the predominantly black precincts in Georgia and Maryland, Harris should have kept them and instead been less certain of his predictions. We will see shortly how the failure to increase the margin of error in suspect data also explains some of the problems psephologists faced in 2000.[54]

Estimates of Votes

But choosing an appropriate sample is just one part of the projection process. The other major component is estimating the vote based on the sample. Mitofsky and Edelman (2002) described the estimation procedure used by CBS from 1967 to 1988 and by all networks from 1990 to 2004. The psephologists did not use linear regression because they wanted to have an estimator that worked better with small samples and thus could be used as the sampled precincts reported their returns. Thus they chose ratio estimators. Ratio estimators resemble a linear regression but with *CONSTANT* constrained to equal zero. In estimating a linear regression as with UNIVAC above, the psephologist needs to estimate two parameters, *CONSTANT* and *SLOPE*. In contrast, with a ratio estimator, the psephologist needs to estimate only one parameter, the ratio. The more parameters a psephologist estimates, the more data he or she needs to have, so by using ratio estimators, psephologists can provide projections with less data.

Ratio estimators are also easy to compute and explain. Suppose a psephologist named Hector has the returns from a random sample of Ohio's precincts in 2004. The total vote for Kerry across the sampled precincts is 200,000. Hector believes that the best estimate from past elections of the vote for Kerry in the precincts in Ohio is the vote for Gore in 2000. The mean vote for Gore across the same sample of precincts was 180,000. The ratio would be 200,000/180,000 = 1.11, which means that Kerry is receiving across the sample precincts approximately 1.11 times the vote Gore received. Then this ratio is multiplied by the official vote Gore received in 2000 in Ohio to get the estimated vote for Kerry in the state. In Ohio in 2000, Gore received 2,183,628 votes, so the prediction from the ratio estimate is 2,423,827.

Remember that the observed Kerry vote is a random variable, and thus the ratio estimate is a prediction of the mean value of the distribution of possible Kerry vote totals in Ohio, not a prediction of the actual vote. The prediction is that the actual vote Kerry will receive is a random draw from a distribution with a mean at 2,423,827. But suppose that Hector took a different random sample? Then he would have a different sample mean. We can imagine that Hector can take many random samples from the population of precincts and that there is a distribution of sample means that Hector will find. We know from statistical theory that the mean of these randomly drawn sample mean predictions is an unbiased estimator of the mean of the observed values of Kerry's total vote in Ohio.

But Hector cannot take a lot of samples and derive the estimate across samples because doing so is costly; he might as well just wait for all the precincts to report their results. Hector wants to make an estimate based on one random sample and one estimate. How far is his estimate likely to be from the true population mean of Kerry's vote totals? We use the concept of standard error to describe how far the sample mean might be from the true population mean. Hector can calculate the standard error of his estimate by using the data from his sample and the past election data. If the standard error is small, it is likely that his sample mean is close to the true population mean, but if the standard error is large, it is likely his sample mean is far from the true population mean. A normal practice is to take the predicted estimate and add the standard error to that estimate to get an upper value for the prediction and to substract the standard error to get a lower value for the prediction. But it is important to remember that the true population mean can lie outside that range; it is just not likely. One reason psephologists like ratio estimators using past votes is that if the votes are correlated with past votes, the error in the estimate is less than it would be if they did not use past votes; that is, they just extrapolate from the sample to make predictions about the rest of the state.[55]

Princeton professor John Tukey was another statistician involved in making estimates on election night. According to Brillinger (2002), who worked with him for NBC from 1962 to 1980, he and his team used voting history, preelection poll results, and political scientists' predictions to compute base values. They compared these base values with county returns as they came in and complete results from selected precincts. The selected precincts were considered "barometric" or "swing-o-metric" and selected in order to provide the best possible random sample of voters. While Tukey's use of nonrandom samples of precincts was problematic, the estimation approach he used was an early example of what we now call empirical Bayesian statistics, an approach that a number of political scientists are now using to understand elections more generally.

Empirical Bayesian statistics comes from the same theory of decision making we assumed Arthur, Dimitri, and Charlotte used in chapter 8. Suppose Hector takes a modern empirical Bayesian approach. His first step is to specify the joint probabilities of observing what he knows (past elections, polls, political scientists' opinions) and what he does not know (the election outcome). As new data (county returns and complete results from selected precincts) come in, he calculates the conditional probability of various outcomes of the election given the new data, following Bayes's rule. Then he evaluates the fit of the model to the overall data and considers whether it makes sense. Brillinger (2002) noted that for Tukey the uncertainty of his estimates (which he developed using a different basis) were just as important as his point predictions and that predicting turnout was often more of a problem than predicting how individuals would vote. HI currently uses Bayesian approaches, along with more traditional approaches, to analyze its survey results.[56]

Enter Polls, Exit Tukey

Exit polls were first conducted in 1967 at CBS by Warren Mitofsky. Originally they were used by the statisticians to get a better idea about what to expect in an election; they were seen as guideposts rather than consequential sources of data. The idea was simple—exit polls allowed a pollster to eliminate the responses of nonvoters, which can lead pollsters to make errors in predictions based on preelection polls; the exit poll could give the pollster a better handle on how voters were actually choosing and also allow him or her to control for last-minute preference shifts.

Soon exit polls evolved into an analytical tool, allowing the networks to know how different types of voters, like women and blacks, were choosing between candidates and the issues that mattered to voters and giving the political analysts more to discuss in their election coverage. Whereas analysts had previously inferred from the returns of precincts dominated by particular groups how different groups of voters were choosing, such inferences were problematic and suffered from an ecological fallacy, as discussed in chapter 5. For example, just because a precinct has a majority of blacks, it is impossible to know just from looking at the aggregate vote totals what percentage of support a candidate has among blacks. One way to try to get around this problem is to look for precincts that are extremely segregated— where the percentage of one racial group is nearly 100 percent. However, we cannot assume that voters in highly segregated precincts will have the same preferences as voters of the same racial group who live in less segregated precincts. Exit polls allow the analyst to find out about voters' preferences at the individual level directly. However, exit polls can also suffer from the same problem. In 2004, some observers argued that exit polls overstated the Latino vote for Bush because Cuban Americans constituted a greater percentage of polled voters due to an overselection of precincts with Cuban-American voters.[57]

In exit polling, interviewers are given an interviewer rate. Suppose that the interviewer has a rate of five. Then he or she approaches every fifth voter. Selected voters are asked to fill out a short survey, which are then collected in a ballot box. If the designated voter is "missed" by the interviewer—if the interviewer cannot reach him or her due to physical constraints at the polls or the voter refuses to answer the survey—the interviewer records basic information on this voter (approximate age, race, gender) and starts his or her count over and approaches the next fifth voter. Thus the total number of voters the interviewer approaches is endogenously determined by turnout. Exit interviewers call in their survey results periodically during the day. In 2004, results were called in three times—shortly before noon local time, in the late afternoon, and during the last hour before the polls closed.

Exit polls became more than just a tool for analysis when in 1980 NBC substituted exit-poll analysis for the work of Tukey and his statisticians—and projected the Reagan win earlier than any other news network.[58] Using only actual reported votes from sampled precincts, ABC announced the Reagan win at 9:50 P.M., and CBS did not announce it until 10:20, after Carter conceded. Since then, exit polls have been used by all the networks in making election-outcome projections. But the increased pressure to call elections early using exit polls made election-night coverage much more expensive during a period (the 1980s and 1990s) when there was growing pressure for news reporting to be profitable, as discussed in Hamilton (2004).

The networks had formed a cooperative with AP to collect the national election returns from nonsampled precincts in 1964, but each network still had its own army of data collectors for its sampled precincts and its own exit-poll interviewers. Exit polls were conducted at only a subset of the randomly sampled precincts, for which early returns were gathered, due to the higher cost of interviewing. Mitofsky and Edelman noted that each network was spending approximately $6 million on exit polling in 1988. For 1990, the networks decided to pool their efforts and created an external polling operation headed by Mitofsky and Edelman, reducing each network's contribution to $2 million. In 1993, this operation was combined with the existing service that provided tabulated returns on election night, and the joint organization was called Voter News Service (VNS). VNS had other clients for the exit polls and returns, including newspapers like *The New York Times*. In 2004, VNS was replaced, but exit polling was still conducted as a pooled enterprise, using the same basic methodology devised by Mitofsky and Edelman with Waksberg's assistance. Exit polling and analysis of sample precincts' results were conducted by a collaboration of Edison Media Research and Mitofsky International (Edison-Mitofsky), and the AP independently tabulated the actual election returns.

The creation of an independent exit-poll organization that provides data to the networks fundamentally altered the nature of election-night projections in three ways: (1) the decision to project a winner in a given state became a decision made by the networks independent of the pollsters' analysis of the exit polls, (2) exit-poll data began to be released to clients on election day before it could be compared to actual results and errors could be corrected, and (3) the dominance of one primary source magnified the impact of errors in the data. Those three changes led to many of the problems in election-night coverage in 2000 and 2004.

How Election Night Works

"Make no mistake. The Election Night broadcast occurs in a cauldron of competitive heat—heat that comes from within each individual and within each network, all burning to be the best and to be first," summarized the authors of an investigation into CBS's coverage of election night 2000 (Mason, Frankovic, and Jamieson 2001, p. 15). Konner (2003, p. 11) quoted Tom Johnson, former chairman and CEO of the CNN News Group, about the atmosphere on election night in 2000: "The competitive drive to be first played a powerful role. It's more important to be right, but in the pressure of the election, there is a raw competitive race to be first, like athletes on the playing field." Konner pointed out that "time pressures are the whole reason for the use of exit polls and other devices in calling the winners of states before the actual computation of complete returns is known." That competitive heat and resulting time pressure led to the wrong projection of the winner in Florida—first Gore, then Bush—in an extremely close presidential contest that was not settled until weeks after election day and ultimately depended on the votes in that state. In retrospect, neither projection should have been made on election night. What went wrong?

The process of determining whether to project that a candidate has won a state began with the exit-poll data. After each call from the interviewers at the selected precincts, the analysts at VNS and, later, Edison-Mitofsky took the data and computed the ratio estimators and the corresponding predicted votes for the candidates. In Florida in 2000, VNS selected 120 out of 5,885 precincts in their sample, 45 of which had exit interviewers. They interviewed 4,356 voters and had staffers at 67 county offices. After the polls closed in a state, VNS and, later, Edison-Mitofsky also collected the reported vote from the larger group of sampled precincts in the state (those with an interviewer and those without, as the pollsters' representative went to each precinct and collected those vote totals and called them in to New York). So in Florida in 2000, VNS heard from the 120 precincts sampled in the hours after the polls closed. VNS used the data both to adjust the exit-poll data for biases and to augment that data and compute newly revised ratio estimators and predicted votes. Later in the evening, VNS received tabulated statewide data county by county, which were also incorporated when possible into the predicted vote. Note that in Florida, because part of the panhandle is in the central time zone whereas the majority of the state is in the eastern time zone, the polls closed at different times. Therefore, a projection decision was sometimes made while some precincts were still open. In 2000, the networks called Florida for Gore approximately ten minutes before the polls closed in the western part of the state.

What rule did VNS (and, later, Edison-Mitofsky) use to make a projection decision? The pollsters examined the difference in the percentage of the vote for the two leading candidates and estimated the standard error of that difference. They computed a t-statistic, which is the ratio of the percentage difference divided by the standard error. According to statistical theory, if this ratio is greater than or equal to 2.6, there is a 99.5 percent probability that the leading candidate is the winner or a 200-to-1 chance that the leading candidate is the winner. Intuitively, this makes sense: if the difference between the candidates is over two and a half times the estimated error in the prediction, it is highly unlikely that the leading candidate is not going to win the state. For example, in 2004 in Minnesota after the third call of exit-poll data, Kerry was estimated to be leading Bush by 14.3 percent of the votes with an error of 3.6 percent. The t-statistic for the state was then 3.97, and thus Minnesota was projected a Kerry win after the exit-poll data were in. In contrast, in Iowa in 2004 after the third call of exit-poll data, Kerry was leading by an estimated 1 percent with an error of 2.5 percent. The t-statistic for the state was 0.4, and thus Iowa was too close to call.[59] These procedures have worked very well. According to Mitofsky and Edelman (2002), while they worked for CBS alone (from 1967 to 1988), they made five mistakes out of fifteen hundred elections, and during the 1990s VNS had only one error in about seven hundred projections.

Although VNS and, later, Edison-Mitofsky provided the data, estimates, and projections, the networks made their own decisions about whether to project a state as a win by a candidate. That was not the original setup, however; when the networks began their collaboration to gather exit-poll data, they allowed for the exit pollsters to make the projections. But in 1994, ABC hired its own decision team and made its own calls, declaring wins in governors' races in Texas (George W. Bush) and New York (George Pataki) and the loss of Oliver North in Virginia's Senate race while the other networks were not able to do so. From then on, all the networks hired their own decision teams, including a number of political scientists, such as Professor Christopher Achen of the University of Michigan, who worked for ABC in 2000. So, for example, in 2004 the pollsters gathered and analyzed the data and made their predictions, but each network made its own decision whether to call states like Minnesota and Iowa for Kerry or Bush.

What Went Wrong in 2000

At 7 P.M. eastern time, 95 percent of Florida's polls were closed. The exit-poll data alone showed a close race between Gore and Bush. VNS waited for the sampled precinct data to come in, which was checked against the exit-poll data. As the data came in, VNS saw that Gore had a lead. At 7:40 P.M. on the computer screens of their clients and the networks, VNS signaled that statistically Gore was leading (the t-statistic was greater than or equal to 2.6) but they were checking the data further. NBC and CBS did not wait for VNS's decision and projected the state for Gore at 7:48 P.M. and 7:50 P.M., respectively. At 7:52 P.M. VNS estimated that Gore had a lead of 7.3 percent with a t-value of 3.8, VNS declared the state for Gore. At 8:02, ABC projected a Gore win in Florida.[60]

In the end, the results in Florida showed Bush and Gore in a statistical dead heat. So the 7.3 predicted difference was in error. That error came primarily from four sources. First, the pollster underestimated the size of the absentee vote in Florida. They estimated that the absentee vote would reduce Gore's lead by 1 percent, to 6.3 percent, which had a t-statistic of 3.3. But the absentee vote actually reduced Gore's lead by 1.7 percent. The second source was that the exit polls that had not been verified by actual returns were biased in favor of Gore whereas the pollsters believed that the bias was in favor of Bush. In Kentucky, they had found the exit polls to be biased in favor of Bush, and for the small subsample of exit-poll precincts for which the pollsters had returns, they appeared to show that the exit polls were biased in favor of Bush.

The third problem was that the pollsters' estimation procedure understated the magnitude of the sampling error, since they computed the estimates without all the sample precincts available; they had only the ones that had been turned in by the time the polls closed in the eastern part of the state. They were working with incomplete data but were assuming that the sampling error was the same as it would be if the data were complete. The last problem was their choice for the past vote in the ratio estimator. If they had used either the 1996 presidential race or the 1998 senatorial race, the ratio estimator would have predicted a closer race, with t-statistics less than 2.6. But they chose the 1998 governor's race because it was, given the returns and poll numbers available, the closest in correlation, and thus the ratio estimator was likely to have the smallest error. Notice that if VNS had not understated the error in the estimates or used a different past race, the state would not have been called for Gore. Although there may have been some bias in the exit poll in Gore's favor, the bias resulted in a false call only because the error in the estimates was understated and the 1998 governor's race was used as the past election in the estimation. If the error had been correctly stated and a different past election had been used in the ratio estimation, the bias in favor of Gore would not in itself have led to the false projection.

After the networks made the call for Gore in Florida, actual returns began to show that the race was much closer than estimated. The networks and VNS retracted their calls of Florida before 10:30 P.M. As other states returns became available, it became clear that the outcome of the presidency would depend on who won Florida. For a while VNS estimates showed a race too close to call. But at 2:10 A.M., tabulated vote returns from VNS showed that Bush had a lead of 51,433 votes, with 97 percent of the precincts counted. VNS estimated that Gore would need 63 percent of the estimated 179,713 outstanding votes in order to win. Furthermore, Gore was estimated to be able to reduce Bush's lead by only 20,000 in counties that were going in Gore's favor, and Bush was expected to gain even more votes from the returns that had not yet been tabulated, so it seemed highly unlikely that Gore would win. Although VNS and AP never called the state for Bush, all three networks did so within a few minutes of one another.

Yet, again, the calls were in error because the figures the networks were using were incorrect. Arguably, it was a more serious error than the first one because it also meant calling the presidential race for Bush, which in turn led to Gore's preliminary concession, which he later retracted. This error had two sources. First, the Bush lead was the consequence of vote-counting errors in Florida—a 20,000-vote mistake in Volusia County and a 4,000 one in Brevard County. Bush's lead at 2:15 A.M. should have been reported as 27,000 votes, not 51,000. Significantly, AP did not call the state for Bush because it had a backup data source for vote tabulations in the state, and those tabulations showed a smaller Bush lead, even with the errors in the two counties. As AP Florida bureau chief Kevin Walsh recalled, "I think everyone was affected by that erroneous data. However, our vote totals in all the counties were far ahead enough of VNS' that it affected us less. We were recording votes so fast in the Miami bureau that the Volusia problem did not have as dramatic an impact on the overall Bush margin for us as it did for VNS."[61]

The second source of the error was in the estimate of the outstanding vote. There were 359,000 votes not yet tabulated, about half of which would come from Palm Beach County, where Gore was leading. The VNS model for estimating the outstanding vote was a simplistic extrapolation of the returns already available. It assumed "that the outstanding precincts in each county will be of average size and will vote in the same way as the precincts that have already reported from that county" (Mason, Frankovic, and Jamieson 2001, p. 24). But in Florida in 2000, that was not the case. Bush ended up winning Florida with only a 537-vote margin, after the U.S. Supreme Court ruled against Gore's plea to have additional ballots counted.

In summary, the calls giving Florida first to Gore and then to Bush were a consequence of failures of VNS methodology. Those failures were magnified because all the networks relied almost exclusively on the same data source. Yet the failures did not need to lead to the problematic projections for Bush. The false calls for Bush occurred because the networks independently made their decisions, had few other data sources, and were under the pressure of competition. As Mitofsky and Edelman (2002, p. 178) summarize:

> While the network analysts, along with the country, were focused on the closeness in Florida where slight changes in the vote were highly significant, the VNS people doing the tabulation were disconnected from the national drama and were focusing on keeping the data flowing as accurately as possible in all of the states. . . . If the network analysts had had access to the entire trail of inputs into each county, they might have discovered and questioned that vote drop themselves and given the closeness of the race, might have waited.

Similarly, if the network analysts had had additional sources of data, as the AP did, they may also have been more cautious in their projections. Finally, the desire of the networks to make the calls was intense. NBC decision-desk head Sheldon Gawiser was on the phone with Murray Edelman at VNS shortly after 2 A.M. He repeatedly asked Edelman why he could not make the call. Not happy with the answer, he broke the connection. Fox News called Florida for Bush at 2:16 A.M., NBC at 2:17 A.M., CNN at 2:18 A.M., and CBS at 2:20 A.M.[62]

In 2004, Edison-Mitofsky instituted a number of changes to correct for the statistical and data-collection problems: (1) they improved their estimate of absentee and early voters and surveyed them in advance of the election; (2) they added a correction in their method of calculating the error in the predictions to account for the use of incomplete data from the samples; (3) they used more than one past election in their calculations of the ratio estimator; (4) they revised their model of predicting the outstanding vote; (5) they instituted more quality-control measures to catch errors in counties' vote reports to prevent mistakes like those in Volusia and Brevard Counties from leading to false projections; and (6) they increased the amount of data available to their clients to help them make more informed decisions. Finally, in 2004, AP handled vote tabulations by county. But even though those statistical changes did lead to better reporting and projecting on election night, new questions were raised in 2004 about the process of election projection when exit-polls results were leaked early in the afternoon, suggesting that Kerry would win.

What Went Wrong in 2004

By comparison with 2000, 2004 was amazingly smooth in terms of election projections. The states too close to call were not projected until a sufficient number of votes could be tabulated accurately. The troubling issue was the exit-poll results. Why did they seem to have a Kerry bias? Was it a bias on the part of the pollsters, or was it evidence that the election outcome itself was suspect? First, we need to be careful about the definition of *bias*. An exit poll is simply a sample of the voters participating at a precinct on a given day. But after the election, the exit-poll results can be checked against the tabulated results. The difference between the tabulated results and the exit-poll results is called a within-precinct error (WPE). Lots of things can cause WPE: (1) the selection of the sampling precincts might be biased, (2) the data might be contaminated during collection and processing, (3) vote tabulations could be fraudulent or subject to voting-machine errors, (4) factors relating to interviewer-subject relations could lead to systematic differences in who chooses to respond to the survey, or (5) for some unknown reason, respondents with a particular preference may be more likely to complete the survey.

A January 19, 2005, postelection evaluation by Edison-Mitofsky found little evidence that the WPE in 2004 was caused by the first three potential causes but did find that there were a number of aspects of interviewer-respondent relations that led to higher levels of WPE. Specifically, errors were higher when the interviewer was younger and a student. If interviewers had a large precinct to cover, and thus a greater interviewer rate, the error was also higher, perhaps reflecting the tendency of interviewers to select respondents nonrandomly. And compared with the 2000 election, more than twice as many interviewers reported that they had to stand more than fifty feet away from the polling location and thus were not able to take a random sample of voters leaving the precinct as easily. The pollsters stated that they planned to undertake a number of measures to reduce those sources of error in future exit polls.

The problems with the exit polls highlighted the difficulty of having one source of exit-poll data provided to many clients and the potential for a leak of the results without statistical interpretation. The early results also placed a greater weight on the responses of women, who were more likely to support Kerry. While those weights were corrected later on election day and before the results were used for analysis or projecting outcomes, they increased the popular perception that Kerry was winning the election. The media outlets have announced that in the future they will withhold the distribution of exit-poll information within their organizations until 6 P.M. eastern time on election day. Edison-Mitofsky have stated that they plan to help their clients with the security necessary to control the release of the data and to provide more guidance about the potential for WEP.

Forecasting Elections before Campaigns Begin

Both public opinion polls and election markets provide measures of how individuals view an election during the campaign and can be used as predictions. However, they understandably tend to work best close to an election. But is it possible to predict an election before a campaign even begins? Moreover, is it possible to use political theories about long-term influences on voters to predict election outcomes? Political scientists since Lazarsfeld

have believed that there are factors that are independent of election campaigns and the candidates themselves that affect how individuals vote in
presidential elections. In particular, if voters choose retrospectively based on
the economy, as we have noted evidence suggests, then we should be able
to use the economy to predict presidential elections months in advance, using data on past voters' decisions and the economic situation. A number of
researchers have investigated that possibility.

Ray Fair's Economic Model

 One of the first academics to investigate the relationship between the state
of the economy and presidential elections was Princeton economist Orley
Ashenfelter, who used the earlier analysis of Kramer (1971), which found an
empirical relationship between economic growth and presidential elections,
to predict that Nixon would win the 1972 election with 60 percent of the
vote.[63] To estimate economic growth, Ashenfelter used work previously
done by Yale economist Ray Fair. Fair became interested in the enterprise
and came up with his own predictions in future elections.[64] Now, more than
thirty years later, Fair is known worldwide for his presidential-election predictions.
    Fair (1996) described the basics of his empirical approach to predicting
presidential elections. The theory behind the predictions is that voters
choose solely based on the past economic performances of the two major
political parties. Using data from 1916, he estimated what measures of economic performances worked best to predict the votes in the presidential
elections in the past. He argued that his results show that voters look only at
the economic performance of the current party holding the presidency and
ignore the economic performance of the opposition party the last time it
held the presidency. In 2000, Fair, like other psephologists, estimated that
Gore would win, but unlike the political scientists he predicted a very close
race (in January 2000, he predicted Gore would receive 51.6 percent of the
two-party vote; Gore received 50.3 percent of that vote).
    After each election, Fair adds the data from that election and reestimates
the relationship between the economic variables and the election outcome.
The equation is like the equation UNIVAC used to estimate votes in 1952,
but with more variables on the right side of the equation. Thus, he estimates
different slopes for different variables. This is the equation Fair used to predict the 2004 election:

$$VOTE = 49.61 + 0.691 \cdot GROWTH - 0.775 \cdot INFLATION + 0.837 \cdot GOODNEWS + 3.25 \cdot INCUMBENT - 3.63 \cdot DURATION - 2.71 \cdot PARTY$$

VOTE = the Republican share of the two-party presidential vote, *GROWTH*
= the annual rate of growth of the real per capita gross domestic product

(GDP) in the first three quarters of 2004; *INFLATION* = the annual rate of growth of the GDP deflator in the first fifteen quarters of the Bush administration; *GOODNEWS* = the number of quarters in the first fifteen quarters of the Bush administration in which the annual rate of growth of real per capita GDP was greater than 3.2 percent; *INCUMBENT* = 1 if an incumbent is running for reelection, 0 otherwise; *DURATION* = 0 if the incumbent party has been in power for one term, 1 if the incumbent party has been in power for two consecutive terms, 1.25 if the incumbent party has been in power for three consecutive terms, 1.5 if the incumbent party has been in power for four consecutive terms, and so on; and *PARTY* = 1 if the incumbent president is a Democrat and –1 if the incumbent is a Republican. Fair's equivalent of the estimated constant term is 49.61, and each of the numbers multiplied by the variables *VOTE, GROWTH*, and so on, is the estimated slope.[65]

Although Fair emphasized the economy in his model, the variables *INCUMBENT* and *PARTY* combined capture the incumbency advantage in the election. That is, since in 2004 Bush was running as an incumbent, Fair estimated that that alone would increase the Republican vote share by 3.25 + 2.71 = 5.96 percent. The theoretical assumption behind those figures is that for a given state of the economy, voters will vote retrospectively for an incumbent president who is known rather than take a chance on an unknown opposition candidate. The variable *DURATION*, on the other hand, has a less theoretical basis: it simply suggests that voters like an alteration in party power. For example, in 2008, the Republican candidate would not be an incumbent, so *DURATION* and *PARTY* would reduce his or her vote share by 3.63 – 2.71 = 0.92.

In February 2004, Fair predicted Bush would win by a sizable margin, 58.7 percent of the two-party vote, yet Bush received only 51.6 percent. Macroeconomic Advisers, a forecasting firm in St. Louis, estimated an economic model similar to Fair's, in which vote shares are a function of income growth in the six to nine months before the election as well as the inflation rate and housing starts. Its model also predicted a sizable victory for Bush. Both Fair and Macroeconomic Advisers suggested that the error in their predictions was due to the Iraq war. Joel Prakken, an economist for the firm, told *The Washington Post*: "These models don't know anything about insurgents lining up Iraqi army recruits and executing them. They don't know anything about tons of missing explosives. I think the economy is the most important thing most of the time, but I do not expect the kind of romp for Bush that the economic models predict. It's much too messy this time around."[66] Fair noted that the error in the prediction for 2004 shows a big problem with what we can learn from the success or failure of election-forecasting models. Fair (2004, p. 9) concluded:

> The large error in 2004 means that some other factors were important. Since there are many possible factors, it is not possible to test that one particular factor

is responsible for most of the error in an election. There are many stories and one observation. My personal view is that were it not for Iraq and with the economy as it was, Bush would have come close to the equation's prediction, but again this cannot be tested. What one can say, however, is that conditional on the vote equation being a good approximation, the Democrats did well. Bush should have won by more than he did, and so the Democrats need not be wringing their hands about the demise of the party.

On November 3, 2004, using his 2004 equation, Fair suggested a prediction for 2008. Plugging into his equation the facts that there will be no incumbent, so INCUMBENT = 0, that the Republicans will have been in office for two terms, so DURATION = 1, and that the economy is moderately good (GROWTH = 3.0, INFLATION = 3.0, and GOODNEWS = 2), the vote share predicted for the Republicans is 50.1. As Fair summed up:

> So the main message for 2008 is that the election will be close if the economy is moderately good. It would take a quite strong economy for the equation to predict a comfortable Republican win, and it would take a quite weak economy for the equation to predict a comfortable Democratic win. The Democrats clearly have a much better shot in 2008 than they had in 2004 according to the equation.[67]

Adding in Data on Voters

Before Fair created his famous economic model of elections, a government researcher in the Department of Agriculture during the Great Depression, Louis Bean, decided to take the statistical approach he was using to understand agricultural economics and apply it to forecasting elections. Bean also believed that the economy is a big factor in elections, but he thought that long-term economic forces were more important than short-term ones. Moreover, like Fair, he felt that what he called anomalies—such as issues, events, and other forces—could affect the presidential-election outcome. To control for those affects, unlike Fair, Bean used a combination of economic statistics and past election results combined with voters' preferences. Bean did not conduct polls but used information gathered from ones taken in the Department of Agriculture. According to Salsburg (2001), Bean joked to Gallup that he might one day run a poll and call it the "Galloping Bean pole." In fact, Bean beat Gallup, becoming famous in 1948, when he foretold that Truman would win reelection in his book *How to Predict Elections*, published earlier that year.[68]

Unfortunately, Bean's model did not fare as well in predicting elections after 1948. But his approach of combining economic statistics with measures of voters' opinions is the approach taken in most political scientists' election-forecasting models beginning in the 1980s.[69] Fair criticized this forecasting method, although he acknowledged that the approach might lead to better results. He contended that measures of voters' opinions from surveys is sampling ahead of time what voters intend to do in an election; in his opinion, they do not measure causal factors that underlie what determines how individuals will vote.[70] Political scientists, however, see those variables as serving as proxies for causal factors that matter outside the economic variables that Fair emphasized. For example, Wlezien and Erikson (2001) based their forecasting model on empirical evidence that voters' choice for president is a function of economic variables like growth of per capita disposable income and leading economic indicators measuring the state of the economy on election day and survey data like evaluations of candidates as measured by the NES (which they saw as capturing candidates' positions on issues and perceived valence qualities beyond economics). But since the NES data come from postelection surveys, they could not use those data for forecasting purposes. They thus estimated that the evaluations are largely capturing voters' opinions of incumbents and that surveys measuring presidential approval can serve as a proxy for those evaluations.

In October 2004, *PS: Political Science & Politics*, the journal of record of the American Political Science Association, published a symposium of seven presidential-election forecasts by academic political scientists Alan Abramowitz, James Campbell, Christopher Wlezien and Robert Erikson, Thomas Holbrook, Michael Lewis-Beck and Charles Tien, Brad Lockerbie, and Helmut Norpoth. These forecasting models all represented tests of various theories of how individuals vote in presidential elections. All the models, like Fair's, had some expectation that incumbency gives presidents an advantage in reelection. With the exception of Norpoth's model, all assumed, also like Fair's model, that the state of the economy would be a major factor in presidential voting. Three of the models, however, incorporated subjective, or voters', evaluations of the economy, either in place of Fair's objective measures (Holbrook and Lockerbie) or combined with them (Lewis-Beck and Tien). The reason for incorporating subjective measures is that they may better capture what voters perceive about the state of the economy, which may be different from the actual state of the economy. But the use of subjective measures limits the way in which many past presidential elections can be used in the estimate since such measures do not generally exist prior to the 1950s.

With the exception of Norpoth's and Lockerbie's, all of them, like Wlezien and Erikson (2001), also contained some measure of voters' opinions, and with the exception of Campbell's model, the measure used was the president's job-approval rating; Campbell instead used Gallup polls on voters' preferences in the election. Using voter-opinion data also limits the number of past elections that can be used in the estimate. While Norpoth's model did not use such poll results, his approach was that vote percentages in early primaries predict success in presidential elections, so in a sense he also used a measure of voters' preferences. That allowed him to use presidential elections since 1912 in his estimate. Thus, with variation across models, political science forecasting models, like Fair's, generally assume that the economy and incumbency are important in presidential elections, but (like Wlezien and Erickson 2001) they assume that there are also other ideological factors that determine voting, and to control for these, they use some measure of voters' opinions, typically from polls.

Interestingly, as noted above, political science models significantly overestimated Gore's vote share in 2000. Yet in 2004, their estimates were mostly closer to the outcome than Fair's. The median forecast for Bush's vote share was 53.8 across the models; Abramowitz predicted 53.7; Campbell, 53.8; Wlezien and Erikson, 51.7 to 52.9; Holbrook, 54.5; Lewis-Beck and Tien, 49.9; Lockerbie, 57.6; and Norpoth, 54.7. What are we to make of the differences? It is noteworthy that Lockerbie's model, which was primarily based on economics, had the highest predicted vote share, close to Fair's. Clearly in 2000, the economy as measured by Fair mattered more than the voter-opinion data suggested, and in 2004, the voter-opinion data mattered more than the economy.

Data Mining?

As noted above, Fair reestimated his model after each election, a normal practice for psephologists making predictions based on historical data on the economy and public opinion. In the summer of 2000, as such models were predicting a big win for Gore, journalist Ira Carnahan wrote in *The Weekly Standard* that there was a problem in evaluating whether such models really were successful, since failed models tended "to disappear, with only the most accurate ones surviving to be counted in statistics that measure the success of forecasting."[71] Carnahan pointed out that previous models had failed to predict the first president Bush's loss in 1992 and overestimated the size of Clinton's margin in 1996. Of course, the problem for psephologists is that presidential elections are held only every four years and reliable economic data are not available for the majority of those elections. Fair's 2000 model was based on twenty-one elections, whereas most political science models were based on data post 1948, which means that they were based on only thirteen elections (some models, like Lockerbie's, were based on even fewer). These are precious few observations on which to base a prediction, compared with the estimate on election night using exit polls! So it is very difficult not to want to use new data in order to have a larger sample for the estimate. One way to avoid the data-mining problem is to estimate the model based on a limited sample and then "predict" known outcomes with the model estimated with less data. Fair performed such a diagnostic test on his model, but the political science models have less ability to do such out-of-sample predictions, given the data limitations they have to begin with (Norpoth being an exception).

What Do We Learn about Elections from Psephology Failures?

While occasionally psephologists spectacularly fail in their election predictions, in terms of our understanding elections, their efforts have led to an improved understanding of the process and, significantly, how we can best study that process. In general, the work on election prediction shows that voters' preferences appear to change during campaigns, often in ways difficult to predict, even with detailed knowledge of past voters' behavior. These results support our earlier analysis of how campaigns can affect voters' preferences. It is noteworthy that betting markets perform as well in predicting elections as polls from randomly drawn samples or empirical models based on political science theories of voting. This suggests that the competitive market process of information aggregation on political matters does lead to predictions with little bias, supporting the argument that a mass media market of information in which biases are heterogeneous can lead to a less biased perspective overall, as noted in chapter 8. Furthermore, there is support for the theory that in presidential elections, voters' choices are heavily influenced by the state of the economy, but the economy is not everything. Finally, the failures of polls both before and during elections show that measuring public opinion in surveys is exceedingly difficult, something we will address below, and that choosing a random sample and proper estimation procedure, correcting for the margin of error, can be important if we are going to use surveys to understand voters' preferences.

Do Elected Officials Read Polls?

Moral Values

In early October 2003, North Carolina Republican representative Cass Ballenger talked to journalists about the stresses of living in Washington that had led to his amicable separation from his wife after fifty years. He noted that a large Muslim advocacy group, the Council on American-Islamic Relations (CAIR), had leased a building opposite Ballenger's Washington, D.C., home. The Associated Press summarized Ballenger's concerns: "In the post 9–11 environment in Washington, his wife, a homemaker, was anxious about all the activity at CAIR, including people unloading boxes late at night and women 'wearing hoods,' or headscarves, going in and out of the office building on New Jersey Avenue." Ballenger concluded: "That's 2½ blocks from the Capitol and they could blow it up."[72]

CAIR was not happy with Ballenger's remarks and decided to sue for libel, accusing him of making false and defamatory statements that harmed its reputation. But the U.S. attorneys representing Ballenger said that his comments were made in the course of legislative business and in an "interest to continue as an effective representative of those who elected him to office." If the comments were made as part of his official duties, then, according to the 1948 Federal Tort Claims Act, Ballenger is immune from tort liability. Why was explaining the marital separation so important to Ballenger? According to his attorneys, values voters. The attorneys wrote in their legal brief: "North Carolina residents listed 'Moral Values' as the single most important issue in the election [in exit polls in 2004]." U.S. Attorney Kenneth Wainstein summarized: "Results from the 2004 election leave little doubt that matters relating to marriage and family matter greatly to North Carolina voters, including those voters within the state's Tenth Congressional District."[73] After the interview, Ballenger decided not to run for reelection in 2004. While the exit poll was conducted after Ballenger had made his decision, other polls had shown that such issues mattered to North Carolina's voters. Did voters' concerns about moral values lead Ballenger to retire? More generally, what is the relationship between public opinion polls and elected officials' choices?

Presidential Polling

Our discussion of polls has so far considered how elected officials use them to gauge and predict their likely chances of winning. But polls also ask voters questions about issues. How do their responses affect the behavior of elected officials like Ballenger and other candidates for elected office? One person reading the Gallup polls in the early 1940s was FDR. Roosevelt was of course not the first president or elected official to be concerned with public opinion. Rottinghaus (2003) described how during the administration of Herbert Hoover, officials systematically collected and analyzed newspaper editorials from across the nation in an attempt to judge public opinion on particular issues. Rottinghaus noted (p. 542) that the "Herbert Hoover Presidential Archive contains 6 linear feet of the administration's editorial analysis reports on 346 issues during a 4 year period."

Presidential life changed with the advent of scientific polling, as Geer (1991, 1996) and Rottinghaus (2003) have discussed. The ability of presidents after Hoover to use polls not only gave them a more scientific measure of public opinion but also allowed them to discern public opinion on issues that were not already the subject of editorial opinions—that is, to estimate opinion about possible actions and policy issues at an earlier stage in their decision making. As documented by Eisinger and Brown (1998), FDR used polls conducted by Gallup; Emil Hurja, a Department of Interior employee and Democratic strategist; and Hadley Cantril, director of the Office of Public Opinion Research at Princeton University, to find out what the public thought about many topics before proposing policy changes. For example, FDR's lend-lease program was preceded by extensive information provided by Cantril on the public's willingness to support aid to Britain. In a number of cases, Cantril also provided FDR with advice on how to persuade the public to support his policies. In a discussion of a plan to establish refugee camps in the United States for individuals persecuted by Nazis, for instance, Cantril gave Roosevelt information on the chief reasons the public would oppose such a plan and how best to counter them.[74]

Poll use intensified in later administrations. Jacobs and Shapiro (1994, 1995, 2000) examined the use of polls in the Kennedy, Johnson, and Nixon administrations. Taking a psychological approach to voters' preferences, they contended that the presidents used polls as part of a process of focusing the public on particular issues, or agenda setting, much as we noted George W. Bush appeared to do in early 2004 when he emphasized gay marriage as an issue as the war in Iraq deteriorated (as discussed in chapter 5). Murray and Howard (2002) studied the expenditures of presidents Carter, Reagan, George H. W. Bush, and Clinton on private White House polls. They found that although all four presidents used public opinion polls throughout their terms, during the first three years of their terms Reagan and Clinton used them much more extensively than Carter and Bush. Preliminary analysis suggests that George W. Bush also uses public opinion polls in his decision making. Foyle (2004) presented evidence that public opinion concerns delayed Bush's push to invade Iraq after the attacks of September 11 and influenced the justifications he used for the invasion.

Congressional Polling

Whereas there has been extensive study of presidential use of polls, few scholars have systematically studied the use of polls by other elected officials. Jacobs and others (1998), surveying congressional staff members during the summer of 1994 about their use of public opinion polls, with special attention to the current health-care debate, found a mixed picture. For example, they found that average legislators minimize the impact of polls on their own behavior. That fits with the findings of Cook, Barabas, and Page (2002) and Paden and Page (2003) that presidents and members of Congress rarely mention polls or poll results in their public speeches and debates. But Jacobs and others (p. 27) found that congressional leaders use polls in the formation of policy behind closed doors for three purposes:

> First, polls "enable members to find out what the public is thinking" in order to "build on areas of support" or challenge pockets of opposition. An aide to a legislator specializing in health care explained that polls showing a majority approved of the Clinton plan told his office that "we needed to educate the public regarding what we didn't like about the plan." Second, "polls help to focus and define messages." For instance, two-thirds of our respondents used polls to identify the most effective language or words for framing their policy decisions. Third, polls provided symbolic or rhetorical ammunition for bolstering the legislator's position. About two-thirds of the respondents indicated that polls were helpful in justifying a legislator's public position.

The researchers summarized (p. 39): "Like modern presidents, congressional leaders have come to use information about public opinion as a tool to influence the policy choices of marginal legislators. Much like presidents, recent leaders now commission private polls and focus groups through their parties and use them to devise and defend strategies."

Retrospective Voting and Public Opinion Polls

Do Polls Influence Policy?

While elected officials appear to both measure public opinion and try to influence it by choosing which issues to emphasize or how to present issues, to what extent do public opinion polls influence the choices that elected officials make while in office? For example, in our simple model of retrospective voting in chapter 9, voters evaluate elected officials based on the policy outcomes and how close they are to their preferred choices. We emphasized how voters use retrospective voting to control for moral-hazard and adverse-selection problems. In terms of adverse selection, we argued that voters' use of retrospective voting increases the likelihood that the candidates who choose political careers agree with voters' preferences. Thus, our model of retrospective voting suggests that elected officials both respond to public opinion polls and make choices that are in agreement with them in order to secure votes in forthcoming elections.

As reviewed in Manza and Cook (2002), a large number of studies have found that policy choices and policy activities appear to respond to public opinion. These studies range from cross-state comparisons in which researchers exploit variations in voters' preferences to macro-level dynamic models of U.S. policy making to individual case studies of policy choices over time. At the state level, Erikson, Wright, and McIver (1993) compared public opinion ideology scores with policy liberalism across states and found that states with a more liberal (or conservative) public tend to enact more liberal (or conservative) policies. At the global level, Erikson, MacKuen, and Stimson (2002) estimated a macro-level dynamic model of U.S. policy making in which they looked for changes in public mood in terms of overall liberalism or conservatism as reflected in public opinion polls on policy activity in terms of congressional voting, presidential policy stances, Supreme Court rulings, and so on. They found both direct and indirect effects (primarily through elections) of public opinion on policy. That is, as the public mood, as measured by opinion polls, becomes more liberal (or conservative), policy activity becomes more liberal (or conservative). Individual case studies of domestic social policy, such as the work of Burstein (1985, 1998), Weaver (2000), Jacobs (1993), and Quirk and Hinchliffe (1998), found substantial effects of public opinion on policy choices over time at the federal level. Jones and Baumgartner (2004) found that the agenda and attention of

Congress are highly congruent with issues that voters say are important in public opinion polls.[75]

Do Elected Officials Influence Polls?

Andrew Card, George W. Bush's chief of staff, told reporters in June 2001: "We are not driven by polls. We know polls are important, but they usually don't measure policy. They measure marketing of policy: it's how you say things, rather than what you say."[76] Card's comments seem contrary to the empirical results noted above, suggesting that instead of policy following polls, polls follow policy. Hill and Hurley (1999, 2003) contended that the empirical studies that focus on a unidirectional model of the public opinion that leads to policy choices fail to account for the fact that elected officials can also influence public opinion. They argued that the appropriate model should consider both directions of interaction.

We have already noted that by providing voters with information during election campaigns, candidates, interest groups, and the mass media can change voters' preferences for the candidates. If voters know only a little about an issue, then information can similarly change their preferences on that issue as they revise their positions. By selecting the information they provide, elected officials can influence those positions even if they are biased, much as biased mass media outlets can influence public opinion, as we discussed in chapter 8. In an extensive study of congressional policy making on issues compared with public opinion polls, Hill and Hurley (2003) found that whether polls follow policy or policy follows polls, or both, depends on how complicated the issue is and whether it divides the two major parties. They find that for uncomplicated issues that are not the focus of divisions between the major parties, policy follows public opinion. When simple issues are the focus of divisions between the major parties, the relationship goes both ways: public opinion influences policy, but policy makers also influence public opinion. For complex issues that are not the focus of party divisions, elected officials tend to ignore public opinion. If, in contrast, complex issues are the focus of party divisions, elected officials largely influence public opinion rather than public opinion influencing elected officials. This makes sense with an information story: if voters are less informed about complex issues, then elected officials' ability to structure the public debate on those issues is likely to influence public opinion much more than public opinion will influence the elected officials, as we saw with the mass media in chapter 8.

When Elected Officials and Voters Disagree

Sir Winston Churchill famously disliked political polls, remarking that "nothing is more dangerous than to live in the temperamental atmosphere of a Gallup poll, always taking one's temperature. There is only one duty, only one safe course. And that is to be right and not to fear to do or say what you believe to be right."[77] In our simple model, voters always know the policy outcomes when choosing whether to reward or punish elected officials; what they do not know is the degree to which the official is responsible for the policy outcomes. Suppose, however, that voters know policy choices but not necessarily the policy outcomes. What happens when the elected official and the public agree on the desired policy outcome but disagree on the best policy to achieve that outcome and voters choose retrospectively based on the elected officials' proposals?

Suppose Rudy Giuliani has been elected president and is serving his first term in office. Giuliani believes that the best policy for improving the economy is a flat income tax, one that taxes individuals at all levels of income at the same rate and eliminates many of the exemptions and progressivity of the current tax system. He has support for the proposal in Congress and figures that he can get it passed. But he knows that most voters are uncertain about the outcome of changing the tax system or oppose it outright (for example, *The New York Times*/CBS News poll of January 14–18, 2005, found that 29 percent of respondents favored a flat tax, 33 percent opposed it, 36 percent reported that they did not know enough to have an opinion, and 2 percent did not respond). If he proposes changing the tax system in his first term, he faces the possibility that the policy outcome he expects the tax change to cause (a better economy) will not result before the election and that voters will, using retrospective evaluations, choose his opponent. He figures also that even if the new system has an effect on the economy, if he has time, he can persuade the public to be more supportive of the change. Knowing that public opinion is against him, should he go ahead and advocate the flat-tax proposal because he believes it is the best choice, or should he give up on the proposal and adopt a tax policy with greater public support even though he thinks it is not as good a choice?

Canes-Wrone, Herron, and Shotts (2001) argued that presidents' choices on whether to follow public opinion even when they disagree will depend on their chances for reelection and how close they are to reelection. Suppose that Giuliani is in his second term. Then the researchers contended he will ignore public opinion and propose the policy change that he thinks is best. If he is in his first term but expects to win reelection handily, he will also ignore public opinion. Similarly, if he is in his first term but has little hope of winning relection, he will ignore public opinion. But if he is in his first term and he faces a close contest for reelection, then as the election approaches, he is less likely to ignore public opinion. That is, he may think that by the time he faces reelection, it will be clear that his policy is the best one and therefore ignoring public opinion is okay. Or he might think that during the course of his term he can persuade the public to agree with him. But if it is close to the reelection, he thinks that the policy choice can make a difference to his prospects, and there is insufficient time to wait for the outcome to please voters or try to change public opinion, he is more likely to follow public opinion.

Do Presidents Pander?

Canes-Wrone and Shotts (2004) tested that theory using budget proposals made by presidents in their first terms and responses to public opinion polls. They examined eleven budgetary issues on which legislative negotiations occurred between 1972 and 1999, and they compared the previous year's enacted budget on an issue with the president's proposed budgetary allocation and determined whether the president proposed an increase in spending, a reduction in spending, or no change in spending. They also have for these same issues and years responses to the following survey question (p. 691), asked by the National Opinion Research Center and the Roper Organization: "We are faced with many problems in this country, none of which can be solved easily or inexpensively. I'm going to name some of the problems, and for each one I'd like you to tell me whether you think we're spending too much money, too little money, or about the right amount on [the particular problem]." The researchers calculated a measure of policy congruence between the president and public opinion. If the president proposed an increase (or decrease) in the budget for an issue and more respondents preferred an increase (or decrease) than a decrease (or increase) in spending, they labeled the president's policy and public opinion on the issue congruent. In all other cases, they labeled the president's policy and public opinion on the issue to be incongruent. Canes-Wrone and Shotts used popularity or approval ratings of presidents to measure their prospects for reelection.

The raw percentages of policy congruence follow the patterns predicted by Canes-Wrone, Herron, and Shotts. That is, for presidents who are in the second half of their first terms and have average popularity ratings, for whom policy choices are expected to be pivotal in their reelection bids, policy choices are congruent with public opinion 77 percent of the time. In contrast, presidents who are not worried about reelection have less congruent policy choices. For presidents who are in the second half of their first term and have low (or high) popularity ratings, who would be expected to lose (or win) reelection regardless of their policy choices, policy choices are congruent 53 (or 55) percent of the time. Similarly, for presidents in first half of the first term, the congruence of policy choices is unrelated to popularity. That is, they have policy choices that are congruent 33 percent of the time if their popularity is low, 47 percent of the time if their popularity is average, and 45 percent of the time if they are highly popular.

While those results are supportive, Canes-Wrone and Shotts analyzed the degree of policy congruence controlling for other factors. For example, the data may simply reflect differences in presidents or issues. The researchers showed that the results are significant even controlling for such effects. They found (p. 699) that "if a president's initial popularity is five points below average in the second half of his term, a 10-point decline reduces the likelihood of policy congruence by 20%" and that if the president's initial probability "is five points above average, a 10-point decrease in approval decreases the likelihood of policy congruence by 16%." They also found that for presidents whose probability is about average, the likelihood of policy congruence is 55 percent higher in the second half of their first term than in the first half.

Is this pandering? In chapter 9, we contended that the problem facing voters was to force elected officials to choose in the interest of voters and that retrospective voting was a good thing. In our previous analysis, the problem facing voters was uncertainty about the policy choices, but they knew the policy outcomes. But the perspective in Canes-Wrone, Herron, and Shotts and Canes-Wrone and Shotts is that retrospective voting causes presidents to pander to public opinion in making policy choices rather than make policy choices they think are best to achieve desirable outcomes. If the president is right about the best policy to achieve a given outcome, retrospective voting causes harm and we should prefer that presidents not pander; if the president is wrong, then retrospective voting is a good thing and we want presidents to pander. Retrospective voting results in presidents with just average electoral support making unpopular policy choices only when the time is available for those choices to be consequential in policy outcomes or the president can explain his policy preferences. In this sense, retrospective voting forces presidents to face the judgment or their unpopular policy choices at election time, after outcomes are more likely to be realized or their explanations provided. Those presidents who are not worried about reelection, either because of other choices they have made or because they are in their final term, will not be influenced by retrospective voting should they choose to promote unpopular policy choices.

What Do Public Opinion Polls Tell Elected Officials?

Moral Values Redux

One reason we might prefer that elected officials not pander to public opinion polls is that we are suspicious of what those polls measure. While pre-election predictions from polls can be tested in a unique way against the actual outcome, general polls of public opinion on issues are not subject to such a test. When we ask respondents their opinion on abortion, for example, we cannot have them subsequently vote on the issue in a consequential manner and compare the results. Furthermore, as we saw in chapter 5 when we compared the abortion question in the NES survey with the one asked by *The New York Times*/CBS News poll, different types of questions elicit different types and distributions of responses. Public opinion polls appear most precise when the question is simple and clearly stated, as when respondents are asked about their anticipated vote. As noted above, Hill and Hurley (2003) found elected officials most responsive to public opinion on simple issues. Thus, questions like "Do you approve or disapprove of the current president?" or thermometer ratings on elected officials and groups, and so on, can give us measures of voters' attitudes that are probably as truthful as questions about who voters will choose in an upcoming election.[78]

But when questions are complex and involve a multitude of factors and choices that are sometimes oversimplified or not comprehensive, evidence suggests that responses to surveys can depend on question wording, order, and context. The 2004 exit poll asked voters nationwide: "Which *one* issue mattered most in deciding how you voted for president? (Check only one.)" and gave seven options. Five percent of voters chose taxes; 4 percent, education; 15 percent, Iraq; 19 percent, terrorism; 20 percent, the economy or jobs; 22, percent moral values; and 8 percent, health care. As Ballenger's attorneys noted, of those who mentioned moral values, 80 percent voted for Bush, the winner in the presidential election. Ballenger's attorneys were not the only ones who used the exit-poll results to conclude that concern about moral values was the most important issue in the 2004 election. After the election, newspapers headlined the poll results, and television, radio, and magazine commentators used them as their principal explanation for Bush's victory.[79]

But were moral values all that concerned those who voted for Republicans like Bush in 2004? The tenth congressional district in North Carolina is largely rural, blue collar, and Republican, and it was suffering as the 2004 election approached; some estimated that it had lost forty thousand jobs in the past three years as furniture factories and textile mills had closed. In December 2001, Cass Ballenger had reluctantly cast a deciding vote in favor of giving President Bush the authority to negotiate global trade agreements and submit them to Congress for only a yes or no vote even though many voters in his district saw the measure as a potential contributor to further job losses in the area.[80] When Ballenger ran for reelection in 2002, he received less than 60 percent of the vote in the general election for the first time since he first ran for the seat, in 1986. Ballenger's decrease in support emboldened potential Republican challengers, and several began to announce that they would challenge him in the 2004 primary.[81] Although moral values may have received the most responses in North Carolina (24 percent), the economy or jobs was next highest (21 percent). And there is that funny thing called margin of error in opinion polls. In state polls, the estimated error was 4 percent, and in the national poll it was 2 percent. Statistically, economy or jobs was equally important to North Carolina voters and to voters nationwide. Faced with Republican challengers in the primary, Ballenger chose not to run for reelection.[82]

Furthermore, there is considerable confusion about what voters mean by moral values and why they picked that choice on the exit poll. Gary Langer, director of polling for ABC News, was on the committee that designed the questions for the exit poll. He opposed the structure of the question but was outvoted. He pointed out after the election that four of the options on the question "played to John Kerry's strengths: economy/jobs, health care, education, Iraq. Just two worked in President Bush's favor: terrorism and taxes. If you were a Bush supporter, and terrorism and taxes didn't inspire you, moral values was your place to go on the exit poll questionnaire."[83]

Supporting Langer's argument, other polls show that when given more choices, voters did not choose moral values as often. Just prior to the election, a *USA Today*/CNN/Gallup poll asked voters to rate each of a list of ten issues separately, one after the other, in terms of its importance to their votes. The top three issues based on the percentage saying they were "extremely important" were terrorism, Iraq, and the economy. Moral values was approximately tied with three other categories that followed: health care, education, and Social Security.[84] The Pew Research Center surveyed two groups of voters from November 5 to 8, 2004; some were given the same question as that in the exit poll, in which voters are constrained to pick only one of the options listed, whereas others were given the option of offering any answer. The responses from those constrained to choose an option resulted in 27 percent choosing moral values; 22 percent, Iraq; 21 percent, the economy or jobs; and 14 percent, terrorism. The first responses from those who could offer any answer (respondents were allowed to mention more than one option) were different: 25 percent mentioned Iraq; 12 percent, the economy or jobs; 9 percent, moral values; 8 percent, terrorism or security; 5 percent, honesty or integrity; 9 percent, opposition to the other candidate; 3 percent each, abortion and health care; 2 percent each, the direction of the country, the candidate's religiosity or morals, the candidate's strength or leadership, foreign policy, and a desire to see no change of course; 1 percent each, Social Security, taxes, the environment, the Supreme Court, gun control, and education; 8 percent, other factors; and 5 percent did not know or chose nothing or everything. Gay marriage and marriage were mentioned only as a second choice and only by 2 percent of respondents; similarly, stem-cell research was mentioned only as a second choice and only by 1 percent of respondents. These results show that moral values was important, but not necessarily the most important factor in how voters chose in 2004.

Silent Voices

While poll results can vary significantly with the wording of the question and the complexity of the issue, many social scientists argue that when aggregated, they provide an appropriate measure of public opinion, a better measure than is available through other forms of public input, such as participation in elections or in interest groups or directly lobbying and contacting elected officials. It is believed that through aggregation, simple biases, differences in question wording, and so on, wash out, and so by examining a host of polls from random samples of the entire public, elected officials are able to figure out what voters want. For example, Verba (1996, p. 3) argued: "Sample surveys provide the closest approximation to an unbiased representation of the public because participation in a survey requires no resources and because surveys eliminate the bias inherent in the fact that participants in politics are self-selected . . . surveys produce just what democracy is supposed to produce—equal representation of all citizens."

However, a constant and growing difficulty in surveys is the fact that even though participation appears virtually costless as compared with other forms of participation, individuals often choose either not to participate at all or not to respond to particular questions, as discussed earlier in this chapter. Moreover, as we noted, the problem of nonresponse is growing. If the nonrespondents have preferences that are different from those who respond, then the results of the survey can be biased. Edison-Mitofsky, in their evaluation of the exit polls in 2004, found that even controlling for all the variables that might have biased the results to suggest a greater proportion of votes for Kerry, there still appeared to be a tendency for Kerry supporters to agree to be in the survey moreso than Bush supporters such that the proportion of poll respondents who supported Kerry was greater than Kerry's percentage of support among voters. This led to a famously biased early prediction, which persisted until the results could be verified against the actual turnout figures. Brehm (1993), for example, found that general interest in politics and the degree to which one possesses political information are causally related to willingness to participate in surveys. Responses also vary in accordance with whether an election campaign is occurring and the stage of the campaign. Surveys by telephone produce a greater nonresponse rate than those conducted face to face. In public opinion surveys for which we do not have the opportunity to validate responses, the omission of nonrespondents may bias the results in ways we are unaware of. Alvarez and Brehm (2002) and Althaus (1998) found that when respondents have low levels of information, their expressed preferences can be significantly distorted.

Even voters who agree to participate in surveys often answer that they do not know or do not have enough information in response to particular questions. What do those sorts of answers really mean? Zaller and Feldman (1992) and Zaller (1992) advanced the idea that when individuals are asked to respond in surveys, they typically do not have ready-made opinions from which to draw judgments and responses. They have "a series of partially independent and often inconsistent" attitudes on issues, and when they respond, they need to organize them into a preference (Zaller 1992, p. 93). This is probably most true for complex political issues about which individuals are rarely forced to think or make choices directly. If this cognitive process is more difficult for respondents who have particular types of preferences, then their preferences are less likely to be expressed and reflected in surveys.

For example, Berinsky (2002) considered the impact that differences in the difficulty of forming opinions on social welfare policy had on survey responses. Previous research reviewed by Berinsky shows that liberals and conservatives in the United States value both capitalism (less government and individualism) and democracy (fairness and equality). Zaller and Feldman (1992) had argued that conservatives can reconcile these two factors in forming an opinion on social welfare policy by coupling opposition to social welfare with support for equality of opportunity (not necessarily outcomes), whereas liberals cannot reconcile them as easily since supporting social welfare policy means supporting big government and less individual control. Berinsky suggested, then, that because of this inherent conflict in values, liberals may be more likely than conservatives to choose "don't know" or "not enough information" on questions about social welfare policy, particularly if they are more limited in their cognitive resources due to lower levels of income and education.

Berinsky evaluated his hypothesis using data from NES surveys. Specifically, he examined the factors that determine whether a respondent to the survey chooses "don't know" or "not enough information" to seven-point questions that gauge public opinion on whether the government should guarantee jobs, provide many more services even if that means an increase in spending, and reduce the income differences between the rich and the poor. He then compared those determinants with the factors that affect how those who choose to answer the questions respond. He found that nonrespondents are most similar to the respondents that choose liberal positions on these questions. For each question in his analysis, 7 equals the most liberal position, and 1 equals the most conservative position. For those who responded, the average on whether the government should provide more services even if it costs more money equals 3.84, but the average of the estimated responses of those who did not respond equals 4.26. Similarly, the average of responses for the question on guaranteed jobs equals 3.5, but the average of the estimated responses of those who did not respond equals 3.9, and the average of responses for the redistribution question equals 3.65, but the average of the estimated responses of those who did not respond equals 4.12. Thus, there is evidence that the answers to survey questions on social welfare policy have a conservative bias because a greater proportion of nonrespondents are liberals.

Elected Officials' Views of Polls

It should not be a surprise, then, that Andrew Card, George W. Bush's chief of staff, says that public opinion polls help only in marketing, not in policy making, and that Jacobs and others (1998, p. 25) found that congressional staff members viewed the nearly endless stream of public opinion polls from the media, party organizations, and lobbyists as unreliable. They believed that polls are compromised by technical limitations. Changing question wordings and biasing sampling can, as one staff member put it, "move a survey from an 80–20 split to a 20–80 split." Moreover, they believed that polls are too crude to tap public sentiment about complex policy issues. For instance, several respondents complained that majority support for universal coverage [in health care] was misleading because of the public's apprehension regarding the means for achieving universal coverage—through higher taxes, for example.

In a survey of 257 state legislators, social service agency directors, and senior advisers to governors involved in public assistance policy making during the early to mid-1990s, Shaw (2000) found that only 21 percent mentioned that they used focus groups or surveys to get public input, whereas a majority mentioned public hearings. Herbst (1998), in interviews with legislative staff members in Illinois, found that they viewed polls as not very useful in policy making. The staff reported that the public is too fickle and uninformed, and polls are too vague to guide them.

While such sentiments may seem odd given the evidence of extensive use of public opinion polls by elected officials and the general congruence of public opinion with policy found in the studies reviewed above, the combination shows how elected officials often seek information from polls in an effort to influence and lead public opinion rather than use them as a guide to follow, particularly for complex issues, much as Hill and Hurley contended. This is not because they don't think that public opinion is consequential with regard to whether they stay in office or because they do not care about public opinion. Jacobs and others (1998) found that 75 percent of congressional staffers with members running for reelection believed that a member's position on health care would need to coincide with constituents' opinion in order for the member to win reelection, and 88 percent believed that their members' positions would so coincide. As Canes-Wrone and Shotts found, presidents facing close reelection contests are more likely to choose policies preferred by voters in polls. Members of Congress, presidents, and other elected officials discount polls because they do not believe they accurately and fully present their constituents' preferences on issues, particularly complex issues, and they believe that these preferences can be changed through their efforts. They are still trying to appeal to voters in order to seek reelection, but they do not believe that the way to do so is by blindly following the preferences that are represented in public opinion polls.

What We Know

We know that psephologists use a variety of methods to predict election outcomes—surveys, betting markets, and estimation models using data from previous elections, the economy, and voters' preferences. Predictions are made months and sometimes years in advance, throughout the campaigns, and even as votes are being counted. Our ability to know voters' preferences in elections has improved significantly through the use of better statistical techniques. However, mistakes happen, and they can lead to inaccurate predictions, which both teach us something about the measurement of preferences and make elections more interesting. Most important, through election prediction, the theories of political scientists face a strong and rare test—an opportunity to learn whether our theories of how voters choose are accurate.

But psephologists are not the only ones who are trying to predict what voters think. Elected officials are as well. However, because estimates of voters' opinions on complex issues can be at best unclear and at worse biased, elected officials see public opinion as measured in surveys more as something to influence than as something to follow. Elected officials appear to make choices more in line with the measures of public opinion when elections are close—anticipating retrospective voting—and when issues are simple. Finally, we know that officials are right—evidence suggests that surveys can be biased in the way they represent voters' preferences.

What We Don't Know:
Other Reasons Why Goodling's Election Was Special

When voters were deciding whether to support Bill Goodling for reelection to Congress (discussed in chapter 9), one of the factors that affected his election was how his district had been drawn. As one that was biased toward Republicans, his toughest competition would be in the primary, not the general election. Why was his district dominated by Republicans? District boundaries in congressional as well as other legislative elections are choices made by elected officials that can fundamentally affect which candidates win those races. Furthermore, knowing that Goodling was only one of 435 members of Congress, voters in his district considered not only his voting record but also his ability to influence policy in general by holding positions of power. Goodling was chairman of the Committee on Education and the Workforce, which gave him influence over congressional bills relating to those issues as well as bargaining power with members of Congress who wished to see legislation passed that was relevant to his committee. Congressional elections have a number of distinctive features, which warrant a chapter in themselves, and we turn to them in chapter 11.

Study Questions and Problems

1. Suppose that Tom wishes to predict the outcome of the governor's race in New Mexico using exit polls. Tom has a limited budget and can visit only a sample of precincts. How should he select the precincts in order to get the best prediction? How should he instruct his employees? Would he do as well if he instead set up an online betting market on the election? Why or why not?

2. What is the difference between the ratio estimators used by Edison-Mitofsky to project states' presidential votes and the linear estimation procedure used by UNIVAC and Ray Fair? What are the advantages and disadvantages of the two approaches? Explain.

3. Is it logically consistent for presidents and members of Congress to claim that they do not follow polls in making their policy decisions even though much evidence shows that these officials read, study, and commission polls? Explain.

4. How would presidential elections be affected if Congress outlawed the use of exit polls? Would that be a good thing or bad thing? How would presidential elections be affected if Congress outlawed betting markets like IEM? Would that be a good or a bad thing? In some countries, preelection polls are not allowed in the weeks before an election. Is that a good or a bad thing? Explain your answers.

NOTES

1. Robert G. Kaiser, "Is This Any Way to Pick a Winner? To Researchers, Election Is All Over but the Voting," *Washington Post*, May 26, 2000.
2. Alicia C. Shepard, "How They Blew It," *American Journalism Review*, January-February 2001, p. 20.
3. Shepard, in "How They Blew It," relates that political scientists Christopher Achen of the University of Michigan and Kenneth Goldstein of the University of Wisconsin, who were working for ABC on election night, expressed discomfort over ABC's decision to call Florida for Gore but did not aggressively stop the network from making the call. Achen told Shepard: "Think how we would have felt if we had really had the courage of our convictions and if ABC hadn't called it. But we didn't. The team was wrong, and I'm part of the team. I don't want to say it wasn't my fault."
4. See Butler (1998). Interestingly, although McCallum named a field known for its statistical emphasis, Butler recalls (p. 453) that he was "a wonderful man but he was almost totally innumerate. . . . In 1951, on Oxford Station, he gave me an astonishingly precise election forecast; I asked him how he had arrived at such exactitude. He replied 'Oh! I thought of some broad figures and then I de-rounded them to give verisimilitude to my guess.'"
5. See, for example, the description of amateur psephologist and Fairfax County, Virginia, Republican supervisor (and congressman) Thomas M. Davis III in John Ward Anderson, "Fairfax's Political Animal: GOP's Davis Builds Base to Unseat Moore," *Washington Post*, May 26, 1991. Richard Withlin, Ronald Reagan's pollster, was labeled "the prince of psephology" by Robert G. Kaiser in "White House Pulse-Taking Pollster," *Washington Post*, February 24, 1982.

6. Ward Morehouse, "Koch: 'How Am I Doing?' " *Christian Science Monitor*, July 26, 1982.

7. In 1800, Thomas Jefferson was evaluating his chances for success in the upcoming presidential election. After consulting with party members in the various states, he concluded that the states were evenly divided, except for Pennsylvania, New Jersey, and New York, and that there was a good chance the result would hinge on what happened in New York. He wrote James Madison (Smith [1952, p. 149]): "In any event we may say that if the *city* election of New York is in favor of the republican ticket, the issue will be republican; if the federal ticket for the city of New York prevails, the probabilities will be in favor of a federal issue." Jefferson's party called itself the Democratic-Republican Party but in the 1820s split into two branches, the Democratic Party (which became the modern Democratic Party) and the Whig Party (which was eventually replaced by the Republican Party). Jefferson's evaluation of his canvass of party members turned out to be correct: the Federalists won in New Jersey, Pennsylvania was tied, and the New York City Democratic-Republican vote resulted in that party's carrying the state and the nation.

8. See Patterson (1993). Lichter (2001) found that 71 percent of network news reports during the 2000 presidential campaign dealt with the horse race. The tendency to discuss predicted vote totals appears to be related to the closeness of the election; in 1996, only 48 percent of stories on the networks focused on the horse race, and in both 1992 and 1988, 58 percent of the stories discussed the horse race.

9. Actually Pearson focused on four parameters, adding in symmetry (a measure of the degree to which the measurements pile up on only one side of the mean) and kurtosis (how far rare measurements scatter from the mean). For a good nontechnical discussion of the work of Pearson and other statisticians, see Salsburg (2001).

10. As discussed in Salsburg (2001), Pearson, Sir Francis Galton, and Raphael Weldon in 1901 created the journal *Biometrika*, which for the next twenty-five years was primarily a repository for samples of populations in biology and measurements of those parameters, with researchers constantly trying to find ever larger samples.

11. *Encyclopædia Britannica Online*, s.v. "Elmo Roper," Encyclopædia Britannica Premium Service, January 15, 2005, http://www.britannica.com/eb/article?tocId=906402.

12. See Salsburg (2001) for a nontechnical discussion of the work of these statisticians.

13. As noted by Hamilton (1984), the *Digest* also failed to take into account the nonresponse factor of those polled. One fourth of Landon supporters returned their cards, but only one sixth of Roosevelt supporters did. Furthermore, the *Digest* used their old list, from 1932, and since lower-income voters were more likely to have moved during the Depression, the mail-in ballots were less likely to reach them.

14. See display ad, *Wall Street Journal*, October 6, 1948, p. 7.

15. George Gallup, "Final Gallup Poll Sees Dewey Safe," *Los Angeles Times*, November 1, 1948. Polling by Gallup and Crossley did continue for a month or so after Roper stopped, and the results suggested that the Dewey lead was disappearing. Crossley published his final poll on October 29 (although the polling was conducted in mid-October), showing that Dewey would win with 49.9 percent of the vote to Truman's 44.8 percent (minor-party candidates Henry Wallace and Strom Thurmond made up the rest of the predicted vote). Gallup's column dated October 31 showed that Dewey would receive 49.5 percent and Truman 44.5 Gallup contended that the bulk of his interviewing had taken

place ten to twelve days before the election. See "Dr. Gallup Explains Why Poll Fell Down," *Los Angeles Times*, November 24, 1948. However, in his column dated October 31, 1948, he remarked that the results included surveys taken up to the Friday before the election.

16. Yet for many years, political scientists continued to argue that campaigns had little effect on voters, as discussed in chapter 7. For example, see Campbell et al. (1960). The assumption underlies many forecasting models that predict elections in advance, as we see later in this section.

17. See "Dr. Gallup Explains Why Poll Fell Down."

18. See Berinsky (2004).

19. Salsburg (2001) presents a nontechnical history of the research of Neyman and Mahalanobis and that at the Census Bureau. This work and the work of statisticians at the U.S. Department of Agriculture was also important for an early-election long-term forecaster, Louis Bean, who we discuss below. See also Berinsky (2004) for a review of the sampling controversies of the time.

20. See Berinsky (2004).

21. See Berinsky (2004).

22. See Gallup (1951). For evidence that pollsters continue to make this argument, see New River Media's interviews with Alec Gallup and George Gallup, Jr., for the PBS program *The First Measured Century* at http://www.pbs.org/fmc/inter views/agallup.htm and http://www.pbs.org/fmc/interviews/ggallup.htm.

23. The method was first proposed by Warren Mitofsky, a statistician then working for CBS. His collaborator, Joseph Waksberg, documented the statistical properties. We discuss Mitofsky's and Waksberg's contributions to election-night predictions later in this chapter; see Waksberg (1978). Further advances occurred in the early 1990s, when statisticians discovered how to use directory lists to truncate some of the steps of the Mitofsky-Waksberg methods and computer technology allowed researchers to build the huge databases of U.S. households necessary for random draws. For a review of this history, see Tourangeau (2004).

24. Berrens et al. (2003) reported that of the households who agree to join the panel, 72 percent allow the Web TVs to be installed, 83 percent of those households complete the profiles needed to be included in the panel, and on average 75 percent of those surveyed respond. According to Berrens et al., KN plans to keep participants in the panel for no more than three years, to avoid the potential that as a respondent is repeatedly surveyed, his or her responses may be affected such that they are no longer representative.

25. Knowledge Networks, "Hoover/Knowledge Networks Polls Achieve High Degree of Accuracy in Predicting California Recall Results," press release, December 17, 2003.

26. See Rhode and Strumpf (2004). These betting commissioners were astute observers of politics. On October 7, 1936, *Washington Post* sports editor Shirley Povich quoted Broadway betting commissioner Jack Doyle's view of opportunity sample polls like the *Literary Digest*'s:

> I'll never forget a straw vote they took in New York before the 1916 election. Some newspaper thought it would be a novel idea to interrogate all the passengers on all trains arriving at Grand Central and Penn stations. Of course, it was no true barometer. They forgot that usually it is only persons of means who travel. But anyway, each day's count was kept. The poll showed, usually, 80 per cent for [Charles Evans] Hughes, 20 per cent for [Woodrow] Wilson. . . . I watched them take the poll one day, then sauntered out to the railroad yard where I met an old gate-tender. He had been reading about the poll and

was not surprised at the figures. "Yeah," he said skeptically. "But remember, the gravel train don't come in here."

The old gate tender was right—Wilson defeated Hughes.

27. See Rhode and Strumpf (2004); "St. Louis Sets Odds of 15 to 1 for Dewey," *New York Times*, October 3, 1948; and "Butte Offers Bettors All Kinds of Election Action," *Los Angeles Times*, October 25, 1948.

28. In 1960, Nevada bookkeepers were apparently forced to stop wagers on the presidential race when prosecutors pointed out a little-known state law against election bets. At the time, odds were 8 to 5 for John F. Kennedy and 6 to 5 for Richard Nixon; see "Election Bets Barred by Old Law in Nevada," *New York Times*, November 4, 1960. Yet betting did continue underground, and in 1964 *The New York Times* reported that a Las Vegas source had given Lyndon Johnson an 8-to-1 chance of reelection; see "Gamblers Vary Election Betting: Certain of Johnson Victory, They Seek Point Spreads," *New York Times*, October 18, 1964. For a report of wagers in Las Vegas in the 1980 contest, see Andrew Beyer, "Political Science of Wagering," *Washington Post*, September 19, 1980.

29. See http://www.biz.uiowa.edu/iem.

30. IEM also runs more complicated election markets on the composition of the House and Senate, and so on.

31. See Berg and Rietz (2005).

32. See Oliven and Rietz (2004).

33. "Election Bets," *Chicago Daily Tribune*, October 22, 1944.

34. See "St. Louis Sets Odds of 15 to 1 for Dewey," *New York Times*, October 3, 1948, and "Butte Offers Bettors All Kinds of Election Action," *Los Angeles Times*, October 25, 1948.

35. See George Gallup, "Marked Parallels in '16 and '48," *Washington Post*, November 14, 1948.

36. See Dan Balz and Mike Allen, "Four More Years Attributed to Rove's Strategy: Despite Moments of Doubt, Adviser's Planning Paid Off," *Washington Post*, November 7, 2004.

37. "How Did Exit Polls Start Avalanche of Inaccuracy?" *Seattle Times*, November 4, 2004.

38. Mark Memmott and Martha T. Moore, "Networks Stay Cautious but Hint at Outcome," *USA Today*, November 3, 2004.

39. Memmott and Moore, "Networks Stay Cautious but Hint at Outcome."

40. Richard Morin, "Surveying the Damage: Exit Polls Can't Predict Winners, So Don't Expect Them To," *Washington Post*, November 21, 2004.

41. In 1908, the *Chicago Daily Tribune* described the procedures used by the AP to gather returns from across the nation and the pressure to report the results on the night of the election:

"Where and how is THE TRIBUNE to get these figures? From its own news service, its hundreds of correspondents, and its thousands of miles of wires from the 20,000 miles of wires leased by the Associated Press, from the 300 operators of these wires, and the 900 or more Associated Press correspondents. . . . At almost every county seat in every state is the Associated Press representative. . . . This year for the first time the Associated Press will cover the two doubtful states, Indiana and Ohio, precinct by precinct. . . . The hardest town in which to arrange for representation has been Valparaiso, Ind. . . . Night bulletin service begins at 4 o'clock in the afternoon. This pressure for early, accurate bulletins weighs heaviest on Associated Press workers, and most important of all these in the eyes of directing heads in the organization is the 6 o'clock bulletin. . . . Other results may come when they can be had; this 6 o'clock bulletin, complete or incomplete, must be filed.

Hollis W. Field, "How the World's Greatest Newspaper Will Receive Returns from the Presidential Election," *Chicago Daily Tribune*, November 1, 1908. Things did not always go smoothly for the Associated Press. In 1884, returns were delayed in New York State, causing the president of Western Union Telegraph to angrily dismiss charges of bias and purposeful delay by his company; see Norvin Green, "The Delayed Returns," *Los Angeles Times*, November 26, 1884.

42. "Crowds at the Bulletins," *New York Times*, November 4, 1896.
43. "Beams in the Sky Will Tell Tale," *Chicago Daily Tribune*, November 7, 1916.
44. See Bohn (1968).
45. See Bohn (1968, p. 271).
46. See Mifosky and Edelman (2002) for a discussion of CBS's estimation program. George Gray, "UNIVAC I: The First Mass-Produced Computer," *Unisys History Newsletter*, January 2001 http://www.ec.gatech.edu/gvu/people/randy.carpenter/folklore/v5n1.html, reports that CBS selected key precincts for the estimate rather than all precincts reporting at a point in time. However, based on accounts of the process it does not appear that the sample was scientifically chosen until pollster Louis Harris was brought into the process in 1964. Moreover, evidence suggests that CBS combined precincts across states in the early elections because unusually high vote totals in states that reported early caused errors in projections of the overall outcome, but if state-by-state regressions had been calculated, those errors would not have happened. For example, in 1954, UNIVAC overestimated the size of Democratic majorities in the Senate and House races because of an exceptionally high Democratic vote in Delaware, and in 1960 the early returns in Kansas increased the size of the Republican vote and led to an early call for Nixon by CBS.
47. See Gray, "UNIVAC I: The First Mass-Produced Computer," and James J. Nagle, "UNIVAC Will Know Poll Result First," *New York Times*, October 31, 1954.
48. Mary Hornaday, "UNIVAC—Conversation Piece," *Christian Science Monitor*, November 15, 1952.
49. See Bohn (1968, p. 271).
50. See Brillinger (2002).
51. See Morganstein, Marker, and Waksberg (2000).
52. In Georgia, the Republican candidate did not have a majority, and the election was decided by the state legislature in favor of the Democrat. See Mitofsky and Edelman (2002) for a discussion of Harris's methods.
53. See Mitofsky and Edelman (2002). Both Harris and Mitofsky and Edelman used measures to control for possible errors in tabulation. According to Mitofsky and Edelman, Harris's method of discarding unusual precinct results led to miscalls in 1966. Mitofsky and Edelman placed lower weights on unusually large results rather than discard them.
54. See Morganstein, Marker, and Waksberg (2000, p. 305).
55. For cases in which the parties' votes in past elections were not correlated with the sample, the estimators substituted the total vote in the past election. For example, if it appears that Kerry's and Gore's votes are not correlated and the past total vote in the sampled precincts in Ohio was 400,000, then the ratio Hector would estimate = 200,000/400,000 = 0.5, which means that Kerry is receiving across the sample precincts approximately one half the official total vote in the sampled precincts in 2000. This ratio is then multiplied by the official total vote in Ohio in 2000 to get the estimated vote for Kerry in the state. See Mitofsky

and Edelman (2002). The ratio estimates were also poststratified according to geography and demographic characteristics, as required by the sampling process.

56. Until recent advances in computer capabilities, empirical Bayes was often analytically difficult. With the new computing power, a growing number of political scientists are taking a Bayesian approach to answering empirical questions. Moreover, the procedures currently in use allow political scientists to better specify the certainty surrounding their predictions. But there is also considerable dispute within the statistical community over the value of Bayesian approaches, and by far the most popular current modal approach to empirical study in political science in non-Bayesian.

57. See Edison Media Research and Mitofsky International (2005).

58. See Brillinger (2002).

59. These data are actually from the estimates produced by VNS's successor, Edison-Mitofsky, and are their estimates based only on the exit-poll data; other estimates included previous poll results.

60. See Mitofsky and Edelman (2002), Mason, Frankovic, and Jamieson (2001), and Shephard, "How They Blew It," for the time line of events.

61. Shepard, "How They Blew It."

62. Shepard, "How They Blew It."

63. See Fair (1996).

64. See Fair (1978).

65. Fair also had controls for a few years for which some economic statistics were not available.

66. Jonathan Weisman, "Is It the Economy? Predictive Models Are Breaking Down in Face of Mixed Messages, Foreign Affairs," *Washington Post*, October 29, 2004.

67. Fair's vote equation and other details of his work can be accessed at "Presidential Vote Equation," Ray C. Fair Web site at Yale University, http://fairmodel. econ.vale.edu/vote2004/index2.htm.

68. For a review of Bean's role in election forecasting, see Rosenof (1999).

69. See Lewis-Beck and Rice (1992), Abramowitz (1988), and Campbell and Wink (1990).

70. Fair similarly criticized forecasting models that use stock-market variables because, he argued, they are determined coincidently with voters' intentions and thus are not casual factors. Fair's vote equation and other details of his work can be accessed at "Presidential Vote Equation."

71. Ira Carnahan, "Picking a Winner, after the Fact: Those Academic Election Forecasters Aren't Nearly as Good as You've Heard," *Weekly Standard*, June 12, 2000.

72. Ballenger also blamed the separation on the fact that lobbyists were no longer allowed to give members of Congress and their spouses meals and theater tickets, which had provided "a social life for [congressional] wives." See "Ballenger Blames Muslims, Lobbyist Limits for Marriage Split," Associated Press State & Local Wire, October 4, 2003.

73. Amy Keller, "Ballenger Attorney Cites 'Moral Values' Exit Poll," *Roll Call*, December 13, 2004.

74. Eisinger and Brown (1998) also reported that Hurja used his polling to help Roosevelt allocate patronage positions within his administration. Hurja's polling methods were a combination of opportunity and quota sampling and thus often contained large errors. He later left the Democratic Party and became a Republican partisan and editor of *Pathfinder* magazine. He predicted wins by Wendell Willkie in 1940, Thomas Dewey in 1944 and 1948, and Dwight Eisenhower in 1952.

75. Manza and Cook (2002) pointed out that these studies may overstate the responsiveness of policy to public opinion because the issues that are the subject of polls are the ones on which the elites are making policy and the issues not measured by the polls are ignored by the elites.
76. Bill MacAlister, "Bush Polls Apart from Clinton in Use of Marketing," *Denver Post*, June 17, 2001.
77. Quoted in Hamilton (1984).
78. However, there still might be biases on issues that appear simple but imply conflicts in internal values due to nonresponse, as we discuss below. It is probably always the case that responses to the question "Whom will you vote for?" is always more accurate for voters than the responses to issues questions simply because choosing a candidate is something an individual who votes knows he or she must eventually do.
79. See Dick Meyer, "How Did One Exit Poll Answer Become the Story of How Bush Won? Good Question," *Washington Post*, December 5, 2004.
80. Paul Nowell, "Ballenger Won't Seek Re-election in North Carolina's 10th District," Associated Press State & Local Wire, December 2, 2003.
81. "Ballenger to Face GOP Rival Attacking for Lost Textile Jobs," Associated Press State & Local Wire, October 26, 2003.
82. Nowell, "Ballenger Won't Seek Re-election in North Carolina's 10th District."
83. Gary Langer, "A Question of Values," *New York Times*, November 6, 2004.
84. Frank Newport, "Bush Voters Support Active Government Role in Values Arena," *Gallup Poll News Service*, November 29, 2004.

Part IV

Federal Elections

11

Congressional Elections

Trying to Make a Difference

Larry Weatherford's son was born with cystic fibrosis and a few hours after his birth required surgery at a different hospital, but his HMO (health maintenance organization) would not pay for the ambulance ride. Furthermore, the HMO refused to pay for the medical equipment the child's doctor said was needed for the child to be healthy enough to stay home instead of in the hospital. Weatherford believed that his problems with the HMO were not unique and that the answer was the passage of a patient's bill of rights in the U.S. Congress. In 1974, when Congress brought oversight of pension and employee benefits under federal law, health insurance companies were protected from lawsuits brought by patients for care-denial decisions.[1] Weatherford not only called for his Oklahoma congressman to work for passage of the bill, but he also decided to run for Congress himself in 2000, to challenge the incumbent in his district.[2] We have already seen that challenging incumbents is difficult, given their advantages in terms of campaign contributions and voters who use retrospective voting strategies. Could Weatherford win? Was it rational for him to enter and compete against an incumbent?

Like Weatherford, Minnesota retail salesclerk Betty McCollum entered politics because of something that happened to a child. Her daughter fractured her skull tumbling off an old-fashioned playground slide in the mid-1980s. McCollum recalled, "I walked her over to City Hall and told the city manager that she was fine and we had insurance to cover our costs, but we've got to fix this stuff now."[3] She then ran for city council, the state legislature, and like Weatherford, in 2000 she ran for Congress (negotiating a thirteen-hour sale in men's shirts and textiles during the primary campaign). She did not have to face an incumbent, only other new candidates like her. Did her political experience help her win the election?

Two years earlier, California dairy farmer Devin Nunes had decided to challenge the congressional incumbent in his district. Like Weatherford's, Nunes's top issue in the campaign was one close to his own experiences—better water management for farming in the Central Valley. Nunes wanted a dam and reservoir at Temperance Flat, California, above Millerton Lake. He believed that the dam would be "vital to continue urban growth, maintain agriculture at current levels and help environmental restoration."[4] But Nunes faced a problem running for office—whereas Weatherford was thirty-three when he filed his candidacy to run for Congress and McCollum was forty-six, Nunes was just twenty-four. The U.S. Constitution requires that members of the House of Representatives be twenty-five years old (and citizens of the United States for seven years). Although Nunes would have turned twenty-five on October 1, before the general election, the county elections officials had told him that his name could not be on the ballot because he was not yet twenty-five. Nunes successfully challenged the elections board and got his name on the June 2 primary-election ballot.[5] Did Nunes, who like Weatherford faced an incumbent, become the youngest member of Congress?

In this chapter, we analyze congressional races such as the ones Weatherford, McCollum, and Nunes entered. We discover that sometimes it is rational to challenge incumbents even given their advantages. We find that political experience can be valuable, but it isn't always. And we discover that youth can be less important than how congressional district boundaries are drawn. While much of the analysis of the U.S. election process we have discussed in chapters 1–10 applies to congressional elections, these elections have a number of distinctive features we will explore as we examine the factors that determined who won the seats Weatherford, McCollum, and Nunes sought. We will begin with a consideration of what determines the number of members of Congress a state has and how the boundaries of congressional districts are drawn.

Apportionment and Membership of the House of Representatives

There are 435 members of the House of Representatives, who are apportioned across the states roughly by population after each national census (which is taken every ten years) and elected every two years from single-member districts. These are the jobs that Weatherford, McCollum, and Nunes desired. Table 11.1 presents the population of each state as estimated in the 2000 census and the apportionment of congressional members across the states; figure 11.1 shows the apportionment of Congress in a map of the United States. Note that the requirement that each state have at least one representative does lead to malapportionment across states. For example, both Montana (population 905,316) and Wyoming (population 495,304) have one representative apiece. After reapportionment takes place, new congressional districts are drawn by state legislatures to reflect population changes within states and the effects of reapportionment.

TABLE 11.1
Apportionment Population and Number of Congress Members by State, as of 2000

State	Apportionment Population	Number of Apportioned Representatives Based on 2000 Census	Changes from 1990 Census Apportionment	Total (%)
Alabama	4,461,130	7	0	1.61
Alaska	628,933	1	0	0.23
Arizona	5,140,683	8	+2	1.84
Arkansas	2,679,733	4	0	0.92
California	33,930,798	53	+1	12.18
Colorado	4,311,882	7	+1	1.61
Connecticut	3,409,535	5	−1	1.15
Delaware	785,068	1	0	0.23
Florida	16,028,890	25	+2	5.75
Georgia	8,206,975	13	+2	2.99
Hawaii	1,216,642	2	0	0.46
Idaho	1,297,274	2	0	0.46
Illinois	12,439,042	19	−1	4.37
Indiana	6,090,782	9	−1	2.07
Iowa	2,931,923	5	0	1.15
Kansas	2,693,824	4	0	0.92
Kentucky	4,049,431	6	0	1.38
Louisiana	4,480,271	7	0	1.61
Maine	1,277,731	2	0	0.46
Maryland	5,307,886	8	0	1.84
Massachusetts	6,355,568	10	0	2.30
Michigan	9,955,829	15	−1	3.45
Minnesota	4,925,670	8	0	1.84
Mississippi	2,852,927	4	−1	0.92
Missouri	5,606,260	9	0	2.07

TABLE 11.1 *(cont)*
Apportionment Population and Number of Congress Members by State, as of 2000

State	Apportionment Population	Number of Apportioned Representatives Based on 2000 Census	Changes from 1990 Census Apportionment	Total (%)
Montana	905,316	1	0	0.23
Nebraska	1,715,369	3	0	0.69
Nevada	2,002,032	3	+1	0.69
New Hampshire	1,238,415	2	0	0.46
New Jersey	8,424,354	13	0	2.99
New Mexico	1,823,821	3	0	0.69
New York	19,004,973	29	−2	6.67
North Carolina	8,067,673	13	+1	2.99
North Dakota	643,756	1	0	0.23
Ohio	11,374,540	18	−1	4.14
Oklahoma	3,458,819	5	−1	1.15
Oregon	3,428,543	5	0	1.15
Pennsylvania	12,300,670	19	−2	4.37
Rhode Island	1,049,662	2	0	0.46
South Carolina	4,025,061	6	0	1.38
South Dakota	756,874	1	0	0.23
Tennessee	5,700,037	9	0	2.07
Texas	20,903,994	32	+2	7.36
Utah	2,236,714	3	0	0.69
Vermont	609,890	1	0	0.23
Virginia	7,100,702	11	0	2.53
Washington	5,908,684	9	0	2.07
West Virginia	1,813,077	3	0	0.69
Wisconsin	5,371,210	8	−1	1.84
Wyoming	495,304	1	0	0.23
Total	281,424,177	435		

Source: U.S. Census Bureau.
Note: The apportionment population includes the resident population of the fifty states, as ascertained by the Twenty-second Decennial Census under Title 13, U.S. code, and counts of overseas U.S. military and federal civilian employees (and their dependents living with them) allocated to their home state, as reported by the employing federal agencies. The apportionment population excludes the population of the District of Columbia.

FIGURE 11.1
Congressional Apportionment after the 2000 Census

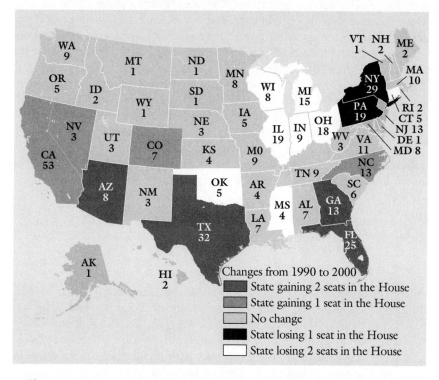

Changes from 1990 to 2000
- State gaining 2 seats in the House
- State gaining 1 seat in the House
- No change
- State losing 1 seat in the House
- State losing 2 seats in the House

Changes in congressional apportionment can affect who runs for Congress and who wins. For example, California dairy farmer Devin Nunes did win election to Congress, but not when he ran at age twenty-four in 1998. In the 1998 election, he lost the Republican nomination by 1,089 votes in a heavily Democratic district in a race against a popular incumbent, Cal Dooley. But after the 2000 census, California gained a seat in Congress, and a new, heavily Republican district was drawn up encompassing Nunes's home. Nunes won his party's nomination in 2002 in California's new congressional district and became the youngest freshman member of Congress in 2003, benefiting from the population growth in his state.

The Constitution does not require that members of Congress be elected in single-member districts, and initially some states used multimember districts and at-large elections to select members of Congress (albeit using plurality-rule or winner-take-all elections). A multimember district is one in which more than one member is elected from a single district. In such elections, voters can vote for as many candidates as can be elected. For example, in a double-member district, voters can vote for as many as two candidates, and the two top winners are elected.[6] At-large elections are those in which an entire state is treated as a district.

In 1842, Congress passed a law requiring the use of single-member districts, although from 1872 to 1929 states were allowed to use at-large elections under certain conditions. In fact, prior to 1968, when at-large elections were again declared illegal, states sometimes used at-large elections to elect new members of Congress if the state had gained a member and not come up with a redistricting plan by the first congressional election after the census. Prior to 1968, states that lost a seat through reapportionment and had not come up with a redistricting plan by the time of the first election after the census had to elect all members in at-large elections, making the entire state a multimember district.[7] Obviously, if members are selected in at-large elections, then the voter who is decisive in determining which candidate wins is the median voter in the state. If all members of Congress are selected in at-large elections, then the median voter in the state will be the decisive voter for determining all the members of Congress from the state.

Redistricting

The Killer D's

Nurses in the neonatal intensive care unit at the University of Texas Medical Branch at Galveston were surprised to be questioned by a Texas Ranger (a state police officer) late on the night of May 12, 2003, about the whereabouts of Craig Eiland, the father of premature twins in their care. Eiland was a respected member of the community, a member of the state legislature, yet the state police were trying to find him. Similarly, Denise Pickett was startled when her seventeen-year-old daughter called her on her cell phone to report that Rangers were at their home that night, questioning the teenager about the whereabouts of her father, El Paso Democratic state legislator Joe Pickett. "I have a lot of respect for police officers so I was just trying to answer their questions as well as possible," Denise Pickett said about her interactions with the Rangers when she returned home. "However, reflecting back I do wish I would have asked them, 'What are you doing in my house without my being there?' "[8]

The Rangers had been called out by the speaker of the state house of representatives, Republican Tom Craddick, to find Eiland and Pickett and forty-nine other Democratic state legislators who had disappeared from the legislature. With that many missing legislators, the house could not act on bills because it lacked a quorum (100 of the Texas state legislature's 150 members). And because the rules of the Texas House of Representatives call for the arrest of members who act deliberately to block quorums, Craddick had called out the Rangers. The majority leader of the U.S. House of Representatives, Texas Republican Tom DeLay, infuriated by the Democratic disappearance, had suggested that federal authorities—the FBI or federal marshals—be brought in to pursue the Democrats, although federal authorities stated that they would not intervene as no federal law had been broken. Learning that one missing legislator, former Texas house speaker Pete Laney, owned a Piper Cheyenne airplane, the Texas Department of Public Safety even contacted a branch of the U.S. Department of Homeland Security to request that it search for the plane, telling officials that it was missing or lost or had possibly crashed and setting off a national controversy over the use of federal funds allocated to fight terrorism in a statewide partisan battle.[9]

Where were the Democrats? The Texas Democrats, labeled the Killer D's (or, according to the Republicans, the Chicken D's), had gone to a Holiday Inn in the southern Oklahoma town of Ardmore (hometown of the Ardmoredillo Chili Cookoff). They believed that they had no choice, as Texas Republicans, with a majority in the state house and senate and control of the governorship, planned to pass a bill redrawing congressional district boundaries in the state. The Democrats returned to the state capitol in Austin on May 16, 2003, after the deadline for action on the redistricting bill had expired, successfully preventing the bill from passing at that time. The flight of the Killer D's made Texas politics not only national, but also international, news.[10]

Checks and Balances, or Why DeLay Cared about the Killer D's

In our analysis so far, we have generally assumed that elected officials operating in isolation make policy choices. But a significant institutional feature of American politics is that elected officials have shared but limited powers to make policy. Policy-making officials are spread across the three branches of government (executive, legislative, and judicial) and across multiple geographic jurisdictions (local, state, and federal). Although each branch has some independent authority, most policy decisions that matter involve more than one branch and more than one geographic jurisdiction. Most state governments have similar structures. The difficulties of the process can frustrate both elected officials intent on carrying out policy promises and the voters who elected them. Texas legislators, both Republican and Democratic, fought over the congressional redistricting bill because they understood that the legislation had implications far beyond their state. How the congressional district boundaries were drawn in Texas would affect which party won the seats and could affect the control of Congress and the ability of President Bush to pursue his agenda. In California, one reason Nunes won election was that the new district was heavily Republican: he could overwhelm his Democratic opponent.

The History of Redistricting

The Old System and Representation Until the 1960s, redistricting in response to new censuses did not always take place, nor was an effort always
made to equalize the size of the districts within a state. For example, in the
1940s congressional districts in Illinois ranged in size from 112,000 voters
to 914,000, and in the 1960s in Georgia they ranged from 272,154 to
823,860 (Stewart 2001, p. 202). Similarly, state legislatures were seriously
malapportioned. Most of these inequities in district size benefited rural voters, since the smaller-size districts tended to be in rural areas, reflecting population growth over time. Thus rural voters were generally overrepresented
in Congress and in state legislatures. Although the more urban a district,
the more likely it would be larger in population, the effect was not linear.
That is, the districts packed with the most voters, and thus most likely to be
underrepresented, were suburban. As Ansolabehere, Gerber, and Snyder
(2002, p. 769) reported:

> In New York state, Nassau, Suffolk, and Westchester counties were more under-
> represented than New York City. In Illinois, Lake and Du Page counties had less
> representation than Cook County (Chicago). In Maryland, the City of Baltimore
> had three times as many legislative seats per person as neighboring Baltimore
> County. Some rural counties were also badly underrepresented in some states.
> Tennessee, for example, gave fewer legislative seats per capita to rural counties in
> the eastern half of the state.

In terms of partisanship, Republican voters were more likely to be in the
suburban districts, so the malapportionment of population across districts is
generally believed to have benefited the Democratic Party.[11]

There is evidence that the malapportionment in state legislatures affected
the distribution of public expenditures, suggesting that there may have been
similar inequities between rural and suburban areas because of the malapportionment of congressional seats. Following the approach of David and
Eisenberg (1961), Ansolabehere, Gerber, and Snyder (2002) constructed a
relative representation index in state legislatures for each county in the
United States. This index measures the number of state legislative seats per
person in a county relative to the number of seats per person in the state. If
the county has an index of 1, then the county is represented according to a
one-person, one-vote rule. Indexes higher than 1 indicate a county that is
overrepresented in the state legislature, and indexes lower than 1 indicate a
county that is underrepresented. The researchers then statistically examined
whether differences in the index led to differences in state spending transfers
to counties. They found that in 1960 there was a strong positive relationship
between the index and state transfers to counties—overrepresented counties
received larger state transfers and underrepresented counties received
smaller transfers. They also compared how increases in the index over time

affected public expenditures and found a significant positive relationship between the change in intergovernment transfers to counties between 1960 and 1980 and the change in the index of representation—as a county's representation within the legislature increased, the county's transfers from the state increased, and as representation decreased, transfers decreased. This evidence suggests that unequally sized districts meant not only unequal representation but also unequal distribution of public resources.

The Redistricting Revolution   In 1962, the United States Supreme Court ruled in *Baker v. Carr* that the malapportioned Tennessee legislature violated the equal protection clause of the Fourteenth Amendment to the Constitution. Two years later, in *Wesberry v. Sanders*, the Court ruled that congressional districts must be drawn to a one-person, one-vote standard. As Cox and Katz (2002) pointed out, the 1964 ruling placed the judiciary in a new, important role in congressional redistricting. Before *Wesberry v. Sanders*, if a state could not come up with a new districting plan after a census, it could just continue to use the old district boundaries even though they were unequal. If the state had gained a district, it could elect the new member at large even though doing so violated the 1842 law; if a state lost a member and did not redistrict, all members of Congress from the state would be elected at large. If a state lost a district, redistricting would eventually be absolutely necessary, and if the state legislature and the governor could not come up with a new districting plan, the courts might get involved. But after the *Wesberry* decision, states that did not redistrict after a census faced court involvement in choosing the new district boundaries (regardless of whether a district was lost). While a principal concern of the judiciary in redistricting cases is making sure the one-person, one-vote rule is followed, since the passage of the Voting Rights Act in 1965, the courts have also considered the racial and ethnic fairness of district boundaries. Most recent court involvement in redistricting has focused on the issue of minority representation, and we discuss the factors involved in chapter 15.

Ostensibly, there are certain desirable goals for drawing district boundaries: (1) that districts not be strung out over a great distance, making it difficult for voters and representatives to interact ("compact"), (2) that geographic areas be connected to one another ("contiguous"), and (3) that existing political boundaries be preserved. These properties, however, are often secondary in designing congressional district boundaries, as states try to respond to the interests of minorities, partisan issues, and in particular, incumbents or certain potential challengers. Doing so is called gerrymandering, after the actions of Governor Elbridge Gerry of Massachusetts, who drew a state senate district in 1811 that joined two Federalist areas to create a Jeffersonian district in the middle. Figures 11.2 and 11.3 show the districts approved for the state of Georgia and for the Atlanta area for the 2002 election. Notice that these districts, drawn primarily by Democrats in order to increase their number of congressional seats, often split county lines, creat-

FIGURE 11.2
Georgia's Congressional Districts, Effective for the 2002 Election

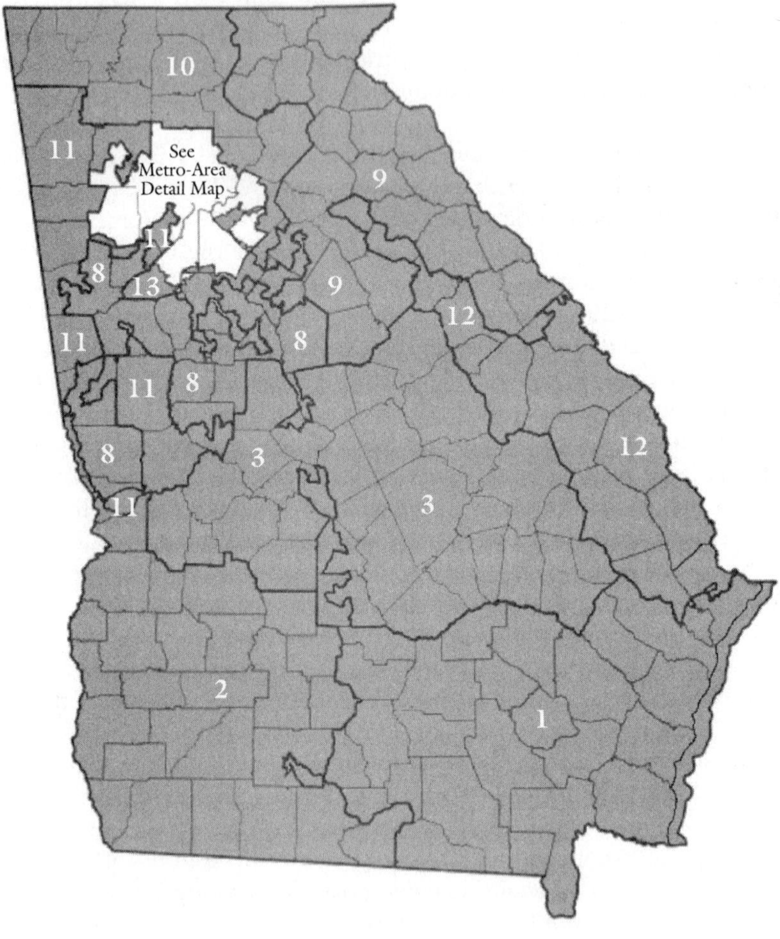

Source: Carl Vinson Institute of Government, University of Georgia (August 2002).
Note: See figure 11.3 for the metro-area detail map.

ing shapes that hardly seem to maximize compactness and contiguity. In particular, district 13, designed to be a new Democratic district, was noted to be one "that would be familiar only to Pascual Perez, . . . the Atlanta Braves pitcher who missed a scheduled start against the Montreal Expos on June 30, 1982" because he got lost on the interstate loop around the city, circling Atlanta twice while searching for the stadium and thus being known as Perimeter Perez.[12]

FIGURE 11.3
Metro-Area Detail, of Georgia's Congressional Districts, Effective for the 2002 Election

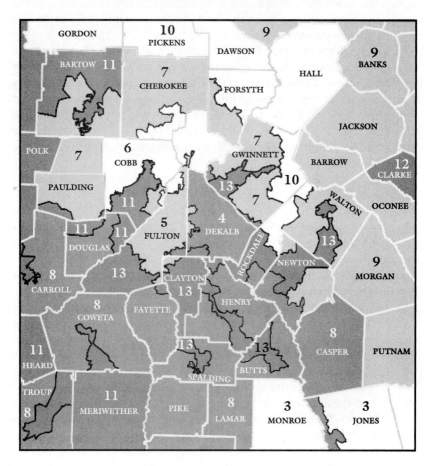

Source: Carl Vinson Institute of Government, University of Georgia (August 2002).

Gerrymandering

Partisan Bias versus Responsiveness

Drawing Responsive Districts Without a doubt, drawing congressional districts, since it determines the voters in congressional elections, is a hotly debated issue, particularly if a state gains or loses a congressional district. States sometimes sue the federal government, claiming that the apportionment of districts is unfair (that the census undercounted its population). But the main battles over congressional district lines are within states and focus on partisan control and protecting the ability of incumbents to get reelected. While Nunes won election to Congress in 2002 from a heavily Republican district, the Democratic-dominated state legislature (and Democratic governor) in California had not given the Republicans the additional seat granted through apportionment. Democratic leaders drew new boundaries designed to reelect the thirty-two incumbent Democrats and added a Democratic seat in Los Angeles County. According to the *Daily News of Los Angeles*, "Republicans were offered a chance to keep their delegation total at 20. All they had to do was jettison Rep. Stephen Horn, R-Lakewood, a moderate veteran of competitive races in a Democrat-dominated district, in return for a safe GOP seat in the Central Valley."[13] Nunes got a seat, and Horn retired rather than run in a now-Democratic-dominated district against Democrat incumbent Grace Napolitano.

In the Democratic-designed districts in California, even though Republican candidates for Congress received 46.37 percent of the two-party vote in 2002, only 37.74 percent of the fifty-three representatives elected were Republicans. If the members elected had been proportionally allocated to the parties in California according to vote share, there would have been at least four more Republicans in Congress. Having the ability to control districting appears to give Democrats in California greater representation in Congress than they have support among voters.

However, dismissing this difference as pure bias on the part of Democrats engaged in aggressive gerrymandering would be premature. Democrats could theoretically design districts that would give them all the seats in California. That is, suppose the Democrats took their 3,731,081 voters in 2002 and distributed them across the fifty-three congressional districts, so that there would be approximately 70,398 Democratic voters in each district (with about thirteen districts having one fewer voter) and also distributed the 3,225,666 Republican voters evenly across the districts, so that there would be approximately 60,862 Republican voters in each district (with about twenty-one having one fewer). Essentially, if each district were a microcosm of the state's partisan balance in Congress, the Democrats could win all the seats.[14] Such a districting plan would be highly "responsive" in that if there was a change in the preferences of about 10,000 voters in each district, then all the seats would immediately switch from Democratic control to Republican control. Technically, a districting plan is responsive if a party receives more seats when its power increases. Of course, Democrats did not design such districts, even though they had control over the districting process. It is not hard to imagine why, given the physical constraint of drawing districts that are contiguous and the desire to maintain some compactness.

Moreover, designing districts that are highly responsive is risky for the majority party, as the district lines will be in place for a period of time, during which the partisan preferences of voters can change. Consider the situation in Michigan, which has fifteen congressional districts. In 2002, Republican congressional candidates received 1,474,178 votes, and Democratic congressional candidates received 1,507,174 votes, with Republicans winning 49.45 percent of the two-party vote and Democrats winning 50.55 percent. If it were possible to distribute these voters evenly across all fifteen districts, there would be a difference of about 2,000 votes in each district. With such a small margin, a swing in voters' preferences could easily switch a district from Democratic to Republican. All the districts would be highly competitive, and parties would be uncertain at election time which candidate would win. Responsiveness can be dangerous.[15]

Drawing Biased Districts In Michigan, even though the vote count is so close and Democratic candidates receive a slight majority of congressional votes, Republicans represent nine of the fifteen districts, or 60 percent in 2002. So 49.45 percent of the voters in Michigan are represented by 60 percent of the state's members of Congress. When the two-party vote share is approximately 50/50, as it was in Michigan in 2002, and one party has a significantly greater number of seats, as the Republicans did, there is said to be a positive partisan bias benefiting that party.[16] Republicans had controlled redistricting in Michigan in 2000, with a Republican governor and Republican majorities in the state house and senate. Democrats had elected a majority of the state's congressional delegation for three decades, and in 2000 there were nine Democrats to seven Republicans (a 56.25 percent Democratic majority in the House from Michigan). But Michigan lost a seat through reapportionment, and Republican control of redistricting reduced Democratic seats by three. In three districts, six Democratic incumbents faced each other in the 2002 election (Lynn Rivers lost the Democratic primary to John Dingell, Jim Barcia ran for the state senate rather than take on Dale Kildee, and David Bonior ran unsuccessfully for governor instead of competing against Sander Levin; Dingell, Kildee, and Levin were all elected in the general election).

Plainly, Republicans in Michigan preferred having a plan that allowed some Democrats to be elected but was biased in their favor to one that had a high level of responsiveness but zero bias and might have meant that they won zero seats with a 50/50 division, given the slight advantage Democrats held in Michigan in 2002 in the congressional elections. Cox and Katz (2002) argued that parties prefer both greater degrees of bias and greater degrees of responsiveness but recognize that these can have a trade-off. The trade-off is evident in Michigan. Republicans achieved their partisan bias by reducing the responsiveness of the districts—the districts they created were not mirrors of the state. They packed Democratic voters into districts in which incumbents would have to face each other, leaving more opportunity for Republicans to be elected in districts where their voters were not as concentrated as Democratic voters, with a lower vote margin but enough of one to make the districts safe for Republican candidates.

Given the difficulty and danger of designing districts that are highly responsive (mirrors of the state) and the trade-off between partisan bias and responsiveness, if a party is able to control the redistricting process, the "textbook" plan is to pack as many of the other party's voters into a few districts (large majority districts for the other party)—called concentration—while spreading out the party's own voters to have safe but not huge majorities in the rest of the districts—called "dispersal."[17] This provides the party with partisan bias, as was the case with the Republicans in Michigan even though Democrats held a slight advantage in the statewide vote in Congress.[18]

Gerrymandering and Policy

Within-Party Policy Differences Our analysis of redistricting so far has assumed that basically all Democratic candidates and voters in the state have the same policy positions or preferences and that all Republican candidates and voters in the state have the same policy positions or preferences (though different from those of the Democrats). But of course this is not true, as within each party and across states there is variation in policy preferences. In Michigan's new fifteenth congressional district, where Representatives John Dingell and Lynn Rivers faced each other in 2002 in the Democratic primary, there were differences in their policy positions. Dingell was viewed as more socially conservative, with ties to the National Rifle Association. Rivers, on the other hand, favored gun control. Dingell opposed partial-birth abortion and Rivers favored full abortion rights.[19] Whereas both were probably more liberal than the Republican candidates in the state at the time, the differences in their policy positions show that arbitrarily assuming that voters viewed them identically or that Democratic voters are identical in their policy preferences, as our analysis of redistricting does, is an oversimplification.

The Game between the States National Republican Congressional Committee chairman Tom Davis and White House aide Karl Rove were calling Pennsylvania state house majority leader John Perzel in 2001. They were concerned about events in Georgia—where Democrats were going to pass a congressional redistricting plan that would likely cost Republicans some seats in Congress that Davis and Rove had been counting on. Why call Perzel about a problem in Georgia? In Pennsylvania, Republicans dominated redistricting, with control over both state houses and the governorship even though the state was largely evenly divided between Democrats and Republicans (in 2000, Al Gore received 51 percent of the state's vote to George W. Bush's 46 percent). But there were some divisions among Republicans over how to draw the congressional lines. One plan was largely drawn by the state senate with the help of Pennsylvania Republican senator Rick Santorum and congresswoman Melissa Hart, which was anticipated to give Republicans an edge of thirteen to six, sacrificing some powerful Democratic incumbent members of Congress. Perzel, from Philadelphia, was good friends with Philadelphia members of Congress and worried that the city would lose influence in the U.S. House under the state senate's plan. He had therefore proposed a plan that was not expected to have the same partisan bias. Perzel must have listened to Davis and Rove. A compromise was designed, leading to a twelve-to-seven Republican majority in Congress from Pennsylvania (Barone and Cohen 2003, pp. 1350–51)—and making up for the Republican loss in Georgia.

Our analysis of redistricting also ignores the fact that congressional districting by a state is part of a larger process involving other states, a game in which the parties are engaged in redistricting in each state in order to affect the balance of power within Congress as a whole. That is, we saw in chapter 5 how the policy preferences of voters in different states vary even if they are in the same party. A Republican from New York is different in her policy preferences from a Republican from Alabama. What should matter to the gerrymandering in a state, then, is how the congressional delegation from that state affects national policy, and thus the gerrymanderer has to recognize the effect of his or her choices on the choices of other gerrymanderers and what happens in the House of Representatives as a whole.

A Model of Gerrymandering Shotts (2002) analyzed the general game between state gerrymanderers who choose district boundaries in order to move national policy closer to their own preferences. Each voter in each state is assumed to have preferences on policy like Charlotte's in chapter 4. That is, each voter has an ideal point for policy, and as policy moves away from that point, his or her utility declines symmetrically. Each state's gerrymanderer is also assumed to have an ideal point for policy. The gerrymanderers must allocate the voters in equal-size districts that must include at least one voter with each policy preference (thus capturing the constraints of geography and information facing gerrymanderers in allocating voters). Each district is assumed to elect a member of Congress whose ideal point is equal to that of the district's median voter. The policy choice within Congress is assumed to equal the median policy preference of all the members elected to Congress from all the states. In chapter 4, we saw how the voter in an election whose ideal point is at the median of all voters' ideal points is pivotal in deciding which candidate wins election. When there is a choice between two options in a legislature and the decision is by majority rule, the median legislator is pivotal, and the proposal that comes closest to his or her ideal point will get the majority of the votes. Shotts also considered situations in which the pivotal legislator is not the median legislator because of advantages in agenda control that the majority may have or because of rules that require a supermajority to pass legislation.

Shotts showed that there is an equilibrium in this game, in which there is a unique national policy position in the House of Representatives. In all states where the gerrymanderer's ideal point is less than this national policy position, the gerrymanderer will design districts to maximize the number of representatives whose policy positions are less than the national policy choice, and in all states where the gerrymanderer's ideal point is greater than this national policy position, the gerrymanderer will design districts to maximize the number of representatives whose policy positions are greater than the national policy choice.

While the national equilibrium policy is unique, there are actually many different plans that each state can design that would be optimal. For example, suppose that Nebraska is apportioned three members of Congress. Without Nebraska's delegation, the other 432 members of Congress have policy positions as follows: 216 liberal members have policy positions equal to 25; 1 moderate member has a policy position equal to 50; and 215 conservative members have ideal points equal to 75. There are actually two median points in Congress, at 25 and 50 (see the discussion in chapter 4 on determining median points).

Now consider the choices before a gerrymanderer named Neal who is in charge of drawing the district boundaries in Nebraska. Suppose he is a liberal with an ideal point at 25. Assume that there are 1,080 voters in

FIGURE 11.4
Redistricting Plan That Mirrors a State's Political Makeup

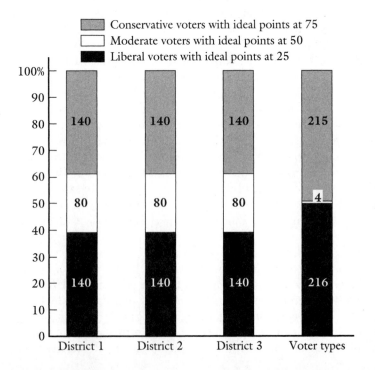

Nebraska—420 liberal voters with an ideal point at 25; 240 moderate voters with an ideal point at 50; and 420 conservative voters with an ideal point at 75. The median voter in the state is a moderate voter with an ideal point at 50. Suppose Neal must divide the state into three districts of 360 voters. If he designs three districts that are "mirrors" of the state, each district will have 140 liberals, 80 moderates, and 140 conservatives, with the moderates at the median. The state would elect three representatives with ideal points at 50. This would ensure that the national median is also at 50 (now the distribution in Congress would be 216 liberals, 4 moderates, and 215 conservatives). Figure 11.4 presents this districting plan.

Now suppose Neal redesigned the districts so that one district has 40 liberals, 20 moderates, and 300 conservatives and two districts have 190 liberals, 110 moderates, and 60 conservatives, as shown in figure 11.5. The ideal point of the representative in the district dominated by conservative voters is 75, and that of the representatives in the two districts dominated by liberal voters is 25. Congress would now have 218 liberals, 1 moderate, and 216 conservatives, with a national median at 25.

FIGURE 11.5
One Redistricting Plan with a Liberal Bias

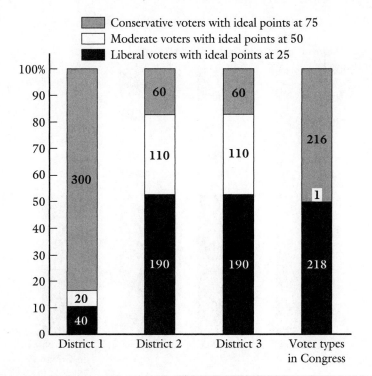

Helping Out Incumbents and Other Candidates But that is not the only way Neal could design the three districts to have the same national effect. For example, he could design one district with 10 liberals, 10 moderates, and 340 conservatives (leading to the election of a conservative), another district with 190 liberals, 160 moderates, and 10 conservatives (leading to the election of a liberal), and the third with 220 liberals, 70 moderates, and 70 conservatives (also leading to the election of a liberal), all with the same effect on the national median. This plan is shown in figure 11.6. Note that gerrymanderers actually work with larger populations and so they have a large number of choices in designing districts to affect the national median. Therefore, it is possible for them both to choose between a number of optimal designs for districts in order to meet other goals, like protecting particular incumbents or benefiting a new candidate for Congress, and to satisfy geographic constraints while still achieving the desired effect on policy. In fact, to the outside observer, many redistricting battles look like fights between incumbents of the same party who want to be sure they are in a district with a lot of their supporters. Because so many different

FIGURE 11.6
Another Redistricting Plan with a Liberal Bias

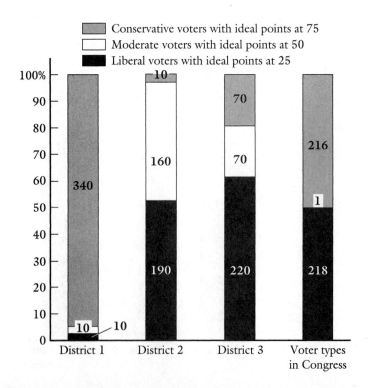

plans can satisfy partisan goals, incumbents and party members are likely to engage in internal bickering about the details of the plan.

Maximizing Party Advantages In our example, since Neal's delegation is pivotal in determining the median voter in the House of Representatives, all that matters is that he sends representatives who are more liberal than conservative; sending the greatest number of liberal representatives is not the issue. It turns out, however, that since this is a game across states, we would expect that when there is an equilibrium in the game (that is, each gerrymanderer is doing the best he or she can to meet his or her partisan goals given what the other gerrymanderers are doing), each state's gerrymanderer will want to maximize the number of legislators with his or her preferences.[20] Thus, in the game across states, gerrymanderers will want to maximize their partisan advantages.

One interesting implication of the analysis is that if one group, liberal or conservative, has greater control over the gerrymandering across states, that group can affect the national median. So in the game among states, if states with liberal gerrymanderers have a greater number of total districts than the states with conservative gerrymanderers, the national median will be liberal, and vice versa. Thus, dominating gerrymandering nationwide by one group can lead to a bias in favor of that group nationally.

Partisan Gerrymandering and Polarization Some have suggested that partisan gerrymandering is one of the causes of the increasing polarization of members of Congress, reviewed in chapter 5.[21] The reasoning is simple and can be clearly inferred from the preceding example. If Neal designed the districts in Nebraska to be microcosms of the state, then all of the members of Congress from Nebraska would have an ideal point equal to 50. But if Neal designed the districts in order to achieve a partisan advantage, the representatives elected from the state would be polarized. Thus, partisan gerrymandering clearly leads to polarization. However, for partisan gerrymandering to explain increasing polarization, there must be an increase in partisan gerrymandering. There are two reasons why this may have occurred: First, the one-person, one-vote court ruling has led to regular redistricting in many cases in which redistricting might not otherwise have occurred. Thus, boundaries have changed more often, allowing partisanship to influence them on a more regular basis. Second, technological advances have made it easier to both measure voters' preferences (much as they have increased the mobilization of voters) and fine-tune the location of district boundaries for optimally gerrymandering. As we discuss below, there has been a noticeable increase in partisan gerrymandering between censuses, suggesting that the phenomenon is on the rise.

Courts and Redistricting

The Effects of the Redistricting Revolution on Partisan Bias There is evidence of national partisan biases over time, which are affected by the national control over gerrymandering. Erikson (1972) and Cox and Katz (2002) showed that prior to the Supreme Court rulings against malapportionment in the early 1960s, gerrymandering across states led to a Republican partisan bias in nonsouthern states (during this period, southern states were dominated by the Democratic Party). Cox and Katz estimated that from 1946 to 1960, there was an overall pro-Republican bias in nonsouthern of states between 6 percent and 6.4 percent. This is somewhat remarkable since, as we noted earlier, malapportionment hurt the Republican Party because Republican voters were more likely to live in underrepresented districts. Yet the district boundaries often changed little over this time and tended to benefit Republican candidates.

Things begin to change in the 1960s, however. Cox and Katz reported (p. 60): "The Republican advantage in the North begins to erode noticeably in 1962, when California, Massachusetts, and Pennsylvania replaced Republican plans; . . . by 1966, the Republican advantage was largely gone." Cox and Katz argued that the erosion of the Republican advantage in nonsouthern states occurred as the consequence of three factors: (1) the dominance of the Democratic Party over state legislatures in the 1960s; (2) the new role to be played by the courts in evaluating redistricting plans; and (3) the dominance of Democrats in the federal judiciary. Because of the one-person, one vote decisions, redistricting could not be avoided, and even in states where Republicans were in control of redistricting or the state government was divided, state legislators recognized that court supervision might ensue if they did not redistrict or if there was a challenge to the plan they designed. Cox and Katz pointed out (p. 81) that the

> highest courts supervising redistricting action in the largest Republican-controlled states—Michigan 1964, Ohio 1968, New Jersey 1968, and New York 1968–1970—all had Democratic majorities. Perhaps Republican politicians in these states worried that, if they passed a plan without perfectly equal-population districts, the court would invalidate it—especially if the enacted plan produced heavy pro-Republican bias. To the extent that achieving the equal-population standard was costly, in order to get Democratic courts to accept some population discrepancies, Republicans in these states might have reduced the level of bias in their plans.

Cox and Katz examined thirty cases from 1964 to 1970 in which it was easy to measure the partisanship of the court and the state gerrymanderer in order to determine whether there was a bias in the courts' likelihood of accepting a redistricting plan, holding malapportionment constant, if the court and the gerrymanderer were associated with the same party. They estimated that for two plans that are identical in malapportionment, the plan considered by a "friendly" court (one whose members belonged to the same party as the gerrymanderer) was accepted 75 percent of the time, whereas a plan considered by an "unfriendly" court (one whose members belonged to a different party from the gerrymanderer) was accepted 35 percent of the time.

Is Partisan Gerrymandering Unconstitutional? While those results suggest that court partisanship can play an important role in affecting gerrymandering—and did in the 1960s—the evidence is unclear as to whether such factors are important in current battles over gerrymandering. The cases in the 1960s that Cox and Katz examined were taken to the courts because of the one-person, one vote requirement, which previously had not been enforced in redistricting plans; they were not taken to the courts because the plans had been drawn to advantage a political party. But given that parties, as we have seen, have an incentive to engage in partisan gerrymandering, is such gerrymandering itself an unconstitutional violation of the equal protection clause of the Fourteenth Amendment?

Davis v. Bandemer After the 1980 census, Indiana Republicans controlled the redistricting process in their state and designed districts for the state legislature that benefited their party. In the 1982 election, Democrats received 51.9 percent of the vote for the state house but only 43 percent of the seats and 53.1 percent of the votes for the state senate but only 52 percent of the seats. In two counties with multimember house districts, Democrats received 46.6 percent of the vote but only 14.29 percent of the seats. Democrats challenged the district boundaries as a violation of the equal protection clause, and the case ended up in the Supreme Court as *Davis v. Bandemer*. In 1986, six of the nine Supreme Court justices ruled that cases of partisan gerrymandering could be justicable under the equal protection clause (that is, the Court could consider whether partisan gerrymandering violated the Constitution). However, four of those six justices also contended that in Indiana, Democrats were not so adversely affected as to allow them to declare the plan unconstitutional. The problem before the judges was that since the Constitution does not require proportional representation, the Court needed more evidence than the simple fact that there was a partisan bias in redistricting to prove that the gerrymandering was an equal protection violation. As Justice Byron White wrote:

> The mere fact that an apportionment scheme makes it more difficult for a particular group in a particular district to elect representatives of its choice does not render that scheme unconstitutional. A group's electoral power is not unconstitutional diminished by the fact that an apportionment scheme makes winning elections more difficult; . . . unconstitutional discrimination occurs only when the electoral system is arranged in a manner that will consistently degrade a voter's or a group of voters' influence on the political process as a whole.

Interestingly, although Republicans in Indiana had drawn the districts that gave them a bias, from 1984 to 1990 Democrats gradually built up their percentage of state legislators, using those districts. By 1988, the Democratic vote for the state house was 47 percent, but Democrats controlled 50 percent of the seats, and the Democratic vote for the state senate was 45 percent, but Democrats controlled 52 percent of the seats.

An Unknown Standard Although the Supreme Court opened the door to considering partisan gerrymandering a violation of equal protection, courts have generally not declared such plans unconstitutional even when they might have a partisan bias to do so. In Michigan, Democrats challenged the 2001 Republican plan unsuccessfully in federal court. The three-judge panel ruled "that any disputes with the congressional map can be addressed through the political process. The Legislature will change the map after the 2010 Census, as it does every 10 years."[22] All the members of the three-judge panel had been appointed by Democratic presidents (U.S. District Court judge Julian Cook and chief judge of the U.S. Sixth Circuit Court of Appeals Boyce Martin were appointed by President Carter, and U.S. District Court judge David Lawson was appointed by President Clinton). In chapter 15, we consider the partisan effects of racial gerrymandering and the courts' role in those instances that have caused a great deal of controversy. There is little evidence in those cases, however, that the rulings by the courts have been motivated by partisanship. In June 2003, the Supreme Court (in an opinion supported by justices appointed by Republicans and the same coalition that voted in favor of Bush in the Gore-Bush case) ruled that a district court that had declared unconstitutional a districting plan designed by Democrats in Georgia for the state legislature had failed to consider all the relevant factors. The Supreme Court vacated the lower court's judgment, a victory for Democrats in the state.

As noted earlier, Tom Davis and Karl Rove did get their Pennsylvania colleague John Perzel to draw boundaries that made up for the Republican loss of seats in Georgia. But just as Republicans challenged the Democrats' plan in Georgia, so Democrats challenged the Republicans' plan in Pennsylvania. The case against the Pennsylvania plan reached the Supreme Court, where the justices further muddied the waters of partisan redistricting. On April 28, 2004, the Court ruled against the Democrats in *Vieth v. Jubelirer.* Four justices (Antonin Scalia, William Rehnquist, Sandra Day O'Connor, and Clarence Thomas) concluded that the Pennsylvania district boundaries were constitutional and, in general, partisan gerrymanderers were nonjusticable; that is, there are "no judicially discernible and manageable standards for adjudicating such claims," voting to overturn the *Bandemer* decision. Four other justices (John Paul Stevens, David Souter, Ruth Bader Ginsburg, and Stephen Breyer) concluded that partisan gerrymanderers were justiciable; that is, the justices voted to direct the lower court to consider the case of partisan gerrymandering in Pennsylvania. However, each justice gave different standards for how the lower court could make its decision. The swing vote was Anthony Kennedy, who concurred with the plurality upholding the lower court's decision (that the boundaries were constitutional) but did not affirm an overturning of *Bandemer*. That is, Kennedy left open the possibility that there might be a manageable constitutional test down the line and suggested that it might be drawn from the First Amendment. The ruling thus did not lead to an overturning of *Bandemer*, but it did not provide any clear guidance to those drawing district boundaries on how to avoid a future ruling of partisan gerrymandering.

The Policy Effects of Redistricting Control in the '90s So far we've discussed a lot of theory of redistricting, some anecdotes, and some court cases. What about general empirical evidence? Do the drawers of congressional boundaries attempt to affect the policy choices in Congress, as Shotts's theory suggests? Table 11.2 summarizes the relationship between partisan control over redistricting in the 1990s, the ideological leanings of a state, and whether the majority of members of Congress from a state were more conservative or more liberal than the median voter in Congress from 1999 to 2000. States are classified as conservative or liberal using ideology scores constructed from public opinion poll data by McIver, Erikson, and Wright (2000). The ideology scores of Poole and Rosenthal (1997) for members of Congress, discussed in chapter 4, are used to determine whether the majority of members of Congress in a state were more liberal or more conservative than the median member of Congress. Not unexpectedly, the more liberal a state, the more likely it is that the majority of the members of Congress from that state will be liberal, and the more conservative the state, the more likely it is that the majority of its representatives will be conservative. In the conservative states, 59.09 percent had a majority of members of Congress who were conservative, and in the liberal states, 66.67 percent had a majority of members of Congress who were liberal.

Yet the percentage does vary according to the party controlling redistricting. For example, in the liberal states in which Democrats controlled redistricting, 71.43 percent of the states had a majority of liberal members of Congress, and in the conservative states in which Republicans controlled redistricting, 80 percent of the states had a majority of conservative members of Congress. Party control over redistricting also appears to limit the extent to which the ideology of a state influences the ideology of the state's members of Congress. When Democrats controlled redistricting in conservative states, 44.44 percent of the states had a majority of liberal members, compared with 0 percent when Republicans controlled redistricting. When Republicans controlled redistricting in liberal states, 33.33 percent of the states had a majority of conservative members, compared with 14.29 percent when Democrats controlled redistricting. Of course, the data here are limited, and it is inappropriate to draw strong conclusions about the effects that control of redistricting have on the ideological composition of a state's con-

TABLE 11.2
Redistricting in the 1990s and Ideological Positions of Congress Members, 1999–2000

	Liberal-Conservative Balance of Congressional Delegation			
Partisan Control over Redistricting	States in Which Majority of Members Are Liberal	States with Balanced Membership	States in Which Majority of Members Are Conservative	Total
	Conservative States			
Democratic control	4 (44.44%)	1 (11.11%)	4 (44.44%)	9 (100%)
Biparatisan control	1 (12.5%)	2 (25%)	5 (62.5%)	8 (100%)
Republican control	0 (0%)	1 (20%)	4 (80%)	5 (100%)
Total	5 (22.73%)	4 (18.18%)	13 (59.09%)	22 (100%)
	Liberal States			
Democratic control	5 (71.43%)	1 (14.29%)	1 (14.29%)	7 (100%)
Bipartisan control	8 (72.73%)	0 (0%)	3 (27.27%)	11 (100%)
Republican control	1 (33.33%)	1 (33.33%)	1 (33.33%)	3 (100%)
Total	14 (66.67%)	2 (9.52%)	5 (23.81%)	21 (100%)

Note: Information applies only to states with more than one district. Information on redistricting is from Barone (1998). State classified as having Republican-controlled redistricting are Alabama, Idaho, Illinois, Indiana, Kansas, Maine, New Hampshire, and Utah. States classified as having bipartisan redistricting are Arizona, California, Colorado, Florida, Iowa, Louisiana, Michigan, Minnesota, Mississippi, Nebraska, Nevada, New Jersey, New York, North Carolina, Ohio, Pennsylvania, South Carolina, Washington, and Wisconsin. States classified as having Democratic-controlled redistricting are Arkansas, Connecticut, Georgia, Hawaii, Kentucky, Maryland, Massachusetts, Missouri, New Mexico, Oklahoma, Oregon, Rhode Island, Tennessee, Texas, Virginia, and West Virginia.
Note: Totals are approximate.

gressional delegation; they do suggest, however, that control over redistricting does influence that composition.[23]

Middecade Redistricting

The Killer D's Redux If party control over a state has changed since the last redistricting, the new leaders will want that control reflected in the new congressional boundaries. That is why Michigan's delegation in Congress switched from majority Democratic to majority Republican between 2000 and 2002. In California, Republicans have not been able to dominate redistricting since 1951 and had little choice but to accept the Democratic plan in 2000, giving up Stephen Horn's seat. A different story unfolded in Texas. After the 1990 census, Texas was apportioned three new congressional seats. In 1991, Texas Democrats controlled the state house and drew what has been called "the shrewdest gerrymander of the 1990s" (Barone and Ujifusa 1999, p. 1448). Eight Republican incumbents were packed into districts that had a large majority of Republican voters, while the remaining twenty-two districts were structured to give Democrats a slight majority and a slight advantage (Democrats won twenty-one of those seats in 1992).[24] Yet in 1992, the popular vote in all races for Congress in Texas was 48 percent Republican. Over the 1990s, Republican vote totals increased, and in 1996 Republicans won the popular vote in the state's congressional races by 54 percent but won only thirteen of the state's thirty congressional districts. The district lines drawn by the Democrats in 1990 had resulted in the state's Democratic voters' having a greater voice in Congress per voter than their numbers in the state, much as the nation's rural voters benefited before the Supreme Court forced states to abide by the one-person, one vote rule.

After the 2000 census, Texas gained two congressional districts. But Democrats still controlled the state house, and although Republicans controlled the state senate and the governorship, plane owner and Texas house speaker Pete Laney kept redistricting from coming to a vote in the house, resulting in a three-judge federal court stepping in and drawing the new districts. The court kept intact many of the existing boundaries from the 1990s. Under the court-designed plan, Democrats controlled seventeen congressional districts in the state, whereas Republicans controlled fifteen, even though the majority of the congressional popular vote was Republican. But in 2002, Democrats lost control of the Texas state house for the first time in 130 years. One of the Texas Republicans in Congress, majority leader Tom DeLay, wanted to increase his majority in Congress, and other Texas Republicans believed that the Democratic control over the congressional districts was inappropriate, given the domination of the state by Republicans. Thus, DeLay and other Texas Republicans proposed a redrawing of the congressional district boundaries, which many estimated would allow the Republicans to win four to seven seats from the Democrats.

That was the situation when the Killer D's revolted and fled to Oklahoma so that the state legislature would not have a quorum, killing the measure— but only temporarily. Texas governor Rick Perry called a special session for the summer, and after another escape by the Democrats, this time to New Mexico, the Republicans were able to pass a revised congressional district plan, which was approved by the Justice Department. Democrats challenged the Texas plan in the courts, and a three-judge federal panel affirmed the Republican plan. But the Texas case may be the one that will lead to greater clarification on the constitutionality of partisan gerrymandering. On October 18, 2004, without comment, the Supreme Court ordered the three-judge panel to review its decision in light of the Court's April 28 decision on *Vieth*. At this writing, the panel has not made a ruling, yet regardless of the ruling most observers expect the decision will be appealed to the Supreme Court. (The Texas gerrymandering question is also relevant to the debate over minority representation in Congress, as discussed in chapter 15.)

Other Middecade Redistricting Efforts While the plight of the Texas Democrats was broadcast by all the news networks and published in international newspapers, Colorado, with slightly less publicity, also redrew its congressional district lines in May 2003 to benefit Republicans, reflecting the increase in power of that party in the state after Republican Bill Owen won the governorship, which had been held by Democrats. Like those in Texas, the boundaries in Colorado after the 2000 census had been drawn by a federal district judge because Republicans controlled the state house but not the state senate or the governorship and the two parties could not agree on a plan. Democrats promised to try every legal measure available to them to challenge the new Colorado districts. They challenged the new plan, and on December 1, 2003, the Colorado Supreme Court ruled that

> Colorado's Constitution allowed only one round of congressional redistricting after each 10-year census [and] . . . that the Republican-controlled Legislature exceeded its authority . . . when it tried to replace a map imposed by a federal court in 2002 after the House and Senate deadlocked. "Having failed to redistrict when it should have, the General Assembly has lost its chance to redistrict until after the 2010 federal census," the court wrote.[25]

While Colorado's constitution stymied Republicans, in February 2005 Georgia's Republicans, who had not been in control when the state's congressional district boundaries were drawn, were floating new plans that would benefit their party. Republicans weren't the only ones trying to make gains in Congress between census years; in 2003, Democratic legislators in the majority in New Mexico and Oklahoma (where Democrats had recently gained control of formerly Republican governorships) also talked of redrawing congressional district lines to benefit Democratic candidates. But in February 2004, New Mexico governor Bill Richardson took redistricting off the table. And in Oklahoma, efforts to redistrict have met with a lack of interest beyond a few legislators.[26]

The Backlash In the 2004 state legislative elections in California, 153 seats were contested. But not a single one changed party hands. "What kind of democracy is that?" Arnold Schwarzenegger complained in his state of the state address in January 2005. Arnold blamed redistricting. He concluded: "The current system is rigged to benefit the interests of those in office and not those who put them there. We must reform it."[27] Arnold argued that California should adopt a bipartisan method of redistricting, as is currently used in a number of states. For example, Iowa law requires that districts be drawn by a nonpartisan body, which must produce districts that are compact and contiguous and disregard partisanship and incumbency. The legislature can only accept or reject the plan and cannot make any amendments. As a result, even though the legislature was controlled by Republicans, three Republican congressional incumbents faced strong challenges in 2002. Since 1991, three states—Arizona, Idaho, and Alaska—have switched to bipartisan commissions. In February 2005, the public interest group Common Cause reported that reform efforts were under way in at least seven other states (Colorado, Florida, Georgia, Maryland, Massachusetts, Pennsylvania, and Rhode Island). At this writing, it is unclear whether the Arnold Schwarzeneggers or the Tom DeLays will win in the battle over redistricting reform.

Does Gerrymandering Give Incumbents an Advantage?

Primaries and Incumbent Losses

In most states, new congressional districts are drawn to protect incumbents. Congressional incumbents rarely lose. In the 2002 congressional race (the first one after the 2000 redistricting), only 6 of the 383 incumbents who did not face another incumbent in their reelection contest were defeated. Protecting incumbents goes hand in hand with creating districts in which parties have sizable advantages—that is, in which they are not responsive—which is the complaint of Arnold Schwarzenegger about California's legislative districts. But incumbents can still be challenged in their parties' primaries, and sometimes they lose.

In Michigan In 1992, Michigan Republican Peter Hoekstra launched an

improbable campaign . . . against Guy Vander Jagt, 26-year incumbent and chairman of the National Republican Congressional Committee since 1975. Hoekstra saved up vacation time and took a county-by-county bicycle tour of the district.

With an earnestness that rang true, Hoekstra called for citizen, not career, politicians, refused PAC money and supported abolishing PACs; advocated 12-year term limits; and promised to uphold family values and to oppose abortion—

popular positions in his district (Barone, Cohen and Ujifusa 2001, p. 782). Hoekstra defeated Vander Jagt in the primary and went on to win the general election easily in the heavily Republican district. According to political analyst Charles Cook, "Vander Jagt had worn out his welcome in his district even though he held a powerful party post in Washington and traveled the country on behalf of other Republican candidates."[28]

In California In 2000, California Democratic state senator Hilda Solis took on the incumbent Democratic congressman, Matthew Martínez, who had "lost support among feminist and labor activists by voting for a ban on late-term abortions and fast-track trade authority and helped to stall gun control" (Barone, Cohen, and Ujifusa 2001, p. 242). Two other congressional incumbents were defeated in primaries in 2000—New York congressman Michael Forbes, who had switched from the Republican Party to the Democratic, was defeated in the Democratic primary by Regina Seltzer (who lost to Republican Felix Grucci in the general election), and Utah Republican Merrill Cook was defeated in the Republican primary by Derek Smith (who lost to Democrat Jim Matheson in the general election). Forbes was seen by voters as a member of neither party, and Cook was known for throwing temper tantrums and engaging in feuds. It is noteworthy that in these cases, voters not only rejected the incumbent in the primary, but also rejected the replacement nominee of the incumbent's party in the general election (Barone, Cohen, and Ujifusa 2001, pp. 1048, 1535).

In Alabama In 2002, Alabama Democrat Earl Hilliard and Georgia Democrat Cynthia McKinney lost primary contests in races that were largely seen as referenda on their records as Congress members. In a contest that attracted much national attention, Hilliard, who is African American and represented a district with a majority of black voters, was defeated by Arthur Davis, also African American. While Hilliard believed that Davis's campaign contributions from outside the district, notably from New York Jewish groups that were angry with Hilliard's pro-Palestinian stance, were the source of Davis's victory,[29] Davis claimed the outcome reflected local issues that had been ignored by Hilliard. Hilliard relied on the support of major state-level black-led political action groups and national black political figures and his history of involvement with the civil rights movement. In contrast, Davis used campaign contributions both to communicate with local voters and to build a grassroots network among political and community leaders in the district. Davis "hired people with extensive connections in the community as well to visit churches and neighborhood meetings or to simply walk with the candidate around town and introduce him." Even County

Commissioner Albert Turner, Jr., whose political organization helped carry his county for Hilliard, recognized that local issues in the race were important to voters and were a major reason why Hilliard was defeated. He concluded: "No longer can you say you marched on the Selma bridge and that gets you in office and keeps you in office. . . . The day of who's the blackest is over. It's about production now."[30]

Of course the ability of challengers to defeat an incumbent depends on the extent to which party nomination contests are open to voters, as discussed in chapter 4. From 1982 to 1996, the average number of major-party congressional candidates in states with closed primaries was 3.15, while the average number of major-party congressional candidates in states with either open or semi-closed primaries was 3.43, numbers that, using statistical analysis, are significantly different, suggesting that there is more competition in states with more open primary systems, reflecting a greater ability by voters to control incumbents in these states.[31] Comparing just those congressional races with an incumbent running, a situation that would depress the incentives for candidates to enter races, we find that the average number of major-party congressional candidates in states with closed primaries was 2.78, but in open or semi-closed primaries the average number of major-party congressional candidates was 3.046, also significantly greater.[32]

Forcing Incumbents to Face Each Other

The examples above demonstrate that gerrymandering does not give incumbents a free ride; they must still please their constituency in primaries. Furthermore, redistricting, through the changes necessitated by apportionment, can force incumbents out of office. In 2002, eight congressional contests pitted two incumbents against each other, and thirty-five incumbents chose either to run for another office or to retire from Congress rather than challenge another incumbent.[33] When redistricting forces incumbents to face each other or retire from Congress, party leaders can use the new lines to influence the incumbent who is likely to win the battle. As we saw, they can do this while still engaging in partisan gerrymandering. When Mississippi lost a congressional seat after the 2000 election, the new districts lines were drawn such that Republican incumbent Charles Pickering faced Democrat Ronnie Shows in 2002. A Democratic-dominated state court first drew up a plan that favored Shows. But three Republican federal judges threw out the plan because it had not been cleared by the Justice Department according to the Voting Rights Act of 1965 (further discussed in chapter 15) and drew a plan favorable to Pickering. Democrats took the case to the Supreme Court, which ruled that a federal court could block a state plan that had not been cleared. With the new plan, Shows lost to Pickering in 2002.

Sometimes party elites use new district boundaries to disadvantage an incumbent in their own party whom they prefer to see defeated. That happened to Gary Condit in California in 2002; his district was redrawn by

Democratic Party leaders to include areas not previously covered and voters who were likely to know only about Condit's involvement in the case of the mysterious disappearance and murder of twenty-four-year-old Washington intern Chandra Levy, which was not likely to help his reelection. Condit lost the Democratic primary in the new district.

Why Do Incumbents Win?

If redistricting is not the source of the incumbency advantage in Congress, what is? In earlier chapters, we discussed many of the reasons why incumbents are advantaged in elections—how voters are more likely to prefer a known incumbent to an unknown challenger, how voters might rationally reelect incumbents in order to solve problems of moral hazard and adverse selection, and how campaign contributors may prefer to give to incumbents in order to receive services or favors, thereby increasing their electoral chances as well. With elections every two years, members of Congress, if they want to keep their job, are sometimes viewed as constantly running for reelection. The short term forces voters to evaluate them often and gives voters ample opportunity to vote retrospectively, as discussed in chapter 9. Ansolabehere and Snyder (2002) examined state-level offices in executive branches (where geographic boundaries are of course constant) and found the incumbents had a similar advantage (they contended that incumbency in state executive-branch offices is higher than in legislatures), further suggesting that the factors discussed earlier, which apply to many elected officials, may be the source of an incumbency advantage in Congress.

Finally, Cox and Katz (2002) contended that what appears to be an incumbency advantage for Democrats in congressional elections is simply an artifact of incorrect empirical analysis. The logic of their argument is complex and best explained after we consider more fully the decision making of candidates (both challengers and incumbents) when they choose to run for office. We will do that in the next section and then return to Cox and Katz's claim.

The Decision to Run

The Expected Utility of Running

Before Hilda Solis became an incumbent member of Congress (she was easily reelected in 2002 and won reelection in 2004 with 85 percent of the vote), she had to win election and, before that, decide to run. What are the factors that determine whether someone runs for Congress? Since the choice of whether or not to run for Congress involves choosing whether to take an action that has an uncertain outcome, we can use the concept of expected utility to examine the choice before potential candidates. Consider the choice before a potential candidate for Congress, Frans. Frans will choose to run for

Congress if the expected utility from doing so exceeds the opportunity cost of running. The expected utility depends on the probability he is likely to win and the utility he would receive from winning, as well as the opportunities if he loses. The opportunity cost depends on the cost of running for Congress and the benefits Fans would derive from other occupations. We have discussed previously many of the costs of running for office in terms of getting on the ballot and how they vary across states (see chapter 4).

Formally, Frans will enter the race if the following is true (where P represents his probability of winning; U_W, the utility Frans receives if he wins; D, the utility he receives from running for office in itself; and C, the opportunity cost of running for office):

$$PU_W + D > C$$

Frans's probability of winning of course depends on his positions on issues and who his potential opponents are and their positions on issues. Because incumbents have advantages in elections independent of policy positions (as discussed above), then the probability of winning against an incumbent is lower for potential candidates. The easiest way to avoid running against an incumbent is getting the chance to run in a newly created district without an incumbent. Democrat Eddie Bernice Johnson was chairwoman of the Texas state senate's committee on redistricting in 1991, when Democrats were in charge of redistricting and needed to devise three new congressional districts. Johnson helped devise the plan that is the basis for the current district lines that Tom DeLay changed. But Johnson is no longer in the state senate—after drawing up a new congressional district in her hometown of Dallas, she ran for Congress in that district and won. While Devin Nunes did not help design the new district in California that he was elected from, he did gain from the fact that the district had been designed as a safe seat for a Republican. The hard part for him was getting the nomination because he faced two strong opponents (which we will discuss further in chapter 14). Minnesota retail salesclerk Betty McCollum, a Democrat, did not run for Congress in a new district, as Nunes and Johnson did, but the incumbent member of Congress, Bruce Vento, was diagnosed with lung cancer and did not seek reelection, dying in office a month before the general election. Moreover, Vento had anointed McCollum as his successor, and the district had been heavily Democratic since 1948, when Eugene McCarthy was selected to represent it. Yet McCollum faced unexpected problems from a third-party candidate in the general election, which we will also discuss in chapter 14.

Political Experience and the Decision to Run

While policy positions are important and a potential candidate's choices on policy influence his or her chances of election, there is evidence that voters also consider candidates' experience and background when nonincumbent candidates are running for Congress. That is, candidates who have political experience, particularly elected experience, are more likely to win election than those who do not have such experience, regardless of whether the challenger faces an incumbent or not. The three congressional candidates we discussed at the beginning of this chapter had varying degrees of political experience. Larry Weatherford had not held elected office but was the chief of staff of the state insurance department. Devin Nunes had been elected to the College of the Sequoias board of trustees and, more significantly, been appointed by President George W. Bush as California state director for the U.S. Department of Agriculture. Betty McCollum had the most political experience, having served for five years in the North St. Paul City Council and for eight years in the Minnesota House of Representatives and having been elected three times to the post of assistant leader of the Democratic Party in the Minnesota House of Representatives.

Table 11.3 presents a summary of the political experience of the nonincumbent major-party candidates for Congress in 2000 and their corresponding electoral success, as well as the type of competition they faced. Of the 814 candidates, 49.6 percent won primaries, but only 5 percent won the general election. If the nonincumbent had no political experience, he or she won the primary 44.5 percent of the time but the general election only 1.4 percent of the time. If the nonincumbent was a state legislator, however, like Betty McCollum, his or her odds were much higher. Of the 80 state legislators who ran for Congress as major-party candidates, 71.25 percent won primaries, and 28.75 percent won the general election. Nonincumbents with a small amount of political experience, like Devin Nunes, typically do similarly better than those without any experience. In Nune's contest in 1998, his opponent for the Republican nomination, Cliff Unruh, while older (forty-eight), also had minimal political experience, having worked with small businesses through the U.S. Chamber of Commerce. Nunes came very close to defeating Unruh, with 48.26 percent of the vote.

TABLE 11.3
Nonincumbent Major-Party Congressional Candidates in Primaries and General Elections, 2000

Candidates' Political Experience	Total Number of Candidates	Candidates Who Won Primary	Candidates Who Won General Election	Candidates Who Faced No Incumbent
Former member of Congress	7	4	1	0
Local Official	80	48	3	29
Party Official	27	18	3	7

State Legislator	80	57	23	41
State Official	9	5	2	4
No political experience	611	272	9	125
Total	814	404	41	206

Abramson, Aldrich, and Rohde (2003) presented data on the success of challengers in general elections as a function of political experience in 2002. The data are presented in Table 11.4. The table shows a similar result—that candidates with experience in state legislatures have a higher probability of success than those without that experience, particularly in races without an incumbent running.

TABLE 11.4
Political Experience of Nonincumbent Major-Party Congressional Candidates in General Elections, 2002

Candidates' Political Experience	Candidates Who Faced an Incumbent		Candidates Who Faced No Incumbent	
	Total	Candidates Who Won General Election	Total	Candidates Who Won General Election
State legislator or member of Congress	21	2	37	26
Other elected official	26	0	21	10
No elected office	256	2	37	13
Total	303	4	95	49

Source: Abramson, Aldrich, and Rohde (2003).

The higher success of candidates with political experience can result from a number of factors. Voters might use knowledge of a candidate's past choices in lower-level political offices to better control for principal-agent problems, as discussed in chapter 9 (voting retrospectively), and that might advantage such candidates over unknowns with no political record. We also expect that those candidates with political experience who choose to run are the ones whose past choices are close to those preferred by voters. McCollum had a record and had made policy decisions that voters could measure and judge, whereas Weatherford was all promise. In addition, potential candidates with political experience have developed ties to political elites and campaign contributors (their political offices can help them provide services and favors to contributors even though they are not in Congress), which can help them amass the campaign resources needed to communicate with voters and mobilize them at election time. Having run for office in the same part of the state, McCollum already had contacts whom she could ask for campaign resources, and she already had contacts with voters. Essentially, challengers with political experience may have some of the advantages that incumbents have in terms of retrospective voting and campaign resources. McCollum was much closer to an incumbent than Weatherford or Nunes was.

Table 11.3 also provides a profile of major-party candidates by political experience when there is an open seat in Congress—that is, when no incumbent is running. Whereas 20 percent of the candidates with no experience entered open-seat races, 51 percent of the state legislators entered those races. But since there are many more races with incumbents than without, this sort of comparison does not tell us much. Another way to think about the data is to compare the types of candidates in races with an incumbent with the types in races without an incumbent. In races with an incumbent, 80 percent of the challengers had no political experience, but in races without an incumbent, 60 percent of the candidates had no political experience. In non-open-seat races, 6.4 percent of the candidates were state legislators, but in open-seat races, 20 percent were state legislators. Thus, nonincumbent candidates are much more likely to have political experience in open-seat races than in non-open-seat ones.

Of course, there are exceptions to the political-experience rule, as former Nebraska Republican state chairman John Gale and Nebraska state board of education member Kathy Wilmot discovered when they ran for an open seat in Nebraska's third congressional district. They were defeated by a candidate with no political experience but with an unbeatable tie to Nebraska voters: former University of Nebraska head football coach Tom Osborne, who had won three national championships and lost only three games during his last five years as coach. Of the major-party candidates for Congress in 2000, twelve had experience in television or radio, of which eight won primaries (a 66.67 percent success rate compared with a 44.5 percent rate for candidates without experience). Only one achieved a general-election win, however, Republican talk-radio-show host Mike Pence in the second district in Indiana, an open-seat contest. Celebrity status does seem to advantage candidates, particularly in primaries, but does not ensure victory. It is important to remember that Tom Osborne campaigned hard for his election, and celebrities, like all other potential candidates, can lose. Former local news anchorman Rich Rodriguez and former baseball player and ESPN broadcaster Jim Rooker failed in their 2000 bids for Congress.[34]

The Game between Challengers

   Weatherford and Watts Larry Weatherford had little political experience
before running for Congress (and was not a celebrity), and our analysis
would suggest that he was less likely to win election because of that. But he
had other disadvantages as well. He ran as a Democrat in a heavily Republican district, and he ran against a popular incumbent, J. C. Watts. As the
only black Republican in Congress, Watts was highly valued by national and
Oklahoma Republicans. Moreover, he had not neglected his voters, turning
down a seat on the House Committee on Appropriations "so that he could
continue to work on local issues on Armed Services and keep jobs at Tin-
ker," the air force base in his district. "He worked for $3.6 million to help
build the dome on Oklahoma's Capitol, . . . and for funds to preserve old
buildings on the University of Science and Arts of Oklahoma in Chickasha.
. . . He worked for the national weather research center in Norman and
for advanced trainers for air traffic control at the FAA center in Oklahoma
City" (Barone, Cohen, and Ujifusa 2001, p. 1257). Unlike Guy Vander
Jagt or Matthew Martínez, Watts had a record with local voters that made
them want to keep him. Although Larry Weatherford did have an issue
with Watts's lack of support for the Patient's Bill of Rights, that issue
was not strong enough with the voters in Oklahoma's fourth district to offset Watts's strong record in the community. Weatherford had no competition for his party's nomination and thus won the Democratic primary by
default, yet he received only 54,808 votes in the general election to Watt's
114,000.
   In 1996, Watts, like Goodling in chapter 9, had promised voters that he
would serve a limited number of terms. Watts promised to retire in 2000,
but with the urging of voters and family, he decided to run again. Nevertheless, his talk of retirement was no doubt known to potential challengers
like Weatherford, and most expected that he would soon retire. Therefore,
many were not surprised when Watts chose to retire in 2002. Furthermore,
potential challengers also knew that in 2001 the new census would come
out and the state would be drawing new district boundaries. Potential challengers are likely to anticipate that this event can mean a challenger's higher
probability of winning as new district lines reflect new partisan balances or
changes in population. But Weatherford did not challenge Watts in 2002.
Instead, he and two other former Democratic opponents of Watt's gave
their support to Darryl Roberts, who had served in the state senate for sixteen years and had been a marine officer in Vietnam, a candidate with much
more political experience than Weatherford. Why did Weatherford run in
2000 but not in 2002? Why had Roberts not run in 2000?

   Why the Weak Run When the Strong Sit We have examined the entry
choices that potential candidates make as independent decisions, but clearly
the decisions are interdependent. Both Weatherford and Roberts had a

choice of whether to run in 2000 or wait until 2002, and the outcome depended on their joint choices, as they both knew. To understand how these choices are interrelated and to understand Weatherford's and Roberts's decisions, we can use the following simple example. We make the following assumptions:[35]

1. Weatherford (assuming he wins the primary) will defeat Watts in the general election with a 25 percent probability. Weatherford (assuming he wins the primary) will defeat a nonincumbent Republican nominee to replace Watts in the general election with a 40 percent probability.

2. Roberts (assuming he wins the primary) will defeat Watts in the general election with a 30 percent probability. Roberts (assuming he wins the primary) will defeat a nonincumbent Republican nominee to replace Watts in the general election with a 45 percent probability.

3. Democratic primary voters strongly prefer Roberts to Weatherford because of Roberts's experience, and in a head-to-head primary contest Roberts will win with an 80 percent probability.

TABLE 11.5
Hypothetical Probabilities of Winning in the Challenger-Entry Game

	Probability of Winning Primary	Probabiity of Winning General Election	Probability That Seat Will Be Open in 2002 (Which Matters If Roberts or Weatherford Plans to Run in 2002)	Probability of Winning General Election Once in the Race
Probability of Roberts's getting elected if				
both Roberts and Weatherford run in 2000	0.8	0.3		$0.8 \cdot 0.3 =$ 0.24
Roberts runs in 2000 and Wetherford runs in 2002	1.0	0.3		$1 \cdot 0.3 = 0.3$
Roberts runs in 2002 and Weatherford runs in 2000	1.0	0.45	0.75	$1 \cdot 0.45 \cdot 0.75$ $= 0.3375$
both Roberts and Weatherford run in 2002	0.8	0.45	1.0	$0.8 \cdot 0.45 \cdot 1$ $= 0.36$

CH. 11   CONGRESSIONAL ELECTIONS

Probability of Weatherford's getting elected if

both Weatherford and Roberts run in 2000	0.2	0.25		$0.2 \cdot 0.25 = 0.05$
Weatherford runs in 2000 and Roberts runs in 2002	1.0	0.25		$1 \cdot 0.25 = 0.25$
Weatherford runs in 2002 and Roberts runs in 2000	1.0	0.4	0.7	$1 \cdot 0.4 \cdot 0.7 = 0.28$
both Weatherford and Roberts run in 2002	0.2	0.4	1.0	$0.2 \cdot 0.4 \cdot 1 = 0.08$

TABLE 11.6
Payoff Matrix for Game between Weatherford and Roberts

		Weatherford's Choices (%)	
		Run in 2000	Run in 2002
Roberts's Choices (%)	Run in 2000	24, 5	30, 28
	Run in 2002	33.75, 25	36, 8

The first number is the probability of Roberts's winning; the second is the probability of Weatherford's winning.

These assumptions yield the probabilities of winning for the entry decisions of Weatherford and Roberts as shown in table 11.5 and the payoff matrix for the game between them as given in table 11.6

We can solve the game between Weatherford and Roberts using Nash equilibrium, also used in chapter 2. An equilibrium will exist when both Roberts and Weatherford are making the best choices given what the other is doing. First consider the optimal choices of Roberts given Weatherford's choices. If Roberts knows for sure that Weatherford will run in 2000, he will prefer to wait and run in 2002, when his probability of winning is higher, 33.75 percent in 2002 compared with 24 percent in 2000. If Roberts knows for sure that Weatherford will run instead in 2002, again Roberts will prefer to wait and run in 2002, when his probability of winning is higher, 36 percent in 2002 compared with 30 percent in 2000. Thus, whatever Weatherford does, Roberts prefers to run in 2002. What about Weatherford? Since Weatherford knows that Roberts's optimal strategy is to run in 2002 instead of 2000, his optimal response is to run in 2000, as his probability of winning is 25 percent in 2000 but only 8 percent in 2002, when he might lose the primary to Roberts. The interesting aspect of the game between strong and weak potential candidates is that weak challengers, like Weatherford, are more willing to challenge incumbents who are harder to defeat, whereas strong challengers, like Roberts, typically wait until the seat is open and they will not face a strong incumbent.

Complicating the Story One factor that our simple analysis ignores is that the cost of running can also be higher for more politically experienced competitors since they often have to give up a position in order to run for office. Politically experienced potential candidates are often making politics their main career and as such need the support of party leaders and campaign contributors for a longer time period. Running when they have less chance of winning can tax that support, reducing the availability of it when they may have a better chance to win. Voters may view repeated election losses as signals that the candidate has undesirable qualities, and to counter principal-agent problems, they may be less willing to support the candidate simply because of these losses. These are factors that can cause a politically experienced candidate to forgo running when the chances are less likely that he or she will win and the opportunity to run again in the near future with a higher probability of winning is a strong possibility. This leaves an opportunity for candidates with less political experience to run in the tough races that politically experienced challengers forgo. The key is that Weatherford has more of a chance of winning against the incumbent than he does if he waits *because* the more politically experienced potential candidate, Roberts, is likely to run in the future.

Of course, our analysis simplifies the complex negotiations between potential challengers within the same party. Contrary to the implicit assumption in the game above, where Weatherford and Roberts must choose between running in 2000 and in 2002, Weatherford could have run in 2002. Roberts had run for Congress two times previously, and some previous challengers of Watt's had competed with Roberts for the nomination. Attorney Ben Odom, who had been Watts's opponent in 1998 but had no political experience, challenged Roberts in the Democratic primary. Despite the costs of running and losing, as discussed above, candidates do "repeat" their entry after early losses, as Roberts and Nunes did. Mack (1998), analyzing the success rate of repeat challengers in congressional races, found that repeat challengers can improve on their own vote totals in subsequent races, although there is little evidence that they do better than those who have not run previously.

Redistricting and Incumbency Advantages Redux

Recall that Cox and Katz (2002) contended that the empirical evidence that Democratic incumbents are advantaged in congressional elections may be a misunderstanding of the data. They pointed out that incumbents also make a strategic decision about whether to stay in office and that they are more likely to retire voluntarily when the probability of winning their district is low for any candidate from their party (independent of the candidate's own personal qualities). For example, Representative Horn of California retired rather than run for his party's nomination in his newly shaped district, which advantaged Democrats. The Republican candidate who ran in his place, Alex Burrola, lost. Thus, if we measure how well incumbents do in congressional races relative to their parties' candidates in open-seat races, what will look like the effect of incumbency may simply be a result of their strategic retirement in anticipation of a tough race for any candidate from their party in their district. The incumbents who run choose to do so when the support for their party is strong and the open-seat races are in districts that are hotly contested.

What would determine a tough race? If the incumbent sees that there is a strong challenger from the other party who is likely to enter, he or she may retire, be "pushed out," or—in Horn's case—sacrificed. Then the nominee of the incumbent's party faces the strong challenger and has a harder time winning. Thus, Cox and Katz argued that if we just compare how incumbents do with how nonincumbents do, we overstate the advantage of incumbency. Cox and Katz (2002) asserted that after the one-person, one-vote Supreme Court decision forcing states to redistrict after each census, it became easier for incumbents and challengers to "coordinate" the decisions of whether or not to run. That is, both knew that after redistricting the ability to be reelected could change significantly for the incumbent and the state could either gain or lose a district, also changing the political landscape that the incumbents faced—perhaps forcing them to face constituents unfamiliar with their records (as happened to Condit in California) or campaign in districts with a different partisan balance (as happened to Horn). Knowing that challengers might take advantage of these factors, incumbents may be more likely to retire strategically right after redistricting. Before the advent of regular redistricting, coordination between strong challengers and incumbents would have been less likely, leading to more head-on contests between them. It is well-known that after the one-person, one-vote decision, the incumbency advantage increased. Cox and Katz maintained that the increased coordination ability is one reason why incumbency advantages increased, since incumbents who knew they would face strong challengers knew it would happen at a particular time and were better able to coordinate their retirement with the challenger's entry.

Cox and Katz measured incumbency advantages by using controls for the strategic effect and claimed that Democratic members of Congress in the 1970s and 1980s had little incumbency advantage while Republicans had a sizable advantage. Why the difference in incumbency advantage by party? During this period, the Republican Party was in the minority in the House of Representatives. According to Cox and Katz, this meant that the utility of being a Republican in Congress was significantly less, so that the candidates attracted to replace retiring Republicans were of a lower quality.[36] On the other hand, majority status for Democrats would attract more politically experienced, higher-quality candidates. This means that nonincumbent Republicans did particularly poorly in open-seat congressional races, and thus the difference between the performance of an incumbent Republican and that of his or her replacement was large, leading to a large incumbency advantage, even when using Cox and Katz's controls for the strategic entry or exit of strong challengers.

In summary, the entry decisions of candidates in U.S. House elections are influenced by the redistricting schedule, the party controlling redistricting, and the performance and potential exit decisions of incumbents, as well as the entry decisions of potential candidates. What may appear to be a strong advantage for incumbents in congressional elections may simply reflect differences in party strength in Congress as well as incumbents' strategic exit decisions coordinated through regularized redistricting.

Senate Elections

One of Louisiana Democrat Mary Landrieu's Republican challengers in 2002 (discussed in chapter 1) was former Congress member John Cooksey. Like eight of his colleagues, he chose to run for the Senate instead of Congress that year. But he lost, as Landrieu was reelected. Three of his colleagues who ran for the Senate did win—Saxby Chambliss of Georgia, John Sununu of New Hampshire, and Lindsey Graham of South Carolina. While the majority lost, in this sense Senate elections are a lot like House elections—political experience can make it easier to win. Table 11.7 presents a summary of the political experience of nonincumbent major-party candidates for the U.S. Senate in 2000. There are many fewer Senate races, so there are fewer candidates. Candidates with political experience tend to have higher levels of experience than do candidates in House races—for example, six former governors ran for the Senate in 2000. The one candidate who ran without political experience and successfully won nomination and the office was Jon Corzine in New Jersey (Hillary Clinton is classified as having party experience, and because Mel Carnahan died before the election and voters knew his wife, Jean Carnahan, who would be appointed in his place, he is classified similarly). Present and former members of Congress are likely in ten out of twelve cases to win Senate primaries when they enter Senate contests but less likely than state officials or governors to win general elections. This no doubt reflects the advantages of holding statewide office when running for the Senate. While a good percentage of Senate candidates are present or former state legislators, they do less well than candidates with higher levels of political experience. Notice that incumbency seems to be less of a deterrent for high-quality challengers and that

TABLE 11.7
Nonincumbent Major-Party Senate Candidates in Primaries and General Elections, 2000

Candidates' Political Experience	Total Number of Candidates	Candidates Who Won Primary	Candidates Who Won General Election	Candidates Who Faced No Incumbent
Member of Congress both present and former)	12	10	3	1
Former senator	1	1	0	0
Local official	7	2	0	0
Party official	7	5	2	1
State legislator	16	2	0	0
State official	6	4	2	1
Governor	5	4	4	2
No political experience	85	11	1	1
Total	139	39	12	6

high-quality challengers defeated a fair number of incumbents in 2002.[37]

While having political experience matters in Senate races, in other ways Senate elections are distinctive. Members of the Senate must be thirty years old and U.S. citizens for nine years. In contrast to members of the House, members of the Senate are elected for staggered six-year terms. That is, every two years, approximately one third of the Senate is up for reelection. Thus there is a longer time between voters' evaluations of incumbent senators than between their evaluations of incumbent representatives. Senators represent entire states, and each state has two (who are elected in different election years). So while the Senate is elected from double-member districts, each Senate election is separate, unlike a traditional multimember district. Even if retirement or death leads to the election of two senators from the same state in the same election year, the races are technically separate, with separate candidates, as when Barbara Boxer and Dianne Feinstein competed for the two Senate seats in California in 1992–while Boxer was running for an open Senate seat with a full six-year term, Feinstein's race was for the remaining two years of Pete Wilson's unfinished term.

As we noted earlier, it is not unusual for a single state, like Iowa, to have two senators, like Grassley and Harkin, whose policy positions on many issues are quite different. We pointed out that because senators are typically elected separately in different years, moderate voters might prefer to elect senators who cancel out an extremist on the other side of the ideological divide. Furthermore, we saw that senators are in general drawn to choose policy positions closest to the party position in their state in order to seek reelection (see chapter 9) and that members of the House of Representatives who seek upward mobility are more likely to be successful if they have chosen policy positions close to the party position in their state as well (see chapter 4).

Are Congressional Races Special?

In many ways, the factors that influenced both the decision to run and the electoral success (or lack of success) of Weatherford, McCollum, and Nunes in Congress and Cooksey and Landrieu in the Senate would have been the same if those candidates had been potential candidates for mayor, governor, or president. That is, the difficulties of facing an incumbent and the advantages of political experience (or celebrity) are similar. The requirement of periodic redistricting and reapportionment across states does make House races different, as we have seen, and affects the choices candidates have open to them. Members of Congress can find their districts taken away from them when the legislature meets, as Stephen Horn did, and given, in a new form, to a nonincumbent, like Nunes.

Sharing Power Once former football coach Tom Osborne was elected to Congress, he held eight meetings with farmers around Nebraska. At each meeting, two farmers were elected to meet at Kearney, Nebraska, to formulate a consensus farm policy. Barone, Cohen, and Ujifusa (2001, p. 939) reported: "After they produced their policy, Osborne said, 'Now we'll see where this meshes with the people in Washington. We're not going to reformulate a national farm policy, but we may be able to move people in our direction.'" Osborne knew that while he was a Republican and his party was in the majority, he was still just one of 435 members of the House of Representatives and lucky to get a seat on the Committee on Agriculture. Any changes in farm policy would have to result from more than just his and his constituents' efforts.

The fact that each state has two senators also can affect which candidates will be successful. One reason Republican congressman Greg Ganske was unsuccessful in his campaign to defeat Democratic senator Tom Harkin in Iowa may be that Iowa voters like balancing out the liberal Harkin with the more conservative Grassley. But an additional significant factor that affects both House and Senate elections is that once in office, officials find that making policy to please voters is a complex process, and the ability of an incumbent to do so depends on which party is in the majority in Congress and how power is shared.

Constituency Services Although Tom Osborne and his constituents cannot determine by themselves the nation's farm policy, there are ways in

which Osborne can help his constituents, perhaps mitigating their dissatisfaction with overall national policy and increasing his chances of reelection.
As Cain, Ferejohn, and Fiorina (1987) argued, members of Congress can
help their constituents with the vast and complicated federal bureaucracy—
they can do casework. Thus, members of Congress have a unique position as
intermediaries between constituents and the federal government. As such,
they typically maintain a staff in their district as well as in Washington just to
handle constituents' problems. Constituents, then, when they vote retrospectively for or against an incumbent member of Congress, evaluate not
just the incumbent's position on the issues and how he or she voted but also
how effectively he or she provided constituent services. These services are
like the valence issues discussed in chapter 5, and thus if incumbents are
seen to be more effective in providing them, they can have an electoral advantage.

Not All Members Are Equal

The Benefits of Being in the Majority Former Republican congressman
Mickey Edwards once compared his life on the Hill to that of his Democratic colleague Dick Gephardt:

> As a Democrat, [he] set agendas; as a Republican, I reacted to them. As a Demo-
> crat, [he] helped to set the terms for debate, deciding what, if any, amendments
> would be considered when legislation reached the House floor; as a Republican, I
> pleaded with the Rules Committee for a chance to offer alternatives. As Demo-
> crats, [he] and his party's committee chairmen decided who would be allowed to
> testify before congressional committees and on what bills; as a Republican I had to
> fight to get conservative views heard.[38]

Why did party make such a difference? Edwards served in Congress during
the forty years (1954–94) when the Democratic Party was in the majority.
Fenno (1997, p. 9, italics in the original) summarized the relationship between majorities and minorities in the House: "The two crucial structural
features of the majority-minority relationship are first that *the majority party
organizes* and runs the House and second that *the minority party adapts* to
the governing majority." The majority rarely consults with the minority on
scheduling of legislation. The majority party controls the organization of the
House, the selection of committee leaders, the jurisdiction of committees
and their size, the allocation of staff resources, and the internal procedures
of committees.[39] It is because being in the majority in Congress is so important that we see Texas Democrats running off to Oklahoma and Colorado
Republicans passing redistricting measures between census years.

Michigan Democratic representative John Dingell, who served with Edwards as a member of the majority party and subsequently as a member

of the minority, agrees with Edwards. Barone, Cohen, and Ujifusa (2001, p. 813) reported: "Asked what he had learned about being in the minority, he said 'Avoid it at all costs.' " Yet minority members of Congress are not completely powerless. Dingell ran for reelection in 2002 even though he had to defeat a fellow representative, Lynn Rivers, to do it, suggesting that he still valued the office and hoped his party would gain a majority. In 2005, Republicans outnumbered Democrats in the House of Representatives, with 232 Republicans to 202 Democrats, with 1 independent, Vermont's Bernard Sanders, who voted with the Democrats. In 2005, there were forty-four Democratic senators, one independent (James Jeffords, who voted with Democrats), and fifty-five Republicans.

Being Pivotal The extent to which majority parties dominate congressional policy choices is one of the more hotly debated questions in current American political science research.[40] As noted previously, however, in majority-rule situations, the voter at the median of voter preferences is pivotal in deciding outcomes. This can give moderate members of both parties majority and minority power. Moderate members of Congress and the Senate recognize the power that being close to the center gives them. Barone, Cohen, and Ujifusa (2001, p. 1106) noted that New York Republican representative Sherwood Boehlert "seems to relish the pivotal position he occupies in the House: as the Republican margin has shrunk [Democrats made gains in 2000], his voice and vote have become more important. 'This is the moderate moment,' he said in April 2000. 'Our time has come.' "

Although being moderate appears to give Boehlert apparent power over policy, a number of factors complicate this simple conclusion. First, many legislatures require supermajorities for the passage of bills—in Congress, if the president vetoes a bill, it must be passed by a two-thirds majority to override the veto. This factor shifts the pivotal voter away from the median when Congress wishes to make a policy choice that the president dislikes. Furthermore, since the majority party can control the agenda and membership on committees, it can structure the choices that are presented to the floor, further lessening the influence of moderates and the minority party.

In the Senate, voting can also be delayed by debate. The term *filibuster* describes the occasional consequence of this right—a filibuster occurs when a senator takes the floor and talks endlessly for strategic reasons. Traditionally, the advantage of filibustering has been that a senator can prevent legislation from being passed by monopolizing the Senate's time, preventing senators from carrying on other business as well as enacting the objectionable bill. The goal is to make the supporters of the bill in question voluntarily remove it from the Senate agenda.

Until 1917, the right to unlimited debate could not be abridged. In 1917, however, after a filibuster by a few senators prevented passage of a bill proposed by President Woodrow Wilson to arm U.S. merchant ships in response to the war in Europe, the president and the public demanded change, and the Senate adopted rule XXII, which provides for cutting off debate in the Senate, or cloture. Originally, rule XXII required a two-thirds majority of the Senate and was rarely used. Currently, cloture requires a three-fifths majority of the Senate membership (sixty senators). It is used more than before, but often cloture petitions are filed in advance of a debate. In the 1970s, the Senate adopted the practice of allowing legislation to proceed on different tracks, so that a filibuster could be paused and unrelated Senate business could continue. This lowered the cost of a filibuster for both a senator and the Senate. Nonetheless, the filibuster gives minorities significant power to delay legislation they do not like, and the pivotal voter can be the voter whose ideal point is at the three-fifths-majority point.

Seniority, Elections, and Incumbency

The Seniority System

Sherwood Boehlert was not only pleased with his status as a moderate in a closely divided Congress, but he was also proud of his seniority in Congress. He argued: "It's pretty easy to sum up why it's useful to be a high-ranking Member of Congress: the more seniority you have, the more you can help your constituents. . . . Thanks to my seniority, I've had the good fortune of attaining some key positions in the House of Representatives."[41] While we noted above that members and chairs of committees are chosen by the majority party, giving that party agenda control over the policies before the committees, another important factor in determining who gets positions of power on committees is seniority—or the number of terms that a member of the House has served. The seniority system developed in the 1910s and was dominant in determining positions of power from about 1912 until the 1970s reform movement. It was a two-part arrangement. The first part was a system whereby once a member of Congress had a position on a committee, he or she could not be involuntarily taken off that committee. That is, once a member was on a committee, he or she had a property right to a place on it. The second part of the seniority arrangement was an understanding that the member of a committee with the longest continuous service got to chair the committee whenever the chair became open.

   The seniority norm led in effect to a system in which, after initial placement on a committee, a member of Congress who succeeded in securing reelection could move toward a position of power (a chair) as older, longer-serving members chose to run for higher office or retire. Why might members of a committee prefer such a system? One factor in enacting legislation in Congress that we have largely ignored is the pork barrel, or distributive, nature of much congressional legislation. That is, consider the choices facing a congressional committee whose members must decide on the allocation of military bases across the country. A military base placed in a member's district can substantially increase income in that district by providing the associated civilian jobs and support services for the base. We have discussed J.C. Watts's efforts to make sure the air force base in his district was not closed, and we noted his claim that he gave up a position on the Appropriations Committee (which Osborne would have loved to get) in order to serve on the House Armed Services Committee.[42]

Seniority and Pork Barrel Politics

Suppose that a committee consists of three members, Adams, Barkley, and Campbell, each from a congressional district in a different state, and the committee wants to build nine more military bases.[43] It is straightforward to show that the members of the committee, who all prefer to build as many bases in their state as possible, face a problem in allocating the bases. That is, suppose Adams proposes that each get three bases in his or her state. But Campbell might propose that Barkley have four bases, he five, and Adams none. Campbell and Barkley would each vote for Campbell's proposal, and Adam's proposal would receive only one vote. Campbell's proposal will defeat Adams's. But then Barkley may propose that she, Barkley, have five bases, Adams three, and Campbell one, which would defeat Campbell's proposal. But Adams could counter with a proposal that he, Adams, have five bases, Campbell two, and Barkley two, which would defeat Barkley's new proposal. The making of proposals and counterproposals can potentially go on forever without a solution.

The problem facing the committee members is commonly called the paradox of voting, and we discuss it and how it affects American politics in more detail in chapter 14. For now, we will focus on one way in which the paradox can be avoided. That is, suppose the committee uses the following rule to make decisions: the chair of the committee, chosen by seniority, has the right to make a proposal on how to allocate the bases, and if his or her proposal is refused, the bases are uniformly distributed across the three states (each state receives three bases). We call the default option the reversion allocation of bases. Suppose the three legislators differ in seniority, with Adams currently in his third term in office, Barkley in her second term, and Campbell a freshman, or in his first term. By seniority, then, assume that Adams is the chair of the committee. He knows that if his proposal is defeated, each will get three bases in his or her state. If Adams wants to come up with a proposal that gives him more than three bases, he needs only two votes to win. Because he has one vote, he need only convince either Barkley or Campbell to vote with him. Either will vote for the proposal if it gives him or her at least four bases (one more than the reversion proposal). But if Adams gives both four bases, he has only one left, which is hardly preferable to him. If Adams chooses to give four bases to only one, Barkley or Campbell, he can have five for himself and defeat the reversion proposal. Suppose Adams uses seniority to determine whether Barkley or Campbell gets the four bases. Then his proposal will be that Barkley gets four, he gets five, and Campbell gets zero. His proposal will pass.

Of course, the seniority system that gives Adams the right to make the first proposal works only if the committee members are willing to vote for that system over some other allocation rule. One alternative might be that the chair is determined by a random draw in which each member has an equal chance of attaining the position and then the committee member getting the extra base, so that the chair can win his or her majority, is also chosen randomly. How many bases could each member expect to get in such a system? One third of the time a member would get to be chair and receive five bases, another third of the time a member would get to have four bases, and the last third the member would get zero bases. The expected number of bases would be $(1/3) \cdot 5 + (1/3) \cdot 4 + (1/3) \cdot 0 = 3$. Clearly, both Adams and Barkley prefer the seniority system to such an alternative if they are risk neutral or risk averse.

Seniority as a Reason to Vote for Incumbents

For voters, the seniority system also leads to clear advantages to reelecting incumbents. For example, suppose that voters in Adam's district have a choice between him and an opponent. Voters know that if they reelect Adams, he will be advantaged by the seniority system (as Boehlert tells his constituents they will be advantaged by his seniority), their state will get more bases, and Adams will vote for the seniority system. Similarly, voters in Barkley's district will choose her over an opponent who would then be in his or her first term, and voters in Campbell's district will vote for him on the chance that either Adams or Barkley will be defeated or will retire, knowing that Campbell is still advantaged over a new member by having served one term. Seniority distribution of resources and incumbency can then work hand in hand and can be hard to dislodge once they take root.

Although the analysis above shows how a seniority system can be used effectively to solve the paradox of voting that is inherit in issues of resource distribution, it is also possible for seniority to thwart the goals of the majority party if the senior members of the party have preferences for policy choices that are at variance with those of the majority in the party. In the 1970s, many new Democrats (whose party was in the majority) believed that the seniority structure was problematic for achieving their policy goals as a whole because senior members did not always share these goals. As a result, Democrats instituted two noted reforms in the system: (1) committee assignments were taken away from the majority-party membership (which at the time was the Democratic Party) of the Committee on Ways and Means and given to a party committee dominated by the Speaker of the House and other majority-party leaders, and (2) an automatic ballot was instituted to ratify nominees for committee chairs, leading to greater violations of the seniority norm. Note that when the majority party voted on whether to use the seniority system, the majority preferred it. A leader has the flexibility to work for what might be best for the party as a whole, however, so by giving themselves power over the committees and the chair assignments, the leaders were able to make choices that benefited the party's policy goals but violated seniority. In the 1990s, when Republicans gained control of the House of Representatives, they also wanted to give the party majority more control over policy and so instituted stronger controls on the role of seniority and term limits for committee chairs. In general, while seniority is a factor in allocating positions of committee power, it is not the current determining factor, and increasingly the loyalty of potential committee chairs to majority-party policy preferences plays a significant role.

Party Control, Positions of Power, and Upward Political Mobility

Republican Representative Nick Smith from Michigan, who retired from the House in 2004, had decided to vote no on the Medicare bill presented before Congress on November 22, 2003, because he believed it was too expensive. According to a posting he made on his Web site the next day, "Because the leadership did not have the votes to prevail, this vote was held open for a record two-hours-and-51-minutes as bribes and special deals were offered to convince members to vote yes." Smith also claimed that after being personally lobbied by Speaker Dennis Hastert (Republican from Illinois) and by Tommy Thompson, secretary of health and human services, "other members and groups made offers of extensive financial campaign support and endorsements for my son Brad who is running for my seat. They also made threats of working against Brad if I voted no." Smith said his son told him to stay with his no vote.[44] In September 2004, the House Ethics Committee concluded that majority leader Tom DeLay had offered a political favor to Smith for his vote and admonished DeLay but took no further action.[45]

In chapter 4, we noted that most elected officials are career oriented and that most candidates for office have some elective experience. We also observed how lower-level elected officials might be induced to make choices that please party elites, who influence nominations for higher-level offices when they make choices retrospectively. We saw that members of the House, for example, whose policy choices in the House are closest to the overall party position in the state are more likely to run for the Senate and to be their party's nominee in the general election.

In legislatures like the U.S. House of Representatives, where power is unevenly distributed, some members, through committee chairs and other positions, have greater agenda control than other members. This power can affect the policy choices as well as the distributive benefits, or pork, that the legislator can bring to his or her district. When seniority determines how these positions of power are distributed, representatives have an incentive to continue to please their district voters and their district party elites (in order to achieve reelection) if they anticipate that achieving power through seniority in Congress has a higher expected utility than running for a higher elective office. And, as we noted, voters and party elites have an incentive to reelect incumbents who are more likely to have the extra power accorded by seniority.

If, by contrast, the majority party pays attention to loyalty to its preferences as a whole in allocating positions of power and other resources, as well as seniority (as in the current Congress), then representatives may have to balance out the preferences of the voters and party members in their district with the preferences of the party majority in the House. While what Smith was allegedly offered to vote the way his party leaders preferred was support for his son's congressional campaign, if he was not retiring it might have been a coveted committee membership or chair or position of power within the party organization. If these two preferences coincide (if the preferences of voters in a representative's district coincide with those of the party leaders in Congress), it is almost as if the member of Congress were "destined" for power within the House.[46] For others, district voters and party elites may be willing to accept some deviation from their preferences so that their representative can achieve power for the distributional benefits, or pork, that power can bring to the district. However, if the majority party's position is far from the preferences of the voters in the district, power seeking by a representative may be impossible and lead to defeat if he or she makes policy choices that are at variance with his or her constituents' preferences—he or she is a "doomed" member.

For example, in the 1992 election, Democratic representative Marjorie Margolies-Mezvinsky of Pennsylvania promised her constituents that she would vote against any tax increases. But in 1993, because of pressure from Democratic House leaders (then the majority party in the House), who needed her vote to pass a tax measure, she broke that promise and was defeated in the 1994 election. Republican representative Cass Ballenger (discussed in chapter 10) faced a similar dilemma when he voted for free trade despite the job losses in his district. Thus, making choices to please the majority-party elites in the House might help a member achieve a position of power, but only if the representative's voters are willing to go along with the choices. In some cases, an ambitious politician from a district in which the preferences of voters are far from those of the party elite in Congress and for whom both achieving a position of power and winning reelection are not possible may choose upward political mobility to further his or her career instead of staying in the House of Representatives. Moore and Hibbing (1998) analyzed the retirement decisions of members of Congress from 1960 to 1996. They found that members who were less likely to achieve positions of power through seniority and those whose policy positions were far from the average party position in the House were more likely to retire, ceteris paribus (all other factors being equal).

What We Know

While this chapter is primarily about congressional elections, we also gain from the discussion some general knowledge about the relationships between incumbents and challengers. We know why weak challengers may take on incumbents when strong ones will not, and we have seen how this phenomenon increases the advantages incumbents appear to have. Evidence also suggests that successful challengers are likely to have political experience in lower-level offices, supporting our earlier observation that voters use retrospective voting when candidates attempt to compete for higher-level offices. More specifically with respect to legislative elections, we know that the advent of regular redistricting after each census has made it easier for congressional incumbents and strong challengers to coordinate entry and exit. When weak incumbents retire rather than face a difficult election, that coordination may also create the illusion that incumbents have an electoral advantage. We know that drawing district boundaries in congressional and other legislative elections can affect both the elections and the balance of power between the major parties. We also know that partisan officials in control of redistricting have an incentive to maximize districts they control, and evidence suggests that partisan control of redistricting does influence congressional delegations. Finally, we know that voters might be willing to vote for incumbents because of the advantages incumbents may receive in the distribution of district-specific benefits as their seniority increases, but if the preferences of voters in a district are far from those of the majority party in Congress, their representative faces the difficulty of choosing between pleasing party leaders and pleasing voters.

What We Don't Know: Moving Down the Street

In spring 2003, nine Democrats declared their candidacy for the nomination of their party for the presidential election of 2004: former Vermont governor Howard Dean, North Carolina senator John Edwards, Missouri representative Richard Gephardt, Florida senator Bob Graham, Massachusetts senator John Kerry, Ohio representative Dennis Kucinich, Connecticut senator Joe Lieberman, former Illinois senator Carol Moseley-Braun, and activist and civil rights leader Al Sharpton. Of these nine, seven are current or former members of either the House or the Senate. Although each of them had successfully competed and won office in the U.S. Congress, they knew that presidential elections in the United States have their own unique features that can affect which candidate wins election. In the next chapter, we analyze how presidential contests work, beginning with the nomination battle that the candidates fought.

Study Questions and Problems

1. In the game between Weatherford and Roberts in this chapter, how would Weatherford's and Roberts's choices on whether to compete against Watts in 2000 change if they thought that there was a 10 percent probability that Watts would decide to drop out of the race a week before the general election, at a point when no other candidate could enter the race and Watts's challenger would win by default?

2. Suppose Sandy is a Democratic leader designing the congressional districts in his state and ideologically his ideal point is at 40. His state had 120 voters with ideal points at 80, 210 voters with ideal points at 60, and 120 voters with ideal points at 40. He has three districts to design. Without his delegation, there are 216 members with ideal points at 60 and 216 members with ideal points at 50.

   a. Can Sandy gerrymander the districts in his state to affect the median voter in Congress?

   b. How does your answer change if Sandy is a conservative gerrymanderer with an ideal point at 80?

   c. How do your answers to 2a and 2b change if Sandy is from a small state with only two congressional districts? (Assume that without his delegation there are 217 members in Congress with ideal points at 60 and 216 members with ideal points at 50.)

   d. If Sandy's state has only one congressional district, he cannot use gerrymandering to affect the congressional median. What implication about the representation of liberal and conservative voters in Congress can you draw from the fact that the size of a state can facilitate gerrymandering?

3. In this chapter, we discuss how the congressional seniority system can solve the problem of voting on the redistribution of resources and how that system might be perpetuated. Consider an alternative system, in which Adams, Barkley, and Campbell are given agenda control over proposals to distribute air force bases according to how often they vote with the majority-party leadership on general policy issues. The majority party's ideal point is at 40. The ideal point of the median voter in Adams's district is also 40, but the median voter's ideal point in Barkley's district is 60, and in Campbell's district it is 90. Under such a system, would voters be willing to reelect incumbents at the same rate as they would under a seniority system? Would voters prefer the alternative system or the seniority system? Which system would candidates prefer? Which system fits reality better, and why?

NOTES

1. Under the federal law, the Employee Retirement Income Security Act of 1974, or ERISA, patients can sue for the dollar value of services found to have been improperly denied but not for damages resulting from the denial. ERISA also preempted existing state laws that allowed for such suits; thus, Weatherford could not sue in state court.
2. Ron Jenkins, "HMO Issue Tailor Made for Democrats," Associated Press State & Local Wire, September 1, 2000.
3. Curt Brown, "McCollum Draws on Experience in and out of the Political Arena," *Minneapolis Star Tribune*, October 25, 2000.
4. John Ellis, "Congress Races Fail to Stir Up Interest," *Fresno Bee*, October 6, 2002.
5. Lewis Griswold, "Young Candidate Put on 20th District Ballot," *Fresno Bee*, February 4, 1998.
6. In some states, voters were required to vote for as many candidates as there were offices—that is, to select a "full slate"—in an effort to reduce the influence of minority voters. In chapter 15, we discuss these measures and why they were discontinued.
7. See Cox and Katz (2002).
8. Karen Masterson, Armando Villafranca, Michael Hedges, and R. G. Ratcliffe, "DeLay Backs Federal Aid to Track Down Walkouts," *Houston Chronicle*, May 14, 2003.
9. Jay Root and Maria Recio, "Homeland Agency Defends Search for Missing Democrat's Plane," *Fort Worth Star-Telegram*, May 16, 2003.
10. See David Rennie, "Yessiree, These Democrats Mean Business," *London Daily Telegraph*, May 15, 2003.
11. See Erikson (1972) and Cox and Katz (2002).
12. Jim Wooten, "Our Opinion: Democratic Coup under Gold Dome," *Atlanta Constitution*, September 2, 2001.
13. "GOP leaders also agreed not to challenge the reapportionment plan in the courts, as they had in 1981 and 1991." See Bill Hillburg, "Fixing to Retain the Seats: Most House Races a Done Deal," *Daily News of Los Angeles*, October 20, 2002.
14. There are a lot of theoretical problems with assuming that the voters would vote the same way in these new districts, as voters may be voting Republican in one district because they are happy with their particular Republican representative's stature in the House of Representatives (he or she serves on an important committee for the district), but they might be willing to vote for a Democratic representative who does not have that particular experience. Votes for Democratic representatives may be similarly changed in the new districts with different candidates. But the point is the same—to the extent that a party can measure voters' preferences for parties' candidates independent of such effects and the party controlling the redistricting has the majority in the state, designing districts that are like the state in preference distribution maximizes the members elected by the party (giving the party complete control over the state's delegation).
15. Michigan is obviously a state where competition between the two parties is intense. In 2000, Democratic presidential candidate Al Gore received 51.3 percent of the vote, and in 2004 John Kerry received 51 percent. In 2002, Democrat Jennifer Granholm was elected governor with just 51 percent of the vote, but Republicans controlled both houses of the state legislature.
16. This is the definition used by Cox and Katz (2002); see also Erikson (1972).
17. See Cain (1985) for an analysis of different types of plans.
18. Gilligan and Matsusaka (1999) showed that as the population of a state in-

creases and/or the number of districts declines, partisan bias is likely to increase. Gelman and King (1994) examined the effects of partisan control on redistricting in state legislatures and found that redistricting results in both increases in responsiveness (because of increased uncertainty in election outcomes) and partisan biases that benefit the party in control of redistricting. Besley and Case (2003) also found evidence of a relationship between partisan bias in state legislatures and partisan control of redistricting.

19. See Nedra Pickler, "Dingell and Rivers Work to Motivate Divided Democratic Voters in Michigan Primary," Associated Press State & Local Wire, August 4, 2002, and Nedra Pickler, "Dingell-Rivers Contest Features the Elder Statesman vs. the Woman Who Overcame Adversity," Associated Press State & Local Wire, July 20, 2002.

20. More precisely, Shotts's (2002) analysis demonstrated that in equilibrium, liberal gerrymanderers maximize the number of representatives from their state whose ideal points are to the left of the unique equilibrium in national policy, and conservative gerrymanderers maximize the number of representatives from their state whose ideal points are to the right of the unique equilibrium in national policy.

21. See, for example, Adam Nagourney, "States See Growing Campaign for New Redistricting Laws," *New York Times*, February 7, 2005.

22. See Nedra Pickler, "Court Dismisses Democratic Lawsuit against Redistricting," Associated Press State & Local Wire, June 7, 2002.

23. A probit analysis of whether a state's congressional delegation is majority conservative as a function of the control over redistricting and the ideology of the state shows that control over redistricting is significant at the 6.4 percent level (ideology is significant at the 0.7 percent level). An estimation where the dependent variable is the percentage of conservative members of a state's congressional delegation shows that control over redistricting is significant at the 1.3 percent level, also controlling for ideology.

24. These district boundaries were challenged as racial gerrymandering by six Texas voters in 1995–see *Thomas v. Bush* (1995) and *Bush v. Vera* (1996)—and the Federal District Court for the Southern District of Texas declared three districts' boundaries unconstitutional. The Supreme Court affirmed this ruling, and the district court redrew the boundaries when the legislature failed to act in time for the next election. We discuss issues of minority representation in more detail in chapter 15.

25. Carl Hulse, "Colorado Court Rejects Redistricting Plan," *York Times*, December 2, 2003.

26. See Loie Fecteau, "Dems Want to Redraw Districts," *Albuquerque Journal*, February 19, 2003; John Williams, "Redistricting Fight Spilling Over: Democrats in Oklahoma, New Mexico Resisting GOP Drive," *Houston Chronicle*, May 16, 2003; Jim Myers, "Redistrict Fuss Not an issue," *Tulsa World*, January 18, 2004; and David Miles, "Richardson Won't Add Redistricting," *Albuquerque Journal*, February 13, 2004.

27. John M. Broder, "Schwarzenegger Proposes Overhaul of Redistricting," *New York Times*, January 6, 2005.

28. John W. Mashek, "Midwest Primaries Extend Incumbents' Slump," *Boston Globe*, August 6, 1992.

29. Jeffrey McMurray, "Hilliard: Runoff Loss Just the Beginning of Black, Jewish Conflict," Associated Press State & Local Wire, June 28, 2002.

30. Vicki McClure and Tom Gordon, "Davis' Win Seen as Sign Voters More Independent: Historically Influential Black Groups Backed Hilliard," *Birmingham News*, June 27, 2002. Cynthia McKinney was defeated by Denise Majette in a controversial race between African Americans in a district with a large black mi-

nority population (formerly created as a black majority district). The two candidates split the black vote, with Majette receiving the votes from black precincts in high-income areas and McKinney winning votes in poorer neighborhoods; see Ben Smith and Mae Gentry, "Majette Win Reflects Racial, Economic Shifts in DeKalb," *Atlanta Journal-Constitution*, September 1, 2002. Majette won by building a coalition of whites and high-income black voters who were unhappy with McKinney's focus on national issues.

31. The standard error for closed primaries is 0.0510497, and for semi-closed or open primaries it is 0.0534652. The t-statistic for the comparison of mean is −3.7391. See Gerber and Morton (2004).

32. The standard error for closed primaries is 0.0362135, and for semi-closed or open primaries it is 0.0425176. The t-statistic for the comparison of means is −4.7846. See Gerber and Morton (2004).

33. The eight contests in which incumbents faced each other were in Connecticut district 5, where Republican Nancy Johnson defeated Democrat Jim Maloney in the general election; Georgia district 2, where Republican Bob Barr lost in the primary and Democrat Sanford Bishop then won the general election; Indiana district 7, where Republican Brian Kerns lost in the primary and Democrat Julia Carson won the general election; Michigan district 15, where Democrat John Dingell defeated Lynn Rivers in the primary and then won the general election; Mississippi district 3, where Republican Charles Pickering defeated Democrat Ronnie Shows in the general election; Ohio district 17, where both James Traficant and Tom Sawyer were defeated by fellow Democrat Timothy Ryan (Sawyer in the primary and Traficant in the general election as an independent); Pennsylvania district 12, where Democrat John Murtha defeated Frank Mascara in the primary and then won the general election; and Pennsylvania district 17, where Democrat Tim Holden defeated Republican George Gekas in the general election. Incumbents who ran for another office include Bob Riley (Alabama), Saxby Chambliss (Georgia), Rod Blagojevich (Illinois), Greg Ganske (Iowa), John Cooksey (Louisiana), John Baldacci (Maine), Robert Ehrlich (Maryland), Jim Barcia (Michigan), David Bonior (Michigan), John Sununu (New Hampshire), Lindsey Graham (South Carolina), John Thune (South Dakota), Van Hilleary (Tennessee), Bob Clement (Tennessee), Ed Bryant (Tennessee), Ken Bentsen (Texas), and Thomas Barrett (Wisconsin). Incumbents who retired from Congress in 2002 without running for another office include Sonny Callahan (Alabama), Bob Stump (Arizona), Stephen Horn (California), Bob Schaffer (Colorado), Dan Miller (Florida), Carrie Meek (Florida), Tim Roemer (Indiana), Marge Roukema (New Jersey), Joe Skeen (New Mexico), Benjamin Gilman (New York), John LaFalce (New York), Eva Clayton (North Carolina), Wes Watkins (Oklahoma), J. C. Watts (Oklahoma), Bob Borski (Pennsylvania), William Coyne (Pennsylvania), Dick Armey (Texas), and James Hansen (Utah). Of these, Stump would have faced fellow incumbent John Shadegg if he'd run in the new district that contained most of his old district; Horn would have faced Grace Napolitano; Chambliss would have faced Mac Collins; Roemer would have faced Mark Souder; Ganske would have faced Tom Latham; Barcia would have faced Dale Kildee; Gilman would have faced John Sweeney; LaFalce would have faced Amo Houghton; Watkins would have faced Frank Lucas; Borski would have faced Phil English; Coyne would have faced Michael Doyle; and Barrett would have faced James Sensenbrenner.

34. Rodriguez won the Republican primary and went on to challenge California Democratic incumbent Cal Dooley but lost in the general election; Rooker lost the Democratic primary in a crowded open-seat contest in Pennsylvania.

35. See Banks and Kiewiet (1989) for a formal exposition of this game.

36. For evidence on this, see, for example, Gilmour and Rothstein (1993) and Ansolabehere and Snyder (1997).
37. Tom Carper defeated incumbent William Roth in Delaware, Debbie Stabenow defeated Spencer Abraham in Michigan, Mark Dayton defeated Rod Grams in Minnesota, Mel Carnahan defeated John Ashcroft in Missouri, George Allen defeated Charles Robb in Virginia, and Maria Cantwell defeated Slade Gorton in Washington.
38. Mickey Edwards, "A Tale of Two Reps: Study in Contrasts," *Boston Herald*, January 10, 1995.
39. See Fenno (1997). Binder (1997) and Dion (2001) present analyses of how the majority parties control the House.
40. For different points of view on this subject, see Aldrich (1995), Cox and McCubbins (forthcoming) and Krehbiel (2000).
41. See the statement on Boehlert's Web page, Congressman Sherwood Boehlert, http://www.house.gov/boehlert/welcome.shtml, July 17, 2002.
42. Of course, military bases have some detrimental effects, but we will assume here that the effects from the standpoint of the districts are all positive.
43. The example that follows is based on the analysis of McKelvey and Riezman (1992).
44. Nick Smith, "A Medicare Showdown," United States Congressman Nick Smith, November 23, 2003, http://house.gov.nicksmith/col.31123.htm.
45. Charles Babbinton, "Ethics Panel Rebukes DeLay," *Washington Post*, October 1, 2004.
46. For a formal analysis of this argument, see Kanthak (2002).

~12~

Presidential Primaries

Skipping Around or Sitting in Place?

On Sunday, October 19, 2003, retired army general Wesley Clark and Connecticut senator Joseph Lieberman, both candidates for the Democratic nomination for president in 2004, pulled their campaigns out of Iowa, where the first contest of the nomination season was to take place on Tuesday, January 20, 2004. Instead, they would focus on the New Hampshire primary, scheduled for January 27, and the primaries and caucuses in seven states on February 3. Political experts were surprised at the decisions. Jenny Backus, a Democratic strategist who was neutral in the contest, noted: "The harsh reality of a Democratic primary is you have to put numbers on the board. You have to wonder where and when those numbers start racking up [for Clark and Lieberman]."[1]

Clark and Lieberman knew that historically, winning Iowa has not meant winning the nomination—for example, the first Iowa Democratic caucus, in 1972, selected Edmund Muskie, who lost the nomination to Iowa's second-place finisher, George McGovern; in 1980, the first president Bush won the Republican caucus but lost the nomination to second-place finisher Ronald Reagan; in 1988, both Robert Dole and Dick Gephardt won their parties' contests but lost the nomination to Iowa's third-place finishers, the first president George Bush and Michael Dukakis; and in 1992, winner Tom Harkin lost the nomination to Bill Clinton (who received only 4.1 percent of the Iowa caucus vote). Thus, in five out of the ten contests in which no incumbents ran, winning Iowa did not seem to matter. Moreover, never before had so many states been holding contests so packed together. Mounting a campaign across those states was costly. Both candidates were having trouble raising money, compared with former Vermont governor Howard Dean, the current front-runner. Why not concentrate their limited resources and time on states also voting early, albeit not first, that the candidates felt they were more likely to win. Why not pick and choose?

Like Clark and Lieberman, in late fall 2003 John Kerry was behind and having serious trouble raising campaign funds. As we discussed in chapter 6, Kerry lent himself money to keep his campaign going. He made the opposite decision of Clark and Lieberman—he put all his efforts into Iowa, both time and money, and did not campaign aggressively in the other states. His campaign staff in New Hampshire "shuddered at the idea of not having their candidate in the Granite state during the key weeks before the primary."[2] Political pundits also criticized Kerry, as they did Clark and Lieberman. In an editorial in the *Boston Herald*, Wayne Woodlief wrote:

> Kerry's gamble in Iowa is risky. Candidates who have relied on Iowa to bail them out in the past have exhausted their resources there and had little left to sustain a campaign anywhere else. That's why ex-Gov. Michael Dukakis, a better money-raiser, was able to outlast Rep. Richard Gephardt and the late Sen. Paul Simon after they finished one-two ahead of him in Iowa in 1988. Dukakis mercilessly blitzed Gephardt with tough 'flip-flop' ads in other states and the Missouri congressman was too cash-poor to fire back.[3]

It turned out that Clark and Lieberman had made bad decisions and Kerry had made a good one, as we will see. In 2004, winning the Iowa caucuses mattered more than ever, particularly because the primaries were so compressed. Why was this true? How had the presidential primary schedule become so compressed? How does such compression affect which candidates are selected as nominees? In this chapter, we answer these questions. We begin with the process of getting on the ballot for the presidential primaries.

What It Takes to Get on the Ballot in the Primaries

The Rules

The formal qualifications for presidential candidacy are contained in Article II, Section 1, of the Constitution, which limits the presidency to natural-born citizens who have lived in the United States at least fourteen years and who have reached the age of thirty-five (so Devin Nunes could not have run for president in 2004). There is some dispute as to the meaning of "natural-born," namely, whether children born to U.S. citizens abroad are eligible, but no candidate has ever directly challenged this issue. The

Twenty-second Amendment to the Constitution (ratified in 1951) limits presidents to two terms.

As we discussed in chapter 1, presidents and vice presidents are elected through the Electoral College system, rather than elected directly by voters. Originally Electoral College members were selected by state legislatures, but currently they are selected directly by voters. We discuss the effects of the Electoral College system on candidates' and voters' choices in presidential elections in chapter 13. But first the candidates must get on the ballot. Although the election is national, state electoral laws govern issues of ballot access. The difficulty of attaining ballot access in all fifty states is a strong impediment to minor-party and independent candidates for the presidency— we will discuss minor-party and independent candidates more fully in chapter 14.

To get on the ballot as a major-party candidate, a candidate must first win the nomination of a major party, which may mean getting on the ballot in the many state primaries, as state primaries now largely determine who wins the nomination. The process of getting on state primary ballots can be extremely difficult and expensive, as Republican senator John McCain discovered in 2000.

The Experience

On a snowy day in January 2000, Republican senator John McCain stood in front of the Russian consulate in New York City. In an appearance on NBC's *Tonight Show with Jay Leno* in 2002, he recalled his reason for calling a press conference there: "I don't know if you remember or not, Russian elections were taking place at that time, and they had three or four names on the ballot. . . . New York State had only one on the ballot."[4] Republican George W. Bush had built a huge campaign chest in 1999 and had the nationwide support of Republican Party leaders. New York Republican governor George Pataki (called Comrade Pataki by McCain) was one of those supporters. And in New York State, to get on the ballot statewide for the March 7 presidential primary, a candidate had to get a petition signed by at least 0.5 percent of a party's voters, or 1,000 Republican Party members in each congressional district, in thirty-seven days between December and early January. With thirty-one congressional districts, this meant 15,500 Republican voters signing petitions. Moreover, in heavily Democratic congressional districts, there were few registered Republicans to draw from (in the eleventh district, for example, there were only 15,872 registered Republicans at the time of the primary). Finally, even if a voter was verified as a registered Republican, his or her signature could be struck from the list if the voter had failed to list his or her town or city in addition to a residence address. McCain was having trouble meeting these qualifications, and his name was not on the ballot in all areas of the state when he spoke before the consulate.

Bush's supporters in New York knew the difficulties and how they could make it even tougher for McCain. *The New York Observer* reported that in December, New York State Republican Party chairman William Powers "sent out a memo admonishing Mr. Bush's district coordinators: 'To ensure that Bush delegates get on the ballot in your Congressional district, your goal is to collect six times the signatures required by the election law.' "[5] Why six times the minimum? Because Bush's supporters knew that names on his list would decrease the number of names available for challengers like McCain. They also knew that there would be legal challenges to the signatures, and they planned to do some challenging themselves. The cost of such legal battles is sizable; in 1996, Senator Bob Dole's campaign budgeted $700,000 for post-petition challenges.[6] With less money than Bush and little support among Republican leaders in the state, McCain did feel as though he was in Siberia instead of Manhattan.

Anticipating the battle, McCain's supporters asserted in December that they would sue to get access. After McCain surprisingly defeated Bush in the New Hampshire primary, McCain's criticism of Bush and Pataki began to stick to candidate Bush, and Bush sent the signal to Pataki to back down. Pataki announced that all Republican candidates would be allowed to have their names on the ballot for the New York primary. So the names of Bush, McCain, Alan Keyes, and even Steve Forbes (who had dropped out of the race) appeared on the ballot. About the same time, addressing McCain's supporters' court case, U.S. District Court judge Edward Korman declared the ballot-access rules unconstitutional.

But voters like Angelo Fatta had trouble finding the candidates' names on the ballot. Since voters were really voting for delegates pledged to support a candidate at the national convention, the names of the delegates appeared on the ballot along with those of the candidates. Unlike the Democratic ballot in New York State, on which candidates' names were larger than delegates' names, the candidates' names were much smaller than the delegates' names on the Republican ballot. Fatta, like a number of other voters, could not find his preferred candidate's name and, according to *The Buffalo News*, "ended up backing George W. Bush. 'I admit it, I didn't read the fine print.' Fatta said."[7] McCain lost the New York primary and withdrew from the presidential contest two days later.[8]

Hyperspeed

As McCain discovered, getting on the ballot was just part of the war; the main battle was winning the primary, and even with the voting problems in New York, on the first Tuesday in March, McCain lost not just in New York but in California, Georgia, Maine, Maryland, Missouri, and Ohio, winning in Connecticut, Massachusetts, Rhode Island, and Vermont for a much smaller delegate total than Bush (eleven states voted on the same day on both coasts and in the South and the North). The support Bush built in 1999 was extremely difficult for a challenger to stop, particularly in the highly compressed primary calendar. In the presidential contests in the 1970s, the presidential primaries were spread out in the months prior to the national conventions. Candidates could spend weeks focusing on one state at a time. But McCain did not have that luxury, and voters on the second Tuesday of March were irrelevant in the contest. In 2000, even a state like Texas, which had moved its primary to the second Tuesday in March in 1988, found that its votes did not matter in the Bush-McCain contest, as McCain had withdrawn five days before the state voted (although anticipating a large number of votes for Bush in Texas and other southern states probably led to McCain's withdrawal before Bush had enough delegates to win the convention, which may imply that Texas voters did make a difference).

In 2003, the Texas primary date was an issue before the state legislature. Shortly after the Killer D's came back to Austin from Oklahoma in May 2003 (see the discussion in chapter 11), a bill that passed the Texas state senate would have moved the state's presidential primary from the second Tuesday in March, March 9, to the first Tuesday, March 2. The March 9 date conflicted with the scheduled spring break in most school districts in the state, and the election would therefore cost more, as the state would have had to pay to open the schools, where many voted, and hire additional security. Moreover, ten other states, including sizable New York and California, would be voting on March 2, and by March 9 the nomination contest could be over. Only two of the thirty-one state senators showed up to vote on the bill, but no one objected and the vote was recorded 31–0 (if they give their prior approval, Texas state senators can be recorded as voting even if not physically present).[9]

But after the congressional redistricting battle was finally won by Texas Republicans in October 2003, Republicans pushed through a bill returning the primary date to March 9. Republicans claimed that they would not get final approval of the new congressional plan until January (because Texas is a "covered" jurisdiction under the Voting Rights Act, the plan had to be approved by the Justice Department, a topic we discuss in chapter 15), and it would be impossible to schedule in the candidates' filing times, ballot printing, and the thirty days that overseas Texans who are members of the military are given to vote. But Democrats criticized the plan as undemocratic and worried about its hurting the ability of Texas voters, particularly minority voters, to influence the outcome of the contest for the Democratic presidential nomination.[10]

Texas was not the only state considering moving earlier in the primary schedule in 2003. On May 28, Tennessee state lawmakers sent the governor a bill to change their primary from March 9 to Feb. 10. The *Chattanooga Times Free Press* reported: "U.S. Rep. Harold Ford Jr., D-Tenn., called the change of primary 'a positive thing. It'll get all the candidates paying more attention to us.' "[11] Earlier in the month, Wisconsin had voted to move its primary date from April to February 17. The *Milwaukee Journal Sentinel* reported: " 'Nothing is guaranteed' by the earlier date, acknowledged the state Democratic chairwoman, Linda Honold, but she hopes and expects the state will have significance. 'I just can't imagine by the third Tuesday in February, with nine candidates to sort through, they're going to have it all figured out by then.' "[12] But beating Wisconsin, Tennessee, and Texas, Arizona's Democratic governor Janet Napolitano moved her state's primary to February 3 (and vetoed a bill from the Republican-controlled state legislature to abolish the primary because of the state budget crisis). Table 12.1 presents a list of the states that moved their primary dates forward for the nomination contest in 2004.

TABLE 12.1
States that Moved Their Presidential Primary or Caucus Date for 2004

2004 Date	*Jurisdiction*	*2000 Date*
January 13, 2004	District of Columbia	May 2, 2000
February 3, 2004	Arizona	February 22, 2000 (Republicans); March 7, 2000 (Democrats)
	New Mexico	June 6, 2000
	Missouri	March 7, 2000
	South Carolina	February 19, 2000 (Republicans); March 9, 2000 (Democrats)
	Oklahoma	March 14, 2000
February 7, 2004	Michigan	February 22, 2000 (Republican); March 11, 2000 (Democrats)
	Washington	February 29, 2000
February 10, 2004	Virginia	February 29, 2000 (Republicans); June 3, 2000 (Democrats)
	Tennessee	March 14, 2000
February 17, 2004	Wisconsin	April 4, 2000
February 24, 2004	Idaho	May 23, 2000
	Utah	March 10, 2000

Watching the jockeying for dates, the Democratic presidential candidates and their campaign managers geared up for a nomination process in 2004 that would be more compressed than that of any previous year. Anticipating the race, Chris Lehane, then a worker for Massachusetts senator John Kerry, remarked, "I think things will move in hyperspeed."[13] Lehane was right. Kerry surprised pundits by winning New Hampshire, Iowa, and then most of the remaining states in the early contests.

By the time Texas had its 2004 primary, although ten Democrats were on the ballot, only one major candidate, John Kerry, was still active. John Edwards, Kerry's last major opponent, after failing to stop Kerry sufficiently in the Super Tuesday contests of March 2, canceled planned visits to San Antonio and Dallas on Wednesday, March 3, and returned home to North Carolina to withdraw from the race. In an Associated Press report, Edwards's spokesman in Texas, Kelly Fero, complained about the movement of the primary date: "While Republicans say the date change was necessary to allow enough filing time for congressional candidates, Fero said the Republicans just wanted to prevent a parade of Democratic presidential candidates from coming to Texas and pointing out Bush's failings. 'That was a stated goal of the Republicans. They wanted to take Texas out of play.' "[14] If Texas had been in play, would Edwards have done better in the contest with Kerry? Moreover, how did such a primary calendar develop? How did the slow, leisurely pace of the 1970s primaries change to "hyperspeed"? To understand how it occurred, we need to examine the evolution of the presidential nomination system.

What It Takes to Get Nominated

When Conventions Made Real Choices

The World before Primaries The history of early presidential electoral politics is intricately connected to the story of the development of the American party system and excellently reviewed elsewhere.[15] Here we highlight the way in which parties' processes of nominating candidates for the presidency evolved into the present front-loaded system and the resulting concerns of policy makers.

Initially the early American parties worked through caucuses that were composed of party members serving in Congress who met to choose nominees for president. As the mass political party developed, however, it became clear that those representatives' choices were not electable and were affected by the limited membership of the caucuses. Parties gradually turned to national conventions, therefore, drawing delegates from state parties, which had developed over time along national-party divisions. By the 1840s, national mass electoral parties, really confederations of the state parties, had evolved, and the process of choosing nominees for the presidency by national conventions of delegates from the state parties had taken hold. The important effect of this period for our current system is that it established the role of parties as more than legislative caucuses—and cemented the role of states and individual voters, at first indirectly, in the presidential nomination process.

Primaries in a Supporting Role

The Advent of Presidential Primaries The advent of presidential primaries in 1901 changed the process of presidential nominations, although party leaders retained ultimate control over nominations until after 1968. Direct primaries were an innovation of the Progressive movement and were used widely by the turn of the century for nominations for statewide office. As Jewell (1984, p. 7) explained, direct primaries served different purposes in northern and southern states. In the West and Midwest, direct primaries were attractive for two reasons: "a theoretical belief in direct democracy" and

> because the primary offered the best vehicle for wresting control over the parties—and nominations—from conservative forces. The Progressives concentrated most of their efforts on the Republican Party, which was the normal majority party in most states. The Democratic Party usually offered a poor alternative, both because of voter loyalties to the Republican Party and because Democratic leadership was often conservative and/or ineffective.

The South, in contrast, used direct primaries with participation restricted to whites in order to maintain white Democratic control over the region, as discussed by Kousser (1974). The conservative southern Democratic leadership feared that factions within the party might break away and mobilize black voters. They established the norm that unsuccessful white candidates would not challenge the nominees in general elections. Since blacks were largely Republican and other measures, such as poll taxes and literacy tests, had restricted black voters' turnout, the direct primary allowed the white Democratic Party to maintain control by handling dissent within its ranks. The success of the use of primaries in the South to unify white voters in the Democratic Party is illustrated by the analysis of McCarty, Poole, and Rosenthal (2005), who found that in the 1950s in the South, income had virtually no effect on the partisanship of voters in NES surveys—both rich and poor southern whites identified themselves as Democrats during this period. (We discuss the "white primary" more expansively in chapter 15.)

Direct primaries were first extended to presidential nominations in 1901, when Florida passed a law allowing state parties to conduct direct primaries to select national convention delegates.[16] In 1905, a year after the national Republican Party rebuffed Governor Robert La Follette's delegates for others chosen in caucuses controlled by party elites, Wisconsin enacted direct primaries for presidential nominations. The early use of presidential primaries was a natural extension of the desires of the new state leaders to either secure dominion from old state party leadership, as in Wisconsin, or maintain white Democratic domination in the South. Presidential primaries were much more prevalent in northern states than southern ones at the time, however. The first modern presidential primary law that resembles the ones used now was enacted in 1910 in Oregon, where voters chose between both competing candidates and slates of delegates. By 1912, California, Illinois, Indiana, Massachusetts, Nebraska, New Jersey, New York, Pennsylvania, and South Dakota had instituted presidential primaries. In his attempt to take over the Republican Party in 1912, Theodore Roosevelt competed in those primaries, winning nine. He was unsuccessful at the convention, however, because of the dominance of William Howard Taft's supporters among the delegates.[17]

The idea of presidential primaries replacing state conventions was definitely popular among some policy makers and academics. In 1915, in the *American Political Science Review*, Francis Dickey called for national presidential primaries. President Woodrow Wilson, in his first annual message after election, also advocated expanding the role of primaries. Nonetheless, Wilson's desired legislation was not enacted and in fact only states explicitly regulate the parties' procedures for nominating candidates; there is no regulation of nominations at the federal level.[18]

The Decline of Primaries Despite continued growth in presidential primaries (reaching a peak in 1916, with twenty Republican primaries accounting for 58.9 percent of delegates to the national convention), they declined in use in the 1920s.[19] As Palmer (1997, p. 68) remarked, presidential primaries "had not produced candidates with mass popular appeal and had proved time-consuming and often prohibitively expensive. The prospect of unwanted nominees foisted by ignorant voters on reluctant party leaders dimmed its luster still further, while to most party officials the primary represented an open invitation to fratricidal conflict."

It is interesting that while some states eliminated primaries, others used methods of restricting choices so that primaries could still be used for statewide offices but had less of an effect on presidential nominations. Caesar (1982, p. 24) noted that some states retrenched from Progressive reforms by "the de factor insulation of the primaries from the national focus through laws that barred delegates from specifying on the ballot which candidate they preferred; and the development of a tradition in some states, enforced by the power of the state parties, of running favorite sons in the primaries." Many existing presidential primaries never specified the names of the presidential candidates on the ballot but listed only the delegates.[20]

It appears then that the motivations behind the use of primaries for statewide offices in the late nineteenth and early twentieth centuries did not translate well to the presidency. That is, primaries were used in the South to prevent white factions of the Democratic Party from breaking out and joining with black Republican voters within the states, but racial solidarity was less an issue in presidential nomination contests in those states where state-level races were sufficient for the unification desired.[21] Presidential primaries, even during the heyday of the Progressives, were used on a much more limited basis in the South. As Progressives decreased in strength in Republican states, their ability to wrest control, never sufficiently strong at the national level, diminished. Thus, presidential primaries declined.

<u>Making Primaries Count and Premonitions of Front-Loading</u> Nevertheless, primaries did continue to play a role in presidential nominations, and that role increased over time. Norpoth's (2004) presidential forecasting model, discussed in chapter 10, predicts winners of the elections based on performance in presidential primaries. Norpoth found a significant relationship between success in primaries and predicted vote share in the general election from 1912 to the present. Palmer (1997) reported that in 1928 Al Smith and Herbert Hoover used primaries, in one case to demonstrate that a Catholic could receive votes outside New York State and in the other to squash a possible opponent. In 1932, Franklin D. Roosevelt attempted to use primaries to discourage Smith. Wendell Willkie's lack of success in Wisconsin's 1944 primary hurt his chances for selection as the Republican nominee. Most notably, in 1948, Harold Stassen of Minnesota came close to using primary victories combined with media publicity to take an underdog route to nomination.

Stassen's success induced midwestern states such as Indiana, Montana, and Minnesota to revive their presidential primaries by 1952. Palmer (1997) argued that not just the increase in primaries but the candidacy of Dwight Eisenhower marked "a pivotal year in the emergence of the modern campaign process." He noted (p. 69): "The candidacy of General Eisenhower was launched by the New Hampshire primary of March 1952. In this and succeeding primaries, the general's backers demonstrated their candidate's popular appeal to national and state Republican Party leaders and to the electorate at large. Eisenhower's victories proved crucial for delegate accumulation and in wresting the nomination from Robert Taft at the convention."

But Eisenhower's success was not the only one influenced by presidential primary victories after World War II. Adlai Stevenson, despite receiving the Democratic nomination in 1952 without participation in primaries, attained the nomination in 1956 after defeating Estes Kefauver in the California primary. As with Willkie in 1944, he entered the primaries to demonstrate that he could win despite loosing as his party's nominee in the previous presidential election. In 1960, John F. Kennedy used primaries to demonstrate his electability to Democratic Party leaders. Richard M. Nixon was a winner in Republican primaries in both 1960 and 1968. Barry Goldwater used success in primaries to achieve the Republican nomination in 1964. The first rejection of a primary winner since 1956, that of Eugene McCarthy in 1968, was, as Epstein (1986) stated, "in extraordinary and politically disastrous circumstances."

More telling than the relationship between primary winners and nomination choices from 1956 on is the fact that from 1948 for Republicans and from 1952 for Democrats, nominations were decided on the first convention ballot. Party leaders increasingly appeared to make commitments prior to the conventions. Thus, conventions were becoming less significant in determining the nominee—that is, the negotiation and bargaining was occurring *before* the convention and whether by primary victories or high standings in polls, nominees were expected to demonstrate that they had public support. The nomination determination was occurring earlier in the electoral season and was influenced by primaries. State party leaders began to make commitments and negotiate earlier, a premonition of front-loading.

<u>The Impact of the Mixed System</u> Current problems in presidential primaries are partly a consequence of developments during the mixed period. Three such developments are important:

- Parties, their nomination processes, and elections in general are largely regulated at the state level. This makes any kind of national reform of the presidential nomination process difficult. It is a reason why front-loading has occurred—states may all prefer that contests be spread apart, but because they see that their own self-interest is served by moving their primaries closer to the front of the season, all primaries end up bunched together.
- Conventions largely ceased to be the place where nominations were settled—gradually candidates were nominated on the first ballot. This meant that delegates were being "promised" prior to conventions and that the process by which delegates were promised became more important for securing a nomination.
- National political parties, with formal staffs and goals, gained power. However, the relationship between the national parties and the candidates became complex since national party rules can have an effect on which candidates are selected.

Primaries in a Starring Role

Reforms That Mattered Much has been written about the post-1968 Democratic reforms in delegate selection and the consequences those reforms have had for the presidential nomination process.[22] In general, the post-1968 period has led to the dominance of primaries in determining presidential nominees. Other changes during the post-1968 period, of course, have had a contributing influence on presidential campaigns, such as campaign finance legislation (discussed in chapter 6) and changes in the national news media (discussed in chapter 8). But the arrival of national rules controlling how state parties select delegates has had a profound effect. Interestingly, although only the Democrats officially reformed their presidential nomination system, the Republican Party was also significantly affected,

primarily because individual state regulations apply to both parties. Therefore, changes in state laws instituted to respond to Democratic reforms also
affected Republican primaries.

The changes in the rules post-1968 are rather complicated and have been
manipulated over time. The principal original goal of these reforms was to
open up the process by which nonprimary states chose delegates to a
broader spectrum of party members. This was mainly accomplished by the
requirement of participation by rank-and-file party members, either through
direct primaries or through the encouragement of such participation in the
caucuses and conventions, the alternative to primaries. Yet there were significant variations over time, which are instructive. First, while there is a definite preference over the thirty years for delegate choice in the Democratic
Party to be proportional to vote totals, there are also consequential devia-
tions over time in the degree of proportional representation and the tendency to reintroduce a role for party leaders. The first reform commission of
the Democratic National Committee (DNC), McGovern-Fraser (1969–72),
eliminated the unit rule and required that at least 75 percent of each state
delegation be selected at a level no higher than that of congressional districts. The Mikulski Commission (1972–73) required proportional representation, with a few exceptions, forcing California, for example, to change
from winner-take-all to proportional representation. Candidates were required, however, to meet a 10 percent threshold of votes to be allocated
delegates, which was later increased to 15 percent. The Winograd Commission (1975–78) permitted states with at-large delegates to set their own
thresholds, with a 25 percent threshold for delegates chosen at the district
level, but banned winner-take-all primaries for the 1980 election. The Hunt
Commission (1981–82) allowed some states to have winner-take-all primaries, allowed "winner-take-more" primaries, in which winners got extra
delegates, and created "superdelegates" (14 percent of the total number of
delegates) for the 1984 convention, who were chosen on the basis of party
status or public office. The Fairness Commission (1984–85) increased the
number of superdelegates for the 1988 convention but lowered the threshold for candidates to 15 percent of the delegates. In 1992, winner-take-all
and winner-take-more primaries were banned yet again. Palmer (1997,
p. 75) noted:

> The DNC's prevarication over this issue was symptomatic of the vulnerability of
> successive rules reviews to the whims of powerful candidates such as Carter, Mon-
> dale, and Jesse Jackson. It also demonstrated the importance that delegate alloca-
> tion was deemed to have in determining the dynamics of primary momentum.
> Proportionate allocation, the commission believed, would take the edge off Iowa
> and New Hampshire by slowing the pace of delegate accumulation and forcing
> candidates to spread their resources more evenly. The presence of winner-take-all
> primaries later in the contest was, conversely, seen as essential in persuading can-
> didates not to fold their tents after discouraging early results.

While the Democratic Party has gone back and forth over whether to allow winner-take-all primaries, Republicans, have been agnostic on the issue, and as a consequence, more Republican primaries are winner-take-all. State leaders see an advantage in having winner-take-all primaries, as they make their state a larger prize for candidates to compete over. Republicans also allow for open primary participation of nonparty members if a state chooses, while the Democratic Party has either banned outright or allowed only a few open primaries. Thus, while both Democratic and Republican primaries have become dominant in determining the nominees of their parties and subject to many of the same state regulations, there are important party differences in the way presidential primaries are held. Winner-take-all elections can allow a candidate to gain large delegate counts more quickly, leading to shorter contests. Furthermore, as noted in chapter 4, Gerber and Morton (1998), found that in more open primaries, members of Congress are more moderate relative to the voters in their districts, suggesting that presidential nominees may be affected by the difference. Certainly many argued that John Edwards's greater vote totals in open primaries like Wisconsin's (discussed in chapter 4) and McCain's success in Michigan in 2000 could be partly attributed to sincere crossover voting by members of the opposition party or by independents.

Primaries Rise Again As mentioned in the preceding section, the writing of the first set of reforms was largely dominated by members of the DNC and their staff. Ironically, the reformers believed that by making state and local caucuses more open, there would be a decline in the demand for presidential primaries and primaries might actually decrease in use and influence. Reformers expected and wanted greater use of caucuses, which require voters to participate at a different level—that is, discussing candidates in small groups with other voters—a town-hall-meeting idea of democracy. Instead, many states opted to add direct primaries and in some cases caucuses that are more like elections than the ideal of the reformers (for example, as discussed in chapter 3, Michigan's Democratic Party used Internet and early voting for its 2004 caucus, making it easier for voters to vote without the personal interaction of going to the caucus location).

Caucuses did not increase for a number of reasons. First, the caucus process under the new rules is more complicated to manage, with participation required first at the precinct level, then at a county convention, and finally in a statewide convention. The difficulty of satisfying those detailed requirements added the specter of a state's delegation being refused a role at the convention, as Richard Daley's Illinois delegation was in 1972. Second, there is an advantage to states from the media exposure of a primary election—there is a greater degree of voter participation since participation is less costly in terms of time, and thus in general it becomes a larger contest with more interest shown by the electorate. Finally, state party leaders may fear that ideological extremists—supporters of particular candidates—will dominate caucus choices, leading to candidates who will be less successful with the general public. There is evidence that caucus participants are less representative of the general electorate than primary voters; in particular, they are stronger partisans and more ideological.[23]

The increase in the use of presidential primaries after 1968 is startling given that the last increase in presidential primaries had occurred in 1956, when Florida Republicans and the District of Columbia first held primaries. In 1968, only sixteen states and the District of Columbia had presidential primaries: Alabama, California, Florida, Illinois, Indiana, Massachusetts, Nebraska, New Hampshire, New Jersey, New York, Ohio, Oregon, Pennsylvania, South Dakota, West Virginia, and Wisconsin. By 1972, six more states had switched to presidential primaries: Maryland, Michigan, New Mexico, North Carolina, Rhode Island, and Tennessee. By 1976, seven more states had switched—Georgia, Idaho, Kentucky, Montana, Nevada, Texas, and Vermont—while only New Mexico switched back to a caucus-convention system. Arkansas made its optional primary compulsory. In less than ten years, the number of states holding presidential primaries had almost doubled.

This trend continued through 1980, when thirty-five states and other convention constituencies (such as Guam and the District of Columbia) in the Democratic Party and thirty-four in the Republican Party used presidential primaries. However, 1984 did experience a decline, as a number of states dropped their primaries and only twenty-five Democratic and thirty Republican states and other convention constituencies held presidential primaries. Yet by 1988 those numbers had almost rebounded to previous levels. Since 1988, the number of Democratic primaries has leveled off while the number of Republican primaries has continued to increase substantially. By 1996, thirty-six states were holding Democratic presidential primaries and forty-three were holding Republican presidential primaries.

The number of delegates selected by presidential primaries rather than caucus conventions experienced a similar strong increase. In 1968, 37.5 percent of Democratic delegates and 34.3 percent of Republican delegates were chosen by presidential primaries. By 1976, those percentages were 72.6 percent and 67.9 percent, and in 1980 they were 71.8 percent and 76 percent. In 2004, only 16.66 percent of Democratic delegates were superdelegates. It is striking to note that although the reforms were written and devised to change the Democratic Party, they also affected the way in which Republican Party delegates are chosen in that by 1996, 88.3 percent of Republican delegates were selected through presidential primaries. This is partly because both parties are affected by changes in state regulations, which are required to satisfy the national Democratic Party's requirements.

Nevertheless, Republicans have continued to use some methods by which voters' preferences and delegate selection are disconnected. Some states formerly had a legal ban on the identification of a delegate's presidential candidate. While the national Democratic Party had achieved full compliance

with a prohibition on this type of primary by 1976, Republican primaries in
Illinois, Mississippi, New York, and Pennsylvania used this type of primary in
1980 (as noted earlier, in 2000 in New York the candidates' names, although listed, were much smaller than the delegates' names). Republicans
have not attempted to reduce winner-take-all primaries. In 2000, over half
of the Republican primaries were winner-take-all, some used winner-take-all
if a candidate received a majority of the vote and proportional representation
if not, and about one fourth used proportional representation. Thus,
Republican contests benefit early front-runners more than Democratic contests do since mathematically a candidate can build a majority quicker even
through close wins.

Another significant difference between the two national parties exists in
the voters allowed to participate in the delegate-selection process. While the
Democratic Party has attempted to restrict participation in primaries and
caucuses to party members (requiring, with some few exceptions, closed primaries or caucuses), the Republican Party has allowed somewhat more open
primaries and caucuses, allowing for crossover voting by nonparty members.
Moreover, Republicans, unlike Democrats, do not have superdelegates.
Thus, Democratic controls suggest that delegates are chosen by a more representative group of rank-and-file party members and party elites, while Republican controls allow for delegates to be chosen by a wider distribution of
the general electorate.

Spaced-Out Primaries, 1972–84

While the increase in primaries is the most notable aspect of the plebiscitary
system, there are substantial differences over time in how they have been organized. Two types of plebiscitary candidate nominations have occurred:
nomination contests in which voting is sequential and drawn out and nomination contests in which voting is closer to simultaneous, as in a virtual
national primary (after voting by Iowa and New Hampshire) because of
front-loading of primaries earlier and earlier in the schedule. The first contests under the new system, in 1972, 1976, and 1980, were clearly more
drawn out than the later ones, of 1988–2004, with 1984's contest a mixture. In the first contests, it became apparent that the schedule of primaries
mattered, and this realization led to manipulation of the schedule and front-
loading.

When Sequence Did Not Matter In the later years of the mixed period,
while demonstrating public support through either polls or primaries was
crucial for securing the presidential nomination of the major parties and evidence exists that much of the bargaining occurred prior to the national
convention, the sequence and schedule of primaries were not as big an issue
as they were to become post-1968. The proliferation of primaries made the
sequence in which they were scheduled important. Prior to 1972, since pri-

maries did not determine the outcome, candidates could pick and choose which ones to enter and seek support from convention delegates based on poll results as well as primary outcomes. The key is that during the mixed period, candidates for the nomination not only entered primaries to gain votes at the convention (to achieve direct popular support, which gained a set of delegates) but also used polls and other mechanisms to influence state party leaders (who determined the vast majority of the delegates). Polls and other mechanisms could play an important role pre-1972, and the sequence of the primary outcomes was less important. States scheduled primaries to fit their own electoral calendars, which varied because of state-specific calendar issues, such as harvest times, local holidays, and so on.

Post-1968, primary delegate votes have been a greater percentage of the outcome. But the mechanics of caucus-convention choices have also been significantly different, since rank-and-file members have been given greater roles in determining delegate choices. With greater participation by rank-and-file party members, both through direct primaries and in caucus conventions, the majority of delegate votes are now in the hands of these members rather than in the hands of party leaders. This has meant that unless a state's voters could choose early enough in the process, before one candidate got a majority of the delegates, their votes would not be consequential. Theoretically, if two or more candidates are in a close contest for the nomination through the end of the primary season, the votes of a state scheduled late in the season could make a difference in the outcome. But over the years, candidates have become "winners" earlier and earlier in the season, a phenomenon popularly called momentum. States that wait until late in the season to vote are increasingly inconsequential.

When Sequence Became Important, or the Story of the Killer Bees The Killer D's (discussed in chapter 11) were not the first Texas Democratic state legislators to walk out rather than vote on a bill they disliked. On May 18, 1979, twelve legislators walked out of the Texas state senate (ten hid out in an Austin garage studio apartment). Why? Former Texas governor John Connolly was going to run for president in 1980 as a Republican.[24] But Lieutenant Governor Bill Hobby and other conservative Democrats in Texas were worried. The presidential primary in the state would be held in May, at the same time as the primary for state legislators and members of Congress. If conservative Democrats crossed over in Texas's open primary to vote in the Republican contest for Connolly, then the Democratic primary would be dominated by liberals, who would vote against the conservative Democrats.

Hobby came up with a solution. Texas would have two primaries, one for president, held in March, and then a second one for state and congressional races, in May. That way the conservative Democrats could vote in both primaries. Of course, liberal Democrats did not like this idea at all, and the Republicans (in the minority in the state at the time) were also eager to have the presidential primary in May since they wanted more conservative Democrats to join the Republican Party. Hobby gave in to the Killer Bees, as the opposition to Hobby was called at the time, and the split-primary idea was defeated, as was Connolly, who withdrew from the presidential race on March 9, 1980, when he was decisively trounced by Ronald Reagan in the South Carolina primary. Connolly, despite spending millions, having come in to the campaign with the most money, won only one delegate.[25] Having a primary late in the season was costly for Texas in 1980, since by the time voters voted, their favored candidate was no longer in the race. By 1988, Texas had moved its primary to March.

FIGURE 12.1
Compression of Republican Primaries

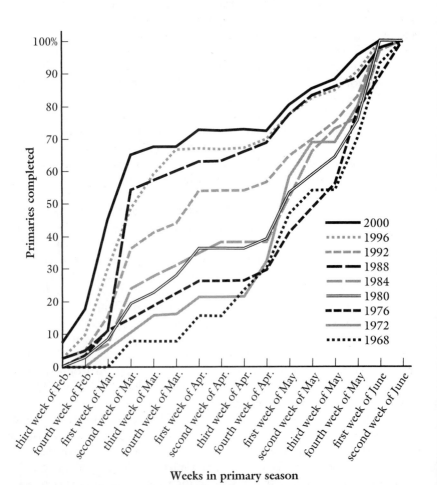

Weeks in primary season

FIGURE 12.2
Compression of Democratic Primaries

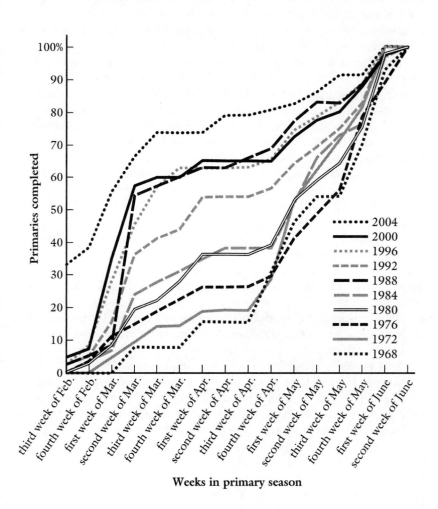

Weeks in primary season

Front-Loaded Primaries, 1988–2004

Texas was not the only state that moved up its primary date in 1988. Figures 12.1 and 12.2 show how the percentage of primaries held by week in the primary season has risen over time (2004 for Republicans is omitted since Bush had very little opposition). The figures show how primary front-loading began to increase in 1988. There is also ample evidence that candidates with the ability have attempted to manipulate not just ballot-access rules but the scheduling of primaries to their advantage, as Connolly's supporters tried to. For example, in 1992, Arkansas governor Bill Clinton induced Georgia governor Zell Miller to get Georgia's Democratic primary moved so that it would be held a week earlier, helping Clinton win the nomination (Barone, Cohen, and Ujifusa 2001, p. 432).

As Palmer (1997 p. 78) remarked: "With the formation of the Winograd Commission in 1976, primary scheduling became a target for candidate organizations seeking to mold the timetable to their political advantage, and post-Mikulski reform bodies soon degenerated into intraparty squabbles between the most influential candidates of the period." Democratic national reforms have generally led to a shorter primary season. The Winograd Commission shortened the Democratic primary season from six to three months, while the Hunt Commission reduced the period of time between the Iowa caucuses and the New Hampshire primary from thirty-six days to eight.[26] In contrast, until 1996, the national Republican Party had not attempted to control the primary schedule.[27]

Perhaps the first example of front-loading was not the movement of a primary to an earlier date but the placement of Iowa's caucuses in 1972 ahead of New Hampshire's historic first-in-the-nation primary. Iowa's caucuses became an important early stomping ground for candidates, and publicity followed, which is why Clark's and Lieberman's decisions not to campaign there were surprising to many political experts.[28] At first, states resisted front-loading. It began in earnest with the first southern regional primary, labeled Super Tuesday, held on the second Tuesday in March in 1984. While the first Super Tuesday involved a total of nine states (five primaries and four caucus conventions held simultaneously), in 1988 twenty-one states and convention regions held primaries or caucuses on one Super Tuesday, resulting in the selection of 31.4 percent of Democratic delegates and 33.1 percent of Republican delegates simultaneously.[29]

The year 1992 did show a decline in front-loading in presidential primaries, as shown in figures 12.1 and 12.2. Yet these graphs are misleading since they omit caucus states. Despite the decrease in front-loading of primaries in 1992, thirty-one states (more than half) held primaries or caucuses by the end of March of that year. Moreover, front-loading of primaries was reinvigorated in 1996, with nearly equal the compression of primaries in 1988. Notably, delegate compression in 1996 superseded 1988 levels because of front-loading. Arizona, Delaware, and Louisiana, with varying degrees of success, attempted to hold either caucuses or primaries in advance of or extremely close to Iowa and New Hampshire. New England states held a "Junior Tuesday" of primaries prior to Super Tuesday. Most substantially, large states such as California, Ohio, and New York moved their primary dates closer to the beginning of the primary season. California's primary was held in June in 1988 and 1992, but in 1996 its 165 Republican delegate votes and 422 Democratic delegate votes were determined in the fourth week of March. Ohio's primary (67 Republican delegate votes and 172 Democratic delegate votes) was in May in 1988 and 1992 but on "Big Ten" Tuesday, March 10, in 1996. New York's primary (102 Republican delegate votes and 289 Democratic delegate votes), in April in 1988 and

1992, was held on March 7 in 1996, two days after Junior Tuesday. As discussed above, in scheduling the 2004 contests, states continued the front-loading (see table 12.1). In summary, by 1996 the plebiscitary system had evolved, through front-loading, to a virtual national primary for the states after Iowa and New Hampshire. States front-loaded their primaries because over time later states found the outcome virtually decided before they voted—that is, early wins or successes were turned into big wins, and competing candidates dropped out. Contests were decided before later voters had a chance to choose. Thus, states bunched their contests toward the beginning of the season, shortly after those of Iowa and New Hampshire.

Why did later states become inconsequential? Mathematically it was always possible for a close contest to be decided at the end of the primary season rather than at the beginning if candidates who were behind could have successes later. But candidates like Connolly and others dropped out after early losses, or if they stayed in the contest, they failed to be successful. While it is true that the winners in Iowa and New Hampshire did not always become the nominee, as noted at the beginning of this chapter, it became increasingly true that early success in these states and others meant that later states were simply too late. Skipping Iowa, as McCain did in 2000 and Clark and Lieberman did in 2004, was deemed a mistake, and it hurt.

How the Current System Works

Do Voters Learn during Primaries?

Susan Crotto, a forty-year-old schoolteacher from Keane, New Hampshire, was not sure whom to vote for in the upcoming primary after she learned the results in Iowa. She summarized her dilemma: "I really thought Clark was the best person to beat George Bush until the Iowa caucuses."[30] Twenty-one-year-old Sean Luther, a political science major at Clemson University in South Carolina, also looked to the results in Iowa, as well as those in New Hampshire, in thinking about whom to vote for in South Carolina's primary a week after New Hampshire's. A newspaper report noted Luther's conclusion: " 'The big thing New Hampshire showed us is that Clark isn't as popular as he thought, and Lieberman . . . just totally blew it.' Luther had liked former Vermont Gov. Howard Dean's stance on issues. Then he heard his screaming concession speech in Iowa. 'I was totally turned off.' "[31] Luther decided that he was leaning toward John Edwards or John Kerry.

As noted in chapters 7, 8, and 10, initial research on presidential-election campaigns in the 1940s by sociologists such as Paul Larzarsfeld suggested that voters did not alter their preferences much during the campaigns and concluded that campaigns and the mass media had a minimal effect on voters' preferences. Similarly, early research conducted once primaries became important in the nomination process also suggested that nothing much happened during the primaries as well. For example, in a study of voters' information levels during the 1980 primary season, Keeter and Zukin (1983) argued that there was little evidence that voters "learn" during primaries. However, recent analysis shows a different story. Bartels (1988) and Popkin (1991) demonstrated that during presidential primary campaigns, voters' information levels do change in response to campaign events and news-media reports. Norrander (1989, 1993) showed how voters' preferences for candidates develop during nomination contests.

In earlier chapters, we discussed how voters can use a Bayesian learning procedure to update their evaluations of candidates as they gain information and how voters' preferences can change as a result of new information. Using that approach, Alvarez and Glasgow (1997) applied a Bayesian model of voter learning to the 1976 and 1980 primary-election campaigns. Using data on both media reports and voters' evaluations they found support for their model. Interestingly, they showed that in 1976 voters demonstrated a high level of learning about Jimmy Carter when he began as an unknown but much less in 1980, when he ran as an incumbent, despite the fact that in both cases the amount of substantive information provided about Carter during the campaign was large. Similarly, examining 1984, Bartels (1988) found that at the beginning of the campaign, voter evaluations of Walter Mondale were initially better formed (that is, they were based on Mondale and his campaign positions) than were the evaluations of Gary Hart (which were based more on anti-Mondale sentiment), but during the course of the campaign the evaluations of Hart became more like the evaluations of other candidates (that is, they were based on Hart and his campaign positions).

Learning by Voting in Presidential Primaries

The preceding literature and chapters 7 and 8 discuss how voters can learn from campaign messages and events in election campaigns. Yet those mechanisms cannot explain why later primaries became increasingly inconsequential in determining which candidates were nominated in the 1980s and 1990s. In presidential primaries, voting is sequential. This means that voters learn how others have chosen before they choose. Voters are doing more than just making their estimates of candidates' policy positions and qualities more precise and therefore stabilizing preferences during the primary season based on traditional campaign messages and events—they are also using the choices of earlier voters in that process. Hence, the information conveyed to later voters in presidential primaries is fundamentally different from, as well as more complicated than, the information conveyed in other election campaigns.

How do earlier voting decisions convey information to later voters? Later voters can learn two types of information from earlier voting in presidential primaries: (1) information about a candidate's policy positions or general qualities and (2) information about how successful a candidate can be in defeating the "opposition," or the expected candidate in the general election. As we discussed in chapter 4, voters in primaries care about their expected utility. If there is uncertainty about the ideal point of the median voter in the general election, these voters will weigh the closeness of a candidate's policy positions against the probability that the candidate can win in the general election (the candidate's electability), and the weights and estimates they will place on these matters will also vary with the information they have. We saw how voters Bob Peter, Jana Jayroe, and George Hollman in the South Carolina primary in 2004 varied both in the weight they placed on electability versus policy and in their uncertainty over which of the candidates would be most likely to win in the general election (for example, although Jayroe thought Edwards or Kerry might be more electable, she was willing to support Dean, whose policy positions she preferred, because electability was not as important to her; in contrast, Peter chose Kerry over his first choice, Clark, because of electability issues; and Hollman chose Edwards both for electability and policy preferences).

What we did not discuss in chapter 4 was how these South Carolina voters were forming their impressions of the candidates after learning about the voting in Iowa and New Hampshire. How did that voting affect their impressions of the policy preferences of the candidates and their chances of winning in November? Since this is a complicated process, we will divide it into two parts. First we will consider how later voters can learn about the candidates' policy positions through sequential voting, ignoring electability (that is, we assume voters are myopic and are just looking for the candidate to win the nomination who would give them the highest utility given what other voters are doing). Then we will consider how voters learn about electability.

Learning about Policy

Voters in Iowa To see how voters can learn about policy positions of candidates when voting sequentially, we will work through a simple model. Suppose that there are three types of voters: liberals, moderates, and the conservatives. The voters are divided into states, which will vote sequentially, as in the presidential primary system. Iowa voters will choose first, then New Hampshire voters, then voters in the rest of the states. The winner of the election is the candidate who gets the most votes of all the votes combined. The voters know that candidates can be one of three types as well, a liberal, a moderate, or a conservative. Assume that liberal voters have ideal points where a liberal candidate's policy position is located, moderate voters have ideal points where a moderate candidate's policy position is located, and conservative voters have ideal points where a conservative candidate's policy position is located. Then liberal voters' first preference is a liberal candidate, their second preference is a moderate candidate, and their last preference is a conservative candidate. Conservative voters have the opposite preferences. Moderate voters' first preference is a moderate candidate and see both a liberal or a conservative candidate as equally bad.

Now suppose that there are three candidates, named Libby, Manny, and Connie. Libby is a liberal, Manny is a moderate, and Connie is a conservative. However, voters in Iowa, who will vote first, don't know the policy positions of all the candidates, but they do know the policy position of one of the candidates. Why might this be the case? We can think of the candidate they know as the candidate who is well-known because he or she has run in past campaigns or because he or she is from Iowa (as Tom Harkin was) or a nearby state, like Missouri (as Dick Gephardt was) or because he or she is the incumbent president or vice president (as Al Gore was). There are three possibilities: (1) the voters know for sure that Libby is a liberal but are uncertain about the positions of Manny and Connie; (2) the voters know for sure that Manny is a moderate but are uncertain about the positions of Libby and Connie; or (3) the voters know for sure that Connie is a conservative but are uncertain about the positions of Libby and Manny.

How will the Iowa voters choose? Assume that no voting type is a majority and the Iowa voters are just voting according to their policy preferences. In the first case, when Libby's policy position is known and Manny's and Connie's positions are unknown, liberal voters are likely to vote for Libby, and the other types will randomize their votes, choosing between Manny and Connie. If the liberals are large enough as a voting group, Libby can win. Similarly, in the third case, when Connie is the one candidate whose policy position is known, conservative voters will be likely to vote for her and the other types will randomize, choosing between Libby and Manny. If the conservatives are large enough as a voting group, Connie will win. The second case is a bit more complicated and depends on how risk averse voters are. If voters are risk averse, then Manny will get votes from all types and will win even if the group of moderate voters is not sizable. This is because the liberal and conservative voters would be willing to vote for their second preference, Manny, over the lottery between a liberal and a conservative. If the group of moderates is sizable, then Manny is even more likely to win.

In summary, who wins in Iowa in our simple example depends on the distribution of voters' preferences and which candidate is better known by the voters. If a particular ideological group has a majority in Iowa and one candidate has a policy position that is close to the group's position and the candidate is better known than other candidates, that candidate will be advantaged and is most likely to win in Iowa. If voters are risk averse and a moderate candidate is better known than the other candidates, the moderate candidate is likely to win Iowa. Moreover, the moderate candidate will win with a larger percentage of the vote than a liberal or conservative would receive if one or both were well known because the moderate candidate attracts the votes of all types of voters.[32]

We can see this effect in the Iowa caucuses in 2004. Kerry was not doing well in Iowa in December as compared with Dean (who had built up support through the Web) and Gephardt (who had campaigned there in previous years and is from a neighboring state). Kerry decided that he needed to put an all-or-nothing effort into getting to know the voters in Iowa, meeting one-on-one with as many as possible. Clark and Lieberman chose not to campaign heavily in Iowa, and voters there knew less about them than they knew about Kerry, Dean, Edwards, or Gephardt. Kerry was not doing well there before he decided to spend extra time in the state. As Iowa's voters got to know him as well as Gephardt and Dean, they revised their preferences, favoring him more. Edwards also benefited from the time he spent in Iowa. Clark and Lieberman, however, by not spending time there, did not gain votes. Obviously, being well-known in itself is not why Kerry beat Gephardt, Dean, and Edwards, who were also spending time in Iowa. Kerry won because when Iowa voters got to know Kerry, Edwards, Gephardt, and Dean better, they discovered that they most preferred Kerry and their second preference was Edwards. The Iowa voters might have found either Lieberman or Clark more attractive instead, but they did not have the chance to find out.

Voters in New Hampshire and Later States It is obvious that being better known advantaged Kerry in Iowa, but why did it advantage him in New Hampshire? And why did doing well in New Hampshire advantage Kerry further in South Carolina? New Hampshire voters had some idea of the preferences of Iowa voters and knew the results of Iowa's caucuses. They also had some information about the candidates, but it was a bit different from the information that Iowa voters had. How could this be? We can imagine that one candidate's home state is close to New Hampshire (as was the case for both Kerry and Dean). The New Hampshire voters heard about the outcome of voting in Iowa through the news media. Given that they also may have had some idea of what those voters were like, they could update themselves on what the Iowa voters knew about the candidates. They could "learn" from the horse-race results.

Similarly, South Carolina voters had some idea of the preferences of Iowa and New Hampshire voters and knew the results of both Iowa's caucuses and New Hampshire's primary. And they also had some information about the candidates, different from that known to Iowa and New Hampshire voters. One candidate's home state might be close to South Carolina (as was the case with Edwards), or there might be a group of voters who know the candidate for other reasons (such as the high percentage of voters in South Carolina with military-service experience who knew Clark from his previous job as a general and also know something about the preferences of those in the military). As with the New Hampshire voters, the South Carolina voters heard the outcome of voting—in both Iowa and New Hampshire—through the news media. Given that they also may have had some idea of what those voters were like, they could also update themselves on what those voters knew about the candidates. They, too, could learn from the horse-race results.

How might the "learning" from the horse-race results work? Suppose that the voters in Iowa are known to be largely liberal and they split their votes between Libby and Manny, not really voting for Connie at all. The voters in New Hampshire can infer that there is a high probability that Connie is conservative and that Libby and Manny are probably either moderate or liberal. Suppose the New Hampshire voters also know for sure that Libby is liberal because she is from a nearby state, having served as governor there and instituted liberal policies. Therefore, Manny is the only unknown candidate to them. How to vote? If they are liberal, their choice is easy—they would vote for Libby and not be significantly affected by what they learned from how Iowa voters chose. But if they are moderate, they may want to vote for Manny, as there is some probability that Manny is a moderate (and they would infer from how Iowa voters chose that Connie is conservative, and they would know that Libby is liberal). And if the New Hampshire voters are conservatives, they can use the information they gained from the Iowa voters' choices to vote for Connie. Similarly, voters choosing in later-voting states, such as South Carolina, can learn from the voting in both Iowa and New Hampshire.

In this example, voters learn about the ideological positions of the candidates from earlier voting, so that, depending on the distribution of preferences, winning a first primary may not always help a candidate win later. The winner in Iowa will win in our example if Democratic voters in Iowa are like those in the rest of the nation; if voters are different across states, then the later voters will have a chance to update their knowledge based on the voting in Iowa and perhaps make different choices. As we saw earlier, in 50 percent of the cases historically, the winner in Iowa has not gone on to win the nomination. In those cases, later voters were either ignoring the Iowa results or using them to conclude that the Iowa winner was not their preferred candidate.

However, those cases are all from 1992 and before. In the last three presidential contests, which have been more front-loaded after Iowa and New Hampshire than before, winning in Iowa has been essential. To understand why, consider how voters can learn about electability through the presidential primary season.

Learning about Electability We can think of all voters across states as trying to pick a candidate with the same quality—the perceived ability to beat Bush in November—and using the information they gain to choose the one they believe has that quality. Suppose now that voters do pretty much know the candidates' policy positions on the issues and that the majority of voters see these positions as close enough not to make a big difference—that is, the majority of voters would prefer any of the three (Libby, Manny, or

Connie) to their likely opponent in the general election, whom we will call Harry. The majority of voters want to select the most electable of the three candidates. However, each candidate does have some group of voters who prefer him or her so much that they are willing to vote for him or her even if there are serious doubts about electability (like Jayroe in South Carolina). Some voters will almost always vote for Libby, another group will almost always vote for Manny, and another group will almost always vote for Connie.

Suppose that voters face a potential information problem—that is, they may not know which of the three candidates are electable. So imagine the problem facing the Iowa voters in our story—there are three candidates, Libby, Manny, and Connie. One may be electable, two may be electable, or all three may be. Conversely, one or more may be unelectable. Libby and Manny decide to campaign in Iowa, and Connie decides to forgo campaigning and wait. Suppose that Iowa voters learn that Libby is electable and Manny is not, and Connie they don't know about. The majority vote for Libby, and Connie and Manny get only the support of those who vote for them independent of whether they are electable. Libby wins Iowa.

In the meantime, Connie has been campaigning in New Hampshire, and voters there have discovered that Connie is indeed electable. Libby and Manny have been campaigning some, but not as much. So some of the voters, although perhaps not all, have figured out that Libby is electable and Manny is not. They know that the majority of Iowa voters picked Libby and did not vote for Manny, reinforcing the view that Libby is electable and Manny is not. Should the majority of New Hampshire voters, who mainly care about electability, choose Connie or Libby, given that both are likely to be electable? If they split their votes, Manny may win, which would make the majority of voters unhappy. So even though they don't see much difference between Libby and Connie, they need to coordinate on behalf of one (either Libby or Connie) to be sure that Manny, who they have good reason to believe is unelectable, loses. An easy way to coordinate is to focus on the winner in Iowa, Libby, plus doing so reduces further the chances of Manny's winning the nomination. (We discuss coordination in multicandidate races like this one in more detail in chapter 14).

Now what about the voters in South Carolina and the other seven states voting a week later? They haven't seen the candidates nearly as much as Iowa and New Hampshire voters have, so they have much less information on electability. Although there is a week between New Hampshire and their elections, the seven states (South Carolina, Missouri, Delaware, Oklahoma, Arizona, New Mexico, and North Dakota) are larger and spread out across the nation. Thus, these voters do not get to know the candidates that well, but they know that Connie and Manny have lost twice and that Libby has won twice. They can infer that both Iowa and New Hampshire voters figured Libby was electable. They don't know for sure whether Connie or Manny is unelectable. But why take the chance? So in the states that vote after Iowa and New Hampshire, voting for Libby, for the majority who care about electability, is an easy choice even if they have some information that Connie is electable. Connie, who is electable and who could have done better if she had campaigned in Iowa, loses again.

One important piece of our analysis is the effect of early wins in Iowa and New Hampshire on the ability of candidates to raise resources. As noted in chapter 6, contributors who give resources for policy reasons will give in order to maximize their expected utility, much as voters will. If they see that the candidates are ideologically similar, then they will want to give to the candidates they perceive as most electable as well. The contributors, then, also "learn" about electability from the early voting, and the candidates who do well can benefit from that. Contributors who give resources for favors or access will want to coordinate on behalf of a winner as well, albeit for different reasons (as discussed in chapter 6). Early winners receive; losers don't. The advantage in campaign contributions is amplified by the fact that candidates' needs for resources increase with the number of states they have to cover in their campaigning—as they have to plan larger events, mailings, television and radio ads, and so on. The expenses of campaigning are higher if a candidate is perceived as more of an unknown simply because of a failure to win in the early contests, for the candidate has to spend more to convey to voters his or her qualities.

The 2004 Democratic Primaries Of course, our story in an oversimplification of what happened in the 2004 Democratic presidential primaries. Yet it does provide an explanation of why campaigning in Iowa is particularly important for candidates in a year like 2004, when electability is seen as an important factor for voters, and why it was desirable for voters to coordinate on their choice of one candidate whom they saw as electable even if they also recognized that some of the other candidates could also be electable and they liked them as well.

Recall how Kerry withdrew from all later states to concentrate on Iowa, while Clark and Lieberman decided to hope that by campaigning in states that voted later, they could win there and make the race competitive. Moreover, in the last days of the campaign in Iowa, Kerry emphasized his service in Vietnam in campaign commercials, suggesting that he would be a strong competitor for Bush on war issues. Iowa voted before the controversies over Kerry's service surfaced. Kerry's efforts paid off—he won in Iowa. While that win was probably also related to his policy positions, evidence suggests that many voters chose him because of the perception that he was more electable. In the caucus exit poll, participants were asked what they believed was the most important quality in choosing a candidate. Twenty-nine percent cited that the most important quality was that the candidate "takes strong stands"; 26 percent chose the response that the candidate "can beat Bush"; 22 percent, that the candidate "cares about people"; 15 percent, that the candidate has the "right experience"; and 1 percent chose the response that they voted because of "endorsements" received by the candidate. Of those who chose that the candidate "takes strong stands" as the most important quality, 31 percent chose Dean; 26 percent, Kerry; and 23 percent, Edwards. But of those who chose "can beat Bush" as the most important quality, 37 percent chose Kerry, 30 percent chose Edwards, and 21 percent chose Dean. Similarly, on the response "right experience," which is arguably related to the voter's perception of the probability of a candidate's electability, Kerry did exceptionally well, with 71 percent, compared with 18 percent for Gephardt.

In the New Hampshire primary exit poll, voters were asked simply whether the most important determinant of their vote was the candidate's ability to beat Bush or the candidate's stances on the issues. While the majority of voters chose issues (57 percent) to beating Bush (33 percent), of those who mentioned beating Bush, 56 percent voted for Kerry and of those who mentioned issues as most important, Dean and Kerry tied with 29 percent, with the other candidates dividing the total. Interestingly, the candidate who received the second highest total from voters who most cared about beating Bush was Clark with 16 percent, as compared with Dean's 14 percent, Edwards's 11 percent, and Lieberman's 2 percent. Clark also came in third in the race behind Kerry and Dean. These results suggest that New Hampshire voters did perceive Clark as electable, something they learned while he campaigned in the state, since they did not know much about him prior to the campaign, but that the combination of Kerry's closeness on issues and perceived electability made Kerry a better choice. Even though Clark had campaigned more in New Hampshire than Kerry, who was not in the state until after Iowa, the Iowa results helped him convey that he was electable, and thus voters were still willing to perceive him as such.

In the voting on February 3, Kerry won five of the seven states, with South Carolina going to Edwards and Clark barely winning Oklahoma after spending considerable time and effort in that state. In South Carolina, Edwards's win (with 45 percent of the vote) and Kerry's not-far-behind second-place finish (with 30 percent) similarly illustrates the importance of perceptions of both electability and policy in how voters chose. Of those surveyed in exit polls who claimed that beating Bush was the most important determinant of the vote—32 percent—Kerry and Edwards tied with 42 percent. Of those who said that the most important determinant of their vote was a candidate's stance on issues—59 percent—42 percent chose Edwards, and only 22 percent chose Kerry. In Oklahoma, although Clark officially won, the outcome was close to a three-way tie between Clark, Edwards, and Kerry. Again, most of those surveyed in the exit polls stated that issues were the major determinant in their vote choice (63 percent), but a sizable number also chose beating Bush (27 percent). Of those who mentioned beating Bush, 47 percent chose Kerry, while of those who stated that stance on issues was most important, only 19 percent chose Kerry.

These results suggest that even in the states where Kerry lost, he had a significant number of supporters who saw him as more electable than the other candidates. In states where Kerry won, sizable majorities of voters who viewed beating Bush as the most important determinant of their votes chose Kerry. Moreover, Kerry's support was higher among those voters than it was among those who voted on issues. Consider, for example Missouri, where Kerry won with over 50 percent of the vote. Of those who felt the most important determinant of their vote was beating Bush, 68 percent chose Kerry, but of those who felt the most important determinant of their vote was the candidate's stance on issues, only 39 percent chose Kerry. Thus, by February 3, the majority of Democratic voters saw Kerry as the most electable candidate, and a sizable portion of his support came from that perception.

After those primaries, Lieberman dropped out of the race. Voters saw him as neither close to them on issues nor electable. Clark stayed in for the February 10 primaries, but he had so little money his campaign staff gave up their paychecks to run television ads in Tennessee.[33] Nevertheless, Clark came in third in the state behind Kerry and then Edwards. Of the voters in Tennessee who chose based on electability, 59 percent chose Kerry, while the voters who chose based on issues roughly split their votes between Kerry, Edwards, and Clark. Clearly, the perception that Kerry was more electable helped him defeat both Clark and Edwards in the state. Kerry's wins helped him raise money to campaign in the other states, winning twenty-seven out of thirty primaries by Super Tuesday. Kerry went from having no money to raising $270,000 a day in February to almost a $1 million a day in March. By contrast, Edwards, his last major opponent, began to see his cash dry up, and by the time he dropped out, he had only $1 million in the bank and twice as much in debt.[34]

Edwards dropped out after the primaries on March 2. He had hoped to do well in Georgia, but he received only 41 percent of the vote to Kerry's 47 percent. Although 50 percent of those Georgia voters who said in exit polls that issues were the most important determinant of their vote chose Edwards, Kerry garnered 68 percent of the votes of those who said that beating Bush was the most important factor. Although more voters said they cared more about issues than about beating Bush (53 percent to 35 percent), the strength of Kerry's support among those who cared about electability helped him win Georgia.

The Michigan Democrats' use of early voting in their caucus provides a nice illustration of how voters were influenced during the primary season. Figure 12.3 shows how the support for the candidates in Michigan changed during the voting period, mirroring the choices in earlier primaries. At the beginning of the voting period, Gephardt and Dean dominated. Gephardt's strength reflected his strong union ties and Dean's his support among younger Internet voters and unions. Prior to Iowa's caucuses on January 19, Clark had begun to show growth in support, and to a much lesser extent Kerry's vote totals grew as well. After Iowa, where Kerry won, Edwards came in second, Dean came in third, and Gephardt withdrew, support for Kerry and Edwards developed; however, Kerry's support clearly expanded at a faster

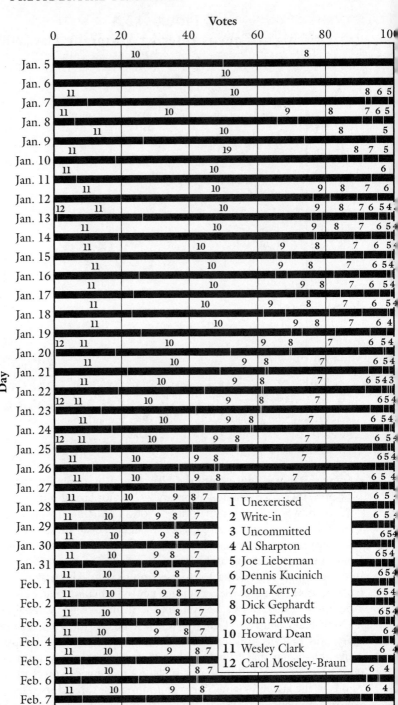

Figure 12.3
Michigan Caucus Voting by Candidate and Day, 2004

1 Unexercised
2 Write-in
3 Uncommitted
4 Al Sharpton
5 Joe Lieberman
6 Dennis Kucinich
7 John Kerry
8 Dick Gephardt
9 John Edwards
10 Howard Dean
11 Wesley Clark
12 Carol Moseley-Braun

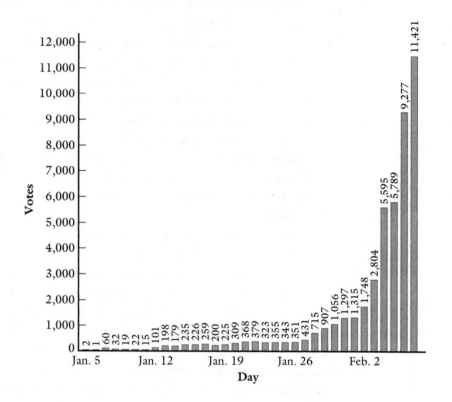

FIGURE 12.4
Michigan Caucus Internet Voting by Day, 2004

rate, reaching its height before the New Hampshire primary, then receding a bit before the caucus date of February 7, but not taking him out of the lead.

Note, however, that the majority of votes in Michigan were cast in the last week of the campaign; see figure 12.4. Hence, even though Dean led early on, it was during a period when very few voters were casting ballots. Recall from our discussion of early voting in chapter 3 that most voters who are undecided wait until closer to the election to vote. This makes sense, as voters wait to see whether they will learn new information that will change their vote. One of the reasons Kerry took the gamble of not campaigning much in New Hampshire until after Iowa, just before the New Hampshire primary, was that his pollster had told him that most New Hampshire voters were unlikely to make up their minds until right before primary day. According to New Hampshire exit polls, 54 percent of voters made up their minds in the last week and 35 percent in the last three days. Thus, he felt he still had a chance to sway those voters and would do better if he showed success in Iowa.

Problems with Learning by Voting

Iowa and New Hampshire Voters Are Different The process described in this chapter gives a lot of influence to voters in Iowa and New Hampshire if later states' voters and contributors believe that those voters can judge electability. Yet these states are not mirrors of the nation, and because of that their influence has been strongly criticized. Why should "tiny New Hampshire with its elderly population, its large French-speaking minority, its backward economy, and its lack of statewide communication other than the wildly idiosyncratic *Manchester Union-Leader*" have such influence? (Polsby 1983, p. 173) Such criticism may reflect prejudices that are unfounded, but there is objective evidence that New Hampshire is ideologically different from many other states. One important aspect of New Hampshire politics is that the state's two parties are highly polarized. Wright, Erikson, and McIver (1993) measured the degree of polarization between the two major political parties across states and found that New Hampshire's is the sixth highest in the nation, suggesting that in both parties the average party member is more extreme than the average party member in most other states. Keeter and Zukin (1983) also concluded that New Hampshire Democrats are more liberal and Republicans more conservative than national party members.

New Hampshire is also greatly Republican. Prior to the 2004 election, New Hampshire had two Republican senators, two Republican representatives, and a Republican governor (in 2004, Democrat John Lynch defeated incumbent governor Craig Benson). Erikson, Wright, and McIver (p. 55) measured the effect of living in New Hampshire versus that of living in Arkansas (in the early 1990s, a highly Democratic state) and concluded:

> The difference in party identification produced by the difference between the political cultures of Arkansas and New Hampshire (40.8 points) approaches the partisan consequence of being Jewish instead of Protestant (55.9) or of being black instead of white (59.4)! And remember that the state coefficients are derived from an analysis in which all major demographic variables are controlled. These differences in state effects on partisanship are *not* a function of the measured state demographics.

While the ideological differences between Iowa voters and the "average" American are not as strong, the rural, agriculturally dominated Iowa economy no doubt influences the issues that Iowa voters consider important, which can also potentially affect their policy choices.

Does Nonrepresentativeness Matter? In what way does it matter whether Iowa and New Hampshire voters are different ideologically from other voters? As we saw above, if later voters know that they are, they can use the information to reject the choices of Iowa and New Hampshire voters in favor of candidates they like better. This has apparently happened, as Iowa and New Hampshire winners have lost nomination contests. However, it is less likely to occur if voters also value electability and contributions are related to electability. How? Suppose Iowa voters know that both Libby and Connie are electable but Manny is not. They also know that Libby is a liberal and Connie is a conservative, and they would prefer a liberal to a conservative. So they vote for Libby over Connie. Libby wins.

Later voters are now getting mixed signals; they learn that Libby is electable, and they also suspect that she is a liberal. Suppose that because primaries are compressed, they don't have the time to learn much about Connie or Manny. They care about electability, so they will focus on Libby as well, even if they think there is some possibility that either Connie or Manny is ideologically closer to them and electable—because they don't know this for sure and want to avoid choosing a candidate who is unelectable, they end up picking Libby. The Iowa voters' ideological preferences with a compressed primary schedule, then, can affect which candidates later voters choose. If the early voters are different ideologically from the later voters but the later voters have less ability to gather their own information and care about electability just as the early voters do, early voters can affect the ideological position of the nominee. There is evidence that Iowa voters felt Edwards was electable and New Hampshire voters felt Clark was as well, but in both states Kerry was preferred to those candidates by voters who cared most about issues, suggesting that the ideological preferences of Iowa and New Hampshire voters may have influenced the outcome in Kerry's favor.

How the Current System Works: The Evidence

Data Problems

While the preceding analysis has sketched out how later voters in primaries can learn about unknown candidates and thus advantage them, as well as empirical evidence of voters' learning and the suggestion of momentum in these primaries, we lack enough data to say that the primary system itself influences the types of candidates elected. The story of Kerry in 2004 "seems" to fit the data, but that is hardly an empirical test. It is what is called a "just so" story: the theory explains the story, but there are lots of alternative theories that could explain the story of Kerry's nomination just as well. Ideally, we would like to evaluate the theory using data from many different nomination contests, much as we would want to use more than just one surveyed voter after an election to determine voters' preferences. Ideally, too, we would like to draw a random sample of nomination contests and, using statistical analysis to control for nonrandom factors, determine whether our theory works. But we don't have such an option. We have the opportunity sample of a few nomination contests since 1972, when primaries became consequential. As King (1993) argued, the common practice of using the president as the unit of analysis in presidency research is extremely unlikely to yield reliable empirical conclusions because the number of observations available is far too few. He calculated that at least a number of centuries would need to pass before we would have enough observations, even using all the former presidents as observations. It would be thus quite a long time before we could say something that makes statistical sense of the history we observe. Moreover, since the system has changed over the years and will continue to do so, it is highly improbable that we will ever be able to do a proper empirical analysis of the effects of the primary system on which candidates are nominated.

Experimenting with Primaries

In order to address the data problem, Morton and Williams (1999, 2001) analyzed a series of laboratory elections designed to represent two election systems—sequential voting, as in presidential primaries, and simultaneous voting, as in a single national primary. There were three candidates—as in our example above—which we again call Libby, Manny, and Connie (in the experiment, the candidates were given the names Blue, Green, and Orange, and the names and types were randomized between election periods). To induce subjects to have preferences for the candidates, the subjects were paid according to which candidate won, but how much they were paid varied. That is, some subjects would get $1.10 if Libby won, $0.90 if Manny won, and $0.15 if Connie won. Other subjects got $1.10 if Connie won, $0.90 if Manny won, and $0.15 if Libby won. Still other subjects got $1.10 if Manny won and $0.90 if either Libby or Connie won. However, in the elections, voters were given information about only one of the candidates. That is, they were told what their payoff was for one of the candidates but not what it would be for the other two (they knew what the possibilities were, but not for sure).

Morton and Williams conducted 250 laboratory elections. In some of the elections, the subjects voted simultaneously, and in others they were divided into two groups and voted sequentially. Not surprisingly, in the simultaneous voting, the candidate who was revealed to the voters (the well-known candidate) was much more likely to win than the candidates who were unknown. In the sequential voting, the early voters were told the identity of one of the candidates. In some cases, the early and later voters were similar (that is, the number of voters who preferred Connie or Libby or Manny was the same in both groups of voters), while in other elections the early voters were more likely to prefer Connie and the later voters were more likely to prefer Libby. Later voters were told two things—the outcome of the early voting and the identity of a different candidate. Later voters also knew the early voters' payoffs. In some cases, they knew how the different payoff groups of early voters voted, not just how the whole group voted. The laboratory elections were designed to capture the reality of primaries in which voters hear "horse-race" information—how an early state, say, New Hampshire, voted—and also have some idea about the preferences of the voters in the early state. For example, exit polls and news reports often convey information about how women vote versus how men vote or how different ethnic groups vote.

In the sequential-voting elections, Morton and Williams found that early voters tended to choose "informatively"—that is, it was generally possible for later voters to infer what the early voters knew, given the horse-race information and the information that they had on one of the candidates. This was also evident because later voters were less likely to choose their least preferred candidate than were early voters or voters in the simultaneous-voting elections, who did not have the horse-race information. There was also evidence that candidates who were well-known were more likely to win in the simultaneous-voting elections than they were in the sequential-voting elections, where later voters could use their information to affect the outcome and advantage another candidate. The moderate candidate, Manny, was more likely to win in the simultaneous-voting elections when he was known to the voters, but when he was not known in the beginning, he was more likely to win in sequential-voting elections.

Finally, Morton and Williams found that nonrepresentative early voters were able to influence the outcomes significantly if they knew who their favored candidates were—their favored candidates (when known) were more likely to win than other candidates. This did seem to have a momentum-like effect. Later voters appeared not to learn as much from nonrepresentative early voters' choices as from detailed information about representative early voters' choices. But when early voters were nonrepresentative, there was a slight increase in the probability that moderate candidates would win.

Morton and Williams conclude that when voter information is asymmetrically distributed across voters, the representativeness of early voters can affect the electoral outcome, an argument against allowing nonrepresentative states to vote first. Furthermore, the argument that later primary voters learn from early primary voters' choices was supported only on a limited basis, when voters received detailed horse-race information about early voters' choices, as in exit polls, and early voters were representative. On the plus side for the current primary system, however, moderate candidates were more likely to win in sequential voting when they were not well-known at the beginning, suggesting that moderate candidates can benefit from sequential voting if they are not well-known. This might explain the ability of Bill Clinton to win the Democratic nomination in 1992 by performing well in the early primaries, although not winning them. Recall that primaries in 1992 were more drawn out than those in the previous contest.

Views of the State of Primaries

Should There Be a Return to Convention Rule?

The dominance of direct primaries has had numerous critics and supporters, particularly in the 1980s. Polsby (1983) argued that the reforms have led to less desirable nominees and problematic consequences for the role of parties in American politics. He noted that the openness of both the caucus process and primaries gives a stronger role to activists who may be ideologically extreme—"purists"—and has significantly reduced the roles played by party leaders. Keeter and Zukin (1983) contended that voters are making choices that are uninformed and thus worse than those that would have been made by party elites. Epstein (1986), in contrast, observed that the evidence on the types of candidates is based on too few data points, that the old process has led to a number of disastrous nominees, and that the other consequences are more complex. And we have already reviewed the evidence from Alvarez and Glasgow (1997), Bartels (1988), and Popkin (1991), according to which voters learn through the primary process. Finally, Stone and Abramowitz (1983), based on surveys of party activists selected from caucuses in 1980, demonstrated that they are not purists but are also concerned with the electability of candidates.

Using Superdelegates

Regardless of whether the critics of the plebiscitary system are correct or not, most observers recognize that it is highly unlikely that the presidential nomination process will move from rank-and-file participation back to control by party leaders in restricted caucuses and conventions. Even the addition of superdelegates has not led to much change, since many of them make commitments to particular candidates prior to the conventions. Consider the experience of Ohio representative Sherrod Brown, a superdelegate to the Democratic National Convention in 2004. Initially he pledged his support to his colleague in Congress Dick Gephardt. But when Gephardt withdrew, he started to think about other candidates. In mid-February, according to an Associated Press report:

> Kerry spoke to Brown about the senator's views on trade, manufacturing and jobs—issues especially dear to Brown's blue-collar northeast Ohio district. Brown said a conversation was also scheduled with Edwards, but that fell through and was never rescheduled. Brown . . . endorsed Kerry. The lobbying for endorsements is "part of the business," Brown said. "But what I got out of this is it gave me a chance to explore their views on issues and what needs to be done in the state.

Although Brown gave Kerry his endorsement in late February, most superdelegates "are more bandwagon-jumpers than trailblazers," waiting until

ANALYZING ELECTIONS

the Super Tuesday results to make their decisions.[35] It is unlikely that the nomination contest will become the exclusive domain of political elites again.

The central question currently facing reformers is whether to legislate formal procedures for candidate nominations at the federal level. As we have seen, the trend has been toward a virtual national primary, with states frontloading their primaries and caucuses extremely close to the first-in-the-nation Iowa and New Hampshire contests and in some cases attempting to challenge their opening status. Front-loading seems to advantage well-known front-runner candidates. On the other hand, when primaries are drawn out, there is empirical evidence that voters learn information about candidates that allows them to make what may be more informed decisions. Political pundits have argued that drawn-out primaries give candidates a chance to be "seasoned," so that they will be better able to face critical questions before the general-election campaign. As *New York Times* columnist and PBS commentator David Brooks noted after Kerry won the nomination: "Kerry rose and really nobody has gone after him in any serious way. So he will emerge into very unfamiliar territory. Massachusetts is not like America. And he will face criticism [of] his record, about his personality, that he has never faced before. I think it is the short loading of this process that [he] will be remembered for."[36] Kerry did face such criticism, from the Swift Boat Veterans and from Bush after securing the nomination. If primary voters in later states had had more time to evaluate Kerry, would their choice have been different? On the other hand, drawn-out primaries give early voters, who may not be representative of the general national-party membership, an opportunity to perhaps influence the results of the later voting.

How Can Primaries Be Reformed?

A number of reformers take as a given the plebiscitary system of presidential nominations and address the question of how to devise a more "sensible" alternative. Essentially the free-for-all in scheduling that has resulted in frontloading and earlier and earlier campaigning is viewed as costly to both candidates and states alike. Reform in the guise of regulation that would make the primary system easily understood and "fairly" scheduled has been proposed by a number of policy makers. The two principal alternatives are a set of spaced-out regional primaries and one single national primary.

Regional primaries would be scheduled two to three weeks apart, with an order at first randomly determined to some extent. Although regional primaries have endogenously arisen, as in the southern Super Tuesday primaries, the eastern states' Junior Tuesday, and the movement toward western primaries as a bloc early in the season, these have also been part of the front-loading process as groups of states have jockeyed for a bigger role in the nomination process. A standardized regional primary system, in contrast, is expected to increase the length of time between primary elections. Regional primaries are believed to be an advantage in that candidates would be able to campaign in one area of the country at a time, and voters may gain information in the process. Regional primaries are an enforced sequential voting process. One variant of regional primaries was approved by the National Association of Secretaries of State (NASS) on February 12, 1999. It is a rotating system of four regions with Iowa's and New Hampshire's contests held prior to the regional contests. It remains to be seen whether the plan will ever be put into effect. At this writing, the NASS is considering whether to continue to push its proposed plan.[37]

At first glance, a national primary would seem to be a legislated version of the result of front-loading. It would take away the roles of Iowa and New Hampshire, however, and if it were held later, during the summer, it could possibly give voters exposure to more candidates than the current front-loaded system does because of the time candidates would have to campaign more broadly, as they do in national elections. It may not be possible, however, for voters to "learn" at a national level about more than one or two well-known candidates. And campaign contributors might play a bigger role as kingmakers since nationwide campaigning would be a daunting task.

What We Know

We know that the process by which we select presidential nominees can have an effect on which candidates are selected. Not all voters get to choose, and the voters who choose are not necessarily representative of those who do not. Voters who choose in primaries care about both the policy choices of the candidates and their chances of winning the general election—electability. Uncertainty over electability and coordination can lead to candidates' being chosen whose policy positions are more representative of early voters than of later ones. If the primary campaign is drawn out, however, later voters can learn from early voters' choices—if they also know something about the early voters' preferences. Nevertheless, many Americans are unhappy with the current process of selecting presidential nominees, and a number of reforms have been suggested. Yet the federal nature of primary regulation, the interests of candidates and parties, and uncertainty about the consequences of change have impeded reform.

What We Don't Know: The Next Step

To win the nomination for president, a candidate has to pay attention to the variations in state rules for getting on the ballot, when voters in different states vote, and how they vote. But the differences between the states also play a part in determining who wins the presidency once the field is narrowed to the party nominees. As noted in chapter 1, presidents in the United States are selected by the Electoral College, not by popular vote, and electoral votes are in almost all the states given by state (Maine and Nebraska allocate electoral votes by congressional district). As a consequence, while voters in New York mattered in the presidential primaries in 2000 (and to some extent in 2004), they were virtually ignored by the candidates during the general elections. In the next chapter, we discover why.

One of the candidates for president in 2004, John Edwards, was elected to the U.S. Senate in 1998. He first took a leading role in major legislation in the Senate in February 2001, the year he began to prepare to run for president. With Senators John McCain and Edward Kennedy, he co-sponsored a bill to regulate HMOs, and in August 2001 the bill passed the Senate. But President George W. Bush opposed the legislation. Did Edwards actually have hopes of getting it passed? The problem illustrates the shared-but-limited-powers feature of American politics. Even if elected, a president does not have the power to make significant policy changes without the consent of Congress and if senators and representatives wish to pass bills opposed by the president, their task can be difficult. We also consider in chapter 13 the relationship between the electoral process and the shared-but-limited-powers feature of American politics. We see why a representative from Georgia required three days of a president's full attention and persuasive powers in regard to the bill that Edwards helped pass in the Senate.

Study Questions and Problems

1. Suppose that in 2008 the secretaries of state are successful and regional primaries are introduced.
   a. How would the use of regional primaries affect the campaign strategies of the following potential presidential candidates: Rudy Giuliani, Jeb Bush, John McCain, Hillary Clinton, Barack Obama, and John Edwards. Which of these candidates would be likely to win the Republican nomination, and why? Which would be likely to win the Democratic nomination, and why?
   b. Suppose, instead, that a single national primary is held in June of 2008. Would your answers to question 1a change, and why?
2. You are the campaign manager for Rudy Giuliani and would like to design a nomination procedure that is most likely to lead to his selection as the Republican nominee. The system must allow all party members across states to participate, although you can vary the date when the different states' voters vote and whether and to what extent non-party members can participate. You can also vary the electoral rules on how delegates are counted (that is, delegates may be allocated by winner-take-all decisions or proportionally by vote), but either all

states must use the allocation rule or states may be allowed to use the rules they prefer (you give the states discretion).

   a. What procedure would you design, and why?

   b. How does your answer change if you are the campaign manager for Jeb Bush? for John McCain? for Hillary Clinton? for Barack Obama? for John Edwards?

NOTES

1. Mark Z. Barabak, "Candidates Bet against History in Skipping Iowa," *Los Angeles Times*, October 21, 2003.
2. John J. Monahan, "Friends Powered Kerry On," *Worcester Telegram & Gazette*, March 7, 2004, and Scott Shepard, "Kerry Campaign Manager's Gamble on Iowa Paying Off in Fight for Presidential Nomination," Cox News Service, February 27, 2004.
3. Wayne Woodlief, "If Kerry Can't Do It in Iowa, He's Finished," *Boston Herald*, December 21, 2003.
4. Randal Archibold, "Pataki and McCain Unite (Teddy Would Have Smiled)," *New York Times*, September 23, 2002.
5. Terry Golway, "Bush Bash," *New York Observer*, March 13, 2000.
6. See the *New York Law Journal*, February 15, 2000.
7. Fatta wanted to vote for Alan Keyes. Tom Ernst, "Ballot Confusion Leaves Some Voters Angry and Perplexed," *Buffalo News*, March 8, 2000.
8. Pataki did help McCain out with his legal expenses, however, with help from New York taxpayers. New York State and the Republican Party each paid $200,000 to cover McCain's legal costs. The Republican Party also paid $50,000 to the Forbes campaign and $40,000 to Alan Keyes's lawyers. See Anny Kuo, "State, GOP to Pay Legal Costs to Put McCain on Primary Ballot," Associated Press State & Local Wire, August 9, 2000.
9. Ken Herman, "No Uproar as Senate Moves Up Primaries," *Austin American-Statesman*, May 29, 2003, and "Legislation Bumps Up Texas' Primary Date, Associated Press State & Local Wire, May 10, 2003.
10. R. G. Ratcliffe, Polly Ross Hughes, Armando Villafranca, and Ruth Rendon, "Remap Plan Gets Approval by House: Both Chambers Vote to Delay 2004 Primaries," *Houston Chronicle*, October 11, 2003.
11. Andy Sher, "Primary Date Switch Lauded by Democrats," *Chattanooga Times Free Press*, May 30, 2003.
12. Craig Gilbert, "Earlier Vote May Bolster State Role: February Primary and Geography Could Lure Democrats Here in '04," *Milwaukee Journal Sentinel*, May 12, 2003.
13. Gilbert, "Earlier Vote May Bolster State Role."
14. Kelly Shannon, "Texans' Role in Democratic Nominee Selection Diminished," Associated Press State & Local Wire, March 3, 2004.
15. See, for example, Aldrich (1995), Epstein (1986), and McCormick (1982). Significant parts of this section are drawn from Morton and Williams (2001, ch. 2).
16. Only Florida Democrats held presidential primaries before 1956.
17. Palmer (1997, ch. 3) reviews much of this history. See also Ranney (1977).
18. There is, however, federal regulation of campaign spending by presidential candidates, as discussed in chapter 6.
19. New Hampshire, Ohio, and West Virginia started presidential primaries in 1916, whereas Alabama's date from 1924 to 1934, restarting in 1940.
20. New Hampshire's primary, for example, although instituted in 1916, did not al-

low voters to express preferences for presidential candidates in their delegate selections until 1949. See Palmer (1997, p. 2).

21. Some southern whites gradually began to vote for and support Republican presidential candidates while maintaining a Democratic Party identity at the state level.

22. See in particular Aldrich (1980), Caesar (1982), Keeter and Zukin (1983), Polsby (1983), and Shafer (1983).

23. See Hagen (1989), Norrander (1989), and Stone, Abramowitz, and Rapoport (1989). Norrander (1993) found that the candidate choices in presidential caucus states are more ideologically extreme than those in states that use primaries.

24. Connolly had switched parties during Nixon's presidency and served as Nixon's secretary of treasury.

25. The liberals had been nicknamed Killer Bees by Hobby during one of their earlier filibusters. He called "the pesky liberals killer bees because 'you never know where they're going to show up next.' " Dave McNeely, " 'Killer Bees' Made Political History: Liberal Senators Hid Out," *Austin American-Statesman*, January 10, 1999. See also Chase Untermeyer, "Texas Politics Would Never Be the Same after 'Killer Bees,' " *Houston Chronicle*, August 22, 1999. Then, too, Texas state troopers were also called out to find the missing legislators, although federal forces were not brought in. The brother of one of the missing senators was arrested when he was mistaken for the senator.

26. Iowa and New Hampshire actually violated the National Democratic Party rules in order to schedule primaries in advance of other New England states in 1984. Yet neither delegation was unseated at the convention. See Palmer (1997, pp. 137–54) for a discussion of the intricate scheduling battles among the two states, the national party, and other states. Because of the complicated battle, the Democratic Party granted exemptions for Iowa and New Hampshire in the subsequent electoral cycles, maintaining their first-in-the-nation status. Other states have challenged these states, notably Louisiana, Arizona, and Delaware in 1996.

27. Republicans attempted to induce states to spread primaries out in 2000, without much success.

28. While New Hampshire has not needed to engage in front-loading, its actions and attempts to maintain its first-in-the-nation status are clearly similar to other states' attempts at front-loading. In 1975, the state enacted legislation requiring that its primary be held on either the second Tuesday in March or on the Tuesday immediately preceding the date on which any other New England state scheduled a similar election. This law was amended in 1995 to require that there be a gap of seven full days between New Hampshire's primary and any other primary. See Palmer (1997).

29. The Southern states that held primaries on Super Tuesday in 1988 were Texas, Florida, North Carolina, Georgia, Missouri, Virginia, Tennessee, Maryland, Louisiana, Alabama, Kentucky, Oklahoma, Mississippi, and Arkansas. Massachusetts and Rhode Island also held primaries on that date. And Washington, Hawaii, Idaho, Nevada, and American Samoa held caucuses.

30. Scott Shepard and Mike Williams, "Undecided Voters Key on Eve of N.H. Primary," *Atlanta Journal-Constitution*, January 27, 2004.

31. Matt Kempner, "Carolinians Weigh Their Choices," *Atlanta Journal-Constitution*, January 28, 2004.

32. Of course, Iowa voters know that they are choosing in a complicated strategic game with the voters of New Hampshire and other states. To the extent that they are forward looking, anticipating the effects their voting can have on later voters, the choices they make may be different. However, it turns out that given the information environment described, they do not have an incentive to vote

against their preferences. These issues are addressed further in Morton and Williams (1999, 2001).

33. "Clark to Withdraw Wednesday," CNN.com, http://www.cnn.com, Tuesday, February 10, 2004.

34. Glenn Justice, "For Kerry, Victories Lead to More Cash and More Spending," *New York Times*, March 22, 2004.

35. Genaro Armas, "Kerry's Superdelegate Lead Forged by Early Outreach and Front-Runner Status," Associated Press, March 1, 2004.

36. David Brooks, *The NewsHour with Jim Lehrer*, March 3, 2004.

37. Marian Gail Brown, "Regional Rotation for Primaries Urged Again," *Connecticut Post*, March 21, 2004.

~13~

Presidential Elections

Going West

In September 2000, Republican candidate George W. Bush's campaign chairman in California, Gerry Parsky, didn't like the assumptions that a lot of journalists and analysts were making about his state's importance in the presidential race. "There is a theory out there that a Republican can win by winning the Midwest," he said. "Our whole focus from the very beginning has been to play to win in California." Yet journalists predicted that Bush would ignore California in the campaign—reporter John Marelius contended: "According to the prevailing electoral vote model, the Midwestern heartland stretching from Pennsylvania to Wisconsin and down to Missouri is the region where the election will be won or lost. . . . There may be occasional sightings of presidential campaign ads in California. In Pennsylvania, Ohio, and Michigan, they're difficult to avoid." California had gone for Democrat Bill Clinton in 1992 and 1996. Both U.S. Senators were Democrats, and the state had a Democratic governor in 2000. Al Gore had double-digit leads in opinion polls in the state over the summer. All the signs pointed to very few Bush sightings in the state.[1]

But Persky was right, and Marelius was wrong: Bush spent a lot of money and time in California during the campaign. He spent $1.5 million on new TV ads in California the week before the election (including a new Spanish-language ad to reach Latino voters in the state), in addition to $1.5 million that the state Republican Party and the Republican National Committee had already spent each week on commercials.[2] He visited the state for a two-day

494

trip that same week and even sent vice presidential candidate Cheney to the state right before the election. In all, Bush spent eleven days in California during the presidential campaign in the fall of 2000, which was more time than he spent in forty-eight other states—only Michigan received more time from Bush (twelve days). Although he did visit the heartland states that pundits predicted he would concentrate on, like Michigan—Pennsylvania for ten days, Wisconsin and Missouri each for eight days, and Ohio for six days—California certainly got more than its expected share of attention.[3]

Why did Bush visit California so often? Although Gore's lead appeared to narrow in opinion polls, Gore still carried California with 53.45 percent of the vote to Bush's 41.65 percent (with minor-party candidates receiving the remainder). Wouldn't it have been better if Bush had spent more time in Florida or another state that was at stake, given how close the electoral vote ended up nationally? Some speculated that Bush's California visits were meant primarily to help out Republican candidates for Congress. Yet two of the congressional candidates Bush spent considerable time campaigning for, Rich Rodriguez and Jim Cuneen, lost to Democrats, Cal Dooley and Mike Honda, respectively. Bush's time and energy in California, in retrospect, was a mistake. In this chapter, we investigate why Bush made this mistake. We find that a candidate's optimal choice in choosing where to campaign has a lot to do with the Electoral College, the procedure we use to elect presidents.

How the Electoral College Works

Faith and the 2004 Election

South Charleston, West Virginia, mayor Richie Robb was unhappy with the criticism he received during the final months of the 2004 presidential campaign. Recalling the remarks after the election was over, he told a reporter for the Associated Press: "There was some pretty strong language I had to put up with."[4] What had caused the mayor to receive such treatment? Robb was one of the 538 U.S. citizens who actually got to vote for the president and vice president in 2004—that is, he was a member of the Electoral College. His name was on the ballot in West Virginia, "pledged" to vote for Bush. And Bush won West Virginia—that is, the Republican electors like Robb won. But Robb was unhappy with Bush. He opposed the Iraq war, and he did not like Bush's tax cuts. As a veteran who had received the Bronze Star for his service in Vietnam, he did not like Bush's criticism of Kerry.

How had Robb ended up an elector pledged to Bush? He had run unsuccessfully for the Republican nomination for governor in the state, and the party leaders had thought that a nice consolation price for the unsuccessful candidates would be to choose them as the party's nominees for electors.

But no one had checked to see whether Robb was a Bush supporter before putting his name on the ballot. A few weeks later, at a Labor Day event at which Robb publicly reiterated his complaints about the president, someone asked him if he was thinking about not voting for Bush, despite his pledge to do so. Robb was surprised, as he hadn't really thought about it. It turns out that West Virginia, like twenty-one other states, does not require that electors fulfill their pledge. Robb began to talk about not casting his vote for Bush as a protest, voting instead for Cheney or another Republican (he said it was highly unlikely he would vote for Kerry). Republicans became concerned. To win the presidency, a candidate must receive 270 electoral votes, and in 2000 Bush had received just 271. If Bush won West Virginia and barely enough other states to receive 270 votes and Robb chose not to vote for him, Robb would keep Bush from winning the presidency. No wonder some of Robb's fellow Republicans were unhappy with him.[5]

Robb was not the first elector to consider not voting as pledged. From the first Electoral College to 2004, there have been 157 such "faithless electors." Seventy-one of them were electors whose candidate died before the Electoral College vote. Most have been individuals lodging a protest, as Robb threatened to do in 2004.[6] In 2000, one of Al Gore's electors from the District of Columbia, Barbara Lett-Simmons, abstained rather than vote for Gore to protest the fact that the district does not have congressional representation. Her protest no doubt added just one more injury to Gore, who had succeeded in winning the popular vote but failed in his effort to become president. As noted in chapter 1, in the United States, voters do not vote directly for president and vice president. Instead, they vote for a slate of electors, called the Electoral College, who are "pledged" to support a presidential candidate and a vice presidential candidate. Each state is entitled to as many electoral votes as the state has senators and representatives combined, for a total of 538 electoral votes for the fifty states and the District of Columbia (the district does not have senators or representatives but by constitutional amendment is granted 3 electoral votes).[7] Table 13.1 summarizes the electoral vote for the states in 2004. In every state except Maine and Nebraska, the entire slate of electors that receives the most popular votes is selected (plurality rule determines the winners in those states). In Maine and Nebraska, the winner of the plurality vote for the whole state receives two electoral votes, and the winner of the plurality vote in each congressional district receives that district's single electoral vote.[8]

The Electoral College has a majority requirement. That is, if no candidate receives an absolute majority of the electoral vote, the names of the top three candidates are submitted to the House of Representatives, where each state may cast one vote.[9] Whether a state's vote is decided by a majority, a plurality, or some other fraction of the state's delegates is determined under rules established by the House. To win, a candidate must receive a majority of the votes cast by the states.

TABLE 13.1
Electoral Votes by State, 2004

State	Number of Electoral Votes	State	Number of Electoral Votes
Alabama	9	Montana	3
Alaska	3	Nebraska	5
Arizona	10	Nevada	5
Arkansas	6	New Hampshire	4
California	55	New Jersey	15
Colorado	9	New Mexico	5
Connectict	7	New York	31
Delaware	3	North Carolina	5
District of Columbia	3	North Dakota	3
Florida	27	Ohio	20
Georgia	15	Oklahoma	7
Hawaii	4	Oregon	7
Idaho	4	Pennsylvania	21
Illinois	21	Rhode Island	4
Indiana	11	South Carolina	8
Iowa	7	South Dakota	3
Kansas	6	Tennessee	11
Kentucky	8	Texas	34
Louisiana	9	Utah	5
Maine	4	Vermont	3
Maryland	10	Virginia	13
Massachusetts	12	Washington	11
Michigan	17	West Virginia	5
Minnesota	10	Wisconsin	10
Mississippi	6	Wyoming	3
Missouri	11		

Note: The total is 538; the majority needed to elect a president is 270.

The Majority Requirement in the Electoral College

Historically, there have been only two elections in which the Electoral College failed to produce a majority, those of 1800 and 1824. In 1800, there was no distinction between presidential and vice presidential candidates: it was specified only that the candidate receiving the majority would become the president. Two candidates from the Republican Party, Thomas Jefferson (who had been designated the party's presidential candidate) and Aaron Burr (who had been chosen to be the vice presidential candidate), received an equal number of votes. Burr, to the anger of many of his party members, refused to defer to Jefferson. With the support of Federalist Alexander Hamilton, Jefferson was elected president. The Twelfth Amendment, ratified in 1804, separated voting for president and vice president to prevent a repeat of the 1800 election. In 1824, four candidates divided the electoral vote (John Quincy Adams, Andrew Jackson, Henry Clay, and William H. Crawford). Although Jackson won the popular vote, Clay threw his support to Adams, and the House of Representatives chose Adams. In return, Adams made Clay his secretary of state, a position believed to be a stepping-stone to the presidency. Clay's support of Adams was famously labeled the corrupt bargain. These two cases illustrate how the majority requirement in the Electoral College has the potential to lead to problematic outcomes. If the Electoral College is divided among three candidates with none receiving a majority, what might happen when voting occurs by state can be difficult to anticipate (as how states' votes will be determined is left uncertain).

It is noteworthy that since 1824, there has always been a winner of the absolute majority of the Electoral College vote for president, and this winner has been a candidate from one of the two major national parties of the time. Because most states use a winner-take-all system to allocate electoral votes, it has been difficult for minor-party and independent candidates to receive electoral votes even when they have strong support nationally. Minor-party and independent candidates typically get a lower share of the electoral vote than the popular vote, although there have been exceptions in cases in which a minor-party or independent candidate has had strong regional support (Strom Thurmond in 1948 received 2.4 percent of the popular vote but 7.3 percent of the electoral vote). Since 1968, there have been a number of third- or minor-party candidates with nationwide support. Only one of these candidates received *any* electoral votes—George Wallace in 1968 received 8.5 percent of the electoral votes because of his regional support, yet that was not enough to challenge the absolute majority of electoral votes received by Nixon and was less than Wallace's popular support of 13.5 percent. Ross Perot, despite receiving 18.9 percent of the vote in 1992, received no electoral votes. Thus, the national parties have been able to use widespread national support such that in most states one of the major parties has a plurality of support, enough to keep minor-party and independent candidates from preventing a major-party candidate from receiving an absolute majority in the Electoral College. (We discuss minor-party and independent candidates more fully in chapter 14).

The Electoral Vote versus the Popular Vote

Whereas all U.S. presidents since 1824 have been able to win with an absolute majority of the Electoral College in the first stage of the process, these candidates have often had less than a majority of the popular vote (they've had only a plurality), and in three noteworthy cases (including 2000) they have not even had that, losing the popular vote.[10] In 1876, the electoral votes from southern states were held in dispute, and although Samuel Tilden is considered the winner of the popular vote, the dispute led to a contested election, which took months to resolve (longer than the time taken to resolve the 2000 election) and resulted in a win by Rutherford B. Hayes, who had the majority of the electoral vote. In 1888, Grover Cleveland received more popular votes than Benjamin Harrison, but Harrison won the electoral vote. And in 2000, Al Gore received a plurality of the popular vote but lost the electoral vote to George W. Bush.

The disconnect between the popular vote and the electoral vote has caused many Americans to criticize the Electoral College, yet although there have been renewed calls for reform since the 2000 election, so far these efforts have not received enough support to be viable. The reasons for the disconnect are clear and twofold: (1) because each state receives at least three electoral votes, smaller states have a disproportionate weight in the Electoral College relative to their population, and (2) because most states use winner-take-all rules to allocate electoral votes, states in which competition between candidates is tight are likely to play kingmaker roles in determining the outcome of the election. Thus, the relationship between the electoral vote and the popular vote is not a direct one-to-one correspondence.

What is the likelihood of a candidate winning the Electoral College vote and losing the popular vote? Katz, Gelman, and King (2002) devised a statistical model using historical data and estimated that the Electoral College vote will differ from the popular vote only when the average vote shares are very close to one half. Stromberg (2002), in simulations of a theoretical model of the presidential campaign process with historical data incorporated (a model we discuss in more detail below), calculated that the probability of electing a president without a plurality of the popular vote is approximately 4 percent, which implies the event's occurring once every one hundred years (as we elect presidents every four years). If you consider only 1888 and 2000 as true cases (in 1876, with the dispute in the South, it is difficult to determine who actually won the popular vote), then once a century is about the actual experience.

The Electoral College and Campaigning

Is It Just Electoral Vote Size?

All states are not equal—not in electoral votes or in partisan balance or in the time candidates spend in them during presidential campaigns. What determines where candidates spend the most time? It seems fairly obvious that states with large electoral votes are important, but if the state—for example, California—seems to be in the other candidate's column, shouldn't a candidate concentrate on getting out the vote in states in which he has more of a chance of winning? Thus, the pundits did not expect Bush to campaign in

California in 2000. In 1992 and 1996, Republican presidential candidates George H. W. Bush (the senior Bush) and Bob Dole did not campaign there. New York and Texas both have large electoral votes, but in 2000 neither state was visited by Gore, Bush, or their vice presidential nominees. Few campaign ads were aired in those areas. So size isn't everything.

To understand what determines where candidates campaign in presidential contests, we consider a model of the process constructed by Stromberg (2002). Although the model is fairly complex, its underlying assumptions are relatively easy to understand. We will first go through the assumptions and then describe Stromberg's predictions and how they match up with the data.

Campaign Visits and Voters

How Campaign Visits Affect Voters We begin by assuming that campaign visits by presidential candidates matter—that they affect how voters will choose on election day. Campaign visits can affect voters' preferences in the same ways that campaign advertising does, as discussed in chapter 7. In this section, we describe the ways in which campaign visits influence voters.

<u>Mobilization</u> First, campaign speeches and rallies help with the mobilization of the candidates' supporters, particularly close to the election, by reinforcing the social benefit of voting as a group to support the candidate. Usually interest groups organize individuals to attend these rallies, and often the rallies are held before prticular targeted audiences (at a meeting of a labor union, for example). In these rallies, candidates often call on voters to help with the mobilization effort and frequently remark on how they plan to win the state they are visiting. In West Palm Beach, George W. Bush urged the crowd: "The voters are there, let's turn them out."[11] We discussed in chapter 3 how Bush's campaign effectively used rally attendants to mobilize voters after a speech and rewarded those who had provided support with special recognition at campaign events. The turnout effect of candidates' visits is probably a big factor in why such visits are seen as helping advantage other candidates in the party. When Al Gore visited Fond Du Lac, Wisconsin, Democratic state assembly candidate Lewis Rosser remarked: "We're definitely hoping for some runover. . . . It energizes the base."[12]

<u>Coordination</u> Second, campaign visits can serve as a coordination mechanism in multicandidate presidential races, particularly if minor-party candidates are trying to convince supporters of the size of their backing. In 2000, Ralph Nader wanted to win at least 5 percent of the presidential vote in order to secure public funding for the Green Party's candidate in 2004. But to do so, he needed to convince voters that it was possible for him to generate that large a share of the vote. He attempted to do that with rallies. The

Minneapolis Star-Tribune reported on a Nader rally in September 2000 at the Target Center in Minneapolis, where organizers hoped to draw a crowd of 15,000 (11,500 showed up): "With little cash, Nader chose cities that have either large college populations or that he thinks are inclined to be liberal and receptive to his anti-corporate, pro-consumer message. News coverage of the campaign has been picking up, with organizations as disparate as the *New York Times, USA Today* and Swedish Television covering the tour; the rally was broadcast on C-SPAN."[13] By the first of November, Nader's use of rallies had built what appeared to be a strong enough following in Minnesota and a few other states to make Democrats worry that he would make the difference in the tight contest between Bush and Gore, taking votes from Gore, even though Nader had raised only $6.5 million by that date (the FEC reports that Bush had raised over $94 million and Gore over $49 million).[14] Nader did get 5.2 percent of the vote in Minnesota, where Gore won 47.9 percent to Bush's 45.5 percent (Nader won 2.74 percent nationwide, failing to meet his objective). (We discuss Nader and other minor-party candidates more fully in the next chapter.)

<u>Psychological Attachment</u> Third, campaign visits can influence voters' psychological attachment to candidates. We discussed how this might work with campaign advertising even if we assume voters are rational. That is, if a voter is indifferent about candidates on policy grounds and he or she gets some tiny bit of utility from a campaign visit, the voter might be more likely to vote for the candidate with whom he or she has had more such contact. Having an instance of physical interaction with a candidate (albeit far removed) may have a greater influence on this psychological attachment than simply viewing the candidate on television. For example, after one of Bush's campaign stops in Fresno, California, voters remarked on the common feelings they felt they shared with the candidate. Voter Kari Vennendall concluded about the reaction she and her friends had to the rally: "We knew he meant what he said. It was heartfelt." Voter Marge Borne reported: "I thought he was great, very clear and concise about how he feels for our country."[15] In Fond Du Lac, one rally attendee hugged both vice presidential candidate Lieberman and presidential candidate Gore.

<u>Signals, Valence Issues, and Endorsements</u> Fourth, campaign visits can also serve as a way of signaling a candidate's ability to perform the job as an elected official (recall our discussion of valence issues in chapter 5). A campaign stop gives voters a chance to observe a candidate firsthand and determine whether in their perception the candidate has the ability to serve as president. When Gore made a round-the-clock campaign blitz on Labor Day of 2000, the workers he visited noted that "they were glad to see Gore also toiling over the holiday weekend. . . . Ray Della Vella, a 36-year-old electrician, said that by campaigning all night Gore was 'showing the work ethic this country needs.' "[16]

In addition, like campaign advertising, campaign visits often involve other political leaders and celebrities, who by their attendance as well as their words endorse the candidate and provide signals on candidate valence issues. Ben Affleck campaigned for Gore in this manner in 2000 (as we discussed in chapter 2) and for Kerry in 2004. In 2004, Kerry was accompanied by Bruce Springsteen in Wisconsin and other states and made Springsteen's song "No Surrender" the campaign anthem. Jon Bon Jovi joined John Edwards when Edwards spoke at the University of Wisconsin at La Crosse. Country music star Lee Greenwood campaigned with Bush. When World Series–winning Red Sox pitcher Curt Schilling had to cancel his appearance with Bush in New Hampshire, Arnold Schwarzenegger was quickly drafted as a substitute. Usually the political leader or celebrity is someone with some connection to the crowd. Gore was also joined by Martin Luther King III, son of civil rights leader Martin Luther King, Jr., when he campaigned before black groups in Memphis. In 2000, Bush campaigned with Republican governor Tommy Thompson and the Oak Ridge Boys in rallies with rural voters in Wisconsin. And in 2004, Bush toured the battleground state of Ohio with Jack Nicklaus, a native of Columbus.

Reducing Uncertainty Fifth, campaign visits may be an opportunity for voters to learn more about a candidate's policy positions, and so on. We discussed earlier how reducing the uncertainty that voters have about candidates can affect their preferences for candidates. In 2000, twenty-one-year-old Pennsylvania voter Patsy Cunningham remarked after seeing Bush at a campaign stop: "That actually made me really start to think, start to want to be politically educated." As a consequence, "she began following issues important to her, such as taxes and foreign policy, and settled on Bush."[17] Candidates discuss campaign issues in visits they make, usually issues that they have been told by their campaign staff the voters in the area are particularly concerned about. In 2000 in Clearwater, Florida, for instance, Bush held a long question-and-answer session at a retirement center because state Republican Party leaders wanted him "to work harder to explain his tax cut, prescription-drug and Medicare proposals" in order to reach the large population of senior citizens who live in the state.[18] In West Virginia, where perceptions of Gore's positions on the environment had alienated some in the mining industry and hunters were worried about the candidate's stance on gun control, Gore spoke directly to a crowd about his thinking on those issues.[19]

Cheap Advertising Sixth, campaign visits allow a candidate to avail himself or herself of "cheap" advertising in local media markets. In 2004, both Kerry and Bush took bus tours through rural communities in battleground states: Kerry went to West Virginia, Ohio, and Michigan, and Bush traveled through Ohio, Iowa, and Wisconsin. Such trips often focus on small towns that are hard to reach by airplane. When a candidate visits a community, there is coverage in the local newspapers and on radio and television stations, coverage that the candidate does not have to purchase. Moreover, the coverage can be greater in rural communities than in a large city such as New York or Los Angeles. Thus, the advertising bang for the buck is higher for a campaign visit to a small community than for a larger one. For example, in 2004, the local La Crosse, Wisconsin, newspaper's front-page headline featured Bush's visit there. According to the *Milwaukee Journal Sentinel*, when Bush visited Lancaster, Wisconsin, "factories, the local parochial school and the public elementary school closed."[20] The candidate or his or her staff and surrogates may grant interviews to local media reporters and thus generate news stories about the candidate. Campaign visits, then, can have a multiplier effect, providing more exposure of the candidate to more voters than the number who actually see the candidate during the visit. A survey of media use by Pew Research Center in June 2004 found that 59 percent of respondents watched the local television news regularly, compared with 34 percent who watched the network television news (CBS, ABC, NBC, or Fox). Much smaller percentages watch specialty news channels regularly.

Empirical Evidence Is there empirical evidence beyond the anecdotes that campaign visits affect voters? King and Morehouse (2004), comparing state-level poll data before and after candidates' visits in the 2000 campaign, found that on average a campaign visit by Bush in a state increased his poll numbers by 1.56 percent in that state and a visit by Gore in a state increased his numbers by 1.4 percent in that state. King and Morehouse also examined Gore's postconvention Mississippi riverboat tour of small Wisconsin, Iowa, Illinois, and Missouri communities. They found that in local polls Gore's percentage of support rose on average 11.5 percent and that the percentage of undecided voters dropped 9.4 points. According to the researchers, Gore also gained national coverage from the trip by the major networks, and *The Christian Science Monitor* reported that Gore was gaining momentum in the race. They also found that the trip had lingering effects on Gore's support in the area. They calculated that the trip generated Gore approximately 16,331 votes in Iowa, a state he won with just over 4,000 votes. Similarly, they estimated that the trip gained him the votes he needed to win Wisconsin as well. Given that the trip only cost $600,000, the payoff was significant. King and Morehouse (p. 4) reported that the value of the trip was not lost on Bush campaign manager Karl Rove, who stated after the election that it was the best tactical move the Gore campaign made—"it was good because it got the candidate 'glowing news coverage in some relatively inaccessible areas of eastern Iowa, and other key battle ground states.' "

In his study of the determinants of presidential vote shares in states, discussed in chapter 7, Shaw (1999) also examined the effect of campaign visits. As with campaign advertisements, because both candidates are campaigning, we need to look not at the effect of one candidate's visit on his or her vote, but at the effect of the difference in the two candidate's visits. That is, if both Bush and Kerry visited Ohio in 2004 the same number of times, we would not expect that their visits would have affected the votes they received in Ohio. But if Bush visited Ohio more than Kerry and campaign visits affect voters, we would expect that Bush would receive more votes than he would have otherwise. Thus, Shaw examined whether the difference in candidates' visits in a state affects the vote share of the candidates in the state in the presidential elections of 1988, 1992, and 1996. His findings were similar to those for campaign advertising—that is, when a candidate visits a state more often than his or her opponent, the candidate's vote share is increased. Moreover, Shaw also found that the effect is greater when the percentage of undecided voters in the state as of September is higher.

Modeling the Effect of Visits on Voters In summary, there are many ways in which campaign visits can positively influence how much support a candidate receives. Thus, it is justified to assume that the more campaign visits a candidate makes to a state, the more utility a voter in the state receives from the election of that candidate. We will now assume that there are two candidates, D and R (sometimes we refer to them in terms of their 2000 incarnation, Gore and Bush). For now, we ignore the impact of minor-party candidates, which we discuss in more detail in chapter 14. In terms of notation, we use d_s^D to represent the number of visits candidate D makes to state s and d_s^R to represent the number of visits candidate R makes to state s. The utility that a voter in state s gets from visits from candidate D is then represented as $U(d_s^D)$ and the utility a voter gets from visits from candidate R is represented as $U(d_s^R)$.

We assume that the effect of visits on utility decreases with the number of visits—that is, visits increase voter utility but at a decreasing rate. Essentially, we are assuming that voters' utility from campaign visits is like Sona's utility from policy in chapter 4—concave.[21] Voters also have policy preferences for the candidates, of course, and we assume that the ideological preference of a voter for candidate R over D is given by the term R. In terms of the 2000 contest, we can think of R as the difference in utility the voter gets from Bush being elected instead of Gore in a state where there are no campaign visits (for example, New York). If R is positive, the voter has a preference for Bush independent of any campaign visits, and if it is negative, the voter has a preference for Gore independent of any campaign visits. Obviously, R will vary by voter and by state.[22]

Adding in Electoral Uncertainty In chapter 4, we noted that often candidates and voters are uncertain about voters' preferences in advance of an election. This is also true in presidential campaigns. To some extent, we can think of voters' preferences for presidential candidates as affected by national shocks. For example, after September 11 many voters were much more concerned about fighting terrorism than they had been before, and this new concern affected their policy preferences. Willingness to increase defense spending and to allow for increased police surveillance went up. If a national that changes voters' preferences occurs during an election, it can obviously similarly affect the outcome. Voters' preferences might also be affected by state-level shocks. For example, late-season forest fires in the West might alter western voters' preferences on some environmental issues, or an unexpected downturn in a state's economy because of a decrease in demand for one of its largest industries might alter the state's voters' preferences for government spending and unemployment insurance. We use η_s to represent a state-level shock in state s. If it is positive, the shock increases the voters' preference for Bush; if it is negative, it increases the voters' preference for Gore. We use η to represent a national-level shock. If it is positive, it increases the voters' preference for Bush; if it is negative, it increases the voters' preference for Gore.

At election time, any shock that is going to occur during the campaign will have occurred. We assume that if a voter is indifferent, he or she will vote for Gore; then a voter will vote for Gore if

$$U(d_s^D) - U(d_s^R) \geq R + \eta_s + \eta$$

If the above equation is not true, the voter chooses Bush.

However, although voters choose individually, we assume that a candidate wins a state's electoral vote if he or she wins the most votes in the state (that is, there is a winner-take-all distribution of electoral votes rather than a proportional distribution) and that states vary in their electoral vote. Thus, the candidate's probability of winning the election is the probability that he will win the most electoral votes, which depends on the probability of winning each state times the electoral votes each state has.

Candidates' Preferences

Given voters' preferences and the distribution of electoral votes across the states, we assume that candidates choose how many days to campaign in each state in order to maximize their expected probability of winning the election. Candidates are obviously in a strategic situation in which each one needs to make the best choices he can make given what the other is doing. Candidates are constrained, however, by the number of days they have to campaign (presidential campaigns historically begin around Labor Day and end on election day—although candidates often campaign as soon as the nomination is secure, and political conventions are today viewed more as free advertising).

Of course, candidates may have other goals in campaigning, such as helping out congressional or senatorial candidates or candidates in state and local races. Although these factors are likely to be important, we assume that candidates first concentrate on maximizing the probability of their own victory, and to the extent that there is leeway in how a candidate does this, he or she also will help out other candidates in other races. So, for example, if Bush wishes to visit California, rather than pick an area of the state at random, he may choose to campaign in a congressional district where a candidate he wishes to help is running, as his 2000 visit to Fresno was meant to help out Rich Rodriguez. At the last minute, Bush added a visit to New Jersey to his 2000 schedule, to help out the Republican candidate for the Senate, Bob Franks. It was an easy add-on, as he was in Philadelphia, on his way to Florida, and he stopped in New Jersey only because a poll showed Franks in a competitive race.[23] But Bush did not take the time to cross the Hudson and visit New York to help out Republican senatorial candidate Rick Lazio, who was running against Hillary Clinton in a tough race, even though it is probably a given that supporters of Lazio wished he had.

Equilibrium Choices

Visit, Countervisit We now have a basic model of campaigning. The next step is to "solve" the model, or discover what the candidates will do in equilibrium—that is, discover the optimal strategy for each candidate, given that his opponent is also choosing an optimal strategy. In solving the model for the equilibrium campaign strategies of the candidates, Stromberg (2002) first found that in equilibrium the candidates should end up visiting the same states. This follows from the fact that the probability of winning for one candidate is just one minus the probability of winning for the other. So if Gore finds it optimal to visit a state because the visit will most increase his probability of winning the Electoral College, it is also probably true that a visit by Bush to that state will most increase Bush's probability of winning the Electoral College as well. In general, the candidates did visit pretty much the same states, as shown in figure 13.1 (Shaw provided Stromberg with this data). The figure shows the percentage of visits by presidential candidates added to one half times the percentage of visits by vice presidential candidates by state for each party. There are some notable exceptions—Gore visited Florida many more times than Bush, and Bush visited California many more times than Gore. Gore also visited Iowa, Wisconsin, and Missouri more than Bush (as part of the riverboat trip), and Bush visited Michigan, Pennsylvania, and Ohio more than Gore. The fact that Bush visited California more than Gore, who visited Florida to a greater extent, a state that became decisive in the election outcome, does lead credence to the ex post conclusion that Bush did not make the right choice in visiting California as often as he did.

Decisive Swing States Stromberg (2002) also found that optimally the candidates should devote more time to visiting states that are likely to be

Presidential Campaign Visits by State, 2000

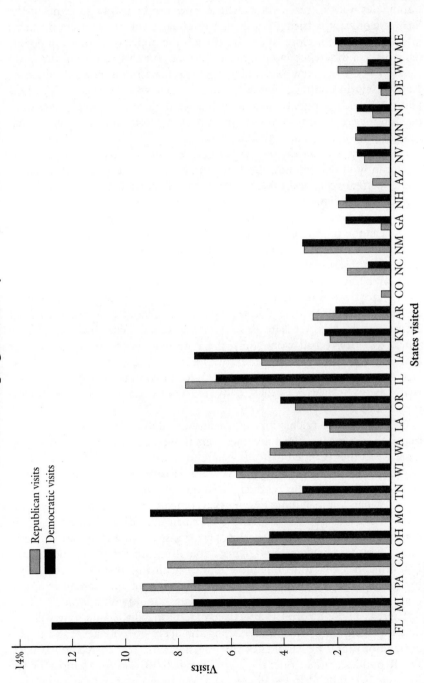

Source:: Stromberg (2002).
Note: Percentage of visits by presidential candidates added to one half times the percentage of visits by vice-presidential candidates.

"decisive swing states."[24] What does it mean to be a decisive swing state? Candidates want to reach voters whose votes can be pivotal in terms of the final outcome. It is fairly obvious that candidates will concentrate on states in which the race is close (swing states) and the undecided voter can potentially make a difference in how the state goes. For this reason, in the 2000 election Texas and New York did not get much attention, nor did Illinois or New Jersey. In contrast, Florida, where the race was close, got a lot of attention. Florida Republicans thought Bush had Florida sewn up in late summer and were surprised when the race got close and Gore ended up campaigning in the state a great deal.

But closeness is not the only factor in determining whether a state counts significantly in determining the outcome. Because states vary in the size of their electoral vote, and for most states the electoral vote is allocated on a winner-take-all basis, not all states have the same probability of being pivotal in terms of the overall outcome, even if the candidates are in equally close races in all the states. For example, in 2004 Bush won New Mexico with just 5,988 more votes than Kerry. New Mexico was clearly a swing state, ex post facto. But if Kerry had won New Mexico, he still would have lost the election because New Mexico had only 5 electoral votes; Kerry needed 270 electoral votes to win (because of the majority requirement), and he received only 252. Another 5 votes would have placed him closer, but not close enough. Another state Bush won was Texas. Texas had 34 electoral votes, so if Kerry had won Texas, the state would have been decisive for him. But there Bush had a comfortable margin of 1,694,213 votes, so Texas was not, ex post facto, a swing state. Ohio, in contrast, ex post facto, was both close—Bush won by 118,599 votes—and decisive, as it had 20 electoral votes.

Of course, these calculations of which states were decisive swing states are made after knowing the outcome, something not possible for Bush and Gore when they planned their campaign visits in the fall of 2000. Stromberg calculated the probability that a state was a decisive swing state using polling and other data that the candidates would have had available on September 1, when campaigning began. We compare these estimates with the actual visits in figure 13.2 (Gore-Lieberman and Bush-Cheney visits are combined). Some of the states that were decisive swing states are not startling—Florida, Michigan, and Pennsylvania. But surprisingly for the experts, California has the fourth highest rating, justifying Bush's visits there—though perhaps not as many times as he went. Hence, on September 1, California looked like a state that both candidates should visit a lot.

There is a strong correlation between the probability that a state will be a decisive swing state, as measured using the September 1 data, and the percentage of times the candidates visit the state; the raw correlation is 0.91. For Republican visits alone, the correlation is 0.90, and for Democratic visits alone it is 0.88.[25] Iowa, Illinois, and Maine received notably more visits than predicted, and Colorado received fewer. These differences between

Predicted versus Actual Presidential Campaign Visits, 2000

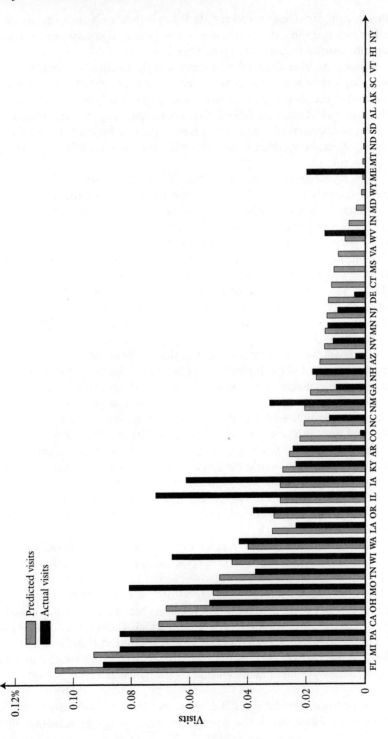

Source: Stromberg (2002).
Note: Utah, Texas, Rhode Island, Oklahoma, Nebraska, Massachusetts, Kansas, and Idaho = 0 for both series.

theory and facts may represent decisions candidates made based on new information during the campaign, as the predicted choices are made based on information available on September 1.

Having decisive electoral votes and a close election are factors affecting whether a state is a decisive swing state, but they are not the only determinants. Yet the theory predicts that some states should be visited more often than their closeness or electoral size would normally predict, either because of the anticipation of national and state shocks or because visiting the states might affect the variance in the national electoral vote. Why?

The Effect of National and State Shocks Suppose that in the national election Bush was expected to receive 60 percent of the vote to Gore's 40 percent. In such a case, individual states are likely to vary in how close they are—some will be close, with the two candidates tied; some will have Gore winning; and some will have an expected vote difference like that for the nation as a whole, with Bush expected to win by 60 percent. In September 1996, Clinton was ahead by 60 percent nationally and in Pennsylvania. But in Texas the race was close. Should Clinton have campaigned in Texas or in Pennsylvania? Clearly, campaigning in Texas was likely to increase his margin in the state and increase his ability to win the election, given the current expectations.

But recall that candidates recognize that national shocks can affect voters' preferences and their probability of winning. Suppose the economy had taken a sudden downturn during the campaign and voters blamed Clinton because he was president. Assume that Clinton faced a situation in which the race was suddenly 50/50 because of that shock. Then it is likely that Pennsylvania was also at 50/50 because the national shock affected all states, whereas Texas was expected to surely go to Dole. Campaigning in Pennsylvania, then, would have been best for Clinton because the state was clearly a decisive swing state, whereas Texas was a lost cause. So, given current expectations, Texas was the better state to campaign in, but if a large national shock had occurred, Pennsylvania would have been more important.

How should candidates balance out the two effects? Recall that voters' preferences are affected by state-specific shocks as well. Stromberg calculated that the probability of being a decisive swing state per electoral vote is highest when a state's forecasted electoral outcome is halfway between 50/50 and the forecasted national electoral outcome. In 1996, this would have meant more often visiting large states in which Clinton was ahead by about 55 percent. In 2000, when opinion polls suggested that Gore had a slight lead, it meant that both candidates should have given weight to states in which Gore was just slightly ahead of Bush (such as Pennsylvania).

Increasing the Variance But of course Gore's small lead over Bush in September 2000 was in the share of expected votes. In actuality, all knew that the vote share might be larger or it might be smaller—that is, there is a margin of error in the estimate, or a variance in the vote share. (Recall our discussion of predicting election outcomes in chapter 10.) The higher the variance, the greater the chance that Bush can still win even though his expected vote share is less than Gore's. Thus, one strategy that Bush should have used was to try to increase the variance somehow, and Gore should have tried to reduce that variance. But how?

It turns out that the variance in the national vote, conditional on the national shock, is the sum of the variances across all the states. Each state's variance is proportional to the electoral votes in the state squared. This means that the effect on total national variance, per electoral vote, is higher in large states. So Bush should have visited large states. But which ones? The variance in a state is also higher the closer the expected result in the state is to a tie. So to increase the variance in a state, Bush would have wanted to visit states in which he was behind so that he could move that state toward an expected tie. Lagging candidates, like Bush in September 2000, should visit states with large electoral votes that are in the opponent's column (which is, of course, reinforcing the effect mentioned earlier).

On the other hand, Gore, the leading candidate, would have liked to reduce the variance. So he would have wanted to increase his defense of states in which he was ahead. In September 2000, the large states in which Gore was ahead were Michigan and Pennsylvania; Bush was slightly ahead in Ohio. Gore should have visited Michigan and Pennsylvania defensively. Thus, the probability that a state is a decisive swing state depends on the effect it can have on the variance of the vote as well as on the expected vote. As we see in figure 13.2, Michigan and Pennsylvania received more campaign visits than Ohio, as predicted. Finally, note that the reason why increasing (or decreasing) the variance may be desirable for a lagging (or leading) candidate is related to the fact that the election has a win-or-lose outcome—that is, it doesn't matter to the candidates by how much they win, just that they win. If candidates cared about electoral vote totals as well or instead, then the prediction about which states to visit would be different, and there would be less of an advantage in affecting the variance.

There are a number of sports analogies that show how lagging teams might take actions to increase the variance around the expected outcome in a last-ditch effort to win. Stromberg mentioned how in ice hockey a team behind might take out its goalie and replace him with offensive players. The team trades a decrease in the expected chance of winning for an increase in the variance around that value. In basketball, players on a team that is losing sometimes intentionally foul a player late in the game because although the player gets a free throw and the chance to score, the losing team gets the ball back and the chance to score. Similarly in football, teams that are behind when a game is close to ending and are facing a fourth down may choose an onside kick, which they can potentially catch and score with, but in many cases the opposing team just catches it, and since that team is closer to its end zone, it is more likely to score or just run out the clock. Another football example is when a quarterback at the end of a game throws what is commonly referred to as the Hail Mary pass, hoping that one of his players will catch it but taking the chance that the other team will catch it and increase its score or run out the clock. And in baseball, a team may pull a pitcher who is doing better than his potential replacement at defending the team against runs and put in a "pitch hitter" who is likely to score a run. One exception to this norm in sports is World Cup soccer, in which a team's place depends on its scores and thus teams care not just about winning or losing their games.[26]

Why California?

Although our analysis helps explain what makes a decisive swing state, the fact remains that the candidates did not always visit the states predicted at the rates predicted or they did not even visit the same states. Bush did go to California more than is predicted in figure 13.1 even though California was predicted to receive a lot of campaign visits by both candidates. One important thing to recognize about the real-world data is that if one candidate does not choose the optimal distribution of visits, the other candidate's optimal strategies are affected. In September 2000, Gore's expected vote share in California was 56 percent. Defensively, Gore needed to visit California because of its large size, since as a slightly lagging candidate in September, if Bush could move California closer to a tie, he would increase the variance in the national outcome. But Gore neglected California and Bush visited it, so the expected vote share moved to Bush's advantage, further increasing Bush's reason for visiting the state. Bush appeared to try to capitalize on this by visiting California even late in the campaign. The strategy was apparently not successful, however, as Bush lost California, and it was costly to him because visits to Florida instead might have shored up his vote there, allowing him to avoid the Florida battle of the ballots after the election.

In Florida, Bush made a strategic error by not visiting a lot, but he did make defensive visits to counter Gore, who recognized early on that it was a highly decisive swing state. Bush's brother had recently been elected governor of the state, and Bush's team believed at the beginning of the campaign that it was a relatively safe state for them because they knew that Cuban Americans were unhappy with the Clinton administration's return of the child Elian Gonzalez to Cuban (when Gore was vice president) and so would be energized against Gore. But Bush was surprised that Gore's choice of Joe Lieberman, the first Jewish candidate for vice president, would carry so much of the state in Gore's direction in opinion polls.[27] Bush made defensive visits to the state, but Gore clearly spent more time there overall. Chuck Reed, a Flagler County businessman, concluded about Bush's increased visits as the campaign progressed: "I know he didn't plan on spending that much time here, but if it's necessary, that's what has to be done. It will make a tremendous difference. It will give the voters a little more closeness to him and his ideas."[28]

Why Albuquerque?

Voters in New York not only didn't see Gore and Bush much in person during 2000, but they didn't see them on television either. Just as candidates strategically choose which states to visit, they also strategically spend money on advertising. Stromberg (2002) also modeled the game the candidates play in advertising across the states. The same sorts of factors that affect candidates' visits also affect their advertising—candidates should advertise more in media markets in which the voters are in decisive swing states. Stromberg found that the model predicted that the two media markets in which most campaign ads should appear were Albuquerque–Santa Fe, New Mexico, and Portland, Oregon, markets that per advertising dollar had the greatest effect on the probability of winning. It turns out that these were the same media markets in which candidates did advertise the most. Why Albuquerque instead of a media market in a state that called for a lot of campaign visits, such as Florida or California? Of the voters in the Albuquerque market, 95 percent lived in New Mexico, and New Mexico was hardly a state with a lot of electoral votes—it had only five in 2000. But with only 1.8 million citizens, it has a high electoral vote per capita (the effect of small states). The race was also very close there—it was clearly a swing state. Furthermore, the cost per ad is one of the lowest in the nation. So the price differential means that the areas of the country where advertising should be high are not always the same as those candidates should visit a lot (although there certainly was more advertising in the states visited a lot, such as California and Florida, than in New York and Texas).

The Electoral Vote and Government Spending

Retrospective Voting and the Electoral College

Thousands of people on a Sunday afternoon in October 2000 crowded the downtown area of East Lansing, Michigan. Usually a slow day for businesses, Troppo Restaurant tripled its sales. Why the increase in business? Democratic presidential candidate Al Gore was holding a rally. According to a news report, " 'People were stuck in front of us for about six hours,' " . . . reported manager Curtis Turner. "Tom Guastello, president of Center Management, said business has increased at his four metro Detroit hotels because of the entourage of reporters and Secret Service agents that follows Democrat Al Gore and Republican George W. Bush as they campaign. 'Being a swing state, we've had a lot of traffic come through, especially in Macomb County," Guastello said."[29]

The fact that candidates are elected by the Electoral College rather than a national popular vote potentially benefits voters in decisive swing states in more ways than bringing customers into restaurants during campaigns. Recall chapter 9, in which we saw how voters might choose in elections retrospectively, according to what they have received in the past from the incumbent. As long as the incumbent is viewed as better than the random draw of a challenger, voters will prefer the incumbent. If an incumbent knows he or she is going to be facing reelection and voters will choose retrospectively, then to the extent that the incumbent can discriminate in the distribution of resources, he or she will want to please the voters in decisive swing states and distribute more resources to them than to voters in other states. This implies that not all voters will be treated equally when federal resources are distributed.

Of course, presidents are limited to two terms, which may mean that the potential for an inequitable distribution of resources across voters nationally is not a large problem. If presidents care about the success of their party's nominee, however, and voters evaluate candidates based on the performance of their party and the incumbent is in their party (if Gore is evaluated on Clinton's record), then the president may find it optimal to distribute resources unequally across voters, according to which voters live in decisive swing states.

Stromberg (2002) pointed out that if the president were elected through direct popular vote and federal resources were distributed across states to influence that vote, the resources would be allocated to influence marginal voters (independents or moderates) nationwide. Marginal or moderate voters are more likely to be in states in which the vote share varies with the national vote share. Stromberg compared the distribution of such voters nationwide and found less variation in them than in the probability of being a decisive swing state according to the Electoral College. This implies that there would be less unequal distribution of resources across states under a direct popular vote for president than there is with the Electoral College.

Empirical Evidence

Is there evidence of incumbent presidents' allocating more resources to expected decisive swing states? There is some evidence of federal expenditure targeting. Mebane and Wawro (2002) examined federal expenditures as a function of a county's support for an incumbent president and found evidence of targeting of expenditures. They did not consider the effects of the Electoral College on those choices, however. Wright (1974) found a positive relationship between per capita New Deal spending and per capita electoral votes. However, one complicating factor in estimating the effect of the Electoral College on federal expenditures is that electoral votes are unequally distributed across states mainly because they are allocated on the basis of the number of senators and representatives each state has, and regardless of size, each state has an equal number of senators. Thus, the evidence Wright finds may be due to overrepresentation of voters in the Senate rather than the Electoral College. A number of researchers have examined the extent to which representation in the Senate and House determine federal expenditures; see in particular Lee (2004, 2003, 2000, 1998). They found that federal expenditures are likely to be unequally distributed because of the overrepresentation of small states. Theory suggests, however, that if the Electoral College is a factor in the distribution of expenditures, then the likelihood that a state is a decisive swing state would be important. At this writing, we are not aware of an empirical study that examines the effect of decisive swing state status on federal expenditures.

Voters and Divided Government

The Saga of Patients' Rights

When he ran for Congress in 2000, Larry Weatherford had a main issue—support for the Patient's Bill of Rights legislation that would allow patients to sue their HMOs, which the incumbent member of Congress did not back and is outlawed by federal law. Weatherford lost, as we discussed in chapter 12, but Republican Charlie Norwood, a dentist elected in 1994 from Georgia, has made patients' rights a significant part of his agenda since 1997. Under the federal Employee Retirement Income Security Act of 1974, or ERISA, patients can sue HMOs for the dollar value of services found to have been improperly denied but not for damages resulting from the denial. Norwood quickly learned (as Osborne told the farmers in Nebraska) that getting legislation passed in Congress is a difficult process. The story of Norwood's attempt to pass a Patient's Bill of Rights is a good illustration of how the president and Congress must negotiate and compromise in order to pass legislation. The fact that they must do so also has important implications for how voters choose in federal elections. The story of the Patient's Bill of Rights also illustrates how both Congress and the president sometimes use their negotiations to communicate with voters.

In 1999, with a large bipartisan majority, Norwood and his co-sponsor, Democratic representative John Dingell, saw their Patient's Bill of Rights pass 275–151 in the House. President Clinton announced his support for the bill, stating that it was "a major victory for every family." But the legislation could not reach the president for his signature unless the Senate also passed the bill, and the Senate passed only a limited version. "For the next year, all sorts of negotiations took place: Republican-Democrat, House-Senate, Congress–White House. But the bill remained logjammed" (Barone, Cohen, and Ujifusa 2001, p. 460). It was this logjam that motivated Weatherford's candidacy. Gore also campaigned on the issue.

Bush became president, replacing Clinton; Republicans controlled both the House (although only by nine votes) and the Senate (only by Vice President Cheney's tie-breaking privileges). The White House started to lobby fellow Republican Norwood on the Patient's Bill of Rights issue, and when the bill was reintroduced in the House in 2001, Norwood was no longer the main sponsor. In March, Bush announced that he had his own plan for patient protection and that he disliked the plan proposed by Dingell that was being considered in the Senate (sponsored by Senators John Edwards, John McCain, and Edward Kennedy). The Senate plan allowed patients who sued their insurance companies after treatment was denied to get as much as $5 million in punitive damages (not a surprising amount, given that John Edwards had been a trial lawyer and opposed any limits on damages). Bush argued that the limit was too high. In a speech before a convention of cardiologists, he declared: "To make sure health care coverage remains affordable, I will insist any federal bill have reasonable caps on damage awards."[30] His press secretary, Ari Fleischer, told reporters that Bush's statement was a "veto pledge," meaning that if the bill came before the president without lower caps than those in the Senate bill, the president would veto it.

In May, Vermont senator James Jeffords announced that he would become an independent and vote with Democrats on organizational issues in the Senate. Democrats were now in the majority and could control the agenda. On June 29, the Senate passed the bipartisan bill with a majority of 59–36 (nine Republicans joined the fifty Democrats).[31] Now the bill would go to the House, and Republicans were apprehensive. If it passed the House—and many worried it would because the House had passed a similar bill in 1999—then "that would force Bush to veto a bill popular with millions of Americans, or to back down before triumphant Democrats."[32] What to do? Would the House, like the Senate, pass the legislation? Would the president then veto the bill? Would Congress attempt to override the veto if that happened? And how does all this relate to elections?

The President and Legislation

Legislation without Congress The Constitution of the United States gives Congress the power to pass legislation and control the national government. However, the Constitution also contains the presentation clause, which requires that Congress present all bills to the president for his or her signature. Furthermore, the president, as head of the executive branch, is involved in the implementation of legislation and has the ability to make executive agreements with foreign countries and issue domestic executive orders in order to implement policy as required by the Constitution. All this gives the president significant power over legislation.

It is useful to reflect on how much the president and the executive branch can do independent of congressional action. After the 2002 midterm elections, President Bush announced a review of all federal rules and regulations. His office began to declare new executive orders and rules at a rate of one every few days, causing many to claim he was bypassing Congress.[33] But actually issuing such orders is normal. Clinton issued fifty-seven executive orders in his first year in office, whereas Bush issued fifty-four. These executive orders and rules have policy implications. Even simple executive-branch decisions on the way to calculate student aid can affect millions of Americans and reduce federal support for education.[34] When the Department of Health and Human Services increased subsidized child health insurance for prenatal care, the rules noted that the fetus should be treated as a child. And in two executive orders issued in December 2002, Bush required that federal agencies not discriminate against religious organizations in awarding money to community and social service groups for programs to help people in need and created new offices for religion-based initiatives in the Department of Agriculture and the Agency of International Development.

Of course, the rules are limited by existing legislation and by the Constitution, and Congress can act to alter executive-branch decisions it dislikes. After the Federal Communications Commission—under the leadership of Michael K. Powell, who was appointed by President Bush—voted along party lines to allow for greater deregulation of media control, a number of senators criticized the decision and immediately introduced legislation to change the ruling, which according to the Congressional Review Act of 1996, Congress can do without approval of the president.[35] Congress did use this power to overturn one of the Clinton administration's workplace ergonomic rules. Nevertheless, executive orders and administrative rule making give the president agenda power independent of Congress.

The Presentation Clause: When Both the President and Congress Want Change Whereas executive orders, rules, and regulations are a way in which the president can bypass Congress, for major legislation Congress must be involved. President Bush cannot cap liabilities for HMOs or legislate patients' rights significantly without such a bill first being passed by Congress. We will use a simple model to understand how this process works. We assume that Congress's preferences on policy can be represented by the ideal point of the median voter in Congress, which we will call C. Although we recognize that the process by which Congress makes decisions is complex, we make the assumption that the median voter in Congress is the one who is "decisive" in passing legislation. We assume that as policy moves away from this point, Congress is less and less happy as a whole (similar to the decline in utility that Charlotte experienced in chapter 4 as policy moved away from her ideal point). Similarly, we assume that the president has a most preferred policy position, P, and that as policy moves away from P, he is less and less happy.

Given the status quo policy position, which we call SQ, and the positions of C and P on a policy issue, when will Congress pass a bill that the president will sign, and what will that bill look like? There are two configurations of these three points that will result in Congress's passing a bill that the president will sign. We will call these cases 1 and 2. Figure 13.3 presents an example of case 1, and figure 13.4 presents an example of case 2. In figure 13.3, the president's most preferred policy position is at 25, Congress's most preferred position is at 40, and SQ is at 45. The president will approve any bill between 5 and 45 because any point in that range is closer to 25 than 45 is. Any bill that Congress presents to the president that is within that range the president will sign. Congress would like to propose a bill that is as close to its most preferred position, 40, as possible. Because the president prefers 40 to 45, Congress can just pass a bill equal to its median voter's ideal point of 40 and the president will sign the bill. Clearly, this was not the case with the Patient's Bill of Rights legislation, as the indications suggest that the president did not want to allow patients to sue as much as Congress preferred.

FIGURE 13.3
Effect of Presentation Clause, Case 1

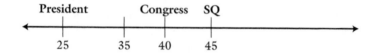

FIGURE 13.4
Effect of Presentation Clause, Case 2

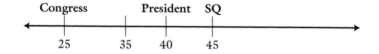

Case 2 is somewhat closer to the disagreement between Congress and the president over the Patient's Bill of Rights legislation. In figure 13.4, the president's ideal point and Congress's median voter's ideal point are reversed; now the president's ideal point is at 40, whereas Congress's is at 25. The president will sign bills in the range of 35 to 45, but Congress's median voter's ideal point is no longer in this range. However, the policy choices that the president prefers to the status quo are also points that Congress prefers to the status quo. Congress will want to propose a bill as close to its ideal point as possible, but one that the president is willing to sign. Assume that if the president is indifferent in the choice between the SQ and Congress's bill, the president will sign Congress's bill. Congress, therefore, will propose a bill at 35, where the president is just indifferent in the choice between the SQ and the bill and is as close to Congress's median voter's ideal point as the president is willing to approve. If case 2 is the situation, we would expect Congress would just alter the legislation to please the president and the president would sign the legislation.

Note that Congress, by having the power to pass legislation, has proposal power. That is, Congress determines the choices the president faces. The president can get his ideal policy preference passed only if that point is equal to the *SQ*. Thus, instead of being able to choose policy from the range of all possible alternatives, he can choose only whether to accept Congress's proposed bill or the *SQ*. Through Congress's power to set the agenda, a multitude of choices has been reduced to only two choices. No doubt this is frustrating to a president like Bush, who has his own ideas about what legislation should be passed.

When Only Congress Wants Change In both cases 1 and 2, the president and Congress's ideal points are on the same side of the status quo— that is, Congress and the president agreed that the status quo should be changed. What happens if the president and Congress do not agree that the status quo should be changed? Figure 13.5 presents an example of this situation. Here the president's ideal point is at 25, the status quo is at 45, and Congress's ideal point is at 80. Unlike cases 1 and 2, there is no overlap between the points that the president prefers to the status quo (points less than 45) and the points Congress prefers to the status quo (points greater than 45). Clearly, the president will veto any bill that Congress prefers. The president has veto power over legislation, but the veto of a president can be overridden if the House and the Senate pass the bill a second time by a two-thirds or greater vote. However, if a president does not sign a bill within ten days, it automatically becomes law. But if the president chooses not to sign a bill during the last ten days of a legislative session, the limit will expire after Congress is out of session, and the bill is vetoed, in what is called a pocket veto.[36]

If a veto occurs, what can Congress do? Although the president has veto power, the Constitution allows Congress to pass bills over a presidential veto if a two-thirds majority in Congress is willing to vote for an override. This means that in the case where Congress and the president disagree, the decisive voter in Congress is not the median voter, *C*, but the voter whose ideal point is such that two thirds of the voters whose ideal points are either greater or less than his or her ideal point prefer the bill. In our example, if

FIGURE 13.5
Effect of Presentation Clause, Case 3

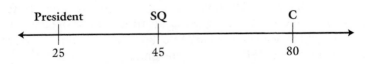

two thirds of the voters' ideal points are greater than some point greater than 45—say, 50—then Congress can choose a bill at that point, and even if the president vetoes it, enough members of Congress will vote to override the veto, passing the bill. If this two-thirds point is less than or equal to 45, there is no bill the median voter in Congress will prefer to SQ that could get enough votes to override a veto.

Congressional-Presidential Negotiation and Elections When is it likely that Congress and the president will disagree, as shown in figure 13.5? Generally, the Congress and the president are more likely to disagree over policy when the two branches of government are controlled by different parties— when there is a divided government. In the post–World War II era, divided government has occurred 60 percent of the time (in thirty-six out of sixty years). Table 13.2 presents a summary of divided and unified governments in the United States during this period. Why would this happen? Why would voters be willing to vote such that the Congress and the president would disagree and reduce the chance of either one having preferred policies enacted? We address this question shortly, but first we discuss how the president and Congress might use disagreement to communicate with voters through presidential vetoes.

Why and When Vetoes Happen

Uncertainty If the president and Congress understand the rules of the game, it seems from the analysis above that we should never observe presidential vetoes. If the two branches agree that the status quo should be changed, they should be able to come to some compromise. If the two branches disagree on changing the status quo and Congress passes a bill with a two-thirds majority, or is likely to, then the president should not veto it, as the veto would be meaningless. If Congress does not have a two-thirds majority, then it should not pass a bill, as it knows the bill will be vetoed. Yet presidential vetoes do occur, although they are rare events. Of the 17,428 bills passed by Congress from 1945 to 1992, only 2.3 percent were vetoed (Cameron 2000, pp. 46–47). Why might this happen? It could occur if members of Congress and the president are uncertain about each other's ideal points.

If some vetoes occur because members of Congress are uncertain about the president's ideal point, then we would expect that when Congress attempts to repass the bill after a veto, there may be some concession made to the president—the bill will be modified to come closer to the president's ideal point. Cameron (2000) analyzed presidential vetoes from 1945 to 1992 and estimated that 80 percent of the time Congress appears to make concessions in repassed bills, suggesting that Congress is updating itself on presidential preferences after a veto (note, however, that Congress repasses a bill only approximately 50 percent of the time).

TABLE 13.2
Divided and Unified Federal Government, 1946–2004

Years	President	House and Senate	Type of Government and Duration
		Party	
1946-48	Truman—Democratic	Both Republican	Divided, 2 years
1948–52	Truman—Democratic	Both Democratic	Unified, 4 years
1952–54	Eisenhower—Republican	Both Republican	Unified, 2 years
1954–60	Eisenhower—Republican	Both Democratic	Divided, 6 years
1960–64	Kennedy, Johnson— Democratic	Both Democratic	Unified, 4 years
1964–68	Johnson—Dermocratic	Democratic	Unified, 4 years
1968–72	Nixon—Republican	Democratic	Divided, 4 years
1972–76	Nixon, Ford—Republican	Democratic	Divided, 4 years
1976–80	Carter—Democratic	Democratic	Unified, 4 years
1980–86	Reagan—Republican	Republican Senate, Democratic House	Divided, 6 years
1986–88	Reagan—Republican	Democratic	Divided, 2 years
1988–92	Bush—Republican	Democratic	Divided, 4 years
1992–94	Clinton—Democratic	Democratic	Unified, 2 years
1994–2000	Clinton—Democratic	Republican	Divided, 6 years
2000–2002	Bush—Republican	Republican House, Democratic Senate	Divided, 2 years
2002–8	Bush—Republican	Republican	Unified, 6 years

Blame-Game Politics and Communicating with Voters

<u>Bush and Norwood</u> But what was the situation facing Congress and Bush over the Patient's Bill of Rights legislation in the spring and summer of 2001? It is doubtful that there was much uncertainty about Bush's position on the issue or the views of Congress because the legislation had been debated and discussed since 1997. Bush's statements seem to imply that the situation was as in case 2, where he was willing to see a change in the status quo in the same direction as Congress, but with liability limits. Congress should have been able to compromise with the president and pass the legislation the president wanted. Yet Congress—or at least the Democrats— didn't seem willing to compromise. The Senate bill did not have the limits, the House was ready to vote on the same bill, and the Republicans did not believe they could stop it. A veto would look bad for the president, as the bill had popular support and Democrats were eager to hold Bush to his threat.

With agenda control over the House, Republican Speaker Dennis Hastert postponed the vote on the bill for a few days, realizing he did not have the votes to defeat it. And Bush invited Charlie Norwood over to the White House to talk about things. *The Washington Post* reported: "Bush spent several minutes lavishly praising the Georgia Republican for his skill in leading a band of rebels that had outmaneuvered Bush. . . . But Bush soon dispensed with the pleasantries. 'So now that I've kissed your [rear end], what do I have to do to get a deal?' Bush asked, according to several sources familiar with the meeting."[37] After a three-day intensive lobbying effort, Norwood caved—on August 1, 2001, he and Bush announced an agreement, and the next day the House passed a bill with the limits on liability Bush wanted. *Time* magazine labeled Norwood its Person of the Week. The game was not over, however. Because of the defection of Jeffords (a legislator Bush had failed to court), the Senate was controlled by Democrats, and the legislation would again go to a conference committee. There was still the possibility that the bill would not be to Bush's liking. "These are not legislative victories until they are signed into law," stated Kori Bernards, a spokesperson for House Democratic leader representative Dick Gephardt.[38]

Did Democrats Really Want a Bill? Why would Democrats in the Senate have pressed to pass a bill that they suspected would be vetoed when a compromise was at hand that would likely have been preferred by both to the status quo? Moreover, because the House had passed a bill Bush liked, even if the Democrats were successful in the conference committee, passage with a two-thirds majority in both houses to overcome a veto was highly unlikely.

An answer might be in the popular support the Democrats knew the bill had with the public. They could use Bush's veto to try to communicate to the public that Republicans opposed patients' rights. If vetoes are a way in which elected officials communicate with voters, then we would expect a relationship between elections and veto occurrence. This relationship is likely to be complex. If members of Congress are using presidential vetoes to communicate with the electorate, then they will pass bills they know the president will veto. They are more likely to do this when the president is a member of a different party from the one dominating Congress. Similarly, if the president is using his veto power to communicate with the electorate, he will veto more bills when he is up for reelection and there is divided government. McCarty (2002) analyzed presidential vetoes from 1829 to 1996 and found evidence that incumbents up for reelection are significantly more likely than lame duck incumbents (incumbents in their last term) to veto legislation if there is a divided government. Similarly, incumbents up for reelection when there is a divided government are significantly more likely to veto legislation (vetoing 200–400 percent more legislation) than incumbents up for reelection when there is a unified government.

In August 2001, because of Democratic strength in Congress, Bush had to work hard to convince Republicans in the House, like Norwood, to support his bill, and he still faced the possibility of Senate Democrats forcing him to veto a conference committee bill. Divided government limited Bush, but it also limited the Democrats. Gephardt called Bush's bill "special-interest legislation" that did "the bidding of the health insurance companies and the HMOs over the interests of the people that we represent."[39] John Dingell, who had co-sponsored the original bill with Norwood, had felt victory was in reach and Bush would either veto or be forced to sign his bill. But divided government worked against him.

The Moderating-Voter Theory

Norwood and Augusta Bush and the Democrats had to deal with divided government because of choices voters made. In the 2004 NES survey, 56.79 percent of respondents said that divided government is a good thing, 22.07 percent preferred a unified government, and 21.14 percent said that it did not matter. To understand why the majority of voters would prefer a divided government, consider some of the voters in Norwood's district. The city of Augusta, Georgia, home of golf's famous Masters Tournament, was part of Republican representative Charlie Norwood's congressional district in 2000.[40] It is one of the more liberal areas of the state. Although Georgia was one of the few states Republican presidential candidate Bob Dole won in 1996, Augusta gave Bill Clinton 54 percent of its vote. In 2000, Gore won 55 percent of the city's vote. Yet in 2000, Norwood won reelection over a Democratic opponent with 53 percent of Augusta's vote (and 63 percent of the vote in the entire district). Clearly, some Augusta citizens were voting Democratic for president but Republican for the House of Representatives. If we assume that all the voters in Augusta who voted for Bush also voted for Norwood, that means that 13 percent of Norwood's votes in Augusta came from voters who had chosen Gore for president (of course, some of Bush's supporters might have voted for Norwood's Democratic opponent, implying an even greater percentage of Norwood voters who also chose Gore).

Like the voters in Iowa who elected both Republican Charles Grassley and Democrat Tom Harkin to the Senate at the same time (as discussed in chapter 5), some voters in Augusta seem willing to support both parties in national elections. Although Norwood had fought for patients' rights before the 2000 election, a position at odds with that of more conservative members of his party, his voting record in general was solidly Republican, earning a 5 from the ADA, and the Speaker of the House, Republican Dennis Hastert, had attended a fund-raiser for him in Augusta during his campaign. Norwood has been a consistent opponent of abortion and gun control (earning him a 0 out of 100 from Panned Parenthood and an A from the National Rifle Association). The League of Conservation Voters, an environmental group, gave him a 10 on a 100-point scale. Gore, by contrast, campaigned in favor of abortion and gun control and placed a significant focus on the environmental positions preferred by the League of Conservation Voters.

Fiorina's Moderating-Voter Theory One theory that has been proposed to explain this tendency is the moderating-voter theory of Fiorina (1992), which was mentioned in chapter 5. According to this theory, voters recognize that policy will be determined by bargaining between the president and Congress. Assuming that the president has some slight advantage in the bargaining process and that elected Democrats are more liberal than elected Republicans, one example of the different policy choices before the voters is represented in figure 13.6.[41] In the example, if a Democrat is elected president and Democrats control Congress, policy is at point *DD*, which is 0 on the graph. If a Democrat is president and Republicans control Congress, policy is at *DR*, 20 on the graph. If a Republican is president and Democrats control Congress, policy is at *RD*, or 60, and if Republicans control both the presidency and Congress, policy is at *RR*, or 80. Fiorina's theory is that voters will recognize these differences and will vote sincerely for the most preferred outcome (assuming they have utility functions like those of Charlotte in chapter 4). This means that voters whose ideal points are between 0 and 10 will vote a straight Democratic ticket, voters whose ideal points are between 10 and 40 will vote for the Democrat for president and the Republican for Congress, voters whose ideal points are between 40 and 70 will vote for the Republican for president and the Democrat for Congress, and voters whose ideal points are greater than 70 will vote a straight Republican ticket.

Although some Republican voters in this example may be voting for a divided government, they do not prefer divided government in itself. What they most prefer is the policy outcome that is closest to their ideal point, and it turns out that given the positions of the political parties and the institutional nature of checks and balances in the federal government, the policy outcome under a divided government is closest to their ideal points on policy. They would be just as happy with a united government at the same policy position.

The Evidence Does Fiorina's theory hold up? Table 13.3 presents a summary of the extent of split-ticket voting by voters' identification of themselves on the liberal-conservative policy dimension in NES surveys for presidential elections from 1980 to 2004. In the surveys, 22.04 percent of respondent's reported splitting their vote between the parties in presidential elections. It does appear that as voters become less ideological, they are more likely to split their votes, a finding that supports the moderating-voter theory. Voters who identify themselves as moderates split their votes 27.88 percent of the time (nonmoderates split their votes 19.74 percent of

FIGURE 13.6
Example of Voters' Preferences in Presidential and Congressional Elections

If voters elect a Democratic president and a majority Democratic Congress, policy will be at **DD**. If voters elect a Democratic president and a majority Republican Congress, policy will be at **DR**. If voters elect a Republican president and a majority Democratic Congress, policy will be at **RD**. And if voters elect Republicans as both president and the majority in Congress, policy will be at **RR**.

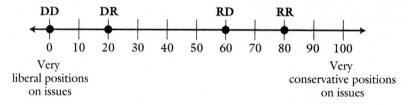

Source: Alesina and Rosenthal (1995).

the time). However, even voters who report that they are either extremely liberal or extremely conservative sometimes split their votes. Extremely conservative voters in the surveys were willing to vote Democratic in both races a surprising 14.12 percent of the time, significantly more often than extremely liberal voters are willing to vote Republican in both contests (1.06 percent of the time).[42]

There are many possible alternative explanations for split-ticket voting besides intentionally moderating voters. In Augusta, liberal voters may have seen that reelecting Norwood was beneficial because he would have more seniority than his challenger and could potentially get more for the city. Alternatively, voters may have been using a retrospective voting strategy, which benefits incumbents. And as noted earlier, because incumbents are more likely to be "known" quantities, voters may prefer them to other candidates whose positions on issues are unknown. If we examine only those surveyed in open-seat congressional races from 1980 to 2000, we find that moderates split their votes 23.2 percent of the time and nonmoderates split their votes 14.62 percent of the time, suggesting that some of the splitting by both moderates and nonmoderates reflects the influence of incumbency, but incumbency is more likely an explanation for the split-ticket voting of nonmoderates. Incumbency may also benefit presidential candidates—and may also lead voters to split their tickets. If we examine just the year 2000, when no incumbent was running for president, and races in which no incumbent was running for Congress, 25 percent of moderates split their votes, compared with 7.41 percent of nonmoderates.

TABLE 13.3
Ticket Voting in Presidential Elections,
as Reported by NES, 1980–2000

Voters Ideological Identity	Voting Choices				
	Democratic President and Democratic Congress	Democratic President and Republican Congress	Republican President and Democratic Congress	Republican President and Republican Congress	Total
Extremely liberal	70 (88.61%)	5 (6.33%)	3 (3.8%)	1 (1.27%)	79 (100%)
Liberal	370 (79.74%)	44 (9.48%)	18 (3.88%)	32 (6.9%)	464 (100%)
Slightly liberal	358 (64.5%)	77 (13.87%)	52 (9.37%)	68 (12.25%)	555 (100%)
Moderate	528 (43.53%)	136 (11.21%)	210 (17.31%)	339 (27.95%)	1,213 (100%)
Slightly conservative	217 (24.69%)	61 (6.94%)	170 (19.34%)	431 (49.03%)	879 (100%)
Conservative	98 (10.19%)	34 (3.53%)	140 (14.55%)	690 (71.73%)	962 (100%)
Extremely conservative	22 (15.38%)	5 (3.5%)	23 (16.08%)	93 (65.03%)	143 (100%)
Total	1,663 (38.72%)	362 (8.43%)	616 (14.34%)	1,654 (38.51%)	4,295 (100%)

Strategic Moderating Voters A number of political scientists have conducted more sophisticated analyses of the extent to which voters appear to split their tickets in order to create a balance between the two parties. The evidence is mixed—some argue that Fiorina's theory is supported, others not, suggesting that incumbency and other factors may be resulting in ticket splitting, not moderate voters balancing between the parties.[43] The data reviewed above show a greater likelihood of split-ticket voting by moderates, although the majority of both moderates and nonmoderates do not split their tickets, and some nonmoderates do. Does this mean that voters are not recognizing that policy is a compromise between the president and Congress and are not moderating between the parties? No. The problem with simply looking at split-ticket voting and concluding that a lack of evidence of such voting implies that voters are not acting intentionally is that voters who prefer divided government might find it strategic to vote a straight ticket, and such voting may be more likely than split-ticket voting to result in divided government. How can that be?

FIGURE 13.7
Sincere Moderating Voters' Choices in Example

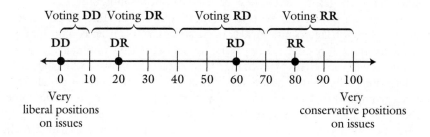

Suppose that in the example in figure 13.6, voters' ideal points are uniformly distributed from 0 to 100. That means that 10 percent of the voters' ideal points are between 0 and 10, 10 percent are between 10 and 20, 10 percent are between 20 and 30, and so on. If the voters vote sincerely for their preferred policy outcomes, then 10 percent (voters with ideal points between 0 and 10) will vote for a Democratic president and a Democratic Congress, 30 percent (voters with ideal points between 10 and 40) will vote for a Democratic president and a Republican Congress, 30 percent (voters with ideal points between 40 and 70) will vote for a Republican president and a Democratic Congress, and 30 percent (voters with ideal points between 70 and 100) will vote for a Republican president and a Republican Congress. These voting choices are shown in figure 13.7. The Democratic candidate for president will get 40 percent of the vote, and the Republican candidate for president will get 60 percent. Congress will also be Republican, with Republican candidates receiving 60 percent of the vote and Democrats 40 percent. Although 60 percent of the voters, all the moderates, are splitting their votes, Republicans dominate the government.

The voters who chose outcome DR cannot be happy, as they received the outcome they preferred the least. Interestingly, it is the outcome that many of Augusta's liberal voters experienced in 2000 even though they had chosen to vote DR. Alesina and Rosenthal (1995), Mebane (2000), and Mebane and Sekhon (2002) presented alternative models in which voters' choices take into consideration electoral outcomes and voters choose the optimal strategy, given what other voters are choosing. They pointed out that in the case of simple sincere voting, the voters whose ideal points are between 10 and 40 are not choosing optimally, given what the other voters are doing. If instead of voting for a Democratic president and a Republican Congress, the voters whose ideal points were between 10 and 40 voted for a Democratic president and a Democratic Congress, they would be better off. Why? The Democratic candidate for president, with 40 percent of the vote, would still lose to the Republican, but now Congress would be majority Democratic (70 percent of the vote for Congress would be Democratic and

30 percent would be Republican). The government would be divided, with a Republican president and a Democratic Congress, outcome *RD,* which is closer to the ideal point of the voters who most prefer *DR* but, by voting sincerely, were getting *RR*. These choices are shown in figure 13.8.

Although it is clear that voters with ideal points from 10 to 40 prefer voting the straight Democratic ticket, to be sure that this is an equilibrium we need to make sure that other voters are also choosing optimally. That is, would any of the other voters change their choices in figure 13.8? First, consider voters whose ideal points are between 0 and 10. There is no alternative, given how the others are voting, that will lead them to an outcome they prefer more. Voters whose ideal points are between 40 and 70 are getting their preferred outcome and have no reason to want to change their choice. Finally, voters whose ideal points are between 70 and 100 cannot improve on the outcome by changing their choice, given what other voters are doing. So in equilibrium, some moderate voters (those whose first preference is divided government) should instead vote a straight Democratic ticket so that they do get a divided government. Not all moderate voters will split their tickets in equilibrium.

FIGURE 13.8
Strategic Modeerating Voters' Choices in Example

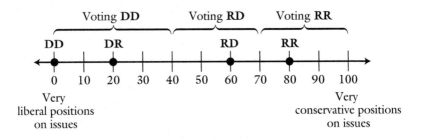

The Empirical Evidence Again This example is simplistic, but Mebane (2000) devised a more general formal model of voting in presidential and congressional elections, in which voters choose optimally to balance tickets based on their expectations about the electoral outcome. Voters have both common knowledge of what that outcome will be as well as private information. Mebane used the model as a basis for a statistical analysis of the NES survey data from 1976 to 1996 and showed that voters do in fact make choices to balance between the House of Representatives and the president and that enough voters split tickets to affect election outcomes. In the empirical analysis, he incorporated other factors that affect voters' choices in the elections—such as incumbency and the state of the economy—as factors that affect voters' preferences and private information (and as we have seen in earlier chapters these factors affect presidential vote choices). Mebane also compared the strategic-choice model with Fiorina's nonstrategic-choice model and found that the strategic-choice model better explained the data. He found (p. 50) that "moderation is almost always a feature of every voter's choices," but as our example showed, moderation "has no direct implication for the numbers of voters who may have been splitting their tickets to try to balance the House position with that of the future president."

Coattails, Incumbency, the Economy, and So On One feature of presidential elections is the so-called coattail effect—according to which an increase in the probability that a party's candidate will win the presidency increases the votes received by the party's candidates for Congress—but the converse does not occur. That is, an increase in a party's congressional vote share does not lead to an increase in the probability that that party's candidate will win the presidency. Mebane (2000) found the same relationship in his empirical analysis. He noted (p. 50) that this relationship "reflects the patterns in which changes have occurred across election periods in ideal points, party positions, partisanship, economic evaluations, and incumbency." As with the coattail effect, Mebane did find that partisanship, economic evaluations, and incumbency do often outweigh concerns about policy in determining how an individual votes. Nevertheless, he concluded that policy-related balancing of voters is frequently large enough to be "an important determinant of election outcomes." His analysis fits with our analysis of economic voting discussed in chapter 9 and 10.

The fact that factors such as partisanship, economic evaluations, and incumbency frequently outweigh policy moderation no doubt helps explain why some nonmoderate voters split their tickets and some moderates choose either to split or to not split their votes when doing so might not be optimal for policy concerns. These were certainly factors that were likely to influence the ticket splitting that appears to have occurred in Augusta, even though it helped result in the outcome of a Republican president and a Republican Congress, which some liberal voters may not have preferred on policy grounds. Norwood's efforts on the Patient's Bill of Rights legislation had given him a lot of stature within Congress, and the visit of the Speaker of the House during the campaign signaled to voters that Norwood would continue to have power in Congress. Compared with his politically inexperienced opponent (also a dentist), Norwood had a lot of advantages.

Midterm Elections

The Moderating Voter and Midterm Elections Liberal voters in Augusta got a second chance to try to get an outcome with greater Democratic control in the bargaining in the federal government. Although they could not vote President Bush out of office, they could make a decision about Norwood, who, like all members of the House of Representatives, faced election again two years later. Typically in these elections, the party of the president experiences a loss of seats. Table 13.4 presents a summary of the seat losses for the president's party in midterm elections from 1946 to 2002. With the exception of the last two midterm elections, 1998 and 2002, the president's party has indeed experienced losses of seats in Congress. If we consider 1946 and 1974 as the equivalent of second terms for administrations, then it appears that historically, presidents in their second term have higher seat losses than those in their first. However, the data is hardly sufficient to reach strong conclusions about seat losses and the effect of presidents' terms. One of the largest losses occurred in Clinton's first term, in 1994. The losses in 1946 and 1974 may have been the consequence of concerns about the change in administration because of death in one case and resignation in the other. And classifying 1950 and 1966 as Harry Truman's and Lyndon Johnson's second terms, respectively, is another judgment call.

Alesina and Rosenthal (1995) showed that a midterm loss for the president's party is to be expected if voters are choosing strategically to moderate policy. That is, when voters make their choices in a presidential election, there is uncertainty about the outcome of the voting. Once the election has occurred, some voters will wish they had made different choices because policy is a result of bargaining between the president and Congress. Consider the following example. Suppose a moderate voter named Esther, who is slightly on the conservative side, would like to have a Republican president balanced by a Democratic Congress. Suppose further that the presidential election is a toss-up, as in 2000, and Esther expects that there is a 50/50 chance the Democratic candidate will win. If she tries to balance the outcome by voting for a Republican president and a Democratic Congress, Esther could end up with a Democratic president and Congress, an outcome that she prefers less than having a full Republican administration. So she votes for the Republicans for president and Congress. Then, in the congressional midterm election, when there is no presidential contest, she can safely vote Democratic to balance out the Republican president if the Republican won, resulting in the president's party receiving a midterm loss. If the Democratic candidate won the presidency, other voters who voted straight Democratic tickets in the presidential-election year can similarly moderate the president by voting Republican for Congress. One implication is that when presidential elections are exceptionally close, midterm losses should be greater.

The Reality Mebane and Sekhon (2002) statistically evaluated Mebane's (2000) moderating-voter model of midterm elections, which has the same prediction as Alesina and Rosenthal's analysis of midterm losses based on NES data from congressional midterm elections. Although Mebane and

TABLE 13.4
Losses of Congressional Seats by the President's
Party in Midterm Elections, 1946–2002

Year	Change in Number of Seats	President's Party	President's Term in Office
1946	−55	Democratic	first*
1950	−29	Democratic	second
1954	−18	Republican	first
1958	−47	Republican	second
1962	−4	Democratic	first
1966	−47	Democratic	second
1970	−12	Republican	first
1974	−43	Republican	first†
1978	−11	Republican	first
1982	−26	Republican	first
1986	−5	Republican	second
1990	−9	Republican	first
1994	−52	Democratic	first
1998	+5	Democratic	second
2002	+6	Republican	first

*FDR had died in office in 1945.
†Nixon had resigned in August 1974.

Sekhon found evidence that midterm losses are a consequence of presidential-election uncertainty, they found that this effect is minor and accounts for only a small portion of the midterm changes in seats. By simulation, they showed that uncertainty alone would result in a midterm loss of about 0.01 to 0.06 percent of seats. Moreover, the results of 2000, when the election was exceptionally close and the president actually experienced a midterm gain, suggest that this effect is also not likely to be significant.

Campbell, (1987) presented an alternative theory of midterm losses that is related to voter turnout and mobilization. He contended that in presidential elections more independent voters with a preference for the president and his party's position are mobilized, and during midterm elections only more committed partisans vote. Thus, the president's party loses vote share in the midterm elections. Mebane and Sekhon (2002) found little support for this explanation, however. They showed that turnout at midterm does not appear to be affected by policy concerns, suggesting that if more voters vote, the outcome would be largely unaffected. If the turnout decision is a strategic choice by the same groups who mobilize voters in general elections, it is not surprising that the difference in turnout is not policy related. What Mebane and Sekhon found instead was that at midterm elections both voters and nonvoters typically have policy preferences that are further from those of the president's party than is the case in the preceding election, although in 1998 the effect was the opposite (their study did not include data from 2002).

Augusta and the 2002 Election Did moderate voters use midterm votes strategically in 2002? If they did so nationally, the effect was overwhelmed by other factors, as the president's party actually gained seats. To see how these factors worked, it is useful to consider Augusta's experience as illustrative of the national trend. Did moderate votes who wanted some Democratic control get a chance to correct for the effect of the unexpectedly close presidential election by voting against Norwood and other Republicans for Congress nationwide? Three events between 2000 and 2002 probably kept that from occurring in Augusta and other areas and led to the Republicans' seat gains nationally. The first was redistricting, the second September 11, 2001, and the third Senator Jeffords's defection.

Redistricting Georgia grew significantly in population in the 1990s and gained two new congressional districts for the 2002 election. Democrats controlled both houses of the state legislature and the governorship, and after much wrangling and a court challenge, congressional district boundaries were totally redrawn. Figures 11.2 and 11.3 present the boundaries used in the 2002 election. Most of Augusta was assigned to one of the new congressional districts, the twelfth, in which the son of one of the leaders of the state Democratic Party ran for office. The new twelfth district includes 81.3 percent of Richmond County (Augusta and Richmond share a combined government) with Norwood's new district containing only some of the city's northern suburbs. As a consequence, Norwood's new district (the ninth) is now heavily Republican, and he won reelection easily, with 72.8 percent of the vote in the district and 78 percent of the vote in the conservative northern suburbs of Augusta. Augusta's experience was not unique. Redistricting across the nation altered voters' incentives and abilities to use midterm elections to moderate Bush's win. Although Democrats controlled the redistricting in Georgia, their effort to increase their seats made Norwood's seat safe—a similar effect in California made it easier for Devin Nunes to win a seat. Sophisticated gerrymandering to advantage the party in control of the state's redistricting significantly affected voters' ability to alter the partisan balance.[44]

What about the district that now comprised most of Augusta? Did the Democratic candidate win as Augusta voters attempted to moderate the all-Republican outcome of 2000? Although the Democratic candidate, Charles Walker, Jr., received 52.2 percent of the vote in Augusta, it was less than Gore had received in 2000 and was not significant enough to win the district (he received 44.8 percent of the vote in the district and lost to Republican Max Burns). The two other events that occurred between 2000 and

2002 probably prevented Democratic candidates from winning in Augusta and across the nation.

September 11 It is obvious that September 11, 2001, and the threat of terrorism made foreign affairs and concerns about fighting terrorism more important in voters' preferences in 2002 than they were during the presidential election of 2000. A postelection poll taken by *USA Today*/CNN/Gallup demonstrated that voters in 2002 also believed that the Republican position on these issues was more desirable than the Democratic one: "57 percent of those polled said Democrats are not tough enough on terrorism, while 64 percent said Republicans are. And 54 percent of Democrats polled said the party needs to moderate its liberal message."[45] Rebecca Dunbar, a forty-nine-year-old in the Denver suburbs who voted for Gore in 2000, told *Washington Post*/ABC News pollsters in September 2002 that she had "come to admire Bush for his handling of the war on terrorism." She remarked: "The international issues are domestic issues right now. Terrorism is the number one issue causing fear and trepidation in the American public. People aren't sure; they don't know if we're capable of defending ourselves, if attacking is right. People are apprehensive."[46]

Georgia Republican congressional candidate Max Burns emphasized Iraq and the fight against terrorism in his campaign and promised that he would help Bush and the Republicans in Congress fight terrorism. Vice President Cheney attended a fund-raising reception for Burns in Augusta. *The Augusta Chronicle* reported that Cheney "spent most of his time . . . delivering a strong message from President Bush about the looming war against Iraq."[47] Other national Republican candidates ran on those issues. The evidence suggests that contrary to the norm in previous midterm elections, with the exception of 1998, voters' policy preferences in 2002 moved closer to those of the president's political party nationally, and that gave the president an increase in seats rather than a loss.

Jeffords's Defection The final event that may have affected voters in Augusta—and nationally—was Jeffords's defection in the closely divided Senate in May 2001. In 2000, the Senate was tied between Democrats and Republicans, and although the ability of Vice President Cheney to vote to break ties gave Republicans control on paper, Democrats demanded and received a greater role in decision making within the Senate in early January 2000. Republicans lost their tenuous control over the Senate through Jeffords's actions, and thus when voters chose in November 2002, Republicans did not have full control over Congress. Not only did voters see the Democratic Party as less capable of dealing with terrorism, but Republican candidates also blamed the delay in passing the measures they wanted to fight terrorism on Democratic control of the Senate.

Still, most of the respondents in the September *Washington Post*/ABC

News poll did say they thought government worked better if Democrats were in control of Congress to check the power of the president, echoing statements made by such voters as Bruce Babcock, an Iowa pharmacist, who reported, "As much as I'd like to see Republicans control it, you've got to have the check and balance."[48] But by the time of the election, voters were more solidly in favor of full Republican control. In the *USA Today*/CNN/Gallup postelection poll, 74 percent of voters said that with one party in charge more things would be accomplished, including the creation of a cabinet-level domestic security department (legislation on the department was before Congress before the election but had not been approved, and a number of Democrats had criticized the lower level of civil service protection for employees that the legislation provided for). When asked whether Republicans controlling the White House and Congress is a "good thing" for the country in terms of foreign affairs, 57 percent of survey respondents said that it was. Even on the economy, united Republican control was seen as desirable by 53 percent of respondents. Between 2000 and 2002, redistricting, Democratic control in the Senate, and the new emphasis on fighting terrorism coupled with belief that Republicans were better able to handle the problem helped Burns in Augusta and led to an unexpected gain by the president's party in 2002.[49]

What Happened to the Patient's Bill of Rights?

Norwood was reelected, and Bush and he had an agreement. Republicans won majorities in both the House and the Senate. Yet the Patient's Bill of Rights legislation remained in limbo. Why? There is a simple answer to this question: September 11. The new war on terrorism and the anthrax mailings to members of Congress significantly dominated Washington affairs for a considerable time. Then, in 2002, when Democrats lost control of the Senate and saw their numbers reduced in the House of Representatives, they no longer had the chance to pass a bill that Bush would veto or be forced to sign to please public opinion. However, Republicans did not seem to be motivated to present the new compromise legislation to the president either. Perhaps the reason was that the situation in the summer of 2001 was similar to that in figure 13.4: Bush and the Republicans preferred no change in the status quo but, recognizing that the Democrats had popular opinion on their side, were willing to go through with what they interpreted as a smallish change to prevent the Democrats from using the issue in the 2002 elections. But as a consequence of the effects of September 11 and Bush's and the Republicans' apparent success in voters' eyes in managing terrorism, a Patient's Bill of Rights was no longer the hot issue in congressional races. At the time this chapter was written the Patient's Bill of Rights appeared to be a dead issue.

More Checks and Balances

States and Patients' Rights

An injury forced Texas oral and maxillofacial surgeon David Sibley to give up his practice in 1985. He decided to enter politics, first becoming mayor of Waco and going to law school. He became a Republican state senator in 1991. Like Weatherford, Norwood, and Edwards, he, too, wanted to enact legislation that would allow patients to sue HMOs for damages when needed care recommended by doctors was refused.[50] In May 1997, he succeeded—the Texas state legislature passed the Texas Health Care Liability Act, allowing patients to sue HMOs in Texas state courts. Sibley's golfing buddy[51] Governor George W. Bush was uncertain whether to sign the bill. It went against the tort reform that he was proud of pushing through the Texas legislature. A number of business interests who had supported him electorally and through campaign contributions opposed the bill. But Bush also had supporters who had pressured him to provide relief for patients, and he worried about voters' demands. He had vetoed a patient protection act two years before. The *Austin American-Statesman* reported: " 'I don't think the public could avoid looking at it [a veto] paired with what he did last time,' said Lisa McGiffert, senior policy analyst for Consumers Union Southwest Regional Office."[52] Expressing concern over the possibility of a bonanza of lawsuits that might result from the bill, Bush decided to let it become law without his signature.[53] By 2004, nine other states—Arizona, California, Georgia, Maine, New Jersey, North Carolina, Oklahoma, Washington, and West Virginia—had passed similar laws.

Bush used Sibley's bill in his campaign for president as evidence of his willingness to work with Democrats and support patients' rights. On October 17, 2000, when presidential candidates Governor George W. Bush of Texas and Vice President Al Gore debated in St. Louis, one of the issues that came up was the Patient's Bill of Rights. Gore summarized his position and his view of Bush's: "I support a strong national patient's bill of rights. It is actually a disagreement between us. The national law that is pending on this, the Dingell-Norwood bill, a bipartisan bill, is one that I support and that the governor does not." But Bush strongly disagreed with Gore's statement:

> Actually, Mr. Vice President, it's not true. I do support a national patients' bill of rights. . . . I brought Republicans and Democrats together to do just that in the state of Texas, to get a patients' bill of rights through. . . . We're one of the first states that said you can sue an H.M.O. for denying you proper coverage. . . . I support a national patients' bill of rights, Mr. Vice President. And I want all people covered. I don't want the law to supersede good law like we've got in Texas."[54]

Limits on What State Representatives Can Accomplish

As we have seen in this chapter, as of the winter of 2005 such a national law had not been passed or signed by Bush. State Senator Sibley seemed to have accomplished what Weatherford, Norwood, and Edwards had not been able to do at the federal level. However, can states enact such laws when Congress chooses not to? When ERISA was passed in 1974, state laws providing for patient protection from insurance company denials were voided. The federal law does not provide for suits for damages, as these state laws do. Was it permissible for the states to provide an additional remedy that the Congress had chosen not to provide for programs regulated by ERISA?

The day after Ruby Calad's hysterectomy in Texas in 1999, she was told that her health insurance company, CIGNA Corporation, would not pay for an additional day in the hospital even though her doctor had recommended the longer stay. She could stay if she paid the charges herself—$1,500 per day. Calad was released but had to return to the hospital several days later and in 2004 needed further corrective surgery because of problems resulting from the initial release. Calad sued CIGNA under the new Texas law, but CIGNA claimed that the suit was a violation of ERISA. As reported by *The Washington Post*, the U.S. Court of Appeals ruled in 2003 "that individuals could sue in state court. Given that decisions on whether to pay for a particular treatment are decisions about both insurance and medical practice, the court reasoned, insurance companies can be held liable under state laws that enforce health care standards."[55]

CIGNA appealed the case to the U.S. Supreme Court, which heard it and a similar Texas case in March 2004. Interestingly, the Bush administration's Justice Department joined the case on the side of the insurance companies, against the Texas state law. Assistant Solicitor General James A. Feldman summarized the administration's view: "To allow states to essentially say, as the state has said here, 'Well, we're going to provide an additional remedy that Congress rejected when it drew that careful balance,' would be to completely undermine Congress's decisions about how this system should be structured."[56] The administration and the HMOs won the case: on June 21, 2004, the Supreme Court ruled unanimously in *Aetna Health Inc. v. Davila* that ERISA does void state laws allowing individuals the right to sue their HMOs.

Sibley's quest for patients' rights at the state level illustrates the complexity of the checks and balances of policy making in American politics. Although we have discussed how voters can try to use their votes in congressional and presidential elections to moderate partisan differences and reach desired policy outcomes, voters also realize that the federal structure of the U.S. government means that the ability of actors to control policy outcomes at both the state and the federal level is limited in many cases. In some cases, nonelected Supreme Court justices end up making decisions that ultimately affect the success of legislators like Sibley in succeeding to provide the policy choices they promised voters. These factors are some of the reasons why voters in U.S. elections have difficulty evaluating the performance of incumbents, as we discussed in chapter 9, and why voters may see participation in the electoral process itself as too costly, given the expected benefits received.

Despite the dying of patients' rights in Congress after September 11, Charlie Norwood remained optimistic: "I just got the easiest district in Georgia. I'm going to be here 10 years, and I'm going to lay it up for them every year."[57] As noted earlier, Norwood's district was made "easy" because Democrats were trying to increase the likelihood of electing more Democratic members of Congress. But Georgia's redistricting was more complicated than that in other states because it was subject to judicial review and a court case—not because Democrats were engaging in aggressive partisan gerrymandering but because of its potential effects on minority representation. In fact, even though Norwood won election in the new district in 2002, the district boundaries were under review by the U.S. Supreme Court, in *Ashcroft v. Georgia* (2003). This was not a new situation in Georgia—the state's congressional district boundaries were redrawn several times after the 1990 census and settled only for the 1996 election. Similarly, North Carolina's congressional district from the 1990s were still under review by the courts after the 2000 census had been completed. The debate over the boundaries centered on fundamental questions of how minority voters are incorporated into the American electoral process. In chapter 15, we explore the issues and see how Norwood benefited.

What We Know

We know that presidential campaigns matter and that campaign visits by candidates can affect their votes much as campaign advertising does. We also know that the Electoral College fundamentally affects how presidential candidates campaign and whose votes are courted. Candidates rarely visit states that are clearly in one candidate's column or those with few electoral votes—unless the election is expected to be exceedingly close, as in 2000 or 2004. Sometimes, though, candidates make mistakes—as Bush did in 2000—and make suboptimal decisions, failing to adapt to changes in polls and their opponent's strategies. We know that when voters choose both presidential candidates and congressional candidates, they sometimes split their votes, suggesting that they may be trying to moderate the major political parties. Yet when valence issues are important, which may have been the case in 2004, voters may choose a unified government. Finally, when the presidency and Congress are controlled by different political parties—or if there is significant disagreement between the two on policy issues even though the same party controls both—both may try to use presidential vetoes as a way of communicating to voters with an eye on future elections.

What We Don't Know: Other Parties and Candidates

In 1990, Democrat David Worley came close to defeating Georgia Republican representative Newt Gingrich in his race for reelection to Congress; he lost by only 983 votes. Defeating Gingrich would have benefited the Democrats—at the time, Gingrich was a powerful leader of his party in Congress, the minority whip. In 1994, Gingrich led the Republican takeover of Congress, where Democrats had held the majority for forty years, and became Speaker of the House. Worley's close race surprised many, mainly because the candidate did not run a single television ad and campaigned only via direct mail. The Democratic Party had given him only $5,000, one tenth of what they had given him when he ran against Gingrich in 1988, and had provided the funds only in the last week of the campaign. Why? If Worley had won, would the Democrats have been able to maintain control of Congress in 1994? But an even stranger consequence of the Democratic Party's refusal to provide Worley with the type of contribution it typically makes in key elections may have been the 2000 election of George W. Bush. In the next chapter, in which we consider how minor parties and independent candidates are involved in U.S. elections, we see why the Democratic Party's choice not to support Worley could have been partly responsible for the loss of the presidency ten years later.

Study Questions and Problems

1. Suppose that the 2008 presidential election is between Barack Obama and Rudy Giuliani. Assume further that the expected votes for each candidate are the same as those received by Kerry and Bush in the 2004 contest, except that in New York Giuliani is predicted to be tied with Obama, and Obama is expected to win very easily in Illinois.
   a. Which states would you recommend that the candidates visit the most, and why? Which states would you recommend that the candidates not visit very much, and why?
   b. Suppose that Obama visits a state he should not visit too much (pick one from your answer above). Should Giuliani change his strategy? Why?
2. Suppose that in 2006, Democrats are able to win control of both houses of Congress, but they do not have enough votes to override a presidential veto. They would like to pass a comprehensive health-care plan for all citizens and resident aliens. Bush most prefers no bill but might be willing to compromise on a bill that covers only citizens.
   a. What sort of expectations about voters' preferences in the 2008 election might lead Democrats to pass the legislation with coverage of noncitizens even though they think it will be vetoed?

b. What sort of expectations about voters' preferences in the 2008 election might lead Bush to sign the legislation even though it covers noncitizens?

3. Suppose you are a Democratic senator who is up for reelection in 2008 and you are trying to decide whether to support Hillary Clinton or John Edwards for your party's nomination for the presidency in 2008. You would like to see the Democrats have a majority in the Senate and control the presidency, but if you had to choose between the two, you would choose being in the majority in the Senate. How might your decision depend on whether you think voters will moderate their choices in the election in the way Fiorina hypothesized or in the way Alesina and Rosenthal hypothesized?

NOTES

1. John Marelius, "Bush Camp Says It Is Ready to Fight for California Voters," Copley News Service, September 17, 2000.
2. Zachary Coile, "Bush Plans Last-Week Push in California: Lead for Gore Slips into Single Figures," *San Francisco Examiner*, October 27, 2000.
3. Data courtesy of Daron Shawn and David Stromberg.
4. Jennifer Bundy, "Robb Says Margin of Victory Was Persuasive," Associated Press State & Local Wire, November 3, 2004.
5. See Dennis Roddy, "The Elector Who Might Not," *Pittsburgh Post-Gazette*, October 10, 2004, and "West Virginia Elector Says He Might Not Vote for President Bush," *USA Today*, October 21, 2004, http://www.usatoday.com/news/politicselections/state/westvirginia/2004-10-21-elector_x.htm.
6. For discussions of the history of faithless electors, see Center for Voting and Democracy, "Faithless Electors," *http://www.fairvote.org/e_college/faithless.htm*, and Bennett (n.d.), ch. 7.
7. Each state, regardless of population, has two senators. The total number of representatives is fixed at 435. After each census, the House of Representatives is reapportioned according to each state's population. Each representative is popularly elected in a single-winner election.
8. In 1824, six states selected their electors in their state legislature, but by 1828 the number had been reduced to only two states, and after 1828 only one state, South Carolina, continued the practice.
9. An absolute-majority requirement means that a majority of the eligible voters must vote for the winner, not just a majority of those who vote, which is the case with most majority requirements in large elections.
10. The presidents who won an absolute majority of the electoral vote but had only a plurality of the popular vote were James K. Polk, Zachary Taylor, James Buchanan, Abraham Lincoln, James A. Garfield, Grover Cleveland, Woodrow Wilson, Harry S. Truman, John F. Kennedy, Richard M. Nixon, and Bill Clinton.
11. Carla Marinucci, "Candidates Take It Down to the Wire: Gore, Bush in Frantic Push across Battleground States," *San Francisco Chronicle*, November 6, 2000.
12. Yvonne Abraham, "A Gore Splash, Aided by Many," *Boston Globe*, November 3, 2000.
13. Bob von Sternberg, "Faithful Hear Nader at Target Center: The Green Party Candidate Appeared with Running Mate Winona LaDuke, Phil Donahue and Michael Moore," *Minneapolis Star Tribune*, September 23, 2000.

14. For examples of the Democrats' worry about Nader, see Lynn Sweet and Scott Fornek, "Nader Won't Back Down," *Chicago Sun-Times*, November 1, 2000, and Bob von Sternberg, "Nader Voters Take Spotlight: In Minnesota and Other Battleground States, Liberal Democrats Are Imploring Those Learning Green to Reconsider," *Minneapolis Star Tribune*, November 1, 2000.

15. John Ellis, Jim Wasserman, and Cyndee Fontana, "Bush Woos Valley Vote: Texas Governor Visits Fresno to Boost GOP Slate," *Fresno Bee*, October 31, 2000.

16. Bennett Roth, "Gore Woos Unions in Swing States in Campaign Blitz," *Houston Chronicle*, September 4, 2000.

17. Rick Hampson, " 'Battleground' Voters Nearing Combat Fatigue" *USA Today*, November 1, 2000.

18. Tom Raum, "Bush Loses Comfortable Edge in a State Now Ranked a Toss-Up," Associated Press State & Local Wire, September 14, 2000.

19. Kevin Sack, "The 2000 Campaign: The Vice President; With Broad Themes, Rivals Seek to Energize Voters," *New York Times*, November 5, 2000.

20. Craig Gilbert, "Candidate Bus Trips Offer More Than Pretty Pictures: In an Era of Parity, Small-Town Votes Can Make a Big Difference," *Milwaukee Journal Sentinel*, May 9, 2004.

21. We do not assume, however, that the utility from campaign visits has a peak, as we assume for utility from policy positions. That is, more campaign visits are always good for the voters, but the additional benefit from an additional visit decreases as the number of visits increases.

22. The subscript is omitted.

23. David M. Halbfinger, "The 2000 Campaign: New Jersey; After a Long Absence, Bush Is Back to Visit," *New York Times*, November 5, 2000.

24. See also Snyder (1989).

25. The correlation between the percentage of combined campaign visits per electoral vote and the predicted percentage per electoral votes is 0.81. Stromberg (2002) also compared his predictions about campaign visits with the choices made by the candidates in 1996, 1992, and 1988. The predictions fare less well in comparison to the actual choices in those races. Stromberg speculated that the lack of success is the result of the unevenness of the races and that the candidates chose to use visits to help out congressional races or for other goals.

26. I thank Sandy Gordon for this insight.

27. This example shows how sometimes candidates appear to use vice presidential picks as strategically as they allocate campaign visits—Gore's campaign probably anticipated the effects of the Lieberman choice on Florida, although of course other factors were important in the choice as well.

28. Rachel La Corte, "Florida Plays Pivotal Role in Presidential Sweepstakes," Associated Press State & Local Wire, October 21, 2000.

29. Amy Franklin, "Capital Focus: Presidential Campaigns Have Cash Registers Ringing in Michigan," Associated Press State & Local Wire, November 5, 2000.

30. "Bush Wants Damage Cap in Rights Bill for Patients: He Threatens Veto of Protection Bill," *Atlanta Journal-Constitution*, March 22, 2001.

31. Interestingly, Jeffords did not support the bipartisan bill but, with Senators Bill Frist, Republican from Tennessee, and John Breaux, Democrat from Louisiana, proposed a bill with lower limits on damages that was defeated 59–36.

32. Jacker Koszczuk, "Patient Rights Bill Passed in Senate over Conservative Objections," Knight-Ridder Washington Bureau, June 30, 2001.

33. Zachary Coile, "Bush Seeks Sweeping Overhaul of Federal Rules: Health Regulations, Environmental Protections among Hundreds of Targets," *San Francisco Chronicle*, December 22, 2002.

34. Greg Winter, "Change in Aid Rule Means Larger Bills for College Students," *New York Times*, June 13, 2003.
35. Stephen Labaton, "Senators Move to Restore F.C.C. Limits on the Media," *New York Times*, June 5, 2003.
36. In 1996, Congress gave the president the power to veto particular items within a bill, and that power was used by President Clinton in 1997. In 1998, the Supreme Court ruled that such power could be given to the president only through a constitutional amendment and that the line-item veto as passed by Congress was unconstitutional.
37. Dana Milbank and Juliet Eilperin, "On Patients' Rights Deal, Bush Scored with a Full-Court Press," *Washington Post*, August 3, 2001.
38. Terence Samuel, "Bush Finally Gets His (GOP) House in Order," *U.S. News and World Report*, August 13, 2001.
39. Samuel, "Bush Finally Gets His (GOP) House in Order."
40. After the 2000 redistricting, only part of the city remained in Norwood's district.
41. This example is drawn from Alesina and Rosenthal (1995).
42. This was true even for respondents outside the South and for elections in the 1990s, although respondents in 2000 and 2004 showed a decline in their willingness to engage in this type of split-ticket voting.
43. See Alvarez and Schousen (1993), Born (1994a,b), Burden and Kimball (1998), Fiorina (1994), Frymer (1994), Garand and Lichtl (2000).
44. In nine states (Florida, Idaho, Kansas, Michigan, New Jersey, Ohio, Pennsylvania, Utah, and Virginia), Republicans controlled both houses of the state legislature and the governorship during the redistricting process, affecting 109 seats in Congress, and in eight states (Alabama, California, Georgia, Hawaii, Maryland, Mississippi, North Carolina, and West Virginia), Democrats controlled the state government, affecting 102 seats. The remaining states had some form of divided government. See Barone, Cohen, and Ujifusa (2001, pp. 1703–5).
45. Richard Benedetto, "Most Favor GOP on Economy, War on Terrorism," *USA Today*, November 12, 2002.
46. Dan Balz, David S. Broder, and Helen Rumbelow, "Poll: War Tops Economy in Voters' Minds; Other Issues Temper GOP Autumn Hopes," *Washington Post*, September 29, 2002.
47. The Richmond County Republican Party chairman, Dave Barbee, summarized Cheney's role in the campaign to voters: "He is a messenger for the president of the United States, and he came here and talked to us about homeland security and what the president was doing for our country and what he needed to do. And also why it's so important . . . that we keep control of Congress." Sylvia Cooper, "Cheney Pays Visit to Support Burns, Vice President Discusses Iraq, Terrorism," *Augusta Chronicle*, October 5, 2002.
48. Balz, Broder, and Rumbelow, "Poll: War Tops Economy in Voters' Minds."
49. Of course, local issues were important in the Georgia congressional race as well. Burns had criticized the Democratic candidate, Walker, for his lack of experience and raised questions about his ethics. The point is that because of redistricting, September 11, and Jeffords's defection, moderate voters had less desire to intentionally vote Democratic to balance out the Republican control.
50. Dave McNeely, "GOP's Workhorse: Texas Sen. Sibley Vows Bipartisanship Can Work," *Austin American-Statesman*, December 12, 1996.
51. "Tee Time with the President," *Austin American-Statesman*, August 23, 2003.
52. A. Phillips Brooks, "Bush Won't Rush to Sign HMO Bill: Measure Poses Dilemma for Tort," *Austin American-Statesman*, May 13, 1997.
53. Megan Rhyne, "75th Legislature in Review: Plaintiffs Bar Doesn't Expect Suit Bonanza from HMO Law," *Texas Lawyer*, June 9, 1997.

54. "Exchanges between the Candidates in the Third Presidential Debate," *New York Times*, October 18, 2000.

55. Charles Lane, "Court to Hear Insurance Case: Patients Seek Right to Sue When Companies Deny Coverage," *Washington Post*, November 4, 2003.

56. Linda Greenhouse, "Justices Hear Arguments about H.M.O. Malpractice Lawsuits," *New York Times*, March 24, 2004.

57. Jeffrey McMurray, "Even with Less Clout, Norwood Hasn't Abandoned HMO Reform Quest," Associated Press State & Local Wire, December 2, 2001. David Sibley left the Texas State Senate in 2002 and became a lobbyist in the state capital. In January 2003, the Texas Medical Association hired him. "Lobbying," *Austin American-Statesman*, January 23, 2003.

Part V
Challenging the Majority

∽14∽

Minor Parties and Independent Candidates

Winning by Division

In California

Republican Devin Nunes first ran for Congress in 1998, when he was twenty-four years old and then again in 2002. Although redistricting had made the new 2002 district safe for Republicans, as discussed in chapter 11, Nunes was not the only potential candidate who decided to compete for the Republican nomination. Two other, more politically experienced candidates joined the race—state assemblyman Mike Briggs and Fresno mayor Jim Patterson. When the race began, Briggs and Patterson were the front-runners. According to our analysis, in chapter 11, of the effects of political experience and the difficulty weak challengers have overcoming them, Nunes should not have won. How did his election happen?

One reason Nunes won was geography. Both Brigg's and Patterson's main support came from Fresno, whereas Nunes's home was in Tulare County, which constituted 57 percent of the district. If Nunes could carry the majority in Tulare and Briggs and Patterson divide Fresno, with Nunes receiving some votes there, Nunes could win. Nunes also had the strong support of Congressman Bill Thomas, a powerful member of the House Ways and Means Committee, and both Briggs and Patterson had baggage along with their experience.[1] Nunes did lose Fresno to Patterson (Patterson received 37.9 percent; Briggs, 30.5 percent; and Nunes, 28 percent) but won Tulare (Nunes, 46.4 percent; Patterson, 27.8 percent; and Briggs,

20.6 percent), winning the district overall with less than a majority of the votes but more than any other candidate (Nunes, 37.1 percent; Patterson, 33 percent; Briggs, 25.7 percent).[2]

In Chicago

Democrat Harold Washington had a similar fight for the nomination for mayor of Chicago in 1983 (recall our discussion of Washington's campaign in chapter 2). Whereas Nune's success was remarkable because of his youth and his limited political experience compared with that of his opponents, Washington's was historic. The first (and only) African American elected mayor of the city, Washington successfully took on the Chicago Democratic political machine and the white establishment by splitting the white vote between two white candidates. He received only 36.65 percent of the vote, but because that was greater than the percentage won by either of his two opponents (incumbent mayor Jane Byrne received 33.55 percent, and then–Cook County state's attorney Richard M. Daley received 29.79 percent), he won the Democratic nomination. It is doubtful that Washington would have won the primary if there had not been a three-way race, given the racial tensions in Chicago at the time.[3]

Almost all U.S. elections are winner-take-all contests. Although ten states and a number of cities have majority requirements that mean a candidate cannot win with a simple plurality, as Washington and Nunes did, in most cases it takes only a plurality of the vote to win election. Yet close three-way contests, such as those that allowed Nunes and Washington to win, are relatively rare in U.S. elections, particularly in general elections (both of these examples involved primary contests). The reasons for their rarity are also, reason for the lack of success of minor parties in electing candidates and the reason designing legislative districts has come to be viewed as the main way to increase the representation of minority voters. In this chapter, we explore these reasons. But first we need to understand how elections with more than two candidates work. Thus we begin with the story of an unusual three-candidate race for the Senate.

Voters' Choices in Three-Candidate Elections

The Christine Jorgensen of the Republican Party

In 1970, voters in New York State faced a dilemma. The Republican candidate for the Senate, Charles Goodell, wasn't acting like a Republican. He was denouncing the Vietnam War and the Republican president, Richard Nixon. A minor political party, the Liberal Party, often viewed as being to the left of Democrats in the state, had publicly given Goodell support. The Republican vice president, Spiro Agnew, called Goodell the "Christine Jorgensen of the Republican Party," in reference to Jorgensen's highly publicized sex-change operation.[4]

But whereas the Liberal Party had supported Goodell, the Democratic Party had its own candidate, Richard Ottinger, and there was even a third candidate, James Buckley, running as a nominee of another minor political party, the Conservative Party, who was publicly supported by a number of prominent Republicans. How were Republican voters supposed to vote in the election if their own national party leaders were denouncing the state party's candidate, who was receiving support from liberals? How were Democratic voters supposed to vote when liberal voters in their state were supporting the Republican candidate and not the Democratic candidate? How were voters who thought of themselves as more leftist liberals supposed to vote?

New York's 1970 Senate Race

In the 1970 New York Senate race, the incumbent was Republican Charles Goodell, who had been appointed to fill the seat of Democratic senator Robert Kennedy after his assasination. In New York, there are other active political parties, particularly the Conservative and Liberal Parties, and New York law allows different parties to nominate the same candidates. That is, a candidate can run as both a Republican and a Conservative, for example.[5] Typically, that is what happened in New York—the Conservative Party nominated the same candidate as the Republicans, and the Liberals nominated the same candidate as the Democrats.[6]

In 1970, however, things were not straightforward. The Republican candidate, Goodell, had taken a liberal stance on the Vietnam War and opposed Republican president Richard Nixon's pro-war policies. The Liberal Party, which also opposed the war, endorsed Goodell as a result. The Democrats chose a candidate from their party's mainstream, Richard Ottinger. And the Conservative Party, dissatisfied with Goodell, chose to nominate a candidate who supported the Vietnam War, James Buckley, brother of the conservative columnist William F. Buckley. As a result, there were two candidates who were perceived as liberals, Goodell and Ottinger, and one conservative, Buckley. In a three-candidate race such as that one, determining how a voter will choose is not as easy as it is in two-candidate races.

A simple way to think of the situation in New York in 1970 is that there were basically three types of voters: voters whose first preference was Goodell (whom we will call G voters), voters whose first preference was Ottinger (whom we call O voters), and voters whose first preference was Buckley (whom we will call B voters). These voters' utility from the three candidates reflect these preferences. For example, assume that the three types of voters' preferences for the three candidates are those given in table 14.1.

G and O voters prefer either Goodell or Ottinger to Buckley, whereas B voters prefer Buckley and are largely indifferent in the choice between

TABLE 14.1
Model of Voters' Choices in the New York
Senate Election, 1970

	First Preference	Second Preference	Third Preference	Voters (%)
G voters	Goodell	Ottinger	Buckley	30
O voters	Ottinger	Goodell	Buckley	30
B voters	Buckley	Ottinger or Goodell	Ottinger or Goodell	40

Goodell and Ottinger. *B* voters are the conservatives who are in favor of the Vietnam War and upset by Goodell's defection from the Republican Party. They see both Ottinger and Goodell as equivalents, since both oppose the war. The *O* voters are Democratic voters who want the Democratic Party to win the seat in the Senate, but they prefer Goodell to Buckley because they oppose the war. The *G* voters are liberals who oppose the war and would like to support the incumbent senator because of his policy positions.

Voting in the Three-Candidate Race in New York

For *B* voters in the three-candidate race in New York, the choice is easy. Because they are indifferent to the choice between Goodell and Ottinger, then it is as if the race were a two-candidate race. Either Buckley wins or someone else wins and they don't care who the someone else is. Hence, they should vote for Buckley as long as there is any chance, even if extremely small, that Buckley is in a close race to win the election. We say that the *B* voters are voting *sincerely* for their most preferred candidate.

However, things are different for *G* and *O* voters. First, consider the *G* voters. They prefer either Goodell or Ottinger to Buckley. Although they most prefer Goodell, if it is likely that Goodell has little chance of winning and Ottinger does have a chance, they will vote for Ottinger instead of Goodell. Similarly, if it is likely that Ottinger has little chance of winning and Goodell does have a chance, *O* voters will vote for Goodell instead of Ottinger. That is, because there are more than two candidates in the race, some voters may find it preferable to vote *strategically* for their second preference rather than their first preference, if they perceive that their first preference has little chance of winning and their second preference has a good chance of winning.

What determines whether a voter will choose sincerely or strategically in a three-candidate election? Consider a voter named Maria, who is an *O*-type voter. We assume that Maria wants to make sure that if her vote makes a difference, it gives her the highest expected utility. When can Maria's vote make a difference? It can make a difference in four possible cases: (1) there

is a close two-way race for first place between Ottinger and Buckley, (2) there is a close two-way race for first place between Ottinger and Goodell, (3) there is a close two-way race for first place between Goodell and Buckley, and (4) when there is a close three-way race for first place between all three candidates. If Maria figures that cases 1, 2, or 4 are more likely than case 3, she will vote sincerely for Ottinger. But if Maria thinks case 3 is more likely than either cases 1, 2, or 4, she will vote strategically. In summary, *a voter will choose sincerely when she thinks that the most likely close race for first place will include her first preference. If the voter thinks that the most likely close race for first place does not include her first preference, the voter will vote strategically for the candidate in that close race she most prefers.* Note that we are not assuming that the voter necessarily thinks that a close race is always likely. What we are assuming is simply that the voter figures that if there is a close race, he or she will choose in such a way as to make a difference. Certainly, the greater the likelihood of a close race in an election, the more we would expect to see voters choosing as we have assumed here.

Election Outcomes in the Three-Candidate Race

Because of the possibility of strategic voting, figuring out what is likely to happen in a three-candidate race like the race in New York in 1970 depends, then, on voters' expectations of which candidate is going to win. As in our analysis of moderating voters in chapter 13, voters will be choosing optimally when their choices make sense given these expectations and what other voters are doing. It turns out that there is no single predicted equilibrium in this three-candidate race—in fact, there are three possible outcomes, and all three candidates have a chance to win. These three possible outcomes and the associated voters' choices are summarized in table 14.2.[7]

The situations in which either Goodell or Ottinger wins are fairly straightforward. For example, Goodell can win if voters perceive that Ottinger is clearly in third place and the contest is mainly between Goodell and Buckley. Then *G* and *O* voters form an *electoral coalition* for Goodell (*G* voters choose sincerely, and *O* voters choose strategically), and Goodell wins. Similarly, Ottinger can win if *G* and *O* voters see him and Buckley as the top competitors and they form an electoral coalition behind Ottinger. But Buckley can win as well because the supporters of Goodell and Ottinger face a problem of coordination. They would like to coordinate in a common electoral coalition on behalf of either Goodell or Ottinger. Unless they can do that, Buckley will win. Such coordination is not always easy, and in New York in 1970 it failed. Goodell received 24 percent of the vote, Ottinger received 37 percent, and Buckley won the Senate race with 39 percent of the vote.

TABLE 14.2
Possible Voting Equilibria in the Three-Candidate Race

	Voters' Choices When Goodell Wins	Voters' Choices When Ottinger Wins	Voters' Choices When Buckley Wins	Voters (%)
G voters	Vote sincerely for Goodell	Vote strategically for Ottinger	Vote sincerely for Goodell	30
O voters	Vote strategically for Goodell	Vote sincerely for Ottinger	Vote sincerely for Ottinger	30
B voters	Vote sincerely for Buckley	Vote sincerely for Buckley	Vote sincerely for Buckley	40
Voters' Expectations	Race between Goodell and Buckley for first place with Ottinger in third place	Race between Ottinger and Buckley for first place with Goodell in third place	Close three-way race between Goodell, Ottinger and Buckley	100

Choosing Whether to Party

Buckley won because Democratic voters were divided on how best to defeat him and Republicans in New York were divided over the Vietnam War. However, although he ran as a Conservative without the Republican Party label, once in office he became the Republican Senator from New York, and when he ran for reelection, he ran as a Republican. He lost to Democratic candidate Daniel Patrick Moynihan. A type of failure of coordination similar to the one that led to Buckley's win was a factor in the primary wins of Nunes and Washington. Republican voters in Fresno divided among the three candidates—if Briggs, for example, had not run, Patterson would probably have gained votes. Similarly, white Democratic voters in Chicago divided their support between incumbent mayor Jane Byrne and Richard M. Daley, giving Washington a chance to win the nomination. But in the general election in California, Nunes won handily, with 70.5 percent of the vote. And although in Chicago the Republican candidate received significant support from white Democrats unhappy with Washington's nomination, Washington was able to gain enough Democratic support to win the mayor's race with 51.72 percent of the vote. Unlike Buckley, he won reelection, with 53.77 percent of the vote, in a race against a Democrat who ran as an independent.[8] Similarly, Nunes won reelection in 2004 with 73 percent of the vote.

Although Buckley, Washington, and Nunes won initially in part because of voter-coordination failures, all three were ultimately working through the two-party system in order to achieve office and eventually won or lost in contests in which the competition was between the two major parties and voters had clear choices. Buckley ran as a Conservative but had Republican support and then ran for reelection as a Republican in a largely two-candidate contest.[9] Both Washington and Nunes, once they gained their party's nomination, were able to win election and, in Washington's case, reelection by relying on the fact that voters in most U.S. general elections coordinate their choices along party lines. None of these candidates saw themselves as working outside the two major parties but instead saw as their goal the building of a large enough majority to win in a race dominated by two parties.

Yet the experiences of Buckley, Washington, and Nunes—the experience of winning first by division—highlight the only route available to minor-party and independent candidates in an American political system dominated by the two major political parties—like former professional wrestler Jesse "the Body" Ventura, who ran for governor of Minnesota in 1998. Ventura made no secret of his contempt for the two major political parties (and some minor-party candidates whom he viewed as extremists). On August 20, 2000, Ventura discussed the presidential-election contest with talk-show host Larry King on CNN:

> VENTURA: But I don't like him [Pat Buchanan, the Reform Party candidate in 2000] politically, because I believe, Larry, for a third party to be successful, you have got to be centrist. You've got to be in the middle, not farther right than the Republicans, as [is] the case of Mr. Buchanan, or farther left than the Democrats, which is the case of Mr. Nader. If you're going to be successful as a third party, my belief is you have got to be centrist. And what I am . . .
>
> KING: But isn't centrist what the Democrats and Republicans, in your opinion, have become?
>
> VENTURA: No, not at all. They try to be. They're still left and right. What they do is they become centrist for an election, because they know it's those independents in the middle that determine who wins.
>
> KING: So you're saying there are no true centrists?
>
> VENTURA: Yes, there are true centrists, but they're left with no choice. Democrats and Republicans are not centrists, because, Larry, I'm fiscally conservative, but I'm socially liberal.
>
> KING: That means—who do you endorse this year?
>
> VENTURA: No one.

Ventura implied that the candidates in the presidential election were not at the median voter's ideal point, something we saw in chapter 4. But Ventura was also arguing that he is conservative on some issues and liberal on others and that being centrist is more than just being in the middle (not liberal or conservative) overall, but something more complicated. In order to understand Ventura's point and how he used the politics of division to achieve office, we need to think about issues in a more complex way, where Ventura's position (liberal on one issue, conservative on another) is possible.

Moving to More Than One Dimension

The Paradox of Voting

So far, we have assumed that the policy choices before voters can be represented along a single liberal-conservative dimension. But most issues that face voters are not so simple. Consider two issues that are often mentioned in election campaigns—government control over the economy and legalization of abortion. To think graphically about voters' choices on those issues, we need to be able to represent a voter's utility in a two-dimensional space, as in figure 14.1. Positions on abortion are measured along the horizontal axis. At position 0, unlimited abortion is allowed; as we move right along the horizontal axis from 0, the level of abortion allowed decreases so that at

FIGURE 14.1
Example of Voter's Utility from Two Issues

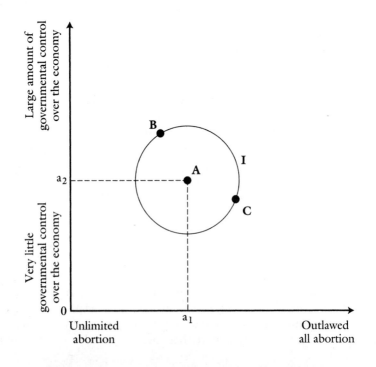

the farthest position on the right, no abortion is allowed. Positions on the economy are measured along the vertical axis. At position 0, there is very little government involvement in the economy, and as we move up the vertical axis from 0, the degree of government control of the economy increases so that at the highest position there is a great deal of control over the economy. We can think of a single voter—say, Aaron—whose ideal position on the combination of these issues is point A, which corresponds to position a_1 on abortion and a_2 on the economy.

In chapter 4, we represented Charlotte's ideal point in a single-dimension issue space, as seen in figure 4.1. As policy moved away from her ideal point, her utility declined. The same thing is true when we think about Aaron's utility in a two-dimensional space. The way to think about point A is that it is the top of a mountain of utility for Aaron, and as policy moves away from point A, it climbs down the mountain and decreases in utility. The circle labeled I represents a set of points equidistant from A. They are like a set of points that are all at the same altitude on the mountain. Because all the points give Aaron the same utility, we call the curve an indifference curve— that is, Aaron is indifferent between these positions. Aaron is thus indifferent between the combination of policies at point B and the combination of policies at point C. He would prefer, however, policy combinations closer to A, and he prefers B and C to all points farther from A. There are actually an infinite number of indifference curves, just as there are an infinite number of heights of a mountain. For every possible combination of positions on the issues of abortion and the economy, there is an indifference curve and a corresponding level of utility for Aaron associated with that indifference curve, just as every inch of a mountain has a height associated with it.

Now let's add two other voters to our example, Ellen and Tom, as in figure 14.2. The points E and T represent their ideal points and, as with Aaron, these points are like the top of their utility mountains, so that as we move away from them, their utility declines. What happens if we now have two candidates—say, for governor, Ventura and Humphrey—who choose positions in order to win?[10] Where will the candidates locate themselves?

Suppose that Ventura chooses a policy position at point V, which is where the indifference curves for Aaron and Ellen are just touching each other. But Humphrey can easily defeat this position by choosing a policy position at point H, which is closer to Aaron's and Tom's ideal points than V. So Aaron and Tom will vote for Humphrey, whereas Ellen will vote for Ventura. But Ventura can defeat Humphrey by choosing a position at V^*, which is closer to Ellen's and Tom's ideal points, leaving Aaron to vote alone for Humphrey. However, by moving positions Humphrey can defeat this position as well and then Ventura will want to move and on and on. It turns out that there is no equilibrium set of positions for Ventura and Humphrey. That is, for every position that Ventura might take, Humphrey can choose a position that will defeat him. Similarly, for every position that Humphrey might take, Ventura can choose a position that will defeat him.

FIGURE 14.2
Example of the Paradox of Voting

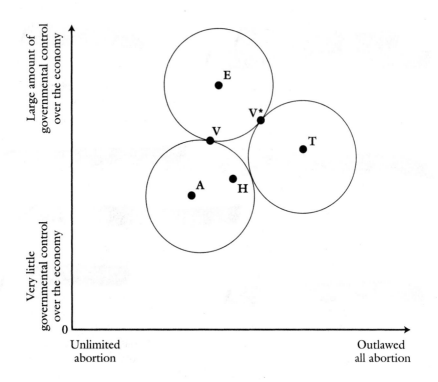

The problem facing the candidates and the voters is what is generally called the *paradox of voting*—the fact that it is easy to construct majority voting situation, like the one described above, in which there is no equilibrium. We saw this paradox earlier, in our discussion of the choices faced by a congressional committee choosing how to allocate military bases (see chapter 11). This is a paradox that has been known for many years—most credit the marquis de Condorcet, a French revolutionary, with its discovery, but more recently we have recognized that Condorcet rediscovered what was already known.[11]

The Paradox of Voting and U.S. Elections

We rarely think about Condorcet's paradox, and it is certainly not often discussed in works on U.S. elections. Why? We often ignore it because the policy choices in U.S. elections can usually be organized in a single liberal-conservative dimension that, although it may vary over time, is usually stable for long periods. How does this work? Consider two issues that divide the two political parties today—restriction of abortion and government control over the economy. Figure 14.3 gives an example of the two parties' positions on these issues at D and R, respectively. The Democratic Party has a position of d_1 on abortion (few restrictions) and d_2 on the economy (high involvement). Similarly, the Republican Party has a position of r_1 on abortion (significant restrictions) and r_2 on the economy (little government control).

FIGURE 14.3
One Example of How Party Positions Define the Liberal-Conservative Dimension

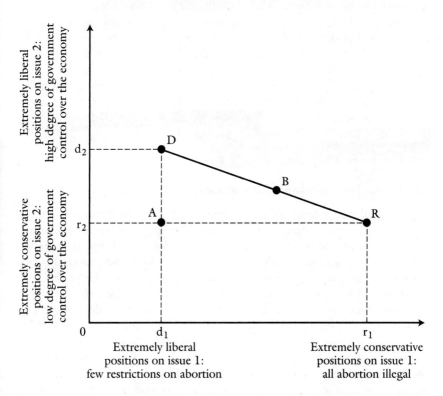

We can think of the policy positions as being determined by the members of those parties through the candidates they have selected and the positions those candidates have advocated. These parties have major status because they have managed to be the dominant two parties in electoral competition. The electoral institutions across the states give them, to varying degrees, easier access to ballots, and both have managed to have a set of existing party members who participate in the process of choosing the party positions. They have a set of voters they have mobilized and existing relationships with campaign contributions and interest groups. We saw in chapter 4 that when working in a single liberal-conservative dimension, if the two major political parties choose their candidates for the general election using some sort of primary process that is principally dominated by party members with more extreme preferences and there is uncertainty about the preferences of voters in the general election, the parties will align at different points in the distribution of preferences. This is also true when policy is multidimensional.[12]

The party policy positions structure the debate over policy. Assume Bob, whose ideal point is at point B, is what is normally thought of as a middle-of-the-road voter, who slightly prefers the Republican Party because it is closer to him ideologically (this is what Larry King meant by centrist in the dialogue with Jesse Ventura). But consider Aaron, whose ideal point is given by point A on the graph (who is more what Ventura thinks of as centrist). Aaron's ideal policy position on issue 1 is the same as the position of the Democratic Party, whereas Aaron's ideal policy position on issue 2 is the same as the position of the Republican Party. In terms of the distance of the points, however, Aaron's ideal point is closer to the Democrats than to the Republicans. Thus, point D is on an indifference curve that is closer to Aaron's ideal point than R is. If Aaron sees his policy choices as between D and R, then he prefers D to R and thus will vote for D even though R's position on issue 2 is at his ideal point.

The Meaning of Liberal and Conservative

We can think of the bold line connecting D and R as the liberal-conservative alignment of issues in the country as defined by the two parties. Some voters' ideal points will be close to that line, like Bob's, and thus their preferences will be easy to describe by the terms *liberal* and *conservative*, as defined by the two major parties. But what about Aaron, who prefers both abortion and less control over the economy? Aaron is not easily characterized in terms of being a liberal, conservative, or moderate. Because Aaron's ideal point is closest to the Democrats, he prefers them. But is Aaron a liberal? a conservative? a moderate? We would usually say that Aaron is a liberal on abortion policy but a conservative on the government's involvement in the economy, using the labels for the parties (Democrats as the liberal party, Republicans as the conservative party) to correspondingly define what it means to be liberal or conservative on these two policy issues. Aaron is like Jesse Ventura (economically conservative and socially liberal).

These definitions are entirely arbitrary. Democrats and Republicans could conceivably have positions like those in figure 14.4, in which Democrats advocate more restrictive abortion and a high degree of government control over the economy and Republicans advocate the opposite. We would then say having restrictions on abortion is the "liberal" position and having fewer restrictions on abortion is the "conservative" position. In figure 14.4, Aaron's preferences (at point A) are consistent with the liberal-conservative dimension established by the party positions, and B is the oddball.

FIGURE 14.4
Another Example of How Party Positions Define the Liberal-Conservative Dimension

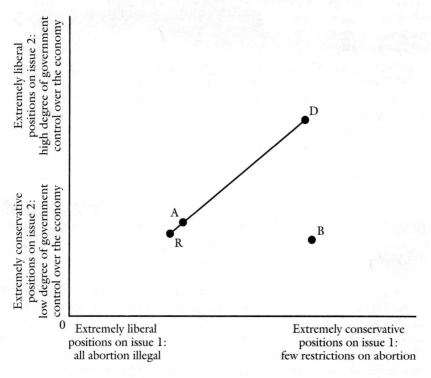

Can Minor-Party or Independent Candidates Succeed in U.S. Elections?

Ventura's Unlikely Achievement

In the Minnesota governor's race in 1998, the Republican candidate, Norman Coleman, was solidly against abortion and for lower taxes and less government control of the economy, the typical *R* position in figure 14.3. The Democratic candidate, Hubert Humphrey III, was opposed to abortion control but in favor of more involvement of the government in the economy, the typical *D* position in figure 14.3. Jesse Ventura was pro-choice on abortion and in favor of fewer taxes, as was Aaron. If Ventura could find enough voters like Aaron, who preferred his positions to both Humphrey's and Coleman's, he could win. He needed only a plurality of the vote—that is, more votes than the other candidates but not necessarily a majority. Yet he needed to convince these voters that they would not be wasting their vote or their time by going to the polls and supporting him. Aaron's second choice would be Humphrey. If Aaron thought Ventura would not get enough votes to win, that he would come in third, Aaron would be better off voting strategically for Humphrey in order to prevent a win by Coleman, his least preferred candidate. Ventura needed voters like Aaron to coordinate on his behalf rather than on Humphrey's. He also needed to attract voters who most preferred him but whose second preference was Coleman—he needed to keep those voters from voting strategically for Coleman. Finally, other voters might prefer Ventura and be indifferent about the choice between Coleman and Humphrey. If they thought the race would be primarily between Coleman and Humphrey and that Ventura had little chance, they would just abstain and not vote. Ventura needed to convince those disaffected voters to turn out; he needed to mobilize them.

Ventura was not just any former pro wrestler. He had already been in politics—he had served as mayor of a suburb of Minneapolis for four years. He also had a radio talk show, on which he had often discussed policy issues and voiced his views on those issues.[13] As we saw in chapter 7, getting voters to know a candidate and his or her policy positions can increase the expected utility that voters get from that candidate's election and can change their preferences. Many minor-party and independent candidates do not have the advantages that Ventura had. According to Dean Barkley, Ventura's campaign chairman, it was this advantage plus his policy positions that motivated Barkley and others to encourage Ventura to run for governor as a minor-party candidate. In October 1997, Ventura and his campaign managers met at Famous Dave's, a restaurant in Ventura's hometown of Maple Grove, Minnesota, and they laid out their plan: to achieve the support of 24 percent of the electorate in the polls by October 1998 (enough support that voters would see Ventura as viable in a race against two other candidates with about 38 percent each—in mid-October, Ventura's support was 21 percent), to be included in all debates, to do well in the debates (again, so that voters would see Ventura as equal to the major-party candidates—so that they would see him as a viable candidate—and would learn his policy positions and observe his ability to handle issues), and finally "to raise $400,000 to $500,000 to spend on paid media for the last 2 weeks of the election to motivate enough of the non-voting public to carry him past the 35% to 38% that would be needed to win" and to "motivate the young voters to vote" (in both cases going after voters who they perceived were not already mobilized by the major political parties and thus were more likely to vote for Ventura if attracted by his positions).[14]

Ventura benefited from a number of aspects of Minnesota's political system in fulfilling his game plan. He was able to participate in a large number of free public forums to debate the issues—many civic associations and interest groups had such meetings (Norman Coleman did not attend many of those early forums because he did not want to be involved in debating Democratic candidates before their primary, when the nomination would be

decided). Ventura was allowed to take part in the later major debates with
Coleman and Humphrey. He also participated in a number of summer festi-
vals and parades. He had fewer money woes than many other minor-party
and independent candidates because Minnesota's public financing system
limited to $2.1 million each the amount the major-party candidates could
spend and allowed Ventura to qualify for public money if he raised just
$35,000 in $50 contributions by the end of August and received more than
5 percent of the vote in the election. But to spend the money before the
election, he needed to get a bank to lend it to him. Banks were reluctant,
but with the help of a Minneapolis City Council member, he received a
bank loan in time to run ads. The ads then attracted more money, bringing
in $10,000 a day (as contributors began to see Ventura as viable).

The final effort that persuaded voters to turn out for him was a seventy-
two-hour tour of areas where his campaign staff estimated the types of voters they needed were most likely to congregate, places where he got free
media coverage. Ventura's campaign did not have the resources to mount
the traditional get-out-the-vote effort of a party organization. As Barkley related, their idea was to

> target the media centers in the areas we needed to reach and as many colleges as
> possible. The campaign dropped everything else to work on this final 72 hour
> drive to victory. We did not know whether or not it would work, but it did. The
> crowds we attracted and the media coverage was better than we had hoped for. It
> could just as easily have been a big flop. It was risky, we knew it, but we pulled it
> off.[15]

Because Minnesota allows voters to register at the polls as well as in advance,
the mobilization of new voters was much easier for Ventura than it would
have been in most other states, which require registration up to thirty days
in advance. With one last television ad before the campaign, showing Ventura as *The Thinker* in Rodin's famous sculpture, Ventura was able to win
with 37 percent of the vote to Coleman's 34 percent and Humphrey's
28 percent (Ventura received more disaffected Democratic support than
Republican).

Ventura's Failure

The year Ventura won office, Minnesota was a state whose economy, like
the nation's, was doing extraordinarily well. When the legislature adjourned
in April 1998, it had disposed of $4 billion in revenue surpluses in the form
of one-time tax rebates, property-tax reductions, education and health programs, and public works projects. Ventura sent out "Jesse checks" to voters
nearly every year. But he had difficulties. He was a "party of one," and the
two major parties controlled the state legislature. An economic downturn
began in the spring of 2001, suggesting a budget shortfall, and with the al-

ready approved tax cuts and rebates, negotiations with the state's largest
public employees union faltered, resulting in a strike of twenty thousand
workers. Public criticism of Ventura's job performance—his moonlighting
as a broadcaster on television and his willingness to use money from the national media to finance a visit to ground zero after September 11—increased. But Ventura tackled these problems head-on. He presented to the
legislature

> a sweeping multi-year budget fix—a mix of tax increases on gasoline and tobacco,
> across-the-board cuts to state government, his own office, local governments and
> schools. . . . It was dead on arrival. Republicans opposed to the tax increase and
> DFLers [Democrats] opposed to program cuts ganged up to ram through a plan
> that balanced the budget by draining much of the state's reserves. When Ventura
> vetoed it, they overrode the veto by overwhelming margins. . . . The master of tri-
> angulation had been sidelined.[16]

It was Ventura against the legislature, and because the two major parties
were united with veto-proof majorities, Ventura lost. The battle became
comical, with the legislature cutting Ventura's security budget. Ventura
closed the governor's mansion (only his twenty-two-year-old son had lived
there) and fired the staff. Even when public funds were restored, he refused
to rehire them. The staff went public with Ventura's son's late-night parties,
food and liquor expenditures, and damage to state-owned furnishings.
Shortly afterward, Ventura announced that he would not seek a second
term. In 2002, Ventura's Independence Party's nominee, Tim Penny, got
only 16.18 percent of the vote to Republican Tim Pawlenty's 44.37 percent
and Democrat Roger Moe's 36.46 percent. The Independence Party candidate for senator got 2 percent of the vote. Minor-party candidates received
3.4 percent of the vote in congressional races in the state. The Independence Party had only one success, the election of state senator Sheila
Kiscaden, who had been in office since 1992 but had switched from the
Republican Party when her local party endorsed a candidate whose position
on abortion was more conservative than hers.

Was It Jesse?

Jesse Ventura's lack of success in building an enduring "third force" in Minnesota politics could be chalked up to the effects of personality and the
economy, but such a conclusion would be shortsighted. When Ventura won
the governorship, he was not the only independent governor in the country—in 1998, Maine's independent governor Angus King was reelected for
his second term. King similarly had been able to win election in 1994 by
taking votes away from the two major-party candidates. Dennis Bailey,
King's campaign spokesman, summarized how King—like Ventura a social
moderate and a fiscal conservative—attracted voters: "Angus owns the big

middle, and the parties have become captives of their extremes, which is something they may have to do to win primaries but is not at all where Maine people are."[17] As a multimillionaire, King was able to finance his election himself and so communicate with voters, and he, like Ventura, was already well-known to the public as host of a television talk show. Whereas King faced difficulties with the state legislature, he benefited from the better economic situation in Maine during his terms and had fewer problems getting the legislature to enact policies he preferred. He had high job-approval ratings throughout his years in office.

Angus King's Legacy

But King was not eligible to run again in 2002. He left office and with his family moved into a recreational vehicle for a tour of the country's perimeter. He was replaced by a Democrat in a contest in which the two non-major-party candidates together managed to win only 11.38 percent of the vote. In the U.S. Senate and congressional races in Maine, no minor-party or independent candidates received votes. One Green Party member, John Eder, and three independents were elected to the 151-seat Maine state house—the rest and all members of the state senate are either Republicans or Democrats.

Eder campaigned hard to get his office, spending a year knocking on doors and meeting nearly every voter and spending hours discussing problems with voters. But he quickly learned that being a party of one does not make life as a legislator easy, as he related: "There is the party stuff, there are issues and then there are relationships. The last one, relationships, that's really the only neighborhood I have to work in. I have no party power. It is just me."[18] Despite representing an urban area, his only committee assignment was agriculture. His proposals had to be "repackaged by Democrats, who then guided the bills to passage." He voted with Democrats "99.9 percent of the time." In this sense, Eder, unlike King and Ventura, is closer to the Democratic policy position than the Republican and thus is in more direct competition with the existing Democratic Party. Democrats clearly saw this and didn't want Eder there. After his election, the legislature voted new district lines, putting the Old Port section of his district, where he resided, into the district of popular incumbent Benjamin Dudley and the West End section into the district of hardworking policy wonk incumbent Edward Suslovic. At first, Eder and his party unsuccessfully challenged the redistricting in the courts. But then Eder recognized that he had a chance of winning with the West End voters, who were largely young, single, mobile, and politically progressive, against Suslovic, a suburban soccer dad. Eder moved to the neighborhood, and he and his party campaigned aggressively. Eder won reelection in 2004 with 51 percent of the vote.

The three independents elected in Maine in 2002 also worked through the major parties to pass legislation and did not attempt to build any formal party organization that would compete with them. In 2004, two of the three won reelection, although one became a Democrat in the process. Although Eder and the lone independent, Richard Woodbury, remain in the state legislature, it is clear that Maine is still a state dominated by the two major parties. Notwithstanding having little of Ventura's baggage, King succeeded as an independent without significantly diminishing the major political parties' control over Maine's politics or the representation of Maine's political preferences in national politics.

How Influential Are Minor-Party and Independent Candidates?

In Presidential Contests

Are King's and Ventura's experiences the norm? Since the Civil War, minor-party presidential candidates have received over 10 percent of the popular vote four times—in 1912, 1924, 1968, and 1992. Votes for minor-party presidential candidates have resulted in seventeen out of forty-one presidents' winning office with less than a majority of the popular vote. In the last forty years, there have been three significant independent or minor-party candidates for president: George Wallace in 1968 with 13.5 percent of the vote, John Anderson in 1980 with 7.1 percent of the vote, and Ross Perot in 1992 with 18.9 percent of the vote and in 1996 with 8.4 percent of the vote.

Although Ralph Nader's vote was only 2.74 percent in 2000, many Democrats believed that Nader's supporters' second choice was Gore. They reasoned that had the Nader voters chosen Gore instead, Gore could have won Florida and other states that were close. Citing exit-poll numbers that suggested that Nader supporters in 2000 would have largely voted for Gore, the *International Herald Tribune* summarized: "It is safe to assume that Nader cost Gore states that Bush narrowly won. In Florida, Nader received 97,488 votes, 1.6 percent of the total, and Bush carried the state by 537 votes. In New Hampshire, Nader won 22,198 votes, 3.9 percent of the total, and Bush carried the state by 7,211 votes. Had Gore won in either state, he would have become president."[19] A Roper poll for Fox News in early March 2004 found that 37 percent of respondents believed Nader's candidacy cost Al Gore the presidency. In April 2004, fifteen progressive and liberal activists sent a letter to Nader, making this argument and asking him not to run in 2004.[20]

Not surprisingly, Nader disputes these claims. First, he argues that Gore lost Florida because of ballot problems and a lack of creative campaigning by the Democrats. Second, he contends that many of his supporters are Republicans and independents who would not necessarily have voted for Gore or even have voted at all. Nader chose to run again in 2004. He has maintained that by drawing out voters and criticizing the Bush administration, he has helped the Democratic Party. He argued in February 2004: "I am persuaded that I will draw far more independents and Republicans who would otherwise have voted for Bush than I would get from the Democratic Party candidate."[21] In 2004, Nader received only 0.38 percent of the vote and did not noticeably affect Bush's reelection.

Although many Democrats see Nader's votes as costing Gore the presidency, some have also suggested that if Pat Buchanan had not been in the race in 2000, Bush might have won more states, making what happened in Florida irrelevant. As Burden forthcoming pointed out, in Iowa, New Mexico, Oregon, and Wisconsin, states won by Gore, Buchanan's vote totals were greater than the difference between Gore and Bush. If Buchanan voters' second choice had been Bush, then the same logic that suggests that Nader cost Gore the election should infer that Buchanan made Bush's win much more difficult. We will consider these issues more expansively below, when we examine empirical evidence on voters' behavior in 2000.

In Congressional Contests

Table 14.3 summarizes the distribution of U.S. senators, Congress members, governors, and state legislators by party affiliation as of February 2005. In Congress, the success of minor-party and independent candidates is rare, although many run. In the 2000 election, 55 percent of the candidates for the Senate and 40 percent of the candidates for the House were independent or minor-party candidates, but only two were elected, Bernard Sanders of Vermont and Virgil Goode of Virginia, both incumbents. Running as an independent was only a step on the way to party switching for Goode, who had first been elected, in 1996, as a Democrat and became a Republican in 2002. Sanders, although an independent, caucuses with Democrats, as does his fellow Vermonter, independent senator James Jeffords (Jeffords had run as a Republican in 2000). In 2002, 72 minor-party or independent candidates for the U.S. Senate and 402 for the U.S. House raised $3.4 million in campaign receipts, as reported by the Federal Elections Commission. Yet only Bernard Sanders won office. Jesse Ventura appointed Independence Party member Dean Barkley to finish out Senator Paul Wellstone's term after his death in 2002, but Barkley was replaced by the newly elected Republican senator, Norman Coleman (Ventura's old foe).

In State and Local Contests

Pockets of Success At the state and local level, minor parties and independent candidates have had more success. In the 1930s, Minnesota's Farmer-Labor Party and Wisconsin's Progressives won gubernatorial elections and legislative majorities.[22] In 1990, former Republican congressman Lowell

TABLE 14.3
Party Affiliation of Elected Officials, February 2005

Officeholders	Democrats	Republicans	Independents or Members of Minor Parties
U.S. senators	48	51	1
U.S. representatives	205	229	1
Governors	22	28	0
State legislators*	3,657	3,658	17

*These figures omit Nebraska because it has a unicameral, nonpartisan legislature.

Weicker formed a third party, called A Connecticut Party, and won the governorship with 40 percent of the vote against Democratic and Republican candidates. That same year in Alaska, former Republican governor Walter J. Hickel won the governorship as a member of the Alaska Independence Party, with 39 percent of the vote. Recently, Socialists have served as mayors of Burlington, Vermont (Sanders before he went to Congress), and Iowa City, Iowa. Although no Libertarians held elected office in 2005, theirs has been arguably the most successful of the existing minor parties in the last fifty years, winning more state legislative elections than any other minor party, with a national vote in the U.S. House elections exceeding 1 percent in 2000 and 2002. Libertarians elected a state legislator in Alaska in 1978, two in 1980, and one in 1984. In New Hampshire, Libertarians elected four state legislators in 1992, two in 1994, and one in 2000. Vermont Libertarians elected a state legislator in 1998.[23]

In 2002, 1,182 minor-party and independent candidates ran for state legislative seats; 21 were successful. None of the 315 minor-party and independents who ran for statewide nonfederal elective office (governor, lieutenant governor, secretary of state, and so on) were successful. Table 14.4 presents details on the seventeen minor-party and independent state legislators serving in February 2005 (excluding Nebraska, where the legislature is unicameral and nonpartisan).

Forcing the Major Parties to Notice Of these state legislators, the ones who have potentially had the biggest impact have achieved that influence by being the swing voters in battles between the two major parties over control of the legislature. Vermont's Progressive Party was the original home of Bernie Sanders, and its members and the independents in the state legislature (which has the largest number of minor-party and independent members of any state legislature) have been the swing voters on issues relating to the organization of the legislature. Because the votes were conducted by secret ballot, however, it is unclear how much influence the Progressives and

TABLE 14.4
Minor-Party and Independent State Legislators, 2005

State	Body	Name	Affiliation	*Known Relationship to Major Parties*
Delaware	House	G. Wallace Caulk, Jr.	Independent	Former Republican incumbent who left party in dispute over executive pay raise
Illinois	Senate	James T. Meeks	Independent	Elected as independent to defeat Democratic incumbent but works with Democrats
Kentucky	Senate	Robert J. Leeper	Independent	Former Democratic incumbent who became a Republican but left the Republican Party in a dispute over partisan decision to violate constitutional election rules
Louisiana	House	Joel C. Robideaux	Independent	Endorsed by some Republicans in state; ran as a conservative
Maine	House	John Eder	Green	Elected as Green but works with Democrats
Maine	House	Richard Woodbury	Unaffiliated	
Massachusetts	House	William Lantigua	Unenrolled	Democrat who ran as an unenrolled candidate to bypass primary competition; ran for reelection as unenrolled candidate in 2004 and beat Democratic challenger
Minnesota	Senate	Sheila Kiscaden	Independence Party	Republican who changed party affiliation after local party officials endorsed another candidate
Vermont	House	Dexter Randal	Progressive	
Vermont	House	Bob Kiss	Progressive	
Vermont	House	David Zuckerman	Progressive	Chair of house agricultural committee
Vermont	House	Winston Dowland	Progressive	
Vermont	House	Sandy Haas	Progressive	
Vermont	House	Daryl L. Pillsbury	Independent	
Vermont	House	Sarah R. Edwards	Democrat Progressive	Elected as a Progressive but works with Democrats
Virginia	House	Watkins Abbitt, Jr.	Independent	Former Democrat who recently declared himself independent and now works with Republicans
Virginia	House	Lacey E. Putney	Independent	Former Democrat who recently declared himself independent and now works with Republicans

Note: Nebraska, which has a unicameral, nonpartisan legislature, is not considered.

independents had. Nevertheless, one of these progressives, David Zuckerman, became chair of the committee on agriculture. More clear is the recent influence of Virginia's Lacey E. Putney, who became an independent in 1967 but recently began to caucus with Republicans, when the makeup of the legislature became forty-nine Republicans to fifty Democrats. By giving his vote to the Republicans, Putney allowed their party to have parity with the Democrats; he was rewarded with a prime committee chairmanship. Putney's experience as a Democrat, then an independent, and then an independent working with Republicans is a route that a number of southern legislators have taken, both in state legislatures and in Congress (as, for example, Virgil Goode had done), with some of them later becoming Republicans. These changes reflect the growing strength of the Republican Party in the South during the 1980s and 1990s and a southern Democratic Party becoming more liberal, changes we discussed in chapter 5.

Like Jeffords in the Senate, some state legislators choose to claim independent status to protest moves by their former party. For example, Wally Caulk of Delaware changed his affiliation from Republican to independent to protest Republican Party legislators' approval of executive pay raises. Similarly, Bob Leeper changed his affiliation from Republican to independent when party members voted to seat a Republican state senator who, the courts had declared, had not satisfied the constitutional requirement for office.

Bypassing Primaries Three of the seventeen state legislators in table 14.4 have worked with major parties but chose to run as independents or minor-party candidates either because of local party opposition to their candidacy or to avoid facing an incumbent in their own party's primary, believing they could defeat that candidate more easily in the general election (Sheila Kiscaden, discussed above, James T. Meeks, and William Lantigua). The use of independent status to bypass primary competition in one's own political party has also been used successfully by a number of past and present members of Congress. For example, the powerful late Massachusettes Democratic representative Joseph Moakley first won office as an independent after having lost the Democratic primary in a previous attempt to win a seat in Congress. Similarly, former Republican representative Ron Packard (who did not seek reelection in 2000) first won office as a write-in candidate, challenging the party's nominee, who had defeated him in the Republican primary after scandalous information about the nominee became public. Current Republican House member Jo Ann Emerson ran as an independent after missing the deadline to file for the primary in the race to replace her husband, Bill Emerson, who had died in office.

The lesson that bypassing the party is a possibility has not been lost on other candidates—William Lantigua remarked during his campaign in 2002: "I'm doing what the late Joe Moakley did." Lantigua chose to run as an independent because he was worried that Hispanic voters, his primary supporters, would have difficulty coordinating in the primary. He explained that "he went independent to get a one-on-one shot at [incumbent Democratic representative Jose] Santiago, skirting a crowded primary in which the Hispanic vote would have been split three ways against an Anglo city councilor who ultimately finished second to Santiago."[24] The option to run as an independent, minor-party, or write-in candidate because a candidate believes he or she has a better chance in the general election will of course vary by states' rules on ballot access. The lower the barriers to choosing those options and the more able a candidate is to convey his or her message to voters without major-party endorsement, the more likely it is that candidates will choose them.

In Georgia, state legislator Buddy DeLoach's decision to run as an independent in order to avoid a possible primary loss ended up "sticking" in a way that surprised him. *The Augusta Chronicle* reported:

> "I saw it strictly as an alternative method of getting on the ballot," Mr. DeLoach said. "But my folks at home saw it as a switch to move out of the Republican Party and become a true independent, no matter how many times I tried to explain it otherwise. It became apparent to me that, having been elected that way, I was going to have to serve that way. Now that I'm here . . . I feel very positive about the move, and I think my constituents feel the same way."

DeLoach, who originally served as a Democratic mayor and then spent several terms in the Georgia state legislature as a Republican, made it clear before his party change that he still saw himself as a conservative. He had little observable trouble as a party of one: " 'People have had some fun with it,' said Minority Leader Lynn Westmoreland, R-Sharpsburg, of Mr. DeLoach's new status as the only independent in the 236-member General Assembly. 'Both sides of the aisle respect Buddy, so it's been taken in good harmony.' "[25] Yet redistricting of the Georgia state legislature forced DeLoach to face a Democratic incumbent, Al Williams, who defeated him.

Giving Up Wins by minor-party and independent candidates are still rare. The vast majority, even at the state and local levels, fail to win, even when they see themselves as major-party candidates in disguise. North Carolina Democrat Gene Gay lost the Democratic primary in an attempt to challenge incumbent Republican representative Sue Myrick in 2000, but because congressional candidates are not required to live in the districts they represent, he then filed as a write-in candidate in a contest with Republican incumbent representative Howard Coble, who had no Democratic competition. Gay received only 632 votes. Other minor-party and independent candidates, once they are elected, find that joining a major party is the only way they can fulfill their goals. The only previous state representative elected as a Green, Audie Bock of California, became a Democrat after failing to be reelected. Bock reportedly told her staffers: "Don't expect doors are going to open to you. You're really going to have to beat your head against the wall every day."[26] Similarly, Maine state representative Troy Jackson dropped his independent status to join the Democratic Party in 2004. According to his Web site, Jackson concluded that "as a member of the party he can more successfully influence state legislative action on small business development and creat[e] high quality jobs that pay a living wage."[27]

Do Voters Vote Strategically?

Evidence of Desertion

As these examples show, voters do not always support the major parties in U.S. elections. As we have seen, many observers believe that Nader's candidacy cost Gore the presidency in 2000, and others have suggested that Buchanan's candidacy made the race more difficult for Bush. Our earlier theoretical analysis shows that when minor-party and independent candidates have little chance of winning, as was the case for Nader and Buchanan in 2000, voters who have preferences for the remaining candidates should vote strategically. We should thus expect voters whose first preference is a minor-party or independent candidate to be more likely to vote strategically than voters whose first preference is a major-party candidate.

Is there evidence that voters who support minor-party and independent candidates choose strategically? Rosenstone, Behr, and Lazarus (1984) found that as elections near, the support such candidates receive in preelection polls generally declines, suggesting that the voters who prefer those candidates are deserting them for their second choice. More concrete evidence on strategic voting can be discerned from responses to the NES surveys. As discussed in chapter 5, the NES surveys voters about their "feelings" about the candidates, using a "thermometer." By comparing the ratings that NES-survey respondents give the candidates, we can get a measure of their preferences for them. For example, consider the 1996 presidential election. The three major candidates were Republican Bob Dole, Democrat Bill Clinton, and Reform Party candidate Ross Perot. If a voter rated Dole at 85, Perot at 50, and Clinton at 40, we could say that Dole was the first preference, Perot the second, and Clinton the third. Sometimes voters rate candidates equally (like the *B* voters in our model of the 1970 New York Senate race).[28] One way to measure the degree to which voters coordinate their votes is to measure how often voters who preferred the minor-party or independent candidate voted strategically for their second preferred candidate. Table 14.5 presents this comparison for the presidential elections of 1968, 1980, 1992, 1996, and 2000.

Note that when a voter's first preference is a major-party candidate, he or she almost always votes for that candidate. Of voters whose most preferred candidate is a major-party candidate, 6 percent or less voted for a minor-

TABLE 14.5
Voting for First Preference in Presidential Elections, by Voters' Preferences, 1968, 1980, 1992, 1996, and 2000

Year	Minor-Party Candidate	Voters Preferring Minor-Party Candidate (%)		Voters Preferring Major-Party Candidate (%)	
		Voting for Minor-Party Candidate	*Not Voting for Minor-Party Candidate*	*Voting for Major-Party Candidate*	*Not Voting for Major-Party Candidate*
1968	George C. Wallace	84	16	96.0	4
1980	John Anderson	57	43	97.0	3
1992	Ross Perot	77	23	94.0	6
1996	Ross Perot	61	39	97.0	3
2000	Ralph Nader	29	71	99.5	<1

Source: Abramson, Aldrich, and Rohde (2002).
Note: Voters who tied in their preferences are excluded.

party candidate. This percentage was lowest when the election contest between the two major-party candidates was closest—for example, in 2000. In that case, less than 1 percent of major-party supporters voted for a minor-party candidate. However, voters whose first preference is a minor-party or independent candidate much more often vote for a candidate who is not their first preference. This tendency has varied over time; it was lowest in 1968 and highest in 2000, when 71 percent of Nader supporters deserted his candidacy.

Interestingly, the three elections in which the tendency was highest (1980, 1996, and 2000) were those in which the minor-party or independent candidate received less than 10 percent of the vote. And the two elections in which the tendency was lowest (1968 and 1992) were cases in which the minor-party or independent candidate received more than 10 percent of the vote. This suggests that the voters were more likely to vote for their first preference when that candidate had a greater vote total, although this is clearly crude evidence.

Nader and the 2000 Election

Survey Evidence If Nader's candidacy cost Gore the 2000 election, then the implication is that Nader's supporters ignored the strategic advantage of voting for Gore and instead voted sincerely for Nader. While the evidence above suggests that Nader's supporters were more strategic than Gore's and Bush's supporters, as well as previous presidential minor-party supporters, there were actually only thirty-three Nader voters in the entire NES sample, an extremely small number from which to generalize. One solution to this problem is to turn to larger Internet-based surveys, such as the KN panel (discussed in chapter 10). As reviewed earlier, KN randomly selects subjects to participate and thus, like the NES, is statistically representative of voters across the country yet surveys a much larger number of individuals, over twenty-nine thousand.

Hillygus (2003) examined the voting decisions of KN respondents who in one or more surveys prior to the election expressed support for Nader—6 percent of the survey respondents. She thus can determine the extent to which these voters "switched" to another choice later as a function of voter ideology. She found that only 28.7 percent of those who reported supporting Nader prior to the election reported voting for him on election day, in comparison with 70 percent of those who reported supporting Bush and 68 percent for those who reported supporting Gore. Thus, the Nader supporters appear to have voted strategically more often than the Bush and Gore supporters.

Closeness and Expressiveness While the evidence suggests that minor-party supporters are more likely to vote strategically than major-party supporters, we would also expect that the tendency will vary and depend on whether a supporter's vote will make a difference in the election. As discussed in chapter 13, in presidential elections the votes that count are the votes in states that can make a difference in terms of the electoral vote—states in which the race is close and the outcome can affect the outcome of the electoral vote. We would expect that the tendency to vote strategically would depend on whether a voter was in such a state.

Consider a minor-party supporter named Cornel. Assume that Cornel receives 1 unit of utility from the election of Nader, 0 from the election of Bush, and u utility from the election of Gore. Assume that $1 > u \geq 0$. If Cornel is indifferent in the choice between Bush and Gore, then $u = 0$, and if Cornel prefers Gore to Bush, then $u > 0$. As u increases, we would expect that Cornel would be more likely to vote strategically for Gore instead of Nader. We would also expect that the closer the election in Cornel's state—that is, the greater the probability that Cornel's vote can affect the outcome of the election in his state—then the more likely it is that Cornel will vote strategically for Gore for a given value of u as long as $u > 0$. We can imagine for a given closeness of an election, there is a threshold value of u, which we label U^*. If $u > U^*$, then Cornel will vote strategically for Gore, and if $u < U^*$, Cornel will vote expressively for Nader. As the race becomes closer, then we would expect U^* to decline. Thus, Cornel is more likely to vote for Gore in battleground states than in states that in which the race not close.

Is there evidence that supports this argument? Hillygus (2003) found that indeed Nader voters were more likely to vote strategically in battleground states. Furthermore, Hillygus reported that when asked their second choice in the surveys, 45 percent of the Nader supporters selected Gore and 26 percent selected Bush. When she compared the ideological positions of the three different types of voters—those for Nader, those for Gore, and those for Bush—she found that Nader and Gore voters had similar preferences, supporting the argument that Nader did take away votes from Gore. However, Hillygus found that some Nader supporters were expressive—they were dissatisfied with both major-party candidates and with government in general, as Cornel is if $u = 0$. Hillygus found that expressive Nader supporters were much less likely to desert Nader for either Gore or Bush.

Nader and Mobilization As Hillygus (2003) recounted, Nader had argued that his campaign would not take away votes from Democrats because he would mobilize new voters, who would vote Democratic in lower-level races. She found evidence that Nader did mobilize new voters—25 percent of his voters had not voted in 1996. Furthermore, they reported that before the campaign, they had not intended to vote, and after the election they reported that they would not have voted if Nader had not been in the race. Yet she found that less than 25 percent of these new voters mobilized by Nader voted Democratic in lower-level races (17.2 percent voted Republican, and the remaining either abstained or voted for minor-party or independent candidates). This evidence suggests that most of the voters newly mobilized by Nader were in fact expressive voters and thus largely indifferent in the choices between the two major parties.

Polls and Outcomes A major problem with comparing voters' intentions with voters' choices as reported in surveys, as Hillygus did, is that many survey respondents tend to report that they voted for the winner even when they had not, as discussed in Wright (1990, 1992, 1993). In 2000, as Herron and Lewis (2004), noted, this was likely to be a particularly difficult problem in analyzing Nader's voters, given the ex post facto controversy over who won the election. Thus, the reports of strategic voting from the surveys are likely to be overstated. One way to get around this problem and uncover evidence that Nader's supporters deserted him is to compare Nader's support in preelection polls with the number of votes he actually received. Burden (forthcoming) made such a comparison across states. He also made the same comparison for other minor-party candidates in 2000 and for minor-party candidates in 1992 and 1996.

Burden contended that if the actual vote for a minor-candidate exceeds that predicted by the poll immediately proceeding the election, there is evidence of a form of strategic voting for minor-party candidates—strategic because the voters might actually prefer one of the major-party candidates but not expecting the election to be close, they vote for the minor-party candidates to also express dissatisfaction with the government—and if the actual vote for a minor-party candidate is less than predicted by the poll before the election, there is evidence of strategic instrumental voting for major-party candidates—strategic voting for a second preference, as we discussed earlier. That is, strategic expressive voters might prefer Gore to Nader and Bush, but because of their unhappiness with the two viable candidates, Gore and Bush, and knowing that Nader has little chance of winning, they vote for Nader to express their dissatisfaction to Gore. Burden found evidence of overall strategic expressive voting in 1992 and 1996 but overall strategic instrumental voting in 2000, particularly in states in which the election was predicted to be close. These results support the analysis of Hillygus.

A Case Study of Florida, Using Actual Ballots In chapter 3, we noted that an examination of ballots from Palm Beach County, Florida, suggests that the butterfly ballot led more than 2,000 voters to vote for Buchanan instead of Gore. Although many observers blame the butterfly ballot for hurting Gore, many also blame Nader, as noted earlier. The analyses of Hillygus and Burden, discussed above, suggest that because Florida was a battleground state and most believed the election would be close, there should have been significant desertion of Nader for the major-party candidates, particularly for Gore. Yet over 97,000 Florida voters chose Nader, significantly more than Bush's slim 537-vote margin of victory in the state. Were these largely expressive voters, as the analyses of Hillygus and Burden would suggest, or would they have supported Gore if the election had been a two-man race? Did Nader cost Gore Florida?

Herron and Lewis (2004) used the actual ballots from the 2000 election in ten Florida counties to investigate the likelihood that voters for Nader in that state would have chosen Gore if Nader had not been in the election. The ballots tell not only how each individual in the county voted in the presidential election but also how he or she voted in the other races in that election—senatorial, congressional, judicial, and so on. Herron and Lewis used a technique similar to that used by Poole and Rosenthal (discussed in chapter 4) to estimate a partisan preference for groups of voters based on their choices across races. That is, recall that Poole and Rosenthal were able to use the set of votes that members of Congress cast on a host of bills to estimate the members' ideological positions on policy. Herron and Lewis used the set of votes on each ballot to estimate voters' ideological positions on parties. However, since they did not have as many votes per individual as Poole and Rosenthal did, they grouped voters together by county, whether they voted absentee or on election day, and presidential preference and estimated each group's party positions. They then estimated the second preferences of the voters in these Florida counties who chose minor-party candidates, and they found that Nader voters in these Florida counties who chose minor-party candidates, and they found that Nader voters were somewhat pro-Democrat and Buchanan voters were somewhat pro-Republican, yet most of them were close to being partisan centrists. This result fits with the analyses of Hillygus and Burden, since Florida was a battleground state, and we would expect that minor-party supporters who had strong secondary partisan preferences would have voted strategically for one of the major-party candidates and that those who actually voted for minor-party candidates would be largely expressive voters who did not have a strong second preference. Fitting with this result, Herron and Lewis also showed that if Nader had not been a candidate, 40 percent of his voters would have chosen Bush, based on their choices in other elections. Nevertheless, Herron and Lewis found that the remaining 60 percent of Nader's voters would have voted for Gore, and thus they argued that the evidence suggests that Nader's candidacy did cost Gore Florida.

This analysis assumes that the Nader supporters in Florida would have voted and not abstained in the two-man race. But the investigation of Hillygus suggested that most of the voters who Nader mobilized in the election were expressive, the type of voter who appears to have voted for Nader in these Florida counties, according to the analysis of Herron and Lewis. Since Herron and Lewis had no data on nonvoters, it is impossible to say whether the Nader voters would have chosen to participate if the election had been a two-man race and that Gore or Bush would have received their votes.

Party Labels as Information and Coordination Devices

This analysis of strategic voting assumes that voters know their preferences, which is probably more likely in presidential contests than in lower-level races. Ventura in Minnesota and King in Maine were successful in large part because they had had a significant public forum for their views on political issues prior to choosing to run for office and during the campaign they had access to financial resources and forums through which to convey information to voters about their policy positions and their capabilities. We already have noted that risk-averse voters who are less informed about a candidate's position are likely to have a lower expected utility from that candidate's winning and are likely to prefer better-known candidates, even if the voter thinks the unknown candidate might have positions closer to those the voter prefers (see chapter 7). As noted in chapter 9, party labels can also serve as a source of information about a candidate's policy positions, decreasing the uncertainty a voter has about the candidate and increasing the voter's expected utility from voting for that candidate (even though, as discussed in chapter 9, empirical evidence suggests these are no substitutes for fuller information).

Candidates who choose to run as minor-party or independent candidates, then, lose that advantage with voters, as voters know less about the minor parties and even less about the positions of an independent candidate a priori. Joe Moakley won as an independent partly because voters knew him— he was already a fixture in the district's politics, as he had served in the Massachusetts state senate. He also was clear about claiming the Democratic Party label even as he ran as an independent. It is not unusual, then, that Progressives are somewhat successful in Vermont—where they already have a reputation with party members in the state legislature and where some cities have had Progressive mayors—but are less successful in other parts of the country.

Party labels can also serve as a coordinating device, helping voters generate expectations about which candidates are likely to come in first or second. Ottinger voters and Goodell voters had difficulty coordinating in 1970 in part because the party labeling that normally occurs in New York State elections, with the Liberal and Democratic Parties coordinating on behalf of one candidate and the Conservative and Republican Parties coordinating on behalf of a different candidate, did not happen. Thus, voters could not rule out a close race among all three candidates. When Ventura ran for governor of Minnesota, he and his advisers knew that the prevailing assumption was that the race would be between the Democratic and the Republican candidates with Ventura a distant third, and they knew that he would have to change those expectations.

Nonpartisan Elections, Majority Requirements, and Coordination

Nonpartisan Elections

After World War II, Sunbelt cities expanded significantly with the growth in oil and other industries. In San Antonio, business leaders were concerned that the machine politics that existed (similar to Plunkitt's rule in New York and Daley's in Chicago, described in chapter 2) would limit the city's ability to provide public services and the infrastructure that the new businesses required. Voters in the city approved a change to an appointed-city-manager form of government, with a city council elected at large in nonpartisan elections (and the council prohibited from interfering with the city manager's day-to-day administration). A nonpartisan election is one in which all the candidates are listed on the ballot without party affiliation if they gained ballot access by either submitting a petition or paying a filing fee (or both). Each council member was elected in a separate contest (with the seats in the council "numbered places" and voters voting for one candidate for each place), and after the election, one council member was selected as mayor.

Until the early 1970s, the new system allowed for the local Good Government League, which was well financed by the business leaders, to put forward a slate of nominees for city council and for voters to coordinate their preferences for those nominees. Because the elections were at-large, it was difficult for the old ward-based political organizations to mobilize enough voters citywide to defeat the Good Government candidates or for alternative organizations to elect more than one or two council members, particularly without the party labels for the voters to use, both as information and as coordinating devices. It allowed for conservative Democrats and Republicans (a small but growing group in Texas at the time) to coordinate on behalf of business-favored candidates to defeat those favored by liberals. In the mid-1970s, when San Antonio's city council adopted district elections but kept the nonpartisan structure, Rosales (2000) contended, the nonpartisan nature of the elections individualized the campaigns in each council district and made elections candidate centered by district, inhibiting the development of a citywide organization.

San Antonio was actually late in adopting nonpartisan elections—one of the first printed ballots in the nation, used in a Louisville, Kentucky, municipal election in 1888, was nonpartisan.[29] By the 1990s, about two thirds of municipal elections and one half of judicial elections in the United States were nonpartisan. Chicago adopted nonpartisan elections in 1997. As noted in our discussion of primary elections in chapter 4, Louisiana uses nonpartisan elections statewide, and Nebraska uses nonpartisan elections to select state legislators. In one sense, by lessening the influence of major-party elites and party labels, nonpartisan elections might be seen as a way for independents and minor-party candidates to achieve office. Certainly, as in San Antonio during the progressive movement, they were used as a method whereby business-establishment leaders and government reformers could take control over a jurisdiction from the existing party machine.

The degree to which nonpartisan elections in state and local contests truly break down major-party influence in those areas is unclear. In some nonpartisan elections, such as those in Louisiana, parties endorse candidates and thus play a role even though the election is officially nonpartisan and a party endorsement is neither required nor part of the process of getting on the ballot. To the extent that candidates seek upward political mobility and recognize that such mobility occurs through major-party nominations for higher-level offices, they are likely to be involved in local major-party organizations. San Antonio business leaders also maintained control over the leadership of the local Democratic Party during the 1950s and 1960s, and that helped them prevent liberals in the party from using it as an alternative organization to the Good Government League.

If nonpartisan elected officials serve in Congress, as do Louisiana's representatives and senators, they recognize that major-party membership (or, at a minimum, some sort of association, as Sanders and Jeffords have) may be necessary to have a role in that body. In Louisiana, nonpartisan elections were instituted as an effort to reduce the likelihood that the state would become Republican as the Republican Party gained power in the South with white support after black voters were enfranchised and became more important in the Democratic Party. As in San Antonio, the idea was that nonpartisan elections allowed conservatives to vote together without taking on major-party affiliations. Voters are less likely to register a party affiliation if participation in party primaries is not part of the electoral process. In 1982, only 6 percent of Louisiana voters were registered as independents (shortly after the state instituted nonpartisan elections), but twenty years later 19 percent of voters were registered without a party affiliation (whereas other states that record party registration have seen little change in the percentage of registered independents over those twenty years).[30]

Nevertheless, only one state legislator in Louisiana is a true independent. The remaining elective offices are filled by party-affiliated candidates. Republicans control the majority of congressional seats in the state, although the senate delegation is divided. And although Nebraska's legislature is selected in nonpartisan elections and the state, like Louisiana, has experienced an upward creep in the number of registered independents and minor-party voters (from 6 percent in 1982 to 14 percent in 2002), the rest of the officials elected in the state are chosen in partisan contests, and minor-party and independent candidates have met with little success. In Chicago, the change to nonpartisan elections was accompanied by an increase in the signature requirement for ballot access—before the change, a Democratic candidate for mayor needed only 2,261 signatures on a petition, but afterward a nonpartisan candidate for mayor needed 25,000 signatures. The effect was a noticeable decrease in the number of candidates running for citywide office of all types.[31]

Louisiana's Spicy Politics

Chicago introduced a majority requirement as well, a common accompaniment of nonpartisan elections, as in Louisiana. If a candidate does not receive a majority of the vote, the two candidates with the highest vote totals face each other in a runoff election. Majority requirements are also used in some partisan elections, as in Georgia. In Louisiana in 1991, the runoff election for governor attracted national attention. The incumbent running for reelection, Republican Buddy Roemer, was unpopular because he had raised taxes after promising not to and had tried to institute a teacher certification program that was extremely unpopular with educators. He had also tried to pass a comprehensive change in the tax structure but failed (see the discussion in chapter 9). Former Democratic governor Edwin Edwards, who had been tried but acquitted on corruption charges, was his opponent.[32] So both Roemer and Edwards had supporters, but neither was seen by the majority of the voters as overwhelmingly desirable.

This in itself no doubt would have attracted some attention, but a third candidate also entered the race, David Duke. Duke was notorious as an active Nazi sympathizer through 1989 and a former leader of the Ku Klux Klan. During the election campaign, he minimized his anti-Semitic and racist statements, which had been part of his rhetoric in the past. He appealed to conservative white voters who felt unrepresented by the major political parties, which they believed were catering to the preferences of more liberal and minority voters.[33] As in the New York Senate race of 1970, all three candidates had vocal supporters—and Duke was perceived to have a potential plurality of the vote (that is, more than either Roemer or Edwards), as he had managed to gain 59 percent of the white vote in an ultimately unsuccessful attempt to challenge Democratic senator John Breaux.[34] Many of the supporters of Roemer and Edwards vehemently opposed Duke. That is, many Roemer supporters' second preference was Edwards, and many Edwards supporters' second preference was Roemer. Like the G and O voters in New York in 1970, Roemer and Edwards supporters faced a problem of coordination. They feared that if everyone voted sincerely, Duke would receive the most votes, as Buckley had, and win election.

Majority Requirements and Coordination

Voters' Strategies The majority requirement, however, made the voters' coordination easier. It meant that even if Duke received a plurality of the vote, as long as he did not receive a majority, he would have to face the second-place finisher in a runoff election. Roemer's and Edwards's supporters did not need to coordinate on behalf of a common candidate and, if they were certain that Duke did not have an outright majority, could let the election determine which of the two candidates made the runoff and then support him against Duke. As expected, none of the candidates received enough votes to win the governorship outright in 1991: Edwards received 34 percent of the vote; Duke, 32 percent; and Roemer, 27 percent.[35] Although Duke did not get a plurality of the vote, as some feared, he did receive enough to challenge Edwards in the runoff. In that election, Roemer's supporters turned largely to Edwards, despite their dislike of him, and Edwards defeated Duke by 61 percent to 39 percent of the vote. The "No Dukes" advocates (who used a modification of the liberal call against nuclear power, No Nukes) coordinated on behalf of Edwards.

Suppose a majority requirement had existed in the 1970 New York Senate race such that if the winner of the plurality did not win more than 50 percent of the vote, the two candidates with the largest share of votes would have to face each other in a runoff election. Would the voters have behaved differently? Consider the B voters. B voters should still vote sincerely for Buckley, as before; the institution of a majority requirement would not change their choices. But what about G and O voters? What happens if G voters vote sincerely for Goodell and O voters vote sincerely for Ottinger? As before, Buckley would receive 40 percent of the vote, Goodell and Ottinger would each receive 30 percent of the vote.

But Buckley would *not* be the winner, as he would have only 40 percent of the vote, less than the required 50 percent. He would have to face either Goodell or Ottinger, who have tied for second place. Because there can be only two candidates in the runoff, there would be some sort of tie-breaking procedure that would select either Goodell or Ottinger (probably a coin toss). Who would win? If Goodell won the coin toss, he would defeat Buckley in the runoff election (both G and O voters would vote for Goodell in the runoff, and Buckley would receive only the B voters' vote). If Ottinger won the coin toss, he would defeat Buckley in the runoff election (both *G* and *O* voters would vote for Ottinger in the runoff, and Buckley would again receive only the *B* voters' votes). With a majority requirement, Buckley cannot win even if the *G* and *O* voters fail to coordinate in the initial election.

One way to think about this analysis is to imagine that in this case the majority requirement works as a coordination device for the *G* and *O* voters. That is, *G* and *O* voters can vote sincerely for their preferred candidates and let the coin toss determine which candidate faces Buckley. Then, once that candidate is chosen, *G* and *O* voters can easily coordinate on behalf of the winner of the coin toss. Initially, however, they do not have to coordinate; the electoral system does it for them. As long as they perceive that Buckley cannot win an outright majority, this is a safe strategy.

Coordination May Still Be Necessary Majority requirements are not a panacea for the coordination problem faced by voters in plurality-rule elections, however. Why is that? Most of our examples have had only three viable candidates. In those cases, we can be sure that at least one of the candidates in the runoff will be a candidate on behalf of whom a majority of the voters would coordinate if they were able to. In our model of the New York Senate race, we can be sure that either Goodell or Ottinger would have been in the runoff and that their supporters would have coordinated on behalf of the one in the runoff. But if there were more than three viable candidates, it is quite possible that the two candidates in the runoff would be less preferred than one of the candidates eliminated in the first stage. When more than three viable candidates exist, voters may find that they still need to coordinate electorally; they cannot rely on majority requirements to solve their coordination problem. To some extent, that may have been the case when Buddy Roemer was elected governor in Louisiana in 1987. He challenged incumbent Edwin Edwards but received only a plurality of the vote, winning 34 percent to Edwards's 28 percent (with Bob Livingston and Billy Tauzin receiving the remainder of the votes). Rather than face a runoff with Roemer, in which he anticipated a loss, Edwards withdrew. Roemer was little known by many voters when he received 34 percent of the vote in the first election. Representatives Bob Livingston and Billy Tauzin, both strong candidates in the state and, like Roemer, members of Congress, were similar in their conservative policy positions. At the beginning of the contest, Livingston was the favorite to beat Edwards, but "during the campaign it became clear that voters had decided that only a Democrat could beat Edwards. . . . In the end they turned to Roemer as the best alternative."[36] Even in the nonpartisan contest for governor of Louisiana, voters used party labels as a way to coordinate. Moreover, when Roemer ran for reelection in 1991, he lost, leading to the Edwards-Duke runoff. Would Livingston or Tauzin have similarly lost in 1991?

Majority Requirements and Independent and Minor-Party Candidates

Although nonpartisan elections might make it easier for candidates to run without party labels and beat existing party candidates, as in San Antonio in the 1950s, majority requirements can reduce the incentive to run for office if a candidate perceives that he or she cannot win with a plurality. Both Jesse Ventura and Angus King won governorships with less than a majority of the vote. A majority requirement would have meant second election contests for them, one-on-one with a major-party candidate who would have had financial backing and sizable party support. Although King may have been successful and certainly won reelection with an outright majority because of the financial resources he had for campaigning, Ventura, who barely managed to borrow from a bank the money he needed to run, would have had more difficulty with a second contest. Majority requirements can disadvantage independent and minor-party candidates, who may lack financial resources to mount a campaign for two elections.

Reflecting the increased cost of achieving a win when there are majority requirements, there were significantly fewer entries in congressional elections from 1982 to 1996 in states with such requirements—the mean number of total candidates in districts with no majority requirements was 4.13, whereas the mean number of total candidates in districts with majority requirements was 3.37.[37] The mean number of independent and minor-party candidates was 0.73 in districts without majority requirements and 0.36 in districts with majority requirements.[38] Although the total number of candidates in gubernatorial races from 1991 to 1998 was unaffected by whether a state had majority requirements, the mean number of minor-party and independent candidates in states without majority requirements was 1.59 and 0.89 in states with majority requirements, which is a statistically significant difference.[39]

Not Unique but Rare . . .

In summary, although there are instances in which American voters fail to coordinate on the electoral coalitions dominated by the Democrats and the Republicans and minor-party and independent candidates sometimes get elected, the vast majority of elected officials in U.S. politics, at almost all levels of government, are members of the two major political parties. Even when their first preference is a minor-party candidate, voters display significant tendencies to vote strategically for major-party candidates, as Nader supporters did in 2000. Minor-party and independent candidates must struggle to make a difference in American electoral politics. If they have advantages like public financing or their own financial resources coupled with prior voter exposure to their positions in a public forum such as a radio or television talk show, as Ventura and King did, or are willing to spend almost all their time campaigning, as Eder did, they can get elected. Nonpartisan elections may increase the probability of election by reducing the role of major parties, but majority requirements can make it more difficult for candidates who have limited financial resources. With luck and the help of elected officials in the major political parties, minor-party and independent candidates can sometimes affect policy once in office (King is proud of his pro-education measures, Ventura is similarly pleased with his tax cuts, and Eder is happy that he managed to get a measure passed that limits pesticide use near schools). But the U.S. electoral system and the need to work with other elected officials once in office make it exceptionally tough for third-party and independent candidates to translate their successes into greater success.

The Implications for Policy Choices

The Liberal-Conservative Dimension over Time

Whereas the parties clearly successfully structure both what we think of as liberal and conservative and our policy choices, these do change over time. When we examined the gender gap in U.S. politics, we saw support for the argument that there has been a change in how the parties and voters perceive themselves on issues of interest to women. How stable has the liberal-conservative dimension been over the course of U.S. history? In general, the liberal-conservative dimension that divides the political parties has been relatively stable for long periods, although it certainly moves about in the policy space.

Poole and Rosenthal (1997) showed that the division between the parties is stable unless a "cross-cutting" issue (an issue that has support and opposition in both parties) becomes "intense." When that happens, they maintained (p. 46), the "dimensional alignments break down and a reorganization of the party system results." Slavery was such an issue and led to the Civil War. Figure 14.5 illustrates how the process takes place. At the top of figure A, the two parties have chosen distinct positions along a single line, the horizontal axis, which is labeled "Old dimension." The center of the two sets of circles represents the party ideal points or positions, and the circles represent the different indifference curves around the party ideal positions, as we discussed earlier in this chapter. The line in the middle, between the two parties' sets of circles, represents the median voter in the general election.

As a new issue begins to become important, because neither party has a defined position on it, it has supporters in both parties, and basically the circles begin to divide into four groups, as in figures B and C. As the parties begin to take positions on the new issue and realign, the four groups again become two, as in figure D and later E. Yet typically we do not see this process happen often, and our party system stays relatively stable for extended intervals. In fact, we normally see mainly gradual changes in party positions rather than the dramatic party breakdown of the Civil War period, when slavery became an "intense" issue. Why?

FIGURE 14.5
How Issue Dimensions Change over Time

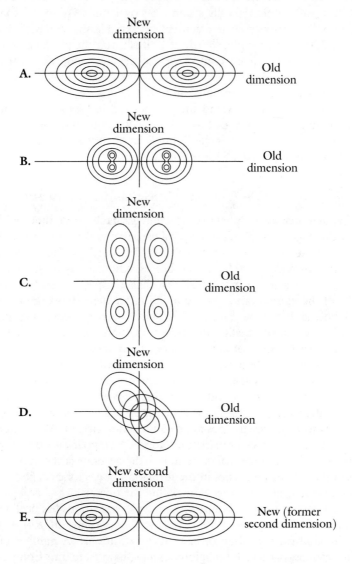

Source: Poole and Rosenthal (1997).

Short-Run Stability

One reason for short-run stability is uncertainty about voters' preferences, which also leads the parties to choose divergent positions. The uncertainty introduces a degree of randomness in policy choices that is somewhat controlled, a sort of alternating of party control that means some relatively stable randomness in policy choices. Voters can also use the multiplicity of elected offices in the country and the different branches of government to balance out or moderate the parties' differences, as we discussed in chapter 13. But policy does typically swing a bit over time. We see that tax and spending policies vary as Democrats replace Republicans who replace Democrats. In 2001, for example, shortly after Bush won the presidency and before the Democrats gained control of the Senate, Congress passed, and President Bush signed, a set of "temporary" tax cuts, including a cut in the inheritance tax. But in the summer of 2002, the Senate, now under Democratic control, refused to extend the cut beyond its beyond its temporary deadline despite the desires of Bush and the Republican-dominated House of Representatives. Then, after the Republican victory in the Senate races in 2002, Republicans passed a $350 billion tax cut.

Longer-Run Stability: The Porousness of American Political Parties

The liberal-conservative dimension changes gradually over time partly because of the "porousness" of our political parties, coupled with our strong institutional status quo bias. Voters who are "left out," as Ventura was, who find themselves "oddballs," have two choices—they can try to get one of the major political parties to move closer to their perspective, leading to a redefining of the liberal-conservative dimension, or they can work outside the major parties and attempt to form a new party or movement (as Ventura did) that they hope will eventually allow them to replace one of the major political parties. Generally, if candidates choose the minor-party or independent route, they eventually become affiliated or work with one of the major parties. Former California Green Party state representative Audie Bock became a Democrat. John Eder has found that his bills succeed if they are repackaged as Democratic measures. But in the process, these legislators are able in varying degrees to influence the positions of the major parties. Although sometimes candidates bypass primaries, a number of political scientists have reasoned that the direct primary system in U.S. elections facilitates the domination of the two major parties in the formation of electoral coalitions by allowing most dissidents to easily work within the two major political parties.[40]

The ability of dissidents to change major-party positions has been evident in the years following the 1973 Supreme Court ruling in *Roe v. Wade*, which declared existing abortion laws unconstitutional. A number of anti-abortion groups, particularly religious groups, have turned to Congress and state legislatures to devise new laws restricting abortion. Similarly, groups supportive of abortion rights became more active politically as well, in order to counter those efforts. In the early 1970s, the two major parties varied only a little in their policy positions on abortion. But over time, Republican and Democratic elected officials have chosen positions on abortion policy that are increasingly divergent, reflecting the influx of activist anti-abortion, "right-to-life" groups within the Republican Party and activist pro-choice feminist groups within the Democratic Party. As these groups have become active in the candidate nomination process, candidates whose positions fit their preferences on the abortion issue have found themselves advantaged and more likely to be selected as nominees and elected to office. These groups have also run their own candidates on minor-party slates, such as the Right to Life Party in New York State. The change over time in response to the internal and external pressures is illustrated in figure 14.6. Adams (1997) measured the percentage of pro-abortion votes by members of the House of Representatives from 1973 to 1994. There was an initial increase in pro-choice votes by members of both parties, but Republican percentages then began to fall slightly, whereas Democratic percentages continued to increase such that by 1994 Democrats voted pro-choice 80 percent of the time and Republicans voted pro-choice 20 percent of the time.

FIGURE 14.6
Pro-Choice Congressional Votes, 1973–94

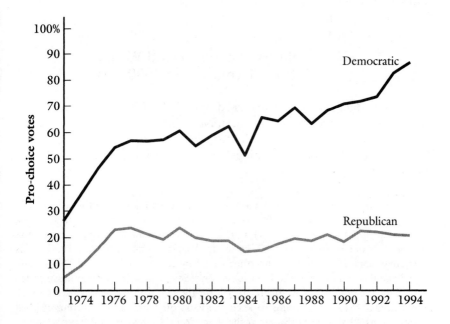

Source: Adams (1997).

The effect of the change in party positions on abortion has meant that voters and candidates who previously supported Republican positions but were advocates of abortion rights faced a dilemma. Minnesota state senator Sheila Kiscaden moved from the Republican Party to the Independence Party in 2002 because her positions on abortion did not fit with that of the local Republican Party leaders, who favored restricting abortion. Other Republicans—for example, Governor Tom Ridge of Pennsylvania—maintained their pro-choice positions but stayed within the party. No doubt some Republicans moved with the party. But Republicans were not the only ones affected; those who favored other Democratic policies but were foes of abortion also had to consider what to do with the realignment. Should they switch parties or switch positions? Some, like Al Gore, changed their policy positions over time. Both groups could no longer easily fit on the liberal-conservative dimension as the Republicans and Democrats became more solidly divided on the issue. The redefining of the parties on the abortion issue gave those who favored abortion and other Democratic policies and those who opposed abortion and other Republican policies a greater voice in the parties as the parties more clearly reflected their preferences, but it lessened the connection between the party positions and other voters, such as Ventura, for example. The dimension changed over time, advantaging the ability of some groups to be represented by one of the two major parties but disadvantaging the ability of other groups of voters. Every voter is not represented in our system all the time. Ventura is right—some voter's preferences are left out.

How Failing to Support David Worley Hurt the Democrats in 2000

In the preceding chapter, we discussed how Georgia Democrat David Worley lost by a slim margin to Republican Newt Gingrich in the 1990 congressional race because the Democratic Party failed to help him in his campaign. Why were the Democrats so stingy? According to a news report, Worley claimed after the election that

> Democrats withheld campaign money from him because he had attacked Gingrich's support of the $35,000 congressional pay raise. Worley's campaign was built around the theme that Gingrich, the second-ranking Republican in the House, is out of touch with his suburban Atlanta district. But, says Worley, his strategy apparently violated the truce called by the Republican and Democratic campaign committees in the House. As congressional leaders tried to muster support for the raise last November, officials for the two national parties tried to allay politicians' fears by agreeing to keep the issue off limits in 1990 congressional campaigns. "I was told privately at the time 'don't do this, or you're not going to get money,' " Worley said in an interview. "I told him to stuff it."[41]

Craig McDonald, former director of Ralph Nader's Congress Watch, and James D. Davidson, chairman of the National Taxpayers Union, supported Worley's claims that in order to pass the controversial pay raise in 1989, a letter of agreement had been signed on November 16, 1989, by Ron Brown, chairman of the Democratic National Committee; Lee Atwater, chairman of the Republican National Committee; Guy Vander Jagt, chairman of the National Republican Congressional Committee; and Beryl Anthony, chairman of the Democratic Congressional Campaign Committee, in which it was agreed not to fund congressional candidates in 1990 who made an issue of the congressional pay raise. When McDonald, Davidson, and Worley complained publicly in October of 1990 as they tried to get resources for Worley's cash-poor campaign, a spokesman for the Democratic Congressional Campaign Committee said that Worley hadn't received money because he had little chance of winning. Worley complained that he was more electable than ever before: "That's what makes this all the more frustrating to me. Now that I'm better established politically . . . I haven't received a penny from the congressional committee since last Nov. 16."[42]

Worley, McDonald, and Davidson weren't the only ones upset by how the pact between the two major parties kept Gingrich from being defeated. Ralph Nader was as well. The political analyst Micah L. Sifry contended that the defeat of Worley because of the major-party agreement may have been the "tipping point" that drove Nader into presidential politics and his full-fledged run for president in 2000, perhaps costing the Democrats the election. Will Nader's run for the presidency lead to the kinds of changes in the political parties that he wants to achieve? In 2004, it was hard to imagine Republican and Democratic congressional leaders signing the kind of letter that they signed in 1989, given the strength of partisan divisions within the country. Sifry argued that some of what Nader wanted to see in the Democratic Party has been happening without him because of the use of the Internet in campaigning: "Citizens and activists have a powerful new way to bind together and amplify their voices as the Howard Dean campaign demonstrated. The Internet genie of mass organization is out of the bottle; all the money-driven top-down parties, candidates and interest groups can't stuff it back in."[43] As the Republican Party responded to anti-abortion activists within the party as well as to Right to Life minor-party candidates, the Democrats have faced pressures from within, from Howard Dean, and from without, from Ralph Nader. It remains to be seen how these activists will affect the policies of the party.

What We Know

We know that the U.S. electoral system is biased against minor-party and independent candidates. Although these candidates can be successful in state and local races, the major political parties have been able to maintain control over almost all federal offices for over one hundred years. Laws controlling ballot access, porous candidate nomination procedures, and the widespread use of winner-take-all elections that select only one winner help the parties maintain this control. As a consequence, voters whose first preference is a minor-party or independent candidate are more likely to strategically choose their second preference when an election is close. Yet evidence suggests that Nader's candidacy in Florida—if we assume that some of his supporters would have voted if he had not been in the race—did apparently cost Gore the state. The difficulties facing minor-party and independent candidates mean that the positions of the major parties typically shape the policy choices before the public—bundling together issue positions and defining how we interpret the meaning of "liberal" and "conservative." Hence, some voters—such as those with preferences like Ventura's—can find that their preferences on issues are not represented by either political party. But the porousness of the political parties can help those voters shape policy over time.

What We Don't Know: The Major Political Parties and Civil Rights

The movement over time in the parties' policy positions on abortion after the 1973 Supreme Court ruling was preceded by a movement on an equally divisive and important issue in American politics, civil rights for African Americans, which we discussed in chapter 5. Carmines and Stimson (1989) showed that before the 1964 election, Senate and House Republicans were consistently more liberal than Democrats in roll-call voting on civil rights for blacks. It was the party of Lincoln and had presided over the emancipation of slaves and the extension of voting rights through the Thirteenth, Fourteenth, and Fifteenth Amendments to the Constitution. The Democratic Party had fought those efforts. Up until 1964, Republican Party platforms devoted more space to civil rights proposals than the Democratic Party platforms did. But after 1964, the parties switched positions in a dramatic, remarkable change. Table 14.6 shows the number of U.S. senators by party affiliation, region, and voting record on civil rights in 1957–58 and 1965–66.

In 1957–58, 90 percent of nonsouthern Republican senators and 100 percent of southern Republican senators took liberal positions on civil rights, but in 1965–66 only 10 percent of nonsouthern Republican senators and 0 percent of southern Republican senators had liberal voting records on civil rights, a dramatic reversal. Although Republicans did not vary significantly by region on civil rights, Democratic senators in the South were significantly more likely to have conservative voting records on civil rights than nonsouthern Democratic senators in both time periods. The division between northern and southern Democratic senators reflects the fact that during

TABLE 14.6
Distribution of Senators on Racial Liberalism and Conservatism by Party and Region, 1957–58 and 1965–66

	1957–58			1965–68		
Region	Senators Voting as Liberals	Senators Voting as Conservatives	Total	Senators Voting as Liberals	Senators Voting as Conservatives	Total
Republicans						
Nonsouth	37 (90%)	4 (10%)	41	10 (36%)	18 (64%)	28
South	5 (100%)	0	5	0	4 (100%)	4
Democrats						
Nonsouth	20 (80%)	4 (20%)	25	37 (90%)	4 (10%)	41
South	1 (4%)	22 (96%)	23	8 (32%)	17 (68%)	25

Source: Carmines and Stimson (1989).

much of the twentieth century, as Poole and Rosenthal (1997) discussed, politics was divided according to two types of issues, economics and civil rights. The two major parties were divided along the economic dimension, whereas the Democratic Party was internally divided by civil rights. Even so, more southern and nonsouthern Democrats adopted more liberal voting records on civil rights in 1965–66 than in 1957–58: 32 percent of southern Democratic senators had liberal voting records in the later period, compared with only 4 percent in the earlier time (the percentage of northern Democratic senators with liberal voting records increased from 80 percent to 90 percent), and this increase meant that a greater percentage of Democratic senators had liberal civil rights voting records (even in the South) than Republican senators.

Thus, the principal source of the switch in positions on civil rights is among Republicans (both northern and southern) and southern Democrats. Northern Democrats had begun to adopt more liberal positions on civil rights as the population of African Americans increased in the North. Table 14.7 illustrates how the percentage of blacks increased from 1930 to 1970 in large nonsouthern cities as southern blacks left the discrimination in the South for economic opportunity in the industrialized northern cities. During the Great Depression of the 1930s, northern blacks began to support the Democratic Party, whose economic positions they found more attractive than those of the Republican Party. As a consequence, black pref-

TABLE 14.7
Blacks in Large Central Cities, 1930–70 (percent)

City	1930	1940	1950	1960	1970
New York	4.9	6.9	9.8	14.7	23.4
Los Angeles–Long Beach	5.0	6.0	9.8	15.3	21.2
Chicago	7.1	8.3	14.1	23.6	34.4
Philadelphia	11.4	13.1	18.3	26.7	34.4
Detroit	7.8	9.3	16.4	29.2	44.0
San Francisco–Oakland	4.9	4.9	11.8	21.1	32.7
Boston	2.9	3.3	12.3	9.8	18.2
Pittsburgh	8.3	9.3	18.0	16.8	27.0
St. Louis	11.5	13.4	5.3	28.8	41.3
Washington, D.C.	27.3	28.5	35.4	54.8	72.3
Cleveland	8.1	9.7	16.3	28.9	39.0
Baltimore	17.7	19.4	23.8	35.0	47.0
Total in Large Central Cities	7.6	9.0	13.7	21.4	30.8

Source: Carmines and Stimson (1989).

erences began to influence northern Democratic positions on civil rights, resulting in the division between northern and southern Democrats, as exemplified in table 14.6.

In 1964, the imbalance began to change in favor of African Americans. The Democratic Party as a whole became more liberal on civil rights than the Republican Party. This switch of the parties, along with unified Democratic control over the federal government, resulted in the passage of one of the most significant pieces of legislation with respect to the American electoral process, the Voting Rights Act of 1965, which has important implications for the way in which U.S. elections work today. We analyze this history of minority voting disenfranchisement and the Voting Rights Act more expansively in the next chapter.

Study Questions and Problems

1. Suppose that John McCain decides to run for president as a minor-party candidate in 2008.
   a. Under what sort of conditions can he win? that is, describe the distribution of voters' preferences across the country, the major-party candidates, campaign finance regulation, and so on.
   b. How would your answer change if McCain decided to run for gov-

ernor of Arizona as a minor-party candidate? if he decided to run for the Senate as a minor-party candidate?

2. Suppose you are a strategist for the Republican Party for the 2008 presidential election and McCain is running as a minor-party candidate.

   a. How does this affect the way in which you mobilize voters? Explain.

   b. How does your answer change if Hillary Clinton is running for president as a minor-party candidate? Explain.

3. Suppose you have positions on issues like those of Ventura—liberal on social issues but conservative on economic issues—and those positions could eventually lead to changes in the meaning of liberal and conservative.

   a. Compare and contrast the benefits of trying to change one of the major party's positions on issues with the benefits of starting a minor party.

   b. If you could push for federal legislation on the electoral process that could lead to the change on issues that you desire, what would that legislation be, and how would it result in your preferred outcome?

Notes

1. Briggs had broken party ranks to cast the deciding vote in the California State Assembly to pass the 2001–02 state budget, angering Republicans not only statewide but also nationally. Although the budget had brought aid to farmers in Briggs's assembly district, which significantly overlapped with the new congressional district, Republicans' anger hindered his ability to attract support within the party. Patterson, as mayor of Fresno, had also made enemies. See *California Journal*, February 1, 2002.
2. Four other candidates received votes in the primary as well.
3. See Grimshaw (1992) for a history of Washington's election.
4. See Bibby and Maisel (1989, p. 47).
5. Candidates who run under more than one party label are called fusion candidates. Some argue that the state election law allowing for fusion candidates a factor makes minor parties more politically viable.
6. When the Liberal Party broke ranks with the Democrats and supported Republican Rudy Giuliani for mayor of New York City over Democrat David Dinkins, it began to lose support from Democrats. In 2002, its candidate for governor received less than the 50,000 votes required to maintain automatic ballot access.
7. For more details on the theory behind these results, see Myerson and Weber (1993).
8. In 1983, incumbent mayor Jane Byrne flirted with the idea of a write-in campaign but ultimately endorsed Washington. She did challenge Washington for the nomination in 1987 but failed. Washington died of a heart attack shortly after his reelection.
9. In 1976, there were a number of minor-party candidates, who received only 6 percent of the vote.

10. One of Jesse Ventura's opponents for the governorship of Minnesota was Attorney General Hubert Humphrey III, known as Skip.

11. See Shepsle and Bonchek (1997) for a detailed discussion of Condorcet's (1785) paradox.

12. See Wittman (1977) and Calvert (1985). The mathematics of how this works is a bit complicated and beyond the scope of this book. But intuitively, the candidates diverge for the same reasons they did in chapter 4. Of course, we are assuming that the members of each party have somehow solved the paradox of voting for themselves. Later in the chapter, we discuss how porousness in the parties leads to some instability in these choices over time. We can think of these positions as largely influenced by status quo biases in the way policy is made, which allows us to think of them as fixed in the short run.

13. Ventura was forced to leave the talk show when he officially filed his candidacy on July 21, because of fears that the Federal Communications Commission would require the station to give equal time to other candidates (Ventura's talk show had given him three hours of air time each day).

14. Dane Smith, "Diary of an Upset," *Minneapolis Star-Tribune*, November 8, 1998.

15. Dean Barkley, quoted in Smith, "Diary of an Upset."

16. In Minnesota, the state Democratic Party is known as the Democratic-Farmer-Labor Party, or DFL. Dane Smith, "Ventura's Roller-Coaster Year," *Minneapolis Star Tribune*, June 23, 2002.

17. A. Jay Higgins, "King Wins Re-election," *Bangor Daily News*, November 4, 1998.

18. Elizabeth Mehren, "A Party of One in Maine," *Los Angeles Times*, June 4, 2003.

19. David E. Rosenbaum, "Nader Plays Down Effect on Democrat Candidate," *International Herald Tribune*, February 25, 2004.

20. Elizabeth Wolfe, "Liberal Leaders Urge Nader to Abandon Bid," Associated Press Online, April 3, 2004.

21. Roy Eccleston, "Defiant 'Spoiler' to Run for President," *Australian*, February 24, 2004.

22. See Jewell and Olson (1982).

23. I thank Richard Winger, editor of Ballot Access News, www.ballot-access.org, for details on these races.

24. Brian C. Mooney, "Politics and Equal Opportunity," *Boston Globe*, October 16, 2002. Lantigua defeated Santiago again in the 2004 general election.

25. Dave Williams, "Caucus Has Lone Member: Assembly Members Adjust to Lawmaker's Status as Only Independent Representative," *Augusta Chronicle*, February 20, 2001.

26. Mehren, "A Party of One in Maine."

27. "Representative Troy D. Jackson—District 1," Maine.gov, http://www.maine.gov/legis/housedems/tjackson.

28. Sometimes voters fail to rate all the candidates, something that happens more often with minor-party or independent candidates. Also, voters often rate at the midpoint candidates they know little about.

29. See Bott (1991, p. 145).

30. See Jewell and Morehouse (2001). Oregon and Nevada saw increases, whereas Kansas experienced a significant decrease; in most states, there was little change. In California, the percentage choosing a minor party or the "decline to state" option grew steadily, from about 5 percent in 1970 to about 20 percent today. I thank Gary Jacobson for pointing this out.

31. Steve Neal, "City Elections Shut Out Challengers, Democracy," *Chicago Sun-Times*, March 5, 1999.

32. In May 2000, Edwards was convicted on corruption charges related to riverboat gambling in the state.

33. Later Duke returned to promoting a neo-Nazi position and self-published an autobiography modeled on Hitler's *Mein Kampf*, called *My Awakening*, in which he calls "Aryans" to action to protect the white European heritage from Jews and nonwhites. Duke pleaded guilty to tax and mail fraud in late 2002 and, like Edwards, at the time of this writing is serving a prison sentence.
34. There were other candidates in the Senate race as well, but they had few supporters and received minimal votes.
35. The total is less than 100 percent because of some votes received by other candidates.
36. David Maraniss, "Edwards Cuts His Losses: Gambling Governor Cedes Louisiana Election," *Washington Post*, October 26, 1987.
37. This difference is statistically significant, with a t-statistic of 8.2709.
38. This difference is statistically significant, with a t-statistic of 12.6658.
39. This difference is significant using a one-tailed test at the 95 percent confidence level with a t-statistic of 1.6806.
40. See Mazmanian (1974) and Epstein (1986). Epstein (pp. 244–45) argued that it is a dynamic that existed prior to the establishment of direct primaries:

> No doubt this use of primaries by voters as well as by aspiring officeholders can be understood as yet another manifestation of the looseness of American party structure and of the tendency of each major party to accommodate considerable diversity. . . . These characteristics antedate the direct primary. Hence the primary may be viewed as the twentieth-century means for confirming the traditional porousness or ready permeability of American parties. I would add, however, that the primary contributes to the porousness as well as confirming it in statutory form. Nothing quite like the American pattern of intraparty electoral competition exists in other nations, and it is not unreasonable to suggest that its absence may help explain why parties in those nations have been less successful than the major American parties in preempting incipient third-party territory.

41. David Dahl, "Democrats' Alliance with Gingrich Was Costly," *St. Petersburg Times*, November 9, 1990.
42. "Party Accord Called Gag on Candidates," *St. Louis Post-Dispatch*, October 26, 1990.
43. Micah L. Sifry, "This Time, Ralph's Run Doesn't Make Much Sense," *Washington Post*, February 29, 2004.

~15~

Minority Voters and Representation

The Dilemma of Representation

"We've propped up white Democrats for long enough. When we get a chance to elect one of our own, we should," argued African American Texas Democratic state representative Ron Wilson. A colleague in the state house, Garnet Coleman, also African American, disagreed: "We can't just be a party of minorities."[1] The disagreement between Wilson and Coleman resulted from the Texas Republican-led congressional redistricting (see chapter 11), in use for the 2004 elections. The new lines made a number of districts with incumbent Democratic members of Congress more Republican and split up the districts of others. The splitting of districts forced white Democratic incumbents Chris Bell and Lloyd Doggett to make a choice—either run in a district that is more Republican leaning and face a tough race in the general election or run in a district that is heavily Democratic but now also largely composed of minority voters and face competition in the primary from a minority candidate (for Bell, an African American challenger; for Doggett, a Hispanic opponent). As Bell summarized: "[Republican house majority leader Delay] drew most of my colleagues' districts to be much more Republican and decided to take care of the others by drawing them into heavily minority districts."[2]

Both Bell and Doggett decided to try to win the minority-dominated districts. Minority voters and leaders were torn. Both Bell and Doggett had achieved some stature in Congress—Bell, although he had been in Congress only one term, had been named the Democratic Party's deputy whip, and

Doggett, who had served since 1994, was a member of the powerful Ways and Means Committee and was one of the leaders of the opposition to the authorization of the use of force in Iraq. Wilson and Coleman disagreed on whether blacks should vote for Bell or his opponent, African American justice of the peace Al Green. Several members of the Congressional Black Caucus visited churches, contacted supporters, and taped radio ads for Green. But African American Tennessee Democratic congressman Harold Ford "criticized fellow members of the Congressional Black Caucus for taking sides against Bell." He commented: "You have an incumbent, and you don't support the incumbent? It was inappropriate."[3]

Similar disagreements were voiced in Doggett's contest; Doggett's opponent, Leticia Hinojosa, stressed her ethnic connection to the voters: "I have lived in both ends of the district and I understand firsthand what the problems of the district are. I share the life experience of the majority of the people who live in this district."[4] Hinojosa ran Spanish-language ads in which an old man questioned how someone who didn't speak Spanish could expect to represent the district.[5] By contrast, the United Farm Workers, whose members are largely Latino, endorsed Doggett and campaigned for him as the incumbent with power.[6] Which is better for minority voters—to support an incumbent white candidate with power in Congress or vote for a minority candidate without congressional experience?

The debate over which candidates minorities should support in Bell's and Doggett's primary contests arises because of the long history of minority disenfranchisement and vote dilution in the American electoral process. In this chapter, we review that history. We will see how as a consequence of it, when district boundaries are drawn for congressional and other legislative elections, gerrymanderers are required to consider how the boundaries affect minority voters, particularly if the state or jurisdiction is one with a known history of minority disenfranchisement. In the 1990s, a number of southern states, including Texas, were forced to devise districts lines that could lead to an increase in the number of minority state legislators and members of Congress. The effects of the "racial gerrymandering" that ensued are one of the more controversial questions in American political science because at the same time that Republicans gained control over Congress, a growing degree of partisanship in Congress took place, as discussed in chapter 5. Did racial gerrymandering, in which minority voters were packed into districts like the ones Bell and Doggett ran in, lead to more Republicans and more conservatives in Congress and in state legislatures as liberal voters became a minority in the remaining primarily white districts? Or did it help minority voters by increasing the number of members of Congress and state legislators with their points of view? In this chapter, we address this question.

What It Was Like

In 1955 in Mississippi, a fourteen-year-old African American boy from Chicago named Emmett Till was murdered (one eye was gouged out and his head was crushed in before he was shot; he was recognizable only by a ring he wore) because he had whistled at a white woman (Williams 1987, p. 44). His murder, though it was noteworthy in that it attracted attention outside the South, was but one event in a long history of white oppression of blacks in the South, which did not end with Till's death. Whereas the identity of the murderers was kept secret, for years blacks had been publicly lynched for minor offenses, with whites collecting postcards and other memorabilia from these occasions.[7] In 1934, the Council of Southern Women for the Prevention of Lynching estimated that 4,751 lives in southern states had been taken through the practice since 1882.[8] Anti-lynching bills passed the U.S. House of Representatives, but they were filibustered in the Senate by southern Democratic senators and never passed by Congress as a whole. In the state of Mississippi, which had the highest percentage of blacks across the states in 1950 (45.3 percent of the population), less than 1 percent of blacks were registered to vote. Because blacks had no voice at the ballot box, there was no way for them to force the senators that supposedly represented them to outlaw the practice.

In 1978, Larry Ortega Lozano died in a Texas county jail. "The sheriff said Lozano committed suicide by banging his head against a cell door. A pathologist said it was homicide after finding 92 injuries to the body, some 'in places where he would have had to be contorted' to inflict injuries on himself. Six to eight lawmen were in the cell with Lozano for 45 minutes before his death."[9] Lozano's death took place at a time when Mexican Americans were citing complaints of discrimination and mistreatment across the country, particularly in Texas. The Texas Ranger Division—the agency that had hunted down the Killer D's (see chapter 11)—has a history of murder and oppression of Latinos as well as blacks in the state. During World War I, Rangers murdered hundreds of Latinos in the border areas. In the 1960s, they harassed Latinos who tried to vote and achieve public office in rural towns in which they were the majority, winning praise from then Texas governor John Connolly for their efforts (Rosales 2000). Vilma Martinez, president of the Mexican American Legal Defense and Education Fund (MALDEF), remarked in 1978: "We are very much an oppressed, discriminated-against group in this country . . . and Texas is our Mississippi."[10]

Texas and Mississippi have changed, however. In Mississippi, blacks vote more than whites and hold political office at the local, state, and national levels. Latinos and blacks in Texas similarly vote and hold positions of power at all levels of government. Although incidents such as the notorious murder of James Byrd in Jasper, Texas, still occur and racial prejudices remain—

divisions between racial and ethnic groups exist in Texas and Mississippi, as they do elsewhere in the nation—no longer is it a matter of course for elected officials—who now sometimes are minorities themselves (the mayor of Jasper was black at the time of Byrd's murder)—to condone or ignore such actions.[11]

The South Today

Texas

In the 2003 Texas legislative session, sixty-one-year-old Texas state representative Chuck Hopson from Jacksonville didn't like the racial profiling he had experienced. He recalled: "The young Republicans, a couple of them, have come up to me to tell me, 'By the way, the Republican caucus has changed to 2 o'clock.' " But Hopson isn't a Republican, he's a Democrat and white, and in the Texas state legislature that's a dying combination (Hopson was one of the Killer D's, discussed in chapter 11). As the reporter Ken Herman wrote: "Once, not so long ago, they roamed in great herds. They controlled the landscape, and the alpha males among them ruled with certainty and swagger. But now, after generations of dominance, they've been reduced to endangered species, and their natural enemies have marked them for extinction."[12] In 2003, of the 127 white Texas state legislators, 22, or 17.32 percent, were Democrats. Of the 54 minority members of the Texas state house and senate, only 2, or 3.7 percent, were Republicans. Twenty years before, there were 106 white Democrats in the Texas state legislature; ten years before, there were 60. Although minority Democratic legislators have increased from 33 in 1983 to 37 in 1993 to 43 in 2003, the rate of increase has not matched the decline in white Democrats (the number of Republican minority legislators hasn't changed much). It turns out that the most underrepresented Texans in the state legislature are white female Democrats—for the first time since 1941 there are none in either the state house or senate (all 22 white female state legislators are Republicans). The Texas state legislature has become divided not only along partisan lines but also along partisan lines heavily influenced by race and ethnicity.

Changes in the South: Voting

The change in Texas is ironic given that the last time Republicans held the majority in the state legislature and the governorship (1869), the Republican Party was a biracial coalition (fourteen of the Republican legislators were black) and Democrats were "lily white."[13] What happened in the intervening 132 years is a tale not just of how the electoral process has changed in Texas but also a tale of how it has changed in the nation at large. In chapters 5 and 14, we discussed how the Republican and Democratic Parties switched their positions on civil rights in 1964, when southern Democrats

began to take more liberal positions on the issue and Republicans in both
the North and the South began to vote more conservatively. The Democratic Party also dominated the national government after the elections of
1964, with majorities in both the House and the Senate and the election of
President Lyndon Johnson. The party fulfilled its promise to black voters—
it passed the Voting Rights Act of 1965, which eliminated many of the barriers that had prevented African Americans from participating in politics in
the South since the end of Reconstruction. Table 15.1 shows the effect of
the Voting Rights Act on the registration of blacks in southern states (which
had been increasing in the post–World War II era). Note that some of the
figures overstate black registration because they fail to account for black
population growth (that is, the denominator is the black voting-age population as of the last census). These figures also fail to account for growing
black disenfranchisement because of imprisonment, as discussed in chapter
2, which may overstate eligible black voters, particularly in the 1994 and
2000 figures.[14]

TABLE 15.1
Estimation of Blacks Registered in the South,
1947–2000 (percent)

State	1947	1956*	1964*	1968*	1976*	1986	1994	2000*
Alabama	1.2	11.0	23.0	56.7	58.4	68.9	66.3	72.0
Arkansas	17.3	36.0	49.3	67.5	94.0	57.9	56.0	60.0
Florida	15.4	32.0	63.8	62.1	61.1	58.2	47.7	52.7
Georgia	18.8	27.0	44.0	56.1	74.8	52.8	57.6	66.3
Louisiana	2.6	31.0	32.0	59.3	63.0	60.6	65.7	73.5
Mississippi	0.9	5.0	6.7	59.4	60.7	70.8	59.1	73.7
North Carolina	15.2	24.0	46.8	55.3	54.8	58.4	53.1	62.9
South Carolina	13.0	27.0	38.7	50.8	56.5	52.5	59.0	68.6
Tennessee	25.8	29.0	69.4	72.8	66.4	65.3	70.0	64.9
Texas	18.5	37.0	45.7	58.4	54.7	56.2	58.5	69.5
Virginia	13.2	19.0	45.7	58.4	54.7	56.2	51.1	58.0
National average	na	na	na	66.2	58.5	64.0	58.5	63.6

Source: Alt (1994), supplemented by figures from the U.S. Census Bureau.
*Presidential-election years.

Changes in the South: Office Holding

The passage of the Voting Rights Act and the advent of the civil rights movement led to an increase in the number of blacks registered to vote as well as
to an increase in their representation in elected offices in the South. Table
15.2 shows the increase over time in the percentage of black members of the

U.S. House and black state legislators in the South from 1970 to 2003. As blacks (and, in Texas, Latinos) began to register and vote in greater numbers, they were more likely to join the Democratic Party in the South, because of its positions on civil rights and economics. Conservative white southerners began to support Republican candidates instead of Democrats, who were now seen as too liberal. Before this switch, Republicans were a rarity in political office in the South, but in the intervening years, Republicans began to succeed in southern elections as they attracted disaffected white Democrats. The percentage of Republicans in southern elected positions increased. The

TABLE 15.2
Black State Legislators in the South, 1970–2003 (percent)

Year	Black Population	State Senate	State House	U.S. House
1970	20.4	1.3	1.9	0
1975	20.4	2.4	6.2	2.8
1980	19.6	3.1	8.3	1.8
1985	19.6	7.2	10.8	1.7
1992	18.8	13.5	14.8	13.6
2003	19.4	15.3	17.2	13

Source: Handley and Grofman (1994, 1998) and Center for Voting and Democracy.

South went from a largely one-party region to a region with viable two-party competition. Table 15.3 presents a summary of the growth in Republican office holding in southern states from 1960 to 1999.

The rise in black office holders (mostly Democrats), coupled with an increase in Republican office holders, is associated with a decline of white Democratic elected officials in the South. In Texas, Latinos constitute a larger percentage of the population than blacks, and they, too, have expanded their voting participation and office holding since the passage of the Voting Rights Act. Longer-term data on office holding by Latinos in Texas are not available, but table 15.4 compares data from 1990 to 2003 in Texas for blacks and Latinos, showing how office holding by both groups has generally increased in the thirteen years. Note that the percentage of the Latino population has risen as well, whereas the percentage of blacks in Texas has stayed constant.

The change that has taken place in the South since 1960 is remarkable—called by some a "quiet revolution."[15] It is a horrendous story of minority disenfranchisement and discrimination as well as an uplifting one of overcoming adversity and making heroic choices. Understanding what happened and how is fundamental to comprehending much about the current electoral system in American politics and current issues concerning the Ameri-

TABLE 15.3
Republican Elected Officials in the South, 1960–99, with Figures for 2003

State	Party of Governor, 2003	Legislative Seats Held by Republicans, 2003	Years with Republican Governors (%)				Average Legislative Seats Held by Republicans (%)			
			1960–69	1970–79	1980–89	1990–99	1960–69	1970–79	1980–89	1990–99
Alabama	R	36	0	0	40	60	1	1	11	28
Arkansas	R	28	40	0	20	40	1	3	9	15
Florida	R	67	40	0	40	20	18	29	33	50
Georgia	R	44	0	0	0	0	8	12	15	33
Louisiana	R	33	0	0	40	40	1	3	10	22
Mississippi	D	30	0	0	0	80	1	4	9	30
North Carolina	D	49	0	40	60	20	19	14	23	39
South Carolina	R	58	0	40	40	80	3	9	21	41
Tennessee	D	45	0	60	60	60	28	37	35	42
Texas	R	59	0	20	60	60	2	10	26	43
Virginia	D	62	20	100	0	80	12	23	29	48

Source: Jewell and Morehouse (2001).

TABLE 15.4
Black and Latino Legislators in Texas, 1990 and 2003 (percent)

	1990	*2003*
Latino		
Population	25.5	32.0
State House	13.3	20.0
State Senate	16.1	23.0
U.S. House	14.8	18.8
Black		
Population	11.9	11.5
State House	8.7	9.3
State Senate	6.5	6.0
U.S. House	3.7	6.3

Source: Handley and Grofman (1998) and Center for Voting and Democracy.

can electoral process. In particular, the rise in the Hispanic population in Texas and elsewhere nationally is part of a growing diversity in ethnic and racial composition in the country that makes the issue of how minorities are incorporated into the electoral process important both historically and currently. In this chapter, we examine this history and the current issues. But we begin with a discussion of the growing diversity and the questions of defining representation.

The Current Rise in Diversity

The U.S. Census Bureau estimated that in 1990 the non-Hispanic white population of the United States was 75.7 percent and, in 2000, 71.3 percent. The Census Bureau projects that by 2060, the non-Hispanic white population will be less than 50 percent of the U.S. population. Most of the recent and projected increase is in the population of persons of Hispanic ancestry. It is estimated that the Hispanic population will be 26.6 percent of the U.S. population in 2060; the non-Hispanic black population is expected to be 13.3 percent; the American Indian population, 0.8 percent; and the Asian and Pacific Islander population, 9.8 percent.

Although the rise in the Hispanic population is a big factor in the decreasing dominance of the non-Hispanic white population, it is significant that other minority groups have not decreased, nor are they expected to, and the wide variety of ethnic backgrounds in American communities has increased, making the country more diverse as a whole. Using the 2000 census data, the newspaper *USA Today* estimated that the chance of two randomly chosen U.S. residents having a different race or ethnicity is 49 out of 100, or almost 1 out of 2, whereas in 1990 this index was 40. But diversity has not just increased overall; it has also increased across states such that many formerly homogeneous states have increased in diversity. In Kansas, for example, the diversity index increased in the ten years between censuses from 21 to 31, and in Texas it increased from 55 to 62. Even in Iowa, one of the most homogenous states, the diversity index rose from 8 to 14.[16] Figure 15.1 shows how the percentage of minorities increased by region in the

FIGURE 15.1
Minorities by Region, 1980–2000

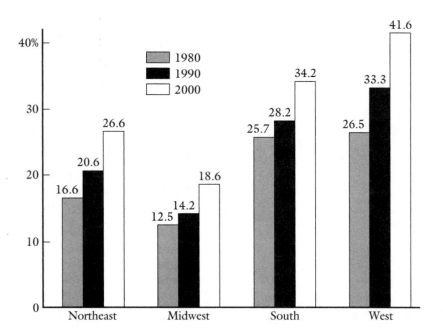

Source: U.S. Census Bureau.

United States from 1980 to 2000. All regions show an increase. What this means is that issues of minority representation, which used to concern mainly urban areas and the South, are now relevant across the nation.

Defining Minority Representation

A chief question in evaluating the extent to which racial and ethnic minorities are incorporated into American politics is, to what degree do elected officials represent these groups once in office? But what is meant by representation? Is there minority representation when elected officials have the same social and demographic characteristics as the groups they represent (*descriptive representation*), or is it when elected officials make policy choices that minority groups prefer (*substantive representation*)? This was the question facing minority voters in the districts that Bell and Doggett were running in. It is important to recognize that the two are not always the same. That is, elected officials from racial or ethnic minorities may represent positions that are not mainstream within those groups. For example, Supreme Court Justice Clarence Thomas has taken positions on issues that are often at variance with the opinions expressed by the majority of African Americans in public opinion polls on issues like affirmative action. In that case, we say African Americans are descriptively represented by Thomas but not necessarily substantively represented by him. Moreover, elected officials from the majority or other groups may take policy positions that are reflective of a racial or ethnic minority, giving the minority group substantive representation but not descriptive representation. Many African Americans stated publicly that President Bill Clinton was the first black president.

Which is more important? It seems fairly obvious that substantive representation is the ultimate goal of voters—to have representatives who reflect their preferences regardless of the representatives' social and demographic characteristics. However, there are two reasons why descriptive representation is likely to lead to greater substantive representation. First, if a minority group is prevented from achieving descriptive representation, majority groups have less incentive to provide minority-group voters with substantive representation. That is, if individuals are prevented legally or financially from competing for office based on social and demographic characteristics, then a representative from the majority does not need to worry about competition from members of that group and can more safely ignore that group's preferences on issues.

Second, to the extent that a representative has discretion once in office (recall the discussion in chapter 9 on the adverse selection problem in elections), then if a representative has particular preferences that are influenced by his or her racial or ethnic identity, he or she may be able to shape policy in directions that he or she prefers. In other words, the extent to which an elected official can shape policy to please his or her own preferences may lead to greater substantive representation for the racial or ethnic group the official identifies with. McCarty, Poole, and Rosenthal (2005) reported that, controlling for measures of constituencies' preferences and partisanship, the race, ethnicity, and gender of a member of Congress has a significant effect on his or her voting behavior. Besley and Case (2003) reported that even controlling for voters' ideological preferences, the presence of more women in state legislatures results in greater family assistance and stronger child-support laws. The identity of representatives does appear to affect policy choices. Thus, having an elected official who is descriptively representative

FIGURE 15.2
Vote Denial, Vote Dilution, and the Representation Link

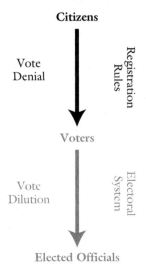

of a racial or ethnic minority group may be more likely to lead to policy preferred by that group than representation by the majority, even if the representatives advocate largely similar positions.

Vote Denial

Whether the goal is substantive or descriptive representation, there are two ways for minority groups to achieve representation in the U.S. political process—by elections and by appointment to nonelective office. Minorities have achieved appointment to the highest levels of nonelective office, especially in recent years—from the Supreme Court to the Department of State—and have achieved the elective offices of senator, governor, and mayor of large urban communities. However, minorities have yet to compete successfully for the highest electoral office, president, and have had only limited success in achieving the positions of senator and governor. One reason for this is that for much of the nation's history the majority purposively prevented minority voters from participating in the electoral process. This has been so at two stages. The first stage is simply denial of the right to vote. The second stage involves structural aspects of the electoral system designed to dilute the strength of minority voters. These two stages are illustrated in figure 15.2.

Direct Vote Denial

There are two types of vote denial: explicit restrictions on voting defined by race, ethnicity, or gender and implicit restrictions, which disproportionately limit voting by race, ethnicity, or gender. Explicit restrictions have been used to prevent voting by various groups in American history. We have already discussed how women did not receive the right to vote until 1919. When the country was founded, many African Americans were enslaved and had no political rights. Although some free blacks were able to vote in the North and even in some southern states before the Civil War, that right actually eroded before the Civil War (by the beginning of the Civil War, free blacks could vote only in New York and the New England states, except Connecticut). The erosion of voting rights for free blacks occurred at the same time that property requirements were reduced for white voters, suggesting that the increased discrimination was both race based and class based. After the war, the Reconstruction Act of 1867 required the former Confederate states to call state conventions to draw up new constitutions guaranteeing voting rights to African American men, and the Fifteenth Amendment, ratified in 1870, prohibited states from denying the right to vote on racial grounds (thus rescinding the restrictions in the northern states).

As a result of the Reconstruction Act, African Americans voted in large numbers—by the end of 1867, more than 700,000 southern blacks were registered and in some southern states were a majority of the electorate. Blacks were elected as senators, representatives, and state officials. Table 15.5 summarizes the number of African Americans elected to Congress as a function of the black population in the Reconstruction period.

American Indians were also directly denied voting rights. Although some American Indians were allowed to vote if Congress deemed them sufficiently "assimilated," full citizenship and voting rights were not given to all American Indians until 1924, when Congress passed the Indian Citizenship Act. Asian immigrants were similarly explicitly denied the right to vote because the Naturalization Act of 1790 restricted citizenships to "whites" (although some Asian Americans were naturalized by friendly officials). Not until 1952, with the McCarren-Walter Act, were the racial restrictions of the 1790 Naturalization Act rescinded and Asian Americans and other immigrants previously deemed "nonwhite" allowed to be naturalized, granted citizenship, and given the right to vote.[17]

Indirect Vote Denial

The African American Experience after the Civil War In 1939, a contractor approached Charles Gomillion and offered to build him a house. Although Gomillion could afford a new house and wanted one, he also wanted something more fundamental than a house. He had lived in Tuskegee, Alabama, since 1934 and had been born a citizen of the United

TABLE 15.5
Blacks in Congress and Black Population
during Reconstruction

State	Blacks in Population (%)	Blacks in Senate	Blacks in House	Total
South Carolina	59	0	8	8
Mississippi	54	2	1	3
Louisiana	50	0	1	1
Florida	49	0	1	1
Alabama	48	0	3	3
Georgia	46	0	1	1
Virginia	42	0	1	1
North Carolina	37	0	4	4
Total		2	20	22

States, yet he had been unable to register to vote. As a professor at the Tuskegee Institute, he could afford to pay the poll tax, which kept most African Americans from voting in Alabama. But the Macon County Board of Registrars, which would have to approve his application, required that two white registered voters vouch for a potential voter's suitability. Even then, the registrars had a great deal of discretion in determining whether a potential voter met the literacy and property requirements. Gomillion had only one voucher, a dry goods merchant. So he agreed to the contract for the house if the contractor, who was white, would appear before the board of registrars and the registrars approved Gomillion's voter registration application. Gomillion's application was approved.[18]

Gomillion's experience was unusual not because it was so difficult for him to be able to vote but because as a black man in Alabama in 1939 he was able to vote at all. After Reconstruction ended in 1876, with the election of Rutherford B. Hayes to the presidency, southern states wrote laws making voting difficult for blacks and rewrote their constitutions, instituting various measures that indirectly denied the right to vote to blacks. Southern states instituted long residency requirements and short registration periods as well as the requirement that new registrants be "vouched for" by two white businessmen, as in Gomillion's case. In Texas, voter registration took place over a four-month period that ended nine months before the elections. Secret ballots and complicated voting procedures were instituted to make it difficult for illiterate voters to cast a ballot.[19] For example, in 1882, South Carolina passed an "eight-box law" that established eight categories of elections with separate ballot boxes for each category. Ballots placed in the wrong box would not be counted. States passed laws and constitutional amendments calling for literacy tests and poll taxes. In the South, these tests were subjective and allowed elected officials to disenfranchise blacks while permitting illiterate whites to vote. Moreover, in the South segregated schools meant lower levels of education for blacks as the spending on African American schools was only a small percentage of the spending per pupil in white schools, which made the effects of these requirements particularly onerous. Finally, southern states enacted the so-called grandfather clause, as in Louisiana's 1898 constitution, which exempted any male or his son or grandson who had been entitled to vote on January 1, 1867 (that is, before the Fifteenth Amendment guaranteed blacks the right to vote), from being denied the right to vote. The grandfather clause was such blatant indirect vote denial that it was declared unconstitutional in *Guinn v. United States* (1915), whereas other measures, like poll taxes and literacy tests, were allowed to continue. Table 15.6 presents a summary of the various measures used by southern states as of 1960 to deny blacks the right to vote.

The White Primary A special type of indirect vote denial instituted in the South during the post-Reconstruction period was the "white primary." As noted earlier, during the latter half of the nineteenth century, a number of states and jurisdictions in both the North and the South began to use direct primaries to nominate candidates for office. We have already discussed how the rules for participation in primaries (whether they are closed to nonparty

TABLE 15.6
Methods of Vote Denial in Southern States as of 1960

State	Literacy Test (Date established)	Poll Tax as of 1960	Residence Requirement
Alabama	Yes (1901)	Yes	12 months
Arkansas	No	Yes	6 months
Florida	No	Abolished before 1948	6 months
Georgia	Yes (1908)	Abolished before 1948	6 months
Louisiana	Yes (1898)	Abolished before 1948	12 months
Mississippi	Yes (1890)	Yes	12 months
North Carolina	Yes (1900)	Abolished before 1948	1 month
South Carolina	Yes (1895)	Abolished after 1948	12 months
Tennessee	No	Abolished after 1948	3 months
Texas	No	Yes	6 months
Virginia	Yes (1902)	Yes	6 months

Source: Alt (1994).

members or open to new voters, independents, and/or members of other parties) can affect the type of candidate elected and the ability of the party to incorporate and respond to changes in the electorate's policy preferences. In the South post-Reconstruction, the Democratic Party used primaries as an indirect method of denying blacks the right to vote. The party declared itself a "private club" and restricted participation to whites. In this way, it attempted to open itself to poor whites (who could potentially form a coalition with poor blacks in the Republican Party) and then instill the norm of coordinating along party lines in the general election, in which party divisions were largely racial. Every state in the South adopted white primaries, with the exception of Tennessee and selected counties in North Carolina. As other measures of vote denial further reduced black voting, the white primary became the "real" general election in these states, further reducing black voting. The South became virtually a one-party state. As noted in chapter 5, the success is illustrated by the fact that income had virtually no effect on southern partisan identification in the 1950s—both rich and poor whites identified themselves as Democrats.[20]

After a long series of court challenges led by the National Association for the Advancement of Colored People (NAACP), the white primary was declared unconstitutional under the Fifteenth Amendment in *Smith v. Allwright* in 1944. The demise of the white primary had an important effect on black voting in the South. In 1940, there were estimated to be about 151,000 black voters in the South (about 3 percent of the voting-age black population), but by 1947 black voting had increased to 595,000 (25 percent) and to 1,238,038 voters by 1956. By November 1964, black registration in the South had doubled since 1952.

The Voting Rights Act Although the white primary was declared unconstitutional in 1944, other indirect measures for denying the vote continued to be used (particularly in the lower South, in Alabama, Mississippi, Georgia, and Louisiana, where the rate of black voting was much below that of white voting) until after the passage of the Voting Rights Act of 1965.[21] The purpose of the Voting Rights Act was to enforce the Fifteenth Amendment. Some sections permanently applied to the entire country, such as section 2, which echoes the amendment's language. The act set out procedures for the attorney general to use to enforce the voting guarantees of the Fifteenth Amendment in all states and authorized the use of federal examiners and observers during voting. The special provisions were applicable for the next five years and applied only to jurisdictions (which could have been counties if a state as a whole did not qualify) where a test or device had been a precondition for registration or voting and in which fewer than 50 percent of the voting-age population registered or voted.[22] In these "covered jurisdictions," literacy tests or devices used as preconditions for voting were suspended. Most important, these jurisdictions had their voting laws frozen, pending federal approval of the proposed changes. Specifically, the covered jurisdictions were required to submit to the attorney general or the District Court for the District of Columbia all planned changes in any "voting qualification or prerequisite to voting, or standard, practice or procedures with respect to voting" that had not been in force before the act was passed. The proposed changes would be cleared after federal scrutiny of the particular facts only if the changes did "not have the purpose and . . . the effect of denying or abridging the right to vote on account of race or color."

In 1970, when the act was amended and extended for another five years, literacy tests were suspended in all fifty states (and the suspension was ruled constitutional by the Supreme Court), residency requirements for federal elections were limited to a thirty-day maximum, and the voting age was lowered to eighteen. The poll tax was outlawed in federal elections by the Twenty-fourth Amendment to the Constitution, and in 1966, in *Harper v. Virginia State Board of Elections*, the Supreme Court ruled that poll taxes in other elections were unconstitutional. Table 15.1 shows the effects of *Smith v. Allwright*, the Voting Rights Act, and the elimination of the poll tax on black voter registration in the South.

The Experiences of Other Minority Groups Literacy tests and restrictions on registration have also been used to indirectly deny the vote to other minority groups, particularly non-English-speaking or illiterate immigrants. Connecticut was the first state to adopt a literacy test, in 1855, with Massachusetts following suit in 1857 and Wyoming in 1889. The tests were designed to reduce voting by immigrants and non-English-speakers who had immigrated to these states.

States with large American Indian populations used five arguments to justify denying Indians the right to vote after the Indian Citizenship Act extended citizenship and, by implication, the franchise to all Indians. First, some states (for example, Minnesota and South Dakota) required that Indians prove they had assumed a "civilized" way of life by severing their relations with their tribe before being allowed to participate in the electoral process. Second, it was contended that residents of reservations who did not pay property taxes should not be able to vote in local and state elections. Third, it was held that the size of the American Indian community in some jurisdictions would give Indians a majority of the vote and thus political control. Fourth, it was argued that as legal "wards" of the federal government (early rulings by Chief Justice John Marshall established that American Indian tribes were not independent political entities but had a guardian-ward relationship with the U.S. government), American Indians were like individuals under legal guardianship, who were generally not permitted to vote (the presumption actually being that wards were mentally handicapped or too young to vote). Finally, it was argued that American Indians were not really "residents" of the state, as they lived on reservations. By the late 1950s, court rulings and pressure at the federal level had discredited these arguments, and American Indians were allowed to vote; Utah was the last state to permit Indians to vote.

In contrast to African Americans, American Indians, and Asian Americans, few Latino Americans were directly denied the right to vote. After the

Mexican-American War, a number of Mexican settlers in Texas and the western states acquired by the United States were granted U.S. citizenship and voting rights by the Treaty of Guadalupe Hidalgo in 1848. Similarly, other Latinos have found the naturalization process easier than Asian Americans have found it. Puerto Ricans, as citizens of a U.S. territory, have full voting rights if they live on the mainland.

However, at the end of the nineteenth century and in the early twentieth century, efforts' were made in Texas to deny Mexican Americans the right to vote. Anglo *patróns* (bosses), typically large landowners who ran ranches along the Rio Grande in a feudal fashion, had mobilized Mexican American voters to choose as they wanted, and the Texas Rangers notoriously served as the bosses' enforcement troops. The practice angered smaller Anglo landowners, and in their attempt to dethrone the large bosses, they instituted indirect methods to deny Mexican Americans the right to vote. Most of the measures involved restrictions on registration like those faced by blacks, but some were obviously aimed at Latino voters. For example, in 1918, the Texas state legislature passed a bill prohibiting interpreters at polls. Similarly, election and ballot materials were to be printed only in English. As with blacks in the South, Latinos attended segregated schools, and such measures, even for long-term residents, made voting difficult.

In *Garza v. Smith* (1970), MALDEF successfully challenged the Texas laws that enabled voting officials to assist physically handicapped voters but not those who were not proficient in English. The 1975 extension of the Voting Rights Act required that bilingual election materials and assistance be available to voters if 5 percent or more of an area's voting-age citizens belong to a single language minority and that language minority's literacy rate in English is less than the national literacy rate. This extension also benefited American Indians, Alaskan Natives, and Asian Americans, who had been indirectly denied the right to vote through the use of English-only election materials and a lack of interpreters.

Vote Dilution

Vote Dilution versus Vote Denial

Vote dilution occurs when the way in which votes are counted is used to dilute or marginalize the votes of minorities. That is, vote dilution occurs when minority groups are prevented from combining their votes in an effectual manner. In some ways, the white primary was both vote denial (by denying African Americans the right to vote in the primary) and vote dilution (by attempting to keep African Americans and poor whites in the South from forming a coalition of voters with common policy preferences). After Reconstruction, southern states used a number of other methods to explicitly dilute African American votes. These measures were used before blacks were effectively disenfranchised through the grandfather clause, the poll tax, the literacy test, and registration limitations—that is, when blacks were still voting in large numbers although northern involvement in Reconstruction had ended with Hayes's election in 1876. Some of these vote-dilution methods were abandoned after vote denial virtually eliminated black voting in the early twentieth century. A number of southern states, however, such as Alabama, in reaction to the growth in voter registration among voters like Gomillion in Tuskegee, returned to them or created new dilution measures after the white primary was declared unconstitutional and, in some cases, after the Voting Rights Act was passed.

Methods of Vote Dilution

What were the methods of vote dilution that southerners used, and how did they work? Specifically, southerners used six methods: racial gerrymandering, annexations, the substitution of at-large districts for single-member districts, full-slate laws and numbered-place systems, the substitution of appointed offices for elected ones, and majority requirements. We discuss the first five methods below and majority requirements later in the chapter.

Racial Gerrymandering and Annexations Recall that from the Civil War period until the 1970s and 1980s, as a consequence of the Republican Party's position on slavery and black political rights in the South, the Republican Party in the South was friendly to and supportive of blacks (almost all blacks in the South were Republicans), whereas southern Democrats desired to reduce the influence of both blacks and white Republicans.[23] To reduce the influence of blacks and white Republicans, southern states in the latter half of the nineteenth century created congressional and legislative districts that packed minority voters and Republicans into concentrated enclaves. Although this may have ensured the election of some blacks or white Republicans, in effect it reduced the total number of blacks and white Republicans elected by changing a district that formerly had a majority of black voters to one with an insufficient number of black voters. For example, South Carolina created a congressional district that comprised two Republican incumbents and went across county lines to pack in black voters. Similarly, Mississippi created a district along the Mississippi River for the length of the state that comprised much of the black population in the state. The consequence of such gerrymandering was a reduction in the number of black and/or Republican representatives.

States also tried to use racial gerrymandering in response to the *Smith v. Allwright* ruling and the Voting Rights Act of 1965, which increased black voting. One such blatant move by Alabama was to redraw the boundaries of the city of Tuskegee to reduce the black voting population from four hundred to five. Charles Gomillion, with the help of civil rights groups, challenged the new lines, and in 1960, in the noteworthy case of *Gomillion v.*

Lightfoot, the Supreme Court declared Tuskegee's new boundaries uncon-stitutional according to the Fifteenth Amendment. In 1966, the Texas legis-lature gerrymandered multimember districts to dilute black votes in the state's most populous county, and Mississippi also engaged in racial gerry-mandering that year. In another noteworthy case, *Allen v. State Board of Elections* (1969), the Supreme Court ruled that efforts like these to dilute black votes, like efforts to deny black votes, had to be pre-cleared under the Voting Rights Act of 1965. In one of his last opinions, Chief Justice Earl Warren stated that the Voting Rights Act "gives a broad interpretation to the right to vote recognizing that voting includes 'all action necessary to make a vote effective.' "[24]

Annexation and redrawing city and local government boundaries had a similar effect on black voters' ability to elect candidates of their choice, by combining black local governments into bigger white-dominated urban ar-eas and thus decreasing black voting strength relative to white voting strength. Annexations to dilute black voting strength occurred after both Reconstruction and *Smith v. Allwright* and the Voting Rights Act. On occa-sion, however, the Supreme Court has supported annexations even if they decrease black voting strength. For example, in *City of Richmond v. United States* (1975), the Supreme Court allowed Richmond to annex a white sub-urb, changing the proportion of blacks in the city from 52 percent to 42 percent, because the city created an electoral system that afforded blacks "representation reasonably equivalent to their political strength in the en-larged community."

Although the historical experience is that racial gerrymandering has been used to hurt the prospects of minorities in elections, more recently, in re-sponse to the Voting Rights Act, white voters have accused states of exces-sive racial gerrymandering to benefit minority voters, and plans approved by the Justice Department have been challenged as discriminatory against whites. We deal with the gerrymandering debates of the 1990s later in this chapter.

At-Large Elections When the Good Government League of San Antonio changed the city's form of government (as discussed in chapter 14), it also chose to hold at-large elections for members of the city council. Although the city's Latino population was sizable, the city's leaders, by commanding a white majority citywide and annexing a white suburban area, largely limited Latino representation on the city council to a small percentage that mostly included Latinos who worked with the Good Government League. At-large districts were also popular in southern states wishing to dilute black votes. After Reconstruction and after *Smith v. Allwright* and the Voting Rights Act, local governments in southern states switched from single-member dis-tricts to at-large districts. For instance, numerous counties in Alabama had switched from at-large to single-member districts after blacks were effec-tively disenfranchised at the turn of the century. But after *Smith v. All-*

wright, these counties began to changed back. Between 1947 and 1971, twenty-five of the state's sixty-seven counties switched from single-member districts to at-large districts. In a special session in 1966, North Carolina's general assembly authorized forty-nine boards of county commissioners to adopt at-large election systems and required all school boards to use at-large elections. In the same year, Mississippi also switched district elections to at-large elections. In *Allen v. State Board of Elections*, however, the Supreme Court declared that these efforts to dilute black votes, like those in racial gerrymandering discussed above, must be pre-cleared.

To understand how replacing single-member districts with at-large districts works to dilute minority votes, consider a simple model of the electoral process. Assume that there are two districts with equal populations (50 voters) and each selects a representative to a state legislature (or city council, and so on). District A has 30 black voters and 20 white voters; district B has 10 black voters and 40 white voters. Suppose that all voters vote by racial lines and in each district a white candidate faces a black candidate. District A elects a black candidate, and district B elects a white candidate.

Now suppose the two districts are combined into one and voters select two representatives. Voters will have two votes, which they can cast for one candidate or two, or they can abstain. Now the voters in the new at-large district, when voting for the four candidates, will elect only the two white candidates, and neither black candidate will be elected. Although this is a stylized example and voters do not necessarily choose purely along racial lines, it shows how the at-large districts in the late nineteenth century and the mid–twentieth century diluted black votes.

The empirical evidence on the effect that the change from at-large to district elections has on black office holding in municipalities in the South is striking. Davidson and Grofman (1994) compared the percentage of blacks in city councils in at-large districts that were changed to single-member districts in eight southern states from the mid-1970s to 1990. Although they found an increase in black office holding in councils in at-large districts during this period, reflecting the increased ability of blacks to register and vote after the passage of the Voting Rights Act, a much sharper increase occurred in municipalities that switched to single-member districts. In cities and towns with a white majority and at-large elections in use at the end of the period, the ratio between the black population and black office holding was approximately one half, meaning that if the black population was 30 percent, 15 percent of the council was likely to be black. In contrast, the ratio for those cities and towns with a white majority and single-member districts was one, meaning that if the black population was 30 percent, 30 percent of the council was likely to be black. It is important to note that those cities and towns that did not change their electoral process were likely to be the ones that were not challenged by blacks for engaging in vote dilution and thus were areas in which whites might have been less likely to engage in bloc voting.[25]

Full-Slate Laws and Numbered-Place Systems In San Antonio, the city council was not just selected at large, but the council positions were also given "numbers" or "places," making each position a separate election. This meant that minority voters could not use single-shot voting to elect a repre-

TABLE 15.7
Voters' Preferences in Example of Single-Shot Voting

	First Preference	Second Preference	Third Preference	Number of Voters
M voters	Mary	David or Rita	David or Rita	54
D voters	David	Rita	Mary	23
R voters	Rita	David	Mary	23

sentative. How did this work? Suppose we have three candidates—Mary, Rita, and David—in an at-large election to select two members of a city council. Mary is the minority candidate, and Rita and David are supported by white voters. We have three groups of voters, *M, D*, and *R*. There are 54 *M* voters, 23 *D* voters and 23 *R* voters. Voters' preferences and the number of each type of voter are given in table 15.7.

Each voter has two votes and can vote for two candidates for the two offices. If each voter does vote for two candidates, *D* and *R* voters will vote for both David and Rita, who will each receive 46 votes; *M* voters will vote for Mary, who will receive 54 votes, and split their remaining votes between David and Rita, who will get approximately 27 more votes a piece. David and Rita are elected even though Mary's supporters outnumber both David's and Rita's supporters combined. However, suppose now that voters recognize they don't need to vote for both candidates—that is, they can vote for just one candidate (or even abstain). *M* voters will vote only for Mary, decreasing the vote share for David and Rita to forty-six each, and Mary will definitely be elected.

With full-slate laws, votes are not counted unless a voter votes for a "full slate," or the same number of candidates as there are positions. Mary's supporters are forced to vote for David and Rita, and Mary is not elected because voters have little choice.[26] However, if there were two minority candidates instead of just one, whom *M* voters prefer to David and Rita, then it would be possible even with the full-slate law for the minority voters to achieve representation. Ballot-access restrictions (which we have discussed) made this unlikely in the South. Southern states clearly used full-slate laws as a strategy to dilute black votes. North Carolina's legislature passed full-slate laws in the 1950s that applied to fourteen counties located primarily in the state's black belt. In 1952, Alabama enacted a full-slate law that applied to every public election, whether statewide or local.

Numbered-place systems, such as that used in San Antonio, similarly forced minority voters to support white candidates when minority candidates were limited in availability—voters had to vote for a candidate for each "place," or city council position, or their votes would not be counted.

Appointed Officials Even more effective as a method of diluting minority voting strength was replacing a locally elected official in a district dominated by minority voters with a state-appointed official (at a time when the state was dominated by white Democratic voters). Many southern states did this with offices such as sheriff, justice of the peace, and so on, after Reconstruction and again after *Smith v. Allwright* and the Voting Rights Act. Significantly for the methods of indirect vote denial that southern states also used, local election officials and boards were appointed at the state level.

The Effects of Vote Dilution in the Late Nineteenth Century

Although anecdotal evidence suggests that vote dilution was used to decrease the ability of African Americans to elect representatives of their choice, what is the empirical evidence that these procedures have the effects predicted? Kousser (1992) examined the post-Reconstruction period, when African Americans were still voting in large numbers. He reported that in the 1880 presidential election (four years after Reconstruction ended), two thirds of black men voted; during the 1880s, 60 percent of black men voted in gubernatorial elections in the eleven southern states; and even in the 1890s, black voter turnout remained high (one half to one third). Yet during this period, the numbers of black elected officials noticeably dropped, as shown in figure 15.3. This suggests that vote dilution did work to decrease the influence of black voters, marginalizing them so that the methods of vote denial could be instituted in the late 1890s and early 1900s. After that, black voter turnout plunged.

Majority Requirements and Vote Dilution

The last southern black member of Congress who had first been elected in the nineteenth century was George White, from North Carolina, who resigned in 1901 rather than seek reelection, knowing he would be defeated. For twenty-eight years, no African American served in the U.S. Congress.[27] For seventy-two years, no African American from the South served in Congress.[28] In 1968, over 20 percent of North Carolina's population was African American, yet no black from the state had served in Congress, and the first African American was elected to the state assembly only in the twentieth century. The state refused to eliminate multimember districts and had

FIGURE 15.3
Blacks Elected to State Legislatures and Congress in Eleven Former Confederate States, 1868–1900

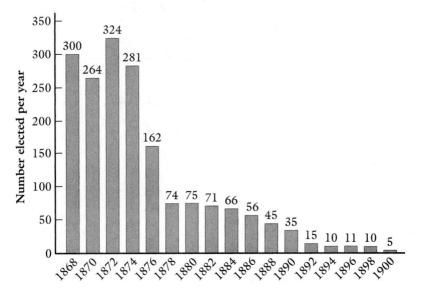

Source: Kousser (1992)

instituted a numbered-place system. That was the situation in 1968, when Eva Clayton chose to be the first African American since George White to run for Congress, challenging the incumbent, L. H. Fountain, whose district was 40 percent black, in the Democratic primary. She lost with only 30 percent of the vote (only 26 percent of blacks in the district were registered to vote).[29]

In 1980, as North Carolina redistricted, blacks thought that maybe this time, for the first time since White, they might be given a chance at winning one of the state's eleven seats in Congress. Although the state had not gained or lost a congressional district in the annual reapportionment across states, population changes within the state meant that districts needed to be redesigned in order to maintain the one-person, one-vote balance required by the Constitution. One of the principal issues was what to do with Durham, an urban area with a sizable black population. Should it go into Fountain's rural district, which it was close to, to make up for the population he had lost? To do so would probably mean that the black percentage might be high enough for an African American to challenge him more successfully than Clayton had. Instead, legislators drew a new district for Fountain, one that looked like a fish hook, a semicircle surrounding Durham. The Justice

Department challenged the new district, however, and the legislature was forced to put Durham into Fountain's district (though it removed another area that would have made the district majority black, keeping the black population high but less than a majority). Fountain chose to retire rather than face a challenge in the primary from Mickey Michaux, a black civil rights leader from Durham.

Two white candidates with significant state legislative and party experience also ran in the Democratic primary, James Ramsey and Tim Valentine. Although blacks were not a majority in the district, it was clear that Michaux would be able to win a plurality of the vote and Ramsey and Valentine would split the remainder. But North Carolina had a majority requirement of 50 percent. Voters whose last preference was Michaux did not need to coordinate (see chapter 14); they could let the majority requirement do it for them. As predicted, Michaux won a plurality of the vote, 44.1 percent, and faced Valentine in a run-off. In the runoff election, voting was largely divided by race, with 91.5 percent of blacks and 13.1 percent of whites supporting Michaux. Michaux lost with 46.2 percent of the vote.[30] North Carolina did not elect a black member of Congress until 1992, when Eva Clayton and Mel Watt won seats. Their stories involve the redistricting battles of the 1990s, which we will discuss shortly.

Michaux's case seems to be an obvious example of how majority requirements can prevent a black candidate from winning when a district has less than a majority of African Americans and voting is largely along racial lines. The only states in the nation that use majority-vote requirements statewide are southern states, and their institution was part of the effort to dilute the strength of black voters. As such, majority requirements have been attacked, and North Carolina lowered its requirement to 40 percent as a consequence of the concern. However, statistical analyses of the use of majority requirements in the South have not found a significant negative effect on minority representation.[31] Blacks have been elected in the South in the face of majority requirements and from districts or areas that do not have a black majority (for example, Andrew Young was elected to Congress in 1972 from a district with a white majority despite a majority requirement; J. C. Watts was similarly elected from Oklahoma to represent a white majority district despite a majority requirement). For this reason, the courts have ruled that majority requirements are constitutional. Many nonsouthern local governments also have majority requirements (like New York City, Los Angeles, and, recently, Chicago), and although some minority advocates have argued that these laws hurt the ability of minority groups to achieve office, the evidence is mixed.

Vote Dilution and Other Minority Groups

The methods of vote dilution have also been applied to other minority racial and ethnic groups. For example, when Texas redrew its state legislative boundaries after the 1970 census, it divided the 150-member body among 79 single-member districts and 11 multimember districts, with the multi-member districts, with the multimember districts in urban areas in which the Latino and African American population was highest. We have already discussed how San Antonio used at-large districts to dilute Latino votes. In South Dakota, an attempt was made to dilute the votes of American Indians by attaching to adjacent counties three "unorganized" counties lying entirely within Indian reservations. The Indians, who were the majority in the unorganized counties, were unable to vote in the adjacent counties, which were controlled by whites. In *Little Thunder v. South Dakota* (1975) a federal circuit court ruled that Indians must be permitted to vote in the adjacent counties.

Vote Dilution, the Fifteenth Amendment, and the Voting Rights Act

One of the big debates about the Voting Rights Act and the Fifteenth Amendment has to do with the extent to which they outlaw or require preclearance for use of the methods of vote dilution discussed above. We noted that in *Allen v. Board of Elections*, Chief Justice Warren ruled that measures that diluted black votes were subject to the Voting Rights Act. However, a number of noted scholars have contended that the purpose of both the Voting Rights Act and the Fifteenth Amendment should be simply to reduce barriers to the act of voting (vote denial). Moreover, some contend that because vote denial has been almost eliminated, there is no further need for the Voting Rights Act. Others have argued that if votes are diluted, then minority and ethnic voters are effectively disenfranchised, and thus the Voting Rights Act and the Fifteenth Amendment require that voting systems be designed to minimize the dilution.

Those who argue that the Fifteenth Amendment and the Voting Rights Act apply to vote dilution face a number of difficult questions:

- What is the evidence of minority-vote dilution? Is proportional representation required to prevent vote dilution?
- What is the evidence of racial discrimination? Do we need to prove intent to discriminate or just results? And if the latter, what do we mean by results?

Court cases addressing the Voting Rights Act and the Fifteenth Amendment in the 1960s and 1970s and the debates over the renewal of the temporary provisions in 1965 (for five years), in 1970 (for five more years), and in 1975 (for seven years) showed much confusion over these issues. *City of Richmond v. United States* (1975) is an example of the problem facing the court. Clearly, the annexation shifted the city's majority population from black to white, diluting black votes. The Court ruled, however, that if the electoral system provided blacks with representation (that is, with single-member districts), the dilution was not a problem. Although the courts were in general willing to consider cases of vote dilution and, in some cases where vote dilution was argued to have occurred, declared electoral laws a violation of either the Voting Rights Act or the Constitution, the courts' rulings and the congressional debate did not provide clear guidelines on how vote dilution was to be addressed and what types of electoral systems were acceptable. It seemed that each case had unique features that had to be addressed individually.

The problem reached a crisis after a sharply divided Supreme Court ruled in *City of Mobile v. Bolden* (1980) that the Fifteenth Amendment applied only to access to the ballot (vote denial) and that proof of intent to discriminate was necessary to show that racial discrimination in voting had occurred. This ruling was a reversal of earlier decisions—*Allen v. Board of Elections, White v. Regester* (1973), *Zimmer v. McKeithen* (1973)—that had not required such proof and held that the Fifteenth Amendment and the Voting Rights Act applied to cases of vote dilution. The crisis caused by the ruling was amplified by the 1980 election of Ronald Reagan (who was anticipated to appoint conservative federal judges and Justice Department officials who might not be committed to fighting voting rights cases) and by the fact that the temporary provisions of the Voting Rights Act would expire in 1982.

Voting rights advocates formed a large coalition across racial and ethnic lines (since in 1975 the act had been extended to language minorities), and Congress passed an amended version of the act in 1982 with veto-proof majorities (as discussed in chapter 13), extending the temporary provisions for twenty-five years. The amended act explicitly states that proof of discriminatory results, rather than intent, is sufficient to substantiate a claim of minority-vote dilution and that electoral systems that can be shown to dilute minority votes are unconstitutional. However, the amended Voting Rights Act also clearly stops short of requiring proportional representation, stating: "Nothing in this section establishes a right to have members of a protected class elected in numbers equal to their proportion in the population." Interestingly, just two days after the amended act was passed, the Supreme Court ruled, in *Rogers v. Lodge* (1982), that circumstantial evidence can be indicative of intent to discriminate under the Fifteenth Amendment (a reversal of *Bolden*). Why did this happen? Chief Justice Warren Burger changed sides, and Justice Potter Stewart, who had written the plurality opinion in *Bolden*, had been replaced by Justice Sandra Day O'Connor, who voted to reverse *Bolden*.

In 1986, when the Court addressed the 1982 amendment in *Thornburg v. Gingles*, a case challenging North Carolina's plans after the 1980 census, it established a three-part test for determining when at-large voting in multi-member districts shows discriminatory results:

- There must be a sufficiently large and geographically compact set of minority voters to constitute a majority in one or more single-member districts.
- These minority voters must be politically cohesive or tend to vote as a bloc.
- Majority voters must vote sufficiently as a bloc "usually to defeat the minority's candidate."

Other factors, such as the lingering effects of discrimination, racially directed campaign appeals, and the use of electoral devices to deny voting, were considered supportive of the case but not essential to it. The Court also made racial bloc voting simple to prove. That is, plaintiffs do not have to prove that voters are voting for reasons of race rather than some other reason, such as religion, party affiliation, age, or a candidate's name identification. All that needed to be shown was that black and white voters voted differently. *Gingles* simplified the decision making in voting rights cases and added predictability. The effects were an increase in voting rights cases, as well as settlements in advance, and a substantial reduction in the use of at-large districts.

Majority-Minority Districts and the Redistricting Debate of the 1990s

The New Majority-Minority Districts

In chapter 11, we discussed how for many years little attention was paid to issues of equity in redistricting, and we noted that in a number of states in both the North and the South congressional and state legislative districts were often unequal in size, with districts often not redrawn after each national census to reapportion the number of voters equitably. A series of court cases in the 1960s—*Gary v. Sanders* (1963), *Wesberry v. Sanders* (1964), *Reynolds v. Sims* (1964)—established the principal of one-person, one-vote, and the requirement that after each census states must redraw district boundaries to best reflect this principal was instituted.

As part of the Voting Rights Act, any redistricting plans in covered jurisdictions are subject to review by the Justice Department, as they are treated like a change in these jurisdictions' electoral systems. For example, the Justice Department made the North Carolina legislature drop the fishhook design for Fountain's congressional district. After the 1990 census, the Justice Department similarly gave the boundaries of the covered states special attention. The initial plans of several states, including Georgia, Mississippi, and North Carolina, were rejected by the Justice Department and the federal courts as eroding minority gains. For example, in North Carolina the initial plan had only one majority African American district out of twelve, or 8 percent, whereas the state was 22 percent African American. The Justice Department called for these states to attempt to "maximize" the number of districts with a majority of minority voters (North Carolina was told to devise an additional majority black district for two out of twelve districts, or 16 percent). The reasoning was that the main way to increase minority representation was to create districts with a majority of minority voters. In order to do so, many states drew congressional district boundaries that were clearly racial gerrymanderings. The new districts elected Clayton and Watt—the first African Americans elected to Congress from North Carolina since George White retired over ninety years before.

The most notorious new districts were in Georgia, Louisiana, and North Carolina. In Georgia, the eleventh congressional district reached across the state to pick up African American voters. In Louisiana, the fourth congressional district combined areas along the Arkansas border with regions in the southern Delta area. In North Carolina, the first and twelfth congressional districts cut across the state, combining black voters. The twelfth district (Mel Watt's) was a particularly obvious instance of racial gerrymandering—it followed I-85 for almost 160 miles, linking minority neighborhoods in different urban areas. For much of its length, the district was no wider than the highway and at some points even narrower. Figure 15.4 illustrates these congressional districts. Although the racial gerrymandering is obvious, less obvious is the fact that the shape of these districts was constrained not only by the desire to maximize the number of majority minority districts but also by the desire to maintain political partisan balance and to benefit incumbents. In fact, the first suit against the twelfth district of North Carolina was filed by the Republican Party, which alleged that the district was an unconstitutional political gerrymander designed to benefit Democrats. Another significant factor was the availability of sophisticated computer technology (both software and hardware), which allowed for gerrymandering to a precise degree not previously available.

Are They Unconstitutional?

These new districts were promptly challenged by white voters as unconstitutional racial gerrymandering. For example, five white voters filed suit against the twelfth district in North Carolina, arguing that the racial gerrymander violated the equal protection clause of the Fourteenth Amendment. The case, *Shaw v. Reno* (1993), reached the Supreme Court, which ruled that a racial gerrymander may, in some circumstances, be unconstitutional and sent the case back to the district court to determine whether the first and twelfth districts had been drawn on the basis of race and, if so, whether the racial gerrymander that resulted was "narrowly tailored to further a compelling governmental interest." Justice Sandra Day O'Connor wrote the majority opinion. As justification for the decision, she stated:

FIGURE 15.4
Majority Black Districts Created in Georgia, Louisiana, and North Carolina after 1990 Census

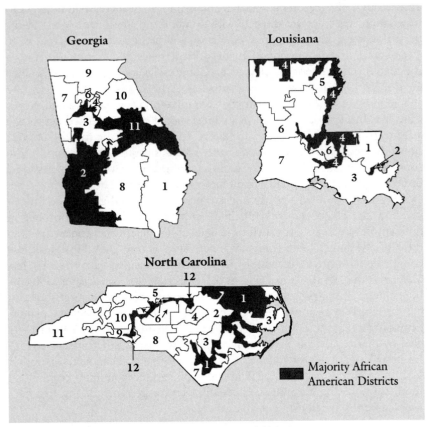

Source: Cartographic Research Lab, University of Alabama.

A reapportionment plan that includes in one district individuals who belong to the same race, but who are otherwise widely separated by geographical and political boundaries, and who may have little in common with one another but the color of their skin, bears an uncomfortable resemblance to political apartheid. It reinforces the perception that members of the same racial group—regardless of their age, education, economic status, or the community in which they live—think alike, share the same political interests, and will prefer the same candidates at the polls. . . . By perpetuating such notions, a racial gerrymander may exacerbate the very patterns of racial bloc voting that majority-minority districting is sometimes said to counteract.

Eventually, after several more court hearings, the twelfth district was redrawn, as were a number of the other majority-minority districts created after the 1990 census. Although the original twelfth district was 54.7 percent African American, the new district was only 44.2 percent African American—no longer majority black (although Latino voters accounted for 6.8 percent of the population). Other redrawn districts ceased to be majority African American, although blacks were close to a majority. Through these court cases, the following formula evolved: Specifically, plaintiffs alleging unconstitutional racial gerrymandering must first prove that race was the predominant factor motivating the redistricting decision. If racial motivation is proved, the strict scrutiny of judicial review is appropriate. According to strict scrutiny, the state is required to prove that the use of racial classifications was narrowly tailored to further a compelling state interest. If it is not proved, then the district boundaries are deemed unconstitutional and must be redrawn.

Although these criteria may seem clear, in actuality the waters of redistricting remain quite murky, as it is difficult to determine whether race is the predominant factor because political gerrymandering can also lead to bizarrely shaped districts, as noted by Justice John Paul Stevens in one of the case of the 1990s.[32] In North Carolina, for example, the redrawn twelfth district and the first district were further challenged by white voters. In *Cromartie v. Hunt* (2000), the federal district court concluded that both districts had been drawn along racial lines for a predominantly racial motive. The Court ruled that the first district was narrowly tailored to achieve the state's compelling interest in complying with the Voting Rights Act, and thus it survived strict scrutiny, but it ruled that the twelfth district was not. In *Hunt v. Cromartie* (2001), however, the Supreme Court reversed the district court. Justice Stephen Breyer, writing for the five-justice majority, stated that "the evidence . . . does not show that racial considerations predominated in the drawing of District 12's boundaries. That is because race in this case correlates closely with political behavior."

Majority-Minority Districts and Other Minorities

Not all of the new majority-minority districts created after the 1990 census to satisfy the Voting Rights Act were in the South or involved African Americans. For example, after the census, the Latino population in Illinois was shown to have increased by 42.3 percent, and even though the state had lost two congressional seats, Latino leaders belived that the increase in the Latino population, particularly in Chicago, justified a new majority Latino district. There was much partisan wrangling, with Republicans favoring the new Latino district, seeing it as an opportunity to hurt Democratic incumbents, who feared such a district would take away their needed support. After Latino leaders received support from the black community, a new Latino district was added. The new district (called the earmuff district—see figure 15.5) combined a Puerto Rican community in the northwest of the city with a Mexican American community in the southwest by a thin loop through white ethnic neighborhoods so that an existing majority African American district was unaffected. Two Latinos ran for the Democratic nomination in the new district, Juan Soliz, a Mexican American former alderman, and Luis Gutierrez, a Puerto Rican alderman, reflecting the diversity within the

FIGURE 15.5
Illinois: Fourth Congressional District, 1992

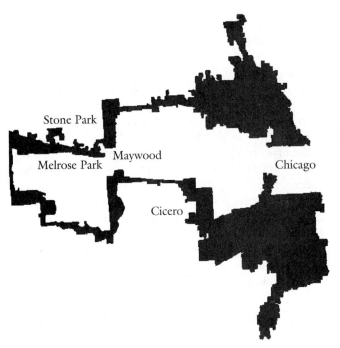

Source: Election Data Services.

Latino community in the district. Gutierrez, better financed and supported by Mayor Daley, won the nomination and defeated a Mexican American Republican in the general election. The district was challenged in federal court, and the Supreme Court declined to hear the case in a 1998 appeal, thereby upholding the district's constitutionality. The district was largely maintained in the 2001 redistricting plan.

A similar situation occurred in New York City when, after the 1990 census, it was revealed that the overall state population had stayed relatively constant but the Latino population had increased by 33.4 percent. Although New York lost three congressional seats, Latino leaders lobbied for a new Latino majority district. As in Illinois, partisan concerns made the task for Latino leaders difficult; they were successful, however. The new plan had two Latino districts: one, in the South Bronx, that was already represented by a Latino, José Serrano, and the new twelfth, which, as in Illinois's fourth district, combined several Latino communities—in the Williamsburg, Bushwick, Sunset Park, and East New York sections of Brooklyn and Corona, Elmhurst, and Jackson Heights in Queens—to create a majority Latino district (see figure 15.6). The new district was 58 percent Latino.

Five Latinos ran for the new seat, as well as a white Democratic incumbent, Stephen J. Solarz, whose district had been carved up in the redistricting. Solarz, who had served nine terms in Congress, argued that he could best give the district substantive representation because his seniority and experience would allow him to provide more for the district. He also had strong name recognition. However, Solarz had notoriously taken advantage of the House bank, and in the scandal that was revealed in the early 1990s voters learned that he had written 743 bad checks. Nevertheless, the potential existed for Latino voters to split their support, thereby allowing Solarz

FIGURE 15.6
New York's Twelfth District, 1992

Source: Election Data Services, Inc.

to be elected. In the Democratic primary, however, Nydia Velázquez received endorsements from top Democratic leaders in the state and city and was able to build a coalition of Latino and African American voters, winning with 33 percent of the vote to Solarz's 27 percent.[33] She then handily defeated the Republican Latino candidate. In 1996, plaintiffs challenged the twelfth district, claiming it had been drawn primarily for racial reasons and as a result was noncompact. A federal district court ruled that the plaintiffs were correct, and the district was redrawn so that it was only 48.6 percent Latino. Figure 15.7 shows the new district (which was largely the same after the 2001 redistricting). The experiences in North Carolina, Illinois, and New York highlight the difficulty of determining both when gerrymandering is sufficiently racially motivated to require strict scrutiny and when a compelling state interest might exist.

FIGURE 15.7
New York's Twelfth District, Redrawn in 1997

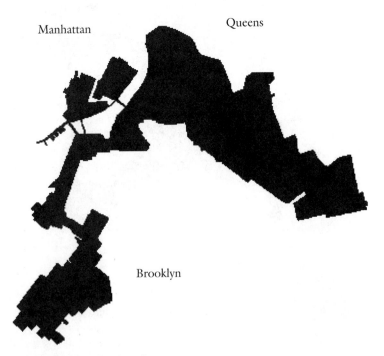

Source: Election Data Services, Inc.

Are Majority-Minority Districts Good for Minorities?

The Effect on State Legislatures

The Theory The creation of majority-minority districts, even though many were later revised, did have the effect of increasing the descriptive representation of minority groups in Congress and in those state legislatures that were also forced to draw boundaries to increase minority office holding. In table 15.2, we saw that between 1985 and 1992 the number of black members of Congress from southern states rose from 1.7 percent to 13.6 percent. Most of that gain was a result of the redistricting that took place after the 1990 census—in 1990, the percentage was only 4.3. In 1990, 12.1 percent of state house members were black; in 1992, 14.8 percent were. In 1990, 9.4 percent of state senators were black; in 1992, 13.5 percent were. Remarkably, although some of the district lines were redrawn in response to court challenges, as seen in table 15.2, the percentages in 2003 are even higher for state legislators and about the same for members of Congress.

As for particular cases, North Carolina's two new African American majority districts resulted in the election of the first black Congress members from the state since 1901, as we noted above. Significantly, as some district boundaries were redrawn, reducing the minority populations to below the majority level, many of the newly elected minority representatives were able to maintain their seats—such as Mel Watt from the twelfth district of North Carolina and Nydia Velázquez from the twelfth district of New York. Others have not fared as well. For example, Cynthia McKinney of Georgia was defeated in the Democratic primary in 2002 after having represented a new minority district since its creation in 1992; her opponent was also African American, however, showing that it is possible for a minority challenger from a district without a majority minority to succeed to office in the South. It is not possible to determine accurately whether minority candidates would have succeeded as well without the creation of these majority-minority districts, which increased descriptive representation initially.

However, many observers expressed concerns that the creation of majority-minority districts has hurt the Democratic Party and resulted in more conservative state legislatures and a more conservative Congress. The intuition is that by taking minority voters from other districts to create new districts, the other districts have become more conservative, and therefore state legislatures and Congress have become more conservative. Lublin (1997) and Lublin and Voss (2000, 2003) made this argument. Lublin and Voss (2000) identified ten congressional seats that Democrats lost because of racial gerrymandering between 1992 and 1994, suggesting that racial gerrymandering may have been a causal factor in the Republican takeover of Congress.

Shotts (2001, 2002, and 2003a) presented an alternative argument, contending that although it may be true that racial gerrymandering has led to more conservative state legislatures, it is not necessarily true for Congress. To understand Shott's line of reasoning, consider a simple model of districting in a state that has three legislative districts and whose minority voters are more liberal than its white voters (this example is drawn from Shotts 2003a). Assume that each district's representative will choose a policy position equal to the ideal point of the median voter in his or her district. Suppose that we can represent policy on a single line, from 0 to 100. Voters in the state are distributed as shown in figure 15.8. Minority voters account for one third of the population, and white voters account for two thirds. Minority voters have ideal points that range from 0 to 40, with the median minority voter's ideal point at M_M, or 20. The triangle with its peak at 20 is the probability distribution of the minority voters' ideal points. White voters, in contrast, have ideal points that range from 40 to 100, with the median white voter's ideal point at M_W, or 70. The triangle with its peak at 70 is the probability distribution of white voters' ideal points. The ideal point of the median voter in the state is at M_s, or 61.2.

Consider two districting plans. In the first, nongerrymandered plan, minority voters are spread evenly among the three districts, such that each one has one-third minority voters and two-thirds white voters. In the second plan, the districts are racially gerrymandered, whereby all minority voters are packed into a single district, and the two remaining districts are 100 percent white. In the first plan, each district has the same median point, 61.2, the median in the state, as both populations are distributed equally across the

FIGURE 15.8
Voters' Preferences in Example of Redistricting

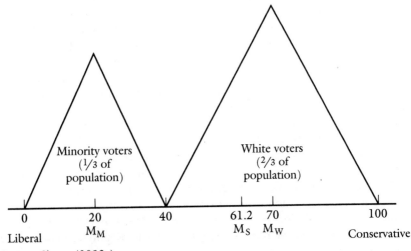

Source: Shotts (2003a).

three districts. So each representative's policy position is the same, 61.2. Under the second plan, however, the policy position of the representative from the majority-minority district is the median of that of the minority voters, 20, and the other two representatives' policy positions are at the median of that of the white voters, 70 (assuming the white voters are equally distributed across the two districts).

Suppose the three representatives serve in a state legislature and the legislature chooses policy outcomes to please its median representative. In that case, the effect of gerrymandering on policy outcomes in the state legislature is clear. In the nongerrymandered plan, the median representative's ideal point is at 61.2, the median in the state. But in the gerrymandered plan, the median representative's ideal point is at 70. In that case the racial gerrymandering has neutralized the minority voters.

The Evidence   The theoretical result is supported by Epstein and O'Halloran's (1999) empirical analysis of the alternative redistricting plans for South Carolina's state senate, which found that creating majority-minority districts can make a state legislature more conservative. This may partially explain why white Democrats are now an endangered species in the Texas state legislature even as many white voters still identify and register as Democrats in the state. Although some, such as Texas Democratic state representative Pete Gallego, might argue that the lack of white Democrats in the state legislature simply reflects a decrease in white voters supporting Democrats statewide, surveys suggest that the decrease in the legislature is sharper. In 2002, exit polls showed that Democratic Senate candidate Ron Kirk received 30 percent of the white vote and Democratic gubernatorial candidate Tony Sanchez received 27 percent.[34] Because both candidates faced popular incumbents, these totals may understate the willingness among whites to support Democratic candidates.[35] According to exit polls in 2004, 25 percent of white Texas voters chose Kerry over home-state favorite Bush. African American Democratic legislator Garnet Coleman argued that the reason for the decrease in white Democrats in the state legislature is redistricting: "It . . . shows that somebody was really smart in drawing maps. They knew how to eliminate, through gerrymandering, districts that would elect Anglo Democrats."[36] How exactly did this happen? Some white Democratic voters have been combined with minority voters in districts with a majority of minority voters, who have elected minority representatives. White Democratic voters in rural areas have been combined with white Republican voters in suburban areas. As Chuck Hopson remarked about the new congressional districts that the Killer D's revolted against, which combined rural Democratic white voters with Republican white voters from the suburbs of Houston or Dallas, giving Republicans a majority: "We'll be represented by people driving fancy cars instead of pickup trucks."[37] Increasing majority-minority districts in the Texas state house and senate, as the analysis above shows, does make the legislature more conservative than the state as a whole and in the process squeezes out white Democrats.

The Effect on Congress

The Theory What happens if the representatives elected in our simple model serve in Congress instead of in a state legislature? In that case, the policy outcome in Congress will depend on the location of the median voter in Congress, which depends on the policy positions of representatives from not just this state but other states as well. Assume that there are 100 other legislators with policy positions 1, 2, and so on, through 100. What happens to the national median under the two plans? Under the nongerrymandered plan, all three legislators from the state have policy positions at 61.2, which is to the right of the center. Thus, the national median of the 103-member legislature is at 52. Under the gerrymandered plan, the state elects one representative at 20 and two at 70, so the median of the national legislature is at 51. The racial gerrymandering has increased the number of liberals elected and shifted the national median and policy to the left. As three conservative moderates are replaced with two conservative extremist and one liberal extremist, the national median is moved to the left.

Although this may seem a small effect, consider the situation in which all states face the constraint of creating majority-minority districts. In states in which there is little difference between minority voters' preferences and white voters' preferences, creating majority-minority districts will not affect the distribution of policy positions of the representatives sent to Congress. So those states in which the median voter's preferred position is less than that of the national median will continue to send representatives to the left of the median in the same proportion. Thus, creating a majority-minority district in New York is unlikely to affect the national median. However, in states (like Texas) where the median voters' preferred position is greater than that of the national median, the creation of majority-minority districts will force the states to send representatives whose policy positions are to the left of the national median, moving the national median to the left. If a large number of states are forced to do this, policy may move to the left. Of course, this analysis oversimplifies the complex game among the states, which we discussed in chapter 11. Shotts (2001, 2002) has analyzed this game and has shown that in the more complicated game the basic intuition that majority-minority districts can move national policy to the left is supported.

The Evidence Does Shott's reasoning have empirical support? Shotts examined the roll-call voting scores of southern members of Congress during the redistricting period, as measured by McCarty, Poole, and Rosenthal (2005). Surprisingly, he found that the percentage of liberals had increased,

FIGURE 15.9
Partisanship and Policy Preferences of Southern Congress Members, 1986–96

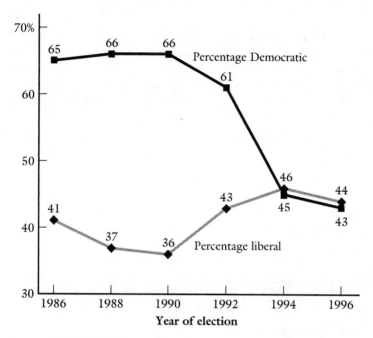

Source: Shotts (2003a)

from 38 percent between 1986 and 1990 to 44 percent between 1992 and 1996. The percentage was calculated by measuring the percentage of members of Congress whose voting records were more liberal than that of the median member of Congress for a given year. The results are shown in figure 15.9. Notice that whereas the Democratic percentage decreased, the liberal percentage increased, reflecting the change in the median voter in the Democratic districts. Southerners increased the percentage of representatives who were more liberal than the national median even as the number of Democrats decreased. Democratic members of Congress who were moderate conservatives were replaced by both Republican conservatives and Democratic liberals, increasing the percentage of liberals from these states.

Lublin and Voss (2003) disagreed with Shotts's analysis of the data—they contended that the percentage of liberals should be calculated by measuring the percentage of legislators who would vote conservatively on median legislation passed in 1994 (that year representing the status quo on current legislation). Using the standard, they found that the percentage of conservatives increased. This change may simply be a shift in overall voters' preferences, however, rather than a consequence of the racial gerrymandering.[38]

FIGURE 15.10
Partisanship and Policy Preferences of Texas Congress Members, 1986–2000

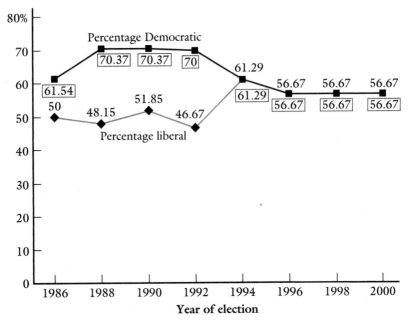

Source: Compiled by author.

The Killer D's Once Again What about Texas, from which Democratic state legislators fled rather than vote on a redistricting plan put forward by the Republican majority? Figure 15.10 presents the same data for Texas members of Congress through 2000. Before 1994, although Democrats accounted for a high proportion of the Texas delegation (around 70 percent), the proportion of members of the delegation who had voting records more liberal than the median voter in Congress was much lower, around 50 percent. In 1994, conservative Texas Democrats were replaced by Republicans and more liberal Democrats. All Texas Democrats had a more liberal voting record than the median voter in Congress, resulting in the Texas delegation's providing more liberal members of Congress than conservative members. When Texas redistricted after the 2000 census, the federal court gave the two new districts to Republicans and designed the remaining districts to facilitate the reelection of incumbents. Democrats maintained control over the same seventeen districts they had controlled prior to the redistricting while the Republicans' control increased from thirteen to fifteen districts, so that the percentage of Democrats from Texas in Congress in 2002 was 53.13.

Looking at these figures, one is not surprised that conservative Republican House majority whip Tom DeLay of Texas and others pushed for congressional redistricting in the state in 2003, in time for the 2004 elections. At a time when the state was becoming more Republican and presumably more conservative, racial gerrymandering was actually leading to a greater percentage of liberals in the congressional delegation. The 2003 redistricting reduced the percentage of Democrats from Texas in Congress to 31.25 percent. One conservative Democratic incumbent, Ralph Hall, switched parties, and other Democrats faced tough contests in Republican-leaning districts. But what effect did the 2003 redistricting have on descriptive minority representation in Texas? Are white Democrats an endangered species in the Texas congressional delegation, as they appear to be in the Texas state legislature?

Preliminary evidence is mixed. In 2004, Lloyd Doggett defeated Leticia Hinojosa in his primary contest and won the general election, but Chris Bell lost to Al Green, and Green defeated Hispanic Republican Arlette Molina in the general election. Thus, the number of minority members of Congress from Texas increased after the election, and the number of liberals decreased. It is important to remember, however, that the reduction of liberals is a consequence not of the requirement of racial gerrymandering but of the redrawing of boundaries to benefit the Republicans, which squeezed out some white Democrats. If Texas Republicans had not been forced to ensure that minority representation was maintained, then according to Shotts's argument, the percentage of liberals from Texas would be even lower (assuming that minority voters are more liberal).

Recall that the point of Shotts's argument is that the requirement of majority-minority districts constrains conservative Republican gerrymanderers but does not constrain Democratic ones. After the 1990 census, Texas had two African American majority districts and seven Latino majority districts. The delegation contained five Latino Democrats, one Latino Republican, and two African American Democrats. The 2000 plan benefited incumbents and gave Republicans the two new districts while maintaining the same distribution of minority districts. This means that the percentage of seats held by minorities decreased—African Americans had 6.5 percent of the seats in 2002 and Latinos had 22 percent, whereas the black population in the state is 11 percent and the Hispanic population is 32 percent. Both minority groups attempted to gain seats in the redistricting process but were rebuffed by the Democratic incumbents in Congress, who knew that such a plan would take voters away from them. According to Nina Perales, regional counsel for MALDEF, Texas Democrats opposed a new Latino district in the Dallas area because it would have affected the district of white Democratic representative Martin Frost. She remarked: "They fought like mad cats to keep us away. Neither Republicans nor Democrats were proposing additional Latino districts."[39] The Democrats would have been able to maintain the same percentage and the same percentage of liberals by replacing white incumbents with new Latino districts with a Democratic majority but chose instead to retain incumbents, making the argument that to do so benefited Latino voters in Texas because the incumbents would, through seniority, have powerful positions. A number of Latinos, like Representative Charlie Gonzalez, agreed with this position. As political consultant Lisa Montoya reasoned: "It makes sense; these people have seniority. They already hold positions of power on different committees. It would take a new member 10 years to obtain the power they already have."[40]

Texas Republicans, in attempting to get the district lines redrawn, used the fact that they were forcing some white Democratic incumbents, like Bell and Doggett, to run in minority districts to try to persuade minority state legislators to support the plan. To pass the plan in the state senate, the Republicans needed a supermajority, which meant they needed two Democratic state senators to support them. Minority leaders were divided on the new plan. In a Houston hearing on the Republican-proposed plan in June 2003, black Democratic state representatives Garnet Coleman and Ron Wilson

> took such bitterly opposing positions that they engaged at one point in a shouting match. . . . Wilson, a member of the House Redistricting Committee, has joined Republicans who say the plan that the committee approved would help blacks by giving them the opportunity to control a third congressional district. . . . But Coleman . . . testified that the plan would reduce black influence in other districts, now held by white Democrats who would lose their seats to Republicans.[41]

Hispanic leaders have similarly expressed divided opinion. For example, Democratic state senator and president pro tem Eddie Lucio "said that he does not like the redistricting proposal put forth . . . [by the Republicans] . . . but would consider a plan that created five Hispanic districts along the Rio Grande. That would result in three more Hispanic districts."[42] Ron Wilson's support for the Republican plan had bitter consequences for him—in his reelection contest of 2004, he lost the Democratic primary to Alma Allen, a member of the state board of education, who campaigned on Wilson's ties to the Republicans in the state house.

The Future of Redistricting

Representative Charlie Norwood (discussed in chapter 13) may have liked the new district boundaries drawn in Georgia for Congress and the state legislature after the 2000 census, but the Justice Department was less happy—not about the odd shapes of the boundaries (recall the perimeter district from chapter 11) but because black votes were spread out across districts more than they had been in the previous plan, particularly in the plan for the state senate. Georgia's state senate plan appeared to have been designed by legislators who understood the logic of Shotts's analysis for state legislatures. That is, Georgia's redistricting was controlled by Democrats who worried that if they created districts to maximize the probability of electing blacks to the state senate, by packing in minority voters they would make it easier for Republicans to win and move the median voter in the state senate closer to the Republicans, actually hurting the minority voters whom the new plan was supposed to help. "The Senator who chaired the subcommittee that developed the new plan testified he believed that as a district's black voting age population increased beyond what was necessary to elect a candidate, it would push the Senate more towards the Republicans, and correspondingly diminish the power of African-Americans overall."[43] Democrats designed a plan that kept the number of majority-minority districts constant but increased what they called influence districts, in which black voters would be significant but not decisive. They created thirteen districts with a majority black population, thirteen more districts with a black voting-age population of between 30 and 50 percent, and four others with a black voting-age population of 25 to 30 percent. Ten of the eleven black state senators voted for the plan, and thirty-three of the thirty-four black state representatives voted for it. No Republicans voted for the plan, and without the black vote it would not have passed.

The Justice Department did not like the plan, as it reduced the black vote in three of the districts from what it had been before. In April 2002, the district court agreed with the Justice Department and ordered that it be rewritten. Georgia legislators shifted black voters back into the three districts. But the case was not over. In August 2002, the attorney general of Georgia, black Democrat Thurbert Baker, appealed the district court's decision to the Supreme Court in *Georgia v. Ashcroft*, and the Supreme Court agreed to hear the case, although a decision was not expected before the 2002 election. As Democrats feared, Republicans won a majority in the state senate in 2002, with thirty seats to twenty-six for the Democrats (the previous breakdown was thirty-two Democrats to twenty-four Republicans). Although Baker was reelected, Republican Sonny Perdue captured the governorship from incumbent Democrat Roy Barnes (whose voter-mobilization tactics are discussed in chapter 2) and after taking office demanded that Baker drop the suit. Baker refused, and Perdue sued him.

In June 2003, the Supreme Court reversed the district court's decision for failing to adequately examine the entire plan and its effect on minority representation as a whole in the state senate, sending it back to the district court to consider these factors. Remarkably, the five justices who had voted to reverse the decision and remand it to the district court were appointed by Republicans. Justice Sandra Day O'Connor wrote the opinion and noted that the Voting Rights Act

> gives states the flexibility to implement the type of plan that Georgia has submitted for preclearance—a plan that increases the number of districts with a majority-black voting age population, even if it means that minority voters in some of those

districts will face a somewhat reduced opportunity to elect a candidate of their choice. . . . While courts and the Justice Department should be vigilant in ensuring that States neither reduce minority voters' effective exercise of the electoral franchise nor discriminate against them, the Voting Rights Act, as properly interpreted, should encourage the transition to a society where race no longer matters.

The decision by the Supreme Court to reverse and remand in *Georgia v. Ashcroft* is widely seen as a victory for Democrats in the state and for the use of "influence" districts. In 2007, the Voting Rights Act will expire, unless it is renewed. What would its expiration mean? As for vote dilution, the Fourteenth Amendment and the equal protection clause will not expire. Nonetheless, states such as Georgia would no longer need to seek preclearance for redistricting plans and other electoral changes, as it did in 2000. Should we not worry about the potential for majority voters to use electoral institutions to dilute minority votes? Will the nation decide in 2007 that race and ethnicity no longer matter in designing districts?

Vote Denial Today

Four mornings a year, Florida governor Jeb Bush and his cabinet sit in a basement room of the state capitol and interview convicted felons like John Eason and Cecil Taylor. Both Eason and Taylor have served their sentences, but according to Florida law, they have been stripped of their right to vote, serve on a jury, or hold public office unless the governor grants them clemency. Unless their rights are restored, many felons also cannot qualify for certain state-issued professional licenses—nursing and contracting licenses, for example. Cecil Taylor, who had been convicted of driving drunk and whose college art teacher came to speak on his behalf, was granted his rights. Bush said to Taylor: "I'm praying that you're not going to start drinking again. When we make these decisions, sometimes it puts us in a little bit of a precarious position in that you could let us down." John Eason, who had been convicted of a lewd act with a child in 1993, wanted a contractor's license so that he could take over his father's business. But Governor Bush declined to grant him his voting rights even though his sister came to vouch for him as a good uncle. Eason, frustrated, wondered: "The government thinks they're doing society a favor by showing that it's still convicting the bad people. But how does it benefit society to keep me down in this way?"[44]

Like Eason, Sukjong Lam was frustrated because she could not vote. In the fall of 2004, Lam had been a legal U.S. resident for four years, and when her son came home with bad grades, she was unable to talk to a teacher or counselor about the problem because even though more than one third of the students in the San Francisco school were, like her, from China, there was only one Cantonese-speaking counselor. Lam believed that if she and other Chinese immigrants could vote in school board elections, the school board would be more likely to provide help for the students and their parents. But she would not be eligible to apply for U.S. citizenship until 2006. Lam supported a referendum on the ballot in the city that fall that would extend voting rights to noncitizens in school board elections.[45] The proposition was narrowly defeated, by 51 percent of voters, who of course did not include Lam.

The Voting Rights Act, subsequent litigation, and court rulings have virtually eliminated the use of indirect methods of vote denial. Most instances of claimed minority-vote denial are isolated cases and in clear violation of federal and state laws. We are unlikely to return to the use of the poll tax, literacy tests, whites-only primaries, and other methods of directly denying minorities the vote. However, two indirect methods of vote denial that affect minorities disproportionately persist—the denial of the vote to felons and ex-felons and the denial of the vote to noncitizens. Although some have called for loosening the restrictions on voting for both of these groups, the efforts have met with little success.

How pervasive is felon disenfranchisement? Only Maine and Vermont allow prisoners to vote. Thirty-three states deny the vote to convicted offenders on parole, twenty-nine also disenfranchise offenders on probation, and fourteen states, like Florida, simply bar offenders from voting for life. These laws have disproportionate effects on African Americans (it is estimated that 1.4 million black males are disenfranchised through them) and, to a lesser extent, Latinos, who make up a disproportionate share of the prison population. Republican governor Bob Riley (whose tax plan was discussed in chapter 9) vetoed a measure passed by the Alabama legislature in June 2003 to allow ex-felons to vote in the state, angering Alabama's black legislators. Riley argued that the restriction was not racially disproportionate since 45 percent of the convicted felons were white.[46]

What is the impact of the disenfranchisement of noncitizens? As noted in chapter 5, after the passage of the Immigration Act of 1965, immigration to the United States increased dramatically, leading to a larger percentage of noncitizens in the population—from 1972 to 2000, the percentage of the noncitizen population tripled. We pointed out that McCarty, Poole, and Rosenthal (2005) showed that the growth in noncitizens, particularly poor ones, has led to a greater difference between the income of the median voter in the electorate and the income of the median worker in the population, reinforcing income inequality in the society. Noncitizens are overwhelming minority members, many of whom enter the country illegally. Figure 15.11 shows the estimated distribution of foreign-born residents by citizenship status and region of birth as of 2004, as measured by the census. Notice that over 60 percent of the U.S. foreign-born noncitizen population is from Latin America, largely Mexico. Yet the naturalization rate for this population and, correspondingly, the likelihood of voting are much lower than for immigrants from other regions. For example, of those who entered the United States between 2000 and 2004, the vast majority are from Latin

FIGURE 15.11
Foreign-Born Residents by Citizenship Status and Region of Birth, as of 2004

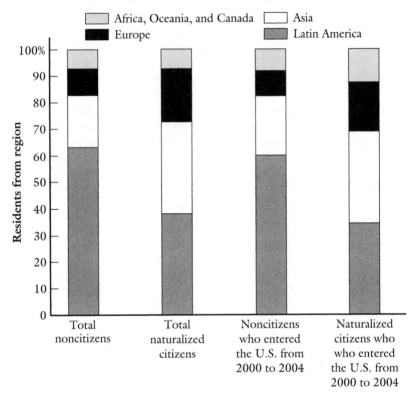

Source: U.S. Census Bureau.

America, yet immigrants from that region make up just under 35 percent of the foreign-born residents who were naturalized by 2004, and immigrants from Latin America make up less than 40 percent of all naturalized citizens. Hence, as immigration has grown, there has been a corresponding growth in Latino noncitizens in the population, which no doubt lessens the political clout of the growing Latino population in general.

Why are Latino immigrants less likely to be naturalized? There are two explanations: (1) some Latino immigrants—particularly Mexican Americans—see their time in the United States as temporary and the return to their place of birth as relatively feasible and (2) many of them enter the country illegally, making it more difficult to achieve citizenship. It is unclear whether this tendency will continue and lead to a further expansion in the number of resident noncitizens.

What We Know

We know that a history of vote denial and vote dilution severely limited the ability of minority voters to participate in elections and have their preferences represented. The Voting Rights Act has profoundly reduced both phenomena, by eliminating much of the vote denial and by regulating how elections are organized in states and localities. Most recently, the requirement that states maximize the number of legislative districts in which minorities are a majority has affected the design of legislative districts, leading to accusations of racial gerrymandering. Theory and evidence also suggest that the requirement has led to more conservatives in state legislatures but more liberals in Congress. However, much controversy remains over whether the federal government should continue to regulate states' electoral procedures to reduce vote dilution and how we measure vote dilution. Furthermore, some argue that the denial of the vote to ex-felons and noncitizens is a form of minority disenfranchisement.

Study Questions and Problems

1. On April 28, 2002, *The New York Times* reported that a town councilman from Stratford, Connecticut, Michael Singh, had resigned after evidence surfaced that he was not a citizen when he registered to vote. Singh was born in Jamaica and moved to the United States with his family when he was one year old. Evidence suggests that, like Singh, other noncitizens are able to register to vote because voting registrars typically have no formal procedure for checking citizenship status. Similarly, in some states with rules against ex-felons' voting, when a potential voter registers, his or her status as an ex-felon is not formally checked. In those states, election officials instead do periodic reviews of the voter rolls, which can vary in intensity and scope.
   a. Why might a state prefer such lax systems of checking voters' qualifications?
   b. How does the laxness of enforcement affect the representation of minorities who are likely not to meet the qualifications or to be suspected of not meeting them?
   c. Would a nationwide uniform voter registration system be a good thing or a bad thing for minority representation?
2. As this chapter is being written, Governor Arnold Schwarzenegger of California has proposed changing the redistricting process in the state so that it will be handled by a nonpartisan commission, in order to reduce partisan gerrymandering and increase the competitiveness of congressional and state legislative races.
   a. If the commission is instructed to maximize the number of Latino

and African American majority districts, how would the representation of voters in California be affected in both Congress and the state legislature?

    b. Would the Republican Party or the Democratic Party benefit more from such a constraint?

  3. One proposed alternative to single-member districts is the election of representatives from a multimember district using cumulative voting. Some small jurisdictions use cumulative voting, and for a number of years Illinois's state legislature was elected using this procedure. With cumulative voting—if two representatives are to be elected—each voter has two votes, which he or she can allocate in one of the following ways: (1) by voting for no candidate, (2) by casting one vote for one candidate, (3) by casting one vote for each of two candidates, or (4) by casting two votes for one candidate. Consider the example in the chapter in which David, Rita, and Mary elect two representatives. If they were using cumulative voting, who would win, and why? How does cumulative voting affect minority representation?

Notes

1. John Williams, "New 9th District Stokes Old Tensions: Bell, Green Trade Allegations in Racially Charged Dem Primary," *Houston Chronicle*, March 5, 2004.
2. Pam Easton, "Candidates Differ on Whether Race Played Role in Primary," Associated Press State & Local Wire, March 12, 2004.
3. Joe Black, "Peacemaker Bell Will Invite Green to Meet Dem Caucus," *Houston Chronicle*, March 19, 2004.
4. Quincy C. Collins, "Four Vying to Represent Redrawn District 25: Political Vets Pitted against Newcomers," *Corpus Christi Caller-Times*, March 6, 2004.
5. Guillermo X. Garcia, "Race Getting Nastier: Negative Ads in District 25 Demo Battle Hitting the Valley Airwaves," *San Antonio Express-News*, March 6, 2004.
6. Suzanne Gamboa, "Democrats Push to Protect Seats in Congress in GOP-drawn Districts," Associate Press State & Local Wire, March 9, 2004.
7. At this writing some efforts are under way to reopen the investigation of Till's murder based on new evidence. See Laura Parker, "Justice Pursued for Emmett Till," *USA Today*, March 11, 2004.
8. "Lynchers in Congress," *Charlottesville Reflector*, June 30, 1934.
9. Bill Curry, "An Unequal Society: Brutality and Segregation Afflict Hispanics," *Washington Post*, March 28, 1978.
10. Curry, "An Unequal Society."
11. The continued racial divide is shown in the 2002 film *The Two Towns of Jasper*.
12. Ken Herman, "Vanishing at Capitol: The White Democrat; As GOP Burgeons, Opposition Members Tend to Be Minorities," *Austin American-Statesman*, March 1, 2003.
13. The Mexican American population in the state was much smaller in that period than it is currently.
14. See Alt (1994) for details on the sources of the figures from 1947 to 1986.
15. See Davidson and Grofman (1994).
16. Haya El Nasser and Paul Overberg, "Index Charts Rise in Nation's Growth," *USA Today*, March 15, 2001.
17. Note that in a few jurisdictions during the nineteenth century, noncitizens were

allowed to vote. To some extent, denying citizenship to Asian Americans and those deemed "nonwhite" was an indirect method of vote denial rather than the explicit method, with its laws against black voting prior to the Civil War.

18. See Norrell (1998, pp. 36–37).

19. Secret ballots were introduced nationwide at this time. Although some scholars contend that the motive for using the secret ballot in the North was to reduce election fraud and bribery (because secret ballots made it difficult for a voter to prove to someone who paid for his or her vote that he or she had fulfilled the bargain), others argue that the motives of both northern and southern states were similar and that northern leaders desired to disenfranchise illiterate or non-English speaking immigrants. See Kousser (1992).

20. See McCarty, Poole, and Rosenthal (2005).

21. The Civil Rights Acts of 1957, 1960, and 1964 also attempted to increase black voting in the South, but they were largely ineffectual as they relied on court-based prosecution and were easily circumvented by southern judges and election officials.

22. Initially covered were Alabama, Alaska, Georgia, Louisiana, Mississippi, South Carolina, Virginia, twenty-six counties of North Carolina, and one in Arizona. In 1965 and 1966, other North Carolina and Arizona counties were added, as well as one each in Hawaii and Idaho. Alaska and some other counties were able to exempt themselves during the 1960s by showing that no test or device had been used to deny or abridge the right to vote on account of race during the last five years. When the act was amended in 1970 to extend the special provisions for another five years, the measure of voting discrimination was changed to the 1968 presidential election and extended for five years. Three boroughs of New York City—Manhattan, Brooklyn, and the Bronx—were added, as well as one county in Wyoming, two in California, five in Arizona, and a number of political subdivisions in Connecticut, New Hampshire, Maine, and Massachusetts. Some counties that had been exempted after 1965 were re-covered in 1970—four election districts in Alaska, a county in Idaho, and several counties in Arizona. In 1975, the act was further extended for seven years, and the coverage formula was amended to include those states and counties with a substantial language-minority population and English-only voting materials. This captured the entire states of Arizona, Alaska, and Texas and jurisdictions in Colorado, South Dakota, California, Florida, and North and South Carolina. In 1982, the act was extended for twenty-five years.

23. It is noteworthy that this was not necessarily true nationally. Some northern Democrats, although supporting the suppression of black political rights in the South, supported integration and black civil rights in their northern states, and some northern Republicans supported suppression of black civil rights in their states but opposed such suppression in the South. See Kousser (1992).

24. See *Allen v. State Board of Elections*. After the passage of the Voting Rights Act, the racial and ethnic effects of gerrymandering became an important political issue. The debate has centered on whether it is appropriate to gerrymander districts racially in order to increase minority representation rather than dilute minority votes. We discuss this recent issue later in the chapter.

25. Handley and Grofman (1994) compared the percentage of blacks elected to state legislatures from 1975 to 1985 based on whether the state legislature used multimember districts. They, too, found a higher percentage of blacks elected in state legislatures that used single-member districts than in those that used multimember districts, controlling for other factors that affected black representation at the time.

26. Although we assume that M voters split their votes between David and Rita equally, it is possible for M voters to coordinate on either David or Rita and al-

low Mary to come in second. For example, if they all decide that Rita is their second choice, Mary would get 54 votes, Rita would receive 77, and David would get only 46. But with a failure of coordination of just 9 voters (who might prefer David), Mary will still come in last.

27. In 1928, Oscar De Priest was elected from Illinois (the Chicago district).
28. In 1972, Andrew Young was elected from Georgia (the Atlanta district), and Barbara Jordan was elected from Texas (the Houston district). Jordan became the first African American woman in Congress from the South.
29. See Kousser (1999) for a review of the North Carolina experience.
30. See Kousser (1999).
31. See Bullock and Johnson (1992).
32. In *Hunt v. Cromartie* (2001), Justice Stevens, in his concurrence, wrote that a "bizarre configuration is the traditional hallmark of a political gerrymander."
33. Other candidates received the remaining votes.
34. R. G. Ratcliffe, "It's a Grand Old Sweep," *Houston Chronicle*, November 6, 2002.
35. Governor Rick Perry was fulfilling the term of George W. Bush, so technically he was not an incumbent. Some have suggested that white support was lower for these two candidates because of anti-minority biases, since Kirk is African American and Sanchez is Hispanic and both brought up issues relevant to minority voters in the campaign, driving whites away.
36. Herman, "Vanishing at Capitol."
37. Gary Susswein, "Redistricting Lessens Clout of Rural Areas," *Austin American-Statesman*, May 15, 2003.
38. Shotts (2003b) responded to the criticism of Lublin and Voss (2003).
39. Gromer Jeffers, "Voting with the Enemy on Redistricting?" *Dallas Morning News*, June 29, 2003.
40. Suzanne Gamboa, "Map Redrawing Provides Anticlimactic Outcome to Latino Hopes," Associated Press State & Local Wire, November 20, 2001.
41. Don Mason, "Hearings Enliven Redistrict Debate," *Houston Chronicle*, June 29, 2003.
42. Jeffers, "Voting with the Enemy on Redistricting?" Republicans were also alleged to have promised badly needed funding for medical school complexes in El Paso and the Rio Grande Valley, areas represented by Democratic state senators. See Guillermo X. Garcia, "Hearings Underscore Tensions on Redistricting," *San Antonio Express-News*, June 29, 2003.
43. See syllabus to *Georgia v. Ashcroft* (2003).
44. Abby Goodnough, "Fighting for Florida: Voting Rights of Florida Felons Scrutinized after 2000 Election," *New York Times*, March 28, 2004.
45. "Proposition F in California Would Let Non-Citizens Vote in Local School Board Elections," *Tavis Smiley*, NPR, October 19, 2004.
46. For a discussion of the relationship between race and felon disenfranchisement, see Behrens, Uggen, and Manza (2003).

~16~

The Future and Analyzing Elections

The 2008 Presidential Contest

As I write this chapter, it is three years until the next presidential election. In that election, voters like Fannie Jeffrey will be mobilized by groups—both benefit seeking and office seeking. Some voters may choose via the Internet. Others, newly registered, like Nora Galowitch in 2002, will vote for the first time. Candidates will choose policy positions in order to attract those voters—as Jeb Bush did in 1998—as well as those who will determine which candidates are nominated in direct primaries. Interest groups like the Culinary Workers in Las Vegas will provide candidates with campaign contributions, both to elect the candidate whose policy positions they prefer and to pay for the private favors that the candidates can provide. Candidates will spend those funds in attempts to influence voters by running campaign ads in places like Albuquerque.

Voters like Patsy Cunningham will attempt to use what information they have about the candidates' past records to decide whether to support them in the future. There will be referenda and initiatives on issues like abortion, gun control, tax changes, and gay marriage, and maybe for some voters there will be a recall election of their governor, as there was for Gray Davis, or their mayor, as there might have been for Dianne Feinstein. Some voters will also be choosing judges and prosecutors with little information beyond their sentencing choices and conviction rates, and some voters will be choosing public utility commissioners, knowing only how much their electricity costs.

Members of Congress like Charlie Norwood and Tom Osborne will run for reelection, or voters will choose between new candidates—such as Larry Weatherford, Betty McCollum, and Devin Nunes—for open seats; in some cases, as in Texas, the district boundaries may be different from those of the previous congressional election. State legislators like David Sibley as well as governors like Rick Perry and state-level elected officials will be on the ballot in some states. There will be minor-party and independent candidates like Angus King and Jesse Ventura, probably for all offices, and some will surprise voters and political experts by succeeding. And there will be something unexpected that will happen because the outcome of an election depends on the choices of voters on a given day (or period of days, when there is absentee and early voting), and predicting those voters' preferences perfectly is never possible. Psephologists will make predictions—some will be correct, some will not. Who would have predicted before November 2000 that a presidential contest would end up in the Supreme Court?

The result of the 2008 presidential election, like the result of the 2000 election, discussed in chapter 1, will shape American politics for the next four years. It will affect whether a Patient's Bill of Rights is passed by Congress and how voters choose in the midterm elections of 2010, as well as how America deals with threats of terrorism and war and many other aspects of life in the United States.

The Message and What We Know Redux

As noted in the introduction, this book has a message. It has the purposive message that current political science theory about the electoral process combined with empirical evidence can help us understand many aspects and features of U.S. elections. It also has the message of my perspective. Throughout the book, we have discussed the actors in elections—voters, candidates, party leaders, campaign contributors and interest group leaders, elected officials—with the presumption that each is making the choices that best meet his or her goals, albeit sometimes seemingly not rationally from the perspective of the observer. We have also seen the ubiquitous role of institutions in affecting the decisions of these actors.

We have observed as well the flaws in the electoral system, as discussed in the introduction. Voters in Florida who used the butterfly ballot in 2000 probably did not have their votes counted as they wished. If forces cause those who participate to become polarized on policy issues, as some evidence suggests has happened in recent years, it may become more difficult for voters to enact moderate policies; instead, candidates will become polarized even when moderate voters are a plurality of the electorate. Voters' concerns over nonpolicy or valence issues can also result in the election of more extreme candidates. We have seen as well that campaign finance regulation has not reduced the use of private money to finance election campaigns, and we have seen that incumbents' advantages in raising resources can give them advantages in elections. Many voters are not well informed about candidates' actions and have little incentive to become informed. Evidence suggests that the information about elected officials provided to voters by the media is sometimes biased. Moreover, sometimes the information that voters do have leads them to reward (punish) elected officials for actions that may not have been (may have been) optimal. Elected officials are similarly sometimes in the dark when trying to figure out voters' preferences, and the process of measuring public opinion and predicting elections is not easy and to some extent is becoming less so—leading to more uncertainty. We have seen that gerrymandering can reduce the ability of some voters to elect representatives of their choice and can lead to a state legislature or delegation to Congress that has an ideological bias that is not representative of the state. Separation of powers, majority control of Congress, and federalism can limit the influence of voters through their representatives in Congress and state offices. The dominance of the two major political parties can limit the representation of preferences of those voters whose preferences do not easily fit with the standard liberal-conservative division on issue positions. Although the use of vote denial and vote dilution to limit the ability of minorities to participate in elections has been significantly reduced, in the process new questions have arisen about the effects of using race as a criterion in gerrymandering and about the restrictions on voting that affect some groups more than others.

I believe this is a realistic appraisal. Yet I am optimistic. The frequency of U.S. elections means that candidates need to appeal to voters frequently—particularly voters whose preferences are at the median of the distribution. Although participation is costly and the cost may result in extremists' having a greater say and influencing policy choices, there are incentives for groups of voters to mobilize when they believe their preferences are not being considered, as has been the case historically and continues to be—for example, with the noncitizen voters in San Francisco pushing for the right to vote in school board elections. When challengers can advertise incumbents' records, voters can learn and make more informed decisions. Efforts to provide challengers with extra resources when they face opponents who are wealthy is one way of mitigating the effects of campaign funds on elections. Even biased information can allow voters to be more informed about politics and make better decisions, if preferences are heterogeneous or voters are seeking unbiased information. Some states, like Iowa, use neutral methods of redistricting. And victories by minor-party and independent candidates in local and state elections can give voters whose preferences are not aligned with either major party the chance to express them.

I am optimistic as well because of the changing nature of the electoral process. We continually grapple with the process—with what the role of money in campaigns should be; how to deal with voters' low levels, and perhaps biased sources, of information; how to best design legislative districts that change with changes in the population while giving all voters, minorities included, the chance of representation; and where to draw the lines that determine who can participate in electoral politics. As I write this chapter, the Federal Election Commission and Congress are deciding how to treat campaign expenditures by 527s and how to deal with other new factors in campaigns, such as Web logs. In some states, battles are still being fought over how congressional district lines will be drawn in response to the 2000 census, boundaries that will be redrawn again after the 2010 census. Other states, like California, are considering the adoption of neutral methods of redistricting. Some states are contemplating changing the rules that affect voter registration, ballot access, and how primaries are run. There are proposals to eliminate the Electoral College, hold a national presidential primary, institute terms limits for members of Congress, relax the restrictions on felons' and noncitizens' voting, and institute national referenda and initiative procedures, as well as to make many other changes in the electoral institutions at the federal, state, and local levels of government. Such changes would affect how elections are conducted, which voters vote, how candidates choose positions and which candidates win, and the ability of the major political parties to continue to dominate U.S. elections. As noted in the introduction, change has risks as well as advantages. Sometimes solutions have unintended consequences—the reforms of the presidential nomination process enacted by the Democratic Party were not anticipated to lead to the highly front-loaded primary system that existed in 2004. But whether we wish it to or not, the electoral process will change.

References

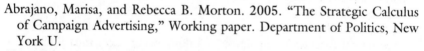

Abrajano, Marisa, and Rebecca B. Morton. 2005. "The Strategic Calculus of Campaign Advertising," Working paper. Department of Politics, New York U.

Abramowitz, Alan I. 1988. "An Improved Model for Predicting Presidential-Election Outcomes." *PS: Political Science & Politics* 21(4):843–47.

Abramowitz, Alan I. 2004. "When Good Forecasts Go Bad: The Time-for-Change Model and the 2004 Presidential Election." *PS: Political Science & Politics* 36(4):745–46.

Abramowitz, Alan I., and Walter J. Stone. 1984. *Nomination Politics: Party Activists and Presidential Choice.* New York: Praeger.

Abramson, Paul R., John H. Aldrich, and David W. Rohde. 2002. *Change in Continuity in the 2000 Elections.* Washington, D.C.: Congressional Quarterly Press.

Abramson, Paul R., John H. Aldrich, and David W. Rohde. 2003. *Change and Continuity in the 2000 and 2002 Elections.* Washington, D.C.: Congressional Quarterly Press.

Adams, Gregory D. 1997. "Abortion: Evidence of an Issue Evolution." *American Journal of Political Science* 41(3):718–37.

Adams, James D., and Lawrence W. Kenny. 1986. "Optimal Tenure of Elected Public Officials." *Journal of Law & Economics* 29(2):303–28.

Aldrich, John H. 1980. *Before the Convention.* Chicago: U. of Chicago Press.

Aldrich, John H. 1995. *Why Parties? The Origin and Transformation of Party Politics in America*. Chicago: U. of Chicago Press.

Aldrich, John H., and William T. Bianco. 1992. "A Game-Theoretic Model of Party Affiliation of Candidates and Office Holders." *Mathematical & Computer Modelling* 16(8–9):103–16.

Alesina, Alberto. 1988. "Credibility and Policy Convergence in a Two-Party System with Rational Voters." *American Economic Review* 78(4):796–806.

Alesina, Alberto, John Londregan, and Howard Rosenthal. 1993. "A Model of the Political Economy of the United States." *American Political Science Review* 87 (March):12–33.

Alesina, Alberto, and Howard Rosenthal. 1995. *Partisan Politics, Divided Government, and the Economy*. Cambridge: Cambridge U. Press.

Alt, James. 1994. "The Impact of the Voting Rights Act on Black and White Voter Registration in the South." In Davidson and Grofman, *Quiet Revolution in the South*, pp. 351–77.

Alterman, Eric. 2003. *What Liberal Media? The Truth about Bias and the News*. New York: Basic Books.

Althaus, S. L. 1998. "Information Effects in Collective Preferences." *American Political Science Review* 92 (September):545–58.

Alvarez, R. Michael. 1997. *Information and Elections*. Ann Arbor: U. of Michigan Press.

Alvarez, R. Michael, and John Brehm. 2002. *Hard Choices, Easy Answers: Values, Information, and American Public Opinion*. Princeton, N.J.: Princeton U. Press.

Alvarez, R. Michael, and Garrett Glasgow. 1997. "Do Voters Learn from Presidential Election Campaigns?" Working paper. California Institute of Technology, Pasadena.

Alvarez, R. Michael, and Matthew M. Schousen. 1993. "Policy Moderation of Conflicting Expectations: Testing the Intentional Models of Split-Ticket Voting." *American Politics Quarterly* 21(4):410–38.

Ansolabehere, Stephen, John de Figueiredo, and James Snyder. 2003. "Why Is There So Little Money in U.S. Politics?" *Journal of Economic Perspectives* 17:105–30.

Ansolabehere, Stephen, and Alan S. Gerber. 1996. "The Effects of Filing Fees and Petition Requirements on U.S. House Elections." *Legislative Studies Quarterly* 21:249–64.

Ansolabehere, Stephen, Alan S. Gerber, and James Snyder. 2002. "Equal Votes, Equal Money: Court-Ordered Redistricting and Public Expenditures in the American States." *American Political Science Review* 96 (December):767–77.

Ansolabehere, Stephen, and Shanto Iyengar. 1995. *Going Negative: How Political Advertisements Shrink and Polarize the Electorate*. New York: Free Press.

Ansolabehere, Stephen, Shanto Iyengar, Adam Simon, and N. Valentino.

1994. "Does Attack Advertising Demobilize the Electorate?" *American Political Science Review* 88 (June):829–38.

Ansolabehere, Stephen, Erik Snowberg, and James Snyder. 2004. "Statistical Bias in Newspaper Reporting: The Case of Campaign Finance." Working paper presented at the annual meetings of the Public Choice Society, Baltimore.

Ansolabehere, Stephen, and James Snyder. 1997. "Money, Elections, and Candidate Quality." *Legislative Studies Quarterly* 22:124–24.

Ansolabehere, Stephen, and James Snyder. 2000. "Valence Politics and Equilibrium in Spatial Election Models." *Public Choice* 103(3–4):327–36.

Ansolabehere, Stephen, and James Snyder. 2002. "The Incumbency Advantages in U.S. Elections: An Analysis of State and Federal Offices, 1942–2000." Working paper. Massachusetts Institute of Technology, Cambridge.

Ansolabehere, Stephen, James Snyder, and Charles Stewart. 2001. "Candidate Positioning in U.S. House Elections." *American Journal of Political Science* 45(1):136–59.

Aragones, E., and Thomas R. Palfrey. 2002. "Mixed Equilibrium in a Downsian Model with a Favored Candidate." *Journal of Economic Theory* 103(1):131–61.

Arnold, R. Douglas. 2004. *Congress, the Press, and Political Accountability.* New York: Russell Sage Foundation.

Ashworth, Scott. 2003. "Campaign Finance and Voter Welfare with Entrenched Incumbents." Working paper. Princeton U., Princeton, N.J.

Atkin, Charles K., Lawrence Bowen, Oguz B. Nayman, and Kenneth G. Sheinkopf. 1973. "Quality versus Quantity in Televised Political Ads." *Public Opinion Quarterly* 37:209–24.

Atkin, Charles K., and Gary Heald. 1976. "Effects of Political Advertising." *Public Opinion Quarterly* 40:216–28.

Austen-Smith, David. 1987. "Interest Groups, Campaign Contributions, and Probabilistic Voting." *Public Choice* 52(2):123–39.

Austen-Smith, David, and Jeffrey S. Banks. 1989. "Electoral Accountability and Incumbency." In *Models of Strategic Choice in Politics.* Ann Arbor: U. of Michigan Press.

Banks, Jeffrey S., and John Duggan. 2000. "A Multidimensional Model of Repeated Elections." Working paper. U. of Rochester, Rochester, New York.

Banks, Jeffrey S., and Rodney Kiewiet. 1989. "Explaining Patterns of Candidate Competition in Congressional Elections." *American Journal of Political Science* 33(4):997–1015.

Banks, Jeffrey S., and R. K. Sundaram. 1993. "Moral Hazard and Adverse Selection in a Model of Repeated Elections." In William A. Barnett, ed., *Political Economy: Institutions, Information Competition, and Representation.* Cambridge: Cambridge U. Press.

Barnett, James D. 1912. "The Operation of the Recall in Oregon." *American Political Science Review* 6 (February):41–53.

Barnouw, Erik. 1979. *Sponsor: Notes on a Modern Potentate*. Oxford: Oxford U. Press.

Baron, David. 1989. "Service-Induced Campaign Contributions and the Electoral Equilibrium," *Quarterly Journal of Economics* 104(1):45–72 February.

Baron, David. 1994. "Electoral Competition with Informed and Uninformed Voters." *American Political Science Review* 88 (March):33–47.

Baron, David. 2004. "Persistent Media Bias." Working paper. Stanford Graduate School of Business, Stanford, Calif.

Barone, Michael. 1998. *Almanac of American Politics*. Washington D.C.: National Journal.

Barone, Michael, with Richard E. Cohen. 2003. *The Almanac of American Politics 2004*. Washington, D.C.: National Journal.

Barone, Michael, with Richard E. Cohen and Grant Ujifusa. 2001. *The Almanac of American Politics 2002*. Washington, D.C.: National Journal.

Barone, Michael, and Grant Ujifusa. 1999. *The Almanac of American Politics 2000*. Washington, D.C.: National Journal.

Bartels, Larry M. 1988. *Presidential Primaries and the Dynamics of Public Choice*. Princeton, N.J.: Princeton U. Press.

Bartels, Larry M. 1992. "The Impact of Electioneering in the United States." In D. Butler and A. Ranney, eds., *Electioneering*, pp. 244–77. New York: Oxford U. Press.

Bartels, Larry M. 1993. "Messages Received: The Political Impact of Media Exposure." *American Political Science Review* 87 (June):267–85.

Bartels, Larry M. 1996. "Uninformed Votes: Information Effects in Presidential Elections." *American Journal of Political Science* 40(1):194–230.

Bean, Louis H. 1948. *How to Predict Elections*. New York: Alfred A. Knopf.

Behrens, Angela, Christopher Uggen, and Jeff Manza. 2003. "Ballot Manipulation and the 'Menace of Negro Domination': Racial Threat and Felon Disenfranchisement in the United States, 1850–2002." *American Journal of Sociology* 109(3):559–605.

Bendor, Jonathan, Daniel Diermeier, and Michael M. Ting. 2003. "A Behavioral Model of Turnout." *American Political Science Review* 97 (May):261–80.

Bennett, Robert. n.d. *Taming the Electoral College without Constitutional Amendment*. Unpublished manuscript.

Berdahl, Clarence. 1942. "Party Membership in the United States, I." *American Political Science Review* 36 (February):16–50.

Berelson, B. R., Paul F. Lazarsfeld, and W. N. McPhee. 1954. *Voting: A Study of Opinion Formation in a Presidential Election*. Chicago: U. of Chicago Press.

Berg, Joyce, Robert Forsythe, Forrest Nelson, and Thomas Rietz, "Results from a Dozen Years of Election Futures Markets Research," forthcoming in *The Handbook of Experimental Economics Results*, Charles R. Plott and Vernon L. Smith, editors. Amersterdam: Elsevier Science.

Berg, Joyce, and Thomas A. Rietz. 2005. "The Iowa Electronic Market: Lessons Learned and Answers Yearned." In Paul Tetlock and Robert Litan, eds., *Information Markets: A New Way of Making Decisions in the Public and Private Sectors.* Washington, D.C.: AEI-Brookings Joint Center.

Berger, Mark, Michael C. Munger, and R. F. Potthoff. 2000. "The Downsian Model Predicts Divergence." *Journal of Theoretical Politics* 12(2):228–40.

Berinsky, Adam J. 2002. "Silent Voices: Social Welfare Policy Opinions and Political Equality in America." *American Journal of Political Science* 46(2):276–87.

Berinsky, Adam J. 2004. "American Public Opinion in the 1930s and 1940s: The Analysis of Quota-Controlled Sample Survey Data." Working paper. Department of Political Science, Massachusetts Institute of Technology, Cambridge.

Berinsky, Adam J., Nancy Burns, and Michael W. Traugott. 1998. "Who Votes by Mail? A Dynamic Model of the Individual-Level Consequences of Vote-by-Mail Systems." Working paper. Center for Political Studies, University of Michigan, Ann Arbor.

Berrens, Robert P., Alok K. Bohara, Hank Jenkins-Smith, Carol Silva, and David L. Weimer. 2003. "The Advent of Internet Surveys for Political Research: A Comparison of Telephone and Internet Samples." *Political Analysis* 11(1):1–22.

Besley, Timothy, and Anne Case. 1995. "Does Electoral Accountability Affect Economic Policy Choices: Evidence from Gubernatorial Term Limits." *Quarterly Journal of Economics* 110(3):769–98.

Besley, Timothy, and Anne Case. 2000.

Besley, Timothy, and Anne Case. 2003. "Political Institutions and Policy Choices: Evidence from the United States." *Journal of Economic Literature* 4(1):7–73.

Besley, Timothy, and Stephen Coate. 1997. "An Economic Model of Representative Democracy." *Quarterly Journal of Economics* 112(1):85–114.

Besley, Timothy, and Stephen Coate. 2003. "Elected versus Appointed Regulators: Theory and Evidence." *Journal of the European Economic Association* 1(5):1176–1206.

Bibby, John F., Cornelius P. Cotter, James L. Gibson, and Robert J. Huckshorn. 1990. "Parties in State Politics." In Virginia Gray, Herbert Jacob, and Robert B. Albritton, eds., *Politics in the American States*, 5th ed. Glenview, Ill.: Scott Foresman.

Bibby, John F., and L. Sandy Maisel. 1989. *Two Parties—Or More?* Boulder, Colo.: Westview Press.

Binder, Sarah. 1997. *Minority Rights, Majority Rule: Partisanship and the Development of Congress.* Washington, D.C.: Brookings Institution.

Bohn, T. W. 1968. "Broadcasting National Election Returns—1916–1948." *Journal of Broadcasting* 12(3):267–86.

Bohn, T. W. 1980. "Broadcasting National Election Returns, 1952–1976." *Journal of Communication* 30(4):140–53.

Bolton, Patrick, and G. Roland. 1997. "The Breakup of Nations: A Political Economy Analysis." *Quarterly Journal of Economics* 112(4):1057–90.

Born, Richard. 1994a. "Split-Ticket Voters, Divided Government, and Fiorina's Policy Balancing Model." *Legislative Studies Quarterly* 19:95–115.

Born, Richard. 1994b. "Rejoinder." *Legislative Studies Quarterly* 19:126–29.

Bott, Alexander J. 1991. *Handbook of United States Election Laws and Practices: Political Rights.* New York: Greenwood Press.

Bovitz, Gregory L., James N. Druckman, and Arthur Lupia. 2002. "When Can a News Organization Lead Public Opinion? Ideology versus Market Forces in Decisions to Make News." *Public Choice* 113(1–2):127–55.

Bowler, Shawn, and T. Donovan. 2002. "Do Voters Have a Cue? Television Advertisements as a Source of Information in Citizen-Initiated Referendum Campaigns." *European Journal of Political Research* 41(6):777–93.

Boylan, Richard T., John Ledyard, and Richard D. McKelvey. 1996. "Political Competition in a Model of Economic Growth: Some Theoretical Results." *Economic Theory* 7(2):191–205.

Boylan, Richard T., and Richard D. McKelvey. 1995. "Voting over Economic Plans." *American Economic Review* 85(4):860–71.

Brady, Henry E. 1996. "Strategy and Momentum in Presidential Primaries." In John R. Freeman, ed., *Political Analysis*, vol. 5. Ann Arbor: U. of Michigan Press.

Brehm, John. 1993. *The Phantom Respondents: Opinion Surveys and Political Representation.* Ann Arbor: U. of Michigan Press.

Brians, Craig Leonard, and Martin P. Wattenberg. 1996. "Campaign Issue Knowledge and Salience: Comparing Reception from TV Commercials, TV News, and Newspapers." *American Journal of Political Science* 40(1):172–93.

Brillinger, David. 2002. "John W. Tukey: His Life and Professional Contributions." *Annals of Statistics* 30(6):1535–75.

Brinkley, Douglas. 2004. *Tour of Duty: John Kerry and the Vietnam War.* New York: William Morrow.

Brody, Richard. 1978. "The Puzzle of Political Participation in America." In A. King, ed., *The New American Political System*, pp. 287–324. Washington, D.C.: American Enterprise Institute for Public Policy Research.

Buell, Emmett H., Jr. 1991. "Meeting Expectations? Major Newspaper Coverage of Candidates during the 1988 Exhibition Season." In Emmett H. Buell, Jr., and Lee Sigelman, eds., *Nominating the President*, pp. 150–95. Knoxville: U. of Tennessee Press.

Bullock, Charles S., III, and Loch K. Johnson. 1992. *Runoff Elections in the United States.* Chapel Hill: U. of North Carolina Press.

Burden, Barry C. 2004. "Minor Parties in the 2000 Presidential Election." In Herbert F. Weisberg and Clyde Wilcox, eds., *Models of Voting in Presidential Elections: The 2000 U.S. Election*, pp. 206–27. Stanford, Calif.: Stanford U. Press.

Burden, Barry C. forthcoming. "Minor Parties and Strategic Voting in Recent U.S. Presidential Elections." *Electoral Studies.*

Burden, Barry C., and David C. Kimball. 1998. "A New Approach to the Study of Ticket Splitting." *American Political Science Review* 92 (September):533–44.

Burstein, P. 1985. *Discrimination, Jobs, and Politics.* Chicago: U. of Chicago Press, 1998.

Burstein, P. 1998. "Bringing the Public Back In: Should Sociologists Consider the Impact of Public Opinion on Public Policy?" *Social Forces* 77(1):27–62.

Butler, David. 1998. "Reflections on British Elections and Their Study." *Annual Review of Political Science* 1:451–64.

Caesar, James W. 1982. *Reforming the Reforms: A Critical Analysis of the Presidential Selection Process.* Cambridge, Mass.: Ballinger.

Cain, Bruce. 1985. "Assessing the Partisan Effects of Redistricting." *American Political Science Review* 79 (June):320–32.

Cain, Bruce, John Ferejohn, and Morris P. Fiorina. 1987. *The Personal Vote: Constituency Service and Electoral Independence.* Cambridge, Mass.: Harvard U. Press.

Caltech-MIT Voting Technology Project. 2002.

Calvert, Randall. 1985. "Robustness of the Multidimensional Voting Model: Candidates' Motivations, Uncertainty, and Convergence." *American Journal of Political Science* 29(1):69–95.

Cameron, Charles M. 2000. *Veto Bargaining: Presidents and the Politics of Negative Power.* Cambridge: Cambridge U. Press.

Cameron, Charles M., and James M. Enelow. 1992. "Asymmetric Policy Effects, Campaign Contributions, and the Spatial Theory of Elections." *Mathematical and Computer Modeling* 16(8/9):117–32.

Campbell, Angus, Philip E. Converse, Warren E. Miller, and Donald E. Stokes. 1960. *The American Voter.* New York:John Wiley & Sons.

Campbell, James E. 1987. "The Revised Theory of Surge and Decline." *American Journal of Political Science* 31(4):965–79.

Campbell, James E. 1992. "Forecasting the Presidential Vote in the States." *American Journal of Political Science* 36(2):386–407.

Campbell, James E. 2000. *The American Campaign: U.S. Presidential Campaigns and the National Vote.* College Station: Texas A&M U. Press.

Campbell, James E. 2004. "Forecasting the Presidential Vote in 2004: Placing Preference Polls in Context." *PS: Political Science & Politics* 36(4):386–407.

Campbell, James E. 2004. "Introduction—The 2004 Presidential Election Forecasts." *PS: Political Science & Politics* 36(4)733–35.

Campbell, James E., and James C. Garand. 2000. *Before the Vote: Forecasting American National Elections.* Thousand Oaks, Calif.: Sage Publications.

Campbell, James E., and K. A. Wink. 1990. "Trial-Heat Forecasts of the Presidential Vote." *American Politics Quarterly* 18(3):251–69.

Canes-Wrone, Brandice, Michael C. Herron, and Kenneth W. Shotts. 2001. "Leadership and Pandering: A Theory of Executive Policymaking." *American Journal of Political Science* 45(3):532–50.

Canes-Wrone, Brandice, and Kenneth W. Shotts. 2004. "The Conditional Nature of Presidential Responsiveness to Public Opinion." *American Journal of Political Science* 48(4):690–706.

Carey, John W., Richard G. Niemi, and Linda W. Powell. 1998. "The Effects of Term Limits on State Legislatures." *Legislative Studies Quarterly* 23:271–300.

Carmines, Edward G., and James A. Stimson. 1989. *Issue Evolution: Race and the Transformation of American Politics.* Princeton, N.J.: Princeton U. Press.

Carmines, Edward G., and James A. Stimson. 1992. "Party Politics in the Wake of the Voting Rights Act." In Grofman and Davidson, *Controversies in Minority Voting.*

Caro, Robert A. 1981. *The Years of Lyndon Johnson.* Vol. 1, *The Path to Power.* New York: Alfred A. Knopf.

Charlesworth, James C. 1948. "Is Our Two-Party System Natural?" *Annals of the American Academy of Political & Social Science* 259:1–9.

Clarke, Richard A. 2004. *Against All Enemies: Inside America's War on Terror.* New York: Free Press.

Coate, Stephen. 2004a. "Political Competition with Campaign Contributions and Informative Advertising." *Journal of the European Economic Association* 2(5):772–804.

Coate, Stephen. 2004b. "Pareto-Improving Campaign Finance Policy." *American Economic Review* 94(3):628–55.

Coleman, James S., E. Heau, R. Peabody, and L. Rigsby. 1964. "Computers and Election Analysis—*The New York Times* Project." *Public Opinion Quarterly* 28:418–46.

Condorcet, Marquis de. 1785. *Essai sur l'application de l'analyse à la probabilité des décisions rendues à la pluralité des voix.* Paris: l'Imprimerie.

Congressional Quarterly. 1982–94. *America Votes.* Washington D.C.: Elections Research Center, Congressional Quarterly Press.

Cook, Fay Lomax, Jason Barabas, and Benjamin I. Page. 2002. "Invoking Public Opinion: Policy Elites and Social Security." *Public Opinion Quarterly* 66:235–64.

Cook, Rhodes. 1989. "The Nominating Process." In Michael Nelson, ed., *The Elections of 1988.* Washington, D.C.: Congressional Quarterly Press.

Cook, Rhodes. 1997. "CQ Roundtable: GOP Wants a Revamp of Primary Process." *Congressional Quarterly*, August 9, 1942.

Cooper, Alexandra, and Michael C. Munger. 1996. "The (Un)Predictability of Presidential Primaries with Many Candidates: Some Simulation Evidence." Paper presented at the annual meetings of the American Political Science Association, San Francisco.

Coulter, Ann. 2002. *Slander: Liberal Lies about the American Right.* New York: Crown.

Cox, Gary W. 1997. *Making Votes Count: Strategic Coordination in the World's Electoral Systems.* Cambridge: Cambridge U. Press.

Cox, Gary W., and Jonathan N. Katz. 2002. *Elbridge Gerry's Salamander: The Electoral Consequences of the Reapportionment Revolution.* Cambridge: Cambridge U. Press.

Cox, Gary W., and Mathew McCubbins. Forthcoming. *Legislative Leviathan Revisited.*

Cukierman, Alex, and Allan H. Meltzer. 1986. "A Theory of Ambiguity, Credibility, and Inflation under Discretion and Asymmetric Information." *Econometrica* 54 (September):1099–1128.

Daniel, K., and John R. Lott, Jr., 1997. "Term Limits and Electoral Competitiveness: Evidence from California's State Legislative Races." *Public Choice* 90(1–4):165–84.

David, Paul T., and Ralph Eisenberg. 1961. *Devaluation of the Urban and Suburban Vote.* Charlottesville: U. of Virginia Press.

Davidson, Chandler, and Bernard Grofman. 1994. *Quiet Revolution in the South.* Princeton, N.J.: U. of Princeton Press.

Delli Carpini, Michael X. 1984. "Scooping the Voters? The Consequences of the Networks' Early Call of the 1980 Presidential Race." *Journal of Politics* 46(3):866–85.

Dickey, Francis W. 1915: "The Presidential Preference Primary." *American Political Science Review* 9(3):467–87.

DiMaggio, Paul, John Evans, and Bethany Bryson. 1996. "Have Americans' Social Attitudes Become More Polarized?" *American Journal of Sociology* 102 (3):690–775.

Dion, Douglas. 2001. *Turning the Legislative Thumbscrew: Minority Rights and Procedural Change in Legislative Politics.* Ann Arbor: U. of Michigan Press.

Domke D., D. P. Fan, M. Fibison, D. V. Shah, Steven S. Smith, and M. D. Watts. 1997. "Term Limits and Electoral Competitiveness: Evidence from California's State Legislative Races." *Journalism & Mass Communication Quarterly* 74(4):718–37.

Downs, Anthony. 1957. *An Economic Theory of Democracy.* New York: Harper & Row.

Duverger, Maurice. 1954. *Political Parties.* New York: John Wiley & Sons.

Edison Media Research and Mitofsky International. 2005. *Evaluation of Edison/Mitofsky Election System 2004.* January 19. http://www.exit-poll.net/election-night/EvaluationJan192005.pdf.

Edlund, L., and Rohini Pande. 2002. "Why Have Women Become Left-

Wing? The Political Gender Gap and the Decline in Marriage." *Quarterly Journal of Economics* 117(3):917–61.

Eisinger, Robert M., and Jeremy Brown. 1998. "Polling as a Means toward Presidential Autonomy: Emil Hurja, Hadley Cantril, and the Roosevelt Administration." *International Journal of Public Opinion Research* 10(3):237–56.

Epstein, David, and Sharon O'Halloran. 1999. "Measuring the Electoral and Policy Impact of Majority-Minority Voting Districts." *American Journal of Political Science* 43(2):367–95.

Epstein, Leon. 1986. *Political Parties in the American Mold*. Madison: U. of Wisconsin Press.

Erikson, Robert S. 1972. "Malapportionment, Gerrymandering, and Party Fortunes in Congressional Elections." *American Political Science Review* 66 (December):1234–45.

Erikson, Robert S., Michael B. MacKuen, and James A. Stimson. 2002. *The Macro Polity*. Cambridge: Cambridge U. Press.

Erikson, Robert S., Gerald C. Wright, and John P. McIver. 1993. *Statehouse Democracy*. Cambridge: Cambridge U. Press.

Evans, John. 2003. "Have Americans' Attitudes Become More Polarized?—An Update." *Social Science Quarterly* 84:71–90.

Fair, Ray C. 1978. "The Effect of Economic Events on Votes for President." *Review of Economics & Statistics* 60:159–73.

Fair, Ray C. 1996. "Econometrics and Presidential Elections." *Journal of Economic Perspectives* 10:89–102.

Fair, Ray C. 2004. "A Vote Equation and the 2004 Election." Ray C. Fair Web site at Yale University. http://fairmodel.econ.yale.edu/vote2004/vot1104a.pdf.

Feddersen, Timothy J. 1992. "A Voting Model Implying Duverger's Law and Positive Turnout." *American Journal of Political Science* 36(4):938–62.

Feddersen, Timothy and Wolfgang Pesendorfer (1996). "The swing voter's curse." *The American Economic Review* 86(3):408–24.

——— (1997). "Voting behavior and information aggregation in elections with private information." *Econometrica* 65(5):1029–1058.

——— (1999). "Abstention in elections with asymmetric information and diverse preferences." *American Political Science Review* 93(2):381–398.

Feddersen, Timothy J., and Alvaro Sandroni. 2002. "A Theory of Participation in Elections with Ethical Voters." Working paper. Managerial Economics and Decision Sciences Department, Northwestern University, Evanston, Ill.

Feld, Scott, and Bernard Grofman. 1991. "Incumbency Advantage, Voter Loyalty, and the Benefit of the Doubt." *Journal of Theoretical Politics* 3(2):115–37.

Fenno, Richard F., Jr. 1997. *Learning to Govern: An Institutional View of the 104th Congress*. Washington, D.C.: Brookings Institution.

Fey, Mark. 1997. "Stability and Coordination in Duverger's Law: A Formal

Model of Preelection Polls and Strategic Voting." *American Political Science Review* 91 (March):135–47.

Filer, John, Lawrence W. Kenny, and Rebecca B. Morton. 1991. "Voting Laws, Educational Policies, and Minority Turnout." *Journal of Law & Economics* 34(2, pt. 1):371–93.

Filer, John, Lawrence W. Kenny, and Rebecca B. Morton. 1993. "Redistribution, Income, and Voting." *American Journal of Political Science* 37(1):63–87.

Finkel, S. E. 1993. "Reexamining the 'Minimal Effects' Model in Recent Presidential Campaigns." *Journal of Politics* 55(1):1–21.

Fiorina, Morris P. 1973. "Electoral Margins, Constituency Influence, and Policy Moderation—Critical Assessment." *American Politics Quarterly* 1(4):479–98.

Fiorina, Morris P. 1981. *Retrospective Voting in American National Elections.* New Haven, Conn.: Yale U. Press, 1999.

Fiorina, Morris P. 1992. *Divided Government.* New York: Macmillan.

Fiorina, Morris P. 1994. "Response to Born." *Legislative Studies Quarterly* 19:117–25.

Fiorina, Morris P., with Samuel J. Abrams and Jeremy C. Pope. 2005. *Culture War? The Myth of a Polarized America.* New York: Pearson/Longman.

Foley, D. 1967. "Resource Allocation and the Public Sector." *Yale Economic Essays* 7:45–98.

Forsythe, Robert, Roger B. Myerson, Thomas A. Rietz, and Robert J. Weber. 1993. "An Experiment on Coordination in Multicandidate Elections: The Importance of Polls and Election Histories." *Social Choice & Welfare* 10 (July):223–47.

Forsythe, Robert, Forrest Nelson, George R. Neumann, and Jack Wright. 1992. "Anatomy of an Experimental Political Stock Market." *American Economic Review* 82(5):1142–61.

Forsythe, Robert, Thomas A. Rietz, and Thomas Ross. 1999. "Wishes, Expectations, and Actions: A Survey on Price Formation in Election Stock Markets." *Journal of Economic Behavior & Organization* 39 (May):83–110.

Foyle, Douglas C. 2004. "Leading the Public to War? The Influence of American Public Opinion on the Bush Administration's Decision to Go to War in Iraq." *International Journal of Public Opinion Research* 16(3):269–94.

Francis, Wayne, and Lawrence W. Kenny. 1999. *Up the Political Ladder: Career Paths in U.S. Politics.* Thousand Oaks, Calif.: Sage.

Francis, Wayne, Lawrence W. Kenny, Rebecca B. Morton, and Amy Schmidt. 1996. "Evidence on Electoral Accountability in the U.S. Senate: Are Unfaithful Agents Really Punished?" *Economic Inquiry* 34(3):545–67.

Frank, Thomas. 2004. *What's the Matter with Kansas? How Conservatives Won the Heart of America.* New York: Metropolitan Books.

Franken, Al. 2003. *Lies and the Lying Liars Who Tell Them: A Fair and Balanced Look at the Right.* New York: E. P. Dutton.

Frankovic, Kathleen A. 2003. "News Organizations' Responses to the Mistakes of Election 2000: Why They Will Continue to Project Elections." *Public Opinion Quarterly* 67:19–31.

Frymer, Paul. 1994. "Ideological Consensus within Divided Government." *Political Science Quarterly* 109(2):287–311.

Gais, Thomas. 1996. *Improper Influence: Campaign Finance Law, Political Interest Groups, and the Problem of Equality.* Ann Arbor: U. of Michigan Press.

Gallup, George. 1951. "The Gallup Poll and the 1950 Election." *Public Opinion Quarterly* 15:16–22.

Garand, James C., and M. G. Lichtl. 2000. "Explaining Divided Government in the United States: Testing an International Model of Split-Ticket Voting." *British Journal of Political Science* 30 (January, pt. 1):173–91.

Garramone, Gina M., Charles K. Atkin, Bruce E. Pinkleton, and Richard T. Cole. 1990. "Effects of Negative Political Advertising on the Political Process." *Journal of Broadcasting & Electronic Media* 34(3):299–311.

Geer, John G. 1991. "Critical Realignments and the Public-Opinion Poll." *Journal of Politics* 53(2):434–53.

Geer, John G. 1996. *From Tea Leaves to Opinion Polls: A Theory of Democratic Leadership.* New York: Columbia U. Press.

Gelman, Andrew, and Gary King. 1993. "Why Are American Presidential Election Campaign Polls So Variable When Votes Are So Predictable?" *British Journal of Political Science* 23 (October):409–51.

Gelman, Andrew, and Gary King. 1994. "Enhancing Democracy through Legislative Redistricting." *American Political Science Review* 88 (September):541–59.

Gentzkow, Matthew. "Television and Voter Turnout." Working paper, University of Chicago Graduate School of Business. 2005.

Gentzkow, Matthew and Jesse M. Shapiro. "Media Bias and Reputation." Working paper, University of Chicago Graduate School of Business. 2005.

Gerber, Alan. "Rational Voters, Candidate Spending, and Incomplete Information: A Theoretical Analysis with Implications for Campaign Finance Reform," working paper, Institutional for Social and Policy Studies, Yale University. 1996.

Gerber, Alan S., and Donald P. Green. 2004. "Do Phone Calls Increase Voter Turnout? A Field Experiment." *Public Opinion Quarterly* 68:489–89.

Gerber, Elisabeth R. 1996. "Legislative Response to the Threat of Popular Initiatives." *American Journal of Political Science* 40(1):99–128.

Gerber, Elisabeth R. 1999. *The Populist Paradox: Interest Group Influence and the Promise of Direct Legislation.* Princeton, N.J.: Princeton U. Press.

Gerber, Elisabeth R., and Rebecca B. Morton. 1998. "Primary Election Systems and Representation." *Journal of Law, Economics & Organization* 14(2):304–24.

Gerber, Elisabeth R., and Rebecca B. Morton. 2004. "Electoral Institutions and Party Competition: The Effects of Nomination Procedures on Electoral Coalition Formation." Working paper. New York U.

Gilligan, Thomas W., and John G. Matsusaka. 1999. "Structural Constraints on Partisan Bias under the Efficient Gerrymander." *Public Choice* 100(1–2):65–84.

Gilmour, J. B., and Paul Rothstein. 1993. "Early Republican Retirement— A Cause of Democratic Dominance in the House of Representatives." *Legislative Studies Quarterly* 18(3):345–65.

Goldberg, Bernard. 2002. *Bias: A CBS Insider Exposes How the News Media Distort the News.* Washington, D.C.: Regnery.

Gordon, Sanford C. and Cathering Hafer. 2005. "Flexing Muscle: Corporate Political Expenditure as Signals to the Bureaucracy." *American Political Science Review* (May).

Gordon, Sanford C., Catherine Hafer, and Dimitri Landa. 2005. "Consumption or Investment: Campaign Contributions and the Structure of Executive Compensation." Working paper. Department of Politics, New York U.

Gordon, Sanford C., and Gregory A. Huber. 2002. "Citizen Oversight and the Electoral Incentives of Criminal Prosecutors." *American Journal of Political Science* 46(2):334–51.

Graber, D. 1984. *Processing the News: How People Tame the Information Tide.* New York: Longman.

Grimshaw, William J. 1992. *Bitter Fruit: Black Politics and the Chicago Machine, 1931–1991.* Chicago: U. of Chicago Press.

Groeling, Tim, and Samuel Kernell. 1998. "Is Network News Coverage of the President Biased?" *Journal of Politics* 60(4):1063–87.

Grofman, Bernard, and Chandler Davidson, eds. 1992. *Controversies in Minority Voting: The Voting Rights Act in Perspective.* Washington, D.C.: Brookings Institution.

Grofman, Bernard, and Neil Sutherland. 1996. "Gubernatorial Term Limits and Term Lengths in Historical Perspective, 1790–1990." In Bernard Grofman, ed., *Legislative Term Limits: Public Choice Perspectives,* pp. 279–87. Boston: Kluwer.

Grofman, Bernard, and Lisa Handley. 1998. "Estimating the Impact of Voting-Rights-Act-Related Districting on Democratic Strength in the U.S. House of Representatives. In Bernard Grofman (Ed.), *Race and Redistricting in the 1990s.* New York: Agathon Press, 51–67.

Groseclose, Timothy. 2001. "A Model of Candidate Location When One Candidate has a Valence Advantage." *American Journal of Political Science* 45(4):862–86.

Groseclose, Timothy, S. D. Levitt, and James M. Snyder. 1999. "Comparing Interest Group Scores across Time and Chambers: Adjusted ADA Scores for the U.S. Congress." *American Political Science Review* 93 (March):33–50.

Groseclose, Timothy, and Jeffrey Milyo. 2003. "A Measure of Media Bias." Working paper. Department of Political Science, U. of California, Los Angeles.

Grossman, Gene M., and Elhanan Helpman. 1996. "Electoral Competition and Special Interest Politics." *Review of Economic Studies* 63(215):265–86.

Grossman, Gene M., and Elhanan Helpman. 1999. "Competing for Endorsements." *American Economic Review* 89(3):501–24.

Hadley, Arthur T. 1976. *The Invisible Primary.* Englewood Cliffs, N.J.: Prentice Hall.

Hagen, Michael G. 1989. "Voter Turnout in Primary Elections." In Peverill Squire, ed., *The Iowa Caucuses and the Presidential Nomination Process.* Boulder, Colo.: Westview Press.

Hamilton, James T. 2004. *All the News That's Fit to Sell.* Princeton, N.J.: Princeton U. Press.

Hamilton, Jean Marie. 1984. "A Primer on Polls." *Northwest Orient* 35 (February).

Hamilton, R. H. 1988. "American All-Mail Balloting—A Decade's Experience." *Public Administration Review* 48(5):860–66.

Handley, Lisa, and Bernard Grofman. 1994. "The Impact of the Voting Rights Act on Minority Representation: Black Officeholding in Southern State Legislatures and Congressional Delegations." In Davidson and Grofman, *Quiet Revolution in the South,* pp. 335–50.

Handley, Lisa, and Bernard Grofman. 1998.

Harvey, Anna. 1998. *Votes without Leverage: Women in American Electoral Politics, 1920–1970.* Cambridge: Cambridge U. Press.

Herbst, Susan. 1998. *Reading Public Opinion: How Political Actors View the Democratic Process.* Chicago: U of Chicago Press.

Herrnson, Paul S. 1997. "Two-Party Dominance and Minor-Party Forays in American Politics." In Herrnson and Green, *Multiparty Politics in America.*

Herrnson, Paul S., and John C. Green, eds. 1997. *Multiparty Politics in America.* New York: Rowman & Littlefield.

Herron, Michael C., and Jeffrey Lewis. 2004. "Was Ralph Nader a Spoiler? A Study of Green and Reform Party Voters in the 2000 Presidential Election." Working paper. Department of Government, Dartmouth College, Hanover, N.H.

Herron, Michael C., and J. S. Sekhon. 2003. "Overvoting and Representation: An Examination of Overvoted Presidential Ballots in Broward and Miami-Dade Counties." *Electoral Studies* 22(1):21–47.

Highton, B., and Raymond E. Wolfinger. 1998. "Estimating the Effects of the National Voter Registration Act of 1993." *Political Behavior* 20(2):79–104.

Hill, Kim, and Patricia Hurley. 1999. "Dyadic Representation Reappraised." *American Journal of Political Science* 36(2):351–65.

Hill, Kim, and Patricia Hurley. 2003. "Beyond the Demand-Input Model: A Theory of Representational Linkages." *Journal of Politics* 65(2):304–26.

Hillygus, D. S. 2003. "Stand by Your Man? Assessing the Dynamics of Nader Support in Election 2000." Working paper. Department of Government, Harvard U., Cambridge, Mass.

Holbrook, Thomas M. 2004. "Good News for Bush? Economic News, Personal Finances, and the 2004 Presidential Election." *PS: Political Science & Politics* 37(4):759–61.

Hotelling, Harold. 1929. "Stability in Competition." *Economic Journal* 39 (March):41–57.

Huber, Gregory A., and Sanford C. Gordon. 2004. "Accountability and Coercion: Is Justice Blind When It Runs for Office?" *American Journal of Political Science* 48(2):247–63.

Husted, Thomas, Lawrence W. Kenny, and Rebecca B. Morton. 1995. "Constituent Errors in Assessing Their Senators." *Public Choice* 83(3–4) 251–71.

Imai, Kosuke. 2005. "Do Get-Out-the-Vote Calls Reduce Turnout? The Importance of Statistical Methods for Field Experiments." *American Political Science Review* 99 May).

Irvine, Reed, and Cliff Kincaid. 2001. "Post Columnist Concerned about Media Bias." Accuracy in Media. http://www.aim.org/media_monitor/A900_0_2_0_C.

Jackson, John E. 1983. "Election Night Reporting and Voter Turnout." *American Journal of Political Science* 27(4):615–35.

Jacobs, Lawrence R. 1993. *The Health of Nations: Public Opinion and the Making of American and British Health Policy.* Ithaca, N.Y.: Cornell U. Press.

Jacobs, Lawrence R., Eric D. Lawrence, Robert Y. Shapiro, and Steven S. Smith. 1998. "Congressional Leadership of Public Opinion." *Political Science Quarterly* 113(1):21–41.

Jacobs, Lawrence R., and Robert Y. Shapiro. 1994. "Issues, Candidate Image, and Priming: The Use of Private Polls in Kennedy's 1960 Presidential Campaign." *American Political Science Review* 88 (September): 527–40.

Jacobs, Lawrence R., and Robert Y. Shapiro. 1995. "The Rise of Presidential Polling: The Nixon White House in Historical Perspective." *Public Opinion Quarterly* 59:163–95.

Jacobs, Lawrence R., and Robert Y. Shapiro. 1995–96.

Jacobs, Lawrence R., and Robert Y. Shapiro. 2000. *Politicians Don't Pander: Political Manipulation and the Loss of Democratic Responsiveness.* Chicago: U. of Chicago Press.

Jamieson, Kathleen Hall. 1996 *Packaging the Presidency: A History and Criticism of Presidential Campaign Advertising.* New York: Oxford U. Press.

Jennings, M. Kent, and Laura Stoker. 1997. *Youth-Parent Socialization Panel Study, 1965–1997: Youth Wave Iv, 1997.* Ann Arbor, Mich.: Interuniversity Consortium for Political and Social Research.

Jewell, Malcolm E. 1984. *Parties and Primaries: Nominating State Governors.* New York: Praeger.

Jewell, Malcolm E., and David Breaux. 1988. "The Effect of Incumbency on State Legislative Elections." *Legislative Studies Quarterly* 13:495–514.

Jewell, Malcolm E., and David Breaux. 1991. "Southern Primary and Electoral Competition and Incumbent Success." *Legislative Studies Quarterly* 16:129–43.

Jewell, Malcolm E., and Sarah M. Morehouse. 2001. *Political Parties and Elections in American States,* 4th ed. Washington, D.C.: Congressional Quarterly Press.

Jewell, Malcolm E., and David M. Olson. 1982. *American State Political Parties and Elections,* rev. ed. Homewood, Ill.: Dorsey Press.

Jones, Bryan D., and Frank R. Baumgartner. 2004. "Representation and Agenda Setting." *Policy Studies Journal* 32(1):1–24.

Kahn, K. F., and John G. Geer. 1994. "Creating Impressions: An Experimental Investigation of Political Advertising on Television." *Political Behavior* 16(1):93–116.

Kanthak, Kristin. 2002. "Top-Down Divergence: The Effect of Legislative Rules on Candidate Ideological Placement." *Journal of Theoretical Politics* 14(3):301–23.

Kanthak, Kristin, and Rebecca B. Morton. 2001. "The Effects of Primary Systems on Congressional Elections." In Peter Galderisi and Mike Lyons, eds. *Congressional Primaries and the Politics of Representation.* Lanham, Md.: Rowman & Littlefield.

Katz, Jonathan N., Andrew Gelman, and Gary King. 2002. "Empirically Evaluating the Electoral College." Social Science Working Paper 1134. California Institute of Technology, Pasadena.

Keefe, William J. 1998. *Parties, Politics, and Public Policy in America,* 8th ed. Washington, D.C.: Congressional Quarterly Press.

Keeter, Scott, and Cliff Zukin. 1983. *Uninformed Choice: The Failure of the New Presidential Nominating System.* New York: Praeger.

Kenny, Lawrence W., and John R. Lott, Jr. 1999. "Did Women's Suffrage Change the Size and Scope of Government?" *Journal of Political Economy* 107 (December):1163–98.

Kenney, Patrick, and Tom W. Rice. 1994. "The Psychology of Political Momentum." *Political Research Quarterly* 47:923–38.

Kernell, Samuel. 2000. "Life before Polls: Ohio Politicians Predict the 1828 Presidential Vote." *PS: Political Science & Politics* 33(3):569–74.

Kessel, John H. 1988. *Presidential Campaign Politics,* 3rd ed. Chicago: Dorsey Press.

Key, V. O., Jr. 1964. *Politics, Parties, and Pressure Groups,* 5th ed. New York: Thomas Y. Crowell.

King, David C., and David Morehouse. 2004. "Moving Voters in the 2000 Presidential Campaign: Local Visits, Local Media." Working paper. John F. Kennedy School of Government, Harvard U., Cambridge, Mass.

King, Gary. 1993. "The Methodology of Presidential Research." In George C. Edwards III, John H. Kessel, and Bert A. Rockman, eds., *Researching the Presidency: Vital Questions, New Approaches*, pp. 387–414. Pittsburgh: U. of Pittsburgh Press.

Klinkner, Philip A. 2004. "Red and Blue Scare: The Continuing Diversity of the American Electoral Landscape." *Forum* 2(2), article 2.

Knack, Stephen. 1992. "Civic Norms, Social Sanctions, and Voter Turnout." *Rationality & Society* 4(2):133–56.

Konner, Joan. 2003. "The Case for Caution: The System Is Dangerously Flawed." *Public Opinion Quarterly* 67:45–18.

Kousser, J. Morgan. 1974. *The Shaping of Southern Politics: Suffrage Restrictions and the Establishment of the One-Party South, 1880–1910.* New Haven, Conn.: Yale U. Press.

Kousser, J. Morgan. 1992. "The Voting Rights Act and the Two Reconstructions." In Grofman and Davidson, *Controversies in Minority Voting*, pp. 135–76.

Kousser, J. Morgan. 1999. *Colorblind Injustice: Minority Voting Rights and the Undoing of the Second Reconstruction.* Chapel Hill: U. of North Carolina Press.

Kramer, Gerald H. 1971. "Short-Term Fluctuations in U.S. Voting Behavior, 1896–1964." *American Political Science Review* 65 (March):131–43.

Krehbiel, Keith. 1998. *Pivotal Politics.* Chicago: U. of Chicago Press.

Krehbiel, Keith. 2000. "Party Discipline and Measures of Partisanship." *American Journal of Political Science* 44(2):212–27.

Lau, Richard R., and Gerald M. Pomper. 2002. "Effectiveness of Negative Campaigning in U.S. Senate Elections." *American Journal of Political Science* 46(1):47–66.

Lazarsfeld, Paul F., B. R. Berelson, and H. Gaudet. 1944. *The People's Choice.* New York: Columbia U. Press.

Ledyard, John. 1984. "The Pure Theory of Large Two-Candidate Elections." *Public Choice* 44(1):7–41.

Lee, Frances. 1998. "Representation and Public Policy: The Consequences of Senate Apportionment for the Geographic Distribution of Federal Funds." *Journal of Politics* 60(1):34–62.

Lee, Frances. 2000. "Senate Representation and Coalition Building in Distributive Politics." *American Political Science Review* 94 (March) 59–72.

Lee, Frances. 2003. "Geographic Politics in the U.S. House of Representatives: Coalition Building and Distribution of Benefits." *American Journal of Political Science* 47(4):714–28.

Lee, Frances. 2004. "Bicameral Institutions and Geographic Politics: Allocating Federal Funds for Transportation in the House and Senate." *Legislative Studies Quarterly* forthcoming.

Leigh, Andrew, and Justin Wolfers. 2005. "Competing Approaches to Forecasting Elections: Economic Models, Opinion Polling and Prediction Markets," working paper, Wharton, University of Pennsylvania.

Lewis-Beck, Michael S. 1988. *Economics and Elections.* Ann Arbor: U. of Michigan Press.

Lewis-Beck, Michael S., and Tom W. Rice. 1992. *Forecasting Elections.* Washington, D.C.: Congressional Quarterly Press.

Lewis-Beck, Michael S., and Charles Tien. 2004. "Jobs and the Job of President: A Forecast for 2004." *PS: Political Science & Politics* 37(4)753–58.

Lichtman, A. J. 2003. "What Really Happened in Florida's 2000 Presidential Election." *Journal of Legal Studies* 32(1):221–43.

Lichter, S. Robert. 2001. "A Plague on Both Parties: Substance and Fairness in TV Election News." *Harvard International Journal of Press/ Politics* 6(3):8–30.

Lipset, Seymour Martin, Martin A. Trow, and James S. Coleman. 1956. *Union Democracy.* New York: Free Press.

Littlewood, Thomas B. 1998. *Calling Elections: The History of Horse-Race Journalism.* Notre Dame, Ind.: U. of Notre Dame Press.

Lockerbie, Brad. 2004. "A Look to the Future: Forecasting the 2004 Presidential Election." *PS: Political Science & Politics* 37(4):741–44.

Londregan, John, and Thomas Romer. 1993. "Polarization, Incumbency, and the Personal Vote." In William A. Barnett, Melvin J. Hinich, and Norman J. Schofield, eds., *Political Economy: Institutions, Competition, and Representation.* New York: Cambridge U. Press.

Lott. John R., Jr., and Kevin A. Hassert. 2004. "Is Newspaper Coverage of Economic Events Politically Biased?" Working paper. American Enterprise Institute, Washington, D.C.

Lowry, D. T., and J. A. Shidler. 1995. "The Sound Bites, the Biters, and the Bitten—An Analysis of Network TV News Bias in Campaign '92." *Journalism & Mass Communication Quarterly* 72(1):33–44.

Lublin, David Ian. 1997. *The Paradox of Representation.* Princeton, N.J.: Princeton U. Press.

Lublin, David Ian, and D. Stephen Voss. 2000. "Boll-Weevil Blues: Polarized Congressional Delegations into the Twenty-first Century." *American Review of Politics* 21 (Winter):427–50.

Lublin, David Ian, and D. Stephen Voss. 2003. "The Missing Middle: Why Median-Voter Theory Can't Save Democrats from Singing the Boll-Weevil Blues." *Journal of Politics* 65(1):227–37.

Lukas, Anthony J. 1998. *Big Trouble: A Murder in a Small Western Town Sets Off a Struggle for the Soul of American.* New York: Simon & Schuster.

Mack, W. R. 1998. "Repeat Challengers—Are They the Best Challengers Around?" *American Politics Quarterly* 26(3):308–43.

Magleby, David B. 1987. "Participation in Mail Ballot Elections." *Western Political Quarterly* 40(1):79–91.

Magleby, David B. 2000. *Dictum without Data: The Myth of Issue Advocacy and Party Building*. Provo, Utah: Center for the Study of Elections and Democracy.

Maisel, L. Sandy, Cary T. Gibson, and Elizabeth J. Ivry. 1998. "The Continuing Importance of the Rules of the Game: Subpresidential Nominations in 1994 and 1996." In L. Sandy Maisel, ed., *The Parties Respond: Changes in American Parties and Campaigns*, 3rd ed. Boulder, Colo.: Westview Press.

Manza, Jeff, and Fay Lomax Cook. 2002. "A Democratic Polity? Three Views of Policy Responsiveness to Public Opinion in the United States." *American Politics Research* 30(6):630–67.

Markin, Karen M. 1995. *Ballot Access 4: For Political Parties*. Washington, D.C.: National Clearinghouse on Election Administration, Federal Elections Commission.

Markus, G. B. 1988. "The Impact of Personal and National Economic Conditions in the Presidential Vote: A Pooled Cross-Sectional Analysis." *American Journal of Political Science* 32(1):137–54.

Mason, Linda, Kathleen Frankovic, and Kathleen Hall Jamieson. 2001. *CBS News Coverage of Election Night 2000: Investigation, Analysis, Recommendations*. CBS News. http://www.cbsnews.com/htdocs/c2k/pdf/REPFINAL.pdf.

Matsusaka, John G. 1992. "Economics of Direct Legislation." *Quarterly Journal of Economics* 107(2):541–71.

Matsusaka, John G., and Nolan M. McCarty. 2001. "Political Resource Allocation: Benefits and Costs of Voter Initiatives." *Journal of Law, Economics & Organization*, 17(2):413–48.

Mayhew, David R. 2002. *Electoral Realignments: a Critique of an American Genre*. New Haven, Conn.: Yale U. Press.

Mazmanian, Daniel A. 1974. *Third Parties in Presidential Elections*. Washington, D.C.: Brookings Institution.

McCarty, Nolan. Not dated. "Presidential Vetoes in the Early Republic," working paper, Woodrow Wilson School, Princeton University.

McCarty, Nolan M., and Timothy Groseclose. 2000. "The Politics of Blame: Bargaining before an Audience." *American Journal of Political Science* 45(1):100–119.

McCarty, Nolan M., Keith T. Poole, and Howard Rosenthal. 2005. "Polarized America: The Dance of Ideology and Unequal Riches." CIG working paper 5. Center on Institutions and Governance, U. of California, Berkeley.

McCormick, Richard P. 1960. "New Perspective on Jacksonian Politics." *American Historical Review* 65 (January):288–301.

McCormick, Richard P. 1982. *The Presidential Game: The Origins of American Presidential Politics*. New York: Oxford U. Press.

McDonald, Michael P., and Samuel L. Popkin. 2001. "The Myth of the Vanishing Voter." *American Political Science Review* 95 (December):963–74.

McIver, John P., Robert S. Erikson, and Gerald C. Wright. 2000. "Public Opinion and Public Policy in Temporal Perspective: A View from the States." Working paper. Department of Political Science, U. of Colorado Boulder.

McKelvey, Richard D., and Peter C. Ordeshook. 1985. "Elections with Limited Information—A Fulfilled Expectations Model Using Contemporaneous Poll and Endorsement Data as Information Sources." *Journal of Economic Theory* 36(1):55–85.

McKelvey, Richard D., and Raymond G. Riezman. 1992. "Seniority in Legislatures." *American Political Science Review* 86 (December):951–65.

McLean, Ian, and Arnold B. Urken, eds. 1993. *Classics of Social Choice*. Ann Arbor: U. of Michigan Press.

Mebane, Walter. 2000. "Coordination, Moderation, and Institutional Balancing in American Presidential and House Elections." *American Political Science Review* 94 (March):37–57.

Mebane, Walter, and J. S. Sekhon. 2002. "Coordination and Policy Moderation at Midterm." *American Political Science Review* 96 (March): 141–57.

Mebane, Walter, and Gregory J. Wawro. 2002. "Presidential Pork Barrel Politics." Working paper. Department of Government, Cornell U., Ithaca, N.Y.

Media Dynamics. 2001. *TV Dimensions*. New York: Media Dynamics.

Meltzer, Allan H., and Scott F. Richard. 1981. "A Rational Theory of the Size of Government." *Journal of Political Economy* 89 (October):914–27.

Mitofsky, Warren J. 1998. "Was 1996 a Worse Year for the Polls Than 1948?" *Public Opinion Quarterly* 62:230–49.

Mitofsky, Warren J., and Murray Edelman. 2002. "Election Night Estimation." *Journal of Official Statistics* 18(2):165–79.

Moncrief, Gary, Richard G. Niemi, and Lynda W. Powell. 2004. "Time, Term Limits, and Turnover: Trends in Membership Stability in U.S. State Legislatures." *Legislative Studies Quarterly* 29:357–81.

Moore, M. K., and J. R. Hibbing. 1998. "Situational Dissatisfaction in Congress: Explaining Voluntary Departures." *Journal of Politics* 60(4):1088–1107.

Morganstein, David, David Marker, and Joseph Waksberg. 2000. "A Conversation with Joseph Waksberg." *Statistical Science* 15(3):305–6.

Morton, Rebecca B. 1991. "Groups in Rational Turnout Models." *American Journal of Political Science* 35(3):758–76.

Morton, Rebecca B. 1999. *Methods and Models: A Guide to the Empirical Analysis of Formal Models in Political Science*. Cambridge: Cambridge U. Press.

Morton, Rebecca B., and Charles M. Cameron. 1991. "Elections and the Theory of Campaign Contributions: A Survey and Critical Analysis." *Economics & Politics* 4:79–108.

Morton, Rebecca B., and Roger B. Myerson. 2003. "Decisiveness in Contributors' Perceptions." Working paper. Department of Politics, New York U.

Morton, Rebecca B., and Kenneth C. Williams. 1999. "Information Asymmetries and Simultaneous versus Sequential Voting." *American Political Science Review* 93 (March):51–67.

Morton, Rebecca B., and Kenneth C. Williams. 2001. *Learning by Voting.* Ann Arbor: U. of Michigan Press.

Morris, Edmund. 2001. *Theodore Rex.* New York: Random House.

Mullainathan, Sendhil, and Andrei Shleifer. 2005. "The Market for News." *American Economic Review.*

Murray, Shoon Kathleen, and Peter Howard. 2002. "Variation in White House Polling Operations: Carter to Clinton." *Public Opinion Quarterly* 66:527–58.

Myerson, Roger B., Thomas A. Rietz, and Robert J. Weber. 1998. "Campaign Finance Levels as Coordinating Signals in Three-Way Experimental Elections." *Economics & Politics* 10:185–217.

Myerson, Roger B., and Robert J. Weber. 1993. "A Theory of Voting Equilibria." *American Political Science Review* 87 (March):102–14.

Nardulli, Peter F. 2004. "Handicapping the 2004 Presidential Election: A Normal Vote Approach." *PS: Political Science & Politics* 37(4):813–20.

National Motor Voter Coalition. 1996. *First Year Report on the Impact of the National Voter Registration Act, January 1, 1995—December 31, 1995.*

Niemi, Richard G., Harold W. Stanley, and R. J. Vogel. 1995. "State Economies and State Taxes—Do Voters Hold Governors Accountable?" *American Journal of Political Science* 39(4):936–57.

Niven, D. 2001. "Bias in the News—Partisanship and Negativity in Media Coverage of Presidents George Bush and Bill Clinton." *Harvard International Journal of Press/Politics* 6(3):31–46.

Noggle, G., and L. L. Kaid. 2000. "The Effects of Visual Images in Political Ads: Experimental Testings of Distortions and Visual Literacy." *Social Science Quarterly* 81:913–27.

Norpoth, Helmut. 2004. "From Primary to General Election: A Forecast of the Presidential Vote." *PS: Political Science & Politics* 37(4):737–40.

Norrander, Barbara. 1989. "Ideological Representativeness of Presidential Primary Voters." *American Journal of Political Science* 33(3):570–87.

Norrander, Barbara. 1993. "Nomination Choices: Caucus and Primary Outcomes, 1976–88." *American Journal of Political Science* 37(2):343–64.

Norrell, Robert J. 1998. *Reaping the Whirlwind: The Civil Rights Movement in Tuskegee.* Chapel Hill: U. of North Carolina Press.

Oliven, Kenneth, and Thomas A. Rietz. 2004. "Suckers Are Born but Markets Are Made: Individual Rationality, Arbitrage, and Market Efficiency on an Electronic Futures Market." *Management Science* 50(3):336–51.

Oliver, J. Eric. 1996. "The Effects of Eligibility Restriction and Party Activity on Absentee Voting and Overall Turnout." *American Journal of Political Science* 40(2):498–513.

O'Neill, John E., and Jerome R. Corsi. 2004. *Unfit for Command: Swift Boat Veterans Speak Out against John Kerry*. Washington, D.C. Regnery.

Osborne, Martin J., and Al Slivinski. 1996. "A Model of Political Competition with Citizen Candidates." *Quarterly Journal of Economics* 111(1):65–96.

Overbye, E. 1995. "Making a Case for the Rational, Self-Regarding, Ethical Voter . . . and Solving the Paradox of Not Voting in the Process." *European Journal of Political Research* 27(3):369–96.

Paden, Catherine, and Benjamin I. Page. 2003. "Congress Invokes Public Opinion on Welfare Reform." *American Politics Research* 31(6):670–79.

Palfrey, Thomas R. 1989. "A Mathematical Proof of Duverger's Law." In Peter C. Ordeshook, ed., *Models of Strategic Choice in Politics*, pp. 69–92. Ann Arbor: U. of Michigan Press.

Palfrey, Thomas R., and Keith T. Poole. 1987. "The Relationship between Information, Ideology, and Voting Behavior." *American Journal of Political Science* 31(3):511–30.

Palfrey, Thomas R., and Howard Rosenthal. 1983. "A Strategic Calculus of Voting." *Public Choice* 41(1):7–53.

Palfrey, Thomas R., and Howard Rosenthal. 1985. "Voter Participation and Strategic Uncertainty." *American Political Science Review* 79 (March):62–78.

Palmer, Niall. 1997. *The New Hampshire Primary and the American Electoral Process*. Westport, Conn.: Praeger.

Paolino, Philip. 1996. "Perceptions of Candidate Viability: Media Effects during the Presidential Nomination Process." Paper presented at the annual meetings of the American Political Science Association, San Francisco.

Paolino, Philip. 1998. "Voters' Perceptions of Candidate Viability: Uncertainty and the Prospects for Momentum." Paper presented at the annual meetings of the Midwest Political Science Association, Chicago.

Patterson, Beeman C. 1969. "Political Action of Negroes in Los Angeles: A Case Study in the Attainment of Councilmanic Representation." *Phylon* 30(2):170–83.

Patterson, Samuel C., and Gregory A. Caldeira. 1985. "Mailing In the Vote: Correlates and Consequences of Absentee Voting." *American Journal of Political Science* 29(4):766–88.

Patterson, Thomas E. 1980. *The Mass Media Election: How Americans Choose Their President*. New York: Praeger.

Patterson, Thomas E. 1993. *Out of Order*. New York: Alfred A. Knopf.

Patterson, Thomas E., and Wolfgang Donsbach. 1996. "News Decisions: Journalists as Partisan Actors." *Political Communication* 13:453–68.

Peltzman, Samuel. 1992. "Voters as Fiscal Conservatives." *Quarterly Journal of Economics* 107 (2):327–61.

Persson, Torsten, and Guido Tabellini. 1990. *Macroeconomic Policy, Credibility, and Politics.* Chur, Switzerland: Harwood Academic.

Petrocik, J. R. 1996. "Issue Ownership in Presidential Elections, with a 1980 Case Study." *American Journal of Political Science* 40(3):825–50.

Pew Research Center for the People and the Press. *The 2004 Political Landscape: Evenly Divided and Increasingly Polarized.* Pet Research Center for the People and the Press. http://people-press.org.

Polsby, Nelson W. 1983. *The Consequences of Party Reform.* Oxford: Oxford U. Press.

Polsby, Nelson W., and Aaron Wildavsky. 1971. *Presidential Elections: Strategies of American Electoral Politics,* 3rd ed. New York: Charles Scribner's Sons.

Poole, Keith T., and Howard Rosenthal. 1997. *Congress: A Political-Economic History of Roll-Call Voting.* New York: Oxford U. Press.

Popkin, Samuel L. 1991. *The Reasoning Voter.* Chicago: U. of Chicago Press.

Prat, Andrea. 2002. "Campaign Advertising and Voter Welfare." *Review of Economic Studies* 69(4):999–1017.

Puglisi, Ricardo. 2004. "Being *The New York Times:* The Political Behavior of a Newspaper." Working paper. London School of Economics.

Quirk, P. J., and Hinchliffe, J. 1998. "The Rising Hegemony of Mass Opinion." *Journal of Policy History* 10(1):19–50.

Ranney, Austin. 1977. *Participation in American Presidential Nominations, 1976.* Washington, D.C.: American Enterprise Institute for Public Policy Research.

Rhode, Paul, and Koleman S. Strumpf. 2004. "Historical Presidential Betting Markets." *Journal of Economic Perspectives* 18:127–42.

Ridout, Travis N., Michael Franz, Kenneth Goldstein, and Paul Freedman. 2002. *Measuring the Nature and Effects of Campaign Advertising.* Department of Political Science, U. of Wisconsin, Madison. http:polisci.wisc.edu/~tvadvertising/reliability.pdf.

Rietz, Thomas A. 1998. "Three-Way Experimental Election Results: Strategic Voting and Coordinated Outcomes and Duverger's Law." Working paper. U. of Iowa, Iowa City.

Riker, William H. 1982. "The Two-Party System and Duverger's Law: An Essay on the History of Political Science." *American Political Science Review* 76 (December):753–66.

Riker, William H. 1988. *Liberalism against Populism.* Chicago: Waveland Press.

Riker, William H., and Peter C. Ordeshook. 1968. "A Theory of the Calculus of Voting." *American Political Science Review* 62 (March):25–42.

Riordon, William L. 1994. *Plunkitt of Tammany Hall.* New York: St. Martin's Press.

Roberts, K.W.S. 1977. "Voting over Income-Tax Schedules." *Journal of Public Economics* 8(3):329–40.

Robinson, Michael J., and Margaret Sheehan. 1983. *Over the Wire and on TV: CBS and UPI in Campaign '80*. New York: Russell Sage Foundation.

Rogoff, Kenneth. 1990. "Equilibrium Political Budget Cycles." *American Economic Review* 80(1):21–36.

Rogoff, Kenneth, and Anne Sibert. 1988. "Elections and Macroeconomic Policy Cycles." *Review of Economic Studies* 55(1):1–16.

Romer, Thomas. 1975. "Individual Welfare, Majority Voting, and the Properties of a Linear Income Tax." *Journal of Public Economics* 4(2):163–185.

Rosales, Rodolfo. 2000. *The Illusion of Inclusion: The Untold Political Story of San Antonio*. Austin: U. of Texas Press.

Rosenfield, Margaret. 1994. *Innovations in Election Administration*. Vol. 9, *Early Voting*. Washington, D.C.: National Clearinghouse on Election Administration, Federal Election Commission.

Rosenof, Theodore. 1999. "The Legend of Louis Bean: Political Prophecy and the 1948 Election." *Historian* 62 (Fall):63–78.

Rosenstone, Steven J. 1983. *Forecasting Presidential Elections*. New Haven, Conn.: Yale U. Press.

Rosenstone, Steven J., Roy L. Behr, and Edward H. Lazarus. 1984. *Third Parties in America: Citizen Response to Major Party Failure*. Princeton, N.J.: Princeton U. Press.

Rosenstone, Steven J., and John Mark Hansen. 1993. *Mobilization, Participation, and Democracy in America*. New York: Macmillan.

Roth, Alvin. 1995. "Introduction to Experimental Economics." In John Kagel and Alvin Roth, eds., *The Handbook of Experimental Economics*. Princeton, N.J.: Princeton U. Press.

Rottinghaus, Brandon. 2003. "Limited to Follow: The Early Public Opinion Apparatus of the Herbert Hoover White House." *American Politics Research* 31(5):540–56.

Royko, Mike. 1971. *Boss: Richard J. Daley of Chicago*. New York: New American Library.

Rusk, Jerrold G. 1968. "The Effect of the Australian Ballot Reform on Split Ticket Voting: 1876–1908." Ph.D. diss. U. of Michigan, Ann Arbor.

Salsburg, David. 2001. *The Lady Tasting Tea: How Statistics Revolutionized Science in the Twentieth Century*. New York: W. H. Freeman.

Schansberg, D. E. 1994. "Moving Out of the House—An Analysis of Congressional Quits." *Economic Inquiry* 32(3):445–56.

Schmidt, Amy, Lawrence W. Kenny, and Rebecca B. Morton. 1996. "Evidence on Electoral Accountability in the U.S. Senate: Are Unfaithful Agents Really Punished?" *Economic Inquiry* 34(3):545–67.

Schneider, William. 1997. "And Now the GOP Is Rewriting Its Rules." *National Journal* 12 (April):734.

Schuessler, Alexander A. 2000. *A Logic of Expressive Choice*. Princeton, N.J.: Princeton U. Press.

Severin, Werner, and James Tankard, Jr., 1992. *Communication Theories: Origins, Methods, and Uses in the Mass Media.* New York, Longman.

Shafer, Byron E. 1983. *Quiet Revolution: The Struggle for the Democratic Party and the Shaping of Post-Reform Politics.* New York: Russell Sage Foundation.

Shaw, Daron R. 1999. "The Effect of TV Ads and Candidate Appearances on Statewide Presidential Votes, 1988–1996." *American Political Science Review* 93 (June):345–61.

Shaw, Greg M. 2000. "The Role of Public Input in State Welfare Policymaking." *Policy Studies Journal* 28(4):707–20.

Shepsle, Kenneth A. 1991. *Models of Multiparty Electoral Competition.* Chur, Switzerland: Harwood Academic.

Shepsle, Kenneth A., and Mark S. Bonchek. 1997. *Analyzing Politics: Rationality, Behavior, and Institutions.* New York: W. W. Norton.

Shotts, Kenneth W. 2001. "The Effect of Majority-Minority Mandates on Partisan Gerrymandering." *American Journal of Political Science* 45(1): 120–35.

Shotts, Kenneth W. 2002. "Gerrymandering, Legislative Composition, and National Policy Outcomes." *American Journal of Political Science* 46(2):398–414.

Shotts, Kenneth W. 2003a. "Does Racial Redistricting Cause Conservative Policy Outcomes? Policy Preferences of Southern Representatives in the 1980s and 1990s." *Journal of Politics* 65(1):216–26.

Shotts, Kenneth W. 2003b. "Racial Redistricting's Alleged Perverse Effects: Theory, Data, and 'Reality.' " *Journal of Politics* 65(1):238–43.

Simon, Adam. 2002. *The Winning Message: Candidate Behavior, Campaign Discourse, and Democracy.* Cambridge: Cambridge U. Press.

Sloth, B. 1993. "The Theory of Voting and Equilibria in Non-cooperative Games." *Games & Economic Behavior* 5(1):152–69.

Smith, Charles W. 1952. "Measurement of Voter Attitude." *Annals of the American Academy of Political & Social Science* 283:148–55.

Smith, R. L. 2002. "A Statistical Assessment of Buchanan's Vote in Palm Beach County." *Statistical Science* 17(4):441–57.

Snyder, James. 1989. "Election Goals and the Allocation of Campaign Resources." *Econometrica* 57 (May):637–60.

Snyder, James M. 1990. "Campaign Contributions as Investments: The U.S. House of Representatives, 1980–1986." *Journal of Political Economy* 98, 1195–1227.

Snyder, James M., and Michael M. Ting. 2002. "An Informational Rationale for Political Parties." *American Journal of Political Science* 46(1):90–110.

Sorauf, F. J. 1992. "Politics and Money." *American Behavioral Scientist* 35(6):725–34.

Spilliotes, Constantine J., and Lynn Vavreck. 2002. "Campaign Advertising: Partisan Convergence or Divergence." *Journal of Politics* 64(1):249–61.

Stein, Robert M. 1998. "Early Voting." *Public Opinion Quarterly* 62:57–69.

Stein, Robert M., and Patricia A. Garcia-Monet. 1997. "Voting Early, but Not Often." *Social Science Quarterly* 78:657–71.

Steinbicker, Paul G. 1938. "Absentee Voting in the United States." *American Political Science Review* 32 (October):898–907.

Stewart, Charles. 2001. *Analyzing Congress.* New York: W. W. Norton.

Stewart, Charles. 2005. "Residual Vote in the 2004 Election." Caltech-MIT Voting Technology Project Working Paper. California Institute of Technology, Pasadena.

Stokes, Donald E. 1963. "Spatial Models of Party Competition." *American Political Science Review* 57 (June):368–77.

Stone, Walter J., and Alan I. Abramowitz. 1983. "Winning May Not Be Everything, but It's More Than We Thought: Presidential Party Activists in 1980." *American Political Science Review* 77 (December):945–56.

Stone, Walter J., Alan I. Abramowitz, and Ronald B. Rapoport. 1989. "How Representative Are the Iowa Caucuses." In Peverill Squire, ed., *The Iowa Caucuses and the Presidential Nomination Process.* Boulder, Colo.: Westview Press.

Stratmann, Thomas. n.d. "Contribution Limits and the Effectiveness of Campaign Spending." Working paper. Department of Economics, George Mason U.

Stromberg, David. 2002. "Optimal Campaigning in Presidential Elections: The Probability of Being Florida." Working paper. Stockholm U.

Stromberg, David. 2004a. "Mass Media Competition, Political Competition, and Public Policy." *Review of Economic Studies* 71(1):265–84.

Stromberg, David. 2004b. "Radio's Impact on New Deal Spending." *Quarterly Journal of Economics* 119(1):189–221.

Strumpf, Koleman S. 2002. "Strategic Competition in Sequential Election Contests." *Public Choice* 111(3–4):377–97.

Sutter, Daniel. 2004. "Can the Media Be So Liberal? The Economics of Media Bias." *Cato Journal* 20 (Winter):431–51.

Taylor, Humphrey. 1999. "Comparing Online Survey Results with Telephone Survey." *International Journal of Market Research* 42(1):51–63.

Taylor, Humphrey, John Fremer, Cary Overmeyer, Jonathan W. Siegel, and George Terhanian. 2001. "The Record of Internet-Based Opinion Polls in Predicting the Results of 72 Races in the November 2000 U.S. Elections." *International Journal of Market Research* 43(2):127–37.

Tourangeau, Roger. 2004. "Survey Research and Societal Change." *Annual Review of Psychology* 55:775–801.

Traugott, Michael W. 1992. "The Impact of Media Polls on the Public," In Thomas E. Mann and Gary R. Orren, eds., *Media Polls in American Politics*, pp. 125–49. Washington, D.C.: Brookings Institution.

Traugott, Michael W. 1997. "An Evaluation of Voting-by-Mail in Oregon." Paper prepared for the Workshop on Voting-by-Mail, U. of Michigan, Ann Arbor, and the League of Women Voters, Washington, D.C.

Traugott, Michael W. 2001. "Assessing Poll Performance in the 2000 Campaign." *Public Opinion Quarterly* 63:389–419.

Troy, Gil. 1996. *See How They Ran: The Changing Role of the Presidential Candidate*, rev. and expanded ed. Cambridge, Mass.: Harvard U. Press.

U.S. Federal Election Commission. 1999. *Federal Elections*. Washington, D.C: Information Division, Federal Election Commission.

Vavreck, Lynn. 2001. "The Reasoning Voter Meets the Strategic Candidate: Signals and Specificity in Campaign Advertising, 1998." *American Politics Research* 29(5):507–29.

Verba, Sidney. 1996. "The Citizen as Respondent: Sample Surveys and American Democracy." *American Political Science Review* 90 (March):1–7.

Waksberg, Joseph. 1979. "Sampling Methods for Random Digit Dialing." *Journal of the American Statistical Association* 73(361):40–46.

Walker, Jack. 1983. "The Origins and Maintenance of Interest Groups in America." *American Political Science Review* 77 (June):390–406.

Wand, J. N., Kenneth W. Shotts, J. S. Sekhon, Walter Mebane, Michael C. Herron, and Henry E. Brady. 2001. "The Butterfly Did It: The Aberrant Vote for Buchanan in Palm Beach County, Florida." *American Political Science Review* 95 (December):793–810.

Weaver, R. K. 2000. *Ending Welfare As We Know It*. Washington, D.C.: Brookings Institution.

West, Darrell. 2000. *Air Wars: Television Advertising in Election Campaigns, 1952–2000*. Washington, D.C.: Congressional Quarterly Press.

Whitehead, Ralph, and Joel Weisman. 1974. "Is LaSalle Street Grooming the Black Mayor?" *Chicagoan* 1 (August).

Williams, Juan. 1987. *Eyes on the Prize: America's Civil Rights Years, 1954–1965*. New York: Viking Penguin.

Wilson, Woodrow. 1966. "First Annual Message." In *The State of the Union Messages of the Presidents, 1790–1966*, vol. 3, pp. 2544–50. New York: Chelsea House.

Witt, J. 1997. "Herding Behavior in a Roll-Call Voting Game." Working paper. Department of Economics, U. of Amsterdam.

Wittman, Donald A. 1977. "Candidates with Policy Preferences: A Dynamic Model." *Journal of Economic Theory* 14 (1):180–89.

Wlezien, Christopher, and Robert S. Erikson. 2001. "After the Election: Our Forecast in Retrospect." *American Politics Research* 29(3):320–28.

Wlezien, Christopher, and Robert S. Erikson. 2004. "The Fundamentals, the Polls, and the Presidential Vote." *PS: Political Science & Politics* 37(4):741–51.

Wolfers, Justin. 2002. "Are Voters Rational? Evidence from Gubernatorial Elections." Working paper. Stanford Graduate School of Business, Stanford, Calif.

Wolfers, Justin, and Eric Zitzewitz. 2004. "Prediction Markets." *Journal of Economic Perspectives* 18:107–26.

Wolfinger, Raymond E., and Jonathan Hoffman. 2001. "Registering and Voting with Motor Voter." *PS: Political Science & Politics* 34(1):85–92.

Wolfinger, Raymond E., and Peter Linquiti. 1981. "Tuning In and Turning Out." *Public Opinion Quarterly* 4:56–60.

Wolter, K., D. Jergovic, W. Moore, J. Murphy, and C. O'Muircheartaigh. 2003. "Reliability of the Uncertified Ballots in the 2000 Presidential Election in Florida." *American Statistician* 57(1):1–14.

Woodward, C. Vann. 1951. *Origins of the New South*. Baton Rouge: Louisiana State U. Press.

Wright, Gavin. 1974. "Political Economy of New-Deal Spending—Econometric Analysis." *Review of Economics and Statistics* 56:30–38.

Wright, Gerald C. 1990. "Misreports of Vote Choice in the 1988 NES Senate Election Study." *Legislative Studies Quarterly* 15:543–563.

Wright, Gerald C. 1992. "Reported versus Actual Vote: There Is a Difference and It Matters." *Legislative Studies Quarterly* 17:131–143.

Wright, Gerald C. 1993. "Errors in Measuring Vote Choice in the National Election Studies, 1952–1988." *American Journal of Political Science* 37(1):543–63.

Wright, Gerald C., Robert S. Erikson, and John P. McIver. 1993. *Statehouse Democracy: Public Opinion and Policy in the American States*. Cambridge: Cambridge U. Press.

Zaller, John R. 1992. *The Nature and Origins of Mass Opinion*. New York: Cambridge U. Press.

Zaller, John R., and Stanley Feldman. 1992. "A Simple Theory of the Survey Response: Answering Questions versus Revealing Preferences." *American Journal of Political Science* 36(3):579–616.

Zimmerman, Joseph F. 1986. *Participatory Democracy: Populism Revived*. New York: Praeger.

Index